Internal Audit Handbook

Henning Kagermann
William Kinney
Karlheinz Küting
Claus-Peter Weber
(Eds.)

Internal Audit Handbook

Management with the SAP®-Audit Roadmap

In cooperation with:
Corinna Boecker
Julia Busch
Oliver Bussiek
Margaret H. Christ
Petra Eckes
Markus Falk
Penelope Sue Greenberg
Bernhard Reichert
Manfred Wolf

Translated from German by:
Ziggie Keil

Springer

Professor Dr. Henning Kagermann
SAP AG
Dietmar-Hopp-Allee 16
69190 Walldorf
Germany

Professor Dr. Karlheinz Küting
Institut für Wirtschaftsprüfung
Universität des Saarlandes, Campus
Gebäude B4 1
66123 Saarbrücken
Germany

Professor William Kinney, Ph.D.
McCombs School of Business
University of Texas at Austin
1 University Station B6400
Austin, Texas 78712
USA

Professor Dr. Claus-Peter Weber
Institut für Wirtschaftsprüfung
Universität des Saarlandes, Campus
Gebäude B4 1
66123 Saarbrücken
Germany

Additional material to this book can be downloaded from http://extras.springer.com.

ISBN 978-3-642-43039-8 ISBN 978-3-540-70887-2 (eBook)

DOI 10.1007/978-3-540-70887-2

Softcover re-print of the Hardcover 1st edition 2008

Cover design: WMX Design GmbH, Heidelberg

Printed on acid-free paper

9 8 7 6 5 4 3 2 1

springer.com

Preamble by the Institute of Internal Auditors

It's plain and simple: Internal auditing is anything but plain and simple. It is a rapidly changing profession with high standards. Internal auditing is unique to the organization and culture in which it is performed, and requires an in-depth understanding of that organization's culture, policies, and procedures.

Today's professional internal auditors more closely resemble coaches and educators than did their predecessors. They watch for efficiencies, economies, and effectiveness and make recommendations for improvement when they find gaps. Internal auditors assess risks—financial, operational, strategic, compliance-oriented, and reputation-related—to ensure an organization's system of control is strong. They evaluate processes and determine what's working and what's not. And internal auditors' main job function is to help management and the board to meet goals and objectives.

Such a broad and dynamic profession requires its members to be ever watchful for new and better ways of doing things. The Insitute of Internal Auditors (IIA) and The IIA Research Foundation are both committed to enhancing the professionalism of internal audit practitioners and elevating the profession all around the world. This includes expanding the proficiency and performance of internal auditors, as well as building broad awareness of the value the internal audit activity brings to an organization and its myriad stakeholders.

Clearly, this handbook is consistent with these two goals. It sets the stage by defining internal auditing, relating to the *International Standards for the Professional Practice of Internal Auditing,* and describing recognized frameworks for internal control and risk management. It explores internal audit methodology and provides helpful information on scope, integration, analysis, and quality.

Written for management, board members, chief audit executives, and staff internal auditors, the concepts presented on the pages that follow put the complexities of internal auditing into language that is understandable and relevant.

Trish Harris
Director, Communications
The Institute of Internal Auditors, Inc.

Foreword

Everything starts with an idea, and this book is no exception. At first, the various thoughts and discussions were focused on the original intention to "merely" create a job introduction for new Internal Audit employees. This plan has since evolved into a comprehensive, up-to-date presentation of the tasks and challenges facing Internal Audit, in a format and on a scale hitherto unrivalled in the market.

There are very few units in the company that have been subject to such a major change process in recent years as Internal Audit. This applies irrespective of company size as corporations adapt to developments in information technology, corporate governance, legal requirements, and global best practices. For large corporations, the change process typically involves restructuring, expanding, and internationalizing the existing department, while smaller and medium-sized companies face the challenges associated with setting up such a department for the first time. For this reason, we have not produced this book with a specific audience or sector in mind. Rather, we have tried to present the idea of Internal Audit so comprehensively that readers can get from it the information they require for their particular situations.

The target audience of this handbook could not be more varied, and we hope that a large cross-section of managers and employees from Internal Audit, compliance, risk, and corporate management will benefit from reading it. Apart from the auditors themselves, this book should also appeal to those who have contact with Internal Audit within or outside their own company, with the aim of giving them insight into the tasks and responsibilities of this department. In this context, it is our particular concern to eradicate, once and for all, the outdated notion of internal auditors as controlling box checkers, not much loved by the rest of the company, and instead to present the highly varied, interesting, and increasingly international range of tasks of Internal Audit as a navigator in the company. Finally, we hope this book will make an important contribution to teaching (internal) auditing at universities.

The introductory information provided in Section A gives a comprehensive overview of the principles of internal auditing. It places audit work in the overall context and deals with organizational issues as well as the practice of audit and consulting work. Section B describes the Audit Roadmap, the process model of Internal Audit at SAP®. The chapters in Section C provide fictitious, practice-based examples of how Internal Audit at SAP AG deals with selected audit topics. Section D revisits some focus areas and special topics for a more detailed discussion.

The summarizing key points at the beginning of each chapter are to give readers a concise overview of the topics dealt with in the chapter. The same applies to the enclosed CD containing templates to put specific elements of theory into practice.

With the Hints and Tips at the end of most chapters we hope to provide useful impulses for practical audit work.

As mentioned earlier, this handbook is intended to satisfy a variety of users with different information requirements. Nevertheless, the information generally makes reference to examples from the organizational structure of SAP AG and its internal audit service provider GIAS (Global Internal Audit Services), although in specific cases we depart from company-specific names and structures to make the information more generally accessible. With regard to SAP-specific terminology and situations, e.g., the organizational position of Internal Audit under the CEO or reference to SAP AG's local subsidiaries, we ask readers to apply the information provided to their personal situations as required. This also holds for adjustments resulting from certain company forms and the application to other legal forms of information relating to the German *Aktiengesellschaft* (stock corporation).

This guide incorporates the latest status of discussion, although we have to bear in mind that the whole topic is subject to constant development. Some issues of the future have already been touched upon, but will require further development and consolidation. It remains to be seen how changes will shape the future of Internal Audit.

As the scale of work suggests, this book could not have been published without the dedicated efforts of a large team of people, who worked hard over the past few months to help this project succeed. We would like to say a special thank you to Margaret Christ, Penelope Sue Greenberg, and Bernhard Reichert for their dedication in revising and editing the English translation of this handbook, which first appeared in German as *Handbuch der Revision*. Thanks also to Ziggie Keil for translating the work into English. We would also like to acknowledge the original authors of the German edition: Corinna Boecker, Julia Busch, Petra Eckes, Oliver Bussiek, Markus Falk, and Manfred Wolf. We also wish to thank Christine Benner for her organizational work, for producing numerous graphics, and for looking after the CD design. A word of thanks also to Dorothee Brechtel and Adelheid Röben, who read and reread each chapter with tireless dedication, contributing to factual and linguistic quality assurance and making many valuable suggestions. We are also grateful to the following Internal Audit employees of SAP AG for their work on specific chapters: Julio M. Arevalo, Thorsten Caspari, Önder Güngör, Miang Ngee Lau, Christian Müller, Mark Scavillo, Maria Eliana Testolin, Zoltan Vagvoelgyi, and Kai Zobel. Other departments of SAP AG also gave us plentiful support by reading the text and providing critical feedback. Thanks also to the employees from Global Communications, Corporate Legal, Corporate Financial Reporting, Global Risk Management, Global Compliance, HR Business Partner, Project Management Office Finance & Administration, Corporate Controlling, Controlling, and Global Purchase Organization of SAP AG, and the Office of the CFO. We would like to thank Dr. Matthias Heiden for coordinating the reviews and for making many valuable suggestions. The staff of Springer-Verlag, especially Dr. Werner A. Müller and Ruth Milewski, deserve our thanks for the excellent and smooth cooperation.

We also wish to sincerely thank Trish Harris, Director of Communications at the Institute of Internal Auditors, for agreeing to write a preamble to this handbook.

We would be delighted if this new handbook enjoyed a positive reception in both corporate practice and at universities. We look forward to your critical feedback and suggestions for improvement, which we will incorporate in our next edition. Please e-mail any comments to audithandbook@sap.com.

Walldorf, Austin, and Saarbrücken, August 2007

Henning Kagermann
Karlheinz Küting
William Kinney
Claus-Peter Weber

Note to Users

This internal audit handbook has been written for different target audiences and therefore addresses different interest groups. It is comprised of five sections and includes a CD with examples and templates. Read in its entirety, the handbook is a complete guide to a modern internal audit department. However, depending on your personal knowledge and available time, you may prefer to approach the content selectively. To this end, each chapter starts with Key Points, which provide a concise overview of the topics discussed within the chapter. The Hints and Tips at the end of most chapters are to provide helpful suggestions for day-to-day audit-work. The following table shows the contents that each section of the guide covers and lists possible target groups.

Section	Contents	Target groups
A	General and specific topics	All interested parties, especially general managers, Boards of Directors, managers and specialized employees of Internal Audit
B	Description of the SAP® Audit Roadmap	Internal Audit managers and employees
C	Operational aspects of audit execution	Internal Audit employees and operational managers
D	Applied specialist knowledge	Audit employees and interested parties with a high level of professional knowledge or expertise
E	Conclusion	All

The included CD provides a visual depiction of the Audit Roadmap at SAP, which is dealt with extensively in Section B of the guide. The content of the CD is presented in two different modes. With the "View" function, you can display selected topics from Section B, including the different templates used. With the "Edit document" mode, users can complete templates by entering their own details and then save them to their own hard disks for subsequent use. For this reason, the CD is particularly valuable for practical audit work.

Finally, this handbook is intended for use by internal audit departments from around the world. However, when describing Internal Audit and corporate governance in general, we focus on U.S. rules and regulations. In addition, in the chapters that specifically address SAP practices, we refer to the two-tiered Board system which is standard in Germany. This two-tiered Board comprises an Executive Board, which consists of the managing directors, and a Supervisory Board, which consists of shareholder representatives and employee representatives. However, wherever it seems expedient we refer to either the "Board of Directors" or only the "Board".

Contents

List of Abbreviations

ABAP	Advanced Business Application Programming (the SAP® programming language)
AG	*Aktiengesellschaft* (legal form of a German stock corporation)
AICPA	American Institute of Certified Public Accountants
AktG	*Aktiengesetz* (German Stock Corporation Act)
ARB	Accounting Review Bulletin (US-GAAP)
AS	Auditing Standard
AUD	Australian Dollar
B2B	Business to business
BilReG	*Bilanzrechtsreformgesetz* (German Accounting Legislation Reform Act)
BSC	Balanced scorecard
CAE	Chief Audit Executive
CIA	Certified Internal Auditor
CD	Compact Disc
CEO	Chief Executive Officer
CFO	Chief Financial Officer
CHF	Swiss Francs
CIS	Contract Information System
COBIT®	Control Objectives for Information and related Technology
COSO	Committee of Sponsoring Organizations of the Treadway Commission
COSO ERM	COSO Enterprise Risk Management
COSO IC	COSO Internal Control
CPI	Continuous process improvement
DCGK	*Deutscher Corporate Governance Kodex* (German Corporate Governance Code)
DDIC	Data Dictionary
DSO	Days sales outstanding
DVD	Digital Versatile Disc
e.g.	for example
ed.	edition
eds.	editors
EITF	Emerging Issues Task Force (US-GAAP)
et al.	and others
etc.	et cetera
EUR	Euro
FU	Follow-up

GBP	British Pound
GCAF	Global Contract Approval Form
GIAS	Global Internal Audit Services (internal audit department at SAP AG)
G/L	General Ledger
HGB	*Handelsgesetzbuch* (German Commercial Code)
HIPAA	Health Insurance Portability and Accountability Act
HR	Human Resources
i.e.	that is
ICS	internal control system
ID	Identification
IFRS	International Financial Reporting Standard(s)
IIA®	Institute of Internal Auditors
IIR	*Deutsches Institut für Interne Revision* (German Institute for Internal Auditing)
Impl.	Implementation
ISACA	Information Systems Audit and Control Association
ISO	International Organization for Standardization
IT	Information Technology
J-Sox	Japanese Financial Instruments and Exchange Law
KonTraG	*Gesetz zur Kontrolle und Transparenz im Unternehmensbereich* (German Act on Control and Transparency in Business)
KPI	Key Performance Indicator
Mgmt	Management
MM	Materials Management
NDA	Non-disclosure agreement
No.	number
NYSE	New York Stock Exchange
PC	Personal Computer
PCAOB	Public Company Accounting Oversight Board
PO	Purchase Order
PR	Purchase Request
QAR	Quality assurance review
QG	Quality Gate
Ref.	Reference
RRA	Revenue Recognition Assurance
SAB	Staff Accounting Bulletin (US-GAAP)
SAF	Solution Addendum Form
SAP® AIS	SAP® Audit Information System
SC	Status check
SEC	Securities and Exchange Commission
SOP	Statement of Position
SOX	Sarbanes-Oxley Act

SRM	Supplier Relationship Management
TPA	Technical Practice Aids
TransPuG	*Transparenz- und Publizitätsgesetz* (German Transparency and Disclosure Act)
UK	United Kingdom
U.S.	United States (of America)
US-GAAP	United States Generally Accepted Accounting Principles
USD	US-Dollar
VAT	Value-added Tax
vs.	versus
WBOT	Workbench Organizer and Transport System
ZAR	South African Rand

List of Figures

A Conceptual Basis of Internal Audit

B The SAP®-Audit Roadmap as a Working Basis for Internal Audit

C Examples from Audit Practice at SAP

D Special Topics and Supplementary Discussion

A Conceptual Basis of Internal Audit

1 Nature and Content of Audits

1.1 General Definition of Audit

KEY POINTS

- During audits, an independent party compares the existing condition to predetermined criteria (such as US-GAAP, or the policies and procedures of the organization).
- Audits serve two important control functions. Firstly, they are detective control mechanisms by which auditors identify and investigate variances or deviations from predetermined standards. Secondly, they are used as preventive control mechnisms because the expectation of an audit should deter individuals from engaging in fraudulent financial reporting or making careless errors.
- In the course of their evaluation, auditors identify business risks and evaluate the effectiveness and efficiency of the control systems designed to avoid, reduce or eliminate those risks. Auditors should also be aware of the risk of fraudulent activities.
- The primary goal of auditing is to serve the company by providing an independent and objective evaluation of the organization's adherence to operational, financial and compliance policies, guidelines and regulations.
- Likewise, audits are performed to protect the interests of third parties, such as investors and creditors.

Auditing in General

In general, auditing is defined as a systematic process of objectively obtaining and evaluating evidence regarding the current condition of an entity, area, process, financial account or control and comparing it to predetermined, accepted criteria and communicating the results to the intended users. The criteria to which the current state is compared may be a legal or regulatory standard (such as the Sarbanes Oxley Act), or internally generated policies and procedures.

Internal Control

Internal control is defined as,
"*a process affected by an entity's Board of Directors, management or other personnel – designed to provide reasonable assurance regarding the achievement of objectives in the following categories:*
(1) reliability of financial reporting,
(2) effectiveness and efficiency of operations, and
(3) compliance with applicable laws and regulations" (COSO 1992).
Further, the Institute of Internal Auditors (IIA) defines control as, "any action taken by management to enhance the likelihood that established objectives and goals will be achieved" (Sawyer et al. 2003). Controls may be preventive (to deter undesirable events from occurring), detective (to detect and correct undesirable events which have occurred), or directive (to cause a desirable event to occur). A control system is the integrated composition of control components and activities that are used by an organization to achieve its objectives and goals.

Objectives of Audits

Audits are part of the overall control system of an organization and provide several important control functions. Firstly, they can serve as detective control mechanisms – that is, through their audit investigations, auditors may identify and evaluate errors or omissions, or variances between the current condition and predetermined criteria. Secondly, audits can be a preventive control mechanism, such that errors, misstatements and fraudulent activities do not occur in the first place. Finally, the results of audits should be used to identify and propose any potential improvements to the audited entity.

Audit Procedures

Audits entail comparing the current, existing condition of a process, organization, division or account to predetermined, accepted criteria. A variety of audit procedures may be used. Audit procedures are the activities that the auditor performs to obtain sufficient, competent evidence to ensure a reasonable basis for the audit opinion. Examples of some audit procedures available to auditors include: observation of personnel or procedures, physical examination of assets, inquiries or interviews with personnel, confirmation with outside parties, recomputation or recalculation of data, examination of documents, and analytical procedures.

Preserving the Interests of Third Parties

The final objective of audits is to preserve the interests of various third parties, including investors and creditors. In this regard, audits must comply with the standards of the third parties and any applicable regulations. For example, from an accounting perspective, audits of financial reporting must focus on the accuracy of the organization's financial statements and must be performed in accordance with the standards of the Public Company Accounting Oversight Board (PCAOB). Alternatively, audits of internal controls over financial reporting provide an assessment of the risks and controls relevant to the operations affecting the financial reporting process and financial data and should be based on a formal control framework, such as the COSO Internal Control Integrated Framework (see Section A, Chapter 1.2 and 1.3). Internal control assessments should also be performed in accordance with the guidance of the PCAOB.

LINKS AND REFERENCES ↗

- COMMITTEE OF SPONSORING ORGANIZATIONS OF THE TREADWAY COMMISSION (COSO). 1992. *Internal Control Integrated Framework.* New York, NY: AICPA.
- INSTITUTE OF INTERNAL AUDITORS. 2004. *Standards for the Professional Practice of Internal Auditing.* Altamonte Springs, FL: The Institute of Internal Auditors.
- KEITH, J. 2005. Killing the Spider. *Internal Auditor* (April 2005): 25–27.
- MESSIER, W. F. 2003. *Auditing and Assurance Services: A systematic approach.* 3rd ed. Boston, MA: McGraw-Hill.
- PUBLIC COMPANY ACCOUNTING OVERSIGHT BOARD (PCAOB). 2004. *Auditing Standard No. 2: An Audit of Internal Control Over Financial Reporting Performed in Conjunction With an Audit of Financial Statements.* http://www.pcaobus.org/Standards/Standards_and_ Related_Rules/Auditing_Standard_No.2.aspx (accessed May 31, 2007).
- RITTENBERG, L. E. AND B. J. SCHWEIGER. 2005. *Auditing: Concepts for a changing environment.* 5th ed. Boston, MA: Thompson.

- ROBERTSON, J. C. AND T. J. LOUWERS. 1999. *Auditing.* 9th ed. Boston, MA: Irwin/McGraw-Hill.
- SAWYER, L., M. DITTENHOFER, AND J. SCHEINER. 2003. *Sawyer's Internal Auditing.* 5th ed. Altamonte Springs, FL: The Institute of Internal Auditors.
- SEARS, B. 2002. *Internal Auditing Manual.* New York, NY: Warren, Gorham & Lamont.

1.2 Definition of Internal Audit

KEY POINTS

- Internal auditing is an independent, objective assurance and consulting activity designed to assess the effectiveness of the control environment, add value, and improve an organization's operations.
- In the past, Internal Audit was regarded as merely focused on financial and accounting matters, but today its role has developed to include active risk and control evaluations and is considered integral to the corporate governance process.
- The internal audit function is part of the internal monitoring system of the organization and therefore should be positioned within the organization such that the independence of internal auditors can be guaranteed. Ideally, Internal Audit should report functionally to the Audit Committee of the Board of Directors and administratively to the Chief Executive Officer (CEO) of the organization.
- Generally, an internal audit is a multi-step process aimed at determining whether existing processes and procedures (the condition) comply with applicable rules and regulations (the criteria) or deviate in any way from these criteria.
- The Committee of Sponsoring Organizations of the Treadway Commission (COSO) established the concepts and criteria that an internal audit function should follow in practical terms.

IIA Definition

The Institute of Internal Auditors (IIA), which is the international professional organization that oversees internal audit guidance, certification, education, and research, defines internal auditing as:

[…] an independent, objective assurance and consulting activity designed to add value and improve an organization's operations. It helps an organization accomplish its objectives by bringing a systematic, disciplined approach to evaluate and improve the effectiveness of risk management, control, and governance processes. (IIA Standards for the Professional Practice of Internal Auditing, Glossary)

Transformation of Internal Audit

The IIA's definition demonstrates the transformation that Internal Audit has undergone in recent years with regard to its role and how it is perceived. In the past, Internal Audit was regarded as a management support function that generally focused on financial and accounting matters. Now its role may include active risk management, which – along with traditional auditing – is an integral part of the corporate governance process. Internal Audit no longer focuses only on transactions that occurred in the past to determine whether control systems were effective. Today's internal auditors also look ahead to identify the potential risks that may adversely affect the organization and to evaluate the control mechanisms that will avert or minimize them. Moreover, the activities of internal auditors are no longer limited strictly to audit tasks; management consulting is now considered an important and expanding role for internal auditors. Thus, when internal auditors identify areas for improvement in the course of their regular audit work, they will also suggest recommendations as to how the organization can improve its operations.

Support for Corporate Management

Internal audits allow management to delegate its oversight function to the internal audit department. In larger companies management can not perform the oversight function itself for several reasons, including,

- growing complexity of the operating environment due to automated data processing,
- increased decentralization in physical location and decision-making as a result of globalization or internationalization, and
- its lack of expertise required to conduct efficient, high-quality audits.

Systematic Positioning of Internal Audit

Internal Audit is part of the internal monitoring system of an organization. This system comprises all monitoring measures and precautions put in place within the company to secure assets and guarantee the accuracy and reliability of the accounting system. This task is managed with objective-based and compliance-focused comparisons between the existing condition and the accepted criteria, as required by all applicable policies, regulations, and laws.

Internal Audit in the Context of Legal Requirements

In recent years, internal control has become increasingly important. This is evidenced in the numerous laws, regulations and standards that now require that organizations have an internal audit function or an internal control review. Several of the most influential requirements are described further in Section A, Chapter 1.3.

Internal Audit Process in General

Generally, an internal audit is a multi-step process aimed at determining whether existing processes and procedures (the condition) comply with predetermined rules and regulations (the criteria) or deviate in any way from this standard. Firstly, to perform an internal audit, the auditors must identify and understand the criteria to which the condition must be compared. Secondly, internal auditors collect evidence regarding the existing condition. Thirdly, Internal Auditors analyze and evaluate the evidence. Analysis and evaluation may include (among other activities):

- observation of processes and procedures,
- inquiry of key participants in the processes,
- comparison of current period information with prior year information,
- comparison of current information with budgets and forecasts,
- comparison of current activities with approved policies and procedures,
- sampling and testing the actual performance to the desired performance,
- utilizing computer assisted audit tools to review, compare and analyze large amounts of data.

Fourthly, based on this analysis and evaluation, Internal Auditors draw conclusions about the effectiveness of the control systems and the extent to which the current condition meets the required criteria. Finally, the results of the work and the conclusions drawn by the auditor are communicated to the relevant parties (audited units, management etc.) along with any necessary recommendations for improvement in the form of an audit report. It is management's responsibility to act upon the results of an auditor's evaluation.

Audit Team

An internal audit is generally conducted by a team of auditors (i.e., more than one auditor). As internal audits vary in size and content, the size of the internal audit teams working on each audit also fluctuate. One of the auditors acts as team lead who is responsible for planning and overseeing the audit, as well as communicating with the auditees, while other audit team members execute the audit activities (for the organization of audit teams, see Section A, Chapter 4.4).

Reporting

After the internal audit, the results and findings are reported to the Audit Committee, senior management, and the manager responsible for the audited unit. The results are also shared with the employees concerned. As necessary, other parties with interests in the audit may be informed of the results; these parties may include creditors, strategic partners and external auditors (for reporting on completed audits, see Section B, Chapter 5).

COSO

The Committee of Sponsoring Organizations of the Treadway Commission (COSO) has defined criteria for audits on which the work of Internal Audit should be based. COSO is "*a private-sector organization dedicated to improving the quality of financial reporting through business ethics, effective internal controls, and corporate governance*" (see www.coso.org).

Key COSO Internal Control Concepts

COSO provides criteria for establishing internal control and evaluating its effectiveness. Further, COSO defines key concepts that explain the purpose and performance of internal control as follows:

- *Internal control is a process. It is a means to an end, not an end in itself.*
- *Internal control is affected by people. It's not merely policy manuals and forms, but people at every level of an organization.*
- *Internal control can be expected to provide only reasonable assurance, not absolute assurance.*
- *Internal control is geared to the achievement of objectives in one or more separate but overlapping categories.* (www.coso.org/key.htm)

HINTS AND TIPS

- The internal audit function should remain independent from all other departments within the organization. This allows internal auditors to maintain objectivity as they perform their audit activities.
- Internal auditors should familiarize themselves with their organizational position within the company and when necessary, clearly communicate to their

auditees how they fit in the organization and what their primary service is to the organization.

- Internal Audit must meet the needs of the organization. Therefore, the organization's strategy, objectives, and structure must be understood before determining how Internal Audit will fit into it.

LINKS AND REFERENCES

- COMMITTEE OF SPONSORING ORGANIZATIONS OF THE TREADWAY COMMISSION (COSO). 1992. *Internal Control Integrated Framework.* New York, NY: AICPA.
- COMMITTEE OF SPONSORING ORGANIZATIONS OF THE TREADWAY COMMISSION (COSO). 2004. *Enterprise Risk Management Integrated Framework.* New York, NY: AICPA.
- INSTITUTE OF INTERNAL AUDITORS. 2004. *Standards for the Professional Practice of Internal Auditing.* Altamonte Springs, FL: The Institute of Internal Auditors.
- KEITH, J. 2005. Killing the Spider. *Internal Auditor* (April 2005): 25–27.
- MESSIER, W.F. 2003. *Auditing and Assurance Services: A Systematic Approach.* 3rd ed. Boston, MA: McGraw-Hill.
- REDDING, K., P. SOBEL, U. ANDERSON, et al. 2007. *Internal Assurance and Consulting Services.* Altamonte Springs, FL: The Institute of Internal Auditors.
- RITTENBERG, L. E. AND B. J. SCHWEIGER. 2005. *Auditing: Concepts for a Changing Environment.* 5th ed. Boston, MA: Thompson.
- ROBERTSON, J. C. AND T. J. LOUWERS. 1999. *Auditing.* 9th ed. Boston, MA: Irwin/McGraw-Hill.

1.3 Regulatory and Organizational Framework

KEY POINTS

- Internal audits are subject to a large number of regulatory and organizational requirements. Recent notable regulations and guidance have been developed in the US, Germany, UK, Canada, Japan, China, and Hong Kong.
- Independence of both internal and external auditors is more important than ever before. Therefore, Internal Audit should be an independent staff department.
- The internal audit function can either be centralized or decentralized based on the needs of the organization.

Overview

Audits are subject to a variety of regulatory and organizational conditions. Regulatory standards have undergone particularly rapid development in recent years as a result of several new legislative initiatives.

Regulatory Standards

A number of new regulations have been passed in recent years, which affect not only external auditing, but also the internal audit function. Many standards and legal requirements now address the internal audit process directly, or the internal control structure of organizations. For the internal audit function, the following laws, standards and guidance provide the most explicit directives (details regarding internal audit and internal control are provided below):

- United States:
  - Sarbanes Oxley Act of 2002 (SOX),
  - NYSE Listing Standards,
  - COSO Internal Control Integrated Framework,
  - COSO Enterprise Risk Management Integrated Framework,
  - COBIT® Control Objectives for Information and related Technology.
- Germany:
  - Act on Control and Transparency in Business (KonTraG),
  - German Corporate Governance Code (DCGK),
  - Transparency and Disclosure Act (TransPuG),
  - Accounting Legislation Reform Act (BilReG).
- United Kingdom: The Turnbull Report: Internal Control Requirements of the Combined Code.
- Canada: Canadian Securities Administration Rules.
- Japan: Financial Instruments and Exchange Law.
- China: Code of Corporate Governance.
- Hong Kong:
  - Rules Governing the Listing of Securities on the Stock Exchange of Hong Kong Limited,
  - Rules Governing the Listing of Securities on the Growth Enterprise Market of the Stock Exchange of Hong Kong Limited.

SOX

The Sarbanes-Oxley Act of 2002 (SOX) was enacted by the United States Congress in response to several major accounting scandals in 2001 and 2002. The explicit purpose of the Act is to "protect investors by improving the accuracy and reliability of corporate disclosures made pursuant to the securities laws" (US Congress 2002). The Act is applicable to all publicly registered companies listed on U.S. stock exchanges and under the jurisdiction of the U.S. Securities and Exchange Commission (SEC). This includes any foreign firm that is listed on a U.S. stock exchange. SOX has several sections, the most important to Internal Audit are section 302, requiring the CEO and CFO (Chief Financial Officer) to certify the validity of the financial statements, section 404, which requires that management assess and report on the effectiveness of the internal controls over financial reporting and that the independent external auditor attest to that assessment, and section 806, which protects employees, known as whistleblowers, who report fraudulent behavior (see Section A, Chapter 2.6 and Section D, Chapter 13).

NYSE Listing Standards

New York Stock Exchange (NYSE) Final Corporate Governance Rules require that all listed companies have an internal audit function to "provide management and the audit committee with ongoing assessments of the company's risk management processes and system of internal control" (NYSE 2003). Compliance with NYSE listing standards has been mandatory since November 2003.

COSO IC

The COSO Internal Control Integrated Framework (IC) was developed in 1992 to provide a model for evaluating internal controls and is recognized as the standard against which organizations should measure the effectiveness of their internal control systems. COSO defines internal control as:
A process, effected by an entity's board of directors, management and other personnel, designed to provide reasonable assurance regarding the achievement of objectives in the following three categories:
- *effectiveness and efficiency of operations,*
- *reliability of financial reporting,*
- *compliance with applicable laws and regulations (COSO 1992).*

COSO defines internal control as consisting of five interrelated components:
- control environment,
- risk assessment,
- control activities,
- information and communication, and
- monitoring.

COSO's broad definition of control marks a significant departure from the previously held notion that Internal Audit should be concerned only with retrospective audits of financial and accounting data. Instead, Internal Audit's responsibilities include internal controls over strategy and operating effectiveness and regulatory compliance, as well as reliability of financial reporting (COSO 1992). For more information on COSO IC and its relation to SOX see Section D, Chapter 14.1.2.

COSO ERM

More recently, in 2003, COSO released a framework for enterprise risk management (ERM) that encompasses and enhances COSO IC. COSO defines ERM as:
A process, effected by an entity's Board of Directors, management and other personnel, applied in strategy setting and across the enterprise, designed to identify potential events that may affect the entity, and manage risks to be within its risk appetite, to provide reasonable assurance regarding the achievement of entity objectives (COSO 2003).
An ongoing ERM approach helps management effectively deal with uncertainty and associated risk and opportunity throughout the organization, and therefore helps the organization achieve its objectives. The COSO ERM model is illustrated using a cube, which shows how the objectives, internal control components and organization levels are interrelated.

COSO ERM Cube

COSO ERM expands upon the objectives set forth in the IC framework and provides four categories for an organization's objectives:
- strategic,
- operations,

- reporting, and
- compliance.

Further, COSO ERM describes eight interrelated components that are integrated within the management process:

- internal environment,
- objective setting,
- event identification,
- risk assessment,
- risk response,
- control activities,
- information and communication, and
- monitoring.

COSO ERM clearly affects the entire organization at all levels: the entity as a whole, each division, all business units, and any subsidiaries (COSO 2004).

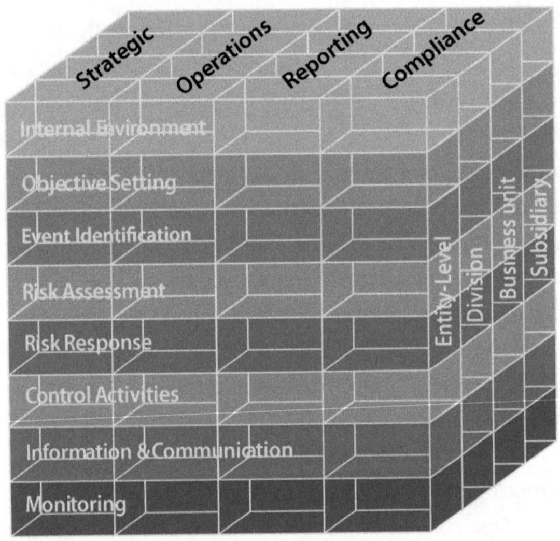

Fig. 1 COSO Cube (ERM)

Adapted from SOX-Online, http://www.sox-online.com/coso_cobit_coso_cube-new.html

Copyright © 2001 by the Committee of Sponsoring Organizations for the Treadway Commission

COBIT® The COBIT® (Control Objectives for Information and related Technology) framework is particularly useful in an organization with a strong information technology environment. The COBIT® framework was issued and is maintained by the Information Systems Audit and Control Association (ISACA). COBIT® supplements

COSO and SOX by focusing on the governance of IT resources and processes. It is especially helpful because it provides a framework and supporting tool set that bridges control requirements, technical issues and business risks (for more information on COBIT® see Section A, Chapter 6.2.5).

KonTraG (Germany)

The German Act on Control and Transparency in Business *(Gesetz zur Kontrolle und Transparenz im Unternehmensbereich – KonTraG)* was introduced in 1998 with the aim of eliminating potential weaknesses in the internal control systems in German public companies, including in the internal and external audit functions. This was achieved primarily be redefining the roles of Executive Board and Supervisory Board (which function in lieu of the Board of Directors in German corporations), as well as the role of the external auditors. The key stipulation requires the Executive Board to ensure that an adequate risk management system and an adequate internal audit function are in place. This law marks the first time that the internal audit function has been codified in German law, thus recognizing its place as an integral part of the financial reporting system.

German Corporate Governance Code (DCGK)

The German Corporate Governance Code (DCGK), which was established in 2005, does not refer to the internal audit function directly, but it does oblige the Supervisory Board of a company to set up an Audit Committee. This Committee is tasked primarily with issues of accounting and risk management including the budgeting and monitoring of the external auditors. The chairman of the Audit Committee "shall have specialist knowledge and experience in the application of accounting principles and internal control processes" (Government Commission German Corporate Governance Code 2006). This establishes the basis for cooperation between the Audit Committee and Internal Audit.

German Transparency and Disclosure Act (TransPuG)

As a result of the German Transparency and Disclosure Act (2002) the Standards of the German Corporate Governance Code have been incorporated into law. Thus Executive Boards of listed companies must confirm annually whether the company complies with the recommendations of the Commission of the German Corporate Governance Code and state which recommendations have not been implemented.

German Accounting Legislation Reform Act (BilReG)

The German Accounting Legislation Reform Act of 2004 *(BilReG – Bilanzrechtsreformgesetz)* has made a significant contribution to strengthening the independence of the external auditors. Specifically, sections 319 and 319a of the *Handelsgesetzbuch* (HGB - German Commercial Code) list a number of advisory services that the external auditors are not allowed to perform for a company if they audit the company. This concept can also be applied to Internal Audit. Here, too, the consulting function has gained importance in recent years and now forms an important part of Internal Audit's responsibilities. On the other hand, however, all internal audit work also must comply with the postulate of independence. If a close relationship between auditing and consulting is regarded as inappropriate for external auditors and is not permitted for this reason, it must be assumed that such a relationship could also damage Internal Audit's effectiveness if auditor independence is not guaranteed and conflicts of interest arise.

The Turnbull Report (UK)

In the United Kingdom the Turnbull Report (Internal Control Requirements of the Combined Code) requires that the Board of Directors "maintain a sound system of internal control to safeguard shareholders' investment and the company's assets." Annually, directors must conduct a review of the effectiveness of the internal control system, including all controls (financial, operational and compliance) and risk management, and must report this evaluation to shareholders. Further, companies without internal audit functions must periodically assess their need for such a function. In general, the Combined Code requires that listed companies disclose how they apply the principles in the code (including those related to internal controls) and confirm that they comply with the code or – where they do not comply – issue an explanation for that deviation. The Combined Code on Corporate Governance was originally issued in June of 1998 and revised in 2005 (Institute of Chartered Accountants in England and Wales 2005).

Rules of the Canadian Securities Administration

In 2004, the Canadian Securities Administrators developed rules to improve investor confidence. The rules require the development of an independent Audit Committee, that has a written charter and communicates directly with the internal audit function (Canadian Securities Administrators 2004).

Financial Instruments and Exchange Law (Japan)

In Japan, the Financial Instruments and Exchange Law, legislation similar to the U.S. Sarbanes Oxley Act, was developed in 2006. This law, nicknamed J-Sox, is effective for fiscal years beginning on or after April 2008. Standards developed by the Business Accounting Council of the Financial Services Agency require all listed companies in Japan to prepare and submit internal control reports based on management's evaluation of internal controls over financial reporting. J-Sox has a broader definition of financial reporting than US SOX, which includes other items disclosed in Securities Reports that use financial statement data. Further, company management must evaluate controls at any affiliates that are consolidated under the equity-method of accounting. Internal controls are to be evaluated using a formal control framework such as the J-Sox framework, which is based upon the COSO IC framework. Finally, the auditor must report on management's evaluation of internal controls.

Code of Corporate Governance for Listed Companies in China

The Code of Corporate Governance for Listed Companies in China was developed by the China Securities Regulatory Commission in 2001. The code requires that one third of the members of the Board of Directors be independent and suggests the (optional) appointment of an Audit Committee. The majority of the Audit Committee members must be independent and one member must be a financial expert. The principal responsibilities of the Audit Committee include overseeing the internal audit function (Chinese Securities Regulatory Commission 2001).

Rules Governing the Hong Kong Stock Exchanges

The Rules Governing the Listing of Securities on the Stock Exchange of Hong Kong Limited and the Rules Governing the Listing of Securities on the Growth Enterprise Market of the Stock Exchange of Hong Kong Limited were established to ensure investor confidence in the market. These rules require that listed companies establish an Audit Committee whose responsibilities include overseeing the financial reporting system and internal control procedures. For listed companies with an internal audit function, the Audit Committee must review and monitor Internal Audit's effectiveness and ensure it has sufficient resources. Further, the Audit Committee must report to shareholders about its review of internal control effectiveness annually (Hong Kong Exchange 2007).

IIA Standard 1100

IIA Standard 1100 clearly states that the organization's internal audit function must be independent, and internal auditors should be objective in performing their work. Independence is achieved through organizational status and objectivity and is a decisive factor in ensuring that internal auditors can perform their tasks in line with requirements. The Chief Audit Executive (CAE) should report to a level within the organization that allows Internal Audit to achieve independence. Ideally, the CAE should report functionally to the Audit Committee and administratively to the CEO of the organization. Further, the CAE should have direct and unrestricted communication with the Board of Directors and Audit Committee. Specifically, the CAE should regularly attend Board of Directors meetings and should have the opportunity to meet privately with the Audit Committee. Independence is strengthened when the CAE is appointed and terminated by the Board of Directors, not management.

Staff Department

To maintain independence, the internal audit function should be managed as a separate staff department without the authority to manage or direct employees of other units. This ensures that Internal Audit does not audit any processes or scenarios that it has been involved in creating. In addition, this organizational structure also enhances the standing of Internal Audit within the organization as all employees of the company accept and respect this department and the work it does. As an independent department, Internal Audit can evaluate operations and provide recommendations for improvement, but cannot implement them. Implementing Internal Audit's recommendations, as well as designing and implementing control solutions, is the responsibility of management.

Centralization vs. Decentralization of Internal Audit Services

Internal Audit must decide whether to establish a centralized or a decentralized internal audit function. This decision depends on the specific needs of the organization. Centralized internal audit services are managed and controlled by one Internal Audit management team with one audit plan for the entire function. The audit activities, tools and reporting methods are standardized for the entire function. A decentralized internal audit function may be organized into multiple divisions, each of which has the authority to develop individual audit plans, design differing audit techniques and division-specific reporting procedures. Alternatively, some organizations may use a hybrid internal audit department with characteristics of both centralized and decentralized internal audit functions. SAP's internal audit department for example is a centrally organized staff department with a decentralized, regional structure, i.e. with teams in Germany, the United States, Singapore, and Japan (see Section A, Chapter 4).

HINTS AND TIPS

- Before beginning internal audit activities, the auditors should be aware of any laws, regulations or applicable standards that relate to the specific audit objectives. For global organizations, this may include international guidance.

LINKS AND REFERENCES

- *Aktiengesetz (AktG) vom 6. September 1965 zuletzt geändert durch Artikel 13 des Gesetzes vom 5. Januar 2007.* http://bundesrecht.juris.de/bundesrecht/aktg/gesamt.pdf (accessed May 31, 2007).
- BUSINESS ACCOUNTING COUNCIL. 2007. *Standard for Implementation of Evaluation and Audit for Internal Control over Financial Reporting.* http://www.fsa.go.jp/en/news/2007/20070420.pdf (accessed May 31, 2007).
- CANADIAN SECURITIES ADMINISTRATORS. March 29, 2004. *New Rules Promote Investor Confidence, Change Issuers' Disclosure and Governance practices.* Press Release.
- CHINESE SECURITIES REGULATORY COMMISSION. 2001. *Code of Corporate Governance for Listed Companies in China.* http://www.ecgi.org/codes/documents/code_en.pdf (accessed May 31, 2007).
- COMMITTEE OF SPONSORING ORGANIZATIONS OF THE TREADWAY COMMISSION (COSO). 1992. *Internal Control Integrated Framework.* New York, NY: AICPA.
- COMMITTEE OF SPONSORING ORGANIZATIONS OF THE TREADWAY COMMISSION (COSO). 2004. *Enterprise Risk Management Integrated Framework.* New York, NY: AICPA.
- FINANCIAL SERVICES AGENCY. 2006. *New Legislative Framework for Investor Protection: Financial Instruments and Exchange Law.* http://www.fsa.go.jp/en/policy/fiel/20060621.pdf (accessed May 31, 2007).
- Gesetz zur Einführung internationaler Rechnungslegungsstandards und zur Sicherung der Qualität der Abschlussprüfung (Bilanzrechtsreformgesetz – BilReG) vom 4. Dezember 2004. *Bundesgesetzblatt* I 65 (9.12.2004): 3166–3182. http://www.bmj.bund.de/media/archive/834.pdf (accessed May 31, 2007).
- Gesetz zur Kontrolle und Transparenz im Unternehmensbereich (KonTraG) vom 27. April 1998. *Bundesgesetzblatt* I 24 (30.04.1998): 786–794. http://217.160.60.235/BGBL/bgbl1f/b198024f.pdf (accessed May 31, 2007).
- Gesetz zur weiteren Reform des Aktien- und Bilanzrechts, zur Transparenz und Publizität (Transparenz- und Publizitätsgesetz) vom 19. Juli 2002. *Bundesgesetzblatt* I 50 (25.07.2002): 2681–2687. http://217.160.60.235/BGBL/bgbl1f/bgbl102s2681.pdf (accessed May 31, 2007).
- GOVERNMENT COMMISSION GERMAN CORPORATE GOVERNANCE CODE. 2006. *German Corporate Governance Code as amended on June 12, 2006 (convenience translation).* http://www.corporate-governance-code.de/eng/download/E_CorGov_Endfassung_June_2006.pdf (accessed May 31, 2007).

- HONG KONG EXCHANGE. 2007. *Rules Governing the Listing of Securities on the Growth Enterprise Market of the Stock Exchange of Hong Kong Limited.* http://www.hkex.com.hk/rule/gemrule/GEM-App15%20(E).pdf (accessed May 31, 2007).
- INSTITUTE OF CHARTERED ACCOUNTANTS IN ENGLAND AND WALES. 2005. *Turnbull Report – Internal Control Guidance for Directors on the Combined Code.* London: The Institute of Chartered Accountants in England and Wales.
- INSTITUTE OF INTERNAL AUDITORS. 2007. *International Standards for the Professional Practice of Internal Auditing.* http://www.theiia.org/guidance/standards-and-practices/professional-practices-framework/standards/standards-for-the-professional-practice-of-internal-auditing (accessed May 31, 2007).
- INSTITUTE OF INTERNAL AUDITORS. 2002. *Practice Advisory 1100-1: Independence and Objectivity.* Altamonte Springs, FL: The Institute of Internal Auditors.
- NEW YORK STOCK EXCHANGE. 2003. *Final NYSE Corporate Governance Rules.* http://www.nyse.com/pdfs/finalcorpgovrules.pdf (accessed May 31, 2007).
- PROTIVITI. 2007. *J-Sox Flash Report – Japanese Guidelines for Interal Control Reporitng Finalized – Differences in Requirements Between the U.S. Sarbanes-Oxley Act and J-Sox.* http://www.protiviti.jp/downloads/flashreport/JSOX_Flash_Report0221E.pdf (accessed May 31, 2007).
- PUBLIC COMPANY ACCOUNTING OVERSIGHT BOARD (PCAOB). 2004. *Auditing Standard No. 2: An Audit of Internal Control Over Financial Reporting Performed in Conjunction With an Audit of Financial Statements.* http://www.pcaobus.org/Standards/Standards_and_ Related_Rules/Auditing_Standard_No.2.aspx (accessed May 31, 2007).
- PUBLIC COMPANY ACCOUNTING OVERSIGHT BOARD (PCAOB). 2005. *Staff Questions and Answers: Auditing Internal Control over Financial Reporting.* http://www.pcaob.org/standards/staff_questions_and_answers/2005/01-21.pdf (accessed May 31, 2007).
- REDDING, K., P. SOBEL, U. ANDERSON, M. HEAD, S. RAMAMOORTI, AND M. SALAMASIK. 2007. *Internal Assurance and Consulting Services.* Altamonte Springs, FL: The Institute of Internal Auditors.
- RITTENBERG, L. E. AND B. J. SCHWEIGER. 2005. *Auditing: Concepts for a changing environment.* 5th ed. Boston, MA: Thompson.
- SAWYER, L., M. DITTENHOFER, AND J. SCHEINER. 2003. *Sawyer's Internal Auditing.* 5th ed. Altamonte Springs, FL: The Institute of Internal Auditors.
- SEARS, B. 2002. *Internal Auditing Manual.* New York, NY: Warren, Gorham & Lamont.
- US CONGRESS. 2002. *Sarbanes-Oxley Act of 2002. 107th Congress of the United States of America. HR 3763.* Washington DC: Government Printing Office.

2 Internal Audit: Meeting Today's Needs

2.1 The Dynamics of the Operating Environment

KEY POINTS •••

- Internal Audit is influenced by a variety of factors, including regulatory and legal requirements, internal expectations, and competitors. Internal Audit can and must meet these factors with flexibility and in accordance with company objectives and the standards established by the professional institutes.
- The external environment and internal factors demand that internal audit functions are integrated within the business processes of the organization.

Global Orientation

To be a viable global competitor in today's business community, organizations must juggle constantly evolving operational processes, a multitude of varying legal requirements and regulations, and the increasing demands of international business relationships. While traditional business activities, such as delivering quality products and services, continue to be decisive prerequisites for business success, global market factors must also be carefully considered. Due to the complexity of the international environment, organizations face stringent time, resource and cost constraints that are more significant than ever before. Operating in a global market provides organizations with exciting opportunities and immense benefits. However, it also introduces risks that must be carefully managed.

International Requirements

To compete in the global marketplace, organizations must comply with rapidly evolving international business regulations, including financial reporting regulations, political, environmental, health and safety provisions, and human rights requirements, among many others. These international requirements are particularly important when organizations operate in multiple nations with different cultural norms, expectations, and behaviors. For example, there is increasing focus of legal standards on consistent, auditable figures. One such legal standard is the Sarbanes Oxley Act of 2002 (SOX) in the U.S. SOX requires that any organization listed on a U.S. Stock Exchange (regardless of its nationality) comply with strict rules which expose management and directors to unique challenges and risks as they oversee operations and reporting.

Internal Design Factors

In addition to the many external requirements that organizations must satisfy, internal factors, such as organizational design and complexity, impact the day-to-day activities of a company. The detailed organization and workflow structures of a company are influenced by its strategic objectives, the skill levels of its employees, the information and communication systems it uses, and the availability of resources necessary to meet its objectives. Further, as an organization grows and changes, the interpersonal dynamics will change as well, which can have a strong impact on its corporate culture and control environment.

Organizational Realignment

All of these factors impact the design of a company's business functions, either directly or indirectly. Moreover, the continuing evolution, expansion and realignment of the operating environment affect not only the productive business functions, but also all supporting units, such as the accounting and legal departments. Internal Audit must also adapt to the evolving goals and objectives of individual company divisions and/or the entire enterprise and must be able to recognize the new risks that emerge as the organization's goals change.

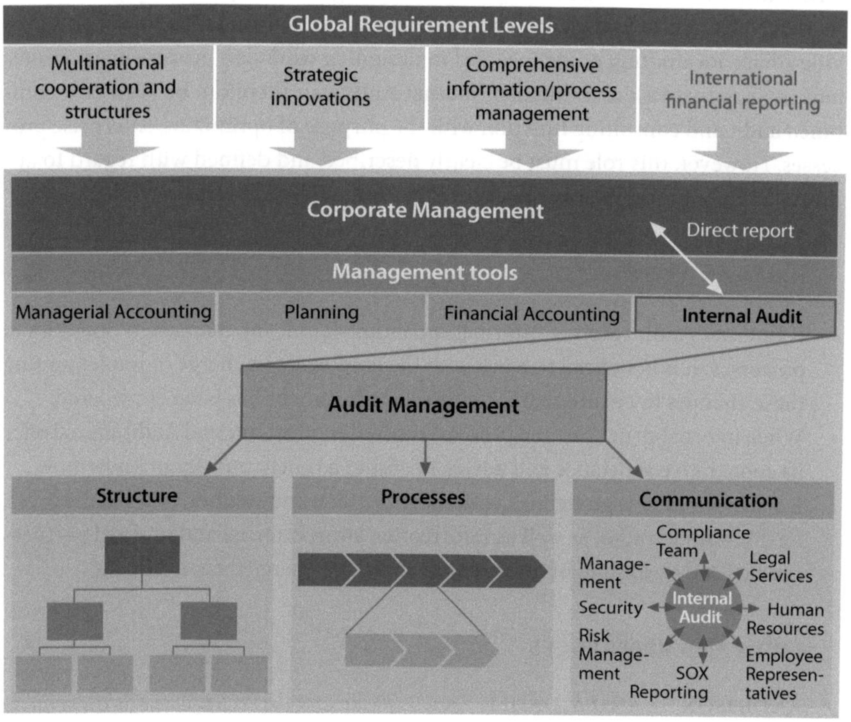

Fig. 2 Functional Position of Internal Audit

Taking Risk into Account

As the organization continues to evolve, managing business change processes becomes a necessary prerequisite for maintaining the enterprise as a going concern. This objective must be pursued with appropriate risk evaluation and mitigation, and the relevant internal controls must be defined. Specific steps in the business change process may include: extending the organizational structure to include new subsidiaries, lines of business or customer bases, adding new processes or changing the existing ones to better meet the strategic objectives of the organization, redeploying employees to new areas of responsibility, and even developing new, often global, guidelines and work instructions. Each of these activities must be rated with regard to its inherent risks before it is implemented. That is, the organization must consider the level of risk that exists within an activity in the absence of an internal control system. The result of this risk analysis forms the basis for implementing appropriate controls and analyzing their risk management effectiveness.

Role of Internal Audit

Internal Audit can provide support in each step of the change management process. Ultimately, the objective remains to evaluate and verify that operational processes comply with regulatory standards and organizational requirements and are performed efficiently and effectively. Additionally, Internal Audit can act as an internal advisor and optimization agent in every stage of enterprise change, thanks to its rich collection of knowledge and experience. Internal Audit can assist and provide advice for drafting guidelines and in designing work and process instructions, and can support risk assessments. Internal Audit can therefore be seen as a combined audit and consulting function with the purpose of optimizing enterprise processes. However, this role must be clearly described and defined with regard to audit requirements and interests to ensure that Internal Audit remains independent.

HINTS AND TIPS

- If Internal Audit receives information about significant changes to operational processes, it is beneficial to work with the employees in charge of implementing these changes to ensure that the control environment has been considered.
- When internal structures and processes are redesigned, Internal Audit should offer its cooperative assistance and advice to ensure a timely transfer of know-how.
- E-mails about new guidelines, articles in corporate magazines, news in the press, on TV, and on radio, as well as information from external and internal partners can be used as sources of information about the changed environment.

LINKS AND REFERENCES

- ANDERSON, U. AND A. DAHLE. 2006. *Implementing the Professional Practices Framework*. 2nd ed. Altamonte Springs, FL: The Institute of Internal Auditors.
- CASCARINO, R. AND S. VAN ESCH. 2005. *Internal Auditing: An Integrated Approach.* Lansdowne, SA: Juta and Co.
- COMMITTEE OF SPONSORING ORGANIZATIONS OF THE TREADWAY COMMISSION (COSO). 2003. *Enterprise Risk Management Framework.* New York, NY: AICPA.
- DELOACH, J. 2000. *Enterprise-wide Risk Management: Strategies for Linking Risk and Opportunity.* London: Financial Times Management.
- INSTITUTE OF INTERNAL AUDITORS. 2006. *Standards for Professional Practice*. Altamonte Springs, FL: The Institute of Internal Auditors.
- MOELLER, R. 2004. *Sarbanes-Oxley and the New Internal Auditing Rules.* Hoboken, NJ: Wiley & Sons.
- SAWYER, L., M. DITTENHOFER, AND J. SCHEINER. 2003. *Sawyer's Internal Auditing*. 5th ed. Altamonte Springs, FL: The Institute of Internal Auditors.
- SEARS, B. 2002. *Internal Auditing Manual.* New York, NY: Warren, Gorham & Lamont.

2.2 Reorientation of the Requirements Profile

KEY POINTS •••

- Due to the constantly changing business environment, Internal Audit is faced with rapidly evolving requirements, to which it must respond effectively.
- Major requirements include international orientation, a fully standardized audit method that captures the full complexity of business activities, and external demands such as new regulation and capital market requirements.

New Requirements

Traditional audits, such as evaluations of the accounting and the purchasing functions, will continue to be an important focus of Internal Audit. However, due to the constantly changing environment described in Section A, Chapter 2.1, Internal Audit also faces continuously evolving requirements and responsibilities, to which it must respond effectively. The following main requirements can be defined:

Global Organization

- It is necessary to have internationally standardized policies and procedures for internal audit services to guarantee globally uniform audit content and audit methods for the entire organization.

Legal Framework

- The inclusion of international accounting standards, especially the United States Generally Accepted Accounting Principles (US-GAAP) and the International Financial Reporting Standards (IFRS), as well as other legal provisions and guidelines, such as national and international corporate governance principles and SOX demand a high level of expertise in a variety of areas.

Complex Audit Topics

- An increasing degree of interaction between business processes requires an integrative design for audit procedures, ultimately involving all levels and areas of management and all enterprise units. Either individually or combined, performance indicators, basic principles, company policies, guidelines, organizational structures and processes, and individual business objects are areas to be audited by Internal Audit.

Internal Control Systems

- Corporate-wide and complex enterprise workflows require the establishment of comprehensive internal control systems, as well as their integration in the financial reporting cycle. Further, a risk management system must be established that is capable of identifying and addressing business risks, and of mitigating, managing, and monitoring them through those appropriate controls.

Networking

- Increasingly, internal and external information systems are networked resulting in greater interdependence between business activities. Mitigating the resulting risk potential requires comprehensive audit concepts for information technology. Auditing these areas involves analyzing both business and technical system details, and requires consideration of the different perspectives of all involved parties.

Best Practice Solutions

- Demands for "best practice" solutions require Internal Audit to expand beyond its traditional auditing activities into consulting and other services. This may include supporting measures that eliminate control weaknesses, as well as participating in follow-up processes (see Section B, Chapter 6).

Flexible Audit Assignments

- As organizations conduct business in a variety of international locations, it is increasingly common for internal auditors to perform audits outside of their home country. Such audits are not only challenging and difficult to complete due to inherent differences in culture, political environment, and business practices of different countries, but they also may require increased employee flexibility and motivation.

Flexible Audit Plans

- The areas or processes to be audited are selected based on the continuous assessment of risks and controls of varying business workflows. This means that spontaneous ad-hoc audits, intended to ensure business operations, are carried out alongside pre-planned, standard, periodic (usually annual) audits. Thus, to manage both employees' capabilities and the audit needs of the organization, flexible planning systems with easily adjustable parameters are essential.

Volume of Requirements

The increasing demands on Internal Audit require specific audit tools, which in turn are also subject to continuous adjustment and refinement with regard to their type, extent, and qualitative purpose. The following handbook is intended primarily to describe in detail the design and use of these audit tools.

Audit Tools

In general terms, the audit tools can be summarized as follows:

- A global organizational structure with centralized lines of reporting helps to ensure the fast, uniform, direct execution of audits along a standardized process model.
- An internally consistent process model will help guarantee the consistency of a globally standardized audit approach.
- Globally coordinated planning uses risk assessment techniques to involve all decision makers (to the extent necessary).
- Globally standardized audit content and work programs provide a cost-efficient foundation for audits, without limiting the possibility to adapt to individual requirements.
- The collaborative audit approach combines the internal audit function with other compliance functions within the organization, such as the risk management function and the internal control system (ICS).
- The formation of audit-specific teams allows the assignment of different numbers of auditors with different skill levels to specific tasks, depending on the size and complexity of the audit in question.
- A formal follow-up process allows the implementation of the recommendations made by Internal Audit to be monitored individually.

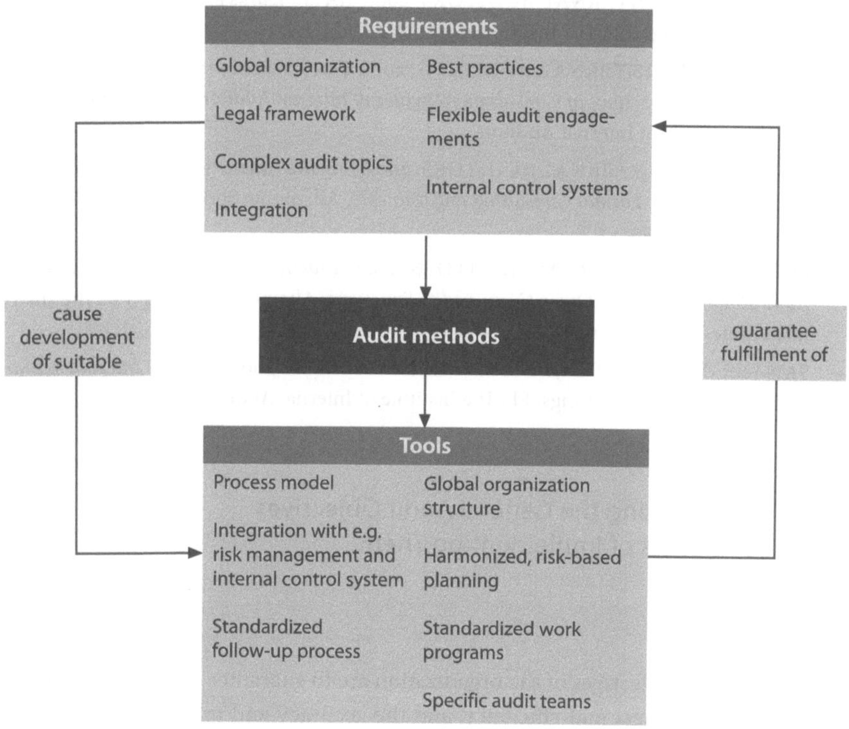

Fig. 3 Audit Requirements and Tools

HINTS AND TIPS

- Documenting a description of all individual audit areas and key risks is useful to ensure that all major influencing factors are taken into account.
- Effective, sufficient communication among all audit participants ensures that everyone has the same understanding of the influencing factors that must be considered.
- An external exchange of information, utilizing all available media, will help Internal Audit develop a complete picture of the existing environment.
- Internal Audit should review all major audit instruments periodically (e.g., through a peer review) to guarantee their consistency.

LINKS AND REFERENCES

- CASCARINO, R. AND S. VAN ESCH. 2005. *Internal Auditing: An Integrated Approach.* Lansdowne, SA: Juta.
- COMMITTEE OF SPONSORING ORGANIZATIONS OF THE TREADWAY COMMISSION (COSO). 2004. *Enterprise Risk Management Integrated Framework.* New York, NY: AICPA.

- INSTITUTE OF INTERNAL AUDITORS. 2006. *IIA Standards for Professional Practice.* Altamonte Springs, FL: The Institute of Internal Auditors.
- INSTITUTE OF INTERNAL AUDITORS. 2001. *Practice Advisory 1000.C1-1: Principles Guiding the Performance of Consulting Activities of Internal Auditors.* Altamonte Springs, FL: The Institute of Internal Auditors.
- INSTITUTE OF INTERNAL AUDITORS. 2002. *Practice Advisory 1000.C1-2: Additional Considerations for Formal Consulting Engagements.* Altamonte Springs, FL: The Institute of Internal Auditors.
- INSTITUTE OF INTERNAL AUDITORS. 2005. *Practice Advisory 1130.A1-2: Internal Audit Responsibility for Other (Non-Audit) Functions.* Altamonte Springs, FL: The Institute of Internal Auditors.
- SAWYER, L., M. DITTENHOFER, AND J. SCHEINER. 2003. *Sawyer's Internal Auditing.* 5th ed. Altamonte Springs, FL: The Institute of Internal Auditors.

2.3 Formulating the General Audit Objectives and Ways of Implementing Them

KEY POINTS •••

- The strategic objectives of the organization are to guarantee compliance, operational effectiveness and efficiency, and the accuracy and reliability of financial reporting.
- Internal Audit must align itself rigorously with these objectives by positioning itself accordingly within the organization and creating a basis for implementing the audit model.
- Information flows, high qualification requirements, the process model, and the audit universe are only a few of the instruments that can be used to meet these general objectives.

Foundation for Audit Mandate

Building on the basic, generally accepted, audit objectives of a globally oriented internal audit function, there are a variety of individual, task specific objectives that Internal Audit must address. However, this chapter will deal with the general objectives of Internal Audit – that is, those that are valid for all organizations. This focus is critical because the general objective framework provides the foundation for deriving the audit mandate, the audit principles, and the audit process model and related detailed work instructions, as well as identifying the task-specific objectives.

Main Strategic Objectives

Internal Audit's objectives and activities must be aligned with the strategic objectives of the organization. These three primary objectives of the organization, as defined in the COSO Internal Control Framework (see also Section A, Chapter 1.3 and Section D, Chapter 14.1.2), are to ensure:

- compliance with laws and regulations,

- reliability of financial reporting, and
- operational efficiency and profitability.

An additional objective, safeguarding of internal controls, may be subsumed under these organizational objectives – alternatively, some organizations consider it an independent objective. Generally, Internal Audit must organize its audit activities based on the principle that the purpose of all audit activities is ultimately to attain these main strategic objectives. Internal Audit and the organization should use risk-based monitoring to support the achievement of these objectives (see Section A, Chapter 6.3).

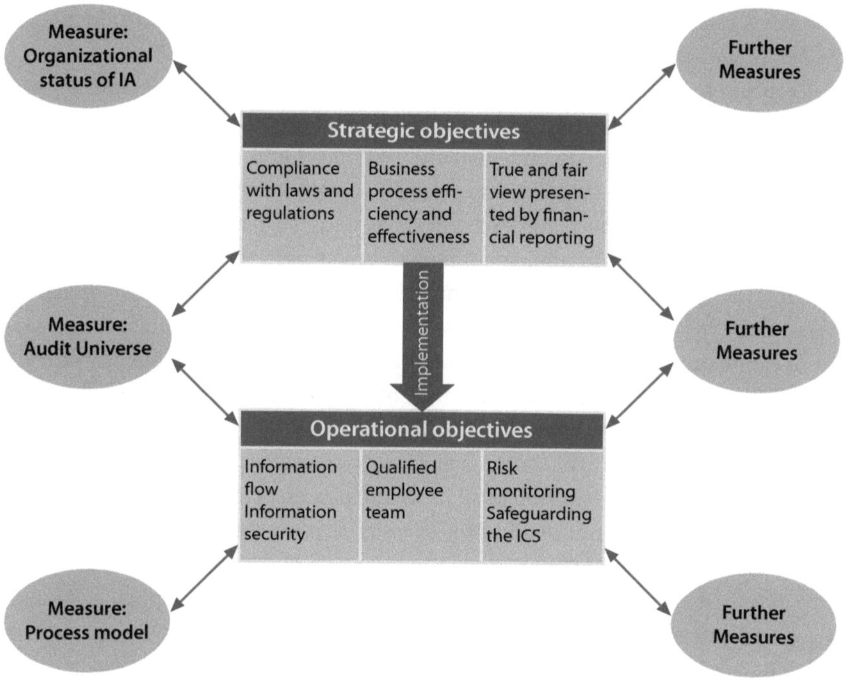

Fig. 4 Strategic and Operational Objectives

Compliance

Providing an independent assessment of business practices' compliance with applicable laws and regulations is one of the most important objectives of Internal Audit. This basic objective influences many task-specific objectives. Compliance requirements are driven by external legal and regulatory requirements, professional practices, contractual relationships with partners and customers and all internal guidelines, instructions, and process descriptions. The compliance objective is closely linked with the objective of ensuring accurate and reliable financial reporting, which also entails legal and regulatory requirements.

Accuracy and Reliability of Financial Reporting

The second strategic objective of the organization, and accordingly, of Internal Audit, is to evaluate the controls which are to ensure the accuracy and reliability of financial reporting. Legal and regulatory requirements mandate that all business and financial information be incorporated to produce a set of figures and disclosures investors and creditors can use to understand the current state of the organization. In the U.S., the Sarbanes-Oxley Act, in combination with the rules of the Public Company Accounting Oversight Board (PCAOB), further requires that all of the processes that affect the financial reporting of an organization be sufficiently controlled to ensure that financial reports are free from material misstatement and fairly present the financial condition of the organization. In this regard, the provisions of SOX have set a trend for the future. According to EU sources, similar guidelines can be expected for European companies following the introduction of the International Financial Reporting Standards (IFRS).

Operational Efficiency and Effectiveness

Ensuring operational efficiency and effectiveness is another important organizational objective. Processes that are essential to ensure the accuracy of financial reporting must be clearly documented and responsibilities must be defined. Internal Audit must ensure that the organization actually performs all essential processes. Internal Audit may also assist in developing and evaluating performance and profitability goals and implementing best practices in the organization. To this end, Internal Audit can perform benchmarking studies and identify best practices from other organizations and help assess the feasibility of implementation. Internal Audit cannot be responsible for implementing these best practices, but can provide this information to management who must make the decision of whether or not to implement new, improved processes.

Risk Monitoring

To ensure that the organization achieves its objectives, Internal Audit should engage in risk-based monitoring of all units and processes that are part of the audit universe, which is the sum of all business units or processes identified as possible audit areas. It is becoming increasingly important to ensure a risk-based audit approach is used, not least due to increasing legal and statutory requirements. For this reason, all phases of the audit process should identify and consider the risk factors of audit objects.

Safeguarding Internal Controls

Another objective closely associated with the risk-based approach is the evaluation of the organization's internal control system. Although this task is not new for Internal Audit, emerging legal requirements for effective control systems have increased its importance. All enterprise units and process flows should be subjected to the internal control system. As a result, the key performance indicators built into the internal control system provide ideal benchmarks for Internal Audit to use during their audit activities (see Section D, Chapter 7).

Information Flow

To meet all these objectives, certain organizational and qualification-related prerequisites must be fulfilled. For example, the internal audit function must be integrated in intra-company information flows without restriction. To ensure that defined objectives are achieved, the entire department must align itself with the respective audit requirements at an early stage. This applies to both the one-time communication of organizational or content-related developments and the permanent exchange of the audit content with complementary departments, such as Risk Management.

Information Security

The requirement for balanced information is extremely important for internal audit services. Audit results must be adequately communicated to the appropriate parties, including management. Accordingly, Internal Audit is part of an enterprise-wide management information system, which reinforces its role as a management tool (see Section A, Chapter 2.5.4).

Auditor Qualifications

Ultimately, the qualifications and flexibility of each auditor are key prerequisites for reaching the objectives described above. Auditors must demonstrate expertise and strong communication skills. Additionally, they must exhibit organizational flexibility and the ability to complete assigned tasks effectively and on time, in order to achieve their designated objectives.

Process Model

Moreover, a highly professional process model is also very important to guarantee consistent audits (see Section B for details). This model must satisfy all theoretical requirements of modern audit workflows in the form of a multilevel phase structure. Flexible reporting structures, an infinitely adaptable system of working papers (see Section B, Chapter 4.2), as well as other forms of documentation are only a few characteristics of decision-oriented audit models. Both the formal rules and individual customization options must be represented in each individual phase of the audit process.

Audit Universe

Another prerequisite for meeting strategic audit objectives is the definition of comprehensive audit topics and the audit universe. A detailed description (or Scope) must be created for each area identified within the audit universe (see Section B, Chapter 2.1). It consists of the specific processes, organizational objectives, guidelines, risks, internal controls and benchmarks for each audit area. By compiling this information, Internal Audit creates a uniform database for globally consistent audits.

Organizational Status

The organizational positioning of Internal Audit in proximity to the Board, as well as to the Audit Committee, creates the necessary independence required to perform the assigned tasks (see Section A, Chapter 1.3). Major characteristics of this relationship include clear lines of communication and opportunities for spontaneous, impartial exchanges between the parties. Regardless of who Internal Audit reports to administratively (e.g., the CEO), Internal Audit must have direct, unencumbered access to the Audit Committee.

Other Audit Objectives

In addition to the main audit-related objectives, Internal Audit can also pursue other operational, non-audit-related objectives. Involvement in internal projects, expert reviews of newly designed solutions, as well as the active initiation of solution steps, such as developing guidelines, illustrate the complexity of the task portfolio of internal audit services (see also Section A, Chapter 7).

LINKS AND REFERENCES ↗

- ANDERSON, U. AND A. DAHLE. 2006. *Implementing the Professional Practices Framework*. 2nd ed. Altamonte Springs, FL: The Institute of Internal Auditors.
- AUMANN, R. 2006. A Multipurpose Manual. *Internal Auditor*. (August 2006): 23–27.
- CASCARINO, R. AND S. VAN ESCH. 2005. *Internal Auditing: An integrated approach*. Lansdowne, SA: Juta and Co.
- COMMITTEE OF SPONSORING ORGANIZATIONS OF THE TREADWAY COMMISSION (COSO). 1992. *Internal Control Integrated Framework*. New York, NY: AICPA.
- COMMITTEE OF SPONSORING ORGANIZATIONS OF THE TREADWAY COMMISSION (COSO). 2004. *Enterprise Risk Management Integrated Framework*. New York, NY: AICPA.
- FRASER, J. AND H. LINDSAY. 2004. *Twenty questions directors should ask about internal audit*. Toronto, CA: National Library of Canada Cataloguing in Publication.
- INSTITUTE OF INTERNAL AUDITORS. 2001. *Practice Advisory 1000.C1-1: Principles Guiding the Performance of Consulting Activities of Internal Auditors*. Altamonte Springs, FL: The Institute of Internal Auditors.
- INSTITUTE OF INTERNAL AUDITORS. 2002. *Practice Advisory 1000.C1-2: Additional Considerations for Formal Consulting Engagements*. Altamonte Springs, FL: The Institute of Internal Auditors.
- INSTITUTE OF INTERNAL AUDITORS. 2002. *Practice Advisory 1110-2: Chief Audit Executive Reporting Lines*. Altamonte Springs, FL: The Institute of Internal Auditors.
- INSTITUTE OF INTERNAL AUDITORS. 2005. *Practice Advisory 1130.A1-2: Internal Audit Responsibility for Other (Non-Audit) Functions*. Altamonte Springs, FL: The Institute of Internal Auditors.
- INSTITUTE OF INTERNAL AUDITORS. 2001. *Practice Advisory 2330-2: Recording Information*. Altamonte Springs, FL: The Institute of Internal Auditors.
- NEW YORK STOCK EXCHANGE. 2003. *Final NYSE Corporate Governance Rules*. http://www.nyse.com/pdfs/finalcorpgovrules.pdf (accessed May 31, 2007).
- PRICEWATERHOUSECOOPERS. 2005. *Audit Committee Effectiveness – What works best*. 3rd ed. Altamonte Springs, FL: The Institute of Internal Auditors.
- PUBLIC COMPANY ACCOUNTING OVERSIGHT BOARD (PCAOB). 2004. *Auditing Standard No. 2: An Audit of Internal Control Over Financial Reporting Performed in Conjunction With an Audit of Financial Statements*. http://www.pcaobus.org/Standards/Standards_and_ Related_Rules/Auditing_Standard_No.2.aspx (accessed May 31, 2007).
- PUBLIC COMPANY ACCOUNTING OVERSIGHT BOARD (PCAOB). 2005. *Staff Questions and Answers: Auditing Internal Control over Financial Reporting*. http://www.pcaob.org/standards/staff_questions_and_answers/2005/01-21.pdf (accessed May 31, 2007).
- SAWYER, L., M. DITTENHOFER, AND J. SCHEINER. 2003. *Sawyer's Internal Auditing*. 5th ed. Altamonte Springs, FL: The Institute of Internal Auditors.
- SEARS, B. 2002. *Internal Auditing Manual*. New York, NY: Warren, Gorham & Lamont.

- SWANSON, D. 2006. The Internal Audit Function, from Step Zero. *Compliance Week.* (December 2006): 69.
- U.S. CONGRESS. 2002. *Sarbanes-Oxley Act of 2002. 107th Congress of the United States of America. HR 3763.* Washington DC: Government Printing Office.

2.4 The Charter as Audit Mandate

2.4.1 Purpose of the Charter

KEY POINTS •••

- The Internal Audit charter establishes the fundamental requirements defined by the Board of Directors and the Audit Committee.
- The charter provides the foundation for regular self-analysis of Internal Audit to determine the extent to which the declared objectives are met.

Audit Mandate

The requirements for Internal Audit are detailed in a clearly defined audit mandate from the Board of Directors and the Audit Committee. This mandate is laid down in the Internal Audit charter and reflects both general and company-specific expectations of these two bodies, which have a decisive influence on Internal Audit.

Charter

The purpose of the Internal Audit charter is to formally document the audit mandate and the powers it grants to carry out internal audit activities on behalf of the Board of Directors and the Audit Committee. The charter should be written in accordance with the IIA Standards for Professional Practice of Internal Auditing (hereafter IIA Standards). The charter defines the framework within which Internal Audit can act independently and should ensure that Internal Audit's responsibilities do not limit its objectivity. Furthermore, the charter should establish the functional and administrative reporting lines of Internal Audit and specify that Internal Audit has direct, unencumbered access to the Audit Committee. The Audit Committee should review and approve the charter annually and appropriate modifications to the charter should be made as the roles and responsibilities of Internal Audit evolve.

Annual Audit Plan

In addition, the charter serves as the foundation for the annual audit plan, which is coordinated with the Board of Directors and the Audit Committee (see Section B, Chapter 2.2). As necessary, the annual audit plan will be amended such that the plan addresses specific audit requests (see Section B, Chapter 2.3). The Audit Committee should review the planned activities of Internal Audit to ensure that they adequately address the risks faced by the organization.

Responsibilities of the Board of Directors

With a carefully developed audit mandate and charter, the Board of Directors can fulfill its responsibility for establishing an effective internal audit function and defining its duties. The Board of Directors must ensure that Internal Audit complies with the audit mandate and charter.

Standard Framework

Internal Audit's responsibility for fulfilling the audit mandate is particularly apparent in that the department carries out its audit activities using a standardized process, making its own activities verifiable as well. Any arbitrary or unjustified activity is prevented by this standardized process. Clearly organized structures and decision-making processes ensure that the audited units are evaluated according to a predefined process. Thus the charter represents a general link between the Board of Directors and Audit Committee, the auditee, and Internal Audit.

The Charter as a Benchmark

Accordingly, the charter should also be perceived as a benchmark providing an ongoing evaluation of audit activities. Regular comparison of the requirements postulated in the charter with the audit activities is absolutely essential to ensure that Internal Audit fulfills the responsibilities entrusted to it by the Board of Directors. As further expectations are raised among other parties and management levels, additional requirements for Internal Audit may arise at any time, and ultimately, may be added to the formal criteria of the charter.

HINTS AND TIPS

- Check the tasks formulated in the charter periodically, and revise them as necessary.
- To clarify the work of Internal Audit and the audits it performs, refer to the responsibilities and tasks defined in the charter.
- The charter is also suitable as a basis for discussion with external units, regarding the tasks and significance of Internal Audit today and in the future.
- If the tasks of Internal Audit are extended or changed, the charter should be used to formalize/codify the corresponding responsibilities. Revise the charter if necessary.

LINKS AND REFERENCES

- ANDERSON, U. AND A. DAHLE. 2006. *Implementing the Professional Practices Framework.* 2nd ed. Altamonte Springs, FL: The Institute of Internal Auditors.
- AUMANN, R. 2006. A Multipurpose Manual. *Internal Auditor.* (August 2006): 23–27.
- CASCARINO, R. AND S. VAN ESCH. 2005. *Internal Auditing: An integrated approach.* Lansdowne, SA: Juta and Co.
- COMMITTEE OF SPONSORING ORGANIZATIONS OF THE TREADWAY COMMISSION (COSO). 2003. *Enterprise Risk Management Framework.* New York, NY: AICPA.
- FRASER, J. AND H. LINDSAY. 2004. *Twenty questions directors should ask about internal audit.* Toronto, CA: National Library of Canada Cataloguing in Publication.
- HERMANSON, D. R. AND L. E. RITTENBERG. 2003. Internal audit and organizational governance. In: BAILEY JR., A. D., A. A. GRAMLING, AND S. RAMAMOORTI, EDS. 2003. *Research Opportunities in Internal Auditing.* Altamonte Springs, FL: The Institute of Internal Auditors.

- INSTITUTE OF INTERNAL AUDITORS. 2001. *Practice Advisory 1000-1: Internal Audit Charter.* Altamonte Springs, FL: The Institute of Internal Auditors.
- INSTITUTE OF INTERNAL AUDITORS. 2001. *Practice Advisory 1000.C1-1: Principles Guiding the Performance of Consulting Activities of Internal Auditors.* Altamonte Springs, FL: The Institute of Internal Auditors.
- INSTITUTE OF INTERNAL AUDITORS. 2002. *Practice Advisory 1000.C1-2: Additional Considerations for Formal Consulting Engagements.* Altamonte Springs, FL: The Institute of Internal Auditors.
- INSTITUTE OF INTERNAL AUDITORS. 2002. *Practice Advisory 1110-2: Chief Audit Executive Reporting Lines.* Altamonte Springs, FL: The Institute of Internal Auditors.
- INSTITUTE OF INTERNAL AUDITORS. 2005. *Practice Advisory 1130.A1-2: Internal Audit Responsibility for Other (Non-Audit) Functions.* Altamonte Springs, FL: The Institute of Internal Auditors.
- PRICEWATERHOUSECOOPERS. 2005. *Audit Committee Effectiveness – What works best.* 3rd ed. Altamonte Springs, FL: The Institute of Internal Auditors.
- SAWYER, L., M. DITTENHOFER, AND J. SCHEINER. 2003. *Sawyer's Internal Auditing.* 5th ed. Altamonte Springs, FL: The Institute of Internal Auditors.
- SWANSON, D. 2006. The internal audit function, from step zero. *Compliance Week.* (December 2006): 69.

2.4.2 Main Contents of the Charter

2.4.2.1 Tasks of Internal Audit at SAP

KEY POINTS •••

The major tasks of Internal Audit at SAP are:
- verifying compliance of business processes and financial reporting with policies, laws, and regulations,
- ensuring an integrated corporate governance approach throughout the organization,
- maintaining a clearly structured reporting system, including company-wide analyses, and
- providing support to optimize business processes and establish new guidelines.

SAP: The Company

Founded in 1972, today SAP is one of the world's leading providers of business software. Measured in terms of its market capitalization, the SAP Group, with its about 100 subsidiaries, is the world's third largest independent software provider. SAP employs more than 39,300 people at sales and development locations in more than 50 countries throughout Europe, the Middle East, Africa, the Americas, and Asia-Pacific. SAP is headquartered in Walldorf, Germany. Its core business is the provision of licenses for SAP software solutions. SAP also markets maintenance, consulting, and training services related to its software solutions. The company cooperates closely with its partners for developing and marketing its solutions portfolio.

SAP AG

SAP AG, a public company, is the parent company of the SAP Group (the Group) and has various roles within the consolidated group:

- It acts as a holding company for the Group.
- It owns most of the SAP software rights. SAP AG therefore primarily generates revenue from licensing fees, which its subsidiaries remit to SAP AG for any software and maintenance the subsidiaries sell to customers. It also directly or indirectly pays for the costs of software development in the Group.
- SAP AG employs most of the development, service, and support staff who work for the Group in Germany.
- In various countries, SAP AG executes software license agreements directly with customers.

Global Internal Audit Services

SAP AG, as a German stock corporation, has a two tiered Board of Directors, with an Executive Board, made up of managing directors, and a Supervisory Board, made up of shareholder representatives and employee representatives.The Supervisory Board oversees and appoints the members of the Executive Board and approves major business decisions. SAP's internal audit department, Global Internal Audit Services (GIAS), is a staff department of the Executive Board that operates throughout the SAP Group and reports directly to the CEO. GIAS is an integral management instrument in the pursuit and achievement of the Group's corporate goals. By providing independent evaluations of business activities and other consulting services, GIAS makes a substantial contribution to risk analysis and management for the entire SAP Group and to the development and monitoring of a functioning internal control system. GIAS is organized as a global department with teams located at various sites throughout the world (for more on the organizational structure of GIAS, see Section A, Chapter 4).

Structure of the Charter

SAP's Internal Audit charter defines GIAS' tasks, organization, and responsibilities. The charter is divided into the actual audit mandate, and further explanations of the organizational and informational arrangements of GIAS and is signed by the CEO and the Chairman of the Audit Committee. While the first part of the charter emphasizes the expectations of the signatories, the second part reflects the basic minimum requirements for meeting the objectives of Internal Audit.

Audits

At SAP, GIAS predominantly focuses on the tasks defined in the charter. In addition, tasks may be added or changed on a case-by-case basis due to SAP's dynamic internal processes, the evolving business environment, and new regulatory requirements such as SOX. This chapter refers to the different tasks only briefly; they are discussed in more detail later in the text. GIAS conducts both scheduled and adhoc audits involving the issues of finance, business processes, information technology, fraud, external business relationships, and management, in addition to more specialized topics. To maintain standards across these different audit fields, the Audit Roadmap, GIAS' standard process model for conducting audits, is to be followed at all times (see Section B, Chapter 1.1).

Corporate Governance

During its audits, GIAS cooperates with other departments in the implementation of corporate governance requirements, coordinating all the individual activities required to meet its objectives. GIAS' findings, in particular, may result in the need to define additional guidelines, policies and procedures or expand existing ones. GIAS regards it as its duty to initiate such documents and accompany their development as part of comprehensive corporate governance.

Compliance of Financial Reporting

In particular, GIAS investigates whether laws and regulations have been followed, including those relating to financial reporting requirements applicable to SAP. In this context, the primary goal is to ensure that all transactions that affect net income or equity are properly recorded and recognized according to US-GAAP which is SAP's primary accounting regime. Of course, all other business transactions are also subject to internal audits.

Risk Management System

GIAS is also responsible for auditing the risk management system at SAP. In Germany, the *Gesetz zur Kontrolle und Transparenz im Unternehmensbereich* (KonTraG – German Act on Control and Transparency in Business) sets specific requirements for risk management (see Section A, Chapter 1.3 for details). The first activity related to these duties is the implementation and application of the risk management system itself, which involves testing the extent to which the organizational prerequisites, personal responsibilities, and process-related activities and documents are available to record the risks in the company correctly and adequately. In addition, GIAS must report the risks identified in its findings to the responsible risk manager. A coordinated procedure is used to ensure that these risks are tracked and controlled jointly by GIAS and the relevant Risk Management employees (see Section D, Chapter 2.2 on cooperation with Risk Management).

Compliance with Code of Business Conduct

During their audits, GIAS also evaluates compliance with the SAP Code of Business Conduct for Executive Board members and employees. This evaluation involves both regular business transactions, such as the purchasing department's vendor relationships, and special activities such as sponsoring sporting events.

Audit Reporting System

GIAS' responsibilities also include the use of a differentiated audit reporting system to convey the main audit results to the responsible persons reliably and promptly (see Section B, Chapter 5). All recipients must be informed of the results of the audit work sufficiently and with the required degree of detail, using various reporting formats.

Consulting Tasks

If necessary, GIAS can also assist in designing new or modified business processes, functioning as either an additional or the sole consulting unit. However, GIAS must perform consulting activities in compliance with the IIA Standards (1000.C1-1) to ensure the preservation of independence and objectivity. In addition, GIAS can also assist with certain in-process issues, and act as a review partner (see Section A, Chapter 7).

Fraud Prevention and Investigation

Internal Audit must always be informed when there is clear evidence or justified suspicion of fraud. Such cases can involve facts that have already been proven or suspicions. It is up to GIAS to investigate and analyze the facts and to identify the persons involved by itself or together with the corporate legal department. It is, however, also possible to call in external support or ask other SAP departments for assistance in such cases (see Section D, Chapter 13). In accordance with the IIA Standards (1210.A2) and the Statement on Internal Auditing Standards No. 3, Internal Auditors may conduct or participate in fraud investigations in conjunction with lawyers, investigators, security personnel, and other internal or external specialists. Further, Internal Audit should assess the alleged fraud to determine if controls need to be implemented or enhanced, to design audit procedures to identify similar frauds in the future, and to maintain sufficient knowledge of fraud. To avoid the occurrence of fraud, Internal Audit should also examine and evaluate the adequacy of the organization's fraud prevention system, perform fraud risk assessments, assess the adequacy of communication systems and evaluate monitoring activities. GIAS, for example, performs preventive audits to reveal potential fraud cases or to identify risk constellations, which may lead to a potential misuse in the sense of fraudulent activity.

Exchange of Ideas

In addition, GIAS promotes and initiates a company-wide exchange of ideas for the ongoing development of successful methods and practices that the auditors observe within the framework of their activities. To this end, GIAS must catalog and communicate these best practices centrally. Enterprise-wide benchmarking with internal key figures, as well as key figures and records from other departments and audited units, promotes the exchange of empirical knowledge and therefore supports the ongoing optimization of business activities (see Section D, Chapter 7 on the Internal Audit performance measurement system).

HINTS AND TIPS

- Before the audit, the auditors must clarify whether the audit request needs to be amended or forwarded to another area of responsibility within the company.
- Auditors must be aware of the ultimate goal of the requested or planned audit activities and of the specified task area at all times.
- Auditors must consider who else may need to be involved in the planned audit. Internal Audit can work in conjunction with other internal divisions or consultants to effectively and efficiently execute audits.

LINKS AND REFERENCES

- ANDERSON, U. 2003. Assurance and Consulting Services. In: BAILEY JR., A. D., A. A. GRAMLING AND S. RAMAMOORTI, EDS. 2003. *Research Opportunities in Internal Auditing*. Altamonte Springs, FL: The Institute of Internal Auditors.
- ANDERSON, U. AND A. DAHLE. 2006. *Implementing the Professional Practices Framework*. 2nd ed. Altamonte Springs, FL: The Institute of Internal Auditors.
- CASCARINO, R. AND S. VAN ESCH. 2005. *Internal Auditing: An Integrated Approach*. Lansdowne, SA: Juta and Co.
- INSTITUTE OF INTERNAL AUDITORS. 2001. *Practice Advisory 1000-C1.1: Principles Guiding the Performance of Consulting Activities of Internal Auditors*. Altamonte Springs, FL: The Institute of Internal Auditors.

- INSTITUTE OF INTERNAL AUDITORS. 2006. *Practice Advisory 1210.A2-1: Auditor's Responsibilities Relating to Fraud Risk Assessment, Prevention and Detection.* Altamonte Springs, FL: The Institute of Internal Auditors.
- SAWYER, L., M. DITTENHOFER, AND J. SCHEINER. 2003. *Sawyer's Internal Auditing.* 5th ed. Altamonte Springs, FL: The Institute of Internal Auditors.
- SWANSON, D. 2006. The Internal Audit Function, from Step Zero. *Compliance Week.* (December 2006): 69.

2.4.2.2 Organizational Foundation

KEY POINTS •••

- The Internal Audit charter must identify the basic organizational framework, including documentation of the organizational structure, the audit organization, and the necessary communication processes.
- The objective of the regulations, which result from the actual audit mandate, is to achieve binding requirements by the Board of Directors and the Audit Committee for the establishment of an effective internal audit function.

Procedural Foundation

The Internal Audit charter should give an extended description of the actual audit mandate providing the procedural foundation for the audit activities performed by Internal Audit. The inclusion of this practical information in the charter accentuates the intention of the Board of Directors and Audit Committee to take account of the organizational requirements of Internal Audit and support the necessary measures.

Role of the Board of Directors

However, although the Board of Directors initiates the establishment of Internal Audit, it assigns all responsibilities for planning and activities directly to the department, and thus to the CAE. This individual is responsible for ensuring that both the organizational and process-related elements of Internal Audit are adequately established within the company.

Charter Parameters at SAP

In detail, the charter for Internal Audit at SAP defines the following parameters for functioning internal audit services:

Organizational Structure

- The description of the organizational structure of GIAS includes the structure of the department itself, its position within the organization and the responsibilities of its employees. Because of GIAS's close relationship with the Executive Board (the members of which are comparable to the managing members of the Board of Directors), it should become clear to everyone in the organization that GIAS is a global, centrally managed department. Additionally, the increasing importance of GIAS' role will result in considerable authority for SAP's regional audit teams. This decentralization of organization and responsibility as well as company-wide process standardization are of highest priority to the Executive Board.

Staff Structure

- From the Executive Board's perspective, this form of organization clarifies the responsibilities of the CAE, thus clearly delegating responsibility for the execution of audit activities to the CAE. The Internal Audit charter provides the necessary authority for this delegation. A qualified staff structure must be defined to implement the individual measures, with the different positions staffed by individuals with distinct levels of expertise and experience. However, it is possible to establish main tasks and competencies for all auditors, regardless of their individual experience (see Section A, Chapter 4.5). These areas are also specified in the charter as a type of extended prerequisite for successful audit work.

Audit Procedures

- Details of the organization of audit work are described in the formal audit procedures, the general requirements for the actual fieldwork, and procedures for reporting audit results. Based on the charter, this organization provides a framework which ensures that the audits are well planned, skillfully executed and well organized so they can withstand quality assurance reviews at any time.

Coordination Process

- The varied nature and complexity of the tasks at hand requires a large measure of both inter- and intradepartmental communication. The internal coordination processes serve primarily to ensure the smooth flow of the audits themselves and the conceptual evolution of Internal Audit. GIAS's global organization, with its various teams, demands an adequate communication system, which is documented in the charter as a requirement for GIAS.

Cooperation

- The regular cross-departmental communication processes consist mainly of cooperation between GIAS and the Executive Board, the Audit Committee, Risk Management, the external auditors, and other external institutions, such as the IIA. From the Executive Board's perspective, these relationships are a decisive element for an effective internal audit function. As a result, the charter accordingly establishes these communication channels and relationships as an extended organizational requirement or attribute.

Framework

The framework for Internal Audit at SAP described above elucidates the Executive Board's demands for the implementation of an effective internal audit function. Based on the documented requirements and specific interrelations, the Executive Board can discharge its responsibilities by referring to the above framework parameters.

HINTS AND TIPS

- When in doubt, auditors should compare each audit request with the contents of the charter.
- The charter should be used as a basis for dispute resolution.

LINKS AND REFERENCES

- ANDERSON, U. AND A. DAHLE. 2006. *Implementing the Professional Practices Framework*. 2nd ed. Altamonte Springs, FL: The Institute of Internal Auditors.

- CASCARINO, R. AND S. VAN ESCH. 2005. *Internal Auditing: An integrated approach.* Lansdowne, SA: Juta and Co.
- HERMANSON, D. R. AND L. E. RITTENBERG. 2003. Internal audit and organizational governance. In: BAILEY JR., A. D., A. A. GRAMLING AND S. RAMAMOORTI, EDS. 2003. *Research Opportunities in Internal Auditing.* Altamonte Springs, FL: The Institute of Internal Auditors.
- INSTITUTE OF INTERNAL AUDITORS. 2001. *Practice Advisory 1000-1: Internal Audit Charter.* Altamonte Springs, FL: The Institute of Internal Auditors.
- PRAWITT, D. 2003. Managing the Internal Audit Function. In: BAILEY JR., A. D., A. A. GRAMLING AND S. RAMAMOORTI, EDS. 2003. *Research Opportunities in Internal Auditing.* Altamonte Springs, FL: The Institute of Internal Auditors.
- PRICEWATERHOUSECOOPERS. 2005. *Audit Committee Effectiveness – What works best.* 3rd ed. Altamonte Springs, FL: The Institute of Internal Auditors.
- SAWYER, L., M. DITTENHOFER, AND J. SCHEINER. 2003. *Sawyer's Internal Auditing.* 5th ed. Altamonte Springs, FL: The Institute of Internal Auditors.
- SWANSON, D. 2006. The internal audit function, from step zero. *Compliance Week.* (December 2006): 69.

2.4.3 The Charter as Part of Internal Audit's Definition Process

KEY POINTS •••

- To ensure that Internal Audit is up to date, a clearly structured process for defining the purpose, authority, and responsibility of the function is necessary.
- It is essential that all steps of this definition process are subject to regular evaluation and are amended as appropriate.
- Because of the rapidly changing environment, Internal Audit must recognize any potential change as soon as possible so that it is promptly translated into appropriate audit activities.

Definition Process

The information provided in the previous chapters shows that the process of defining the purpose, authority, and responsibility of Internal Audit follows a logically organized structure. First, the major objectives for internal auditing services can be derived from the objectives of the organization described above (see Section A, Chapter 2.3). Internal Audit then develops an audit universe covering all risks affecting the organization. This process step must include all expectations, both internal and external. This audit universe provides the frame of reference for formulating the basic audit activities. With these audit activities, Internal Audit achieves the requirements of the audit mandate, and the charter. As the risks facing the organization are continuously evolving, Internal Audit must regularly evaluate whether the specified requirements, identified audit areas, and defined goals and tasks still correspond to the relevant risks (see Section D, Chapter 2.2).

Dynamic Definition Process

The definition process for Internal Audit proves to be dynamic in nature, which must be carefully considered. Adherence to outdated audit goals and tasks will not only harm the efficiency of the audit work, but may also demotivate Internal Audit staff and auditees. Clear and consistent communication is particularly important for maintaining the necessary flexibility. Exchange of information, meetings, presentations, and publications will help all those involved develop an increased appreciation for evolving audit activities.

Structure of the Definition Process

The clear structure of the definition process will provide an end-to-end ordinal framework for both the establishment and the further development of the audit model. Although the details of the definition process are company-specific, the following general rules apply:

- All external influencing factors, such as international financial reporting and process standards, as well as business-law and labor-related policies, must be analyzed regularly and the audit process must be adapted as necessary.
- The catalog of internal and external requirements (e.g., organizational policies and regulatory requirements, respectively) must be evaluated for completeness and, when necessary, extended with international and/or company-specific components (for example, in the case of major reorganizations or acquisitions).
- The strategic, operational, reporting, and compliance objectives of the organization must be carefully considered to ensure that Internal Audit's aims are sufficient to facilitate the attainment of these organizational goals.
- The basic objectives of Internal Audit must be examined critically both with regard to changed or new requirements and externally defined guidelines and standards (e.g, from the Institute of Internal Auditors).
- The charter must be updated regularly.
- All basic operational audit elements, such as organizational/staff structures, audit execution and communication, must be examined critically and adapted if necessary.

Critical Analysis

Taken together, these measures will result in a critical analysis of the charter at least every two years. New requirements from the Board of Directors can be integrated concurrently with this analysis. Further, during the analysis and revalidation of the charter, the CAE, Board of Directors, and Audit Committee can assess the need for additional resources for audit and consulting services. This cyclical definition process is essential to Internal Audit and its work, to ensure that ongoing changes in the framework conditions are ultimately reflected in the audits as well.

HINTS AND TIPS

- Analyze and document changes to legal and internal regulations immediately with regard to their effects on audit content.
- The definition process must be understood as a whole, (i.e., examinations and changes must always be considered as a single step) because the audit assumptions may otherwise be incomplete, outdated or obsolete.

LINKS AND REFERENCES

- ANDERSON, U. AND A. DAHLE. 2006. *Implementing the Professional Practices Framework.* 2nd ed. Altamonte Springs, FL: The Institute of Internal Auditors.
- AUMANN, R. A. 2006. Multipurpose Manual. *Internal Auditor* (63:4): 23–27.
- CASCARINO, R. AND S. VAN ESCH. 2005. *Internal Auditing: An Integrated Approach.* Lansdowne, SA: Juta and Co.
- HERMANSON, D. R. AND L. E. RITTENBERG. 2003. Internal audit and organizational governance. In: BAILEY JR., A. D., A. A. GRAMLING AND S. RAMAMOORTI, EDS. 2003. *Research Opportunities in Internal Auditing.* Altamonte Springs, FL: The Institute of Internal Auditors.
- INSTITUTE OF INTERNAL AUDITORS. 2001. *Practice Advisory 1000-1: Internal Audit Charter.* Altamonte Springs, FL: The Institute of Internal Auditors.
- INSTITUTE OF INTERNAL AUDITORS. 2001. *Practice Advisory 2010-2: Linking the Audit Plan to Risks and Exposures.* Altamonte Springs, FL: The Institute of Internal Auditors.
- PRICEWATERHOUSECOOPERS. 2005. *Audit Committee Effectiveness – What works best.* 3rd ed. Altamonte Springs, FL: The Institute of Internal Auditors.
- SAWYER, L., M. DITTENHOFER, AND J. SCHEINER. 2003. *Sawyer's Internal Auditing.* 5th ed. Altamonte Springs, FL: The Institute of Internal Auditors.
- SWANSON, D. 2006. The internal audit function, from step zero. *Compliance Week.* (December 2006): 69.

2.5 Implementing the Audit Mandate

2.5.1 Internal Audit as an Independent Audit Body for the Whole Company

KEY POINTS

- Internal Audit must carry out standardized audits globally and independently. Organizational standards and procedures for doing so must be developed.
- Other measures are also needed to properly establish an internal audit function that is active throughout the organization. Internal cost/benefit analyses and the general positioning of Internal Audit within the company should also be documented.
- Internal Audit must be able to work independently and objectively. One prerequisite for independence is an appropriate organizational position within the company.

Core Competencies of Internal Audit

The contents of Internal Audit's mandate described in Section A, Chapter 2.4.2.1 must be implemented appropriately. In doing so, Internal Audit can consider different approaches and points of view. We will first examine the "core business" of conducting audits. To guarantee Internal Audit's independence in terms of form and content, a number of procedures and organizational guidelines must be defined in detail. From the Board of Directors' perspective, the following main aspects must be addressed:

- The organizational structure of Internal Audit. This may be defined by function, region/country, line of business, etc.
- Internal Audit's position within the organization, such that the department is able to maintain independence and the auditors are able to carry out their responsibilities objectively. Ideally, this includes reporting administratively to the CEO and functionally to the Audit Committee.
- The definition of the entire audit process, including all internal standards and quality assurance actions.
- Description of all relevant audit fields (e.g. operational audits, financial audits) and the areas within the audit fields.
- Definition of all reporting paths and the content of audit reports.
- Scenarios for extraordinary audit requirements or activities.
- Liaison with other internal and external compliance units, such as risk management and external auditors.

Appreciation within the Organization

Another important responsibility is to boost awareness of and appreciation for Internal Audit throughout the organization. A dialogue should be initiated that emphasizes the advantages of establishing an internal audit department and the benefits derived from such a department and that explains the existing needs and legal requirements for internal audit services. This can take place through information events, internal mailings and memos, audit surveys, and a presence on the company intranet and will help avoid the impression that Internal Audit is merely an end in itself and does not add value to the organization. Indeed, this discussion should focus on Internal Audit's role in the protection and advancement of the organization.

Liaison to External Auditors

The role of protecting the company has gained new importance since the enactment of SOX in the U.S. Internal Audit is a most likely liaison between the independent external auditors and the company in regard to compliance with internal control system requirements. Internal auditors play a crucial role in ensuring the accuracy of the financial reporting system.

Maintaining Independence

It is essential that Internal Audit remain independent. Internal Audit must be enabled to work independently and free from pressure to ensure it can meet its objectives, including assisting the work of the external auditor. IIA Standard 1100 clearly states that the internal auditing activities of an organization must be independent. Independence, which refers to the audit function itself, is necessary to ensure that the internal auditors can be objective. Individual internal auditors are considered objective when they have an "impartial, unbiased attitude and avoid conflicts of interest" (IIA Standard 1120). To be independent, the internal audit function must be appropriately positioned within the company. The IIA Standards do not specifically provide appropriate reporting structures; rather, each organization must make this determination itself. However, at a minimum, the Chief Audit Executive (CAE) should report to an individual in the organization with sufficient authority to promote independence and ensure broad audit coverage, adequate consideration of engagement communications and that appropriate action is taken on engagement recommendations. Ideally, the CAE should report functionally to the Audit Committee, Board of Directors or other appropriate governing authority and administratively to the Chief Executive Officer of the organization. The internal audit department needs sufficient resources to meet its objectives.

Management Consulting Function

With regard to audit findings and recommendations, Internal Audit can provide a management consulting function, which goes beyond providing assurance. When providing consulting services to operational management, audit results that require fast and efficient implementation must be considered. Sometimes it may be necessary to familiarize the manager in charge with the appropriate implementation options.

Operational Support

When the recommendations are implemented, operational details must be identified, organized and certainty must be reached that the recommendations are in line with existing or newly created guidelines. At this stage, Internal Audit often has the role of providing ongoing support, either by sharing its knowledge and experience, or by acting as discussion partner who can assess and optimize suggested solutions.

Internal Audit's Dual Role

Ultimately, Internal Audit performs a dual role. It must exist as a part of the organization, yet not belonging to that organization in an actual operational sense. Despite its independence, Internal Audit is and will remain a part of the company. This applies to both purely technical aspects and personal relationships with employees from other areas. Ultimately, Internal Audit must communicate an image that corresponds to this dual role: auditing with the goal of achieving a win-win situation for everyone concerned. Accordingly, an audit mandate from the Board of Directors is always associated with the challenge of conducting audits by mutual consent, to boost the trust of all involved. It must be clear that Internal Audit does not conduct audits to criticize, but instead to bring about constructive and forward-looking improvements.

Self-Image

This results in a new self-image for Internal Audit. Complex circumstances demanding a high degree of specialized knowledge and highly qualified staff on the one side, and increasingly public demonstrations of responsibility by corporate management on the other, will give Internal Audit a balanced position between the various parties. To achieve this, Internal Audit must have clear principles, distinct processes, and a transparent task spectrum. With this foundation, it will be able to meet the increasing pressure of pursuing its independent audit mandate, while taking differing interests into account.

HINTS AND TIPS

- Internal Audit should consider how other employees perceive the current and future role of compliance, corporate governance, etc. and compare it to how the department presents itself.
- Internal auditors should share ideas for improving audit methods with Internal Audit management.

LINKS AND REFERENCES

- ANDERSON, U. AND A. DAHLE. 2006. *Implementing the Professional Practices Framework*. 2nd ed. Altamonte Springs, FL: The Institute of Internal Auditors.
- CASCARINO, R. AND S. VAN ESCH. 2005. *Internal Auditing: An integrated approach.* Lansdowne, SA: Juta and Co.
- CHAPMAN, C. 2001. Raising the Bar. *Internal Auditor* (April 2001): 55–59.
- HUGHES, P. 2004. Why Internal Auditors Audit. *The CPA Journal* (February 2004): 15.
- INSTITUTE OF INTERNAL AUDITORS. 1997. Internal Audit Independence. *Journal of Accountancy* (January 1997): 8.
- INSTITUTE OF INTERNAL AUDITORS. 2001. *Practice Advisory 1000-1: Internal Audit Charter.* Altamonte Springs, FL: The Institute of Internal Auditors.
- INSTITUTE OF INTERNAL AUDITORS. 2001. *Practice Advisory 1000.C1-1: Principles Guiding the Performance of Consulting Activities of Internal Auditors.* Altamonte Springs, FL: The Institute of Internal Auditors.
- INSTITUTE OF INTERNAL AUDITORS. 2002. *Practice Advisory 1000.C1-2: Additional Considerations for Formal Consulting Engagements.* Altamonte Springs, FL: The Institute of Internal Auditors.
- INSTITUTE OF INTERNAL AUDITORS. 2005. *Practice Advisory 1130.A1-2: Internal Audit Responsibility for Other (Non-Audit) Functions.* Altamonte Springs, FL: The Institute of Internal Auditors.
- MUTCHLER, J., S. CHANG AND D. PRAWITT. 2001. *Independence and Objectivity: A Framework for Internal Auditors.* Altamonte Springs, FL: The Institute of Internal Auditors.
- SAWYER, L., M. DITTENHOFER, AND J. SCHEINER. 2003. *Sawyer's Internal Auditing.* 5th ed. Altamonte Springs, FL: The Institute of Internal Auditors.

2.5.2 Internal Audit as a Component of Corporate Governance

KEY POINTS

- Internal Audit supports compliance within the corporate governance framework in two significant ways. First, Internal Audit is an integral component of the business monitoring system. Second, its fieldwork results in a wide variety of information that can be used to ensure and improve the awareness of and adherence to compliance requirements.
- Internal Audit's responsibilities include the examination of financial reporting and process controls, case-specific individual audits (especially in case of suspected loss to the company or based on a specific request from the Board of Directors), the initiation of guidelines and work instructions, and close cooperation with Risk Management, the external auditors, and – if necessary – the Audit Committee.

Corporate Governance

In recent years, the increasing discussion about corporate governance has had a variety of effects on corporate institutions and management. The impacts range from the creation of new corporate units, such as Risk Management, to modifications of existing functions. The global orientation of companies often goes hand-in-hand with increased notice by the general public. If a company is represented in international markets, the internal and external ethical demands on the company and on its managers should not be underestimated. In this context, a discussion of possible liability of the people responsible is inevitable.

Information Provided by Internal Audit

As a result, the importance of compliant financial reporting and process flows, internal control and risk management systems, and even business functions such as management accounting and auditing, is also increasing rapidly. In particular, Internal Audit can provide important information to control and limit liability, making the risk of unexpected losses easier to control.

Legal Framework and Integration into Corporate Governance

The introduction of SOX has compelled organizations to network all company functions involved in compliance and risk management. As a result of the new legal framework, the exchange of information for ensuring enterprise-wide compliance had to be given the appropriate priority. Internal Audit is involved in the overall corporate governance approach in a variety of ways. The individual relationships can be described as follows:

- **Audit Body of the Board** — As an audit body of the Board, Internal Audit assumes tasks which allow the Board to delegate its responsibilities with regard to its fiduciary and governance responsibilities. This includes tasks aimed at ensuring direct compliance with a corporate governance code (e.g., compliance with rules of conduct).
- **Compliance of Financial Reporting** — Internal Audit conducts numerous fieldwork activities to promote a solid focus on the compliance of financial reporting. It thus contributes significantly to providing reliable information, particularly with regard to accurate, complete and transparent annual financial statements.
- **Auditing the Internal Control System** — Auditing the internal control system (ICS) includes both process evaluations on a sample basis during individual audits and systematic compliance tests to prepare the disclosures stipulated by SOX (see Section C, Chapter 8).
- **Monitoring the Risk Management System** — By monitoring the risk management system, together with the risk management function, if one exists, mutually exchanging information about identified risks, and tracking them jointly, Internal Audit further promotes its integration within the corporate governance framework of a company.
- **Guidelines and Instructions** — To comply with rules and enforce individual measures, it is usually necessary for the Board of Directors to enact appropriate guidelines and instructions. In this context, Internal Audit is responsible for recognizing this need and prompting the responsible departments to formulate these principles. The objective is to create a framework of guidelines to enable (or make it easier for) management to control and test compliance as an element of corporate governance.
- **Board of Directors** — Communication between Internal Audit and the Board of Directors helps to strengthen the role of Internal Audit. To that end, the New York Stock Exchange (NYSE) Listing Standards require that the Audit Committee meet in private with

the CAE periodically. These meetings may relate to the findings of audits conducted or to the requirements that arise directly from the work of the Board.

External Auditors

- There are a number of options for cooperation with external auditors. The findings of ongoing audits can be exchanged regularly. In addition, internal audit reports must be made available to the external auditors. Under certain circumstances, further-reaching cooperation could also be feasible, (e.g. with regard to revenue recognition programs or external auditor reliance on the work performed by Internal Audit for SOX compliance in accordance with Auditing Standard No. 5).

Information Function

- Ultimately, Internal Audit's reports provide a wide variety of information that allows the Board of Directors and management to initiate or perform activities aimed at compliance with corporate governance principles on a case-by-case basis. These activities range from day-to-day business, such as individual staff issues, through fundamental business matters such as financing for major capital expenditure projects or problems related to competition law.

Auditing the Internal Control System

One function takes on a special role in the above catalog of Internal Audit's tasks and functions with regard to enforcing and complying with corporate governance requirements: Audits of the ICS to avoid deliberate or unintentional abuse resulting in losses for the enterprise. Safeguarding the ICS is therefore an important part of almost any internal audit. Examples of internal controls are the segregation of duties, data matches, and plausibility checks on data entries. A distinction can be drawn between a continuous and a discontinuous approach. The aim of all internal controls is ultimately to prevent or identify gaps and errors as far as possible. Internal controls are a process-integrated form of monitoring, while Internal Audit works process-independently. In this regard, Internal Audit has a genuine monitoring role, which means that the control systems installed in enterprise processes must be tested in detail for completeness and effectiveness. These tests include evaluating suitable samples. It is important to note that Internal Audit is not responsible for ensuring that the controls integrated into the processes are actually applied. This is the task of the employee or manager responsible for the process. Especially in global companies, the control processes should be implemented with a networked IT solution. This in turn means that Internal Audit must make provisions for these horizontal processes in its audits by conducting them globally.

Significance of SOX

SOX has increased the importance of internal controls because they form one of the cornerstones of this act. A clearly documented process structure not only identifies the internal controls, but also links them to the applicable risks and the financial accounts affected, and the relevant company processes. Whereas in a traditional ICS, compliance audits primarily test whether the accounting documents (including a physical inventory and the measurement of assets and liabilities) comply with the law, the provisions of SOX are much more far-reaching, because they consider every process that is in any way relevant to financial reporting. Financial reporting compliance has therefore expanded from a focus on the accounting document only to include the underlying processes. This entails changes to the audit approach Internal Audit uses for auditing the ICS (see Section C, Chapter 8).

HINTS AND TIPS

- Audit fieldwork should always integrate information related to compliance, risk management, and internal controls.
- During audit preparation, examine each audit step with compliance in mind.
- Take note of and forward to the individuals or entities responsible any information regarding the need to create, extend, or change internal company guidelines identified during fieldwork.
- Internal Audit must also report any information discovered regarding actual or suspected fraud to the appropriate bodies.

LINKS AND REFERENCES

- BEASLEY, M., AND D. HERMANSON. 2004. Going Beyond Sarbanes-Oxley Compliance: Five Keys to Creating Value. *The CPA Journal* (June 2004): 11–13.
- BROMILOW, C., BERLIN, B, AND J. ANDERSON. 2005. Stepping Up. *Internal Auditor* (December 2005): 52–57.
- BRUNE, C. 2004. Embracing Internal Controls. *Internal Auditor* (June 2004): 75–81.
- CASCARINO, R. AND S. VAN ESCH. 2005. *Internal Auditing: An Integrated Approach.* Lansdowne, SA: Juta and Co.
- COLBER, J. 2002. Furnishing a Context for Internal Auditing. *The CPA Journal* (May 2002): 34–38.
- COMMITTEE OF SPONSORING ORGANIZATIONS OF THE TREADWAY COMMISSION (COSO). 2004. *Enterprise Risk Management Integrated Framework.* New York, NY: AICPA.
- HARRINGTON, C. 2005. The Value Proposition. *Journal of Accountancy* (September 2005): 77–81.
- INSTITUTE OF INTERNAL AUDITORS. 2003. *Internal Audit Reporting Relationships: Serving Two Masters.* Altamonte Springs, FL: The Institute of Internal Auditors.
- INSTITUTE OF INTERNAL AUDITORS. 2002. *Practice Advisory 1110-2: Chief Audit Executive Reporting Lines.* Altamonte Springs, FL: The Institute of Internal Auditors.
- KAPLAN, S., AND J. SCHULTZ. 2006. *The Role of Internal Audit in Sensitive Communications.* Altamonte Springs, FL: The Institute of Internal Auditors.
- KEINATH, A., AND J. WALO. 2004. Audit Committee Responsibilities. *The CPA Journal* (November 2004): 22–28.
- LANGER, D. AND POPANZ, T. 2006. Sustainable Compliance. *Internal Auditor* (February 2006): 54–58.
- MCCOLLUM, T. 2006. On the Road to Good Governance. *Internal Auditor* (October 2006): 40–46.
- PARKINSON, M. 2004. A Strategy for Providing Assurance. *Internal Auditor* (December 2004): 63–68.

- PRICEWATERHOUSECOOPERS. 2005. *Audit Committee Effectiveness – What works best.* 3rd ed. Altamonte Springs, FL: The Institute of Internal Auditors.
- PUBLIC COMPANY ACCOUNTING OVERSIGHT BOARD (PCAOB). 2004. *Auditing Standard No. 2: An Audit of Internal Control Over Financial Reporting Performed in Conjunction With an Audit of Financial Statements.* http://www.pcaobus.org/Standards/Standards_and_Related_Rules/Auditing_Standard_No.2.aspx (accessed May 31, 2007).
- PUBLIC COMPANY ACCOUNTING OVERSIGHT BOARD (PCAOB). 2005. *Staff Questions and Answers: Auditing Internal Control over Financial Reporting.* http://www.pcaob.org/standards/staff_questions_and_answers/2005/01-21.pdf (accessed May 31, 2007).
- RITTENBERG, L. 2002. Lessons for Internal Auditors. *Internal Auditor* (April 2002): 32.
- RITTENBERG, L. 2006. Internal Control: No Small Matter. *Internal Auditor* (October 2006): 47–51.
- SAWYER, L., M. DITTENHOFER, AND J. SCHEINER. 2003. *Sawyer's Internal Auditing.* 5th ed. Altamonte Springs, FL: The Institute of Internal Auditors.
- STERNBERT, R. AND D. POJUNIS. 2000. Corporate Governance. *Internal Auditor* (December 2000): 34–39.

2.5.3 Internal Audit as a Service Unit

KEY POINTS •••

- In addition to traditional audit activities, Internal Audit can offer other audit-related and non-audit-related services.
- The most important concern is that these other services must not cause Internal Audit to violate the principles of independence and objectivity.
- Most important is the decision of whether Internal Audit is authorized, able, and willing to carry out other service activities. This decision will involve a certain amount of self-determination, as well as consideration of the specific business environment.

Expertise

Service activities performed by Internal Audit can create significant value for a company since Internal Audit has wide-ranging experience and company-specific knowledge. Such company specific knowledge gives Internal Audit a competitive advantage over external consultants, which might enable Internal Audit to provide service or consulting activities at a lower cost.

Other Services

Internal Audit is increasingly carrying out other services, in addition to its traditional audit services. These other services can be differentiated into audit-related and non-audit-related services (for more information on other services performed by Internal Audit see Section A, Chapter 7). The differentiation between the two types of tasks is important because each requires a different level of commitment and has a different impact on the independence of the internal audit function.

Audit-Related Services

Audit-related services include pre-investigations, reviews, cost-effectiveness analysis, and implementation support. These services usually do not impact Internal Audit's independence. When, for example, Internal Audit provides support for the implementation of audit recommendations, the auditee is still ultimately responsible for the implementation of those recommendations. As a result, no conflict of interest between auditing and implementation support will arise under normal circumstances.

Non-audit-related Services: Maintaining Independence

When considering whether to offer non-audit-related services, Internal Audit must answer one fundamental question: Does Internal Audit have the authority, the ability and the will to perform non-audit-related activities and if so, to what extent? Internal Audit is authorized to do so as long as its independence with regard to audit activities is maintained. Service activities must not influence decisions, observations, recommendations or findings in connection with fieldwork at any stage of the audit process and the auditors' objectivity must not be compromised. Prerequisites for achieving this impartiality are the targeted selection of the involved auditors, coordination of audit topics, and adherence to an objective audit approach. Non-audit-related services, such as consulting and project management services, must be considered differently. If Internal Audit's expertise is needed, the auditor who carries out these activities cannot be the same individual responsible for subsequent audits of the areas. Decisive factors in determining whether Internal Audit should carry out other service activities are its specific position within the company and the strategic direction that the Board of Directors gives to the internal audit function. Taking on other service activities must be subject to approval by the Board of Directors. To avoid conflicts of interest, the Audit Committee as part of the Board should set unambiguous rules that specify which service activities the internal audit function is allowed to carry out.

Know-How and Self-Image

The extent to which Internal Audit is able to perform consulting activities depends on the technical knowledge available within the department and the amount of time available to perform these activities. Other factors, such as conflicts of interest and organizational policies also need to be considered. Dealing with the question of whether Internal Audit wishes to perform non-audit-related activities may involve a discussion about Internal Audit's self-image and strategy. For the reputation and status of Internal Audit within a company, it may be beneficial to complement the core competency of auditing with these other services. Extending the range of activities will enhance exposure to the Board of Directors, to management, and eventually to all employees. The downside is that too much involvement can potentially affect the reputation and status of the internal audit department with external auditors.

Personal Qualification

Ultimately, the extent to which an individual auditor is willing to carry out non-audit-related service activities will depend on that individual and his or her superiors in addition to any rules set by the Board of Directors. Together they must decide on a case-by-case basis whether the auditor in question is willing and able to perform these tasks. The availability of targeted support and development programs should open new, interesting perspectives for individual career development.

HINTS AND TIPS

- Supporting measures are very useful when implementing the audit recommendations as they convey an additional degree of acceptance.
- Auditors should each decide individually whether and to what extent they want to consider performing non-audit-related service activities. Their personal development program must be aligned based on this decision.
- In the overall planning, the CAE should schedule non-audit-related activities in harmony with the department's targets and the individual goals of each employee.
- Audits must only relate to matters that Internal Audit was not directly involved in creating.
- Internal Audit must keep a brief, ongoing record of services it performs.
- Internal Audit should aim to bill at least part of the non-audit-related services performed.

LINKS AND REFERENCES

- ANDERSON, R. AND S. LEANDRI. 2006. Unearth the Power of Knowledge. *Internal Auditor* (October 2006): 58–64.
- ANDERSON, U. 2003. Assurance and Consulting Services. In: A. D. BAILEY, A. A. GRAMLING AND S. RAMAMORRTI (EDS.). *Research Opportunities in Internal Auditing.* Altamonte Springs, FL: Institute of Internal Auditors Research Foundation.
- ANDERSON, U. AND A. DAHLE. 2006. *Implementing the Professional Practices Framework.* 2nd ed. Altamonte Springs, FL: The Institute of Internal Auditors.
- GROSS, J. 2006. Control Consciousness. *Internal Auditor* (April 2006): 32–35.
- INSTITUTE OF INTERNAL AUDITORS. 2001. *Practice Advisory 1000.C1-1: Principles Guiding the Performance of Consulting Activities of Internal Auditors.* Altamonte Springs, FL: The Institute of Internal Auditors.
- INSTITUTE OF INTERNAL AUDITORS. 2002. *Practice Advisory 1000.C1-2: Additional Considerations for Formal Consulting Engagements.* Altamonte Springs, FL: The Institute of Internal Auditors.
- INSTITUTE OF INTERNAL AUDITORS. 2005. *Practice Advisory 1130.A1-2: Internal Audit Responsibility for Other (Non-Audit) Functions.* Altamonte Springs, FL: The Institute of Internal Auditors.
- MCDONALDS, P. 2003. Staffing today's Internal Audit Function. *Internal Auditor* (December 2003): 46–51.
- RAZZETTI, E. 2003. Internal Auditing. *Consulting to Management* 14 (December 2003): 34–37.
- RICHARDS, D. 2001. Consulting Auditing – Charting a Course. *Internal Auditor* (December 2001): 30–35.
- ROBITAILLE, D. 2004. World-Class Audit and Control Practices. *Internal Auditor* (February 2004): 74–81.

- ROTH, J. 2003. How do Internal Auditors Add Value? *Internal Auditor* (February 2003): 33–37.
- SAWYER, L., M. DITTENHOFER, AND J. SCHEINER. 2003. *Sawyer's Internal Auditing*. 5th ed. Altamonte Springs, FL: The Institute of Internal Auditors.
- SEARS, B. 2002. *Internal Auditing Manual.* New York, NY: Warren, Gorham & Lamont.
- WALKER, P., W. SHENKIR, AND T. BARTON. 2002. *Enterprise Risk Management: Putting it All Together.* Altamonte Springs, FL: The Institute of Internal Auditors.

2.5.4 Trend toward Audit Management as a Corporate Management Instrument

KEY POINTS •••

- As a result of changes in legal requirements and external guidelines, Internal Audit currently has the opportunity to develop from retrospective auditing to become a future-oriented management instrument.
- From a risk and control perspective, Internal Audit can become an integral part of all phases of the corporate management process. In addition, the audit process model typically contains all the essential stages of the corporate decision process.

Development of Internal Audit

Over time, the role of Internal Audit has changed from strictly an "investigative function" to a corporate management instrument. Internal Audit has received relatively little attention in the past. Since its efficiency and effectiveness were not raised as core issues, it was widely perceived as a department of "box checkers." However, increased focus on corporate governance and the introduction of new laws (e.g. SOX) have triggered a change in attitudes. The increasing importance of transparency and reliability has led to an enhancement of Internal Audit's standing because it represents an instrument to help achieve these objectives. For Internal Audit, this presents an opportunity to move past performing only retrospective audit work to a more integrative, process-oriented, forward-looking and global model. On the basis of these elements of integration, focus on the future, and internationality, Internal Audit can expand its position as a corporate management instrument. There are several facts that exemplify this development:

- Individual Internal Audit functions are assigned to the basic phases of the corporate management process.
- The corporate management process of setting objectives, planning, control, monitoring, and information is used within Internal Audit.
- There is a change from purely retrospective to future-oriented auditing.

Integration into the Corporate Management Process

The phases of the basic corporate management and decision process, which are setting objectives, planning, control, monitoring, and information, can be matched to the relevant processes in Internal Audit, almost on a one-to-one basis.

Objectives

- Corporate objectives also have an impact on the audit objectives and contents of Internal Audit. For example, if a main objective of the company is to expand foreign business activities, Internal Audit will, to a certain extent, audit the processes of the units affected by international activities. Conversely, insights gathered as a result of audit work may also have an influence on corporate objectives. For example, if an audit identifies a lack of internal guidelines and instructions, this may be translated into a management objective to improve existing policies and procedures.

Planning

- A company's planning, which is sometimes performed in stages as objectives are being defined, may have a major impact on Internal Audit's annual audit plan. Even if Internal Audit generally conducts its planning independently and with a risk focus, it should take the company's strategic and operational objectives into consideration. For example, if the objective is to support the development of a new product, it is logical that Internal Audit would carefully evaluate quality control and intellectual property requirements.

Control

- The company's business activities can also be controlled with Internal Audit's involvement. The capacities available for ad-hoc audits can be used at short notice to make or validate certain executive decisions. The results of the audits included in the annual audit plan may, in turn, also influence corporate control, because the audit results are made available to management immediately.

Monitoring

- In line with the well-developed follow-up audit process, monitoring the correction of audit findings is becoming increasingly important (see Section B, Chapter 6). This process of implementation monitoring is intended to ensure that the recommendations of Internal Audit are respected and implemented. Implementation monitoring may be closely related to the specific functions of other control units, such as Management Accounting, so cooperation with such units will be mutually beneficial.

Information

- The integration of audit results into the corporate-wide information process is the most important interface with the company's other management instruments. Internal Audit provides reports for all relevant levels of management, including the Board of Directors and the Audit Committee. Depending on their content, these reports may be used as input for Board resolutions, or form the basis for operational implementation instructions for lower levels of management.

Use of the Corporate Management Process

The second fact that underlines Internal Audit's development toward a corporate management instrument is that Internal Audit's organization increasingly resembles that of a strategic business unit. From planning, preparation, and implementation through reporting and follow-up audits, the operational level of the Internal Audit's process model contains all the essential stages of the management process. Because of its phase model, this means that, in purely formal terms, Internal Audit is a management instrument in its own right. A single audit request can be handled according to the same rules as any other strategic decision tool.

Proactive Audit Focus

The third aspect is Internal Audit's evolution from a reactive perspective that focuses on past and present events toward a proactive, future-oriented management instrument. The nature of audits is becoming increasingly preventive, which means that their results can impact the corporate decision process in general or in relation to individual cases. Preventive audits work with assumptions, trends, search functions and criteria, as well as probabilities and approximations. In addition, audit-relevant parameters, such as thresholds, criteria catalogs, statistical distributions and any method that produces key variables, may be used to create a system of early indicators. Once certain thresholds are reached, Internal Audit (automatically or manually) triggers the appropriate fieldwork. This creates a continuous improvement process, which performs its own checks and controls.

Integration of the Audit Process

End-to-end integration of the audit process into the corporate management process completes the shift toward audit management. This turns Internal Audit into an integral part of the corporate management process, which can give rise to synergies. Most importantly, Internal Audit supports the corporate management process in all its phases, but without becoming an operational part of this process and thus running the risk of losing its independence. The diagram below shows how Internal Audit is integrated in the management process.

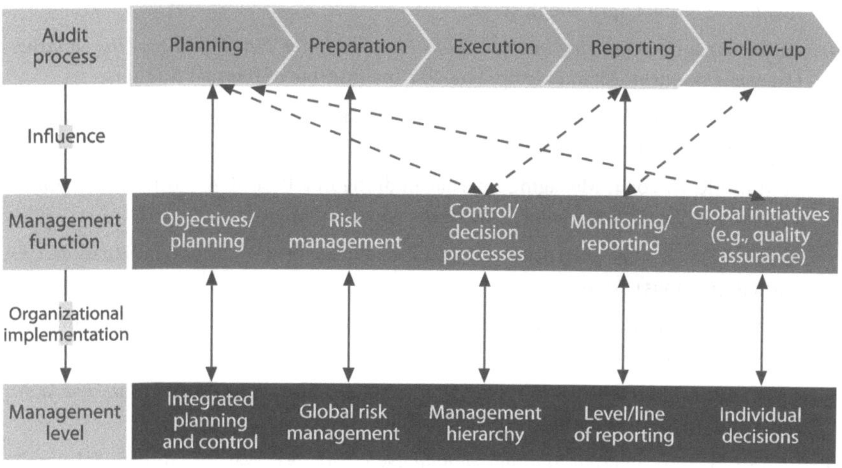

Fig. 5 Integration of Internal Audit in the Management Process

HINTS AND TIPS

- Even though it is useful and necessary to integrate Internal Audit into the corporate management process, its independence must be preserved.

- The management process and management goals guide internal audit activities, because management actions greatly affect company risks. In addition, by focusing on management activities internal auditors can identify areas where they can add most value by generating additional information and guidance for management, and by providing assurance. When performing their work, auditors should thus not limit their activities to working through the audit schedule, but also focus on topics that require proactive audit procedures.

LINKS AND REFERENCES ↗

- ALBIZER, G., J. CASBELL, AND D. MARTIN. 2003. Internal Audit Outsourcing. *The CPA Journal* (August 2003): 38–42.
- CASCARINO, R. AND S. VAN ESCH. 2005. *Internal Auditing: An Integrated Approach.* Lansdowne, SA: Juta and Co.
- CHAPIN, C. AND A. CYTRAUS. 1994. Reinventing the Internal Audit Process. *Ohio CPA Journal* (February 1994): 37–40.
- COMMITTEE OF SPONSORING ORGANIZATIONS OF THE TREADWAY COMMISSION (COSO). 2003. *Enterprise Risk Management Framework.* New York: AICPA.
- DELOACH, J. 2000. *Enterprise-wide Risk Management: Strategies for Linking Risk and Opportunity.* London: Financial Times Management.
- GILL, J. 2005. Believe it or not … the internal auditor is your best friend. *Chartered Accountants Journal* (April 2005): 51–52.
- GRAY, G. 2000. *Changing Internal Audit Practices in the New Paradigm: The Sabarnes-Oxley Environment.* Altamonte Springs, FL: The Institute of Internal Auditors.
- GUPTA, P. 2001. *Internal Audit Reengineering: Survey, Model, and Best Practices.* Altamonte Springs, FL: The Institute of Internal Auditors.
- MOELLER, R. 2004. Managing Internal Auditing in a Post-SOA World. *The Journal of Corporate Accounting & Finance* (May/June 2004): 41–45.
- RICHARDS, P. 1995. Internal Audit vs. Line Management: A Win/Win Situation. *CPA Journal* (July 1995): 63–66.
- ROTH, J. 2002. *Adding Value: Seven Roads to Success.* Altamonte Springs, FL: The Institute of Internal Auditors.
- SAWYER, L., M. DITTENHOFER, AND J. SCHEINER. 2003. *Sawyer's Internal Auditing.* 5th ed. Altamonte Springs, FL: The Institute of Internal Auditors.
- SEARS, B. 2002. *Internal Auditing Manual.* New York, NY: Warren, Gorham & Lamont.
- SERVAGE, J. 2006. Policy and Governance. *Internal Auditor* (August 2006): 83–87.
- SMITH, G. 1999. Why Internal Auditing Must Change to Survive. *The Journal of Corporate Accounting & Finance* (May/June 2000): 11–15.

2.5.5 Internal Audit as a Profit Center Organization

KEY POINTS •••

- Without exception, Internal Audit must be efficient in the resources it consumes.
- Budgets must be efficient, audits must be cost-effective, and variances must be continuously monitored and evaluated.
- If economic efficiency is extended to include revenue, billing options arise for service and consulting activities.
- Another step could involve expanding Internal Audit to be a competence center. This would allow Internal Audit to offer billable services to third parties and to generate revenue.

Use of Resources

Like all other departments, Internal Audit is subject to the basic rules of business. This means that existing resources must be deployed in a targeted, results-maximizing manner and audits must be performed cost-consciously and within the assigned budget. However, deadline and content-related issues can require special or additional audit engagements. In such cases, the management of Internal Audit must ensure that, despite these additional activities, budget limits are adhered to or necessary adjustments explained.

Budget Planning

The CAE is responsible for the entire process of financial control within the internal audit area, although the CAE can also include his or her management team in this responsibility. Employee-related and audit-related budgets form the core of cost-center planning. Important considerations include training and development, travel expenses, as well as audit literature, costs for expert opinions, the involvement of external specialists, and attendance at conferences. Budgets are drawn up within an annual budgeting framework and are based on the number of planned audits as well as expected ad-hoc audits and special projects. The actual costs can be allocated for the entire audit department or divided into regional audit teams. It is also conceivable to allocate audit-related budgets, especially to global audits or audits expected to take a long time. This approach would require all costs to be allocated and – to the extent possible – activities to be traced to the respective audit engagement. Separate budgets for audit-related and non-audit-related services would allow for more specific cost allocation. Allocating costs makes it possible to carry out periodic cost variance analyses for the cost centers at any stage during the fiscal year, and to monitor whether individual audits meet their budgets. Variance analysis could provide a reliable basis for future planning (for more details on cost management, see Section D, Chapter 8).

Profit Center

This cost-based assessment of Internal Audit can be extended to a results-oriented profit center accounting. In this case, however, Internal Audit must ensure that the audits are not under pressure to generate revenue. This also must be reflected in the profit and loss budget, in that profit can only be expected from "service" activities. As a result, the activities of Internal Audit may be divided into "compulsory" activities that cannot be billed and – if possible – billable service activities. The settlement method can be tailored to the respective target group: Intercompany cost transfers for internal customers, and invoices for external customers. Internal Audit receives revenue for its activities in both cases. The objective could be to extend the basis on which the economic efficiency of Internal Audit is measured with regard to budget compliance, or to earn a contribution margin. Of course, additional or supplementary revenue and profit planning – with the corresponding extended variance analysis – will be needed as well, in continuation of the budget planning and cost variance analyses.

Service and Competence Center

Ultimately, this results in Internal Audit also being defined as a kind of service and competence center for audits and other related services. As a result, Internal Audit would also be capable of offering its services to external customers as an extension of its business activities. Joint projects in this regard would make nearly any extension of core competencies – and thus business activities – feasible. As a result, Internal Audit could perform services that go far beyond the typical audit mandate, yet are always derived from its core competencies.

HINTS AND TIPS

- Before the start of an audit, the auditors should ensure that sufficient budget funds and resources are available for the necessary measures.
- Detailed documentation of all costs incurred is essential to enable accurate cost analysis.
- All expenditures and work times by the auditors should be recorded for each audit request for statistical and performance purposes and for potential revenue generation.

LINKS AND REFERENCES

- ANDERSON, U. 2003. Assurance and Consulting Services. In: BAILEY JR., A. D., A. A. GRAMLING AND S. RAMAMOORTI. (Eds.). 2003. *Research Opportunities in Internal Auditing*. Altamonte Springs, FL: The Institute of Internal Auditors.
- ANDERSON, R. AND A. DAHLE. 2006. *Implementing the Professional Practices Framework*. 2nd ed. Altamonte Springs, FL: The Institute of Internal Auditors.
- CASCARINO, R. AND S. VAN ESCH. 2005. *Internal Auditing: An integrated approach.* Lansdowne, SA: Juta and Co.
- INSTITUTE OF INTERNAL AUDITORS. 2001. *Practice Advisory 1000.C1-1: Principles Guiding the Performance of Consulting Activities of Internal Auditors.* Altamonte Springs, FL: The Institute of Internal Auditors.
- INSTITUTE OF INTERNAL AUDITORS. 2002. *Practice Advisory 1000.C1-2: Additional Considerations for Formal Consulting Engagements.* Altamonte Springs, FL: The Institute of Internal Auditors.

- INSTITUTE OF INTERNAL AUDITORS. 2005. *Practice Advisory 1130.A1-2: Internal Audit Responsibility for Other (Non-Audit) Functions.* Altamonte Springs, FL: The Institute of Internal Auditors.
- INSTITUTE OF INTERNAL AUDITORS. 2001. *Practice Advisory 2010-1: Planning.* Altamonte Springs, FL: The Institute of Internal Auditors.
- INSTITUTE OF INTERNAL AUDITORS. 2001. *Practice Advisory 2010-2: Linking the Audit Plan to Risk and Exposure.* Altamonte Springs, FL: The Institute of Internal Auditors.
- SAWYER, L., M. DITTENHOFER, AND J. SCHEINER. 2003. *Sawyer's Internal Auditing.* 5th ed. Altamonte Springs, FL: The Institute of Internal Auditors.
- SEARS, B. 2002. *Internal Auditing Manual.* New York, NY: Warren, Gorham & Lamont.

2.6 Internal Audit and the Requirements of SOX

KEY POINTS •••

- Internal Audit provides audit results which management can use as supporting input to help it meet its SOX certification requirements.
- In a technical consulting capacity, Internal Audit can be involved in preparing the documentation of the processes and internal controls and in ensuring the quality of this documentation.
- SOX impacts the activities of Internal Audit in two areas in particular: financial reporting and the business processes related to financial reporting and their associated internal controls.
- Ensuring SOX compliance is a separate and distinct audit objective for Internal Audit.

Objectives of SOX

The provisions of SOX, including the detailed interpretations provided by the PCAOB, are intended to help ensure compliant financial reporting for companies listed on U.S. stock exchanges and their subsidiaries. The focus is on those areas of a company that are most prone to deliberate misstatements and profit manipulation (i.e., financial reporting and the internal controls of the underlying core business processes).

SOX Provisions

SOX has several provisions that are of specific relevance to internal auditors and for internal control in general.

Section 302

- The Chief Executive Officer (CEO) and Chief Financial Officer (CFO) must certify each quarterly and annual report filed by the organization (Section 302). The certification indicates that the signing officers have reviewed the report and that, based on their knowledge, the report fairly presents the financial condition of the organization and does not include any errors, omissions and is not intended to mislead investors. Further, the certification signifies that the signing officers are responsible for establishing and maintaining internal controls related to financial reporting and disclosure and for performing an annual assessment of those internal controls. The signing officers are also responsible for disclosing all significant deficiencies in the design or operation of the internal controls and any fraud that involves management or employees with a significant role in the organization's internal controls.

Section 404

- Each annual report must include management's assessment of the effectiveness of the internal control structure and procedures of the organization relating to financial reporting (Section 404). The PCAOB, established by SOX, has provided specific guidance to the independent auditors regarding the requirements for the evaluation of management's assessment of internal controls in Auditing Standards (AS) 2. However, it should be noted that the PCAOB has established revised guidance (AS 5) which includes the elimination of the existing requirement that the independent auditor evaluate management's internal control assessment process. The revised guidance requires only that the auditor test the internal controls directly to determine their effectiveness, without evaluating management' assessment process.

Section 806

- SOX also guarantees whistleblower protection to ensure that employees are able to report information regarding potential violations of the Act, any SEC rules, or any activities relating to fraud against the shareholders without fear of adverse consequences (Section 806). Specifically, the act ensures that whistleblowers cannot be discharged, demoted, suspended, threatened, harassed, or discriminated against if they choose to report potential violations. This provision applies specifically to the internal audit function because in some organizations it is Internal Audit's responsibility to receive and process any reported violations and investigate the allegations. Alternatively, many organizations may align whistle-

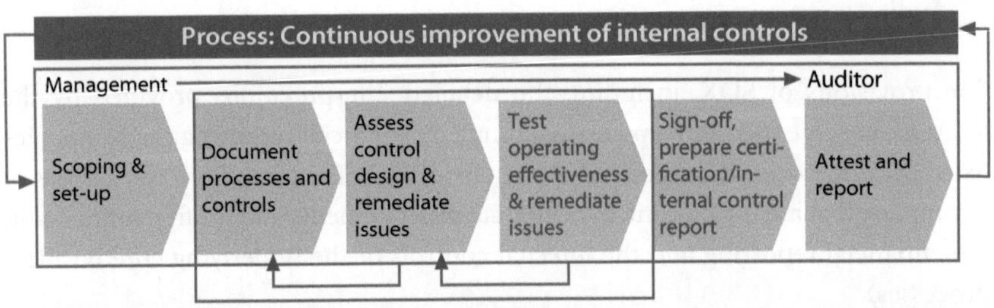

SOX: Section	Requirements	SAP solution
302	The CEO and CFO must certify financial reports	Internal control management tool
404	Report on the adequacy of internal controls	Internal control management tool
806	Whistleblower protection	Report to Audit Committee

Fig. 6 Relevant Requirements of SOX

blower protection under the legal department and may use Internal Audit to assist in investigations of allegations.

New Rules as a Result of SOX

Companies that fall under SOX must integrate the relevant sets of rules into their corporate processes. The most significant provision of SOX for internal auditors is the requirement that financial statement audits now systematically include analysis of business processes related to the financial statements and the relevant internal controls. In a multistage procedure, the functions of the individual process steps must be analyzed, the risks must be identified, and the internal controls must be defined and linked accurately to the appropriate financial accounts. This requires that all process steps be documented in detail and updated annually as part of an internal control evaluation.

Process Responsibility

A number of business units with varying responsibilities are included in the SOX processes. Together with management, the process owners carry the primary responsibility for defining the processes and respective controls. Ultimately, management declares itself responsible for the overall functioning of all process steps and the appropriate controls by certifying under penalty of perjury the accuracy of the financial statements and the system that generated these financial statements.

Support for Implementing the System

As a staff department, Internal Audit can take on two distinct roles with regard to SOX. First, when the system is implemented, it is necessary to ensure that all significant processes have been fully recorded and documented in compliance with the rules, including documentation of all internal controls and the way the risks are linked to financial accounts. Internal Audit can provide support by advising operating units on the basis of its audit experience. Initially, this function should be viewed independently of auditing; it is used as preparation for subsequent audits of the internal control system.

Ensuring SOX Compliance

The second role of Internal Audit is to perform its actual fieldwork. One option is to regard the issue of SOX process controls as a separate audit topic, examining the entire sequence of steps that lead to ensuring SOX compliance. This includes the responsibilities, the quality, and timeliness of the documentation, examining selected core business processes, testing samples of individual internal controls, and the entire information flow between the involved parties, including consultation and cooperation with the external auditors. AS 2 and AS 5 from the PCAOB provide guidance for the external auditors regarding the extent to which they may rely on this work performed by Internal Audit.

Examining the Process Steps

The examination of the individual process steps is in turn divided into several sub-steps: analyzing the process steps and the associated internal controls, and ensuring the quality of the documentation. Some of these audit activities may involve a great deal of work, especially when new operating units participate in the SOX documentation for the first time or comprehensive changes have been made to individual processes. This type of audit requires a modified version of Internal Audit's process model (see Section D, Chapter 14.3.2).

Impact on Standard and Special Audits

SOX is also important for Internal Audit in relation to other audit objects, such as local subsidiaries, internal projects, and initiatives, where the special requirements must be directly integrated into the fieldwork. Testing the internal controls in particular should lead to SOX compliance. The testing procedures are either documented in Internal Audit's own working paper templates or in the original SOX process documentation and may be used as test evidence if necessary. Particularly organizational changes or improvements on the basis of preliminary audits should be included in the work program.

Evidence of the Functioning of Internal Controls

Internal Audit is obligated to gather and document sufficient evidence that the internal controls are functioning. In addition, the Board of Directors must assess the company's SOX compliance and conclude that the internal controls are effective.

Impact of SOX on the Audit Work of Internal Audit

There is no doubt that SOX will have a sustained impact on the audit work of Internal Audit. This has a number of positive effects. First, it makes it compulsory to fully document the core business processes related to financial reporting, including their effects on the accounting system. This is beneficial for Internal Audit because it can structure its work programs on the basis of existing documentation, therefore making processes and internal controls more accessible to audits. Second, it makes the recommendations made by Internal Audit binding, because they no longer relate purely to internal process issues, but evidence of the effectiveness of internal controls must be provided to external financial statement users as part of the management's report on the effectiveness of the internal control structure.

Added Value of SOX Documentation

The results of the SOX documentation may also add considerable value beyond the actual audit work. A comparison of the audited and tested processes and controls applying standardized criteria makes it easier to define optimized processes as standards or benchmarks. Such benchmarks are excellent for use in a knowledge and experience database when backed up by the relevant documentation and scenarios of different procedures. It should be Internal Audit's responsibility to identify and share these optimized processes because their exposure to many different organizational units gives them the best overview of all process alternatives.

Further Impact on Internal Audit

Apart from these fundamental questions about Internal Audit's role and involvement in the SOX processes, there are further tasks that arise in this context. Other tasks may include the introduction of a management code of ethics, the preparation of reports for the Audit Committee, and involvement in developing a reporting system on internal controls. In the context of SOX, Internal Audit also must deal with information received about fraud and ensure adequate cooperation with the external auditors and other compliance functions such as Risk Management.

HINTS AND TIPS

- Take the requirements of SOX into account when preparing for operational audits.
- Consider integrating the assessment of selected controls into the audit steps.
- A dedicated audit scenario should be constructed for the SOX compliance process.
- Use the SOX documentation as a starting point to identify possible areas for process improvements.

LINKS AND REFERENCES ↗

- ANONYMOUS. 2005. Rebalancing Internal Audit in the Sarbanes-Oxley Era. *The CPA Journal* (November 2005): 17.
- D'AQUILA, J. 2004. Tallying the Cost of the Sarbanes-Oxley Act. *The CPA Journal* (November 2004): 6–9.
- DIGREGORIO, D., AND P. CARRUTH. 2002. The Impact of the Sarbanes-Oxley Act of 2002 on Management and Audit Committees. *Journal of Accounting and Finance Research* (Fall 2004): 111–119.
- DOUGLAS, B. 2005. A Guide to Section 404 project management. *Internal Auditor* (June 2005): 61–67.
- DREXLER, P. 2006. Could Sarbanes-Oxley Benefit Non-SEC Registrant Audits? *The CPA Journal* (June 2006): 6–9.
- EDELSTEIN, S. 2004. Sarbanes-Oxley Compliance for Nonaccelerated Filers. *The CPA Journal* (December 2004): 52–59.
- FARGHER, N., AND A. GRAMLING. 2005. Towards Improved Internal Controls. *The CPA Journal* (June 2005): 26–29.
- FARRELL, J. 2003. A Broad View of Section 404. *Internal Auditor* (August 2003): 88–89.
- GEIGER, M., AND P. TAYLOR. 2003. CEO and CFO Certifications of Financial Information. *Accounting Horizons* (December 2003): 357–368.
- GREEN, J. 2006. Section 404 for Small Caps. *Journal of Accountancy* (March 2006): 67–70.
- MARDEN. R., R. EDWARDS, AND W. STOUT. 2003. The CEO/CFO Certification Requirement. *The CPA Journal* (July 2003): 36–44.
- MATYJEWICZ, G. AND J. D'ARCANGELO. 2004. Beyond Sarbanes-Oxley. *Internal Auditor* (October 2004): 64–72.
- MCELVEEN, M. 2002. New Rules – New Challenges. *Internal Auditor* (December 2002): 40–47.
- MILLER, R. AND P. PASHKOFF. 2002. Regulations under the Sarbanes-Oxley Act. *Journal of Accountancy* (October 2002): 33–36.
- O'BRIEN, P. 2006. Reducing SOX Section 404 Compliance Costs. *The CPA Journal* (July 2006): 26–28.
- OWENS, D. 2006. Implementing Sarbanes-Oxley Act Section 404. *The CPA Journal* (April 2006): 6–9.
- PUBLIC COMPANY ACCOUNTING OVERSIGHT BOARD (PCAOB). 2004. *Auditing Standard No. 2: An Audit of Internal Control Over Financial Reporting Performed in Conjunction With an Audit of Financial Statements* http://www.pcaobus.org/Standards/Standards_and_ Related_Rules/Auditing_Standard_No.2.aspx (accessed May 31, 2007).
- PUBLIC COMPANY ACCOUNTING OVERSIGHT BOARD (PCAOB). 2005. *Staff Questions and Answers: Auditing Internal Control over Financial Reporting.* http://www.pcaob.org/standards/staff_questions_and_answers/2005/01-21.pdf (accessed May 31, 2007).

- PUBLIC COMPANY ACCOUNTING OVERSIGHT BOARD (PCAOB). 2004. *Auditing Standard No. 5: Proposed Auditing Standard – An Audit of Internal Control over Financial Reporting that is Integrated with an Audit of Financial Statements.* http://www.pcaob.org/Rules/Docket_021/2006-12-19_Release_No._2006-007.pdf (accessed May 31, 2007).
- RAMOS, M. 2004. Section 404 Compliance in the Annual Report. *Journal of Accountancy* (October 2004): 43–48.
- RITTENBERG, L. AND P. MILLER. 2005. The Good News about Compliance. *Internal Auditor* (June 2005): 55–60.
- SHEIKH, A., AND A. WALLACE. 2005. The Sarbanes-Oxley Certification Requirment: Analyzing the Comments. *The CPA Journal – Special Auditing Issue* (November 2005): 36–42.
- SOBEL, P. 2006. Building on Section 404. *Internal Auditor* (April 2006): 38–44.
- SPILLANE, D. 2004. PCAOB Enforcement: What to Expect. *CPA Journal* (September 2004): 32–35.
- TARANTINO, A. 2006. *Manager's Guide to Compliance.* Hoboken, NJ: Wiley & Sons.
- US CONGRESS. 2002. *Sarbanes-Oxley Act of 2002. 107th Congress of the United States of America. HR 3763.* Washington DC: Government Printing Office.

2.7 Value Added by Internal Audit at SAP

KEY POINTS

- Internal Audit's guiding principle, its mission, specifies the mandate with regard to the added value that is to be created by its activities.
- The main areas where value is added are compliance, improvements to process security (especially with regard to internal controls), and the efficient, target-oriented utilization of the risk management system.
- Internal Audit delivers additional benefits, in that it aims to improve specific aspects of business processes, such as communication links.

Mission and Added Value

If we summarize the attributes of GIAS with regard to the objectives formulated for this department and the tasks involved in the audit mandate, we get a varied picture of contents and forms. A central issue is the all-encompassing basic principle of Internal Audit and the value it adds to the company. The main guiding principle of Internal Audit at SAP is formulated in the mission of GIAS: The mission is to ensure that all activities of the global SAP Group comply with the policies, guidelines, and procedures defined by management. The main areas where value is added are compliance, improvements to process security, especially with regard to internal controls, and the efficient, objective-oriented utilization of the risk management system.

Compliance with Regulations

Similar to the previous descriptions of the objectives and tasks faced by GIAS, this mission once again highlights the different levels on which Internal Audit can be integrated into company processes. The first level is clearly aimed at compliance with all types of internal and external guidelines and regulations, to ensure proper business operations. Here, Internal Audit adds value in the sense of reliability of information generated in the business processes and financial reporting.

Risk Management

On a second level, GIAS cooperates closely with the risk management department in order to identify business risks and suggest ways of keeping these risks to a minimum. This also adds value to the company. The target group of this information is management at any level, but particularly strategic management, which is ultimately responsible for controlling all business risks.

Best-Practice Solutions

Internal Audit can add significant value by developing and sharing optimized process solutions ("best practices") to improve internal controls. As a result, operational management, as well as the individual departments, can identify significant potential for improvement options.

Corporate Culture

There are still other areas where Internal Audit adds value: Improved information and communication flows, reliability and trust in the security and stability of the organization, and the certainty that any inappropriate behavior will be addressed through targeted investigation. In the long term, these benefits will result in increased confidence among employees that arbitrary actions and lack of security have no place in the business environment. Internal Audit ultimately contributes to an ethical corporate culture for the good of all employees.

Equal Treatment

Another important added value regarding the increasing globalization of SAP is the principle fair and impartial work performed by Internal Audit. It reflects the trust that any problem that occurs within the global corporate organization will be solved according to standardized procedures, and irrespective of specific individuals. This awareness will help improve mutual trust among employees, as well as trust in management – especially in the Executive Board.

HINTS AND TIPS

- The overall benefit provided by Internal Audit can be highlighted in meetings and documentation by pointing out the necessity of business optimization, for the greater purpose of company sustainability and competitive advantage in the market.

3 Framework of Internal Audit at SAP

3.1 SAP's Global Audit Approach in the Shape of Global Internal Audit Services (GIAS)

KEY POINTS •••

- The mission statement expresses the basic definition of GIAS' fundamental accountability.
- The global audit approach of Internal Audit at SAP requires that international circumstances are taken into consideration.
- All cultural, legal, statutory, and work-related differences have to be taken into account, and different interpretations of auditing must be considered when operating in an international environment.
- In addition, all organizational prerequisites and procedures have to be defined for each audit so that they agree with all participants' perception of audits.

Mission Statement

The mission statement is a key element of GIAS's definition of itself. The statement specifies the core mandate of Internal Audit, provides a basic definition of the department's fundamental responsibility and is based on a common perception of auditing. The following two objectives are the core of the mission statement:

- that the SAP Group complies with statutory and legal requirements as well as internal guidelines and instructions, and
- that Internal Audit strives to add value by proposing management and organization-related solutions and giving information and recommendations about internal controls and business risks.

Global Standard

It is important that the mission statement, as a definition of Internal Audit's responsibilities, is applied as a global standard by all GIAS teams. The statement provides global guidance which leads to a shared understanding of all processes, responsibilities, and values. The mission statement represents the link between the GIAS Principles and the Charter since it defines the fundamental tasks and forms the basis for the resulting business mandate.

Cultural Differences

The global structure of GIAS gives rise to a number of challenges to implementing the mission statement. Cultural differences are one of the biggest challenge. Both auditors and auditees deal with audits differently, depending on their cultural backgrounds. While there are many countries that deal with the process in a systematic, distanced manner, audits and their findings can have a much different – even personal – significance in other cultural contexts (e.g., in Asia). Accordingly, interpersonal dealings and the communication of positive or negative reports must be straightforward and to the point, and adapted to regional and cultural habits if necessary. It is therefore crucial to show a high degree of sensitivity in dealing with both fellow employees and other parties (for example, employees of the audited unit, external auditors, and partners).

Synchronization of Audit Methodology

A second major challenge is the synchronization of the audit methodology. While in some countries it is possible to achieve objectives quickly through interviews or meetings, in other countries it may be more beneficial to derive the relevant audit facts by studying available documents. Differing styles of communication and discussion, differences in report styles, and divergent procedures for implementing recommendations make a standardized approach difficult to achieve. It is therefore important to select methods and procedures with comparability in mind. A standardized global process model that specifies a binding framework is helpful in meeting these requirements (see Section B). In addition, the management structure of Internal Audit must ensure that an adequate quality assurance system is implemented and practiced. In particular, the documents used by Internal Audit must be harmonized.

Teamwork During Global Audits

In global audits, the audit topic takes precedence over auditors and regions, i.e., co-workers from different regions form a team for the duration of the audit (see Section A, Chapter 6.4). Different time zones and different personal circumstances result in new challenges to audit teams. The global handling of the overall audit, especially the coordination and preparation of the audit results, requires intensive (and often unscheduled) time reserves and needs to be considered in the audit planning.

Team Building

Regular meetings, conferences, and joint events held by GIAS help to create a team spirit, which makes it easier to overcome conflicts and to reach a consensus on potentially divisive issues. Due to the long distances, different time zones, and resource schedules involved, however, such gatherings have to be planned well in advance or, if held spontaneously, with a limited number of participants.

Danger to Efficient Audit Execution

In addition to the issues described above, Internal Audit may face additional challenges that might pose a threat to audit execution. There is always the possibility that an effective audit may be complicated – or even made impossible – by unforseen events (e.g., political developments, inclement weather, and disasters), personal requirements, or changing business needs. As a result of such occurrences an auditor may not be available in time (or at all), which may in turn require changes in the organization of the audit. Accordingly, audits have to be planned with sufficient lead time and contingency plans as far as resources are concerned.

HINTS AND TIPS

- Before auditors start working in a different country, they should familiarize themselves with the local culture and customs.

LINKS AND REFERENCES

- BELL, S. AND M. NARZ. 2007. Meeting the Challenges of Age Diversity in the Age of Diversity in the Workplace. *The CPA Journal* (February 2007): 56–59.
- FINNE, T. 2005. Casting a Wide Net. *Internal Auditor* (August 2005): 29–33.

- LERE, J. AND K. PORTZ. 2005. Management Control. Systems in a Global Economy. *The CPA Journal* (September 2005): 62–64.
- O'REGAN, D. 2001. *Auditing International Entities: A Practical Guide to Objectives, Risks, and Reporting.* Altamonte Springs, FL: The Institute of Internal Auditors.
- RICAUD, J. 2006. Auditing Cultural Diversity. *Internal Auditor* (December 2006): 57–61.

3.2 Structure of the GIAS Code of Conduct

KEY POINTS

- The GIAS Code of Conduct represents a framework of rules of personal conduct, audit principles, and ethical principles.
- The purpose of the GIAS Code of Conduct is to help guarantee a standardized conduct of Internal Audit, both internally and externally, in different audits and in different regions.
- External guidelines by professional associations or internal guidelines developed by other departments or other sets of rules may be used as a basis for the Code.
- Each internal audit department should define its own rules, guided by company-specific conditions and requirements.

Objective of a Code of Conduct

The GIAS Code of Conduct has two objectives. The first objective is to define generally applicable norms of behavior for all aspects and processes of an auditor's work. The GIAS Code of Conduct is intended as a tool and guide for auditors in their dealings with colleagues within the company and with external partners. For Internal Audit to be perceived as a committed, reliable department its employees must conduct themselves fairly, professionally, and with moral integrity in all aspects of business. Internal Audit can only fulfill its task if it is guaranteed that all aspects of an audit are handled objectively. In order to operate within the remits of its role, the department has to make sure that it lives up to the expected levels of honesty, integrity, and transparency in all respects.

Organizational Coherence

The second objective of the GIAS Code of Conduct is to create a globally uniform audit approach. Given the variety of tasks and cultures in which GIAS employees operate, there is a need that all auditors comply with certain standards during their fieldwork. The GIAS Code of Conduct creates such uniform process standards.

IIA Code of Ethics

The IIA has published a Code of Ethics to further promote an ethical culture in the profession. The IIA Code of Ethics has two essential components:

- principles that are relevant to the profession and practice of internal auditing, and

- rules of conduct that describe behavior norms expected of internal auditors.

These rules provide guidance in interpreting the principles for practical application.

Defining the Code of Conduct

Every internal audit department should define a binding Code of Conduct built on such guidance as provided by the IIA or other professional organization but adapt the guidance to company-specific needs. The GIAS Code of Conduct draws on guidance from the following sources:

- the ethical guidelines of the leading professional organizations (e.g., IIA and AICPA),
- general rules and legal requirements (e.g., country or sector specific rules),
- SAP's own corporate guidelines (e.g., Code of Business Conduct and corporate governance rules).

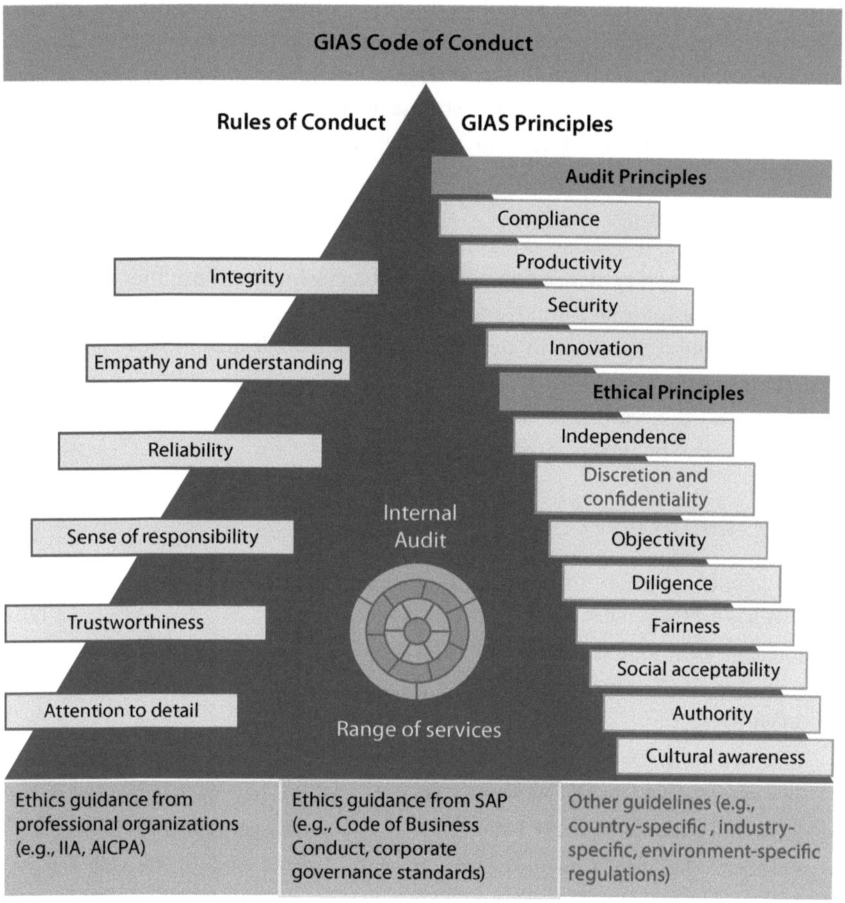

Fig. 7 GIAS Code of Conduct

Rules of Conduct and GIAS Principles

The GIAS Code of Conduct closely resembles the Code of Ethics of the IIA and breaks down into two main categories of individual standards (for more details see Section A, Chapter 3.3):

- The Rules of Conduct, which define the behavior rules for Internal Audit and provide guidance to ensure the integrity of each individual auditor. The rules include attributes relevant to each internal audit employee, such as attention to detail and reliability, which are requirements that are also laid out in SAP's Code of Business Conduct. In addition, more audit-specific conduct requirements, such as sensitivity and understanding, or trustworthiness, are also defined.
- The GIAS Principles, which include both audit and ethical principles, relate to the department in its entirety and apply to the practice of internal auditing.

Staff Department of Company Management

Internal Audit is required not only to comply with its own code of conduct, but also to perform its function as a staff department of company management. This includes that they rigorously investigate any reported contraventions of the Code of Business Conduct, which applies to all employees. In the context of international financial reporting and the ever more stringent control requirements to ensure that processes are compliant, this is an increasingly important task.

HINTS AND TIPS

- Analyze all audit activities critically to establish whether or not they are consistent with the Internal Audit Code of Conduct.
- Discuss doubtful audit activities with the audit lead. It may prove expedient to obtain specific written permission.
- Document the reasons for a particular course of action especially if the audit steps seem to be inconsistent with the Code.

LINKS AND REFERENCES

- ANDERSON, D. 2002. Changing a Culture of Entitlement Into a Culture of Merit. *The CPA Journal* (November 2002): 16.
- BAGGETT, W. 2003. Creating a Culture of Security. *Internal Auditor* (June 2003): 37–41.
- BAGGETT, W. 2007. 7 Criteria for Ethics Assessments. *Internal Auditor* (December 2007): 65–69.
- BERNARDI, R. AND C. LACROSS. 2005. Corporate Transparency: Code of Ethics Disclosures. *The CPA Journal* (April 2005): 34–37.
- BLANK, D. 2003. A Matter of Ethics. *Internal Auditor* (February 2003): 26–31.
- ELIASON, M. 1999. Compliance plus Integrity. *Internal Auditor* (December 1999): 30–33.
- FINAMORE, C. 2005. Common Good, Common Sense. *Internal Auditor* (August 2005): 35–38.

- GRACE, S. AND J. HAUPERT. 2006. How to Make an Ethics Program Work. *The CPA Journal* (April 2006): 66–67.
- INSTITUTE OF INTERNAL AUDITORS. 2006. *Code of Ethics.* http://www.theiia.org/guidance/standards-and-practices/professional-practices-framework/code-of-ethics/code-of-ethics---english/ (accessed May 31, 2007).
- JENNINGS, M. 2003. The Critical Role of Ethics. *Internal Auditor* (December 2003): 46–51.
- MESSMER, M. 2001. Capitalizing on Corporate Culture. *Internal Auditor* (October 2001): 38–45.
- RION, M. AND R. GEBING. 1999. Doing the Right Thing. *Internal Auditor* (December 1999): 33–35.
- VAN WIJK, E. 2004. Iffy Independence. *Internal Auditor* (October 2004): 81–83.

3.3 The GIAS Code of Conduct in Detail

KEY POINTS •••

- While the Ethical and Audit Principles in the GIAS Code of Conduct define the practice of auditing, the Rules of Conduct provide guidance for the activities of individual auditors.
- The GIAS Code of Conduct plays an important role in the career and development planning within the company.

Rules of Conduct

The structure of the GIAS Code of Conduct outlined in the previous chapter distinguishes between the GIAS Principles and the Rules of Conduct. The Rules of Conduct take account of the fact that auditing requires certain personal characteristics in terms of conduct and personal attitude. The most important personal characteristics include:

- integrity,
- empathy and understanding,
- reliability,
- sense of responsibility,
- trustworthiness, and
- attention to detail.

These rules of conduct must be an integral part of the personality profile of each auditor.

Ethical Principles

The GIAS Principles consist of two groups: the Ethical Principles and the Audit Principles (see Section A, Chapter 3.2). The Ethical Principles are:

- independence,
- discretion and confidentiality,
- objectivity,

- fairness,
- diligence,
- social acceptability,
- authority, and
- cultural awareness.

Independence The principle of independence is vital for Internal Audit. GIAS' independence is granted by the CAE's high level access to company management. At SAP AG, the CAE reports directly to the CEO and should meet directly twice a year – or as needed – with the Audit Committee. The CAE may also meet with the Supervisory Board, which oversees the Executive Board. This form of organizational autonomy ensures the necessary independence of audits and prevents other company units from exercising undue influence on GIAS.

Discretion and Confidentiality There is a special relationship of trust between the audit requestor, the auditee, and GIAS. Data and facts discovered by or disclosed to the auditors during the course of the audit must be kept confidential. Only under exceptional circumstances may disclosure be justified for legal reasons (e.g., in the case of police or public prosecutor investigations or as required by the SEC or other regulatory bodies). Such disclosure has to be coordinated with the audit requester and the legal department.

Objectivity Objectivity refers to strict impartiality on the side of the auditors and is vital to ensure high-quality audits. Auditors must not allow themselves to be influenced by personal sympathies or antipathies, subjective opinions of other employees, or by interventions of higher-ranking persons. Auditors need to be aware that personal judgment can be consciously and unconsciously biased. Reviews of findings by other auditors and critical evaluation of one's work can help to ensure objectivity in judgment.

Fairness Closely linked to the principle of objectivity is the principle of fairness. Fairness includes that auditors display appropriate conduct toward all those involved in an audit, that they integrate them adequately, report correctly, and objectively deal with the audit results and documents. In addition, every auditor is obliged to notify the auditee of the consequences of any improper actions and activities.

Diligence Diligence in auditing and reporting is an absolute prerequisite to ensure a high quality audit. Auditors must strive for rigor and extent of their audits at a level that allows them to make high-quality and objective comments on the audit findings, to the best of their knowledge and belief. To ensure a high level of diligence auditors need to maintain a high and up-to-date level of knowledge.

Social Acceptability In an age of formal and informal networks, GIAS must ensure that the audits, and the implementation of their findings, are socially acceptable. Audit activities must not result in encouraging or exacerbating any existing social tensions.

Authority GIAS has to act with authority when necessary and when deemed to be in the best interest of the company. Whenever GIAS acts on its own initiative, the fundamental nature and content of the audit have to be agreed with the CEO first or the Audit Committee if the audit concerns activities of the CEO. As part of its audit mandate, GIAS is authorized to carry out all the necessary activities and request documents without consultation with those involved or their line managers. All auditees have to comply to the best of their knowledge and belief with this procedure. GIAS can act on its own authority with regard to doings of all management levels, so that the set audit measures are at all times supported by the organization as a whole.

Cultural Awareness

Another ethical principle is cultural awareness. In global companies like SAP, national and cultural influences play a major role. The increasing interdependence between cultures must therefore be taken into account in the audit process. Considering cultural differences involves audit teams as well as auditees. Mutual respect for each other and tolerance of different cultures and ways of thinking are an essential prerequisite for successful audits.

Audit Principles

In addition to the above Ethical Principles, the GIAS Principles, as laid out in the GIAS Code of Conduct, include the following practical Audit Principles:

- compliance,
- productivity,
- security, and
- innovation.

Compliance

One of the major tasks of GIAS is to monitor business processes with regard to compliance with regulations. The large number of existing regulations, directives and rules set a very wide-ranging and continually growing framework for audit content and processes. In addition, requirements of countries where stocks are listed on public exchanges apply also to operations abroad.

Productivity

Costs and benefits must be weighted against each other in designing an audit. This means that methods and resources must be used to best serve the intended purpose and budgets should not be exceeded.

Security

Moreover, audit activities must be designed in such a way that they are not detrimental to security interests. Any measures regarded as a potential threat to safety and security by the security department must always be discussed with those responsible. In addition, audit recommendations, and their implementation must consider security-related criteria.

Innovation

As a corporate audit department for one of the world's leading software companies, GIAS has a unique opportunity to use innovative technical solutions for the department's internal processes, and has to ensure that best possible use of SAP solutions is made within the Group as a whole.

General Conclusions

Auditors must strictly abide by the above Principles and Rules of Conduct in their daily work. The management of the department should ensure that these rules are always observed. The GIAS Code of Conduct must be regularly reviewed and adapted.

Personal Employee Development

The GIAS Code of Conduct is important in the context of personal career planning, because it is essential that auditors exhibit the attributes laid out in the Code in order to advance within the department and the organization (see Section A, Chapter 4.6).

HINTS AND TIPS

- When faced with personal attacks or accusations, reference to the GIAS Code of Conduct can help auditors support their actions.
- Make sure that no audit activities are in conflict with the rules and principles of the Code of Conduct.
- Each of the auditor's tasks must be reviewed for compliance with the GIAS Code of Conduct.

LINKS AND REFERENCES

- COLSON, R. 2004. CPA's Responsibilities: Article IV Objectivity and Independence. *The CPA Journal* (June 2004): 80.
- COOPER, C. 2003. One Right Path. *Internal Auditor* (December 2003): 52–57.
- HELPERT, A. 2006. Cultivating a Loyal Workforce. *Internal Auditor* (December 2006): 66–72.
- HUBBARD, L. 2005. A High-Powered Auditor. *Internal Auditor* (February 2005): 26–27.
- INSTITUTE OF INTERNAL AUDITORS. 2006. *Code of Ethics*. http://www.theiia.org/guidance/standards-and-practices/professional-practices-framework/code-of-ethics/code-of-ethics---english/ (accessed May 31, 2007).
- INSTITUTE OF INTERNAL AUDITORS. 2001. *Practice Advisory 1100-1: Independence and Objectivity*. Altamonte Springs, FL: The Institute of Internal Auditors.
- INSTITUTE OF INTERNAL AUDITORS. 2001. *Practice Advisory 1120-1: Individual Objectivity*. Altamonte Springs, FL: The Institute of Internal Auditors.
- INSTITUTE OF INTERNAL AUDITORS. 2001. *Practice Advisory 1130-1: Impairments to Independence or Objectivity*. Altamonte Springs, FL: The Institute of Internal Auditors.
- INSTITUTE OF INTERNAL AUDITORS. 2001. *Practice Advisory 1200-1: Proficiency and Due Professional Care*. Altamonte Springs, FL: The Institute of Internal Auditors.
- INSTITUTE OF INTERNAL AUDITORS. 2001. *Practice Advisory 1210-1: Proficiency*. Altamonte Springs, FL: The Institute of Internal Auditors.
- INSTITUTE OF INTERNAL AUDITORS. 2001. *Practice Advisory 1220-1: Due Professional Care*. Altamonte Springs, FL: The Institute of Internal Auditors.
- MCDONALD, P. 2006. The Quest for Talent. *Internal Auditor* (June 2006): 72–77.
- MUCHLER, J. 2001. *Independence and Objectivity: A Framework for Internal Auditors*. Altamonte Springs, FL: The Institute of Internal Auditors.

3.4 Examples Illustrating the Effectiveness of the Code of Conduct

KEY POINTS •••

- The GIAS Code of Conduct and the auditors' personal expertise and judgment form the basis for Internal Audit activities.
- In conflict situations, it is useful to consult with other employees, primarily within Internal Audit, but also in other departments.
- Sometimes it is expedient to involve a higher hierarchy level.

GIAS Code of Conduct as a Basis for Audits

The Audit Principles, Ethical Principles, and Rules of Conduct collectively form the basis for designing the audit organization and therefore have a significant influence on the organization and workflow structure within Internal Audit.

Fig. 8 The GIAS Code of Conduct as a Basis for Audits

Practical Examples

The fictitious examples, given below, show how the GIAS Code of Conduct can be applied to scenarios prone to conflict during audit activities.

Information Provided by Employees

Employees often approach Internal Audit with reports of shortcomings within the company's organization. Especially unsolicited information has to be examined very carefully for factual accuracy. The following fictitious example emphasizes this. A senior manager approaches a GIAS employee, accusing the human resources department responsible for his unit of being incompetent and unable to work with a simple spreadsheet program to calculate bonuses. The manager also criticizes the lack of support that his division receives from the human resources department. Since the accusations are quite serious, the auditor has to establish whether the manager is simply upset about a single calculation error, or whether there is a systematic failure of the internal controls. If there is such a failure, Internal Audit has to investigate the matter as part of the next scheduled audit, or in very urgent cases conduct an ad-hoc audit. The example shows the importance of being objective, and diligent and maintaining confidentiality and trustworthiness.

Interpersonal Relationships

The open, team-based corporate culture at SAP means that employees forge and maintain close working relationships with each other, sometimes even on a personal level. In some cases, such relationships are extended into the employees' private lives, so that the question arises as to when they start impairing the objectivity that is required professionally. This question is generally relevant for all employees, but in view of the need to judge matters objectively, it is especially important for Internal Audit.

Fictitious Example

The following fictitious example may illustrate this point: A GIAS auditor and an employee of the license administration department have been friends since they both started working for SAP and took part in the same employee introduction program. After a while, the GIAS auditor discovers during a routine internal audit that there are serious non-compliances in the license department, for which his friend shares a large part of the responsibility. Although Internal Audit does not blame any named individuals, the reported shortcomings clearly point to the person responsible.

Possible Solution

If there are close personal ties between the auditor and the auditee, the auditor should in certain cases decline participation in the audit due to bias. This applies particularly to GIAS employees who have joined Internal Audit from other departments. These employees should not participate in audits of their former department, although they usually have excellent expertise in the area being audited. If their participation is unavoidable, other team members should be involved in the audit and in formulating audit findings and recommendations to ensure objectivity and independence.

Conduct Guidelines

The following may be used as guidance for difficult situations:

- Check the plausibility of documents or explanations with professional skepticism and common sense.
- Report any real or perceived conflicts of interest immediately to supervisors and, if possible, excuse yourself from audits where such conflicts occur.
- If possible, resolve the situation in question within the audit team by consulting with colleagues and using their experience and different professional backgrounds.
- Monitor the situation over a certain period of time to follow up the development.
- Document more serious problems, including relevant discussions and decisions, so that the problem and its solution can be reviewed later.
- If necessary, report the situation to Internal Audit management.

Individual Responsibility

By itself, a Code is not able to prevent unethical behavior. All employees are responsible for their own professional actions and have to decide how to deal with difficult situations. However, rules and codes of conduct help create awareness and offer a framework and guidelines in ethically ambiguous situations.

HINTS AND TIPS

- Auditors should have the courage to do what they regard as the right thing, while observing the Code of Conduct.
- GIAS has created a special Roadmap for investigating fraud. It contains the necessary steps to be taken when employees report contraventions of the SAP Code of Business Conduct.
- AICPA has designed a decision tree to help auditors find the appropriate response in cases of conflict.

LINKS AND REFERENCES

- AICPA. 2006. *Ethics Decision Tree.* www.aicpa.org/pubs/cpaltr/sept2002/business/busind1.htm (accessed May 31, 2007).
- AICPA. 2006. *Ethics Decision Tree.* www.aicpa.org/pubs/cpaltr/sept2002/business/busind2.htm (accessed May 31, 2007).

4 Organizational Structure of GIAS

4.1 Organizational Status within SAP

KEY POINTS •••

- At SAP, Internal Audit is a staff department that reports directly to the CEO.
- It is crucial that the organization of Internal Audit at SAP reflect the requirements associated with the global responsibilities that the Executive Board bears.
- The combination of global responsibility and regional structure enables Internal Audit to flexibly carry out a wide variety of tasks.
- At the same time, this approach creates additional opportunities to use Internal Audit's existing global know-how.

GIAS as Corporate Audit

SAP AG is a German corporation under the two-tier Board structure as laid out in the German Stock Corporation Act. SAP AG therefore has an Executive Board with managing directors and a Supervisory Board, which oversees the Executive Board and which consists of shareholder representatives and employee representatives. SAP's Internal Audit is a corporate governance instrument and a staff department the head of which reports directly to the CEO. As a corporate department, it performs services for all business units and regions of the entire SAP Group. This results in a number of requirements in terms of processes and organization.

Global Assurance

GIAS is a management instrument that is established to help ensure that all the liability, supervisory, and administrative duties of the Executive Board with regard to corporate governance are met. Because the Executive Board must demonstrate its universal, all-encompassing awareness of the company, GIAS has to work under this approach without restriction and with the necessary audit volumes. No topic, process, region, or responsibility can be allowed to be excluded from the audit universe (see Section B). The unit structure, distribution of tasks, and overall audit coordination have to be aligned with the requirement that Internal Audit provide global assurance.

Characteristics of a Corporate Audit Organization

GIAS' SAP-wide focus entails a series of characteristics typical of centrally organized and globally operating corporate audit organizations:

Structure

- The first characteristic is the structure of Internal Audit. The department is organized as a horizontal and independent part of the SAP Group. The regional distribution of teams has to reflect the importance of the respective business units and size of the individual regions. Personal preferences for deployment are important, but should not prevail over operational requirements. Although it is centrally managed, Internal Audit has a decentralized, regional structure. All regional teams report to the CAE, who in turn reports to the CEO. This protects all the organizational units of Internal Audit against undue external influence. The structure of GIAS is complemented with cross-regional teams (such as the so-called SOX-team). They operate independently on the global level and report directly to the CAE.

- The second characteristic is the definition and monitoring of central business processes within Internal Audit. GIAS has defined Group-wide audit standards that must be followed by all regions. These standards ensure comparability, uniformity, plausibility, and verifiability of findings and documentation. Centralized reporting lines ensure that these standards are followed, particularly with regard to cultural and personal modifications.

Definition and Monitoring of Central Business Processes

- GIAS has a multilevel reporting system. The highest aggregated reporting level is the Board summary (see Section B, Chapter 5.2.5). The reports for operational management, Corporate Risk Management, and the Executive Board are derived from the individual audit reports. This multilevel reporting structure lies within the responsibility of Internal Audit: All types of reports in the entire organization must be prepared consistently, correctly, and free of influence by external parties. This allows the Executive Board to obtain additional and more detailed information of issues raised in the Board summary down to individual findings if necessary.

Multilevel Reporting

- The CAE coordinates the overall audit planning process (for details, see Section B, Chapter 2; Section D, Chapter 3). In this planning process, the regional teams can name, rate, and prioritize their suggested topics. These inputs together with a multilevel risk analysis lead to a planning proposal, which is then coordinated and discussed with the CEO. This centralized planning approach ensures that the global risk landscape is adequately reflected in the annual audit plan.

Centralized Coordination by the CAE

- The inclusion of additional audit topics in response to audit requests made by individual departments is subject to centralized approval and coordination. In general, every organizational unit and every employee can submit such an audit request. These requests are subject to centralized assessment and approval by the CAE and are agreed with the CEO. This maintains Internal Audit's independence and planning autonomy.

Inclusion of Additional Audit Topics

- Due to the increasingly global focus of business activities, the central coordination of interregional audits is continually gaining importance, for both audits of the organization itself and audits of the actual business environment (major customers, for example). In cases of interregional audits, centralized coordination with the Executive Board, the corporate departments, and the local persons in charge is immensely important.

Central Coordination of Interregional Audits

- Audit work generates significant factual knowledge and potential for effective and efficient solutions to business problems. This knowledge must be made available on a global scale, both for Internal Audit and for all other organizational units. A centralized coordination and organization of Internal Audit helps to make best practice solutions available in a database that is maintained by Internal Audit. Such a collection of data should be administered and maintained centrally for all departments and companies worldwide.

Factual Knowledge and Solution Approaches

- Internal Audit is also increasingly called upon to conduct benchmarking analyses. For such a task, a centralized audit department has the ability to centrally manage, maintain, and analyze comparative data.

Benchmarking

Service and Consulting Activities

- An additional characteristic of centrally organized audit departments is that knowledge resources can be allocated to important audit-related and non audit-related service/consulting activities (see Section A, Chapter 7). Regardless of whether such tasks involve supporting the drafting of guidelines, reviews of central internal projects, or accompanying implementation measures, the use of audit-specific experience in combination with a regional presence will ensure optimal work results. Conversely, it will give subsequent audits a valuable head start with regard to know-how.

Global Structure

The figure below shows the global structure of GIAS within the SAP Group:

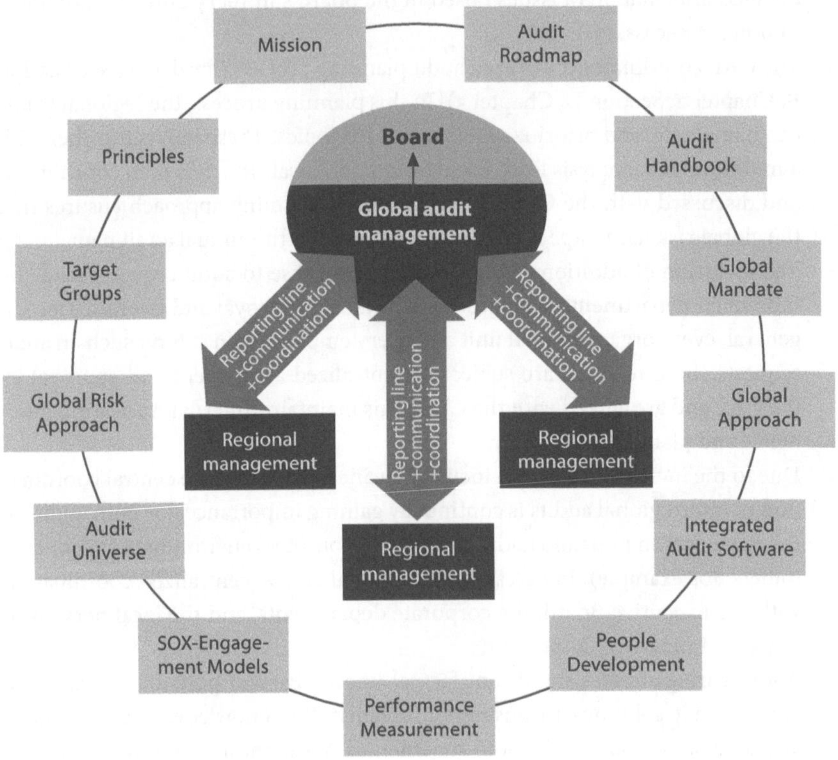

Fig. 9 Global Structure of Internal Audit at SAP

HINTS AND TIPS

- Communication channels and procedures within Internal Audit should be designed to facilitate the exchange of solutions and the optimization of common procedures.
- It is very important to involve regional audit staff in the centralized exchange of information.

4.2 Organizational Structure and Responsibilities within GIAS

KEY POINTS

- Internal Audit at SAP acts as a centrally organized department with a decentralized management structure. The management structure is regional, which results in a large degree of audit responsibility being delegated to the individual regional teams.
- The regional Audit Managers ensure that audits are properly executed and comply with the audit organization.
- A clearly structured communication and meeting structure supports the worldwide harmonization of GIAS across all regional teams.
- The CAE bears overall responsibility for Internal Audit and maintains contact with other governance bodies such as the Audit Committee.

Teams Within GIAS

Internal Audit at SAP is a global department with teams in Germany, the United States, Singapore, and Japan. The individual teams primarily cover audit requirements in their respective regions:

- The team in Germany carries out all audits in Europe, the Middle East, and South Africa, as well as those at the parent company SAP AG.
- The team in the United States is primarily responsible for audits in North and South America.
- The team in Singapore covers audits in Asia and the Pacific region, excluding Japan and Korea but including Australia and New Zealand.
- The team in Japan conducts all audits in Japan and Korea.

Mixed Audit Teams

All audits are based on a uniform, jointly coordinated annual audit plan. As audit requirements are becoming increasingly global, more and more audit teams with auditors from different regions are formed. Working together may either involve exchanging auditors to provide support, to share experiences, and to optimize audits, or establishing specific audit teams who handle a single topic worldwide, either simultaneously or in stages at different locations.

Global Responsibilities of GIAS

The figure below places the global distribution of tasks within GIAS in the overall context of audit work on a global level. This chapter and the following chapters provide details of the distribution of responsibilities as shown in the diagram.

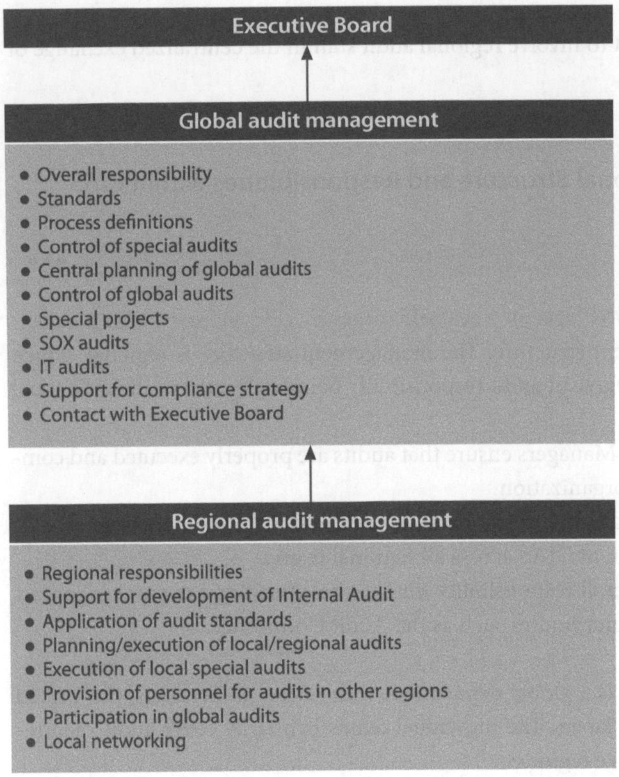

Fig. 10 Distribution of Responsibilities at GIAS

Regional Team Structure

Regional teams consist of auditors from various disciplines and with different levels of experience. The detailed control of these teams is the responsibility of the regional Audit Manager, who is responsible for the team both disciplinarily and functionally. Disciplinary supervision includes all issues that concern terms of employment and performance appraisal. Functional supervision encompasses professional supervision in day to day on the job operations. All issues that regional teams face are decided in direct coordination with the responsible Audit Manager. The only exceptions are escalated issues and tasks or objectives that affect the entire department. In such cases, the regional Audit Manager involves the CAE as the superior line manager.

Meeting Structure

Regular meetings of the Audit Managers and the CAE help to reinforce the management process and reporting structure. At these meetings, the Audit Managers and the CAE discuss and clarify all current issues and future tasks. In addition, weekly bilateral conferences are held between each individual Audit Manager and the CAE. The goal of these meetings is to clarify specific issues that emerge during audits, as well as to jointly identify new, additional audit requirements and topics relevant to the department.

Annual Department Meetings

The annual department meetings represent another important event. At these meetings, all department employees from the different regions meet in one place for several days to discuss and coordinate unresolved issues from audits, along with concepts they have developed and future tasks and objectives. These meetings have the additional benefit of supporting department-wide integration. They provide an important social benefit, since they allow the team colleagues from different regions to get to know each other which lays the foundation for future joint audit activities.

Overall Management

At SAP, the CAE is responsible for the overall management of the department. This means the CAE individually coordinates all regional teams and provides management support to ensure that audit procedures are standardized globally and that global audits are properly coordinated. The CAE also maintains direct contact to all higher authorities, including the Executive Board, the Supervisory Board, and the Audit Committee. In addition, the overall global responsibility for dealings with all other internal and external parties and contacts lies with the CAE.

Regular Meetings with the CEO

In particular, the CAE meets regularly with the CEO to discuss all the major issues faced by Internal Audit with regard to both day-to-day activities and the basic focus of audit tasks. These regularly held meetings are very important for the overall audit work because decisions regarding additional audits – as well as significant measures following from completed audits – are made there. Regularly updated minutes provide a reliable record of what the CEO and the CAE have agreed upon.

Annual Report to the Audit Committee

The Audit Committee, which is a committee of SAP's Supervisory Board, also receives an audit report once a year, which contains information on all important audit-related events. The CAE presents the results, discusses open questions, and fields suggestions in a meeting with the members of the Audit Committee (see also Section B, Chapter 5.4.1).

Planning Levels

As a result, the CAE has to manage several different planning levels:

- overall responsibility for the horizontal coordination of the regional teams,
- further development of the department on a global level,
- main point of contact for all external parties and departments,
- reporting to Executive Board, Supervisory Board, and Audit Committee, and
- department-wide tasks aimed at improving internal organization and communication.

HINTS AND TIPS

- During the audit, information flow to the respective Audit Manager and/or the CAE must be ensured. When in doubt, information should be sent to both parties.

- Regular informal meetings with team colleagues and other regional teams should be held to exchange experiences and information.

LINKS AND REFERENCES

- MARKS, N. 2004. Safeguarding Auditor Objectivity. *Internal Auditor* (October 2004): 37–41.
- BALKARAN, L. 2007. A Solid Reporting Line. *Internal Auditor* (February 2007): 96.
- INSTITUTE OF INTERNAL AUDITORS. 2001. *Practice Advisory 1110-1: Organizational Independence.* Altamonte Springs, FL: The Institute of Internal Auditors.
- INSTITUTE OF INTERNAL AUDITORS. 2001. *Practice Advisory 2020-1: Communication and Approval.* Altamonte Springs, FL: The Institute of Internal Auditors.
- INSTITUTE OF INTERNAL AUDITORS. 2001. *Practice Advisory 2060-1: Reporting to Board and Senior Management.* Altamonte Springs, FL: The Institute of Internal Auditors.
- INSTITUTE OF INTERNAL AUDITORS. 2002. *Practice Advisory 2060-2: Relationship with the Audit Committee.* Altamonte Springs, FL: The Institute of Internal Auditors.
- JOSCELYNE, G. 2004. Balancing Relationships. *Internal Auditor* (February 2004): 35–36.
- TARR, R. 2002. Built to Last. *Internal Auditor* (December 2002): 28–33.

4.3 Structure and Tasks of the Regional GIAS Teams

KEY POINTS

- The regional teams are operational audit units. They possess a high degree of responsibility.
- Audit Managers are in charge of regional teams and responsible for team-specific needs.
- A major focus of regional teams is regional consideration for company specifics and cultural practices. Achieving this goal requires integrating the information channels of the respective region.

Responsibilities of the Regional Teams

Regional teams are responsible for the proper and full execution of all scheduled and ad-hoc audits in their region. In this process, they largely work autonomously – that means, they can schedule and perform all the measures required for proper audit execution. Such wide-ranging freedom is an essential prerequisite for ensuring that Internal Audit can accommodate regional and cultural practices.

Composition of the Regional Team

The regional teams consist of an Audit Manager and a number of auditors with differing areas of expertise and levels of experience. Normally, each regional team will have at least an Internal Auditor, a Senior Auditor, and a Global Auditor (see Section A, Chapter 4.5). However, it is up to the Audit Manager to match the team composition with the requirements of the region.

Challenges Faced by the Regional Team

Aside from their core business of conducting audits, each team is faced with a variety of individual challenges. One challenge beyond the actual audits is to cover the "classic" service activities, as well as additional activities such as consulting, etc. (see Section A, Chapter 7). Some activities arise as a result of regional practices and can include participation in management meetings, discussions with external parties, and cooperation with operating units or other company/audit bodies. Such activities usually involve specific cooperation and are often based on professional relationships developed at a single location. This form of embeddedness in the regional organization, together with informal networking, can create valuable information channels for Internal Audit that a centralized department would find difficult or impossible to achieve.

Responsibility of the Audit Manager

The Audit Manager's responsibilities include budget planning, cost control, the general line management, and coordination of broader issues resulting from the team's work. For these tasks, coordination with the CAE will be just as important as consultation with the central corporate divisions and other regions.

GIAS Network

Despite their independence, the regional audit units remain tied together as part of the GIAS department. This guarantees two things: a uniform, Group-wide audit approach to fieldwork and the actual on-time performance of audits. Auditors from different regions are often involved in time-critical or special audits. Such audits require the planning skills of both the involved Audit Managers and the CAE.

Information Exchange Between Regional Teams and Management

It is particularly important for the regional audit teams to also be in touch with the company's local business managers. To ensure this, GIAS has to communicate with local managers regularly and include local management in its fieldwork. Such cooperation will significantly boost the willingness of the local managers to take the initiative and involve Internal Audit.

HINTS AND TIPS

- Collect and catalog recommendations regarding audits and their organization.
- Auditors have to make sure that all information from their regional teams is also available to the Audit Manager and other GIAS colleagues.

4.4 Structure and Organization of the Audit Teams

KEY POINTS

- An audit team is formed for each audit. Each audit team consists of auditors with the required specific expertise and relevant experience.
- GIAS differentiates between local, regional, and global audits.
- The audit lead, the person in charge of the audit team, is responsible for ensuring that audits are performed correctly, completely, on time and to the defined extent.

- The audit lead's responsibility extends over all audit phases, including planning and reporting.
- Securing the organization of all necessary fieldwork is also under the responsibility of the audit lead.
- The audit team carries out the audit in accordance with the work program and the tasks that are allocated within it. Formal and informal coordination should take place regularly since it is essential for achieving a comprehensive assessment of all relevant aspects of the audit and uniformity of audit results.

The Audit as a Project

Because each audit is an individual activity, audits have project-like characteristics. These project-like characteristics are determined on the basis of criteria such as the audit's uniqueness, time limits, the clearly defined audit request, and specific content-related and organizational objectives and planning. As a result, elements of project control should be applied to audits.

Number of Auditors

Audit teams are formed for each individual audit. An audit is usually performed by at least two auditors at any time; a single auditor is only used in exceptional cases. It is often necessary to include more than two auditors in the audit team.

Levels of Qualification within the Audit Team

The audit team should have a balanced composition at all times. Auditors are assigned to a team on the basis of the required skills and experience, as well as availability and regional or personal suitability. All levels of experience can be represented in an audit team, from Internal Auditor through Senior Auditor to Global Auditor. The team is usually comprised of members with a wide range of qualification levels (see Section A, Chapter 4.5).

The Organization of Audit Assignments

The importance of being able to rapidly form effective audit teams from different locations will continue to increase, because auditors with specific expertise cannot permanently be kept in reserve in all regions, and because auditors usually sign up for local work and may thus be unavailable (at least for some time) for interregional assignments. The Audit Managers and the CAE should demonstrate a considerate approach in assigning employees because interregional assignments usually result in a significant increase in each individual auditor's workload. This increase in workload must be taken into consideration by regional schedules, for example through individual, audit-specific time accounts or blanket time reserves.

Audit Lead

An audit lead is nominated for each audit team as the team leader. The audit lead is responsible for the technical coordination of the audit, and thus for the entire process flow in accordance with the GIAS process model. In addition, the audit lead is responsible for both verifying the quality and ensuring the formal structure of all documentation. Ultimately, the audit lead has to ensure that the audit report is supported by working papers and completed on schedule. Putting different report components together and synchronizing the results to form a consistent opinion are also the responsibility of the audit lead. In case of differences of opinion regarding a specific topic, the audit lead has to ensure that auditors with different opinions ultimately reach a consensus. The audit lead also has to coordinate all audit-related external communication, which includes responsibility for managing appointments with the audited parties, as well as coordinating communication with all the individuals indirectly involved in the audit. All these responsibilities together mean that the audit lead plays a key role in the control and monitoring of the entire audit. Effective scheduling and coordination of the information flow among auditors are major prerequisites audit leads have to meet to ensure a successful audit.

Staffing of Audit Teams

The basic staffing of the audit team is determined during the operational execution planning (see Section B, Chapter 2.4 and Section D, Chaper 3.3). During planning, the available resources are assigned to the time intervals of the scheduled audits. The assignments are preliminary at this point. They are finalized when the actual audits are announced, or at the latest when the operational preparation for the audit begins. By this point, the members of the audit team, as well as the tasks they are assigned to and the time that is allocated for each audit topic, must be determined in detail. The audit team's work program must clearly define the audit objective, the respective audit topics, the fieldwork to be performed, the timelines, and all internal and external dependencies.

Teamwork

During an audit, the audit lead must ensure that the audit team meets regularly (or whenever required) to exchange information and to discuss problems and the progress of the audit. Exchanging working papers, supporting each other during fieldwork, and providing mutual backing for audit findings will help to form a team spirit among audit team members. Other activities that support team work are the joint preparation of opening and closing meetings, reciprocal checks of report components, the joint analysis of interim results, and preparation of the next audit steps.

Regional Audits

Regional audits may be conducted by auditors from different regions (then known as mixed teams). By exchanging personnel between different GIAS teams, the auditors learn about professional development opportunities and mutually benefit from experience and know-how. The composition of the audit team is thus aimed at optimally covering the local and regional audit requirements.

Global Audit Teams

In contrast to regional audits, global audits are always conducted by teams that are comprised of members from different regions. As a result, the topic of the global audit dominates the structure of the team, which means individual auditors are selected and assigned on the basis of their specific knowledge and expertise. With such an approach, global issues can be audited with global representation in different countries, either at the same time or in several stages over time. It is crucial that whenever possible, global audits follow a similar team structure as local or regional audits.

Short-Term Reassignment of Audit Teams

Audit teams usually retain their originally planned composition throughout the entire audit. However, unscheduled changes are possible, when spontaneous events such as personal circumstances or new issues or shifts in emphasis arise during an audit.

HINTS AND TIPS

- Audit teams should be selected based on rational aspects and with personal knowledge and abilities in mind.

- A consistently high level of knowledge among the audit team will allow efficient and reliable audit execution. Achieving this level of knowledge will require commensurate, constant, and coordinated training in audit-specific situations.
- Intercultural aspects and cultural differences as well as cultural knowledge and language skills should be taken into account when composing audit teams. One aim should be to minimize burdens from team composition such as travel.

4.5 Employee Profiles in GIAS

KEY POINTS

- The CAE is responsible for a holistic orientation of the department. This involves making sure that Internal Audit follows guidelines and procedures that are uniform throughout the company, to ensure efficiency, comparability, and quality.
- The CAE is also responsible for basic strategy and the structure of the department.
- The tasks of Internal Audit require a variety of different job profiles within the department. The design of these profiles has to be transparent and uniform, and must include both technical and management-related aspects.
- The different profiles of the auditors contain key tasks that should be the basic foundation for all functional descriptions.
- In addition, each individual job description contains further-reaching requirements, both technical and management-related in nature.

Functions

The following functions by hierarchy exist in the GIAS department:

- CAE,
- Audit Manager,
- Global Auditor,
- Senior Auditor, and
- Internal Auditor.

Personnel Development Concept

The functions listed above describe a career path and are documented in a personnel development concept. Important elements of this concept include the relevant job profiles which lay out the tasks, responsibilities, and authority, as well as expertise and knowledge requirements for each function. Within the framework of the job profiles, a development plan should be drawn up for each job owner according to the employee's individual qualification and performance. Therefore, every step up on the career path reflects the personal experience of the auditor also with regard to professional and leadership qualifications. Each job profile should be documented separately. Such documentation can be used for internal and external job advertisements. Job descriptions should be available to all employees through the intranet.

Activity Areas of the CAE

The CAE is responsible for developing the global strategic direction of the department and a universal audit strategy, which involves the following:

- implementing a secure organizational structure for the department,
- assuming comprehensive management responsibility,
- creating and implementing a general personnel development strategy,
- managing GIAS as an international, multicultural department of different teams, with all staff-related requirements,
- developing process flows within internationally recognized audit standards,
- creating an annual audit plan in close coordination with the CEO and the Audit Committee,
- recording and analyzing audit requests during a year,
- overall coordination, monitoring, and quality control of the audits performed, including communication of audit results to the Executive Board,
- managing and monitoring of escalation processes with regard to audit engagements,
- representing the department at internal and external events,
- interface to and cooperation with internal and external parties,
- supporting the enterprise-wide definition of guidelines, and
- definition and application of key performance indicators within the framework of global benchmarking.

The CAE can suggest audits at his or her own initiative, as well as initiate audits in areas where there is ground for suspicion.

Individual Characteristics

All employees must have a uniform level of expertise and skills with regard to the GIAS audit approach. The structure mapped out in the career path below shows the main additional areas of activity for each position level, broken down by employee profile.

Key Tasks of Auditors

The general tasks in the auditor profiles (first three levels) can be summarized as follows:

- preparing and carrying out scheduled and unscheduled audits from all areas in accordance with audit principles and process guidelines,
- communication of audit results through the appropriate reporting levels,
- monitoring and controlling the follow-up process, including further support, if necessary, in implementing recommendations resulting from an audit,
- close cooperation with other departments, such as Risk Management, as well as external partners to clarify the audit content and monitor audit results,
- support in developing best practice solutions, both for the audit process and in support of other departments and areas,
- rating and analysis of internal process controls and business areas exposed to risk, particularly with regard to regular audits, and if applicable also in coordination with the affected departments, and
- support in designing guidelines and general agreements as requirements for individual business units or the entire company.

Fig. 11 Structure and Tasks by Function within GIAS

Additional Tasks for Senior Auditors

Senior Auditors are, in addition to the above core tasks, involved in special or ad-hoc audits. In most cases, they also serve as audit leads responsible for local and regional audits.

Additional Tasks for Global Auditors

Global Auditors are responsible for globally relevant audit topics. They either represent these topics as interregional technical auditors in all associated audits, or assume the role of global audit leads. This means that they are in charge of colleagues from different regions in a single audit team.

Additional Tasks for Audit Managers

Audit Managers are the regionally responsible heads of organizational audit units, which are organized as cost or profit centers. Audit Managers bear full responsibility for their regional team, in terms of discipline and function. Audit Managers serve as autonomous regional audit executives, but their activities are also centrally aligned and firmly embedded in the overall GIAS department through global integration.

Personal Development

A major consideration of all profiles is the fact that they should merely be seen as a formal framework. Every employee must be able to perform assigned functions individually. The requirements in the profiles represent minimum standards needed to ensure the organizational and professional quality of Internal Audit. Tasks and responsibilities can be extended and intensified at any time, depending on personal ability and interests. Such changes need to be reflected in each individual employee's personal development planning.

HINTS AND TIPS

- Internal auditors should make sure their job descriptions are complete and make suggestions for updates, as well as discuss additional or changes in tasks with the appropriate manager.
- Employees should also be willing to perform tasks that lie outside their job descriptions and document such activities. Based on this documentation, the type and extent of their activities can be examined critically, permitting alternative assignments and new areas of responsibility to be considered.
- The requirements of any position should be discussed with the responsible manager.
- Comparison with similar job profiles in other companies will help recognize potential for changes and improvements in profiles.

LINKS AND REFERENCES

- INSTITUTE OF INTERNAL AUDITORS. 2001. *Practice Advisory 2000-1: Managing the Internal Audit Activity*. Altamonte Springs, FL: The Institute of Internal Auditors.
- INSTITUTE OF INTERNAL AUDITORS. 2001. *Practice Advisory 2040-1: Policies and Procedures*. Altamonte Springs, FL: The Institute of Internal Auditors.
- INSTITUTE OF INTERNAL AUDITORS. 2001. *Practice Advisory 2050-1: Coordination*. Altamonte Springs, FL: The Institute of Internal Auditors.
- INSTITUTE OF INTERNAL AUDITORS. 2001. *Practice Advisory 2050-2: Acquisition of External Audit Services*. Altamonte Springs, FL: The Institute of Internal Auditors.

4.6 Career Paths and Development Potential

KEY POINTS

- The GIAS job profiles are assigned to different career levels. All GIAS functions are therefore linked with each other and form the foundation for a contiguous career path.
- Based on this career path, performance feedback meetings take place for the purpose of performance measurement and development planning. During these meetings, specific measures are defined to either maintain an attained job level or prepare for advancement to the next career level.

- The decisive factor in each auditor's professional development is each individual's commitment. The combination of an employee's commitment and the support of the CAE or the Audit Manager guarantee that career development planning is optimized and translates into professional advancement.
- In addition to development opportunities within Internal Audit, alternative career paths outside of GIAS but within the company are possible.

Job Profile Within GIAS

The GIAS functions listed in the previous chapter are integrated into a prototypical contiguous, transparent career path. The job descriptions for each position form the essence of the GIAS career path (see Section A, Chapter 4.5). The job profiles list all the prerequisites, technical knowledge, and personal characteristics required in a job owner. Every Internal Audit employee must be assigned to one of these positions; otherwise, conscientious performance measurement and development planning will not be possible.

Description of Career Levels

Each career level is described by:

- the required level of knowledge and skills,
- the level of quality and quantity shown in the execution of tasks, documented by ongoing performance measurement,
- the extent of responsibility, and
- acceptance and comprehension of activities both within and outside of GIAS.

Pay Grades

Depending on regional circumstances, the different career levels can be arranged individually in one or more pay grades. The pay grade structure is therefore differentiated by region and by performance level. Respective performance levels should be assigned to corresponding groups worldwide.

Development Potential

The development potential of each individual employee has to be identified, taking the prototypical career path as a foundation. In the annual performance feedback meeting, the performance of each individual auditor and manager is measured, analyzed, and documented jointly. Globally uniform standard documents, such as the GIAS appraisal form, are available for the purpose of measurement, analysis, and documentation, and help record both qualitative and quantitative aspects of audit work. Important factors that are included are the number and type of audits, their quality, and any special tasks performed. The different activity levels create a balanced record of current performance capability and recognized development fields.

Development Plan of Individual Auditors

The professional development of an auditor initially involves identifying and eliminating knowledge deficits and acquiring skills. These measures are intended to establish or maintain the required skills level of the auditor concerned. If the objective is to prepare an auditor for new tasks, a development plan must be established for the next step in the GIAS career path. Such a plan combines different training aspects, such as improvement of technical skills ranging from international accounting to knowledge of modern audit practices, but also language skills and personal abilities such as social behavior, teamwork ability, etc. Such skill acquisition goals are summarized annually in the personal development plan and monitored by the respective auditor together with the line manager.

Development Steps

For the individual auditor, new skill acquisition targets may result in new or additional audit topics, obtaining a professional certification, temporary participation in special audits, global audits, and internal projects or even in moving to a different region. All of these activities significantly expand the horizon of the individual and create a good foundation for professional advancement. Obtaining a professional certification, such as the CIA, CPA, CISA, or CSOX designation, is a step that is particularly suited to improve proficiency and to signal adherence to external ethical and professional standards.

Career Path

Auditors who reach their development goals on time and perform their daily duties satisfactorily can expect to attain the next level in their career path at medium-term intervals of one to three years. The degree of personal commitment of each individual employee is a key factor in this advancement. The question as to whether a career takes a more technical turn or is more management-oriented within the GIAS career path is largely determined individually.

Development Opportunities

Aside from development opportunities within GIAS, auditors also have the option of assuming technical or managerial responsibilities in other parts of SAP. Due to the wide range of experience and knowledge acquired during audit work, Internal Audit represents an ideal qualification platform for working in numerous other areas of the company, particularly in business administration departments or other staff functions. The GIAS employee development system supports individuals who wish to pursue such opportunities.

Future Perspectives

Alternatively, due to the manifold, ever-changing tasks it faces, GIAS can offer exciting long-term perspectives to qualified employees. It is the responsibility of all GIAS managers to emphasize this continually, and to convince the individual auditor of its validity. However, employees have to decide for themselves whether the long-term focus on audit work sufficiently motivates them, or whether they are interested in other enterprise areas.

HINTS AND TIPS

- During the year, Internal Audit staff should verify their achievement of objectives, pose critical questions regarding further education requirements, and discuss topical questions regarding their development directly with their line managers.
- Defining partial and objective goals makes it easier to monitor achievement.
- Auditors should accept tasks that are not necessarily part of their own career focus.
- Career aspects should not be the focus of daily work, but considered in medium to long term planning.

LINKS AND REFERENCES ↗

- HELPERT, A. 2006. Cultivating a Loyal Workforce. *Internal Auditor* (December 2006): 66–72.
- MCDONALD, P. 2006. The Quest for Talent. *Internal Auditor* (June 2006): 72–77.

4.7 The Structure of Timesheets in Internal Audit

KEY POINTS •••

- Timesheets fulfill a number of tasks. Most importantly, they are a crucial planning tool in drawing up a reliable audit plan for each auditor. Other tasks are performance analysis and costing control.
- Timesheets provide information at a glance such as relevant totals for each auditor, and aggregated figures for the entire department.
- On the basis of such information and standard time requirements for individual phases of the Audit Roadmap accurate time values can be calculated for each audit status.
- Timesheets can also be used as a basis for discussion between employee and line manager in performance feedback.

Need to Identify and Structure Available Working Time

Internal Audit is a project-based department. In such departments, it is necessary to identify and structure the available working time for the following reasons:

- To keep the total volume of each time component, such as net working time, productivity and capacity utilization, as well as sick leave and vacation days actually taken, etc., up to date. Current information on the net number of working days available is the basis for scheduling individual audits.
- Standard times can be used to determine the total number of audits that can be executed by each auditor and the whole department.
- By budgeting time and using standard times, a staffing plan based on the capacity for the entire department can be created. Such a plan should cover all auditors with different levels of experience and knowledge, and should take into consideration planned and unplanned absences.
- Creating a staffing plan makes it easier to plan and monitor the audits as a whole as well as the phases of the GIAS process model (see Section B), because the plan identifies how time is allocated within each audit.
- Based on the staffing plan, averages within and across audit categories can be determined for internal and external benchmarking. These averages can be related to other key figures (e.g. performance indicators from previous years or from other internal audit departments). Performance ratios form the basis for additional reports on the department's effectiveness and efficiency (see Section D, Chapter 7).

- In addition, information on the structure and composition of individual assignments facilitates configuring audits with regard to time available, reducing the risk that the complexity of an audit may make it impossible to execute it in time.
- Careful time planning is closely linked to the possibility to bill departments for certain audit activities or services, because time spent on such projects can be determined. The ability to determine time spent and the cost of such time opens up completely new possibilities for internal and external charging.
- Time planning also helps to determine the department's total output. Management can create very detailed reports by breaking down audit categories into individual audits, activities, etc. In addition, by calculating trends and correlations, it is possible to forecast future performance profiles, to determine employee productivity for individual employees, and to identify future staffing requirements.

Development of a Timesheet

There are many ways how capacity-based timesheets can be developed. The most feasible option is to use comparable models from other departments that have project-related activities.

Calculating Auditor Days

An employee's total annual capacity is around 220 to 240 working days, less an amount of non-productive time such as training, vacation, and meetings. Based on experience, a total of around 160 to 180 productive auditor days is available as a basis for planning for each employee.

Creation of Time Profiles for Audit Categories

The next step is to compile a time profile for each audit status, based on the Audit Roadmap, using averages and experience values. According to the Audit Roadmap, a basic audit (see Section A, Chapter 6.6) requires on average 24 days. Given, for example, 160 productive auditor days, an auditor can execute on average 6.5 basic audits a year. By standardizing the time required for status checks and follow-ups (see Section B, Chapter 6), the total number of activities possible per employee and year can be computed using a simple equivalence calculation. Based on our experience, a feasible workload is, on average, four basic audits, four follow-ups, and four audit status checks per year and employee (see Section A, Chapter 6.6).

Problem of Ad-Hoc Audits

Ad-hoc audits pose a special problem with regard to time planning because due to the special requirements of such audits there are usually no standard values to base any planning on. Acceptable standard values can be estimated using values from previous ad-hoc engagements, other planned audits or by making reasonable estimates.

Use of Timesheets in Employee Management

Timesheets can also be used as a performance feedback tool. They form a basis for building a mutual understanding between employee and line manager. Such a shared reference framework makes it easier to discuss and agree on issues such as capacity utilization, exceeded deadlines, schedule changes, or team reorganizations.

HINTS AND TIPS

- All employees should discuss their annual time planning with their line manager and receive an explanation of the scheduled times.
- During an audit, a separate record of unusual events that had an impact on the actual auditing time should be kept.

LINKS AND REFERENCES

- HUBBARD, L. 2000. Audit Planning. *Internal Auditor* (August 2000): 20–21.
- INSTITUTE OF INTERNAL AUDITORS. 2001. *Practice Advisory 2200-1: Engagement Planning*. Altamonte Springs, FL: The Institute of Internal Auditors.
- RIFE, R. 2006. Planning for Success. *Internal Auditor* (October 2006): 25–29.

5 Fundamental Principles of the GIAS Approach

5.1 Employee Profiles and their Interaction in the Audit Process

KEY POINTS •••

- Employee profiles provide formal requirements in terms of the individual functions at GIAS.
- In determining formal requirements it is important to distinguish between disciplinary and technical requirements on one side and social and personal requirements on the other.
- A mix of various skills is necessary to ensure that audits are in compliance with international audit principles.

Employee Profiles

Section A, Chapter 4.5 provides details of individual job descriptions at GIAS. The success of Internal Audit's work can only be guaranteed if the department has employees that fit the job profiles. In determining what skills employees should have and what requirements should be included in profiles the following disciplinary, technical, and social factors should be considered:

- **Disciplinary Structure** Disciplinary factors have to be given consideration. The first disciplinary factor is the internal audit department's disciplinary structure. It ensures to a great extent compliance with audit standards and sets an action framework that is mandatory for all audits and for each employee. The second disciplining factor is the annual audit plan. Compliance with this plan is an important element of disciplinary control.
- **Quality Assurance** Another factor that has to be given consideration is quality assurance. Quality assurance procedures (for details, see Section D, Chapter 5) define in detail who is responsible for the supervision and control of each audit phase. In addition to content, deadlines and formal criteria must also be controlled. The control tasks usually involve the audit lead, the responsible Audit Manager, and, if appropriate, the CAE (see Section A, Chapter 4.5).
- **Social Skills** An internal auditor's social skills need to be considered when filling a function. The way people contribute on a personal level can be critical for how they interact with their colleagues and with employees from other departments. Communication skills, an ability to integrate, and a constant focus on solutions are indispensable behavior patterns.
- **Ability to Cooperate** Internal Audit's ability to cooperate is another important aspect. Cooperation is important in dealing with both technical and personal causes of audit findings in an atmosphere of trust. The personal willingness of employees to cooperate and a positive attitude to interaction with others is a key factor.
- **Information Exchange** Successful audit work needs a well functioning flow of information. Although frankness and clarity are often the only ways to resolve issues, it is sometimes necessary to withhold or anonymize information. Anonymity is especially important when confidentiality, personal data protection, or company interests are

at stake. However, confidentiality requirements should not have an impact on the accuracy of audit results. When confidentiality is concerned, sensitivity is required. Internal Audit's obligation to maintain confidentiality must never be compromised.

Intercultural Cooperation

- Another aspect in formulating profiles is intercultural exposure of each individual GIAS employee. Consideration of such exposure is important especially where mixed audit teams are deployed or global audits in various countries are conducted. It is important to realize what an audit means in a particular cultural group, what importance is attached to it, and what personal conclusions each individual draws from it.

HINTS AND TIPS

- Auditors should obtain information in advance on how audit tasks are distributed in general and make sure that during the audit process the audit team's competency mix adequately matches requirements.
- In addition, auditors should get an idea of the special competencies of their audit colleagues.
- Auditors should try to avoid intersecting responsibilities. Get help from the relevant line manager if necessary to resolve or clarify conflicts.

5.2 Attributes of the Process-Based Approach

KEY POINTS

- The audits conducted by GIAS are increasingly being organized as projects.
- A key requirement for organizing audits as projects is a standardized and clearly structured process model. This process model has to be defined in its individual project phases.
- Main audit phases are planning, preparation, execution, reporting, and follow-up. Every audit has to follow these phases with differing degrees of intensity.
- It has to be generally accepted that the process model with all its standard requirements must be followed in all audits as far as possible.

Project Approach

The large variety of audit topics, and the need to make audits plannable, controllable, and comparable require a project approach to audits. A clear process model is a very useful tool for implementing a project approach because it allows planning and performing an audit seamlessly from beginning to end. A process model has to be based on a standardized approach that covers all standard requirements, and it can be used for every audit and individually adapted as necessary (for details, see Section B).

Audit Roadmap

The standard process model of GIAS, the Audit Roadmap, comprises the following phases:

- Planning,
- Preparation,
- Execution,
- Reporting, and
- Follow-up.

Please refer to Section B for a detailed description of each phase. This chapter explains the reasons for and the advantages of having a process model.

Audit Roadmap as Working Basis

The project character of audits is an important reason for having a standard process model. A standardized process ensures that project-relevant requirements can be implemented easier by providing a sequential model of all necessary audit phases, from planning through execution to preparing the audit report and follow-up activities. Such a model helps to make sure that audits can be reviewed and monitored. However, the individual phases only provide the framework for the audit steps concerned. The included working papers, standard report templates, operational work instructions, and recommendations are of major importance, because they increase the audit reliability of each individual Internal Audit employee. There are very few process steps that the process model does not define, at least in outline. Providing a comprehensive model facilitates comparing individual audits with each other and integrating them into a benchmarking concept. Both process-related key performance indicators and results-based values can be used for key performance indicator (KPI) analysis (see Section D, Chapter 7).

Coordination of Auditors

A process-based approach also facilitates the coordination of individual auditors. Meeting key deadlines in audits, known as milestones, requires a proactive project-based employee management. The process model provides an indispensable basic tool for such a proactive management. The clearly structured phases and their substructures allow Internal Audit management to monitor deadlines, deployment, and reporting, and therefore, to perform comprehensive and sensible audit management.

Performance-Based Audit Execution

A process model opens up the possibility for performance-based incentive systems. Rewards should be given when a milestone is successfully completed. A milestone is successfully completed if all activities required in terms of the standard process model, plus any additional activities needed, have been performed to the required level of quality and within the agreed timeframe.

Phase-Based Quality Assurance

Phase-based quality assurance of the audit process as part of the process model considerably enhances the efficiency of audits. Approval to proceed to the next audit step should only be given when quality assurance has been performed (for details, see Section D, Chapter 5). A process model guarantees an approach that is consistent across all audit phases, while also providing considerable support in ensuring the completeness of the quality assurance process.

Process-Based Approach

The following diagram shows the interrelations within the process-based Internal Audit approach. It also lays out the GIAS Roadmap, which is the working basis for Internal Audit at SAP.

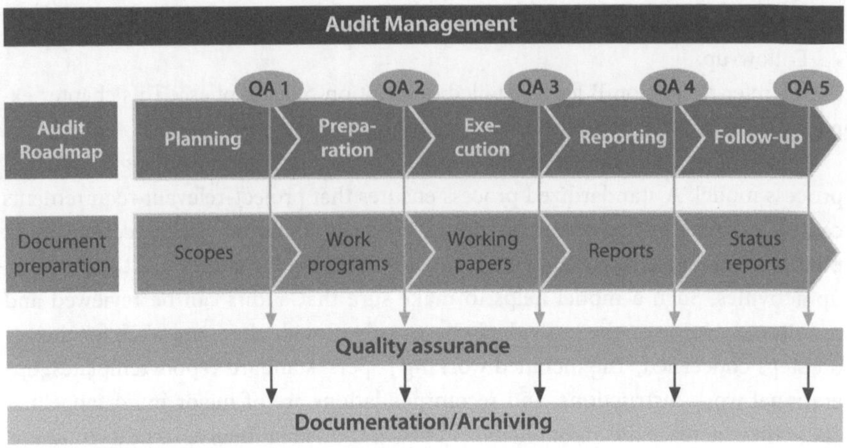

Fig. 12 Process-Based Approach in Internal Audit at SAP

Peer Review

A process based audit model creates the basis for a comprehensive review of Internal Audit. Such a review can be in the form of a peer review, which is a critical evaluation of work by independent colleagues of similar standing (see Section D, Chapter 9) and offers Internal Audit the opportunity to face scrutiny by a committee of outside experts. As part of such a review all process steps must be made available to external third parties for investigation. The process model provides a comprehensive overview of the important performance factors of Internal Audit and helps to structure, plan, and perform peer reviews in an efficient manner. The clear structure of the process model simplifies reviews because assessment criteria can be unambiguously assigned to the relevant phases and process steps. In addition, any improvement potential can be pinpointed accurately and addressed on the basis of clear responsibilities.

Integrated Software Solution

Last but not least, a process-based approach provides the perfect basis to develop or employ IT solutions. Because the content and sequence of steps are accurately described, many of the procedures can be automated (see Section D, Chapter 4).

HINTS AND TIPS

- Every employee should have a thorough understanding of the elements of the GIAS process model. The process model should be applied consistently, and particularly the project approach should be implemented uniformly.

- Standards should be regularly assessed with regard to appropriateness, and if necessary recommendations should be made for optimization. It is useful to review other procedures implemented at official institutions, other companies, or other suitable sources to identify improvement potential.
- Always ensure that each phase is complete and observe the milestones with regard to assuring content quality.
- There should be a regular exchange of views and ideas with those responsible regarding the advantages and disadvantages of the current process model.

5.3 Definition of Audit Content

KEY POINTS •••

- For an efficient and standardized audit execution, audits must be clearly defined in what they cover.
- Uniform content of audits is achieved by defining audit areas and providing information on audit content. At SAP, such a definition is done in Scopes, which are documents describing standard audit content.
- The definition of standard audit content gives auditors the opportunity to familiarize themselves as quickly as possible with new and comprehensive audit topics on the basis of standardized procedures. Familiarity with the relevant Scopes is particularly important because intensive exposure to the material to be audited is an essential prerequisite for a successful audit.
- In addition, audits performed on the basis of Scopes can be compared easier with regard to work performed and results achieved.

Scopes

At SAP, audit content is systematically structured on the basis of comprehensive standard documents known as Scopes. These documents are important tools used to perform efficient and effective audits. The content of each audit field (e.g. operational audits) is defined in a number of Core Scopes (e.g. Purchasing) which in turn are broken down into several Key Scopes (e.g. Purchase Order, Goods Receipt). Scopes contain detailed information about the audit area, including the processes, procedures, risks, and control systems (see Section B, Chapter 2.1). Scopes can have different levels of complexity depending on the audit topic. For example, the audit of an entire department, such as purchasing, or of a corporate function, such as management, requires a much more comprehensive description than the audit of credit card expenses. The scoping phase, which precedes the actual execution of the audit, requires auditors to familiarize themselves in depth with the audit matter.

Creation of Scopes

Section B, Chapter 2.1 describes the content of Scopes in detail. Here, we only point out that the creation of Scopes involves a multi-stage procedure, in which all the facts and the content of an audit area are captured and described according to a standard structure. The following dimensions can be used to map almost all audit-relevant information:

- frameworks set by guidelines, rules, and written instructions,
- organizational units in the company,
- processes that map the interaction between functions, and
- individual process-related objects as the smallest operational units.

Advantages of Scopes

In the context of an integrated process model, the standardized description of audit content based on Scopes presents a number of important advantages:

Standardized, Forward-Looking Description

- A standardized and forward-looking description of audit content allows auditors to familiarize themselves in depth with the material to be audited in advance of the actual audit, thus giving them a foundation of the audit topic. This gives them the opportunity to deal with the audit areas, both in relation to a specific audit and independently of an audit.

Current Condition and Desired Criteria

- The description and definition of audit content specifies not only the current condition but also the desired ideal criteria so that Internal Audit's requirements are already included in the Scopes. When the actual audit is performed, the current and the desired condition are compared, thus ensuring the effectiveness of the fieldwork. This means that existing processes and guidelines are not the only benchmark for audit findings, but are supplemented by the comparison with ideal desired criteria.

Greater Ease of Planning

- The standardized description of audit content also makes audits and the associated costs easier to plan and to control. This allows Intenal Audit to create, edit, and analyze audit assignment schedules with regard to staffing requirements for the audits to be performed, and the time to be allocated. A thorough description also facilitates providing evidence for costs incurred or justifying the need for additional resources.

Standard Audit Content

- Standard audit content is stored in a central database and is available to all employees of Internal Audit. The availability of such standardized content ensures that all auditors always refer to the same Scopes, because Scopes are important prerequisites for preparing the work program (see Section B, Chapter 3.2). It is important to link the audit content with the individual steps of the audit execution, so that work programs are ultimately based on standardized content, which guarantees that each audit is compliant, complete, reliable, and transparent.

Specific Audit Content

The specific content of every audit must be accurately planned and described. There are, however, a number of audits the content of which can only be partially, or not at all, standardized. Examples include specific one-time audits (e.g., the audit of a specific partnership) and audits that arise ad hoc and are firmly linked to specific circumstances. Although it is possible to provide general content descriptions for such audits, the specifics of such audits often evolve during the actual audit preparations as a result of advance analysis and preparatory interviews. In addition, there are audits of topics that have not been covered before or that are subject to non-disclosure obligations. In such cases, the audit content can only gradually be planned as information becomes available.

Highly Integrated Process

Developing standardized audit content should be seen as part of a highly integrated process. Audit findings can be used as feedback for developing Scopes further. This means that each Scope is subject to ongoing change triggered by the audit process itself. In addition, Scopes should be reviewed regularly based on discussions with experts from within and outside the internal audit department and adapted when necessary.

HINTS AND TIPS

- Check Scopes for completeness and discuss any shortcomings with employees responsible for the daily operations of the audit area.
- Internal Audit should have regular discussions about the content and structure of the Scopes. Regular feedback on individual Scopes will ensure that Scopes are current and of high quality.

LINKS AND REFERENCES

- INSTITUTE OF INTERNAL AUDITORS. 2001. *Practice Advisory 2210-1: Engagement Objectives*. Altamonte Springs, FL: The Institute of Internal Auditors.

5.4 GIAS Target Group Structure

KEY POINTS

- Internal Audit is an interactive part of a corporate-wide communication process. For this reason, it collaborates with a large number of internal and external target groups.
- In addition to purely exchanging information, particularly in the form of reports, individual cases may require additional cooperation, such as joint development of solutions.
- Reporting lines for Internal Audit largely follow the organizational structure of the company, which means that the Audit Committee in particular and the CEO are the main focus of the reporting system.
- Other internal target groups also have to be provided with different information. It is important to involve the different target groups in the audit process according to the Audit Roadmap.
- The information provided by Internal Audit is also used by a large number of external groups: External auditors are the most important partners, but many other target groups have to be considered too.

Cooperation Models

There is a large number of groups that either make audit requests to GIAS or that have to be taken into account when information on audits is given. Before conducting audits, these groups may have to be consulted as part of the preparation process. After the audit, it is important that communication with these groups not only includes information about audit outcomes, but also information on optimized business processes. This results in cooperation models for Internal Audit which are described in detail in Section D, Chapter 2.

Internal Target Groups

Separating GIAS's target groups into internal, external, and other units provides the following internal target groups, which are ranked by importance in the "reporting hierarchy":

- Audit Committee and Supervisory Board,
- Executive Board and CEO (or the Board member in charge),
- corporate management,
- regional management/senior management,
- local management/departmental management,
- employees responsible.

Supervisory Board and Audit Committee

The Supervisory Board must be informed of extraordinary audits and audit findings, and it must be included in important decisions, such as the audit planning for the year. The Supervisory Board's Audit Committee receives an annual status report from Internal Audit, which covers all audits that have been performed, significant findings and actions, special projects and initiatives, as well as all basic information about GIAS. The Audit Committee can make audit requests directly, which would lead to additional communication (see Section B, Chapter 2.3).

Executive Board and CEO

The Executive Board and the CEO, as the chairman of the Executive Board, are the highest internal disciplinary unit that receives information on audit findings. In addition to a detailed audit report, GIAS prepares a Board summary (see Section B, Chapter 5.2.5), which outlines the most important audit findings and results. The Board summary contains information that is relevant to the Executive Board, or that requires a Board decision or Board action. At regular meetings held at least once a month, the CAE and the CEO analyze audit findings, follow-up results, and potential escalation cases and determine if any immediate steps need to be taken. In addition, the other members of the Executive Board must be directly informed of any important findings. This reporting system allows for timely and informed decisions to be taken as a result of audit findings.

Corporate Management

Global corporate audit departments should maintain close contact with other global units, for example, Corporate Financial Reporting. There is often an in-depth exchange of information on audit planning and results. Internal Audit can provide valuable support to other departments for the preparation of global guidelines. GIAS can also be contacted regarding the implementation planning of global strategies at the level of operational (local) business units.

Regional Management/ Senior Management

Regional and senior management are usually directly affected by internal audits. Audit findings should be communicated to operational managers who are affected by them. These managers should be given the chance to respond to audit findings. Regional and senior management are charged with implementing the findings of Internal Audit under area-specific aspects.

Local Management/ Departmental Management

For most audit findings, local and departmental management is ultimately responsible for implementing GIAS' recommendations. This reporting level includes those responsible for ensuring that all guidelines and directives are strictly observed in day-to-day operations. Local and departmental management are therefore extensively and actively involved in the auditing process, for example by attending opening and closing meetings. In relation to their areas of responsibility, they are fully answerable for implementing actions that result from audits. Close cooperation with these managers gives Internal Audit the opportunity to have a positive effect on operational and process structures.

Employees

The employees affected by the audit with their functions and duties provide the main point of reference for the audit. During the entire audit process, the employees at the operational level are the auditors' actual contact persons. Once the audit has been completed, the auditees are responsible for actively implementing necessary actions in consultation with their managers. Employees affected by an audit should be able to make suggestions at any time, to obtain advice, and to work with auditors in an open, communicative atmosphere. This cooperation at fieldwork level ensures that all audit findings can lead to appropriate and agreed actions.

External Target Groups

The external target groups can be broken down into external audit bodies and other external cooperation partners, such as customers and suppliers.

External Auditors as External Audit Body

GIAS and the external auditors have numerous joint or overlapping responsibilities, which require regular and detailed exchanges of information and experience (for details, see Section D, Chapter 2.6). The exchange of audit reports, opinions, concepts, and day-to-day issues, in addition to the discussion of solutions to problems discovered in audits, lends special significance to the cooperation between GIAS and external auditors. The more closely the two parties work together in accounting matters, risk and internal control management, and in auditing in general, the better the guarantee of the integrity of the accounting system and the effectiveness of controls.

Importance of the Reporting System for the External Auditors

A differentiated reporting system is critical to efficient cooperation. Due to the general obligation of the Executive Board to disclose and reveal all facts and circumstances which are relevant for the financial statements, external auditors should be given direct access to relevant findings and recommendations made by Internal Audit. To encourage cooperation, internal auditors should, if possible immediately forward all reports directly to the external auditors. By doing so, they can avoid duplication of work and additional costs.

Professional Associations

Professional associations (e.g. the IIA) and standards setters can also be regarded as external target groups of Internal Audit. In this regard a company has to examine to what extent information from Internal Audit could and should be made available to be used as the basis for new statutes. In addition, findings and recommendations from individual audits can be used to define best-practice solutions.

General concepts, e.g., for benchmarking or performance rating on the basis of key performance indicators, can also be developed in cooperation with professional associations or with academia.

Other External Cooperation Partners

To varying degrees, Internal Audit also consults with other external contacts on a case-by-case basis. This often involves the exchange and assessment of papers and documents, or other forms of cooperation before, during, or after an audit. Customers and suppliers are important partners with whom information can be exchanged. Any exchange of information, however, requires legal safeguards for the company such as non-disclosure agreements.

Other Target Groups

Other important contact and target groups include banks and insurance companies, legal firms, or tax consultants, and any relevant public service agencies, including the police and district attorneys' offices. In regard to legal information requirements Internal Audit together with legal council should be involved in drawing up a company-wide document retention policy that considers legal requirements for document retention and information exchange.

General Overview

The following diagram gives a general overview of Internal Audit's possible target groups as explained above.

GIAS target groups		
Internal	**External**	**Other**
• Supervisory Board • Audit Committee • Executive Board • Board member in charge • Corporate management • Regional management/ senior management • Local management/ departmental management • Employees responsible	• External audit bodies, e.g., external auditors, professional associations • Other external contacts e.g., customers, vendors etc.	• Banks • Insurance companies • Law firms • Public authorities • Public institutions

Fig. 13 GIAS Target Groups

HINTS AND TIPS

- Auditors should test each process step along the Audit Roadmap for involvement of the relevant target groups and ensure that all the necessary information is available and all parties concerned have been adequately informed.

5.5 Structure and Content of the Audit Universe

KEY POINTS •••

- Internal Audit possesses a vast array of knowledge. Pooling this knowledge in a comprehensive system results in an audit universe that comprises the process model, audit content, findings and recommendations, key performance indicators, and documentation components.
- The process model and the audit content deal with the methodology and content-related design of audits.
- In the broadest sense, findings/recommendations and key performance indicators are used for evaluating and analyzing audits of any dimension or period.
- Documentation of audits guarantees a fully compliant audit approach by creating primary documents (i.e., documents directly related to audit objects) as well as secondary documents that provide additional information available.
- The next step that follows a definition of the audit universe is the creation of an audit portal as part of an integrated audit management solution.

Definition

The audit universe, as defined at SAP, is the entirety of all practice-related, all theory-based, and conceptual approaches for internal audit services. This definition is broader, than the one commonly used in the internal auditing literature. It is in our opinion important to develop a thorough understanding of audit and communications options, before audit approaches and means for results communication should be defined. Components of the audit universe as defined at SAP are the process model, the audit content, findings and recommendations, key performance indicators, and documentation. The aim of this broad definition is to show that different aspects of internal auditing combine into a comprehensive, harmonious system. As shown below, all aspects have meaningful relations with each other and are important in describing in detail an individually adaptable approach that yields uniformly high quality audit results for a global audit department.

Objective of Fully Comprehensive Documentation

The aim of SAP's audit universe is to provide a comprehensive documentation of tasks and requirements for Internal Audit. This includes descriptive elements such as an audit handbook and a Charter adopted by the Executive Board, plus the entire Audit Roadmap documentation, including all standard templates. In addition to the primary audit documentation, all secondary documentation of upstream and downstream areas must also be included. This comprises all policies and guidelines set by the Executive Board and other management levels, plus detailed work instructions of operational units. Another important area is the comprehensive documentation of processes, including all information on internal controls, risk assignment, and financial accounts. This documentation might be linked to the internal control management tool which is used for the SOX processes. Further documentation that should be included is quality guidelines of individual areas, external quality guidelines, and any audit-relevant laws, directives, and statutes. All secondary documentation should be linked electronically with the audit universe.

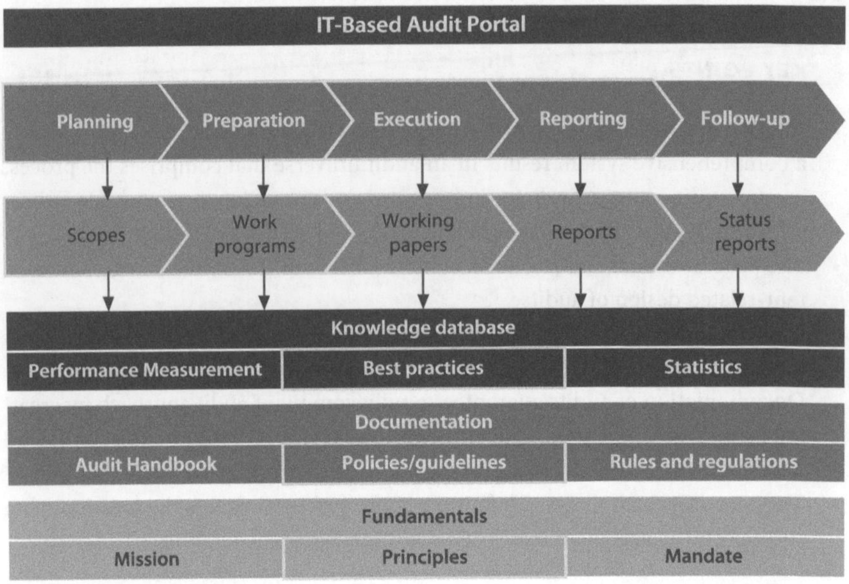

Fig. 14 SAP's Global Audit Universe

Overview The structure of the audit universe is complex, since it integrates different aspects. Detailed information relating to each area is provided in the subsequent chapters. At this stage we will only provide a general overview of the structure.

Addressees The main addressees of the audit universe are all Internal Audit employees and managers. In addition, all members of corporate management and the Audit Committee, plus the parties involved in particular audits and their management, may be considered users. The audit universe also provides a comprehensive source of information on fieldwork to all interested colleagues, managers, or even external partners, provided that the applicable access restrictions are observed.

Standard Methods in the Process Model The audit universe breaks down into the following main components: the Audit Roadmap, the knowledge database, documentation, and the fundamentals. The process model is a method-based approach. The design of the Audit Roadmap reflects the dynamic character of this multi-phase model. It is important to ensure that all procedural and documentation-based approaches and content at any level of detail are available as standard reference for audits. The use of standard methods guarantees that all audits with their respective content are based on a consistent procedural model.

Standard Content: Scopes The above is closely related to developing Scopes (see Section A, Chapter 5.3). Scopes define standards and are available in advance to provide guidance for most audits. Scopes ensure that standard methods are used in conjunction with standard content in most audits, allowing for a high degree of efficiency gains during fieldwork. Individual adjustments and additions will, however, be necessary for each audit. Such adaptations are usually made in the work program. If it is not possible to relate the audit to standardized Scopes, a Scope may be created incrementally. Alternatively, a Scope that is closest to the requirements of the specific audit may be adapted. If the Scope can be reused, it can be submitted as a standard for future audits.

Use of Audit Results

Findings and recommendations made during audits form an important basis for further steps in the audit process, e.g., follow-ups. However, all information gained during an audit and follow-up work can also be used to pursue other objectives. For instance, such data can be used for performance measurement, to provide information on the efficiency of audits and the implementation of the findings in the organization. Information on findings and recommendations can also be incorporated in a knowledge database. Such a database can be useful to document findings and implementation measures with regard to recommendations. It could also be employed to develop optimized process solutions and KPI structures. Database models can help analyze data using a variety of different criteria. Findings and recommendations can be updated in sequence, which allows tracking their significance and frequency over time.

Total of All Key Performance Indicators and Comparisons

A database of findings and recommendations could form the collective basis for any key performance indicator analysis, which allows comparing different as-is situations and their measurement against ideal or to-be situations. KPI analysis can be used to measure Internal Audit's performance, to perform profitability analyses for individual audit objects, and to compile summary reports on all audited units over a certain period. A database also allows performing time-series analysis using statistical tools and generating forecasts (e.g., how many findings are expected for a certain audit volume). This information can be used to identify trends regarding a company's quality awareness and to determine on this basis quality-enhancing measures by introducing appropriate organizational structures. All such arithmetic and statistical algorithms should be included in the audit universe.

Data and Information Pool

The audit universe manifests itself in a comprehensive data and information pool. This pool is not for the exclusive use of Internal Audit. It should be made accessible to all employees and parties involved in the audit as well. To ensure safeguarding of confidential information, access authorization rules should be implemented. Keyword indices and direct access via any search item are as essential in designing the database as are comprehensive links between information in the database. As part of an internet application, the audit universe can provide access to any amount of external information, e.g. from conferences or audit institutes. In addition, the audit universe can be used on an anonymized basis to support the exchange of information between companies.

Audit Portal

An advanced version of an electronic audit universe could take on the form of an audit portal, which is a networked internal audit application. Such a portal should be an important component of an even more extensive corporate governance or compliance portal, which contains a company's overall compliance system. In an ever more dynamic business world, there is an increasing need to make use of this type of fully integrated information platforms. It is the fastest and most efficient way to supplement Internal Audit's knowledge and insights with additional facts and information and deliver it to the units concerned.

HINTS AND TIPS

- Assess all information with regard to its significance for Internal Audit and with a view to inclusion in the audit universe.
- Establish before each audit whether and to what extent there is information relevant to the audit in the audit universe.
- Exchange information with colleagues and external parties about the quality of the audit universe and the data stored there so that suggestions and improvements can be incorporated in the audit universe on an ongoing basis.
- To ensure that a comprehensive information system is user-friendly, it is necessary to tailor content, IT and system support to different user groups.

LINKS AND REFERENCES

- REZAEE, Z., W. FORD AND R. ELAM. 2000. Real-Time Accounting Systems. *Internal Auditor* (April 2000): 62–67.

5.6 Audit Challenges in the Global Corporate Environment

5.6.1 Basis of an International Orientation

KEY POINTS

- Internal Audit should endeavor to balance the interests of all parties involved in an audit.
- In case of conflicts of interest, it is important for auditors to adopt an impartial position and seek guidance from audit management.
- To build trustful long term cooperation, differences in cultural backgrounds should be considered when announcing audit findings.

Internal Position

Internal Audit faces special challenges in a global environment. The first of these challenges is the position of Internal Audit within the organization. The fact alone that GIAS reports administratively to the CEO necessitates great care in how it deals with this "direct line of information." Internal auditors should not derive any tangible or formal advantages from their relationship with the CEO and the Executive Board. At an international level, this perception may be further exacerbated by cultural differences. The relationship of the international subsidiaries with company headquarters is a determining factor in how much attention is being paid to Internal Audit. This assessment is considerably reinforced by the audit mandate, which defines the remit of Internal Audit. The mandate authorizes the department to conduct audits. Internal Audit must use these powers very carefully. Neither threats nor hastily scheduled audits are appropriate means of achieving objectives or getting decisions approved. The fact that Internal Audit has an unrestricted audit mandate should not play a role in day-to-day work or discussions, and the use of these powers should be limited to exceptional circumstances.

Internal Audit Impartiality

Internal Audit is often involved in, or at least affected by, conflicts of interest. It is of utmost importance for auditors to adopt an impartial position in such cases. Even if that may possibly put them at a disadvantage in their efforts to obtain information, strict impartiality is absolutely essential. This does not mean that Internal Audit cannot make use of informal sources or communication channels. Informal sources are often crucial in obtaining important information. To find the right balance between relying on formal and informal sources, particularly internationally, is a significant challenge for each individual auditor and for the managers responsible.

Continuous Balancing of Interests

Maintaining impartiality and balancing sources is closely related to Internal Audit's continuous efforts to balance the interests of all parties involved in an audit. Internal Audit depends on an interactive flow of information. Hence, the information obtained may only be used proactively for audits, not to obtain any kind of advantage. Such a restriction is important because even the hint that Internal Audit may be taking advantage of information must be avoided. Under global aspects, this challenge takes on a special significance because the different cultural groups among which Internal Audit works have very different ways of conducting business. The auditors' independence must not be jeopardized.

Technical Expertise

Another special aspect of a global corporate environment is the increasing speed and frequency of changes mentioned earlier (see Section A, Chapter 2.1). In response to that, the planning of an audit should be based on sound knowledge, although the current speed of change often makes it very hard to be up to date at all times. However, mastering this challenge has almost come to be expected of Internal Audit. Bringing together know-how from different sources is essential in building the audit skills and audit expertise necessary to deal with a high audit density and a large number of different audit topics. Possessing the necessary expertise and competence will help internal auditors gain acceptance within the company.

Dealing with Audit Results

The way audit findings are addressed is critical in ensuring that Internal Audit is accepted by all parties. Although auditors have to apply a certain amount of sensitivity, they also have to address and track audit findings with rigor. Auditors must never present the findings from a position of condescension, but aim to reach general agreement. Establishing and communicating audit findings carries a great potential for conflict. It is therefore important that all involved parties do their utmost to separate the factual from the personal level. To build long term trustful cooperation, different cultural backgrounds have to be taken into consideration when announcing audit findings. This relates not only to the finding itself, but also to the way in which it is communicated, i.e., whether meetings are held only with the auditees, or if line managers are present, whether extensive discussions take place, and how audit findings are documented.

LINKS AND REFERENCES ↗

- O'REGAN, D. 2001. *Auditing International Entities: A Practical Guide to Objectives, Risks, and Reporting.* Altamonte Springs, FL: The Institute of Internal Auditors.

5.6.2 Overview of Global Challenges

KEY POINTS •••

- Internal audit departments that work on a global level have to master a large number of different external and internal challenges.
- The external factors may be taken into account either by applying external rules or specific internal guidelines and principles.
- The internal global challenges affect the structures and processes of Internal Audit in almost all areas. Decentralization aspects have to be considered in this context.
- Audits of outsourced corporate functions particularly in cross-border units are a significant addition to the tasks of a globally active internal audit department.

Complexity of Global Challenges

This chapter addresses the complexity of international challenges that global companies and global internal audit departments face. Such challenges can be broken down into two groups, which are external and internal challenges.

External Challenges

The main external challenges are:

- Environments with different infrastructural characteristics, varying economic policies and diverse cultures, social landscapes, and mentalities: These factors are taken into consideration by creating an appropriate company-political framework and by setting suitable employment contract standards and codes of conduct.
- Different local languages: This problem is addressed by maintaining a standardized terminology throughout the company and by using an internationally accepted working language (e.g., English).
- Different jurisdictions, individual guidelines, compliance principles, and different statutes and articles of incorporation for Internal Audit: These differences are reflected in general legal principles, financial legislation, standards, guidelines, and audit statutes. The problem is addressed by providing access to competent advisors and by making this information available to employees.

Internal Challenges

The main internal challenges and how they are met are:

- Heterogeneous audit landscapes which are addressed by using global audit structures, a global distribution of tasks, and a globally standardized process model.
- Decentralized management structures must be reflected in suitable reporting lines for audit reports, appropriate escalation paths, globally organized information and communication flows, and a globally based benchmarking system.
- The only suitable response to regionally specific audit requirements is a comprehensive Internal Audit product and service portfolio and cooperation with all other auditing units.
- Regional differences in business practices have to be balanced by implementing policies and guidelines, global compliance strategies, by harmonizing audit procedures, and by integrating risk management.
- The response to regionally different requirements in terms of professional and social qualifications of auditors is globally aligned career planning and a globally standardized career path in Internal Audit.
- An appropriate organization of internal processes (e.g. distributing audit announcements, organizing the audit, distributing audit reports, as well as compiling the annual audit plan and determining budget figures) can help counter effects of a decentralized Internal Audit structure.
- Different IT structures can be overcome by implementing a process-based centrally organized or decentralized IT landscape and an internet-based audit portal.
- The risk of individual and therefore diverging audit interpretations in individual regions can be reduced with comprehensive documentation in an audit handbook.

Other Global Challenges

There are other global requirements that a global internal audit department has to master. Due to the dynamic environment, these requirements are subject to constant change. Examples include:

- peer reviews and audit surveys,
- cooperation models, e.g., with external auditors,
- special global process models, e.g., for fraud or information technology,
- global responsibility for topics in the context of Scopes,
- global management conferences (where confidentiality must be guaranteed),
- global profit center organization,
- global structures for regular meetings and discussions,
- global training programs,
- global diversity, and
- global initiatives and internal projects.

Outsourcing

Another focus with regard to globalization may be the audit of outsourced units. Increasing globalization means that services are often outsourced internationally, and the outsourced units may be linked to the organization in different ways (ranging from complete third-party relationships through shared service centers to outsourcing to a subsidiary or partner). The challenge lies in Internal Audit's ability to conduct international audits across companies. The particular feature of such audits is that cooperation on business processes may include outsourced units as well as units within the company. This means that processes, accounting systems, information technology, etc. may have to be audited across company and country boundaries. Audits across such boundaries may entail different time zones and multicultural interests, which means that many of the internal and external challenges listed above particularly apply to these types of audits.

HINTS AND TIPS

- Auditors must inform themselves about the country in which the audit is to be conducted.
- It is important to get as much information as possible about how Internal Audit is perceived in a certain culture.
- It is a good idea to establish personal contacts before an audit.
- Do not try to work against the culture of the country during the audit.

LINKS AND REFERENCES

- LERE, J., AND K. PORTZ. 2005. Management Control. Systems in a Global Economy. *The CPA Journal* (September 2005): 62–64.
- O'REGAN, D. 2001. *Auditing International Entities: A Practical Guide to Objectives, Risks, and Reporting.* Altamonte Springs, FL: The Institute of Internal Auditors.
- RICAUD, J. 2006. Auditing Cultural Diversity. *Internal Auditor* (December 2006): 57–61.

5.7 GIAS Integration Model

KEY POINTS

- The GIAS integration model is intended to help observe all important and necessary framework parameters and assignments during each audit.
- Based on the relevant phase of the Audit Roadmap, the necessary service types have to be identified, and based on that, the audit fields, cooperation partners, and the information to be exchanged have to be defined.
- Although GIAS follows an independent audit process, it is ultimately integrated into the overall business activities.

Basis of the GIAS Integration Model

The main disciplines of Internal Audit interact with each other. These interactions are the focus of the GIAS integration model shown below. Note that permanent and even inevitable relationships exist within the levels. There may be a number of dependencies between the individual levels, which have to be taken into account as fully as possible during the entire audit process.

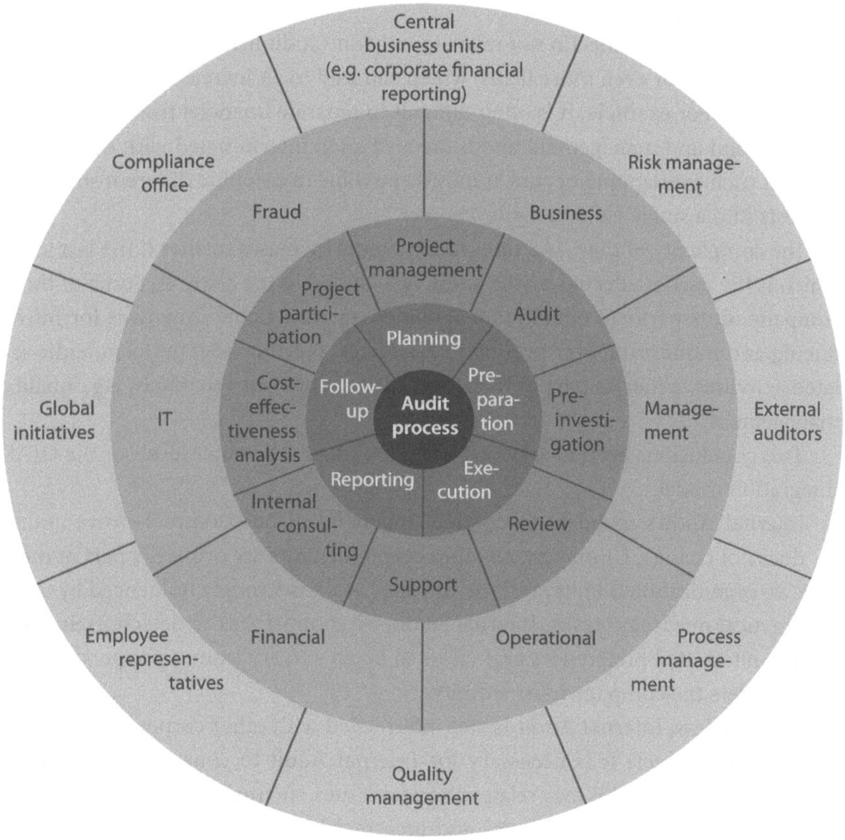

Fig. 15 GIAS Integration Model

Core of the GIAS Integration Model

The audit process is at the core of the GIAS integration model, as represented by the inner circle. It is standard procedure for each audit that each phase of the Audit Roadmap, as mapped in the ring around the "audit process," is completed in full. Exceptions from this rule occur in ad-hoc audits or services, but such exceptions require express consultation with those responsible and must be thoroughly documented with reasons why such an exception occurred.

Content Assignment of Individual Phases

The content of each activity of a phase, or each phase in its entirety, is aimed at certain Internal Audit service types as included in the next level of the diagram. It is also possible to bundle elements of different service types in one phase. For example, even if the planning and preparation phase is for an audit only, audit activities can later be changed into a review, or a review can be added (Section A, Chapter 7.2.3 explains the difference between an audit and a review).

Relation to Audit Fields

In turn, each GIAS service type is related to the next level, which is the main audit fields (see Section A, Chapter 6.2). This means that, in the course of a year, one or several audits, preliminary investigations, reviews etc. can, and normally will, take place in all audit fields.

Complex Audits

However, many audits do not relate to only one audit field but may include elements from two or even more fields, which can lead to an increase in the complexity of audits. For example, it is often difficult to separate financial from operational audits. Fraud and management audits are also often intermingled with other audit fields. If such overlapping occurs, it may be possible to combine different sub-audit requests into a single general audit.

Relation to Outer Level of the GIAS Integration Model

The complexity of the GIAS integration model increases further if the last level, which is the parties affected by the audit, is included in the analysis. Some of these company units perform operational activities, such as global initiatives for introducing and monitoring new products or services. But they also perform audit-related activities, either as part of their operational duties or separately, e.g., quality management.

Independence versus Cooperation

Two conclusions become obvious when looking at the outer levels of the GIAS integration model:

- Internal Audit's mandate to conduct independent and comprehensive audits does not change. Ultimately, all other corporate units are primarily part of their own organizational units, and the way they work is strongly influenced by their practical needs and tasks. Internal Audit, by contrast, has to detach itself from all unit-related preferences and views to be able to act from a perspective that considers the company in its entirety.
- Nevertheless, Internal Audit is still interrelated with other corporate units and in many respects it is necessary for Internal Audit to consult and exchange views with them. This may relate to various issues, such as identifying audit focus areas or avoiding redundancies and incorrect interpretations in the organization.

Overall Network of Interrelations

Auditors and GIAS managers must never lose sight of the network of interrelations between the individual levels shown above. Ultimately it is the right, individual mix of audit phase, service type, audit field (and thus audit content), as well as the cooperation partners that allows Internal Audit to categorize all the requirements it faces in a clear system. If a level is left out, the work may be incomplete or contain errors.

HINTS AND TIPS

- Before starting their activities, auditors have to plan the structure of their approach on the basis of the GIAS integration model.

5.8 Identifying Audit-Relevant Facts

KEY POINTS •••

- Audit requests or leads have to be analyzed to determine whether audit steps or other internal audit services are necessary, or whether the issue should be referred to other departments. This decision can often be made with the help of a few key questions.
- If Internal Audit is found to be responsible for the audit request or lead, it has to be determined whether the audit should be conducted exclusively by Internal Audit, or in cooperation with other departments.

Audits Outside of the Annual Audit Plan

For audits outside of the annual audit plan, the first step is to examine whether the issue in question really is a matter for Internal Audit. If so, then Internal Audit must decide whether to start with a pre-investigation (see Section A, Chapter 7.2.2) or an audit. A useful option is to conduct a review first (see Section A, Chapter 7.2.3). The basic questions are whether the issue warrants an audit, which kind of audit or other service should be considered, and whether Internal Audit is the appropriate unit to handle the task. In addition, Internal Audit should establish whether it would be useful to cooperate with other internal parties or even with external parties, such as law enforcement (see Section D, Chapter 2 for cooperation options). If there is doubt about what course of action to take, it may be expedient to submit a separate audit request, which is then officially assessed and processed accordingly. If the issue does not meet the criteria for an audit, this conclusion must be documented. If appropriate, the issue has to be referred to another department and the Board must be informed.

Criteria for Internal Audit Responsibility

To warrant an audit, at least one of the following criteria has to be met:

- There is a direct Board responsibility, for example if Board policies may have been contravened.
- There is reason to assume that important internal controls are being infringed or are not in place.
- There has been infringement of responsibilities, and this affects the accuracy of financial statement reporting or reporting on internal controls (see Section D, Chapter 14 for more information on this problem).
- There is sufficient reason to suspect fraud.
- There is a reasonable suspicion that there is a significant risk relevant to the company.

Evidence and Pre-Investigations

Although it is certainly possible to make company or sector specific additions to this list, the above criteria give an initial idea of whether or not the issue in question requires further Internal Audit scrutiny. If it is not possible to resolve this question conclusively, an informal search for leads or an official pre-investigation should be started to provide certainty as to whether Internal Audit has to get involved.

Consultation

In deciding this issue, it may also be useful to consult with other departments or functions within the company and to clarify their responsibility. The possibility of cooperation, for example with the human resources department or the legal department, must also be considered.

Involvement of Parties Outside Internal Audit

If other parties are to participate in an audit, it should be discussed and documented at the beginning which party performs which tasks. The assignment is necessary to clarify responsibilities and to help Internal Audit maintain its independence. The findings of all parties should be included as audit findings in the report compiled by Internal Audit. However, it has to be decided on a case-by-case basis to what extent these other parties also make their own recommendations. Different reports or a report with input from different groups should not contain any inconsistencies. Reports that are shared with outside parties, such as external auditors, have to be checked with particular rigor for inconsistencies.

Cooperation

A minimum of consultation and coordination will be achieved if the parties mentioned in the diagram below report audit-relevant matters to Internal Audit (for details, see Section D, Chapter 2), either spontaneously as necessary or, preferably, as part of a regular information exchange. This may create problems in particular for global corporations, because such corporations have multiples of some departments, for example several legal or human resources departments. For this reason, the consultation process between Internal Audit and other departments has

Fig. 16 Cooperation

to be examined from a global perspective as well. Internal Audit therefore faces the challenge of always applying the same benchmarks when identifying and clarifying the facts of an audit and when assigning responsibilities.

HINTS AND TIPS

- If Internal Audit employees receive information personally, they first have to ascertain its validity. If appropriate, they should ask for written confirmation.
- As a rule, all leads have to be taken seriously. Internal Audit employees have an obligation to report any instances when they receive information, at least to audit management.

LINKS AND REFERENCES

- INSTITUTE OF INTERNAL AUDITORS. 2001. *Practice Advisory 2050-1: Coordination.* Altamonte Springs, FL: The Institute of Internal Auditors.

6 Audit Methods

6.1 Content Determinants and Formal Determinants

KEY POINTS •••

- Internal Audit uses a variety of content determinants and formal determinants to identify the appropriate audit method to use for a specific engagement.
- Content determinants include the audit fields and the audit approaches.
- Formal determinants include: the audit category, type, and status of the audit within the audit cycle.
- Thus audit methods are characterized by a framework of standard parameters, which allows auditors to treat different audits according to standard rules. Individual criteria may be added to the predefined standard parameters at any time.

Overview

When planning an audit, Internal Audit must consider several important factors to determine the appropriate audit method to use. Chapter 6 provides an overview of the determinants on which audit methods are based. Additional factors for determining the audit method may be needed. These factors include the period perspective and the distinction between set and freely selectable audit content. These other determinants are described in Section C, where the individual audit fields are discussed.

Content Determinants

For identifying the appropriate audit methods to be used, SAP internal auditors consider several important content determinants and formal determinants. The content determinants of an audit method are described first, followed by the formal determinants. Content determinants include the audit fields and the audit approaches.

Audit Fields

At SAP, the audit universe is divided into six audit fields (for more information on audit fields refer to Section A, Chapter 6.2.1):

- management audits,
- operational audits,
- financial audits,
- IT audits,
- fraud audits, and
- business audits.

Importance of the Audit Fields

In principle, each audit field listed above has the same significance to Internal Audit, as each is exposed to core business risks. These risks are measured by assessing the individual risks as part of the annual audit planning (see Section D, Chapter 3.1.2) and are monitored during the fiscal year through the risk management process. Thus, there may be a different number of individual audits required for each audit field as determined by the annual risk assessment.

Audit Approaches

The content of audits is determined not only by the audit fields but also by the audit approaches that the internal auditors use (see Section A, Chapter 6.3 for descriptions of each audit approach). The different approaches are as follows:
- risk-based audit approach,
- system-based audit approach,
- transaction-based audit approach,
- compliance-based audit approach, and
- results-based audit approach.

Assignment of Audit Approaches to Audit Fields

Each audit field has its own set of specific attributes, thus the emphasis of the audit method is different in each case. Therefore, audit approaches can generally be aligned with the specific audit fields, and standardized combinations can be created for audit methods (for more information see Section A, Chapter 6.3). The correlation identified between audit field and audit approach thus creates a guidance framework for conducting audits, which allows auditors to quickly establish the individual audit steps required.

Formal Determinants

In addition to content determinants, an audit method is also shaped by formal determinants. They include audit category, audit type, and audit cycle. The audit categories are local, regional, and global audits (see Section A, Chapter 6.4). The audit typology defines audits as standard, special, or ad-hoc audits (see Section A, Chapter 6.5). The audit cycle generally consists of the basic audit, a status check, and (up to two) follow-up audits (see Section A, Chapter 6.6).

Merging of Determinants

By combining the audit determinants into a consolidated approach, Internal Audit is able to establish the final design of the particular audit method to use. Thus, for each specific audit, the auditors must consider the following factors:
- assignment to an audit field,
- audit approach,
- audit category,
- audit type, and
- audit cycle status.

The special characteristics of each formal determinant, in combination with the content determinants, allow Internal Audit to identify the appropriate audit method. For example, assume Internal Audit is planning a routine audit of the purchasing process at a regional shared service center and will examine various purchase transactions to determine whether the controls are working effectively. The auditors must define each of the determinants when identifying the appropriate audit method to use, as follows:
- audit field: operational,
- audit approach: transaction-based,
- audit category: regional,
- audit type: standard, and
- audit cycle: basic.

Determination of the Audit Method

The following diagram shows how the audit method is determined by the content and formal determinants with their possible characteristics.

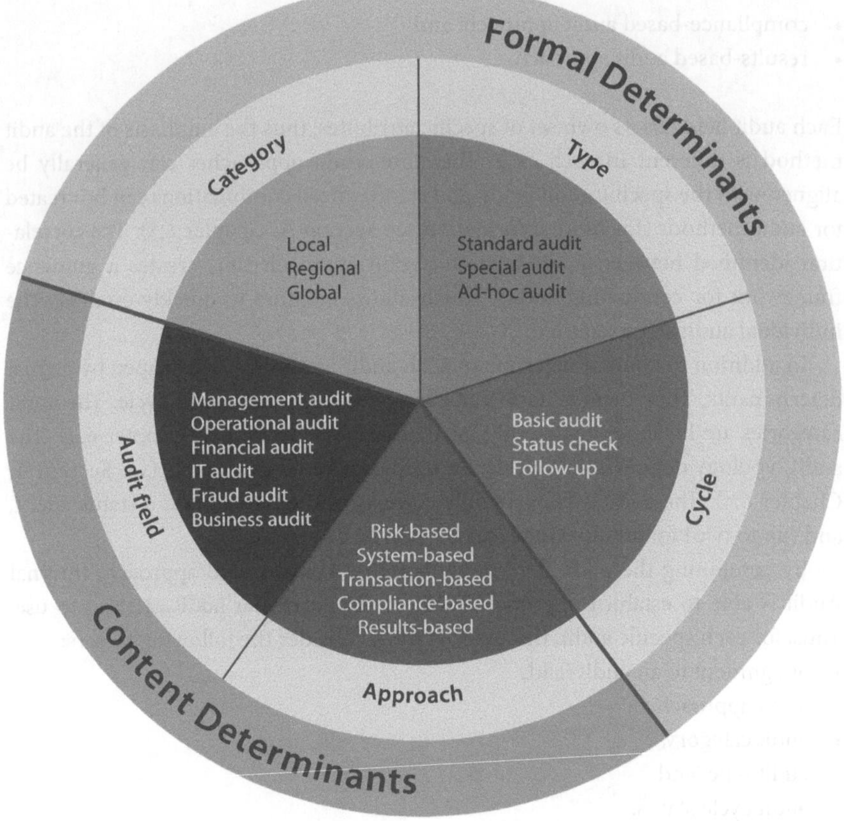

Fig. 17 Determining the Audit Method with Content and Formal Determinants

HINTS AND TIPS

- The differences between the individual audit methods must be clear-cut. Decide together with the Audit Manager in charge which audit method to use in any given case.

6.2 Audit Field Structure

6.2.1 Introduction

KEY POINTS •••

- The audit fields represent the core audit tasks of Internal Audit. Based on the Audit Roadmap, the specific audit methods are applied to the audit fields.
- There are interdependencies between the individual audit fields. It is very rare that an audit will address only one audit field in isolation.
- Increasingly, Internal Audit's work must be viewed from a profitability perspective. Thus, a cost/benefit analysis is frequently performed.

Audit Fields

The audit fields represent the core audit tasks of Internal Audit. Therefore, most audit requests can be classified within the audit fields. Each of these audit fields has several Core Scopes, which in turn contain the Key Scopes at lower levels (see Section A, Chapter 5.3 and Section B, Chapter 2.1).

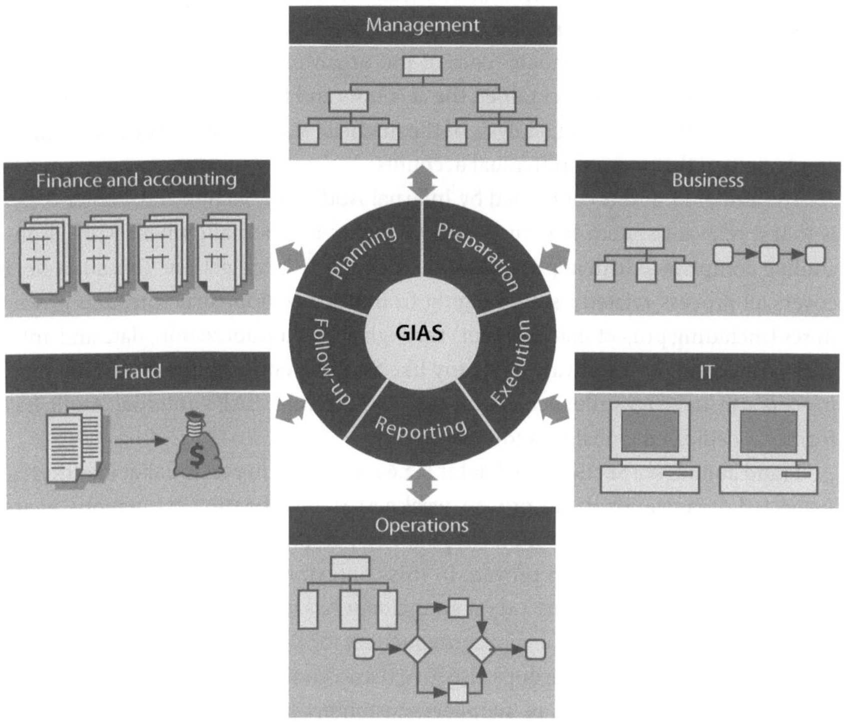

Fig. 18 Overview of Audit Fields

Basics The audit fields shown in the diagram above are audited on the basis of different Scopes using specific audit methods. Ultimately, however, all audits are conducted according to a standard process model, the Audit Roadmap (for details, see Section B).

Interdependencies At first glance, the audit fields appear to be independent of each other, but they do have commonalities. For example, a fraud audit may also include a financial audit. The same applies to business audits. And operational audits are regularly part of any audit (for combined audit topics see Section B, Chapter 5). The rest of this chapter briefly outlines the focus of each audit field. More detailed descriptions are provided in subsequent chapters.

Management Audit As part of a management audit (see Section A, Chapter 6.2.2), Internal Audit tests whether management complies with existing policies, guidelines, and procedures and whether its decisions and the associated internal controls are effective and efficient.

Operational Audit Operational audits (see Section A, Chapter 6.2.3) address issues relating to both organizational and workflow structures. They can affect almost any operational business unit. The audit normally comprises all issues of process design, internal controls, risk cover, and any relevant financial accounts.

Financial Audit The main focus of a financial audit (see Section A, Chapter 6.2.4) is on examining the accounting and financial data of the organization. The focus is different, depending on the audit topic: Either, the accounts and financial data can be audited as a whole on the basis of an analysis of the financial statements, or the audit can be conducted on the basis of individual accounts.

IT Audit The aim of IT audits conducted by Internal Audit (see Section A, Chapter 6.2.5) is to test relevant system structures and processes for their alignment with IT, including compliance with applicable guidelines and risk mitigation. This audit field covers all process-related issues, ranging from organization, structure, and procedures (including project management) through access authorization, data and antivirus protection. In a software company like SAP, the entire software development process can have an influence on IT audits. Therefore, SAP's Internal Audit has formed a dedicated global IT audit team.

Fraud Audit Fraud audits (see Section A, Chapter 6.2.6) are aimed in particular at identifying suspected organizational and process weaknesses, investigating anonymous accusations or specific information on irregularities, or gathering evidence for cases of fraud that have already been proven. In this context, it is of special importance to establish whether and to what extent an incident has led to directly measurable, or at least indirectly related, financial consequences for the company.

Business Audit External business relationships also give rise to audit-relevant issues for Internal Audit, because the network of suppliers, customers, and partners, relations with public institutions and organizations and even government bodies ultimately have a significant influence on the internal processes of a company. A business audit (see Section A, Chapter 6.2.7) is a preventive audit measure conducted in line with the de-escalation strategy. Its main purpose is to ensure that processes, methods, and guidelines within a project are compliant and take third parties into account.

Cost/Benefit Analysis

In today's environment, the effect of Internal Audit's work on profitability is increasingly important. Thus cost/benefit analyses are frequently performed. Cost/benefit analysis can be performed for each of the above audit fields. In doing so, the focus should always be on the audit as a whole, i.e., if a combination of several audit fields is used, all components must be subject to efficiency measurement (for details, see Section A, Chapter 6.7).

HINTS AND TIPS

- At the start of an audit, auditors must be aware of the audit field to which the audit task in question belongs.
- Especially when interdependencies exist, consistent assignment to the audit fields facilitates the structuring of the audit engagement.
- Auditors should try to gather practical experience in all audit fields in order to enhance their personal flexibility and eligibility for engagements.

6.2.2 Management Audit

KEY POINTS

- During a management audit, Internal Audit tests management's compliance with the established policies, guidelines, and procedures.
- Internal Audit also examines the effectiveness and efficiency of management decisions and the associated internal controls.
- The effect of management decisions is a key benchmark of how successfully managers perform their management duties.
- For a variety of reasons, management audits conducted by Internal Audit may lead to difficulties, depending on the corporate culture, the role and importance of management, as well as the managers to be audited and the auditors themselves.

Compliance

When conducting a management audit, Internal Audit must determine whether all the necessary processes and guidelines have been defined in the company, enabling managers to execute their duties according to the established rules. Auditors must also investigate whether managers act in compliance with the established rules and policies.

Efficiency and Effectiveness

In addition, Internal Audit may audit the efficiency and effectiveness of corporate management. Even if managers are very committed to their tasks, it is possible that the company as a whole derives little benefit from their activities. If that is the case, the role of management should be reconsidered and realigned if appropriate. In addition to the financial effects of management's activities, Internal Audit must consider how management's actions affect the motivation and conduct of employees. One of the key points of a management audit is to ensure that management activities are not only duly performed, but lead to the desired results and thus become measurable.

Management Audit as an Audit Field

The two key types of management audits described above (compliance audits and management effectiveness and efficiency audits) make up the complex field of management audits for Internal Audit. During the course of a management audit, the internal auditors should consider:

Process- and Results-based Audits

- Process-based assessment of all aspects of governance as well as a results-based investigation of decision-making within the company as a whole.

Activities in the Interest of the Company

- The extent and the manner in which the managers concerned use the entrepreneurial powers vested in them to the benefit of the company. This includes, in particular, the control of extraordinary management and decision-making situations, as well as crisis management. It involves all the process steps of escalation (and conversely, of course, de-escalation) procedures across various management levels. The audit assesses the existing and required management and communication tools, and how the tools are used to communicate with both superiors and subordinates.

Historical and Forward-Looking Analysis

- Management's past leadership and areas for future improvement, e.g. moving from a problem-based to a solution-based management approach.

Examining the Process Chains

In summary, the main focus of a management audit is the entire management processes, including internal controls. Thus a management audit is mainly about examining all the process chains that managers deal with as part of their strategic and operational tasks. The management audit focuses on the manager's willingness to accept processes and their internal controls and to apply them accordingly. For assessing leadership qualities, employee satisfaction, and the efficiency of the manager's personal management behavior, there are other, more suitable tools, such as management evaluations performed by the human resources department.

Guidelines and Instructions

When implementing these audit requirements, Internal Audit makes use of a number of existing procedures, documents, and external specifications. For example, Internal Audit should examine whether corporate-wide policies and guidelines are implemented and applied. This includes whether each employee has a clear understanding of the company's strategic and operational objectives. It is the only way to justify and enforce certain courses of action among employees and to align and commit all involved parties with the basic objectives of the company. On the one hand, this may involve general principles, such as standard rules of conduct for all employees. On the other hand, however, special guidelines can also be drawn up for individual business areas or operational units and functions, such as general security and IT security.

Legal and Financial Reporting Requirements

Management audits also examine compliance with legal and financial reporting requirements. If these external requirements demand entrepreneurial action and company-internal implementation, the audit work of Internal Audit ensures that the relevant processes are compliant, complete, and correct. This allows Internal Audit to help minimize the company's exposure to legal risks.

Personnel Management

In the context of a management audit, an employee survey or the general motivation of the team assigned to a manager may provide clues as to the degree to which the responsibilities of a management function are met.

Management Controls

The examination of management controls is of high importance for compliance with policies, guidelines, and procedures. Management controls must be established for all activities, including objective-setting, process development and application, decision implementation, and information and documentation activities. Internal Audit must investigate and verify whether these controls are adequately defined and documented and working as intended. This includes management's responsibilities for compiling and tracking minutes and activity lists and maintaining an adequate internal reporting system to the relevant higher and lower ranking management levels. Internal Audit must also ensure that all processes for which management is directly accountable are compliant with the policies of the organization as well as with external requirements (e.g., legal and financial regulations).

Special Challenges of Management Audits

Management audits are characterized by specific challenges. They depend on the corporate culture of the organization and thus the role and importance of management per se, as well as on the personalities of the managers to be audited and the auditors themselves. Due to the required sensitivity, a management audit should be conducted by experienced internal auditors. Ideally, internal auditors who have worked in a management function may be best suited to perform these audits. Other reasons why management audits conducted at the request of the Board present a special challenge for Internal Audit can be summarized as follows:

Mistrust

- Management audits conducted at the request of the Board may be interpreted as a sign of mistrust in management. This may lead to irritation especially if the company's position is healthy on the whole and at first glance there do not seem to be any specific reasons for an audit. This may have a company-political impact, damaging the relationship of trust between the Board and management. It may be very helpful, even before an audit, if the Board of Directors maintains a clear information policy with regard to audits.

Impact on the Standing of Employees

- Managers fear that serious negative findings made by Internal Audit may cause them to lose standing with Internal Audit, the Board of Directors, and perhaps even colleagues and their own employees. For fear of negative consequences, managers may refuse to cooperate or make the auditors' work more difficult. This makes it hard to arrive at objective audit findings, damaging the working relationship between management and Internal Audit and hampering cooperation. In some cultural groups, negative audit findings are interpreted as individual failings at a purely personal level. This may irreparably damage the managers' standing and reputation, especially with regard to their own line managers. This area in particular is where Internal Audit faces the challenge of presenting the results as impartially as possible, supported by examples.

Existing Quality Problems

- If managers already have problems regarding the quality of their work, negative audit reports may further weaken their standing in the company. If that is the case, it is difficult to give the person concerned an objective view of the audit. Internal Audit should then act as a consulting partner and convince managers that, by eliminating the weak points identified by the audit, they may also improve their performance with regard to other success factors.

Manager Personality

- Managers may generally regard their work as confidential and may be reluctant to share their working practices with others. In such cases, Internal Audit must take a sensitive approach so that it can examine the facts on the basis of a personal relationship of trust.

Conflict with Activities of Other Departments

- Management audits may cause problems if they clash with the activities of other departments, such as employee surveys carried out by Human Resources. However, such activities have a different focus and are based on a completely different method. Whereas the investigations of Internal Audit normally focus on management processes and the associated internal controls and risks, evaluations carried out by other departments are aimed at establishing the personal suitability of each manager. It is important to make this distinction clear and to demonstrate this fact on the basis of the audit findings. For this reason, management audits should internally also be referred to as management process audits.

Confidential Information

- Finally, management may be resistant to the audit because being audited requires the manager to reveal information, which may lead to a serious moral conflict for managers. That is, management must decide what information can be given to Internal Audit, and what must be kept confidential. Of course Internal Audit is also required to keep information secret and confidential, but there is a large pool of confidential data that is difficult to deal with in this context. In addition to personal information, this may involve strategic and company-political information or budgeted sales and profit figures.

Summary

Within the context of a management audit, Internal Audit should focus on processes, the associated internal controls and specific individual risks, and how management deals with these risks. Depending on the degree of personal trust, each management audit will develop its own momentum to some extent, which should be handled in such a way that the audit objectives can still be met.

HINTS AND TIPS

- Auditors must familiarize themselves thoroughly with the manager's personality, taking into account any problems from the past.

- Because management audits require sensitivity, the work program should be reviewed by an impartial member of Internal Audit before the commencement of the audit.
- Characteristics typically associated with managers (lack of time, etc.) must not prevent Internal Audit from conducting its audit.
- The sensitivity of management's data must be considered.

LINKS AND REFERENCES ↗

- ANDERSON, U. AND A. DAHLE. 2006. *Implementing the Professional Practices Framework.* 2nd ed. Altamonte Springs, FL: The Institute of Internal Auditors.
- INSTITUTE OF INTERNAL AUDITORS. 2000. *The International Standards for the Professional Practice of Internal Auditing.* Altamonte Springs, FL: The Institute of Internal Auditors.
- INSTITUTE OF INTERNAL AUDITORS. 2001. *Practice Advisory 2120-A1-1: Assessing and Reporting on Control Processes.* Altamonte Springs, FL: The Institute of Internal Auditors.
- SAWYER, L., M. DITTENHOFER, AND J. SCHEINER. 2003. *Sawyer's Internal Auditing.* 5th ed. Altamonte Springs, FL: The Institute of Internal Auditors.

6.2.3 Operational Audit

KEY POINTS •••

- Operational audits can address issues relating to both organizational and workflow structures. They can affect almost all business units.
- Operational audits may examine traditional, corporate-wide, and project-related processes.
- The audit normally comprises several audit steps, which deal with all issues of process design, internal controls, risk cover, and any relevant financial accounts.
- In addition to the actual processes, the controls set up in the company must be examined and verified with suitable tests.

Audits of Core Business Processes

Operational audits include audits along the entire value chain of a company, or specific parts of it. Under the materiality principle, however, a careful selection should be made of the core business processes to be audited and the affected business units. Responsibilities and processes that either are of lesser importance or not exposed to risks that threaten the existence of the company or its business success are included in Internal Audit's annual audit plan according to their risk profile.

Main Objects of the Operational Audit

An initial analysis identifies the following organizational units as common objects of operational audits:

- specific business units (e.g., development, sales, consulting) and their core functions and central tasks,
- central corporate divisions (e.g., Corporate Financial Reporting, Corporate Management Accounting),
- local subsidiaries,
- associates that fall within the remit of Internal Audit due to a majority interest or other legal agreements (in the case of minority interests), and
- other investment relationships (e.g., venture capital participations, joint ventures, etc.).

Objectives

The main function of an operational audit is to improve the organization and workflows of the company. In this regard, a systematic audit focuses on analyzing the organizational structure, as well as individual processes or transactions. The main objective is to ensure that all the organizational solutions of the company are compliant with relevant rules and regulations.

Processes versus Discrete Items

The process-oriented approach focuses on entire processes and organizational units rather than on individual circumstances and transactions. The intention is that this kind of audit should identify underlying risks and their interdependencies and thus pinpoint ways in which the information gained can be used to improve the security, efficiency, and reliability of internal processes. In the above organizational units, Internal Audit therefore examines all business, organizational, and legal issues, responsibilities, authorizations, and procedures, the controls assigned, and the risks to be covered.

Internal Control Audit

Audits of internal controls associated with processes have taken on greater importance now, because SOX requires the CEO and the CFO of companies listed on U.S. stock exchanges to verify, in writing, the existence and effectiveness of key internal controls as part of its reporting to the SEC (see Section D, Chapter 14).

Other Objects of the Operational Audit

In addition to the audit objects mentioned above, there are other areas on which operational audits focus. These areas have strong interrelations between audit objects and process steps. Some main areas are:

- global units (e.g., initiatives, departments),
- person-specific issues (e.g., incentive scheme, pension scheme),
- reviews of external and internal projects with regard to project management, contracts, and project content,
- the entire risk management process, and
- information management between established organizational units and projects/initiatives.

Recording of Processes and Controls

An important prerequisite for efficient operational audits is that Internal Audit document all processes, including controls. This is done at the beginning of the fieldwork for process documentation purposes (see Section C, Chapter 8 and Section D, Chapter 14). In addition to describing each process step, the controls that the company has established for each process are documented, focusing mainly on the following questions:

- What controls exist in the company at the moment?
- Who is responsible for the controls?
- How are the controls documented?
- Are the controls sufficient to cover material risks?

Possible Controls

There are several types of controls that organizations may use, including manual, organizational, automated or programmed controls (see also Section C, Chapter 8). Examples of organizational and manual controls include the segregation of duties, dual control, signature rules, and IT system authorizations. Automated and programmed controls, on the other hand, include consistency and plausibility checks.

Analysis of Business Processes

As part of the audit, Internal Audit performs an analysis of the business processes to identify and highlight their strategic importance, the risks, and controls with a focus on the overall objectives and strategy of the organization as well as in the context of the relevant business risks. In the first instance, the documented process steps required to meet the objectives are analyzed. Here, Internal Audit uses interviews, documents, and guidelines to examine and assess whether the content and purpose of each process make sense. In addition, Internal Audit must establish whether the design of the process is logical, sensible, and effective, whether its structure is clear, and whether it ensures that the intended objective is met.

Content of a Control Assessment

At this stage, the existing and any missing process controls are identified and examined for correct and full implementation. In particular, the audit must establish whether the controls are adequate, sensible, and sufficient for the process concerned, as well as demonstrate and ensure that they function as intended. Under the requirements of SOX, the issue of responsibility for the controls and documenting them is of particular importance.

Process Control

Another step of the operational audit is to examine to what extent the controls identified cover the established or additional process risks so that they can be monitored. Each possible process risk should be monitored and mitigated by at least one corresponding process control. This may lead to additional controls or the development of controls related to other process steps.

Link with Accounting

SOX requires another process analysis step: The adequacy and effectiveness of the controls that have an immediate effect on the accounting figures must also be tested. That is, controls must be established that ensure that financial reporting fairly represents the financial condition of the company.

Staff Interviews

In addition to process analysis, other types of fieldwork are necessary to test process application. In the first instance, discussions should be held to determine whether the employees observe all the guidelines and instructions, whether the flow of information is guaranteed, and the process is practiced as designed. These interviews will demonstrate to what extent the employees are familiar with the processes.

Document Testing

Moreover, examination of documents such as guidelines, contracts, extracts from the commercial register, powers of attorney, etc. should be included in the audit. Thus, an operational audit covers more than testing the internal controls only.

Process Documentation

All process steps, including the internal controls, must be documented fully and in detail. SOX requires that this process documentation (for those processes that affect financial reporting) must be available and up to date at all times. This can be achieved by using a suitable IT tool.

Process and Control Tests

The actual testing of each process and the associated internal controls is another focus of audit work. Various methods can be used. With the help of appropriate sampling procedures, samples of processes are drawn and then tested with regard to the existence and compliance of controls. An alternative method is what is known as the walk-through, where the auditor personally traces a specific transaction or economic event step-by-step through parts of the process or the process as a whole, including all controls. The advantage of this method is that the approach considers all aspects of the process. In practice, a combination of both test methods will ultimately be suitable for conducting the actual audits (see the practical examples in Section C).

Operational Audits and Other Audit Areas

Operational audits may be performed as a separate audit engagement, but it is important to note that they may also be performed in conjunction with an audit of another audit field (e.g., fraud or financial audit). For example, financial audits generally require operational audits to verify and document the validity of the financial data analyzed.

HINTS AND TIPS

- At the start of an audit, the auditor should ask the process owner to explain the process by means of a walk-through.
- Analyze the documentation available for the process carefully. Aim and purpose of the whole process must be clear.
- The auditor should conduct interviews to get the employees' opinion of the process to be examined. Confidential meetings to discuss suggestions or requests made by the employees involved in the process may be a good way to obtain valuable information.

LINKS AND REFERENCES

- ANDERSON, U. AND A. DAHLE. 2006. *Implementing the Professional Practices Framework.* 2nd ed. Altamonte Springs, FL: The Institute of Internal Auditors.
- INSTITUTE OF INTERNAL AUDITORS. 2000. *The International Standards for the Professional Practice of Internal Auditing.* Altamonte Springs, FL: The Institute of Internal Auditors.

- INSTITUTE OF INTERNAL AUDITORS. 2001. *Practice Advisory 2120-A1-1: Assessing and Reporting on Control Processes.* Altamonte Springs, FL: The Institute of Internal Auditors.
- SAWYER, L., M. DITTENHOFER, AND J. SCHEINER. 2003. *Sawyer's Internal Auditing.* 5th ed. Altamonte Springs, FL: The Institute of Internal Auditors.

6.2.4 Financial Audit

KEY POINTS •••

- When performing financial audits, auditors examine both accounting and financial data.
- During an audit, auditors can either examine the financial statements as a whole, or analyze individual accounts and items.
- During financial audits, all applicable legal, tax, and accounting standards must be observed.

Definition

Financial audits are generally defined as an independent evaluation of past accounting data for the purposes of assessing whether this data is appropriate, compliant, and reliable, of protecting the assets of the company, and of expressing an opinion on the effectiveness of the internal control system. As part of a financial audit, Internal Audit examines areas such as the financial accounts of the company, the payroll system, asset management, and the annual financial statements. There are two options in this regard:

- Accounts and financial data can be tested as a whole, based on an analysis of the financial statements, or
- individual accounts and items can be examined specifically using qualified samples.

Analysis of the Financial Statements

If the financial data is to be examined as a whole, it is advisable to analyze the financial statements first. To this end, the data from the balance sheet and income statement to be audited should be compared with the corresponding figures of the previous period and analyzed for any unusual items or discrepancies. In addition to period comparisons, object-related comparisons can also be performed, (e.g., local subsidiaries of similar size and with comparable business activities). The comparison can be made either by using absolute figures or by calculating certain key ratios (e.g., certain accounting ratios like debt/equity ratio, profit ratio, cash flows etc.). Next, the ratios should be compared with external figures, such as corresponding ratios at peer organizations. This may help auditors identify unusual items among the selected variables from the balance sheet and income statement. Depending on what they have observed, auditors must decide whether these comparisons should be continued for each case down to the individual account level, in order to establish the underlying causes of any changes or variances. To evaluate the need for more detailed examinations, permissible ranges for variances must be defined. If a variance exceeds the defined threshold, the audit must continue down to individual accounts. Importantly, thresholds should be set in accordance with the materiality principle so that the audit remains manageable. That is, only material findings should be followed by a more detailed examination.

Items to Be Audited

At a minimum, financial audits should include examination of the following accounts: Noncurrent assets, inventories, receivables, cash and cash equivalents, provisions, liabilities, prepaid expenses, and deferred income from the balance sheet; revenue and certain expenses, such as personnel and travel expenses, training costs, and other expenses from the income statement.

Problem of Revenue Recognition

In global software companies such as SAP, audits of license agreements and consulting contracts are particularly important to ensure that revenue is recognized correctly (see Section C, Chapters 5.2, 5.3 and 9). This often entails complex processes and controls that involve various departments (such as finance, development, product support, training, etc.). Audits focusing on revenue recognition should include the following topics:

- Software license agreements, taking into account issues such as pricing, maintenance, special agreements, legal issues, and accounting policies.
- Any type of consulting contract (for example, fixed-price, or time-and-material projects), taking into consideration legal issues, including accounting policies and the possibilities of individual project reviews.

Items /Accounts

If the examination of accounting and financial data focuses on a targeted analysis of selected accounts and items, the method described for analyzing the financial statements can be used initially. However, the variance limits should be defined more narrowly and accurately so that absolute and relative variances can be detected. Often, specific key variables may be useful (e.g. days overdue, or the discount and credit note ratio). If appropriate, each account is compared and analyzed in turn. Especially in global audits, the careful selection of appropriate subsets or supersets may produce important information (e.g., a summary of balances outstanding from the 50 most important customers). Careful and deliberate evaluation of individual accounts and items should detect the transaction(s) that may be the cause of any inconsistencies identified. However, the principle of materiality can and must be observed in such instances. This means that time and resources for auditing individual transactions are limited and the materiality and efficiency principles must again be applied.

General Rules and Regulations

The accounting function is governed by national and international accounting standards and laws. Companies, such as SAP, that are listed on the U.S. Stock Exchanges must also comply with US-GAAP and the requirements of the SEC. Such companies must undergo financial statement audits performed by independent external audit firms to comply with SEC regulations. In addition to these general standards, companies often have to observe sector-specific regulations and their internal accounting guidelines.

HINTS AND TIPS

- Ahead of a financial audit, auditors should try to identify items that could be critical in the balance sheet and income statement.
- The company's annual report is another document on which Internal Audit can base a preliminary assessment.
- Auditors should look at the documentation of findings from previous audits.

LINKS AND REFERENCES

- ANDERSON, U. AND A. DAHLE. 2006. *Implementing the Professional Practices Framework.* 2nd ed. Altamonte Springs, FL: The Institute of Internal Auditors.
- INSTITUTE OF INTERNAL AUDITORS. 2000. *The International Standards for the Professional Practice of Internal Auditing.* Altamonte Springs, FL: The Institute of Internal Auditors.
- INSTITUTE OF INTERNAL AUDITORS. 2001. *Practice Advisory 2120-A1-1: Assessing and Reporting on Control Processes.* Altamonte Springs, FL: The Institute of Internal Auditors.
- INSTITUTE OF INTERNAL AUDITORS. 2001. *Practice Advisory 2120-A1-3: The Internal Auditor's Role in Quarterly Financial Reporting, Disclosures, and Management Certifications.* Altamonte Springs, FL: The Institute of Internal Auditors.
- INSTITUTE OF INTERNAL AUDITORS. 2001. *Practice Advisory 2120-A1-4: Auditing the Financial Reporting Process.* Altamonte Springs, FL: The Institute of Internal Auditors.
- SAWYER, L., M. DITTENHOFER, AND J. SCHEINER. 2003. *Sawyer's Internal Auditing.* 5th ed. Altamonte Springs, FL: The Institute of Internal Auditors.

6.2.5 IT Audit

KEY POINTS

- The aim of IT audits conducted by Internal Audit is to test relevant system structures and processes for their compliance with applicable policies, guidelines, and standards.
- This audit field covers all process-related issues, ranging from planning and organization, information, and support (including project management) to access authorization, and data and anti-virus protection.
- During the audit, it is important to integrate all relevant (internal and external) guidelines and written documentation.

- The structure of the IT processes should be examined in terms of their overall integration into the entire business process. The main focus in this regard should be on the interaction of organizational and automated controls.
- IT audits can have an internal as well as an external focus.
- The expertise required for IT audits has led to the creation of a separate auditor profile.

Positioning

Information technology is an integral part of all companies. The information made available through the use of IT must meet the requirements of business processes so that business goals can be achieved. A thorough audit of relevant IT-related matters is therefore an essential part of the work performed by Internal Audit. Because IT is such an extensive area, it has established itself as a separate audit field. The following are the main audit objectives in the area of information technology:

- Controls must be in place to ensure that all IT processes (internal and external) include the necessary data processing functions and meet the relevant security standards at the time the system is deployed. Internal Audit should check to ensure that these IT processes operate as designed.
- In addition, these IT processes have to comply with the latest corporate-wide policies, guidelines, and standards as well as legal obligations.

The Changing Face of IT

Like no other aspect of business, information technology is subject to constant change and ongoing development. The innovations in this area are reaching ever greater dimensions. For this reason, Internal Audit faces the permanent challenge of adapting to changes in the technical and software environment as quickly as possible.

Factual Basis IT Audits

A large number of external guidelines and internal rules form an important basis for IT audits. The COBIT® (Control Objectives for Information and related Technology) framework is particularly useful in an organization with a strong information technology environment. The COBIT® framework was issued and is maintained by the Information Systems Audit and Control Association (ISACA). COBIT® supplements COSO and SOX by focusing on the governance of IT resources and processes.

IT Governance Focus Areas

COBIT® is especially helpful because it provides a framework and supporting tool set that bridges control requirements, technical aspects and business risks. The IT governance focus areas in COBIT® reflect the central points of the IT audit discussed later in this chapter.

- Strategic alignment emphasizes aligning IT strategy and operations with the organization's strategy and operations.
- Value delivery ensures that IT delivers the desired benefits.
- Resource management is concerned with the optimal investment in and management of IT resources.
- Risk management includes the transparency of significant IT risks and IT's awareness of the organization's risk exposure.

- Performance measurement tracks and monitors IT's role in strategy implementation, resource usage and process performance.

Responsibility Domains

IT governance may be separated into the responsibility domains of plan, build, run, and monitor. The COBIT® framework labels them Plan and Organize, Acquire and Implement, Deliver and Support, and Monitor and Evaluate, and identifies the processes and activities within each of the domains accompanied by several control objectives.

- Plan and Organize – Provides direction to solution and service delivery. Typical audit questions include:
  - Are the business strategy and IT strategy aligned?
  - Is the organization achieving optimum use of IT resources?
  - Are IT risks understood and managed?
  - Is the quality of IT appropriate for business needs?
- Acquire and Implement – Provides the solutions to be turned into services. Typical audit questions include:
  - Are new projects likely to deliver solutions that meet business needs?
  - Are new projects delivered on time and within budget?
  - Are changes made without upsetting business operations?
- Deliver and Support – Is concerned with the actual delivery of required services and support for those services. Typical audit questions include:
  - Are IT services being delivered in line with business processes?
  - Are IT resources optimized?
  - Is the workforce able to use the IT systems productively and safely?
  - Are adequate confidentiality, integrity, and availability controls in place for information security?
- Monitor and Evaluate – All IT processes should be regularly assessed for quality and compliance with both internal and external control requirements. Typical audit questions include:
  - Is IT's performance measured to detect problems in a timely manner?
  - Are internal controls effective and efficient?
  - Can IT performance be linked back to business goal?
  - Are adequate confidentiality, integrity, and availability controls in place for information security?

Legal Requirements and Internal Guidelines

In addition to the guidelines of the COBIT® framework, legal requirements that recognize the growing concern for privacy must be observed. The Financial Modernization Act of 1999 (also known as the Graham-Leach-Bliley Act) requires financial institutions to adhere to a set of privacy requirements on consumers' personal financial data. The Health Insurance Portability and Accountability Act (HIPAA) introduced privacy and security rules covering personal healthcare records. Internationally, legal requirements such as the German Data Protection Act and rules about the security of user-specific data must be observed. Company-specific internal guidelines and work instructions on technical application-based data handling must also be complied with.

Central Points of the IT Audit

When preparing for and conducting IT audits, Internal Audit has to focus on the following issues:

- Strategic IT planning: This issue includes aspects of a corporate-wide standardized IT strategy, IT-based support of company activities, monitoring the IT market for new developments, and questions relating to the implementability of feasibility studies and system analysis. A critical aspect of strategic IT planning is the alignment of IT goals with business goals.
- Risk management for the IT process: Risks must be identified and their potential impact estimated. The actions taken to minimize risk must be analyzed.
- IT-related infrastructure: This area deals with auditing relevant aspects of physical security, logical access authorizations, and data backup and archiving systems.
- Organization of the IT function: This area primarily looks at aspects of organizational structure and process organization in the information technology function, as well as the distribution of central and decentralized IT tasks, operational IT planning, and the entire change management process. This also includes the resource management of IT assets and performance measurement of the IT function.
- Operational IT processes: Internal Audit has to verify whether the information technology assures the continuity of business processes. The audit may cover all steps, from planning to operational implementation, of the IT process and its subprocesses, including all backup and alternative procedures.
- IT applications: This area looks at the entire development, maintenance, and change process during the in-house creation of software, including all testing and release procedures. At the same time it checks that the software versions used are up to date.
- IT project management: Under this aspect, the overall project framework is tested, including issues of project organization, project planning, and the running of the project, including risk management and financial project control.
- Usage of IT applications: this aspect focuses on examining relevant authorizations, system settings, internal controls and reconciliations, as well as reporting and documentation functions.
- Communication security: This area is a significant aspect of all data communication with external parties and therefore an important object in the work of Internal Audit. It includes auditing the use of anti-virus software and firewalls to protect information technology from outside attacks.
- Data protection functions: Audits of this aspect examine whether all privacy requirements relating to comprehensive data protection are met, including tracing all sensitive data in the system and logging access right changes, access protection, and all aspects of consistent data maintenance.

IT Audit as Operational Audit

The items listed above primarily involve the elements traditionally associated with operational audits. In general, process structures, risks, and internal controls should be examined from an IT perspective as well. This means that inherent technical, organizational, and in some cases even financial-reporting and legal aspects interact as part of the processes.

Alignment with the System

IT audits are conducted on the basis of an extensive IT system environment. In this regard, we differentiate between the following processes:

- purely organizational processes,
- a combination of organizational and IT processes, and
- purely IT processes, i.e. those that run only within the system.

Security-Relevant Levels

When these process types are reflected in the structure of a modern IT landscape, the following security-relevant levels can be distinguished:

- The pure hardware level is characterized by logistical security matters. Here the audit should focus on the extent to which appropriate equipment and buildings security is in place, for example access control, emergency plans, anti-terror measures, and protection from *force majeure*. This also includes the technical aspects of the entire maintenance program and data archiving.
- The operating system level relates to audits in the whole area of system technology, the user concept, failure control, and the relevant authorizations, including access to special operating software functions, such as data backups.
- The application software level also comprises audits of authorization control, system settings, workflows, the structure, nature, and frequency of certain data, figures, and documents, as well as the change service and system archiving. This level also covers interfaces with internal and external systems.
- User guidance and the user interface are also part of an IT audit, because the main parameters of a computer have to be examined, e.g., specific settings or access paths to data sources or internet sites. In some countries (e.g. Germany), however, this requires the employee's explicit permission or a court order if the circumstances are suspicious.

Examining all these levels in sequence will ensure that a complete IT audit is conducted.

Internal Controls in the IT Audit

Internal controls exist both outside of and within the system processes. Here it is important to take the individual steps in a consistent sequence, i.e., the controls must fit together and must be mapped logically and without conflict. The possibilities the system offers for logging individual process steps provide an important basis in IT audits for meeting evidence and documentation requirements. Since the area of information technology has different escalation levels, resulting in different consequences for audit findings, the risks and internal controls have to be particularly closely linked with the relevant process chains. For this reason, risk-based auditing is a core element of the corporate-wide audit approach, especially in the area of IT.

Internal and External Focus of the IT Audit

IT audits can have both an internal and an external focus. Internally, the audit focuses on system-internal business processes. Externally, audits often examine the data of business partners, such as customers and suppliers, but also data communication by e-mail and internet. The examination includes measures to protect the IT system from technical manipulation attempts and virus protection, as well as possible access rights for third parties. Especially internally, Internal Audit has to make sure that the legal and system-related requirements of the technology vendor are respected. In doing so, the responsibilities of individual employees for the whole or part of a process have to be clarified and checked. Any additional internal factors that could have a negative impact on the process also constitute an object of an IT audit conducted by Internal Audit.

Auditor Profile

Due to the expertise that IT audits require, a specific IT auditor profile should be developed. IT auditors must have sufficient know-how to cover the whole area. For this reason, it is essential to conduct adequate training measures for Internal Audit employees.

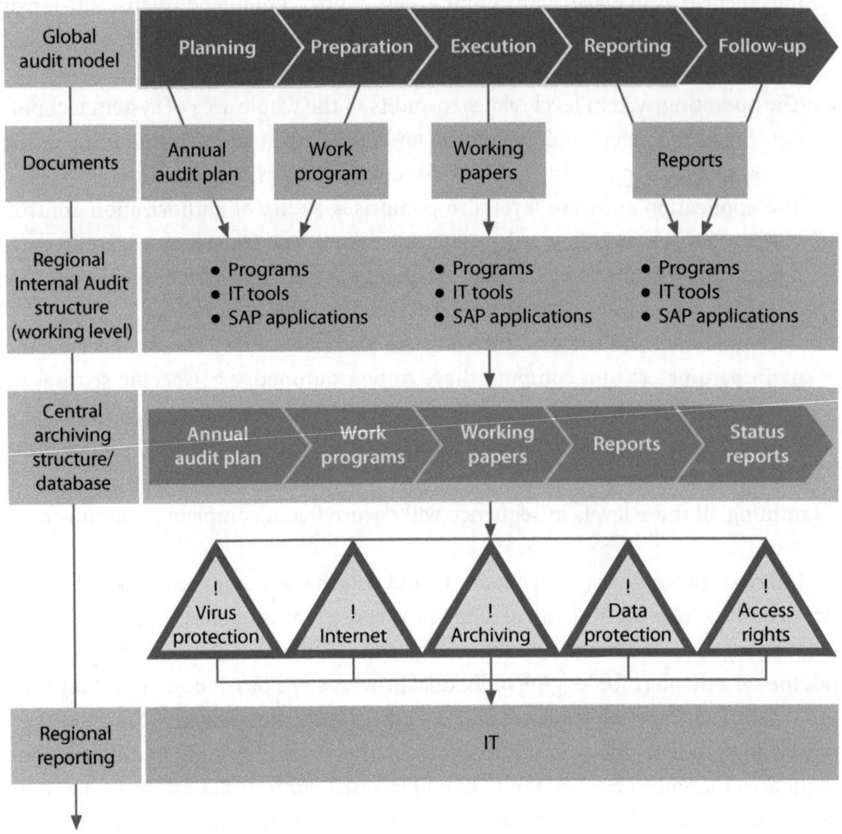

Fig. 19 Audits of the Global IT Environment

Cooperation with the External Auditors

Particularly in IT audits, cooperation with the external auditors is very important, because they have to form an opinion on the reliability and effectiveness of the internal controls. Here, Internal Audit can use the information gathered during its IT audit to resolve relevant issues in advance. The findings may thus contribute to a reduction in the extent of the external audit. Particularly for IT audits in global companies, there are further aspects to take note of regarding a central or decentralized organization.

HINTS AND TIPS

- Auditors should clarify special requirements with regard to access authorizations before the audit.
- Auditors should pay attention to particular weak points in the IT organization and take any unusual items into account when deliberating their findings.

LINKS AND REFERENCES

- CANADIAN INSTITUTE OF CHARTERED ACCOUNTANTS. 2004. *Privacy Compliance, A Guide for Organizations & Assurance Practitioners.* Toronto: The Canadian Institute of Chartered Accountants.
- INSTITUTE OF INTERNAL AUDITORS. 2005. *Global Technology Audit Guide 1: Information Technology Controls.* Altamonte Springs, FL: The Institute of Internal Auditors.
- IT GOVERNANCE INSTITUTE. 2007. *COBIT* 4.1. Rolling Meadows, IL: IT Governance Institute.
- OLIPHANT, A. 2004. *Auditing IT Infrastructures.* Mission Viejo, CA: Pleier Corporation.

6.2.6 Fraud Audit

KEY POINTS

- Most cases of fraud have a short- or long-term financial impact that is more or less directly measurable.
- Generally, the term fraud refers to any kind of attack on a company or its employees.
- Internal Audit must respond to fraud with a self-contained, consistent process model.
- Internal Audit's approach to fraud requires taking preventive measures and investigating suspected or actual cases of fraud.
- The requirements profile for fraud auditors is very broad. In addition to technical knowledge, an interest in forensic audits is recommended.

- During fraud audits, communication with other internal and external parties is very important and must be carefully executed.

Definition

Internationally, there is an increasing trend to refer to all activities driven by criminal intent as "fraud." Examples include attacks on buildings and institutions, violations of data protection laws, damage to the reputation of the company or an employee, corruption, infringement of intellectual property rights, damage to property, trading of confidential information, or non-compliance of financial reporting.

Audit Focus

Fraud audits may focus on fraud prevention or on investigating possible cases of fraud and include the following scenarios (for details, see Section D, Chapter 13).

- Fraud prevention:
  - detection of suspected organizational and process weaknesses, and
  - exact identification of known weaknesses.
- Fraud investigation:
  - investigation of anonymous accusations with or without proof or evidence,
  - investigation of specific information on committed fraud without proof or evidence or naming a suspect, and
  - investigation of proven fraud, where proof exists and/or the suspect is known, but guilt has not yet been established beyond doubt.

Consequences of Fraud

In the context of fraud audits, it is of special importance to establish whether and to what extent an incident has led to directly measurable, or indirectly related, financial consequences for the company. Fraud that can be measured in financial terms must be communicated to the relevant bodies directly and immediately because of the potential impact on financial reporting and the rules of the (international) financial markets. However, fraud that does not have any financial impact must not be overlooked or trivialized, because it may entail damage to the company's reputation, environmental damage, staff resignations, product and service defects, and the associated loss of confidence.

Company-Internal Control Body

In order to categorize possible fraud incidents quickly and reliably and to respond with appropriate action, it is advisable to set up a system that centrally collates all the information and initiates targeted actions. In order to achieve a maximum of security, a control body of this kind should ideally exist outside of Internal Audit, e.g., within the company's legal department. The activities of such a body include the compilation of specific guidelines, the treatment of each incident by forwarding and monitoring it, and a periodic reporting system that keeps detailed information regarding all ongoing and closed cases. In addition, cooperation with other bodies that deal with similar issues should be organized. It may also be beneficial to establish an anti-fraud/anti-corruption program within the organization. An important part of such a program would be a fraud emergency plan, which contains all necessary steps for handling fraud-related matters in a professional, timely, and appropriate manner.

Preventive Audits

Internal Audit's activities in this context comprise much more than merely responding to cases of fraud. The ultimate objective is to protect the company from attacks of this nature. For this reason, Internal Audit must strive to prevent fraud, or at least facilitate early detection. The preventive exclusion of possible misuse involves both identifying potential sources of fraud in general and testing the effectiveness of controls already implemented. Cash flows and any other sensitive area where embezzlement is a direct possibility deserve particular attention. These areas must be analyzed and adequate controls must be established.

Alignment of the Process Model

Internal Audit's process model must be set up accordingly (see Section B, Chapter 7.2). Internal and external communication must be initiated and maintained, and a reporting system should be implemented also with regard to the special requirements on documents that may be used in a court of law. Ultimately, evidence has to be provided to demonstrate that external requirements, such as those imposed on Internal Audit by SOX, are optimally met.

Audit Execution

For investigating fraud, each audit involves an individual procedure with regard to the audit steps to be taken, the audit content, the involvement of third parties, reports, and the necessary follow-up activities. To obtain usable audit results in the shortest possible time, fraud audits normally employ the full range of audit procedures available, from a comprehensive process approach, including Scope and work program, through special, targeted ad-hoc audits. In this process, the body of evidence must be kept as clear-cut as possible.

Requirements Profile for Auditors

In addition to technical expertise, auditors need a certain intuition for irregularities combined with a healthy dose of skepticism and an ability to put themselves into the position of other people. Fraud auditors can come from different technical areas of a company. Ideally, they will at least have basic audit experience in other audit fields, such as operational or financial audits. Fraud audits, however, increasingly also require generalists who can uncover and assess links from both a technical perspective and with an eye for possible criminal motives. Since fraud audits are mostly conducted under time pressure, knowledge and experience in the area to be audited are of great benefit.

Efficiency of Internal Audit

In order to increase the efficiency of the work performed by Internal Audit in this very critical audit field, a separate Scope, a separate Audit Roadmap with specific components, and a ranking list of possible audit segments based on past experience should be set up for fraud in line with the risk potential involved.

Involvement of Other Parties

Relations with other internal and external parties are very important for fraud audits. First and foremost, this includes the legal department, Corporate Security, and Human Resources. The Audit Committee and the compliance officer should also be involved in these processes. Cooperation with the external auditors also must be arranged. Disclosure of incidents of fraud is becoming an increasingly important reporting element for all companies.

Possible Treatment

The whole area of fraud audits is a very complex and sensitive audit field for Internal Audit. For this reason, there is no single correct way of dealing with fraud within the company. The procedure must be determined for each individual case. The following diagram shows possible solutions and the interdependencies that exist in Internal Audit's treatment of fraud.

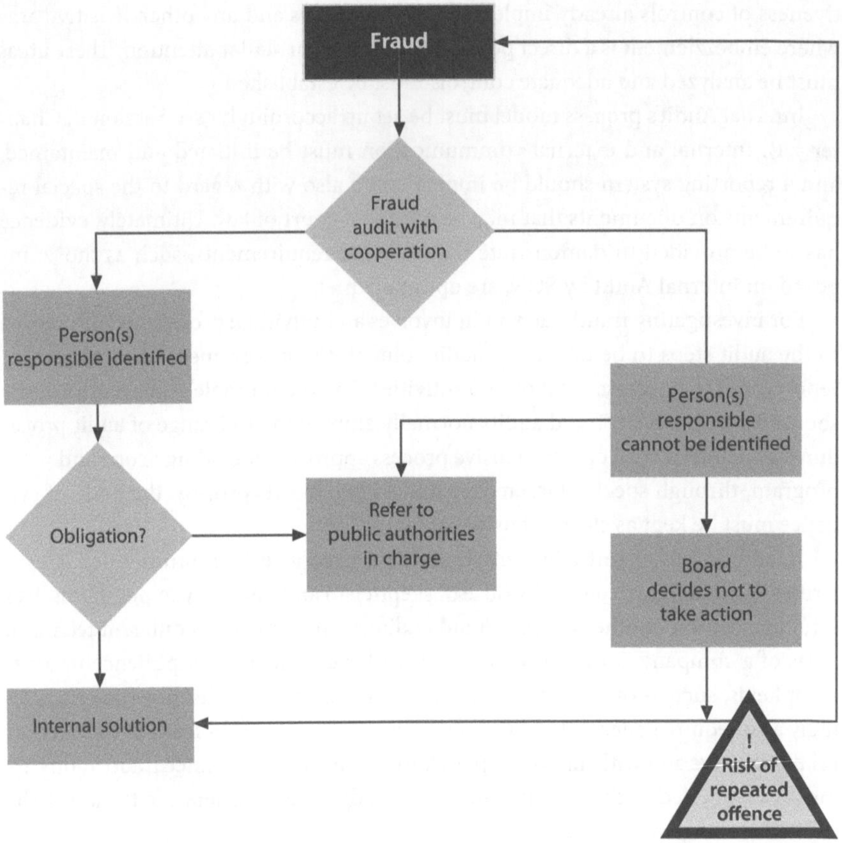

Fig. 20 Possible Treatment of Fraud by Internal Audit

Police and District Attorney

The police and the district attorney could no doubt also be important external parties in this context. Generally, fraud investigations are aimed at identifying unknown perpetrators. If Internal Audit cannot identify them, in consultation with company management and the company's legal department, they may refer the matter to the police and/or the district attorney. This also applies if the investigation has been successful, i.e., Internal Audit has identified the perpetrators and laid a charge against them.

HINTS AND TIPS

- Cases of suspected fraud must get priority treatment in day-to-day auditing, because it is often very important to act quickly.
- Prevent rumors or hasty reactions at any stage in the fraud audit.
- Ensure that the auditors have the necessary documents to hand, because they may be asked to give evidence in a legal dispute.

LINKS AND REFERENCES

- ANDERSON, U. AND A. DAHLE. 2006. *Implementing the Professional Practices Framework.* 2nd ed. Altamonte Springs, FL: The Institute of Internal Auditors.
- INSTITUTE OF INTERNAL AUDITORS. 2001. *Practice Advisory 1210.A2-2: Auditor's Responsibilities Relating to Fraud Investigation, Reporting, Resolution and Communication.* Altamonte Springs, FL: The Institute of Internal Auditors.
- INSTITUTE OF INTERNAL AUDITORS. 2001. *Practice Advisory 1210.A2-1: Auditor's Responsibilities Relating to Fraud Risk Assessment, Prevention and Detection.* Altamonte Springs, FL: The Institute of Internal Auditors.
- SAWYER, L., M. DITTENHOFER, AND J. SCHEINER. 2003. *Sawyer's Internal Auditing.* 5th ed. Altamonte Springs, FL: The Institute of Internal Auditors.

6.2.7 Business Audit

KEY POINTS

- Today, relationships with external parties (such as partners or critical vendors) expose organizations to risk and therefore require Internal Audit's attention.
- The Board or management may engage Internal Audit in audits of these external relationships for a variety of reasons, including de-escalation, legal claims, etc.
- Internal Audit may perform full-fledged audits of these relationships or projects, known as business audits. Alternatively, Internal Audit may perform business reviews, which are less rigorous and require less fieldwork.
- The objectives of business audits or business reviews are generally to ensure compliance with legal, regulatory and contractual requirements and to evaluate risk related to external relationships.
- Internal Audit should seek input from all interested parties to develop a shared responsibility for the success of the relationship and/or project.

Internal and External Perspective

For many years, Internal Audit work has focused on auditing internal processes and organizational units to investigate how effectively departments and their employees interact with each other and their customers as the main determinant of organizational success. While this still applies today, the perspective has shifted somewhat. The increasing reliance upon supply and service chains, both within a company and across different organizations, business sectors and countries, has significantly contributed to broadening the range of factors that determine an organization's success. This trend is set to continue. Ultimately, the network of suppliers, customers, partners, and financial interests as well as relations with public institutions, organizations and governmental bodies has a significant influence on the internal processes of a company and therefore should be in the forefront of Internal Audit's focus. This means that Internal Audit's main audit areas are determined by both internal and external concerns.

Increasing Importance

The importance of audits related to external concerns will continue to increase as organizations' reliance on external partners grows. Management or the Board of Directors may engage Internal Audit to examine these relationships or projects for a variety of reasons:

Interest in Up-To-Date Information

- To effectively manage a relationship or project with outside parties it is imperative that the organization examine current and on-going information. Any significant financial or operational disruptions at any of these organizations may cause (in some cases incalculable) damage to the company's reputation and its market. Damages to an organization's reputation are very difficult to control and are often hard to reverse.

De-Escalation

- Often when organizations engage in projects with outside companies there is a risk of escalation of commitment (i.e., making irrational decisions to justify previous choices). That is, because the organization has entered into the relationship there is a desire to make it work – at all costs. Escalation of commitment often occurs when the project or relationship is not as effective or productive as originally expected and the organization increases the resources dedicated to it in an attempt to improve the likelihood of success. De-escalation activities are designed to counter-act any escalation of commitment tendencies that may exist. The aim of the de-escalation approach is to return to a stable situation internally and to show those involved new ways of reaching their targets.

Legal Requirements

- When an organization partners with other companies it is exposed to increased compliance and regulatory risk because it is also responsible for ensuring that its partner also complies with all applicable legal and regulatory requirements. If a partner fails to comply with applicable requirements, the organization may be liable for damages and subject to sanctions or penalties. Therefore, Internal Audit must carefully examine the relationships and activities of the organizations' partners in a timely manner to ensure legal and regulatory compliance.

Project-Specific Analysis

- Rather than focusing on the specific partner, Internal Audit may also examine a project in which the organization has engaged with its partner. Internal auditors may focus on project-specific issues, such as delays, excess costs, and non performance of services by the contract partner, or significant product or service defects.

Business Audit versus Business Review

For all of the above reasons, the Board may request that Internal Audit conduct a special audit of business objects, also referred to as a business audit or business review. The question as to whether to conduct an audit or a review is usually asked in connection with the extent of the fieldwork that has to be performed. When performing a business audit, Internal Audit examines the entire audit environment in depth using the Audit Roadmap. Alternatively, a business review focuses on recording and analyzing specific key aspects of the relationship or project during limited fieldwork. That is, during a business audit the auditor performs all the individual audit steps, including the necessary documentation. However, during a review, the auditor draws conclusions on the basis of readily available information. Usually, business reviews produce results faster, although the results must be analyzed from the perspective of a review. The advantage of a review over an audit is that it is sooner possible to make the first statements and implement measures. Overall, the results of a business audit include findings and recommendations, whereas a business review only concludes with procedural proposals (for more information, see Section A, Chapter 7.2.3). The rest of this chapter deals with business audits in more detail. In addition to the Board, other parties, (e.g., the legal or contracts department of a company, the sales or consulting officer responsible, other service and support units of the company, and Risk Management) may request an independent audit of the organization's external relationships and projects by Internal Audit.

Features of a Business Audit

A business audit is defined as a preventive audit measure conducted in line with the de-escalation strategy. Its main purpose is to ensure that processes, methods, and guidelines are compliant and working as intended. At the same time, the risks related to the project or partner are examined and, if necessary, appropriate de-escalation measures are proposed. Objectives and content of a business audit must be defined exactly. The audit may focus on legal, contractual, or organizational matters.

Preparing and Presenting the Results

The results of a business audit are prepared and presented in a slightly different manner than are those for a traditional audit. Because of the dynamic nature of the business processes it is necessary to explain interim results and perspectives in a timely manner to management and the employees involved. This means that, apart from the traditional report formats used by Internal Audit, additional memos (see Section B, Chapter 5.3.1) or presentations (see Section B, Chapter 5.3.2) may be needed. This may be of specific importance if the parties concerned need to consider possible actions or costs. However, it is a challenge to communicate interim results, without revealing important findings too early.

Audits Outside the Company

When examining relationships and projects with external parties, it may be necessary to conduct audit activities outside one's own business premises. In this regard, it is necessary to clarify in advance to what extent this is legally possible. Often a "right to audit" clause is included in the contract between the organization and its partner. If such a procedure deserves support, Internal Audit contacts the partner in order to agree the objective and the required action. Generally, relationships with external parties are more productive if the parties are able to cooperate and coordinate such audits without conflict.

HINTS AND TIPS

- For a business audit, auditors should enlist support from other specialist departments and corporate communications.
- During a business audit, auditors should examine all the existing documents for the process, including e-mails.
- During a business audit, auditors must keep themselves informed on an operational level as well as on a strategic level with the latest information from the Board of Directors.

LINKS AND REFERENCES

- ANDERSON S.W. AND K. L. SEDATOLE. 2003. Management Accounting for the Extended Enterprise: Performance Management for Strategic Alliances and Networked Partners. In A. BHIMINI (ED.). 2003. *Management accounting in the digital economy.* London: Oxford Press.
- ANDERSON, S.W., M. H. CHRIST AND K. L. SEDATOLE. 2006. *Managing Strategic Alliance Risk: Survey Evidence of Control Practices in Collaborative Inter-Organizational Settings.* IIA Research Foundation. http://www.theiia.org/research/research-reports/downloadable-research-reports/?i=237 (accessed May 31, 2007).

6.3 Audit Approaches

KEY POINTS

- The risk-based audit approach allows Internal Audit to target its work at areas of critical business risk.
- The audit risk consists of inherent risk, control risk, and detection risk.
- Four audit methods are used under the risk-based audit approach. These methods can be used flexibly in the course of the audit, in response to interim audit results: General risk analysis, analytical fieldwork, system and process based fieldwork, and substantive testing.
- As part of the risk-based audit approach and within the audit methods that its application entails, other audit approaches can be used during audit work, either individually or in combination.
- The system-based audit approach is used to test the effectiveness of the controls and safeguards that have been put in place.
- The objective of the transaction-based audit approach is primarily to detect

transaction errors. This normally means that Internal Audit must use an investigative method.

- The compliance-based audit approach is centered on testing the compliance of any audit object, in relation to meeting a specific requirement.
- The objective of the results-based audit approach is to arrive at a quantified comparison of the audit object's current condition with the relevant criteria, for example legal standards or business guidelines.
- The risk-based audit approach is a key concept that provides a framework for the other audit approaches. The audit objects that are selected and the specific audit activities to be conducted are determined within the framework of the risk-based audit approach. The selection is therefore guided by the risk attached to the audit object and its materiality.

Risk-Based Audit Approach

In principle, an audit approach is a method for developing a certain procedure for an audit, i.e., for formulating the audit strategy. In response to modern corporate structures, the aim of the risk-based audit approach is to allow Internal Audit to tailor its audit work to the areas of business risk. Internal Audit's universality claim of representing permanent control in all areas is giving way to greater focus on audit objects with a high risk potential.

Audit Risk

The following diagram shows that audit risk has two components, error risk and detection risk. Error risk breaks down further into inherent risk and control risk.

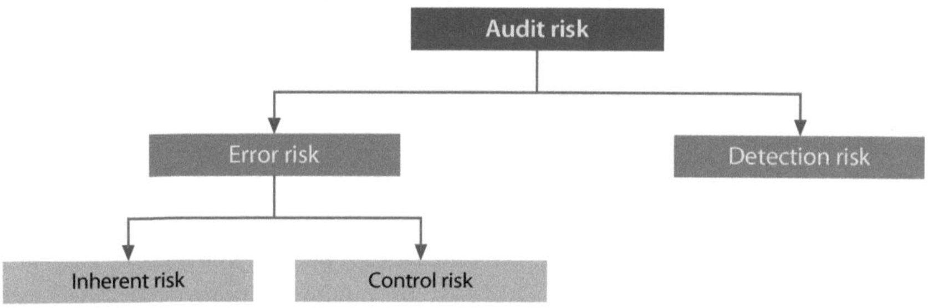

Fig. 21 Audit Risk Components

Inherent Risk

Inherent risk is the risk that is intrinsic to a process and results from the audit object's susceptibility to errors. It comprises macroeconomic, sector- and company-specific factors (e.g., the economic situation, organizational structure, or the company's legal environment, as well as factors specific to the audit object). Factors specific to the audit object include the complexity of work processes in business units and departments and the time pressure to which they are subject. To assess the inherent risk, auditors must have comprehensive knowledge of the company and its environment and use interviews and observations or analyze documents in order to obtain information on workloads, work quality, and techniques in the unit being audited.

Control Risk

Control risk represents the danger that the implemented internal control system does not detect or prevent all relevant errors. There may be two reasons for this: Either, the controls are triggered only after a time delay, which means that any errors are identified too late, or certain aspects are not checked because the internal controls are not effective all the time or there are gaps in their coverage.

Detection Risk

Detection risk is the other main component of audit risk. It quantifies the possibility that in spite of detailed tests, the auditors do not detect material errors, for example because they have selected an insufficient number of samples or inappropriate audit methods. Unlike the other components, auditors can therefore directly influence detection risk by selecting the type and extent of fieldwork.

Audit Risk as the Product of its Components

For reasons of efficiency, only material risks are included in the audit planning. Since the three components of audit risk can offset or reinforce each other, audit risk is determined by multiplying its components:
Audit risk = inherent risk x control risk x detection risk.

Tolerable Detection Risk Levels

Once the overall audit risk acceptable for the audit has been defined and the inherent and control risks have been determined, the tolerable detection risk can be set. Auditors must keep within this risk level by conducting appropriate fieldwork. It is, however, impractical to work out the exact level of risk mathematically, so that general risk categories (low, medium, high) are used in practice.

Risk Analysis

From a risk perspective, four approaches for risk analysis are used as part of the risk-based audit approach:

- general risk analysis,
- analytical audit procedures,
- systems and process based fieldwork,
- substantive testing.

In risk analysis, the areas of business risk are determined and the relevant risks are identified in the overall context of audit risk. The audit objects are determined and the audit is planned on the basis of the results of the risk analysis.

Analytical Audit Procedures

Analytical audit procedures (see Section C, Chapter 3.1) are used to generally assess the risks at process level. The procedures consist of analyzing individual figures and ratios or groups of figures and ratios. They are intended to allow auditors to get an overview of the reliability of the risk management and internal control systems. Analytical audit procedures also help provide a global overview of the processes and controls of the unit being audited and identify any interdependencies. The audit content is divided into audit areas on the basis of this knowledge.

System Audit and Substantive Testing

Detailed system fieldwork helps test the reliability and effectiveness of the internal controls. It is also used to assess the main process risks. These tests are based on a comparison between the applicable standards or company-internal rules and the actual process or situation in the units being audited. Substantive testing is a detailed review of individual material causes of risk or of a specific process.

Flexible Combination of Methods

By combining the above four audit methods in the indicated sequence, the auditors can conduct an audit efficiently with the specified degree of reliability and optimize it with regard to the time and effort it involves. During this process, the reliability of the individual audit statements increases continually from general risk analysis through substantive testing. A significant attribute of the risk-based audit approach is that the combinations of methods can, and have to, be flexibly adapted during the audit in line with interim audit results, i.e., Internal Audit's activities are scaled down or expanded while the audit is being conducted.

Other Audit Approaches

As part of the risk-based audit approach and within the audit methods that its application entails, the auditors can use other audit approaches during their audit work, either individually or in combination. The diagram below shows how the different audit approaches interact, and the text that follows explains the approaches and the interaction between them.

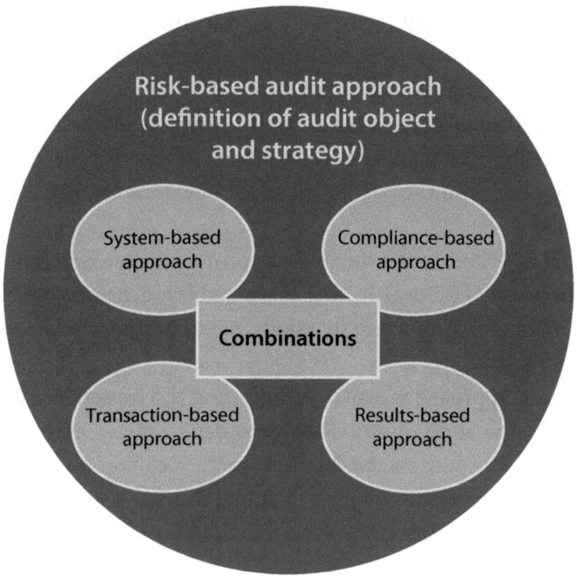

Fig. 22 Embeddedness of Audit Approaches in the Risk-Based Audit Approach

The system-based audit approach should be used to test the effectiveness of the controls and safeguards. The main objective of the system-based audit approach is to give the managers with overall responsibility for corporate monitoring an assurance regarding the control systems used. Any actual or possible weaknesses in the system should be detected and eliminated. The system-based audit approach is generally also based on the risk analysis performed on the company and its processes and procedures.

Characteristics of the System-Based Audit Approach

Audits that follow a system-based approach are similar to process audits and focus on control mechanisms. Although this approach is also intended to detect errors, it focuses on systematic errors during process or transaction handling, not on specific one-time errors. This means that the system-based audit approach is less retrospective and should also be able to produce forward-looking audit results.

Application of the System-Based Audit Approach

Because of its systematic way of dealing with transactions within the company, which requires them to be comprehensively analyzed, the system-based approach is particularly well suited to audit matters related to or impacting on the following topics: Reliability and integrity of accounting, securing of assets, efficiency of transactions, and compliance with legal rules and requirements.

Objective of the Transaction-Based Audit Approach

The objective of the transaction-based audit approach is primarily to uncover transaction errors. In line with this objective, the transaction-based approach often means that Internal Audit has to use an investigative procedure.

Characteristics of the Transaction-Based Audit Approach

Audits that follow the transaction-based approach are best suited to fieldwork such as sample tests and full audits of individual business transactions within the company. They assess whether the relevant processes are performed correctly and the transaction has been handled and recognized properly. Under this audit approach, the controls integrated in the corporate processes are only of secondary importance, because these audits analyze not the general process as a whole, but focus on a specific manifestation. As such, the audit procedure used under the transaction-based approach focuses on the past or present, but can rarely arrive at forward-looking audit results.

Application of the Transaction-Based Audit Approach

Because the focus of audit activities under the transaction-based approach is on a specific transaction, it is best suited to investigating suspected fraud, helping with issues relating to the assessment of management decisions, or supporting customer projects or similar consulting tasks.

Objective of the Compliance-Based Audit Approach

The compliance-based audit approach is centered on testing the compliance of an audit object. Consequently, the audit object is tested to determine whether or not it meets a specific requirement set to establish compliance. Such requirements may include legal standards or company-internal conduct rules, policies, and guidelines. Audits that test whether certain controls or individual control elements are in place are also feasible.

Characteristics of the Compliance-Based Audit Approach

Audit objects may include internal monitoring systems as well as specific processes, process steps, and work results. Note that the compliance-based audit approach leads to an audit statement in the form of a yes-no decision. If the audit object is found to be compliant with the relevant benchmark, this results in a positive audit outcome. However, if the audit finds the audit object to deviate from the relevant benchmark, it is documented as non-compliant. The finding does not comment on the extent of the variance, i.e., the error is not rated.

Application of the Compliance-Based Audit Approach

Since it focuses on following rules exactly or the existence of specified controls or process steps, the compliance-based audit approach is best suited for assessing compliance with legal standards or compliance regulations, assuring the quality of the process structures, or testing whether project targets are achieved as planned.

Objective of the Results-Based Audit Approach

The objective of the results-based audit approach is to arrive at a quantified comparison of the audit object's current condition with relevant criteria, which again include legal standards or company-internal guidelines. This approach is not only about establishing whether or not the audit object meets the benchmark. If any non-compliance with the requirement is found, it should be quantified as far as possible. This applies to both errors in specific procedures and the impact of any control weaknesses that have been identified.

Characteristics of the Results-Based Audit Approach

When the results-based audit approach is applied, audit results are expressed as a quantitative measure, not a yes-no decision. The non-compliances that have been identified can be expressed either as percentages or relative values, or as monetary amounts. If the consequences in the form of a direct percentage or monetary amount cannot be specified, the auditors may alternatively rate the error qualitatively according to its seriousness. Sample testing is particularly suitable for use under the results-based audit approach, not least because of the flexibility of the variables. The results-based approach is also useful where the audit statement is not to be limited to simply confirming compliance, but where the positive aspects are to be quantified. This approach could be used for projects, for example, where the auditors want to report not only the general fact that the objectives have been met, but also that the project was implemented faster and with greater success than planned.

Application of the Results-Based Audit Approach

Since the results-based audit approach focuses on measuring and assessing the variance from the relevant requirements, it is best suited to testing control mechanisms and quality assurance systems. In these types of audit, it is not only important to identify the existence of errors, but also to establish whether they are material and what effect they have. The results-based audit approach is also useful as part of internal consulting activities and for auditing customer projects.

Choice of the Appropriate Audit Approach

In principle, the audit objectives of Internal Audit determine which audit approach is selected. The choice in turn affects the specific audit activities that Internal Audit conducts. Firstly, it is important to clarify whether it is conducting a comprehensive audit of a whole area or only examining certain key issues. If the audit objective is comprehensive, for example, testing the effectiveness of the intended control mechanisms, a system-based approach is advisable. For more specific issues or substantive tests on single transactions or similar, the transaction-based audit approach is more appropriate.

Combination of Audit Approaches

But the system and transaction based audit approaches are not mutually exclusive and can be used in combination with each other. In particular, the auditors can use the transaction-based approach for additional testing under the system-based approach. The reverse procedure, i.e., using the system-based approach as an addition to the transaction-based approach, is normally more difficult and will only rarely be considered a feasible way of achieving the audit objectives. In practice, compliance-based and results-based approaches can also be used in combination, for example to test for the existence of control mechanisms, while at the same time arriving at quantitative statements about whether the intended procedures are fully and appropriately complied with.

Other Possible Combinations

It is also possible to combine the compliance-based audit approach with both the system-based and the transaction-based approach. A combination of the compliance-based with the system-based approach is particularly useful when testing whether control mechanisms or certain process steps exist within process structures. The compliance-based and transaction-based audit approaches can be combined, for example when auditing compliance with specific standards, where a positive or negative audit result without quantification is sufficient. However, if the auditors need to quantify the audit result in a transaction-based audit, they should combine this approach with the results-based approach. When assessing control mechanisms or requirements relating to procedures, it is sensible to combine the system-based and results-based approaches. In such cases, the auditors are testing not only the general effectiveness, but also the materiality of variances from stated requirements.

Risk-Based Audit Approach as a Framework

The risk-based audit approach is a key concept that provides a framework for the other audit approaches: The audit objects are selected and the specific audit activities are determined within the framework of the risk-based audit approach. The selection is therefore guided by the risk attached to the audit object and its materiality. Within the individual steps or audit methods of the risk-based audit approach, the auditors should fall back on other audit approaches that allow them to add specific audit content in the appropriate place within the specified framework. It will depend on the case in question whether the auditors should use the pure forms or combinations of audit approaches. This decision is taken in line with the audit objective on the basis of the specific requirements and circumstances.

Use in IT and Fraud Audits

On this basis, it is also possible to create links between the tasks of Internal Audit and the applicable audit approaches. For the more topical tasks, the assignments are relatively clear. For an IT audit, the system-based approach with results-based elements will normally be best. But a fraud audit will almost invariably use the transaction-based approach in combination with the compliance-based approach, unless it investigates the general effectiveness of a preventive system.

Use in Internal Consulting and Business Audits

In the area of internal consulting, customer projects will tend to be addressed by the transaction-based audit approach, but consulting projects for process improvements will probably require a system-based approach. The same applies to business audits. In most cases, the results-based approach will be more prevalent than the compliance-based approach in these areas, because the quantitative impact of audit findings is very important in internal consulting.

Use in Management Audits

When examining the organizational structure, management audits may use the system-based audit approach, but otherwise the transaction-based approach will be more common. In this audit field, a results focus should commonly outweigh a pure compliance assessment.

Use in Operational and Financial Audits

Since in both operational and financial audits the focus is on processes and business transactions, system-based audit approaches are the preferred choice. In both fields, transaction-based approaches will only be used in individual cases to confirm the results. The adequacy of a compliance-based or results-based approach depends on the audit object in hand, although the results-based approach will probably be used more often.

Audit approach \ Audit field		Management	Operational	Financial	IT	Fraud	Business
Risk-based		X	X	X	X	X	X
Risk-based	System-based	X	X	X	X	x	X
	Transaction-based	X	x	x	x	X	X
	Compliance-based	X	X	X	x	X	x
	Results-based	X	X	X	X	X	X

X = important
x = less important

Fig. 23 Relations between Audit Fields and the Audit Approaches to be Used

Assignment by Risk Orientation

The above diagram explains the relations between audit fields and the audit approaches to be used. For the assignment of possible audit approaches to the task areas, the risk-based audit approach once again functions as a framework. On the basis of risk considerations, decisions are taken about the content of audit objects, which can belong to one main task or to several activities of an audit field. Once the audit objects have been specified and the basic audit strategy has been defined, the audit approach can be chosen.

HINTS AND TIPS

- Auditors should always keep risk-based procedures in mind and act accordingly.
- Risk aspects are also very important when choosing appropriate audit approaches, and it may therefore make sense to consult with risk management.
- Auditors should thoroughly analyze the impending audit request in order to align their method with one or more suitable audit approaches.
- Even after the audit has started, auditors should regularly consider using different or additional audit approaches or audit methods in their work.

LINKS AND REFERENCES

- KEITH, J. 2005. Killing the Spider. *Internal Auditor* (April 2005): 25–27.
- MESSIER, W. F. 2003. *Auditing and Assurance Services: A Systematic Approach*. 3rd ed. Boston, MA: McGraw-Hill.
- RITTENBERG, L. E. AND B. J. SCHWEIGER. 2005. *Auditing: Concepts for a Changing Environment*. 5th ed. Boston, MA: Thompson.
- SAWYER, L., M. DITTENHOFER AND J. SCHEINER. 2003. *Sawyer's Internal Auditing*. 5th ed. Altamonte Springs, FL: The Institute of Internal Auditors.
- SEARS, B. 2002. *Internal Auditing Manual*. New York, NY: Warren, Gorham & Lamont.

6.4 Audit Categories

KEY POINTS

- The audit categories include local, regional, and global audits.
- Local audits focus on local units and processes. They are conducted by the decentralized units of Internal Audit, taking local circumstances into account.
- Audits of topics that are relevant for the whole region are called regional audits. These include audits of a topic performed centrally for the whole region, or on a decentralized basis at different locations in the region.
- Global audits always involve horizontal process chains that affect either different organizational units or the same organizational entity as a global function in different regions and countries.
- All audit standards that have been developed apply without exception to the different audit categories. Deviations from the standards are only allowed in justified exceptional circumstances. The reasons for such deviations must be documented and permission must be obtained from the Audit Manager.

Assignment of Audit Categories to Audit Topics

Three audit categories are differentiated at SAP: Local, regional, and global audits. All audit topics can be assigned to these audit categories. In practice, some audits, e.g., of financial or process topics, are primarily conducted locally, but audits of strategic topics, such as management processes or risk management, are more often audited regionally or globally.

Multiple Assignments

However, the links between audit fields and audit categories are not always clear-cut, and multiple assignments are possible. A financial audit can be conducted locally in an operating unit, but it is also feasible to conduct it on a global level throughout the company.

Definition of Local Audits

Local audits are all audit activities that exclusively cover audit content at a local level, e.g., processes and objects that relate to only one country or those that are to be examined from a local perspective, even though they are globally significant for the entire company. In addition to local subsidiaries, the audit objects of local audits can include joint projects, partnerships, and joint ventures.

Regional Teams at SAP

SAP's Internal Audit is organized in several regional teams with a high degree of autonomy (see Section A, Chapter 4.3). A core task of these regional audit units is to implement the audit standards developed in the various audit categories. Local audits of entities in the area represent a virtually autonomous audit category for regional teams. This gives the audit teams a high degree of responsibility. Regional team members are mainly recruited from among the employees of the region, ensuring that the regionally or locally specific expertise remains within the unit responsible for the region.

Subject of Local Audits

Typical local audits include process and accounting audits, as well as audits of compliance with corporate law (e.g., register entries and articles of partnership). In addition, local audits also examine specific local processes and approval procedures, taking locally relevant legal circumstances into account. This includes audits of local IT processes and IT equipment, as well as specific investigations into alleged or suspected fraud. Ultimately, many elements of the wide field of audit topics may become locally relevant.

Standard Audits versus Special Audits

Under normal circumstances, standard audits will be the type most commonly conducted from a local perspective, i.e., audits that could happen in similar ways at different locations. Special audits with a specific topic focus occur more rarely, if at all, because such unique topics are often encountered only once in the company and are therefore normally not conducted in decentralized units but rather on a global level, e.g. audits of the corporate treasury department (for details on audit typology, see Section A, Chapter 6.5).

Position of Local Audits within the Process Model

Local audits always follow the Audit Roadmap, from planning and preparation through execution, reporting, and follow-up (see Section B). In addition, the whole quality assurance framework must be complied with. Local audits are shaped by the combined influence of centrally specified standard processes and contents on the one hand and their decentralized adaptation and application on the other. Central standards must be applied to the audit to the extent possible, but despite standardization specific local features must be considered.

Information Exchange with Other Parties

Especially in smaller regions, it is important to exchange as much information as possible prior to an audit, because this allows the auditors to identify audit focus areas in a timely manner. This applies to both internal and external contacts, e.g. the local external auditors. Local cultural aspects must also be considered.

Mixed Teams

Local audits are listed in the regional execution plan (see Section B, Chapter 2.2), which must be based on the overall regional capacity for all audits and the available resources to avoid schedules that are too ambitious. Sometimes, however, especially if capacity suddenly becomes unavailable or specialist knowledge is required, there may be additional demand for auditor capacity. In such circumstances, the regional teams should get ad-hoc support from colleagues of other regions. Even when a local audit is conducted by a mixed team, the audit remains local and fully under the responsibility of the regional audit organization concerned, i.e. the regional team and the regional Audit Manager.

Tasks of the Audit Manager

Due to their responsibility for conducting audits in their regions, Audit Managers are also responsible for prioritizing and scheduling each audit. All administrative processes, such as the audit announcement and the distribution of reports, are also performed regionally on the basis of the applicable distribution lists. This affects the managers of the unit being audited at local level in particular.

Definition of Regional Audits

Regional audits focus either on regional matters, e.g. regional management of business partner relations, or on processes centrally organized through shared services centers, e.g., standardized purchasing. This means that under a regional audit, a specific topic is examined in various different locations, either simultaneously or one directly after the other. The audit organization must make sure in each instance that the audits are conducted uniformly and local preferences cannot influence or distort the audit results.

Local versus Regional Audits

The comments on local audits with regard to complying with audit standards and putting the audit team together also apply to regional audits. However, there is a major difference in the way the regional nature of the audit impacts the management of the unit mainly affected by the audit. In the case of regional audits, higher-level (regional) management is responsible for enabling the audit on the one hand and for implementing the audit results on the other. This means that, unlike for local audits, this management level must always be involved in the main phases of the audit itself and the opening and closing meetings.

Value of the Audit Results

Another significant difference is that the results of regional audits may have greater importance for the company than those of local audits. For this reason, it is possible that, in the search for company-wide solutions, critical results of a regional audit will more readily be brought to the Board of Directors' attention because the objective is to release rules and guidelines at senior management level to help harmonization across regional boundaries.

Global Challenges for Internal Audit

International corporate audit departments can and must also face global audit topics (see Section C, Chapter 7). Different audit topics can be identified as challenges for Internal Audit on a global level. They are related to different methods that can or have to be used according to the underlying determinants.

Subject of Global Audits

A global audit of one topic may occur at locations in different regions under one organization with overall functional responsibility. Examples include the global escalation department, the global processing of patents to safeguard intellectual property, or a global purchasing organization. Ultimately, they always involve horizontal process chains that either affect different organizational units or the same organizational unit in different regions and countries. A global audit area may also be a topic whose specific contents are defined by a central unit, which implements and coordinates them in the different countries and regions. Examples include global risk management and globally standardized internal controls, particularly in response to SOX. Global structures of this kind may also be found in development or sales organizations, which are therefore also possible subjects of Internal Audit's work.

Centrally Standardized Audits

From Internal Audit's perspective, it may be sensible to centrally standardize certain topics thus transforming them into global topics for the time of the audit engagement. To ensure that for these topics, audit content, procedures, and expertise are optimized, such audit objects are easier to enforce and coordinate from Internal Audit's point of view if they are managed under the same technical responsibility. The audits in question include primarily management and fraud audits, but also audits of IT processes and information networks. A special feature of these types of audits is that the topics under review are often sensitive and may have a global impact on the entire company.

Thematic Unity

Global audits are seen as a single unit for the whole duration of the audit process. This means that the totality of an audit cannot be broken up, even if it covers areas that differ in terms of content (central functions and decentralized units). In a global audit, the audit topic therefore clearly dominates the regions and forms the focal point of all audit procedures. The whole organization and process of an audit must fall in line with the global topic. The only relevant outcome is a complete and globally coordinated audit result, because only this result will permit the auditors to arrive at findings, recommendations, and conclusions that are appropriate from a global perspective. This means in turn that the audit content must be defined on a global level, not with a local or regional focus.

Reporting Lines

Global audits primarily deal with operational business units that are under uniform global management and therefore have globally standardized processes. The reporting lines to the global level must be clearly defined in this context. Units that are managed on a decentralized basis, yet follow global processes have clear local or regional reporting lines.

Standard Method

Global audits must be treated as a whole not only with regard to content, but also in terms of method in order to ensure audit success. This is why the work program, the working papers, and the reports must always cover all areas of a global audit. Individual parts cannot receive independent treatment, even if they involve different countries or organizational units. Each stage of the quality assurance system should also incorporate the results of all audited units simultaneously. The procedure can only be consistent and deliver a globally cohesive audit result if all audit steps are coordinated across all involved auditors and synchronized with regard to content.

Global Cooperation

Global audits require the auditors involved to communicate and cooperate across continents and time zones and therefore place great demand on the audit lead. Global cooperation also requires that all team members keep to the work program (in terms of timing and organization) and deliver partial results when they are due in order to support the audit lead in conducting a successful audit.

Different Audit Procedures

What makes global audits challenging is the potential conflict between what has been centrally specified and what can be implemented regionally. In such cases, the right balance has to be found in order to get an acceptable audit result. The nature of different global audit scenarios also requires different ways of conducting the audit. In some audits, for example, the central functions will be examined first, followed by corresponding audits in the regions, which are conducted simultaneously or successively. It may be sensible to audit different decentralized units simultaneously so that you can use the mutual exchange of information as a basis for the next steps. Alternatively it may be considered to conclude the audit of one decentralized unit first so that the lessons learned can be applied to improving the audit procedure for further units. The audit lead and Internal Audit management have to decide on a case-by-case basis which procedure is best.

Global Audits and the Audit Roadmap

On the whole, global audits also follow the Audit Roadmap (see Section B), i.e., the audit steps to be taken are integrated into the relevant phases of the process model, although there are some special points to consider when auditing globally which will be discussed in the following paragraphs.

Planning Phase

The planning phase of global audits normally takes longer, because they involve significantly more coordination in selecting the team members and assigning the tasks within the team. Other points to clarify include the entire infrastructure, the organization of meetings, and how information will be exchanged and requirements documented. In addition, global audits may entail a need to inform the various global units of the audit object more comprehensively about the objective and purpose of the audit than in regional or local audits. The auditors must check whether the relevant Scope (see Section A, Chapter 5.3) completely covers the global aspects and update it if necessary.

Audit Preparation

When preparing the work program, the auditors may find that global audits (more often than local audits) require additional technical expertise, e.g., in the form of guest auditors or expert advisors (see Section D, Chapter 10). The schedule to be compiled has to take into account that, due to the great physical distances, meetings and the documentation of working steps are particularly difficult to organize in global audits.

Audit Execution

Global audits do not have any specific requirements in terms of audit execution, but linguistic and cultural needs must be taken into account when creating the working papers and during the closing meeting.

Reporting

During the reporting phase, the audit lead must ensure that all parts of the report are completed on time and are consistent with each other. The amount of work this requires in global audits should not be underestimated. The responsibilities must be defined carefully and clearly to support and to facilitate the subsequent implementation of the audit results.

HINTS AND TIPS

- All involved parties must be aware of the characteristics of the audit category in question.
- Communicate audit-specific information with local and cultural circumstances in mind, using informal channels if appropriate.
- The global audit lead must make sure that the virtual network between all team members is functional.

LINKS AND REFERENCES ↗

- SAWYER, L., M. DITTENHOFER AND J. SCHEINER. 2003. *Sawyer's Internal Auditing.* 5th ed. Altamonte Springs, FL: The Institute of Internal Auditors.
- SEARS, B. 2002. *Internal Auditing Manual.* New York, NY: Warren, Gorham & Lamont.

6.5 Audit Types

KEY POINTS •••

- The audit type is an important determinant of the audit method.
- We can differentiate between standard, special, and ad-hoc audits.
- Each audit type has its own objectives, content, and individual procedures, although it is based on the Audit Roadmap.
- Standard audits most closely follow the Audit Roadmap. They can be planned almost in their entirety and can therefore be performed as often as necessary and at relatively short notice.
- Special audits usually deal with audit objects that occur only once within the company. They also contain many elements of the Audit Roadmap, but they have a larger number of individual elements than standard audits.
- Ad-hoc audits are the most individually structured audits focusing on special topics, or person-specific one-time audits. They are often commissioned by company management. Although they follow the Audit Roadmap in principle, their very individual nature often requires specific steps, fieldwork, and documents during each phase.
- An ad-hoc audit may also readily lead to additional standard or special audits.

Audit Type and Characteristics

The audit type is another important determinant of the audit method. It refers to the differentiation of audits by purpose, content, as well as organization and execution. Three types can be distinguished: standard audit, special audit, and ad-hoc audit. Assignment of an audit to a type results in specific characteristics for the audit that affect each stage of the Audit Roadmap, from the way the audit is planned, the existence of a Scope and work program, the form and timing of audit execution, through the various reporting forms and the follow-up procedure.

Standard Audits

Standard audits investigate objects that have multiple occurrences in the company, so that the topic of the audit comes up repeatedly. This means that the audit can be standardized, i.e., its content and procedure can be applied to any number of similar audit objects. Examples include individual departments in subsidiaries, such as Accounting or Purchasing. But similar processes such as payroll and travel or other expenses can also be specified for standard audits. They are also useful in areas where guidelines, rules, and process standards are to be harmonized. Standard audits are often conducted locally.

Characteristics of Standard Audits in the Audit Roadmap

Standard audits have certain characteristics in terms of the Audit Roadmap (see Section B):

- As part of annual audit planning, they are normally subject to risk assessment and are included in the annual audit plan, if appropriate (see Section B, Chapter 2.2 and Section D, Chapter 3). The audit is announced (see Section B, Chapter 3.1) and the team compiled (see Section B, Chapter 2.4) in line with clear procedures. A Scope, which describes the audit content, exists for standard audits.
- The work program is compiled on the basis of the content of the existing Scope, which means that it can be used for similar audits.
- Certain standard fieldwork activities can also be defined for the audit execution stage, e.g., sample test procedures, interview techniques, or questionnaires.
- All standard reports, from implementation report through Board summary, must be used for reporting under standard audits (see Section B, Chapter 5). One of the reasons for this requirement is that the results of standard audits must be documented and communicated according to fixed rules to ensure compliance with the audit process in the Audit Roadmap. Any individual adaptation at this stage should therefore be reserved for special justified circumstances.
- The same applies to the different phases of the follow-up. For optimization purposes, it is important that the measures and recommendations made by Internal Audit are rigorously implemented, which is why systematic follow-ups are essential.

Execution of Standard Audits

Standard audits are conducted according to clear rules and following standardized steps. For this reason, they are well suited for less experienced auditors to gain experience, in some cases even as audit leads. Standard audits can also serve as a basis for the other audit types, especially special audits.

Special Audits

The topic of a special audit usually occurs only once in the entire organization. Examples include special development departments that develop add-ons with or without a link to a customer project. Like standard audits, special audits are also subject to the whole annual planning process. Special audits are mostly conducted on a global or at least on a regional basis, because their topics are often too specific to be present at local level. They often require specific technical knowledge and special preparation, which must be considered when composing the audit team, because the auditors' technical knowledge and interests can make a key contribution to the success of the audit.

Characteristics of Special Audits in the Roadmap

Special audits require different treatment under the Audit Roadmap (see Section B) than standard audits, at least in part:

- Although they are included in the annual audit plan, they need longer preparation times when they are added to the execution plan. This applies particularly to creating the Scope, a process which should be supported by company-internal or external experts if possible. Sufficient time for building up knowledge among Internal Audit employees is also necessary.
- When the audit is conducted, it may become necessary to use special audit activities or techniques. Such a decision has to be taken on a case-by-case basis.

Pre-structured question catalogs may be helpful. It is important to document work results in the working papers and to disclose references accurately when using additional documents (e.g., contracts, statutes, external guidelines).

- Similar to standard audits, auditors have to ensure that the reports are in line with reporting requirements. The implementation report in particular should be as detailed as possible so that the findings and recommendations can be communicated to all concerned in a comprehensible and clear format. Internal Audit's recommendations are especially important in this regard, because there are no or few comparisons with similar constellations.
- The same applies to follow-ups, where the progress of implementation measures has to be closely monitored.

Execution of Special Audits

Special audits should be conducted preferably by experienced auditors. In addition, it may be necessary to use internal or external experts as guest auditors. Since for special audits fieldwork activities cannot be planned ahead to the same extend as for standard audits, adjustments to the work program may be required during audit execution. Alternative fieldwork activities must be documented in the respective working papers accurately and completely including the reasons for choosing the specific approach.

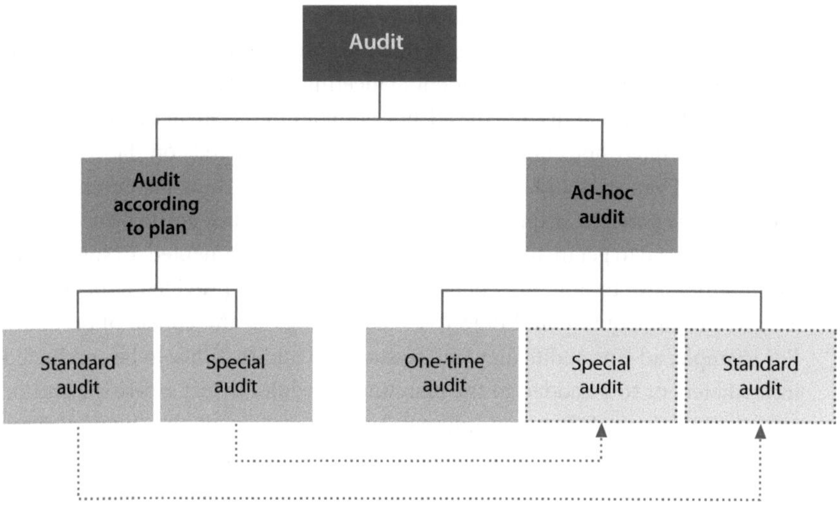

Fig. 24 Audit Types

Ad-hoc Audits

Ad-hoc audits, i.e. audits conducted at short notice, require that resources can immediately be dedicated to issues and tasks that are part of Internal Audit's remit. Examples include sudden problems in day-to-day business operations, in special projects, or with external business relations, or the need to respond to open or anonymous allegations or suspicions of fraud. The content of ad-hoc audits can therefore be very varied. It is also possible that standard or special audits turn into ad-hoc audits if circumstances require immediate action. But those are the exception. Normally, ad-hoc audits are one-time audits of special topics or relating to a particular person, especially in connection with allegations or suspicions.

Characteristics of Ad-hoc Audits in the Audit Roadmap

In relation to the phases of the Audit Roadmap, ad-hoc audits have the following special characteristics:

- Since it is impossible to plan either the content or the number of ad-hoc audits during a year, the amount of time required in the past is the only basis on which an adequate buffer can be built into the annual audit plan. Experience has shown that around 30% to 40% of annual audit capacity should be reserved for ad-hoc audits. Since their timing is uncertain, any ad-hoc audit will lead to an adjustment to the ongoing execution planning. If the ad-hoc audit is to be based on a Scope, this Scope is often created in stages during audit preparation or sometimes even while the audit is being conducted. Especially when one-time audits relate to a person, it is virtually impossible to define a Scope. In order not to waste time before the audit, but still preserve the knowledge and experience gained for similar cases in the future, internal auditors should document the main audit content after the audit, in the form of a Scope if appropriate.
- Preparations for an ad-hoc audit should always include the creation of a work program (even if it is rudimentary) so that the process model can be applied to the audit as fully as possible, in spite of time constraints and mandated content. When one-time audits are investigations on persons, the audit is not announced; in all other cases, a confidential meeting with the main person responsible should be held to discuss the ad-hoc audit announcement beforehand.
- The conduct of ad-hoc audits is very individual and depends on the content to be covered. Even so, standard auditing methods and working papers should be used as far as possible. If special partners such as the police or the district attorney's office need to get involved, the reasons must be documented. In some cases the auditors have to find out whether evidence must be provided to be used in a court of law. Content and objectives may change in the course of an audit: For example, ad-hoc audits may lead to standard audits, either to be conducted immediately or to be added to the planning schedule. Direct escalation and/or information channels between Internal Audit management and the parties responsible, particularly the Board of Directors, are important for ad-hoc audits.
- Some parts of the reporting system follow different rules than that of the other two audit types. Because of its specific content, it may be useful to dedicate a separate column of the special audit report to more detailed information on audit content. Detailed information for a follow-up audit is not necessary, or only to a limited extent, because the release of the findings of ad-hoc audits directly triggers the necessary action, or management initiates a targeted response that does not normally interfere with processes.
- For this reason, ad-hoc audit follow-up can be varied, ranging from a full follow-up to no follow-up at all. In the case of one-time audits, it is often sufficient

if the audit lead and the manager responsible briefly coordinate their response. Irrespective of the procedure used, Internal Audit must always document when a recommended measure has been completed.

Execution of Ad-hoc Audits

Much of the content and organization of ad-hoc audits cannot be planned ahead and often has to be scheduled, prepared, and started at short notice. It is also important to note who is making the request. In principle, anyone can make an audit request, but requests from the Board, higher management levels, the legal department, and internal auditors get special priority, particularly if fraud is suspected. Suspected fraud and requests from the Board are given the highest priority. In some cases, however, an initial analysis of the tasks may show that the request does not fall within Internal Audit's remit, but should rather be dealt with by entities such as the management responsible, the compliance officer, Human Resources, or the legal department (see Section A, Chapter 5.8).

HINTS AND TIPS

- In special audits, it will help the auditors if they can rely on specialist support and discuss the Scope with people who have the necessary knowledge.
- In ad-hoc audits, auditors must gain a clear understanding of the audit content by discussing the audit objectives and content with the requesting party or the person responsible in Internal Audit.
- Even during the audit, it may be expedient to report to the Board of Directors, if the content is time-critical or a response from the people responsible is needed.

LINKS AND REFERENCES

- SAWYER, L., M. DITTENHOFER AND J. SCHEINER. 2003. *Sawyer's Internal Auditing.* 5th ed. Altamonte Springs, FL: The Institute of Internal Auditors.
- SEARS, B. 2002. *Internal Auditing Manual.* New York, NY: Warren, Gorham & Lamont.

6.6 Audit Cycle

KEY POINTS

- The audit cycle is an important formal determinant of the audit method.
- The different statuses (basic audit, status check, and follow-up) are intended to ensure that the audit process is conducted in full, including a check of whether the implementation measures performed have been effective.
- The audit cycle affects the audit types in different ways. It has a major influence on standard and special audits, but ad-hoc audits tend to be more individual in nature.

Three-Phase Process

In addition to the formal determinants already described, the audit cycle is another important factor necessary for defining the audit method. The audit cycle has three stages (also known as statuses): Basic audit, status check, and follow-up. The aim of the multi-stage process is to get away from only looking at the audit process, and to include a check of whether the recommended improvement and implementation measures have been effective. Each audit has to run through the full audit cycle, although the importance of each stage may vary, depending on the case in question. In some cases, the follow-up audit and the ensuing phases are optional (see Section B, Chapter 6.1).

Basic Audit

A basic audit is performed in accordance with planning, the Scopes, and the work program, and the specifications in the audit request, if applicable. It runs through all the phases of the Audit Roadmap and produces findings and recommendations to eliminate any weaknesses identified. The audit results are presented to the auditees and their managers at a closing meeting, and a draft report is forwarded to the parties involved for additional comment. Consultation with the area being audited is intended to create mutual understanding and a shared basis for the subsequent steps. On average, it takes 30 days to conduct a basic audit.

Link between Basic Audit and Audit Type

Although the calculated average completion times are often correct for standard audits, basic audits conducted as part of special audits, especially global ones, often take up to seven weeks. In ad-hoc audits, the duration of the basic audit may be up to two weeks shorter than for standard audits, including reporting. Basic audits are the foundation for the audit cycle, especially for scheduled audits.

Status Check

At least six months should elapse between the basic audit and the next step of the audit cycle, the status check. In case of an escalation process, this timeframe may be reduced. For the status check, Internal Audit asks the persons responsible for the audited area to compile a status update that gives their view of how implementation is progressing. During the status check, senior management evaluates the degree of implementation for each finding and asks the auditees to verify the status on the basis of the implementation report. Problems with the implementation of recommendations can be discussed and recommendations can be adjusted or, in exceptional circumstances, even waived. Internal Audit does not perform explicit fieldwork at this stage. A comprehensive, fully documented check of implementation measures is reserved for the actual follow-up audit.

Execution of Status Checks

Status checks are inserted into the annual audit plan without a separate risk assessment. They are a type of preliminary test intended to find out whether and how Internal Audit's recommendations from the basic audit are being implemented. The basic time required for a status check averages two days.

Link between Status Check and Audit Type

The status check is required for all audit types. In standard and special audits, it is used as originally intended, but in ad-hoc audits it may be applied as a final check for the measures that have been implemented, because under this audit type, recommendations often lead to an immediate requirement for action, and implementation merely has to be confirmed.

Follow-up

Follow-up audits are also included in the audit plan without a separate risk assessment (for details, see Section B, Chapter 6). They should take place approximately six to twelve months after the status check. If an audit is in an escalation process, it may be sensible to perform the follow-up within a shorter timeframe. The follow-up audit is based on the results of the status check. Unlike the status check, a follow-up audit involves fieldwork by Internal Audit because the effectiveness of the implementation measures performed has to be verified beyond doubt. The implementation report of the basic audit constitutes the work program for the follow-up audit. Internal Audit prepares working papers to be used as audit evidence. If implementation is found to be insufficient, this fact must be documented and additional audit findings may have to be added.

Additional Audit Topics

A follow-up audit may give rise to new, additional audit topics, either planned or unplanned. In such cases, the findings of the additional audit work are documented in a new audit report with a separate status.

Execution of Follow-ups

Again, follow-ups should be conducted by the same audit team as the basic audit (or at least by the same audit lead). The design of the follow-up envisages two follow-ups in case there were reasons that made it impossible (or very difficult) to test implementation during the first follow-up (e.g., non-availability of the employees concerned). A second follow-up can also be scheduled if the first follow-up produces unsatisfactory results, i.e. if the identified weaknesses from the basic audit have not been satisfactorily remediated. The second follow-up audit is scheduled approximately six months after the first one. This means that the maximum duration of an audit cycle is approximately 24 months. A follow-up takes around 16 days on average, including all necessary fieldwork.

Link between Follow-up Audit and Audit Type

Follow-ups are normally conducted in the context of standard and special audits. In the case of ad-hoc audits, they only make sense if conducted shortly after the basic audit if at all. The following diagram shows each audit type in relation to the extent of its cycle.

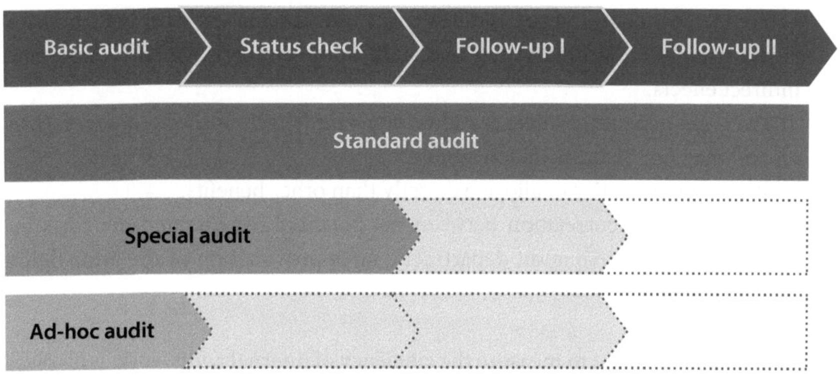

Fig. 25 Extent of the Cycle of each Audit Type

Change in the Organization and Workflow Structures

In connection with the audit cycle, the problem often arises that, since organization and workflow structures in modern (especially global) companies change rapidly, some audited units, e.g., departments or processes, only exist for a limited time. This means that often there is only one audit cycle of Internal Audit that relates to a clearly defined unit requiring the same audit treatment. In such cases, subsequent, separate audit cycles for the audited unit are linked up.

HINTS AND TIPS

- To prepare for a basic audit, auditors should obtain documents from earlier audit cycles of the same audit object.
- Auditors should ensure that the responsibilities and deadlines for implementing measures are clearly defined.
- The audited unit should record all its implementation measures by providing clear evidence, documents, and examples for inclusion in the working papers.
- Auditors should document any deviations from the agreed measures and include reasons.

LINKS AND REFERENCES

- SAWYER, L., M. DITTENHOFER AND J. SCHEINER. 2003. *Sawyer's Internal Auditing.* 5th ed. Altamonte Springs, FL: The Institute of Internal Auditors.
- SEARS, B. 2002. *Internal Auditing Manual.* New York, NY: Warren, Gorham & Lamont.

6.7 Cost/Benefit Analysis

KEY POINTS

- While the cost of an internal audit is easily quantifiable, measuring its benefits is less straightforward since internal audit findings may have both direct and indirect effects.
- The relevant benefits of internal audits often manifest themselves on several levels and may not be immediately visible.
- Cost savings are easier to allocate directly than other benefits.
- By establishing a correlation between the potential benefits and the costs incurred by the internal audit department, an approximation of the profitability can be obtained.

Efficiency Measurement

It can be very important to measure the efficiency of internal audit work. It involves examining the ratio of costs incurred by Internal Audit during the course of a specific audit, or the cost of the entire internal audit department, compared with the actual benefits achieved for the company as a whole, (e.g. through cost savings, reduced risk exposure, etc.). The following criteria can be used to analyze each audit with regard to the benefits it delivers in the short, medium, and long term (for details on cost management of Internal Audit see Section D, Chapter 8):

- cost-related benefits (reducing, avoiding, or limiting costs), and
- monetary and non-monetary benefits (increased sales, improved operating profits, motivation, reputation).

Impact on Costs

Generally, the cost impact of an audit can be seen in the short to medium term. Costs normally respond linearly and usually correlate very clearly and closely with their drivers. They can be quantified, for example on the basis of effective payments made, although direct perception declines as the time between implementing the recommendation and the time of payment increases. In addition, imputed costs can be used as part of the analysis. Normally, imputed costs increase the impact of audit findings in areas more prone to inducing costs, because ineffective internal controls also lead to costs and expenses that could otherwise have been avoided.

Benefits

While the costs related to internal audits and the resulting recommendations are relatively straightforward to determine, the benefits are much more difficult to quantify. First, the benefits often continue over long periods of time. Secondly, it is often difficult to measure benefits and attribute them directly to the processes that have brought them about. Benefits are frequently abstract and the interdependencies between cause and effect are often obscure. A complicating factor is that the effects of qualitative and quantitative benefits sometimes overlap and can thus either reinforce or detract from each other. The more general the benefit analysis, the more difficult it will be to reliably assign indicators that map and explain the causal relationship between an audit activity and its findings on the one hand and the perceptible benefits on the other.

Deriving of Benefits

Before it is possible to quantify any benefits, representative benchmarks must be defined for each audit field (e.g., throughput times, purchasing terms and conditions, contribution margins), applying either direct or indirect measures. Quite possibly, audit recommendations will lead to tangible benefits, such as an improved working atmosphere, greater motivation, or error reduction, which will in turn enhance each employee's understanding of values. There may also be a change in the way effects are perceived externally. An improved position in the marketplace, easier access to finance, and a different public perception, for example, if negative factors are eliminated quickly and with determination and their recurrence is prevented by implementing adequate measures. It is important to recognize that there may be both short-term cost savings and longer-term benefits gained from Internal Audits and the implementation of the resulting control recommendations. Both benefits should be considered when performing a cost/benefit analysis, even though they may overlap sometimes.

Quantifiable Benefits

Including quantifiable benefits in the analysis brings up the most difficult aspect of measuring Internal Audit's efficiency. The main purpose of examining these benefits is to establish a causal link between an audit finding and increased benefit values for a business unit or the company as a whole. A key challenge in this regard is to extrapolate the quantified benefit created by eliminating a process weakness, thus making it visible.

Organizational and Time Delays

With regard to the implementation of audit results organizational effort and time delays should not be ignored. Since each audit field has different content, each must be considered in detail. In business audits (see Section A, Chapter 6.2.7), for example, linear correlations between audit result and increased profits can be established, because there is a direct link between the audit object and the success driver.

Anonymous Cost-Benefit Relationship

Often, the benefit derived from internal audits is unclear, without a direct link to the measurable benefit-related units. Therefore, equivalents must be established by using auxiliary variables to quantify the cost impact and the benefits related to the audit findings.

Standard Cost/Benefit Analysis

To define a standard cost/benefit analysis for each audit field, Internal Audit must define and categorize separate benchmarks (see Section D, Chapter 8 for more on Internal Audit cost management and Section D, Chapter 7 for benchmarking). Thus, Internal Audit is integrated into the business control and decision processes, which results in interdependencies with other disciplines, such as capital investment appraisal, management accounting, and planning.

HINTS AND TIPS

- When preparing for an audit, auditors should investigate whether there are expectations about the audit's efficiency.
- Auditors should discuss the cost savings and benefit potential for each audit with the audit lead or Audit Manager.

LINKS AND REFERENCES

- ANDERSON, U. AND A. DAHLE. 2006. *Implementing the Professional Practices Framework*. 2nd ed. Altamonte Springs, FL: The Institute of Internal Auditors.
- SAWYER, L., M. DITTENHOFER, AND J. SCHEINER. 2003. *Sawyer's Internal Auditing*. 5th ed. Altamonte Springs, FL: The Institute of Internal Auditors.
- SEARS, B. 2002. *Internal Auditing Manual*. New York, NY: Warren, Gorham & Lamont.

7 Other Services

7.1 Introduction

KEY POINTS •••

- Other services that Internal Audit can perform in addition to traditional audit work can be classified as audit-related and non-audit-related other services.
- Audit-related other services include cost-effectiveness analysis, preliminary investigations, reviews, and implementation support.
- Non-audit-related other services include primarily ongoing support, internal consulting, and project management.

Other Services

In addition to the audit activities already mentioned, Internal Audit can perform further services within the company. These other services can be classified into two basic categories: Audit-related other services and non-audit-related other services. The following diagram gives an overview of the other services performed by Internal Audit.

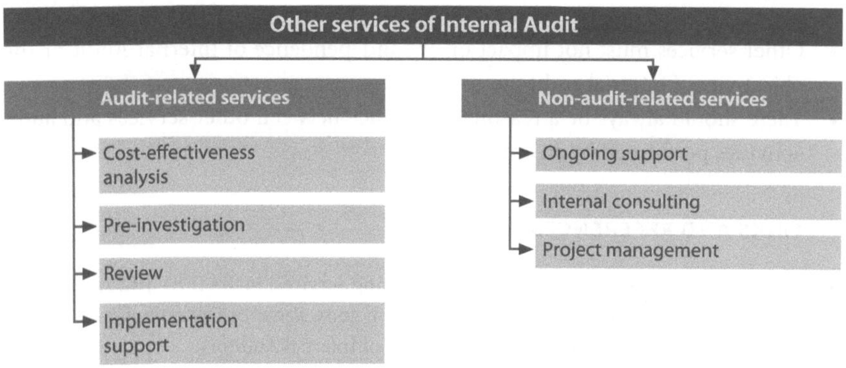

Fig. 26 Other Services of Internal Audit

Audit-Related Other Services

Audit-related other services include cost-effectiveness analysis, pre-investigations, reviews, and implementation support provided by Internal Audit. These services are either fieldwork in the broadest sense or support activities directly resulting from Internal Audit's recommendations.

Non-Audit-Related Other Services

Non-audit-related other services are not directly related to past or future audits. Instead, they involve services provided for longer-term engagements and include ongoing support, internal consulting, and project management.

Reasons for Non-Audit-Related Other Services

Non-audit related other services generally support projects initiated by other core business areas and are therefore primarily performed by employees of these areas. However, there may be a variety of reasons (see Section A, Chapter 2.5.3) that justify the involvement of Internal Audit. One possible objective is to support the area in question from a technical perspective or to provide additional personnel. For Internal Audit, cooperating in these types of projects helps increase employee motivation, provides training for auditors, facilitates the transfer of knowledge, and improves cooperation and communication among Internal Audit and other divisions within the organization.

Independence

The other services performed by Internal Audit should be regarded as completely separate from traditional auditing tasks. Internal Audit's challenge is to reconcile its responsibilities as a staff department that conducts audits with those of a functional department that provides operational support to other areas. Operational support results in interaction with auditing tasks and creates a network of interrelations within the company. Internal Audit therefore must strike the right balance, observing all principles of auditing in order to maintain its independence. Importantly, this includes ensuring that Internal Audit does not assume management responsibilities and that internal auditors do not audit their own work (see Section A, Chapter 2.5.3).

HINTS AND TIPS

- Other services must not impact on the independence of Internal Audit or the objectivity of internal auditors.
- There should always be a reasonable balance between other services and audit activities performed by an employee.

LINKS AND REFERENCES

- ANDERSON, U. 2003. Assurance and Consulting Services. In: BAILEY JR., A. D., A. A. GRAMLING AND S. RAMAMOORTI. (Eds.). 2003. *Research Opportunities in Internal Auditing*. Altamonte Springs, FL: The Institute of Internal Auditors.
- ANDERSON, U. AND A. DAHLE. 2006. *Implementing the Professional Practices Framework*. 2nd ed. Altamonte Springs, FL: The Institute of Internal Auditors.
- CASCARINO, R. AND S. VAN ESCH. 2005. *Internal Auditing: An Integrated Approach*. Lansdowne, SA: Juta and Co.
- INSTITUTE OF INTERNAL AUDITORS. 2001. *Practice Advisory 1000.C1-1: Principles Guiding the Performance of Consulting Activities of Internal Auditors*. Altamonte Springs, FL: The Institute of Internal Auditors.
- INSTITUTE OF INTERNAL AUDITORS. 2002. *Practice Advisory 1000.C1-2: Additional Considerations for Formal Consulting Engagements*. Altamonte Springs, FL: The Institute of Internal Auditors.
- INSTITUTE OF INTERNAL AUDITORS. 2005. *Practice Advisory 1130.A1-2: Internal Audit Responsibility for Other (Non-Audit) Functions*. Altamonte Springs, FL: The Institute of Internal Auditors.

- REDDING, K., P. SOBEL, U. ANDERSON, M. HEAD, S. RAMAMOORTI, AND M. SALAMASIK. 2007. *Internal Assurance and Consulting Services.* Altamonte Springs, FL: Institute of Internal Auditors.
- SAWYER, L., M. DITTENHOFER, AND J. SCHEINER. 2003. *Sawyer's Internal Auditing.* 5th ed. Altamonte Springs, FL: The Institute of Internal Auditors.

7.2 Audit-Related Other Services

7.2.1 Cost-Effectiveness Analysis

KEY POINTS •••

- Cost-effectiveness analysis is part of Internal Audit's range of audit-related other services.
- It can be performed on subjects from different business areas, including cost accounting, investment appraisal, and management accounting.
- Cost-effectiveness analysis can be conducted in pure form, or in connection with audit findings or audit recommendations.
- Finance-mathematical or statistical methods can be used for cost-effectiveness analysis.
- The results of cost-effectiveness analysis offer an ideal basis for further internal consulting by Internal Audit.

Object of the Cost-Effectiveness Analysis

Cost-effectiveness analysis (also commonly referred to as "value-for-money" auditing) focuses on determining whether organizations or programs are managed in an economical, efficient and effective manner. The analysis may relate to audits of legal entities (e.g., local subsidiaries), departments within the organization, or individual projects. Cost-effectiveness analysis uses quantitative data based on actual costs and quantifiable benefits, including future revenues or reduced costs. The data may be obtained from different functions including cost accounting, investment appraisal, and management accounting. Processes and structures are therefore not assessed in qualitative terms, but mapped using suitable indicators. In order to arrive at appropriate conclusions, cost-effectiveness analysis normally uses finance-mathematical or statistical methods.

Objective and Purpose

The main objective of using mathematical and statistical procedures is to make the audit results reliable and to identify and recommend alternative courses of action for the implementation of audit results. Especially in international companies, this kind of financial analysis facilitates discussion and comparison, (e.g., between subsidiaries) on the basis of proven quantitative results.

Main Audit Steps

Cost-effectiveness analysis is conducted as a series of main audit steps as follows:

- clear and unique description of the object to be audited, especially with regard to its efficiency approach,

- motivated selection of the finance-mathematical or statistical methods to be used,
- identification of the base data material (current condition, desired criteria or, if available, planned, budgeted, or forecasted values),
- performance of the actual calculations and alternative calculations for comparison,
- analysis of the (partial) results in the context of the audit content and their aggregation if appropriate, and
- compilation of the findings and recommendations, either at the detailed or the overall company level.

Areas of Use

This auditing procedure can be used in different audit scenarios (see below for a brief description). Each specific case will determine which scenario is used or whether a combination is sensible.

Pure Cost-Effectiveness Analysis

An audit can be announced as pure cost-effectiveness analysis from the outset. To this end, Internal Audit must determine the relevant audit objects, such as the orders a department has received (ranked by profit, loss, or contribution margin generated), all financial transactions of a company (cash flows, key income statement figures, contribution margins), or the key ratios of a capital expenditure project (present value, internal rate of return). Reports at the overall company level are also possible (e.g. an analysis of all fixed-price projects throughout the consolidated group).

Cost-Effectiveness Analysis in Connection with Audit Findings

Another scenario for cost-effectiveness analysis is the calculation of financial ratios in connection with audit findings as an additional analysis. This means that in relation to a finding, cost-effectiveness analysis can be performed to gain additional information and to analyze, modify, or expand existing ratios. Examples include discounted receivables in the area of debtor analysis, comparison of account balances, and maximum/minimum levels of outstanding payments and their extrapolation to the end of the fiscal year, including prior-year and period comparison.

Cost-Effectiveness Analysis in Connection with Recommendations

The results of cost-effectiveness analysis can also be used to support arguments in connection with recommendations. It is particularly important to demonstrate why the recommendations made by Internal Audit can lead to improved business performance. Examples include internal loans and borrowings with excessive maturities, refinancing alternatives, or the effect of alternative compensation/bonus models for senior managers. The recognition of provisions can also be backed with finance-mathematical calculations of cost-effectiveness analysis.

Stand-Alone versus Linked Ratios

The results of cost-effectiveness analysis from the audit scenarios shown above can be treated in different ways. They can be dealt with in isolation. Alternatively, it may be expedient to sensibly link the results thus creating new indicators. The interpretation of these indicators forms the basis for business decisions. Classic models such as the static return-on-investment concept or more up-to-date dynamic discounted cash flow concepts may be used in this regard. The investigation and analysis of the results then tends to focus less on individual figures and more on structured ratio hierarchies and dependencies (for more on ratios, see Section D, Chapter 7.1.2).

Results of Cost-Effectiveness Analysis

The comments on the options for using cost-effectiveness analysis show clearly that this is a varied field of internal audit work. The results achieved can be used as input for internal consulting (see Section A, Chapter 7.3.2). The results have to be adequately communicated to the various management levels, above all the Board of Directors, on the basis of suitable indicators. In addition, a company's external auditors can also use the results in their work.

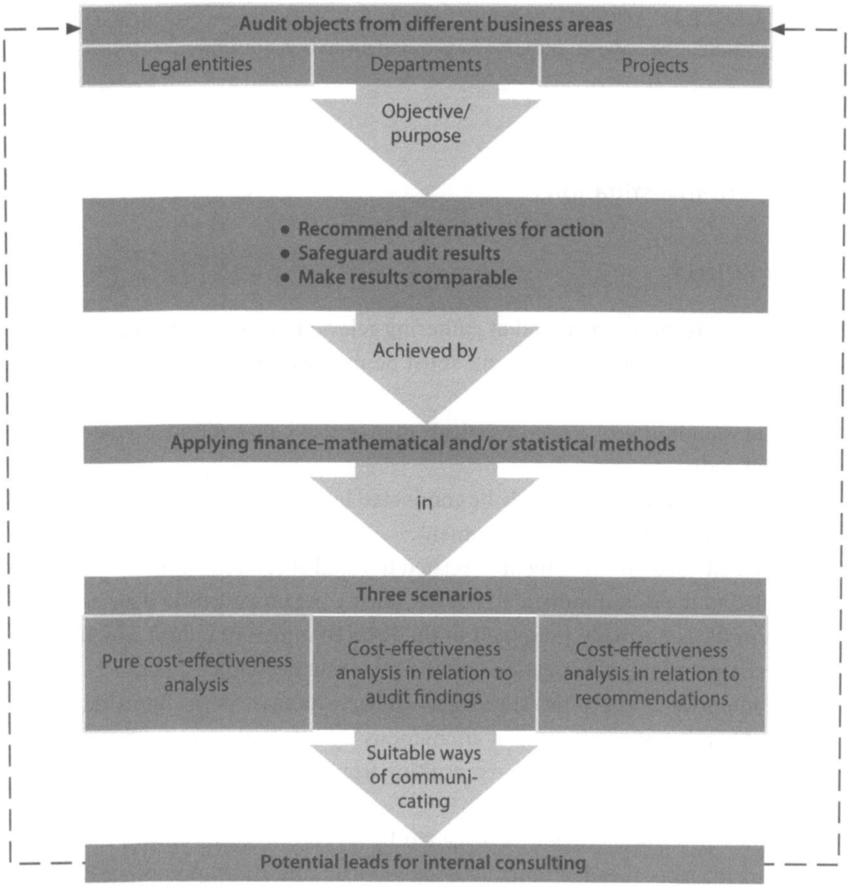

Fig. 27 Cost-Effectiveness Analysis

HINTS AND TIPS

- The potential of appropriate cost-effectiveness analysis should be explored in the context of every audit.
- Under cost-effectiveness analysis, different accounting perspectives (e.g., profitability versus cash flows) should be presented and discussed.

LINKS AND REFERENCES

- LEVY, R. 1996. Managing Value-for-Money Audit in the European Union: The Challenge of Diversity. *Journal of Common Market Studies.* (December 1996): 509–529.
- OFFICE OF THE AUDITOR GENERAL OF CANADA. 2000. *Value for money audit manual.* http://dsp-psd.pwgsc.gc.ca/Collection/FA3-30-2000E.pdf (accessed May 31, 2007).
- U.S. GENERAL ACCOUNTABILITY OFFICE (GAO). 2003. *GAO-03-673G Government Auditing Standards.* http://www.gao.gov/govaud/yb/2003/html (accessed May 31, 2007).

7.2.2 Pre-Investigations

KEY POINTS

- Pre-investigations are aimed at gathering relevant facts quickly and effectively to decide whether a certain topic must be pursued or not, e.g., in response to tip-offs or fraud allegations.
- For new audit topics, a pre-investigation may also help auditors prepare for the actual audit.
- Pre-investigations should only be conducted by experienced auditors, with support from Internal Audit management.
- The results of a pre-investigation related to fraud allegations should be communicated to the Board immediately, even during the investigation if necessary.
- The result is normally presented in the form of a memorandum which details the content of the investigation and the steps that need to be taken.
- The importance of pre-investigations will likely increase in the future due to the possibly increasing amounts of anonymous tip-offs in day-to-day business and the protection of whistleblowers resulting from SOX .

Objective of a Pre-Investigation

Sometimes an audit or review is preceded by a pre-investigation with the aim of clarifying the facts ahead of other audit services by collecting appropriate data and information. On the basis of the insight gained during the pre-investigation, measures are recommended and/or taken directly in order to conclude the case, or Internal Audit may follow it up with further activities, such as an audit or a review.

Distinction from Audit

One difference between a pre-investigation and a regular audit is the initial uncertainty regarding the extent of the investigation. Moreover, it is not clear from the outset whether the investigation falls under Internal Audit's responsibility at all, or whether a different department should be responsible, e.g., the legal department to make use of the attorney-client privilege. However, the general audit principles continue to apply in full.

Reasons for a Pre-Investigation

The main reason for conducting a pre-investigation is to analyze and evaluate the necessity of an audit engagement mostly in response to an ad-hoc request. A pre-investigation may also be triggered by other audits, or may be the result of a whistleblower's tip-off, report, or allegation. In addition, pre-investigations can also be conducted as part of the annual audit plan with the aim of clarifying the audit content in detail before the actual audit starts.

Subsequent Activities

Pre-investigations should normally be conducted immediately and quickly. It may be beneficial to involve an Audit Manager in a pre-investigation so that decisions on subsequent activities can be taken directly. A subsequent activity does not necessarily have to be an audit or a review. If a matter is not ready for auditing, Internal Audit must first create the necessary audit prerequisites, such as guidelines and process descriptions. These should be prepared with involvement by Internal Audit, so that it can contribute all the knowledge it has gained during the pre-investigation and also acquire technical know-how for the subsequent audit.

Team Composition

Pre-investigations should be performed by experienced auditors who can comprehend and evaluate vague information. Further, in some cases, company-political decisions must be taken, thus, extensive experience is a distinct advantage. The investigative team should be kept small so that it can focus its investigation.

Audit Roadmap

Pre-investigations make use of all elements of the Audit Roadmap to the extent possible (for details on the Audit Roadmap, see Section B). However, some areas, such as the Scope, may benefit from being simplified. The creation of a work program is, however, indispensable, and all the steps taken must be duly documented in the working papers.

Reporting

The reporting of a pre-investigation has to be adequate in its details. The investigation team can discuss interim results directly with the appropriate members of senior management and the Board of Directors. Further, if necessary, legal counsel should be notified immediately. If necessary, the Board should be informed of new insights immediately, for example through a priority Board issue (on priority Board issues see Section B, Chapter 5.2.5). The overall report on the pre-investigation can be compiled as a memorandum (see Section B, Chapter 5.3.1). It should primarily present facts and the relevant decision basis so that options for action can be derived. An audit report will only be compiled if a specific recommendation has been made.

Importance of Pre-Investigations

Pre-investigations are likely to become increasingly important to the day-to-day work of Internal Audit as a result of the whistleblower provision included in SOX. This provision (section 806) protects employees' right to reveal irregularities or weak points in the company's accounting system and internal controls without risk of being fired or experiencing discrimination. SOX has also made employees more aware of the importance of compliance. The public's expectations, which are heightened due to greater media exposure, also play a major role. Rapid organizational changes in the company and the introduction of new strategies and initiatives at a global level are also driving the need for pre-investigations. Even if it does not change the importance of the other audit services of Internal Audit, a pre-investigation forms a link between these and other audit disciplines.

HINTS AND TIPS

- Prepare a detailed time schedule ahead of a pre-investigation.
- It is especially important to preserve confidentiality in pre-investigations to prevent rumors.
- Auditors should try to derive and document robust knowledge that can be used in future audits.

LINKS AND REFERENCES

- ANDERSON, U. AND A. DAHLE. 2006. *Implementing the Professional Practices Framework.* 2nd ed. Altamonte Springs, FL: The Institute of Internal Auditors.
- INSTITUTE OF INTERNAL AUDITORS. 2001. *Practice Advisory 1000.C1-1: Principles Guiding the Performance of Consulting Activities of Internal Auditors.* Altamonte Springs, FL: The Institute of Internal Auditors.
- INSTITUTE OF INTERNAL AUDITORS. 2002. *Practice Advisory 1000.C1-2: Additional Considerations for Formal Consulting Engagements.* Altamonte Springs, FL: The Institute of Internal Auditors.
- INSTITUTE OF INTERNAL AUDITORS. 2005. *Practice Advisory 1130.A1-2: Internal Audit Responsibility for Other (Non-Audit) Functions.* Altamonte Springs, FL: The Institute of Internal Auditors.
- REDDING, K., P. SOBEL, U. ANDERSON, M. HEAD, S. RAMAMOORTI, AND M. SALAMASIK. 2007. *Internal Assurance and Consulting Services.* Altamonte Springs, FL: Institute of Internal Auditors.
- SAWYER, L., M. DITTENHOFER AND J. SCHEINER. 2003. *Sawyer's Internal Auditing.* 5th ed. Altamonte Springs, FL: The Institute of Internal Auditors.

7.2.3 Review

KEY POINTS

- Reviews are an independent technique to assess facts and functions.
- A review may lead to an audit or other service from Internal Audit at any time.
- Reviews focus on project-type measures and international structures and processes.

A review is a critical assessment of facts and functions. It is similar to an audit but provides a more general assessment of a matter or function and does not provide the level of detail that is typical of an audit. That is, a review does not examine details and the related evidence but instead focuses on the overall context and basic aspects of the matter or function. In a review, the presentation of evidence is limited to fundamental insights regarding the matter. Similar to an audit, a review can also compare the current condition with the desired criteria, targets, or upstream concept and process levels, thus determining the extent to which projects and processes meet or fall short of these values.

Definition

	Audit	Review
Time	More time	Less time
Approach	Looks at an entire issue or process	Looks at results only
Audit Roadmap	Complete	Complete, but some steps are carried out in simplified form
Documentation	Detailed reports	Presentation of results, supplemented by (selected) reports/action list

Fig. 28 Comparison of Audit and Review

Purpose of the Review

Unlike an audit, a review does not provide or recommend solutions. Instead, its purpose is to identify a need for action or clarification in order to eliminate shortfalls, (i.e. to point out deficiencies and the necessary organizational and methodical steps to arrive at a solution). Generally, the presentation of evidence is very limited, so that the auditor's experience and specialist knowledge form the basis for the assessment. For this reason, a review should always be conducted by experienced auditors.

Use of Reviews

Reviews are appropriate as audit-related services whenever a quick overview of audit content is needed. By the same token, reviews usually involve several parties and focus on very divergent specialist areas. They can also affect external parties like partners and suppliers (see Section C, Chapter 6). The review shares these features with the audit, and it is therefore possible to follow a review with a full audit, especially if the topic or result of the review has identified this as useful or necessary.

Content of Reviews

Reviews are particularly well suited for project-related or highly complex topics. Examples of project-related topics include internal projects (introduction of new systems or reorganization) and external customer and investment projects (joint ventures, cooperation for a specific business purpose). Examples of international review topics include a regional or global outsourcing organization or a shared-service center. A review will provide a comprehensive overview of complex structures and processes within a short time.

Review Process

A review also uses the full Audit Roadmap (see Section B), although certain parts of it, (e.g., the Scope or the work program) are usually simplified in the interest of time. However, detailed documentation is required for each step that has been performed, with reporting (in the form of presentations) often taking place concurrently to execution. Since a review does not involve intensive audit activities, (partial) results should be discussed in detail with those concerned to preclude errors on the part of Internal Audit. A special review report is compiled on the basis of the results presentation, which includes the content, chronological structure, results, and any options for action. In addition, summaries are compiled for management and the Board of Directors and, if appropriate, action items are identified for monitoring outstanding items.

Reviews as a Service Performed by Internal Audit

Reviews should not be a substitute for audits. However, they complete the service range offered by Internal Audit. Reviews are an efficient and selective way of quickly arriving at adequate results for the topic to be investigated. In particular, they are also suitable for preparing or justifying other audit services provided by Internal Audit, (e.g. a basic audit). Therefore, reviews are an important component of Internal Audit's range of service offerings.

HINTS AND TIPS

- Informal discussions at the start of a review will help auditors get an overview of the task at hand.
- Request expert support at the beginning of a review.
- Regard the review as a tool for identifying new audit topics for Internal Audit.
- If possible, present the review results in combination with key ratios to demonstrate the review's business relevance.

LINKS AND REFERENCES

- ANDERSON, U. AND A. DAHLE. 2006. *Implementing the Professional Practices Framework*. 2nd ed. Altamonte Springs, FL: The Institute of Internal Auditors.
- INSTITUTE OF INTERNAL AUDITORS. 2001. *Practice Advisory 1000.C1-1: Principles Guiding the Performance of Consulting Activities of Internal Auditors*. Altamonte Springs, FL: The Institute of Internal Auditors.
- INSTITUTE OF INTERNAL AUDITORS. 2002. *Practice Advisory 1000.C1-2: Additional Considerations for Formal Consulting Engagements*. Altamonte Springs, FL: The Institute of Internal Auditors.
- INSTITUTE OF INTERNAL AUDITORS. 2005. *Practice Advisory 1130.A1-2: Internal Audit Responsibility for Other (Non-Audit) Functions*. Altamonte Springs, FL: The Institute of Internal Auditors.

- REDDING, K., P. SOBEL, U. ANDERSON, M. HEAD, S. RAMAMOORTI, AND M. SALAMASIK. 2007. *Internal Assurance and Consulting Services.* Altamonte Springs, FL: Institute of Internal Auditors.
- SAWYER, L., M. DITTENHOFER, AND J. SCHEINER. 2003. *Sawyer's Internal Auditing.* 5th ed. Altamonte Springs, FL: The Institute of Internal Auditors.

7.2.4 Implementation Support

KEY POINTS •••

- Internal Audit can provide valuable support during the implementation of audit recommendations.
- It is important that the overall responsibility for implementation remain with the management and the employees of the audited area. Thus, Internal Audit does not perform the actual implementation of the audit recommendations, but merely provides support, which may include providing expert opinions or facilitating communication.
- All work performed must be carefully documented.
- Internal Audit must be careful to strike a balance between its position as an independent staff department and its support activities.
- The advantages of providing implementation support are primarily that Internal Audit can build specialist expertise and that recommendations can be effectively implemented.

Reasons for Implementation Support

Although implementation support is not an audit activity, it is an audit-related service that Internal Audit can provide. There are several reasons why Internal Audit may provide support for implementing audit recommendations, new concepts, and strategies. These reasons include auditors' specialized knowledge and expertise, insufficient resources in the department concerned, and extensive coordination requirements. Internal Audit's services may include providing an expert opinion on the processes and structures to be defined or facilitating the communication among those involved. These services help ensure fast, timely, and smooth implementation.

Implementation Report

The implementation report contains any options for action recommended as a result of audit findings (see Section B, Chapter 5.2.3), and it forms the basis for subsequent implementation measures. The implementation report contains information that was jointly discussed at the closing meetings of the audit and during the preparation of the audit report. However, the managers and employees of the area concerned remain responsible for driving the implementation measures. Internal Audit takes on a consulting role and must not be actively involved in the tasks to be performed.

Simple and Complex Recommendations

A recommendation made by Internal Audit may target one particular change, (e.g., the need for a second signature under certain contracts). The employees of Internal Audit act as consultants in such cases, identifying possible solutions. Additionally, it may also become necessary to change or redesign entire processes. In such cases, Internal Audit provides information or advice, while maintaining its impartial role with regard to this audit topic and organizational unit.

Independence

The support work must remain identifiable as such. To maintain independence, Internal Audit must take on only a consulting role, not a deciding role. This requirement must also be reflected in the documentation of the implementation support. Internal Audit must never perform the detailed drafting of the action to be taken or make the final decision about its implementation. If internal auditors did make crucial implementation decisions, or even if such an impression was created, these Internal Audit employees would not be allowed to take part in the follow-up. In principle, however, auditors should work through the entire audit cycle (see Section A, Chapter 6.6) under their own responsibility. Therefore, internal auditors must guard their independence especially when providing implementation support.

Guest Auditors

In some cases it may be beneficial to involve a guest auditor in implementing the recommended action (for more information on guest auditors, see Section D, Chapter 10). This provides even greater assurance that the implementation support provided is impartial. The use of guest auditors is beneficial when no other resources are available or the guest auditor has special expertise or knowledge. Guest auditors and the relevant Internal Audit employees must work in close consultation with each other.

Time Spent

The audit lead and the Audit Manager jointly determine whether and in what form an Internal Audit employee is involved in implementing audit recommendations after the audit has been completed. Together, they must ensure that auditors do not perform the implementation or spend excessive time on this consulting task. The audit resources dedicated to implementation support must be reasonably proportionate to the time for the actual audit (for example, implementation support should not take more than a maximum of 50% of the time it took to conduct the audit).

Documentation

The functional department concerned is responsible for documenting the individual implementation activities. Independently, however, Internal Audit employees should compile minutes or a memorandum detailing their own activities, contributions, and the time spent in order to demonstrate clearly that there is a time limit on these activities. The overall documentation must identify all involved persons and their roles and responsibilities. If there are any disputes during the follow-up, the individual measures can be identified and traced back to the employees involved in their implementation based on the documentation.

Limits of Implementation Support

If possible, Internal Audit should not repeatedly get involved in the same implementation activities and in general avoid providing support in one specific area too frequently. This helps counter the impression that it routinely offers a complete service, including change management, because it is primarily a staff department that reports to the Board of Directors, not an operational service department of the company.

Advantages for Internal Audit

Nevertheless, Internal Audit benefits from providing such services. For example, the knowledge gained can be used directly for preparing new Scopes or revising existing ones (see Section B, Chapter 2.1), thus keeping the expertise available within the audit department. As a result, Internal Audit may be able to respond faster to future audit requests and conduct the audits with greater focus.

HINTS AND TIPS

- Before starting their implementation support work, auditors should get a list of the people responsible for implementation.
- If, during the course of an implementation, a vote is taken, Internal Audit employees must remain impartial.
- Internal Audit employees must never arbitrate.
- If auditors determine that implementation support activities may not be completed in a timely manner, they should communicate these doubts to management early.

LINKS AND REFERENCES

- ANDERSON, U. AND A. DAHLE. 2006. *Implementing the Professional Practices Framework.* 2nd ed. Altamonte Springs, FL: The Institute of Internal Auditors.
- INSTITUTE OF INTERNAL AUDITORS. 2001. *Practice Advisory 1000.C1-1: Principles Guiding the Performance of Consulting Activities of Internal Auditors.* Altamonte Springs, FL: The Institute of Internal Auditors.
- INSTITUTE OF INTERNAL AUDITORS. 2002. *Practice Advisory 1000.C1-2: Additional Considerations for Formal Consulting Engagements.* Altamonte Springs, FL: The Institute of Internal Auditors.
- INSTITUTE OF INTERNAL AUDITORS. 2005. *Practice Advisory 1130.A1-2: Internal Audit Responsibility for Other (Non-Audit) Functions.* Altamonte Springs, FL: The Institute of Internal Auditors.
- REDDING, K., P. SOBEL, U. ANDERSON, M. HEAD, S. RAMAMOORTI, AND M. SALAMASIK. 2007. *Internal Assurance and Consulting Services.* Altamonte Springs, FL: Institute of Internal Auditors.
- SAWYER, L., M. DITTENHOFER, AND J. SCHEINER. 2003. *Sawyer's Internal Auditing.* 5th ed. Altamonte Springs, FL: The Institute of Internal Auditors.

7.3 Non-Audit-Related Other Services

7.3.1 Ongoing Support

KEY POINTS •••

- By providing ongoing support, Internal Audit can acquire expertise necessary for subsequent audits, exchange knowledge with other individuals within the organization, and support other departments in the implementation of new systems and organizational change, or assist with temporary resource shortages.
- Internal Audit can gain practical insight into specific areas of the organization by providing ongoing support.
- Ongoing support should not exceed one year.
- Because providing ongoing support represents a departure from the traditional responsibilities of Internal Audit, these activities must be approved by the Board of Directors.

Points of Departure

Internal Audit may support other departments within the organization in their day-to-day tasks. Ongoing support is often provided to overcome temporary resource shortages or to gain a clearer understanding of certain areas to facilitate future audits. In general, ongoing support should primarily focus on internal control and should last no more than six months. Further, Internal Audit employees should not devote more than 50% of their work time to ongoing support, so that they can continue to perform traditional audit work.

Prerequisites

Generally, ongoing support activities are initiated by the department requiring the support. However, Internal Audit management should inform other managers that the internal audit department can provide these activities. Further, auditors should maintain contact with managers and employees in functional departments to develop the skills that will allow them to perform necessary duties if appropriate. Importantly, before Internal Audit can provide support, certain prerequisites must be met. First of all, the Board of Directors must approve the activities and set necessary limitations.

Documentation

Even though ongoing support does not give rise to many audit elements along the Audit Roadmap, the main content and results should at least be briefly documented. In some cases it is necessary to prepare a special report in the form of a memorandum. For example, if in the course of providing ongoing support an auditor identifies the need for an audit, it may lead directly to an audit request, or the matter may be considered in the next annual audit plan.

Auditors' Personal Preferences

The extent to which specific auditors apply themselves to ongoing support as part of their work is also determined by their personal attitudes toward the topic concerned. That is, if it is one of an employee's specializations or interests, and prospects for personal and professional development can be identified in an attractive working environment, this auditor should be the likely choice to perform the ongoing support. If the planning framework and personnel capacities allow, the audit manager will consider the auditor's request for performing this kind of work.

Acquisition of Detailed Practical Know-How

For auditors who do not yet have extensive professional experience, longer-term support work is a good way of acquiring detailed practical knowledge. Therefore, this kind of work can form part of a general auditor training plan. This gives auditors an opportunity to cover all aspects of a topic and perhaps even develop a new audit topic or establish themselves as audit experts and contacts for this topic. Even experienced auditors should take advantage of such opportunities to become familiar with new topics.

Audit Work in the Supported Area

By providing ongoing support to selected areas, Internal Audit can identify audit topics, gain a better understanding of their content, and ultimately conduct better audits. If the work performed is limited to support, the same employee may generally also audit this area, because with this kind of support, content is not normally redefined or changed. However, if the auditors are actively involved in changing or redefining the content, they should document all the knowledge acquired, but not perform subsequent audits of the area. This applies at least to the audit cycle, i.e. the next two years (see Section A, Chapter 6.6), following the support work to ensure Internal Audit can maintain independence and the auditors can remain objective.

HINTS AND TIPS

- There may be informal ways of identifying an area's requirement for support by Internal Audit.

LINKS AND REFERENCES

- ANDERSON, U. AND A. DAHLE. 2006. *Implementing the Professional Practices Framework.* 2nd ed. Altamonte Springs, FL: The Institute of Internal Auditors.
- INSTITUTE OF INTERNAL AUDITORS. 2001. *Practice Advisory 1000.C1-1: Principles Guiding the Performance of Consulting Activities of Internal Auditors.* Altamonte Springs, FL: The Institute of Internal Auditors.
- INSTITUTE OF INTERNAL AUDITORS. 2002. *Practice Advisory 1000.C1-2: Additional Considerations for Formal Consulting Engagements.* Altamonte Springs, FL: The Institute of Internal Auditors.
- INSTITUTE OF INTERNAL AUDITORS. 2005. *Practice Advisory 1130.A1-2: Internal Audit Responsibility for Other (Non-Audit) Functions.* Altamonte Springs, FL: The Institute of Internal Auditors.
- REDDING, K., P. SOBEL, U. ANDERSON, M. HEAD, S. RAMAMOORTI, AND M. SALAMASIK. 2007. *Internal Assurance and Consulting Services.* Altamonte Springs, FL: Institute of Internal Auditors.
- SAWYER, L., M. DITTENHOFER, AND J. SCHEINER. 2003. *Sawyer's Internal Auditing.* 5th ed. Altamonte Springs, FL: The Institute of Internal Auditors.

7.3.2 Internal Consulting

KEY POINTS •••

- **Internal Audit can perform consulting tasks related to specific long-term projects or general consulting tasks that are independent of specific projects.**
- **Depending on the personal experience and interests of the internal auditor, different levels of consulting tasks can be assumed. These tasks may range from simply giving expert opinions, input into concepts, and solution implementation through actively designing cooperation models and partnerships.**
- **Internal Audit's independence must be safeguarded at all times. Appropriate arrangements must be made, especially in cases where Internal Audit was actively involved in designing the solutions.**
- **The consulting work performed by the internal auditor must be adequately documented.**
- **Consulting work helps Internal Audit develop into a competent partner with employees who have the requisite motivation and expertise.**

Contributing Expertise

Consulting tasks offer internal auditors the opportunity to contribute their expertise in projects outside of the department. In addition to their knowledge and expertise, auditors can provide their analytical and conceptual capabilities to find solutions tailored to the individual project.

Possible Consulting Tasks

There are many different types of consulting projects in which Internal Audit can be involved. In the context of organizational or IT projects, possible consulting tasks include drafting concepts, including acceptance testing, documentation, and internal controls. In capital spending projects, consulting may relate to the compilation of capital expenditure budgets and ongoing financial and organizational monitoring of associated activities. The introduction of special account settlement systems would also be a sensible target for consulting services offered by Internal Audit, with particular focus on compliance, internal controls, and their impact on financial reporting. In the case of restructuring and change management, Internal Audit's consulting work should focus on planning new structures, creating a transition plan, and ensuring that internal controls and risk mitigation strategies are in place in the new organization. Finally, Internal Audit can provide assistance with costing models and cost/benefit analysis for outsourcing and shared service organizations.

Consulting Tasks not Related to Projects

Internal Audit can also provide consulting support that is not directly linked to specific projects. This may include:

- basic analysis to improve information and communication flows,
- creation of early warning systems (e.g., with regard to risks, budgets or revenue),
- assessment of and commentary on problems and suggested solutions,
- mediation associated with the above,

- improvement of decision processes, and
- general support for procedure and conduct recommendations.

Consulting Requests

Often, Internal Audit begins consulting work as a result of a specific request. Such consulting requests can be defined by the Board or by various levels of management and functional departments. Consulting requests initiated by the Board or senior management are generally focused upon strategic matters, which in turn can be transformed into corresponding audits. This may include preparations for a joint venture or for acquiring a share in a company. Internal Audit may also support strategic customer, supplier, and partner selection processes.

Documentation

As in its traditional audit activities, Internal Audit must document the results and consulting methods used in separate working papers. Specific involvement in defining content and joint decisions must also be documented and a brief management summary should be prepared if necessary. These reports are then available for future audits.

Necessary Consultation

Internal Audit's consulting services can add value within the company. Its activities can involve providing an expert opinion or design input. Although design tasks generally increase the motivation and knowledge of those involved, they can pose a significant risk to Internal Audit's independence. Due care must be taken to ensure independence and objectivity are maintained. The Board or the Board member in charge should be consulted prior to consulting engagements (see Section A, Chapter 2.5.3).

Personnel Segregation

When Internal Audit has provided internal consulting services, any subsequent audit must be conducted by a different auditor, preferably from a different team, from those who performed the consulting services. Alternatively, auditors who did perform the consulting services should refrain from auditing that area for at least two years. If for reasons of expertise, the auditors who worked as consultants are to provide expert audit support, they should only work in conjunction with other colleagues. These precautions will help ensure that Internal Audit maintains independence in fact as well as appearance.

Advantages of Consulting

The advantages of consulting work for Internal Audit include enhanced knowledge and skills for the auditors involved and for the internal audit department as a whole. Other important benefits include increased motivation of auditors and a greater general acceptance of Internal Audit throughout the company. That is, performing consulting work can improve the image of Internal Audit to that of a division that adds real value to the organization.

HINTS AND TIPS

- Auditors must be clear about the objectives of the consulting project, especially the extent of their expected contribution.
- Auditors should make realistic estimates of the time requirement and include these requirements in the annual Internal Audit staffing plan.

- When performing consulting activities, Internal Audit should highlight the importance of internal controls in the project or activities.

LINKS AND REFERENCES ↗

- ANDERSON, U. 2003. Assurance and Consulting Services. In: BAILEY JR., A. D., A. A. GRAMLING AND S. RAMAMOORTI. (Eds.). 2003. *Research Opportunities in Internal Auditing.* Altamonte Springs, FL: The Institute of Internal Auditors.
- ANDERSON, U. AND A. DAHLE. 2006. *Implementing the Professional Practices Framework.* 2nd ed. Altamonte Springs, FL: The Institute of Internal Auditors.
- CASCARINO, R. AND S. VAN ESCH. 2005. *Internal Auditing: An Integrated Approach.* Lansdowne, SA: Juta and Co.
- INSTITUTE OF INTERNAL AUDITORS. 2001. *Practice Advisory 1000.C1-1: Principles Guiding the Performance of Consulting Activities of Internal Auditors.* Altamonte Springs, FL: The Institute of Internal Auditors.
- INSTITUTE OF INTERNAL AUDITORS. 2002. *Practice Advisory 1000.C1-2: Additional Considerations for Formal Consulting Engagements.* Altamonte Springs, FL: The Institute of Internal Auditors.
- INSTITUTE OF INTERNAL AUDITORS. 2005. *Practice Advisory 1130.A1-2: Internal Audit Responsibility for Other (Non-Audit) Functions.* Altamonte Springs, FL: The Institute of Internal Auditors.
- REDDING, K., P. SOBEL, U. ANDERSON, M. HEAD, S. RAMAMOORTI AND M. SALAMASIK. 2007. *Internal Assurance and Consulting Services.* Altamonte Springs, FL: Institute of Internal Auditors.
- SAWYER, L., M. DITTENHOFER AND J. SCHEINER. 2003. *Sawyer's Internal Auditing.* 5th ed. Altamonte Springs, FL: The Institute of Internal Auditors.

7.3.3 Project Management

KEY POINTS •••

- There are different ways in which Internal Audit can support or assume project management tasks.
- Internal project monitoring and control are the most important tasks and should relate to Internal Audit's pertinent audit topics, so that expertise can be built or enhanced for subsequent audits.
- Apart from this basic function, Internal Audit employees can also take part in steering committees or provide control and support for project communication.

Project Control and Management Tasks

Another way for Internal Audit to offer non-audit-related services is to participate in or assume project control and management tasks. Although the project lead drives the project in terms of content and makes the relevant decisions, the project manager is responsible for tasks such as time and cost planning. The auditor can take on the role of project staff or of sub-project lead.

Project Implementation

In the case of project management, the individual project steps first must be planned and calculated according to the project phase model. The preparatory work is coordinated among the project team members. Project implementation must be closely monitored, comparing current conditions against desired scenarios and targets, identifying all deadlines, costs, content, or quality variances, and defining and initiating appropriate countermeasures.

Reporting

Project management also requires an adequate reporting system for the project team members and those responsible. Project management always has a financial and a technical/logistical aspect. This chapter does not provide a detailed presentation of the complex issues of project management. A basic description of a similar application, known as audit project management follows later (see Section D, Chapter 11).

Projects

Usually, project management is performed by operational management and the functional executive level. In exceptional cases, Internal Audit employees may also be involved in project management activities. For Internal Audit, the most suitable projects are those whose content is related to one of the department's audit fields. Of particular interest are change management projects and implementation projects to guarantee compliance (e.g., internal control systems as required by SOX, or IT projects with workflow processes).

Objectives and Independence

Similar to internal consulting, project management performed by Internal Audit has two main objectives, the contribution of experience and auditor training. Internal Audit can incorporate the knowledge gained from participating in project management activities into future audits. Importantly, however, there is a need to safeguard Internal Audit's independence, especially because project management means participation in designing procedures rather than implementing them.

Link with the Audit Roadmap

As mentioned earlier, project management services can provide valuable information and ideas for the management of audits. Although the Audit Roadmap is an important basic tool for audit management, it is a procedural model and therefore highly focused on content. For this reason, the Audit Roadmap should be linked with a method for project control which turns the contents of the Audit Roadmap into operational steps of the audit project.

Steering Committees

Another project management service is participation in steering committees. In such cases, an Audit Manager takes part in regular status meetings, receives meeting minutes, and is involved in fundamental decisions regarding project procedures. The most suitable projects are those of value to Internal Audit because of their organizational or content aspects. Examples include the introduction of a global risk management system, the implementation of SOX requirements, or the creation of a shared-service organization.

Communication and Information Support

Another form of project-related support is the control and coordination of communication channels and information flows between regional project teams in global implementation and organization-wide projects. The significance of this task will increase in the future, because different cultural groups must be networked interactively, thus it is important to consider specific regional circumstances. Multi-region projects may be hampered by a lack of communication and support that inhibits the sufficient implementation of all implementation phases and measures simultaneously in all regions. Finally, Internal Audit can provide direct regional support on a one-to-one basis to facilitate the implementation of the project. These forms of project support enhance the perception of Internal Audit throughout the company.

Suitable Employees

In principle, any Internal Audit employee has the option to take on the project management tasks described above; but, functional, methodical, and personal prerequisites and interests should be taken into account. Therefore, these kinds of tasks should be assigned to auditors with extensive project management know-how for the purpose of personal development.

HINTS AND TIPS

- Auditors must be clear about their personal strengths and select their project management function carefully.
- Close cooperation with experienced project managers makes it easier to work successfully.
- Auditors should produce their own personal development plan on the basis of the acquired expertise.

LINKS AND REFERENCES

- ANDERSON, U. AND A. DAHLE. 2006. *Implementing the Professional Practices Framework.* 2nd ed. Altamonte Springs, FL: The Institute of Internal Auditors.
- INSTITUTE OF INTERNAL AUDITORS. 2001. *Practice Advisory 1000.C1-1: Principles Guiding the Performance of Consulting Activities of Internal Auditors.* Altamonte Springs, FL: The Institute of Internal Auditors.
- INSTITUTE OF INTERNAL AUDITORS. 2002. *Practice Advisory 1000.C1-2: Additional Considerations for Formal Consulting Engagements.* Altamonte Springs, FL: The Institute of Internal Auditors.
- INSTITUTE OF INTERNAL AUDITORS. 2005. *Practice Advisory 1130.A1-2: Internal Audit Responsibility for Other (Non-Audit) Functions.* Altamonte Springs, FL: The Institute of Internal Auditors.
- PROJECT MANAGEMENT INSTITUTE (PMI). 2004. *A Guide to Project Management Body of Knowledge (PMBOK Body of Knowledge).* 3rd ed. Newton Square, PA: Project Management Institute.
- REDDING, K., P. SOBEL, U. ANDERSON, M. HEAD, S. RAMAMOORTI AND M. SALAMASIK. 2007. *Internal Assurance and Consulting Services.* Altamonte Springs, FL: Institute of Internal Auditors.
- SAWYER, L., M. DITTENHOFER AND J. SCHEINER. 2003. *Sawyer's Internal Auditing.* 5th ed. Altamonte Springs, FL: The Institute of Internal Auditors.

B The SAP®-Audit Roadmap as a Working Basis for Internal Audit

1 General Introduction

1.1 Structure and Features of the Audit Roadmap

KEY POINTS •••

- The Audit Roadmap is a model for visualizing all phases and process steps of an audit in terms of form and content.
- It is aimed at giving auditors all the necessary standard information on the basis of a standardized, globally binding process model.
- A standard Audit Roadmap helps to achieve uniform audits throughout the company.
- The main phases of the Audit Roadmap are planning, preparation, execution, reporting, and follow-up.
- Each of these phases is divided into sub-phases, which have to be executed in a specified sequence.
- The Audit Roadmap is intended for use as an audit process model for standard audit topics.
- In addition, Audit Roadmaps can be defined for special audit content, specifically for a certain sector, company, or audit.

Aim of the Audit Roadmap

An ordinary roadmap tells drivers how to get to places. In a figurative sense the Audit Roadmap serves the same purpose. The Audit Roadmap provides information on a sequence of events in terms of content and physical arrangement to ensure achievement of an intended audit outcome. A roadmap visualizes a strategy and defines important milestones. The key objective of having an Audit Roadmap is to ensure that all audits conducted by Internal Audit follow a standard process model as far as possible. Even if not all parts of the Audit Roadmap can be used in every audit, the basic structure of the Roadmap adds security to audits and allows for a standardized audit approach throughout the company.

Information Medium

However, the Audit Roadmap is more than a process model. The Roadmap also links audit steps with templates and other documents. In its electronic implementation the Roadmap contains many documents, standard templates, examples, and additional information that auditors can access whenever necessary. The Audit Roadmap must therefore have an in-depth structure that makes it possible to assign documents to each audit step.

Main Phases of the Audit Roadmap

The sequence of steps within the Audit Roadmap is clearly defined. The main areas of the Audit Roadmap are referred to as phases. Each phase represents a self-contained audit section with a clear structure. The main phases of the Audit Roadmap are:

- Planning,
- Preparation,
- Execution,
- Reporting, and
- Follow-up.

Together, these phases lay out a complete audit sequence, ensuring that all necessary audit activities are performed.

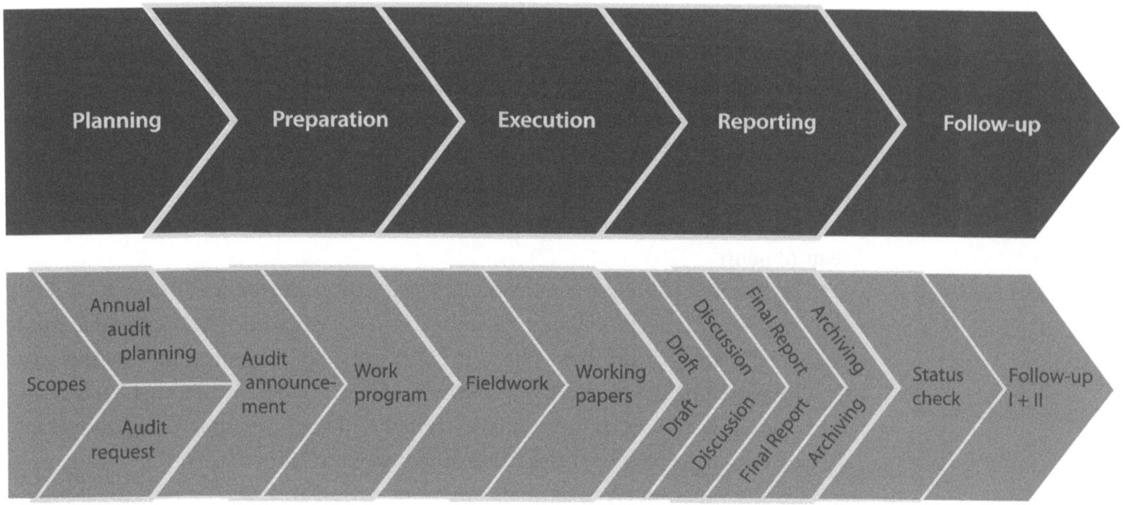

Fig. 1 Structure of the Audit Roadmap

Sub-Phases

For better implementation during the audit, each phase is divided into sub-phases. The sub-phases have to be executed in the same way as the main phases. A sequential work process is necessary because certain measures can only be performed after other operations have been completed. This mandatory sequence of audit steps is intended to ensure that security and quality requirements are met (see Section D, Chapter 5).

Standard Audit Roadmap

The Audit Roadmap exists as a standardized model. Each of its phases contains a large number of specific information. This information includes organizational aspects, such as the description of the opening and closing meetings, as well as audit-relevant documents and standards. In terms of content, the standardized Audit Roadmap covers all audit fields (see Section A, Chapter 6.2). For specific audits, like fraud audits or management audits, the Audit Roadmaps can be modified by replacing, adding, or removing certain standard procedures (see Section B, Chapter 7).

Modification Options

Based on the basic structure of the Audit Roadmap, additional Audit Roadmaps can be drawn up with company-specific and audit-related modifications if needed. For instance, additional question catalogs can be included, or the way the audit is announced can be changed. However, the objective is not to maximize the number of individual Audit Roadmaps, but rather to cover the unique features of special audit topics as comprehensively as possible and to make information on the requirements of such audits available with minimal effort.

Standard Basic Structure

It is mandatory that all internal auditors comply with the standard basic structure of the Audit Roadmap. This ensures that all internal audits, irrespective of when and where they are conducted, follow the same formal framework.

Use in Global Corporate Audit

An important feature of the Audit Roadmap is that it is a process model with a master version that can be updated centrally. This centrally maintained version is the most up-to-date standard and mandatory throughout the internal audit department. Audit-specific copies for the individual regions and audit teams follow this version. This ensures, especially in global corporate audit departments, that all regional teams follow the same audit sequence in preparation for an audit and during an audit. The Audit Roadmap provides the ordinal framework for communicating the necessary individual process steps and documentation requirements.

Quality Assurance

The Audit Roadmap contains quality gates or performance measures such as time and cost budgets. Quality gates function as milestones and conclude audit phases. The start of the next phase is contingent upon passing the quality gate. Quality gates help to ensure that necessary documentation exists, that such documentation is in the correct format and contains all the relevant information. Quality gates link two phases of the Audit Roadmap and can concern different people and involve different types of quality assurance measures. Documents to be examined and released by one person are forwarded either in hard copy or electronically, by e-mail or through the workflow, to the other person. This allows performing quality spot checks without delaying the overall audit process (for details on quality assurance, see Section D, Chapter 5).

HINTS AND TIPS

- Auditors should structure and archive their documents according to the requirements of the Audit Roadmap.
- Auditors should ensure that they are using the latest version of the Audit Roadmap, that they follow the standards it contains, and that they use the documents required by the Roadmap.
- All auditors should use their expertise for the ongoing development of the Audit Roadmap.

LINKS AND REFERENCES

- INSTITUTE OF INTERNAL AUDITORS. 2005. *Practice Advisory 1300-1: Quality Assurance and Improvement Program.* Altamonte Springs, FL: The Institute of Internal Auditors.
- INSTITUTE OF INTERNAL AUDITORS. 2006. *Quality Assessment Manual.* 5th ed. Altamonte Springs, FL: The Institute of Internal Auditors.

1.2 Advantages and Benefits of the Audit Roadmap

KEY POINTS •••

- The Audit Roadmap provides a number of organizational, content-related, and formal advantages as well as benefits with regard to teamwork and cooperation.
- Auditors can use the Audit Roadmap as a communication and guidance medium.
- There are many options for individual use and adaptation of the Audit Roadmap.

Advantages of the Audit Roadmap

The use of a standardized Audit Roadmap offers many advantages for everyday auditing. This chapter summarizes the main aspects.

Complete and Up-To-Date

- Use of the Audit Roadmap helps guarantee that the data is complete and up to date: All auditors can be certain that standard templates and documents are up to date. There is no need for time-consuming searches or for redefining audit documents. Auditors can thus focus on the actual audit.

Shorter Processing Times

- The clear structure of the Audit Roadmap facilitates and shortens both the preparation and the execution of the audit. The formal standardization of the Roadmap also helps auditors to exchange information quickly and efficiently, which creates the potential for time savings at all phases of the audit.

Scheduling and Deadline Monitoring

- The Audit Roadmap makes it possible to plan and monitor audits in detail: Deadlines, costs, and employee assignment can be planned and controlled down to the sub-phase level.

Access Authorization

- Improved planning and monitoring facilitate assigning authorizations and access rights to data and IT systems. This is important especially with regard to confidentiality. Access rights are granted for each phase, based on activities or document types, and defined via role profiles. The resulting authorizations can be entered in the system for each phase, activity, and document type.

Audit Monitoring System

- An Audit Roadmap-based audit procedure facilitates a project-based audit monitoring system. The Audit Roadmap makes it possible to efficiently control the overall audit. Progress is measurable for each phase and for the audit as a whole. This allows identifying deviations in the budget and audit timeline. Auditors in charge for the phase in which the variance occurred are responsible for understanding and explaining these differences. The auditors in turn can respond on the basis of documents or statements that they created in that phase. This timely controlling allows taking necessary countermeasures early.

Audit Analysis

- The Audit Roadmap also facilitates analysis of the content of audit procedures (see Section D, Chapter 7). The audits conducted are reviewed and compared on the basis of results, procedures, phases, etc., both individually and across a sample or all steps taken. Key figures for measuring Internal Audit's efficiency can then be derived and areas for future process improvements in audit work identified. The phase-by-phase comparison of content can be of especially great significance. An integrated quality control system helps to identify any process steps that do not meet the defined expectations, making it possible to respond immediately to any defects identified.

Quality Assurance

- The Audit Roadmap supports the use of a quality assurance system through quality gates. As the audit proceeds, quality gates have to be passed, where the quality of the audit work is checked against clearly defined requirements before advancement to the next process step is possible (for details, see Section D, Chapter 5).

IT Solution for Internal Audit

- The Audit Roadmap guarantees that the procedure used for audits is consistent. These consistent procedures in turn can be supported by IT solutions. The overall administration of documents, including archiving, should be phase-based and run as an integrated part of the IT system to ensure that no documents are missing (see Section D, Chapters 1 and 4).

Individual Design of an Audit Roadmap

- In addition to a standardized Audit Roadmap, it is also possible to create individual Audit Roadmaps for specific groups of topics (see Section B, Chapter 7). For fraud audits, for example, it is possible to plan special activities at the start of the audit, e.g., gathering information in advance or preparing question catalogs for special interview techniques. For management audits, it may be useful to have additional explanatory information or a specific management-based reporting system (e.g. portfolio or trend analysis).

Global Requirements and Integration

- Standardizing procedures is particularly important for corporate audit departments in global companies. The potential conflict between central data maintenance and decentralized processing gives rise to specific requirements. A global process model is necessary to ensure that simultaneous process steps in different regions are coordinated and multi-level approval and quality assurance procedures are in place. Such a process model has to accommodate the different auditors involved, the diverging contents, and the various process levels. In this context, the Audit Roadmap functions as a global integration model, supporting globally standardized processes and personal and cultural integration.

Auditor Qualification

- Standardized processes of a stringent process model, such as the Audit Roadmap, allow auditors to focus on the audit content rather than on administrative issues. As a result, auditors reach higher personal qualifications faster, because their expertise grows faster than with unstructured, non-standardized procedures. Assessment criteria for performance measurement can also be defined more clearly and development potential can be identified more specifically.

Audit Reliability

- Last but not least, an Audit Roadmap contributes to audit reliability and materiality. Among the elements of audit reliability, the completeness of the audit is the most important feature. Other important elements are determined by external standards set by organizations such as the IIA. These standards can be included in an Audit Roadmap as desired criteria, thus aiming at automatic compliance. The same applies to compliance with SOX requirements (see Section C, Chapter 8; Section D, Chapter 14) which are reflected either in the standard Audit Roadmap or in a modified Audit Roadmap. As far as specific audit, test, and documentation steps are required, phase-dependent consistency checks can be integrated into the Audit Roadmap. Such checks could help guarantee that audit results are verified automatically (e.g., the completeness of a sample by testing the findings and/or test cases).

Conclusion

The above list of advantages of the Audit Roadmap in internal auditing is not exhaustive, but the benefits mentioned show that an Audit Roadmap is important for audit work to be efficient.

HINTS AND TIPS

- By comparing procedures with auditors of other companies, auditors can identify best Internal Audit practices.

2 Planning

2.1 Content of Scopes

2.1.1 Integration and Organizational Structure

KEY POINTS •••

- Even though Scopes are integrated into the audit process, they are defined independent of individual audits.
- Core Scopes represent closed business or organizational audit areas, which can be broken down into any number of audit segments, referred to as Key Scopes.
- Scopes have the advantage that they can be used in individual ways and combined with each other in different audits.
- Scopes require regular updating. Audit employees should be assigned responsibility for keeping Scopes current.
- Access authorizations have to be defined for Scopes so that confidentiality is guaranteed.

Positioning of the Scope

Section A, Chapter 5.3 gives a definition of SAP's concept of Scopes and describes the general reasons for using Scopes. This chapter provides a systematic presentation of the details relevant at Audit Roadmap level. With regard to the positioning of Scopes it needs to be noted that, in spite of their integration into the audit process, creating them is independent from any specific audit work because the Scopes are generally and globally available and are normally defined before the actual audit. That is the reason why this sub-phase of the Audit Roadmap has to be addressed first.

Availability

The relevant Scopes should always be available before the work program is compiled (see Section B, Chapter 3.2). For audits that are planned for the first time or conducted at short notice, it is possible as an exception to create the Scope when the actual auditing process is already under way or in its preparation phase. For such audits, creating a Scope makes sense if the audit topic is repeatable and a Scope should be available in the future.

Interrelation between Audit Types and Scopes

There is a functional link between the different audit types and Scopes: For standard and special audits, the Scopes cover a relatively wide range of topics, because these audit types leave sufficient time for research and the creation of Scopes. For ad-hoc audits, which are mostly one-time audits of specific topics or persons, there are generally fewer Scopes available in advance.

Core Scope and Key Scope

Scopes are broken down into Core Scopes and Key Scopes. The Core Scopes represent closed business or organizational audit areas, e. g, purchasing, sales (for audits on sales and purchasing see Section C, Chapter 4.1 and 4.2). Each Core Scope maps out a subsection of an audit field or even the entire audit field (e.g., fraud). Core Scopes in turn break down into individual Key Scopes. This allows dividing a complex audit area into individual audit segments, which can then be handled flexibly. Key Scopes in purchasing for example could be the procurement of third-party services, the vehicle fleet, or delivery processing.

Free Combinations

Key Scopes can be combined with other Key or Core Scopes to define the specific content of an individual audit. It is possible for audits that are based on the same Scope to have different audit objectives or steps. Scopes have the advantage that they can be adapted and used by themselves or combined with each other.

Responsibility for Maintenance and Updates

Scopes require regular updating to ensure that they are current. Scopes are assigned for regular maintenance to one or several auditors, known as Scope owners, on the basis of content, hierarchy, region, or time attributes. The assignment should be rotated at regular intervals. Even though auditors are only responsible for the Scopes assigned to them, they also have to keep themselves informed on other Scopes. There should be a comprehensive review of all Scopes at least once a year. As a result of such reviews, new audit segments may be added or existing ones may be replaced or merged with others.

Access Authorization

Scopes should always be stored centrally. Since only the owners or their deputies should be able to edit them, they have to be protected for editing and access authorizations should be put in place. All persons directly or indirectly involved in audits (e.g., in the functional departments concerned) should have read access to the Scopes. Since Scopes contain comprehensive information about the organization of the company and form the basis for audits, access for non-department employees must be strictly controlled to maintain confidentiality. Access to Scopes for auditees and guest auditors should be decided on a case-by-case basis (see Section D, Chapter 10). Since guest auditors have know-how that could make a valuable contribution to the Scopes, their involvement provides an excellent opportunity to revise existing Scopes or develop new ones.

HINTS AND TIPS

- Auditors should analyze the Scopes for suitability to a specific audit task.
- Auditors should use their individual expertise to develop existing Scopes and forward the relevant information to those responsible.
- It may be useful to exchange information on the content of Scopes with the functional departments to obtain their input.

2.1.2 Templates and How to Use Them

KEY POINTS

- The main elements of a Scope are laws and professional guidelines, the operating functions, the respective processes, and the included specific objects.
- A system of Scope worksheets is intended to facilitate the standardized and systematic development of all Scopes.
- The following types of Scope worksheets exist: Table of Key Scopes, Functions to Processes relationship matrix, Processes to Objects relationship matrix, and the Scope in Detail table.

- Standards are defined for all significant content components of a Scope.
- Scopes need to be consistent within themselves and clearly distinct from each other.

Elements of the Scopes

To cover all the complex types of audit content within a company, Scopes contain the following elements:

- legal and governance provisions, mandated company-internal policies and guidelines,
- descriptions of the organizational operating functions,
- presentation of the relevant business processes and their internal controls, and
- the actual audit objects as verifiable and auditable components of operational processing.

Definition through Worksheets

Scopes have to map the nature and extent of these elements, while also describing the relations among them in both quantitative and qualitative terms. When they are created and when changes are made, Scopes follow a standardized approach which is laid out in standard worksheets. These standard worksheets contain the structure of the Scopes and instructions on how to create them. Each Scope worksheet (see figures below as an example) has different audit perspectives, and use of all the worksheets available within the Scope will maximize the range of applications.

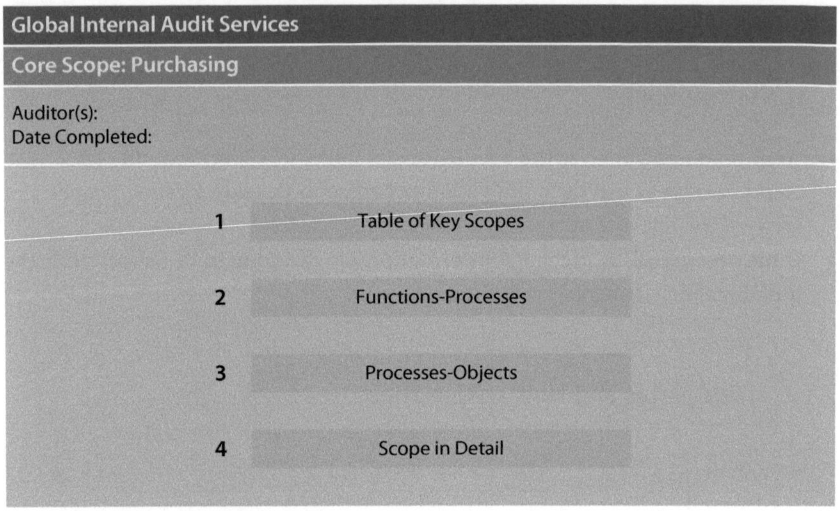

Fig. 2 Core Scope Index

Key Tasks of the Scope Worksheets

As shown in the above figure, the index provides general information and shows the various standard Scope worksheets. Specifically, the sheets have the following functions:

- The "Table of Key Scopes" breaks the Core Scope down into meaningful audit segments.
- The "Functions to Processes" relationship matrix shows which processes affect or run through which operating units and functions.
- The "Processes to Objects" relationship matrix explains which audit objects are affected by a process.
- The "Scope in Detail" table contains all the details specific to each process that could be relevant to an audit.

Global Internal Audit Services
Purchasing
Table of Key Scopes
Mandatory

Key Scopes / Content	Policies/Guidelines/ Procedures	Functions/Operations	Processes	Objects
Purchase Requisition	• Purchasing Global/ Regional/Local Policies and Guidelines • Purchasing Global/ Regional/Local Strategy • Global/Regional/Local Purchase Terms and Conditions • Intercompany Purchasing Policy • Delegation of Authority	• Purchasing Responsibility • Legal department • Departments requesting goods/services	• Vendor Selection • Approvals • Competitive Bidding • Contract Negotiation • Contract Approval • Purchase Requisition creation	• Buyers • Commodity Groups • Quote/bid Logs • Individual and Frame Vendor Contracts • Delegation of Authority • Offer Documentation • Purchase Requisition ....
Purchase Order	• Global/Regional/Local Purchasing Policies and Guidelines • Global/Regional/Local Purchasing Strategy • Intercompany Purchasing Policy • Authorization Policy • Purchasing Guidelines and Procedures	• Purchasing Responsibility	• Approval • Vendor Selection • Creation of Vendor Master Data • Purchase Order Creation • Purchase Order Execution • Purchase Order and Contract Filing	• Approval Documentation • Purchase Order • Vendor Notification • Vendor Contracts • Open Purchase Order Report • Order Confirmation ....
Goods Receipt	....	....	....	....
Purchase Related Accounting	....	....	....	....
Shared Services	....	....	....	....

Fig. 3 Table of Key Scopes

Table of Key Scopes

The Table of Key Scopes provides an overview of the contents of a complex audit area. This is where all the core elements for each Key Scope are defined. The Table of Key Scopes is primarily a summary providing an overview, as well as a checklist for subsequent steps. To prepare the Table of Key Scopes, drafts should be discussed with the relevant functional departments and interested target groups (e.g., the Audit Committee). It is especially important to make a full, one-to-one assignment of audit topics to the Key Scopes. The creation of Scopes should always include a final review to ensure that the Scope is complete and free of inconsistencies.

Global Internal Audit Services
Purchasing
Purchase Requisition
Functions/Operations-Processes — **Optional**

	Processes → / Functions/Operations ↓	1	2	3	4	5	6
		Vendor Selection	Approval	Competitive Bidding	Contract Negotiation	Contract Conclusion	Purchase Requisition Creation
1	Purchasing Responsibility	X	X	X	X	X	
2	Legal Department	X		X	X	X	
4	Departments requesting goods/services		X				X

X = Applicable

Fig. 4 Functions to Processes Relationship Matrix

Functions to Processes Relationship Matrix

The Table of Key Scopes facilitates the creation of assignment matrices. The assignment of functions to processes shown in the above diagram is intended to provide a clear picture of which functions (i.e., organizational units) are run through by a certain process and which processes run within a functional business unit. At the same time this results in a cross-check of the information provided in the Table of Key Scopes: If functions cannot be assigned to processes or vice versa, these elements are either not relevant for the Scope in question, or they may not even exist. The main advantage of assigning functions to processes is that this type of presentation allows selecting any individual item for an audit depending on the audit objective.

Global Internal Audit Services
Purchasing
Purchase Requisition
Processes-Objects

Processes \ Objects		1	2	3	4	5	6	7 (Optional)
		Buyers	Commodity Groups	Competitive Bids	Quote Log	Vendor Contracts	Approval Authority Matrix	Purchase Requisition
1	Vendor Selection	X	X	X	X	X	X	
2	Approval	X	X	X	X	X	X	X
3	Competitive Bidding	X	X	X	X	X	X	
4	Contract Negotiation	X	X	X	X	X	X	
5	Contract Conclusion	X	X			X	X	
6	Purchase Requisition Creation	X	X			X	X	X

X = Applicable

Fig. 5 Processes to Objects Relationship Matrix

Processes to Objects Relationship Matrix

This also applies to the above worksheet, which shows the assignment of processes to audit objects. This refines the way in which audit content can be selectively accessed by another level. The worksheet explains which specific objects are included in a process and which processes an object runs through at different process stages. The information contained in the worksheet has to be logical, i.e., it must be possible to assign at least one audit object to each process. The assignment of processes to audit objects allows looking at partial views, since the spreadsheet shows the processes that an audit object runs through.

Global Internal Audit Services
Purchasing
Purchase Requisition
Scope in Detail

Content		Object Processing (e.g. Workflow Procedures, etc)		Documentation		Internal controls			Impacts
Reference	Item	Input	Output	Data	Process	Risk Area	Control Activity	Document	Optional
P1/O1-O6	**Vendor Selection**	Procedures to ensure objective vendor selection	Vendor Master Data	Bid/Offer, Contract, Vendor Selection List (system)	Bidding, Vendor Selection	Operational Risks	Review, Approve	Vendor Offers, Invitation to Tender, Contract, Vendor Approval	Transparent Vendor Selection, Price-Performance Ratio
P2/O1-O7	**Approval**	Workflow Authorizations, Contract Data, Delegation of Authority	Purchase Requisition	Contract, Purchase Requisition, Vendor Master Data	Approval, Delegation of Authority	Operational Risks	Approve	Purchase Requisition	Transparent Order Process, Control Over Purchasing Activities
P3/O1-O6	**Competitive Bidding**	Procedures to ensure competitive bidding	Vendor Master Data, Purchase Requisition	Bid, Contract, Purchase Requisition, Bid Log	Bidding	Operational Risks	Review, Approve	Vendor Offers, Invitation to Tender, Contract, Vendor Approval	Transparent Bidding Process
P5/P1-2,5-6	**Contract Conclusion**	Contract	Approved and Signed Contract	Contract, Offer, Bid Documentation	Approval Process, Delegation of Authority	Operational Risks	Approve	Contract	Legal Compliance

Fig. 6 Scope in Detail

Scope in Detail

On the operational audit level, more detailed information on each individual process is needed. This information is summarized in the above Scope in Detail table. This worksheet collates, at the level of a specific process, everything that normally belongs to an aspect of fieldwork. First the link to the coordinates of the Processes to Objects table has to be made; the relevant data is listed under Content. The next column shows the input and output information relevant for the process, such as data, organizational information, or specific upstream processes or documents. At this stage, the worksheet should also provide clear information on the actual objective or added value of the process in question. Another column contains Internal Audit's documentation requirements that have to be met to obtain audit reliability. The next column contains information needed to make sure that the internal controls for this process are in place, including areas exposed to risk, the internal controls assigned to them, and the required documentation. This structure has certain similarities to the documentation requirements set out in SOX (see Section D, Chapter 14). The last column of this sheet lists the impact of the processes described (either benefits or disadvantages).

End-to-End Application

It must be possible to read the Scope tables both top down and bottom up, i.e. there must not be any missing components or breaks in the logic between them. For this reason, the Scope owner must maintain and update all worksheets, not only certain parts. If possible, Scopes should always be maintained and updated in their entirety to make sure that they are consistent with subsequent process levels.

Application of Scopes in Practice

A clarification may be necessary to avoid any confusion about the application of the Scope templates. As the content-related part of an audit, the purpose and objective of Scopes is to ensure the completeness of audit-specific work programs. Scopes also allow one to objectively determine observations, findings, and recommendations by providing the criteria against which the current condition of an entity is compared. However, depending on the extent of an audit, the application of all Scope templates described in this chapter may sometimes not be feasible due to time constraints. In practice, the consistent application of all Scope templates will only be possible when it is based on an integrated audit management IT solution.

Table of Key Scopes as a Minimum Requirement

Without such a solution, it is strongly recommended to apply the Table of Key Scopes as a minimum to ensure the completeness of all relevant parts of an audit including the consideration of policies, guidelines, processes, and internal controls. The application of the other Scope templates may be optional depending on the extent of an audit due to the potentially significant work required to complete them. The precise audit content will then be described in detail in the work program only. Most of the relevant processes and internal controls are already described as part of the SOX documentation. Referring to this SOX documentation may help to compile the different line items of the work program and ensure alignment with the structure of processes and controls in the audited area or entity.

Audit Management IT Solution

In the end, the consistent and efficient application of all Scope templates depends on the availability of a fully integrated audit management IT solution. Ideally, such a solution would help:

- to create and permanently maintain and update the Scopes, and
- to link and combine the Scopes with the SOX processes and controls documented in the internal control management tool (see Section D, Chapter 14).

As soon as such an IT solution is available, the entire Scope process can and should become a mandatory part of each planned audit.

HINTS AND TIPS

- Auditors should familiarize themselves with the latest version of the relevant Scopes before the audit.
- Auditors should maintain the Scopes for which they are responsible on the basis of internal and external information and keep them up to date at all times.
- When creating Scopes, auditors should use the appropriate worksheets as templates. Auditors may also find existing Scopes useful as guidance.
- Auditors who, during audit preparation, make additions to the information stored in a Scope should consider whether it is appropriate to update the Scope and, if so, contact the Scope owner.

2.1.3 Overview of Available Scopes

KEY POINTS

- The definition of Scopes allows a quick overview of all important audit topics in the company.
- The creation of Scopes should follow the materiality principle.
- The listed Core Scopes show the audit areas that are important for a global high-tech company with a strongly developed decentralized organization.

Overview of Important Audit Topics

By defining Scopes, Internal Audit can get an overview of all important audit topics in a company within a short period of time. The creation of Scopes should follow the materiality principle, i.e., the main focus should be on corporate areas that are exposed to increased risk and are important in terms of core business processes.

Core Scopes at SAP

Internal Audit has defined the following Core Scopes for SAP, a global high-tech company with strongly developed decentralized structures (in alphabetical order):

- Accounts Payable: Structure, organization, and execution of accounts payable accounting.
- Accounts Receivable: Structure, organization, and execution of accounts receivable accounting.

- Cost Based Activity Charging: Structure and process of cost-based activity charging.
- Custom Development: Additional customer-specific developments, as well as the structure and organization of this area.
- Defense and Security: Organization, processes, and standards in connection with the creation of security-sensitive software.
- Educational Services: Structure, program, and tasks of the educational services area.
- Escalation: Organizational structures and processes in critical customer projects and measures to resolve escalations.
- Fraud: Structure and conduct of fraud audits.
- General Ledger Accounting: Structure, organization, and execution of general ledger accounting.
- Global Communication: Structure and impact of global information and communication processes, both internally and externally.
- Global Initiatives: Global internal projects (e.g., introduction of software) and activities.
- Global Marketing: Structure and organization of global marketing.
- Global Processes: Organizational and process structures of global units, including reporting.
- Global Quality Management: Structure and functions of process-related quality assurance.
- Human Resources with three Core Scopes, which are Compensation and Benefits, Recruiting, and Payroll: Presentation of all organizational HR processes, payroll transactions, and information flows.
- Intellectual Property: Protected patent, trademark, and trade name rights and associated organization.
- IT: Structure, organization, and functions in the IT area.
- Labs: Labs for the development of standard software.
- License Agreements: Overall processing and modalities of all contract types in connection with standard software license sales.
- Management: Structure and functioning of management processes.
- Management Accounting: Structure and functions of global financial and managerial control, including the handling of confidential figures.
- Property, Plant, and Equipment: Structure of property, plant, and equipment recognized in the balance sheet, including general and specific forms of measurement.
- Purchasing: Structure and process of a global purchasing organization.
- Real Estate Property (including construction projects): Construction and management of company real estate.
- Risk Management: Integration into the overall organizational process of the company, including all specific functions and tasks.

- SAP Consulting: Structure, organization, and functions of the consulting service area, including project audits.
- Security of External Data: Dealing with data provided by external parties from a security point of view.
- Shared Services: Service organization for central business processes, taking into account all legal and tax issues.
- SOX: Organization and conduct of audits under the Sarbanes-Oxley Act.
- Subsidiaries: Summary of all business processes that regularly occur in a subsidiary, including organization and responsibilities.
- Third Party Licenses: Structure, process, and impact of integrating and using third-party licenses.
- Travel Management: Structure, processes, and impact of global travel management.
- Treasury: All financial transactions, taking into account all internal and external treasury tasks and the organizational safety and security measures required for this purpose.
- Worldwide Transfer Policy: Types and execution of worldwide transfers of internal employees.

Audit Content and Targets

The Core Scopes listed above represent a comprehensive framework of audit content and targets. Each of them includes up to 15 Key Scopes, which can be combined as required by individual circumstances. The complexity of the data allows GIAS to conduct extensive and very specific audits.

2.2 Annual Audit Planning

KEY POINTS

- Annual audit planning is an integral part of the Audit Roadmap.
- Annual audit planning comprises the creation of risk profiles, the compilation of the audit inventory, as well as the creation of the annual audit plan and of the regional team-based execution plans.

Content of the Annual Audit Plan

In addition to creating Scopes (see Section B, Chapter 2.1), annual audit planning is the second component of the Audit Roadmap independent from any specific audit activities. The culmination of the annual audit planning involves scheduling, i.e. the audits lined up for a year are slotted into the available weeks and months under consideration of personnel capacities. An adjustment of the assignment during the year may affect audits still to be conducted. This chapter gives an overview of the main components of audit planning and their impact on day-to-day audit work. For a more detailed discussion, see Section D, Chapter 3.

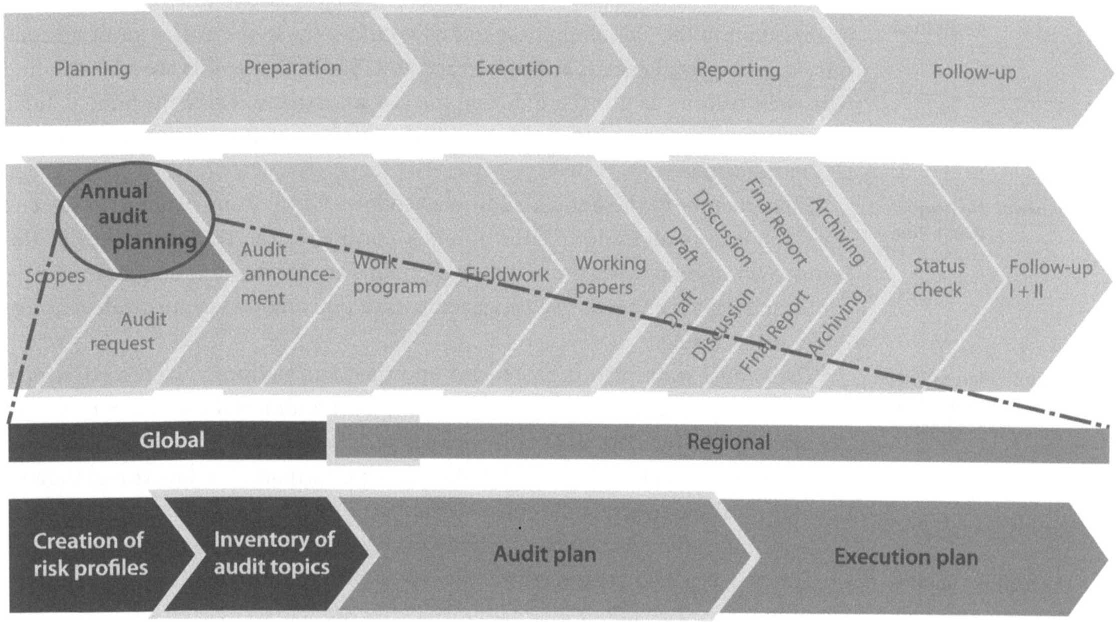

Fig. 7 Overview of the Planning Process

Sub Phases of Annual Audit Planning

The diagram above shows that the annual audit planning phase breaks down into a number of further sub-phases. Annual audit planning begins with the creation of risk profiles for all possibly relevant auditable entities. For all those entities a risk profile is created, and they are subsequently added to the audit inventory. The annual audit plan is then compiled based on the topics in the audit inventory and their respective risk profiles.

Creating Risk Profiles

For each auditable entity a risk profile is created. Each risk profile includes two significant components in a matrix format. The horizontal dimension is based upon the structure of the SOX process groups and ensures the consideration of all relevant processes and controls required for SOX compliance. The vertical dimension denotes so-called risk indicators which allow detailed risk assessment on both the process group and the entity level. The risk-assessment is completed by GIAS as well as by Global Risk Management. Both results are combined and weighted by a predefined ratio. (75% Internal Audit to 25% Risk Management is recommended.)

Creating the Audit Inventory

All evaluated entities are included in the audit inventory with their associated risk levels. The inventory mirrors the total number of risk-assessed entities and is structured by GIAS teams. The annual audit plan is derived from the inventory based upon the priorities given by the risk assessment. This approach enables Audit Managers to continuously map their inventory to the annual audit plan and, if required, address any unforeseeable events and audit needs.

Creation of the Annual Audit Plan

The annual audit plan is the result of several steps (see Section D, Chapter 3). It is important in the planning phase to first consider those audits that must be conducted, taking available capacities into account. Then other audits are added in line with their priority as identified during the risk assessment. Once the annual audit plan is complete, it is presented to the Audit Committee for concurrence and the CEO is informed.

Structure of the Annual Audit Plan

The structure of the annual audit plan follows GIAS' team structure. This ensures the proper allocation of the audits according to the responsibilities of the teams. Within each team, the audit engagements are sorted according to their priorities and appear either as fixed engagements or potential engagements depending on their risk rating.

Audit Plan as Part of the Audit Performance Record

The annual audit plan is embedded into the audit performance record, which provides up-to-date annual statistics of completed audits and the status of audits not (yet) conducted. The audit performance record affords a quick overview of the activities of Internal Audit. At SAP, the audit performance record is maintained centrally, making sure that the entire Group has a uniform understanding of Internal Audit's actual performance requirements (see Section D, Chapter 11.2.1).

Execution Planning

The next step after creating the annual audit plan is the preparation of the actual execution plan. Two points are of importance at the activity-related level:

- The scheduled audits have to be assigned according to the number and skills of the auditors. Qualification, experience, availability, etc. are important for the composition of each audit team.
- The time planning and sequence of the various audits is a closely related issue. The audit performance record has to be consulted to ensure that the scheduled audits can in fact be conducted based on previous performance and time requirements. It is also important to schedule reserve capacities for unscheduled audits. This allows identifying noticeable capacity over- or underutilization in time to make adjustments to the plan.

These steps complete the annual audit planning.

Interaction with the Audit Roadmap

Generally, when completing the annual audit planning, interaction with other phases of the Audit Roadmap should be considered. The following points are important:

- Assigning the relevant Scopes to each audit during the planning phase facilitates matching audit segments with planned audit tasks. Often, a one-to-one relationship exists. Matching Scopes to audits is a good way to find out whether Scopes are available for a specific audit and, if not, what steps need to be taken to create Scopes before the actual audit.
- An audit announcement is sent out at a set point before the start of the audit (see Section B, Chapter 3.1). This is another important reason to complete the detailed planning at an early stage.
- Additional audits may be requested during the year (see Section B, Chapter 2.3). It is therefore possible to have competing planning scenarios. For each case a

decision must be made whether the additional audit request is already covered in the current plan, or whether it should be added to this year's or next year's plan.

Significance of the Annual Audit Planning

The planning is integrated into the Audit Roadmap, both in terms of the general plan and the operational execution plan. Moreover, the audit performance record, mentioned earlier, is one step toward a complete audit-related monitoring system, thus giving the planning data an even greater weight in the control and analysis of variances.

HINTS AND TIPS

- On the basis of the audit topics expected of them, auditors should reconcile their time commitments to optimize their preparations for the planned audits.
- Auditors should prepare personal summaries of scheduled and actually required times and analyze any variances.

LINKS AND REFERENCES

- BEUMER, H. 2004. Starting from Scratch. *Internal Auditor* (August 2004): 79–85.
- HUBBARD, L. 2000. Audit Planning. *Internal Auditor* (August 2000): 20–21.
- INSTITUTE OF INTERNAL AUDITORS. 2001. *Implementation Standard 2010.A1: Assurance Engagements*. Altamonte Springs, FL: The Institute of Internal Auditors.
- INSTITUTE OF INTERNAL AUDITORS. 2001. *Practice Advisory 2010-1: Planning*. Altamonte Springs, FL: The Institute of Internal Auditors.
- INSTITUTE OF INTERNAL AUDITORS. 2001. *Practice Advisory 2010-2: Linking the Audit Plan to Risk and Exposures*. Altamonte Springs, FL: The Institute of Internal Auditors.
- INSTITUTE OF INTERNAL AUDITORS. 2001. *Practice Advisory 2030-1: Resource Management*. Altamonte Springs, FL: The Institute of Internal Auditors.
- KRAMER, J. 1999. Planning for World-Class Audits. *Internal Auditor* (October 1999): 88.
- RIFE, R. 2006. Planning for Success. *Internal Auditor* (October 2006): 25–29.

2.3 Audit Request

KEY POINTS

- Any employee can request an audit or special service from Internal Audit for a variety of reasons at any time.
- Internal Audit reviews requests promptly and discusses the next steps with the Board.

- Depending on the outcome of this assessment, the request may be met immediately, included in future planning or in the audit inventory, or returned to the requestor.

Need for an Audit Request

In addition to the annual audit planning described earlier (see Section B, Chapter 2.2), there is another way in which audits are initiated: audit requests. New events or challenges that the company faces often make it necessary to conduct additional audits (or perform other services). Audit requests are an important tool for the Board to ensure compliance throughout the organization.

Reasons for an Audit Request

Ad-hoc audit requests are submitted for a variety of reasons. The main ones are:

- Circumstances have arisen that make an immediate audit seem sensible. Such circumstances may include general leads or hard evidence of fraud.
- Internal Audit receives unofficial information about matters to be audited. In such cases, Internal Audit can issue an audit self-request.
- Changes in organizational workflows are causing problems. In this case, an audit request may increase the priority of an audit that has already been scheduled or may directly lead to a separate audit.
- The Board identifies the need for an audit, e.g., in connection with critical customer projects.
- Internal Audit is asked for support as part of other services it is performing, for example internal project reviews or project management support, which is particularly important in global projects.

Dealing with an Audit Request

Any company employee can make an audit request. Since this could potentially lead to a flood of requests, Internal Audit has the discretion to decide how to deal with each request. This may mean that a request:

- leads to an immediate audit or other service of Internal Audit,
- is integrated into the annual audit plan, or
- is included in the audit inventory.

As soon as the audit request has been approved and signed by the person responsible, it automatically turns into a binding audit engagement letter for Internal Audit. In rare cases, an audit request may be turned down, although a rejection must be sufficiently justified and documented.

Solid Basis for an Audit Request

An audit by Internal Audit can only be initiated as part of the regular annual audit planning or in response to a duly approved request. This ensures that audits cannot be conducted arbitrarily. Even if Internal Audit acts in response to a self-request, the request will only be accepted after a critical review by Internal Audit management in cooperation with the responsible Board member (e.g., the CEO). The audit request is always assessed with risk exposure in mind. For this reason, each requested audit is subjected to a risk assessment. This may lead to a competitive situation when the current risk assessment of ad-hoc requests are compared with audits the risk assessment of which may have been carried out several months earlier. This means that the request can only be fully judged on the basis of all available information. An audit request template is provided in the figure below.

Global Internal Audit Services (GIAS)

Audit Request			**No.**
Type:	☐ Engagement	☐ Pre-Investigation	☐ Review
	☐ Non-audit-related activities (e.g. Support, Consulting)		
Title:			Location:

Description of requested Audit Service (Requirements) *To be filled out by requesting party*			
Risk Assessment:	☐ Low ☐ Medium ☐ High	Risk description:	
Estimated person-days:		Requested start date:	
Requested by:			
Date:		Signature:	

Will be filled out by GIAS				
Audit Lead:		Auditor(s):		
Related to other GIAS Activities:	☐ No ☐ Yes (please indicate, e.g. other reports, audits, requests)	GIAS estimated person-days:		
Execution:	☐ Immediately ☐ To be scheduled in Audit Plan	Announcement:	☐ Yes	☐ No
		Proposed Time:		

CEO Information				
Date:				
CAE Confirmation				
Confirmed Audit days:		Date:	Signature:	

Fig. 8 Audit Request

Types of Audit Request

An audit request can be used to apply for audits and any other services offered by Internal Audit (see Section A, Chapter 7):

- An engagement request is required for all audits that are not part of the annual audit plan.
- A pre-investigation request is used for preliminary audits.
- A review request is mainly submitted for concept, guideline, and customer project reviews.
- A request for non-audit-related services can be submitted, for example, for internal consulting services to be performed by Internal Audit and for services in connection with internal project management tasks.

To simplify, we use the term "audit request" as a general term for all the above types.

Processing Audit Requests

Internal Audit processes audit requests according to a defined system, which comprises the following steps:

- The requesting unit fills in the relevant form, clearly stating the required tasks and preferred timings.
- Internal Audit checks the request immediately and resolves any queries with the requesting party.
- The CEO receives information about all audit requests.
- The number of auditors and estimated time requirement are assigned to the audit request.
- A copy of the request for the audit concerned or other services to be performed by Internal Audit is sent to the Audit Manager responsible so that preparations can begin. The originals are filed centrally in the office of the CAE.
- If the request is not dealt with immediately, the requesting party is informed of the delay.

Impact of Audit Requests

Requests for audits and other services made in the course of a year may require a dynamic response by adapting the audit plan. As a result, the focus of audits may shift so that Internal Audit can adapt to day-to-day operations and avoid running the risk of auditing matters that have lost relevance. However, audits listed in the annual audit plan should not be cancelled without due consideration because the annual audit plan is the result of careful risk-oriented planning. Cancelled audits should receive high priority in the next year.

2.4 Composition and Role of the Audit Team

KEY POINTS •••

- The composition of the audit team is of key importance.
- It is advisable to select employees who are most likely to accomplish the task at hand not only in terms of expertise, but also personality.

- The choice of audit lead requires particular care.
- Apart from the actual team composition, other aspects, such as requesting support services from other parties, have to be considered.

Organization

Audit teams are composed with consideration to the type, content, and extent of the audit to be conducted. In accordance with the dual-control principle, each audit should be conducted by at least two Internal Audit employees, one of whom has to act as audit lead. This guarantees that the tasks and responsibilities are clearly assigned for each audit.

Audit Lead

The audit lead should be nominated early. In the case of global audits, the end of the audit planning phase is a good time to appoint the audit lead. For all other audits, the appointment should be made well ahead before the audit announcement is sent out (see Section B, Chapter 3.1). However, if the audit lead is nominated too early, changes may be necessary later on. The position of audit lead is a flexible technical coordination role related to a specific audit. The nomination is determined by workloads and efficiency considerations. All suitable auditors should be given the opportunity to prove themselves as audit leads.

General Criteria

The Audit Manager is responsible for selecting the audit teams. The CAE also has a voice in the selection of the team, especially for global audits and audits that are of specific interest to the Board. Individual audit team compositions are outlined for the first time when the annual audit plan is compiled (see Section B, Chapter 2.2). The process of team and topic assignment should take into account the auditors' expertise and experience as well as their main interests and requests for further training. It is useful at this stage to establish employee profiles (see Section A, Chapter 4.5) on the basis of which auditors are assigned to specific audits.

Personal Criteria

When selecting the audit team members, consideration should be given to audit content, cultural group, and linguistic requirements, as well as personal aspects. Although audit teams primarily must be able to meet the requirements of the audit, it is also important that the team members are a good social fit and are able to work together, especially in international assignments. The management of Internal Audit has to deal with the challenge of recognizing these circumstances and taking appropriate actions.

Other Activities

In addition to the basic requirements of audit team composition, a number of other activities have to be performed. Tasks such as the compilation of the work program must be assigned and the need for guest auditors (see Section D, Chapter 10) determined. In addition, it may be necessary to enlist additional team members for consulting and support and to define escalation paths in case problems occur (see Section D, Chapter 6). Lastly, cooperation with external parties has to be coordinated (see Section D, Chapter 2).

Time Considerations

The assignment of tasks must be organized in terms of timing. In particular, dates for meetings and for preparing interim results must be set. For international audits infrastructure has to be considered. The work program should be discussed with the team and individual task areas and milestones have to be defined. A timesheet is a useful tool in this regard; it helps to calculate and provide evidence for each time component (see Section A, Chapter 4.7).

Distribution of Tasks

Each team member must understand the audit process before the beginning of the audit. It is therefore important to hold joint kick off meetings, where important aspects of the audit are highlighted. In addition, the team member responsible for taking minutes should be identified and the manner for presenting interim results should be clarified. Access to sensitive data should be discussed.

HINTS AND TIPS

- Audit leads have to develop an understanding early on of the technical and personal skills required of their audit teams.
- Once the audit lead has been appointed, he or she must have a say in choosing team members.
- Procure any additional resources necessary well in advance.

3 Preparation

3.1 Audit Announcement

KEY POINTS •••

- Audit announcements give Internal Audit and the unit to be audited the opportunity to come to a common understanding on the actual audit and its contents well in advance of the audit.
- Such announcements are advisable within a certain period, depending on the audit or service type.
- Although there are many arguments in favor of audit announcements, it should be critically examined whether announcing the audit jeopardizes audit objectives.
- Whatever the circumstances, announcements have to be in general terms so that the extent of the audit can be supplemented with results from fieldwork or other audits at any time.

Definition

The audit announcement serves an important function as part of the preparations for an audit. The audit announcement gives the departments to be audited and the managers responsible an understanding of audit objectives and breadth of the audit and outlines further test procedures. This creates both an opportunity and an obligation for Internal Audit to announce audits to auditees before the actual audit work commences. The audit announcement is prepared by the audit lead and approved by the Audit Manager.

Areas of Use

In general it must be accepted that Internal Audit, which is an independent body, has the right to conduct audits in response to certain risk situations at any time, even without prior announcement. It is advisable not to announce certain types of audits in advance, but there are other types of audit for which it may be sensible to make an announcement. In particular, all standard and special audits conducted as part of the annual audit plan should be announced. Additional audits initiated by separate audit requests should be announced only if they were included in the annual plan as an exception. An announcement has advantages if Internal Audit strongly depends on support from the unit being audited or if it is conducting audits across different units.

Reasons for Announcing Audits

Reasons for announcing an audit in advance include:

- The announcement gives the parties concerned information about when to expect an audit by Internal Audit. This allows the division to include the audit in their own planning and to ensure that the relevant people and required documents are available.
- The audit content announced gives both Internal Audit and the division to be audited the opportunity to familiarize themselves with the audit objectives at an early stage. This allows the parties to add to the Scope (see Section B, Chapter 2.1), resolve any misunderstandings, and agree on what is being covered, so that no unnecessary interruptions occur during the audit.

- In addition, both parties can agree on procedures for particularly sensitive information and data. Internal Audit may need access to confidential information for its fieldwork. Special access rights to such information may have to be arranged.
- In case of doubt, both Internal Audit and the division to be audited can refer to the audit announcement regarding the content of the audit. However, an announcement must never be understood as a limit to the audit. It should rather be worded in such a way that, although the contents specified are the mandatory minimum for the audit, the actual audit work may be adjusted according to the audit progress and with changing requirements, or if appropriate, at the auditors' discretion.
- Another advantage of announcing an audit is that the audit can not be easily delayed or rescheduled. However, if it turns out that an audit is no longer necessary or has to be postponed, the parties decide jointly how to proceed further.
- Ultimately, announcing audits benefits the auditors because they can maintain a reliable planning schedule. However, if there are unexpected audit requests, some of the audits already announced may have to be postponed, scaled down, or, in rare cases, cancelled altogether.

Content of Audit Announcements

The example below shows the most important information that an audit announcement is intended to address. In addition to giving general audit data and naming the addressees, it also serves to explain the mission of Internal Audit (see Section A, Chapter 3.1) and the objectives and content of the planned audit.

Global Internal Audit Services
Audit Announcement
Conducted in accordance with the International Standards for the Professional Practice of Internal Auditing.

Audit Type:	Audit Title:

Audit Report No:
Audit Status:
Executive responsible:
Date of Audit:
Audit Lead:
Auditor(s):
Distribution List:

Mission and Aims of GIAS:

Scope and Objectives:

Contact:

Fig. 9 Audit Announcement

Time Horizon

Audit announcements are used in different ways, depending on the type of audit. For standard audits, at least two weeks' notice is required before the audit, but individual lead times must be observed for special audits. Local and regional special audits must be announced on average three weeks before the audit. Because global special audits require more comprehensive consultation among the parties involved, they should be announced with at least four weeks' notice.

No Prior Announcement of Ad-Hoc Audits

Because of their special nature, ad-hoc audits usually require that Internal Audit takes immediate action without prior warning. The same applies if the objective is to uncover facts and to secure evidence in this regard. If an additional standard audit has been requested on an ad-hoc basis, an audit announcement should be sent to those affected immediately.

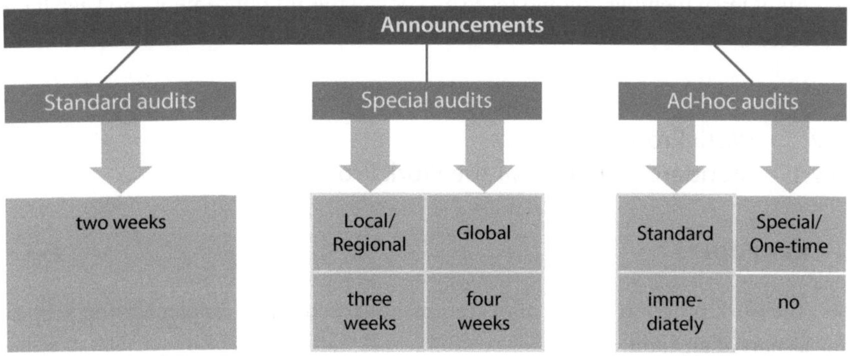

Fig. 10 Timing of Audit Announcements

Addressees

Audit announcements must always be directed to the CEO and the CFO. Depending on the structure and organization of the company, announcements should additionally be sent to operational management and the higher levels of management if their areas of responsibility are affected. All announcements of standard audits are simultaneously sent to the central corporate departments (e.g., Management Accounting, Financial Reporting, Legal, Taxes, etc.). The audit announcement asks operational management of the division to be audited to notify all employees in that division who will be involved in the audit.

Assignment to the Audit Roadmap

The audit announcement is part of the Audit Roadmap and is therefore an element of most audits. In justified exceptional circumstances, it may not be possible (e.g., if certain individuals are suspected) or necessary (e.g., for unannounced license audits) to make an announcement. The system of audit announcements should not make audits too predictable, because a certain element of surprise is necessary for the work of Internal Audit. It is a real possibility that, given enough warning, the division to be audited could manipulate documents or make inappropriate use of facts and information. Such manipulation must be prevented.

Disadvantages of Unannounced Audits

Internal Audit must not create the impression that it suddenly strikes at random in certain departments in order to look for errors. Besides, audits risk being inefficient and ineffective if an unannounced audit causes the division being audited to provide only half-hearted support or none at all. Internal Audit must give consideration to the circumstances of the audit when determining whether to make an announcement. The cultural perception of audits plays an important role in this regard.

HINTS AND TIPS

- Discuss the audit content as defined in the audit announcement with the main person responsible for the audit.
- Audit team members should receive a copy of the announcement and keep it on record.

3.2 Work Program

3.2.1 Standard Structure of the Work Program

KEY POINTS

- The work program is a set of operational instructions for implementing Scopes as part of an audit.
- Each work program has a planning and an implementation component.
- The individual fieldwork activities are described on the basis of the different Scope levels. Completeness is more important than a detailed description, because the actual fieldwork is described in detail in the working papers.
- In addition, there may also be work programs that are not based on any, or only on a very rudimentary, Scope.
- If used repeatedly, work programs can be standardized.

Definition

The work program can be interpreted as a series of instructions for auditors because its function is to divide all the audit material into small packages and to describe the working steps that must be taken. The work program is a link between the planning phase of an audit and its actual execution, i.e., it uses specific instructions to transform the planned audit content into an actual audit process (see Section C, Chapter 3.2.2). In a risk-based audit approach, analytical audit procedures (see Section C, Chapter 3.1) are used to assess and prioritize the audit work generally included in the work program. The basis for this assessment is the Scopes. The goal is to align the detail of the work program with the specific audit task.

Advantages

The work program represents a systematic plan for the audit. It also allows the audit lead to check that the audited content corresponds to the content of the assigned Scopes (see Section B, Chapter 2.1). In addition, it provides a basis for training inexperienced auditors to familiarize them with the objectives of an audit, the Scope, and the test procedures. The audit lead communicates this work program to the auditors involved. A work program can also be used to ensure that the same benchmarks are applied to audits with the same or similar content as audits conducted in the past. This achieves a level of standardization that allows cost and time savings during audit preparation.

Global Internal Audit Services								
Audit Work Program for Audit No.:				Title:				
		Prepared by:						
		Approved by:		Created on:				
#	Key Scope	Area/Object/ Process under Audit	Audit Objectives [1]	Risks (Category/ Sub-category)	Expected Control Activities	Test Procedures	Comment	Working Paper Reference
1								
2								
3								

[1] (according to the IIA)
- Reliability and integrity of financial and operational information.
- Effectiveness and efficiency of operations.
- Safeguarding of assets.
- Compliance with laws, regulations, and contracts.

Fig. 11 The Work Program

Key Scope

The first column of the work program has the heading "Key Scope." It refers to the relevant Key Scope of the Core Scope on which it is based. If the structure is very detailed, the "Area/Object/Process under Audit" column provides the relevant process coordinates from the "Processes to Objects" Scope matrix (see Section B, Chapter 2.1.2).

Risks and Internal Controls

Once the Scopes have been determined, the content of the work program has been defined. It is possible to refer to the standard information or standard parameters of the Scopes in columns 3 through 5 (Audit Objectives, Risks, Expected Control Activities). Since the work program should be tailored to each audit individually, audit-specific objectives can also be included. In addition, further risks and/or internal controls may need to be defined. When determining risks, it is useful to refer to the standard categories and subcategories of the risk management system. In this context, it is also possible to access information relating to SOX audits. In both cases, several entries can be made in the work program. To preserve audit-specific characteristics, auditors should, however, avoid accepting default risks and internal controls without critically questioning their validity (for details on risks and internal controls in the work program, see Section B, Chapter 3.2.3).

Individual Test Procedures

The next column of the work program, the "Test Procedures" column, describes each planned test procedure. Here, auditors have to enter all fieldwork activities that seem sensible from a planning point of view and are expected to occur when the audit is conducted. There is no need to provide great detail, because this is only possible during the actual fieldwork. It is more important to present the fundamental structure of essential test procedures relating to the audit objectives. However, a certain level of completeness is also worth aiming for. The various fieldwork activities listed must be consistent with each other and ultimately define the specific framework for the test procedures to be performed. It may be necessary to name several audit steps for each item of the work program. Usually, the higher the aggregation level of the audit content, the more fieldwork activities will have to be defined. The description of the individual test procedures concludes the planning part of the work program.

Control and Documentation

Next is the area of control and documentation of the actual audit execution. In the Audit Roadmap, these steps are assigned to the audit execution phase which is covered in Section B, Chapter 4. Therefore, only the aspects relevant to the description of the work program are mentioned at this point.

Comment, Working Paper Reference

If fieldwork cannot be performed to the extent planned or at the necessary quality, a note to this effect should be made in the "Comment" column. The "Working Paper Reference" column establishes the link to the working papers (see Section B, Chapter 4.2).

Clear Definition of Processes and Objects

The design of the work program has as an additional objective: to support a clear definition of processes and objects. Proposals for best practice solutions are developed on this basis, allowing comparisons of the model processes with the processes that have actually taken place, either at a global or at a regional level. If the to-be and as-is situations do not correspond, variances may occur, resulting in audit findings.

Work Programs without Link to Scope

It should also be mentioned that there can be work programs that are not linked to a Scope or are linked to a very condensed Scope. This may happen in the case of new topics in ad-hoc audits or audits that can only be detailed step by step in the course of the audit. The key for successfully creating a work program in these cases is very detailed progress planning and monitoring.

HINTS AND TIPS

- Find out beforehand whether any work programs already exist for the upcoming audit, and work through old work programs before the audit and take any relevant insights into account.
- Auditors should try to record all operational information relating to the audit in the work program. This gives them a central document for the entire audit process.

3.2.2 Integration of the Work Program

KEY POINTS

- The work program integrates upstream and downstream stages of the Audit Roadmap, i.e., the Scopes, the fieldwork, and the working papers.
- The relationship between the work program and the Scopes is that the work program assigns the content of the audit material to the planned audit steps. The relationship between the work program and the working papers is centered on giving evidence on the implementation of the audit steps.
- Although both relationship levels define certain dependencies, they offer great flexibility for the individual audit.

Purpose of the Work Program

One of the key features of the work program is its integrative relationship with other elements of the Audit Roadmap. Like a bridge, the work program links the audit content and the Scopes on the one hand with the scheduled audit activities and results on the other. The topics selected for the audit are broken down into work packages and the corresponding test procedures, thus making the audit topics more tangible for the audit and subsequent checks.

Work Program/Scope Relationship

The selection of the main audit contents from the total of all Scopes and their integration into the work program is very important for the success of an audit (for details on the content of Scopes, see Section B, Chapter 2.1). If there is more than one Scope, a decision has to be made to what level of detail the audit is to be conducted. An individual assessment of the timing and the objectives of the audit is made at this stage.

Levels of the Work Program

Another important question is the relationship between the items of the work program and the resulting fieldwork activities. For example, a work program item may contain a detailed description of the actual fieldwork. By putting various separate fieldwork activities together, a higher level is achieved, i.e. the combination into a work package, which can in turn form a work program level.

Combined Work Program Items

It does not happen often that several work program items are combined into a single fieldwork activity, although it may be feasible, especially when circumstances do not (yet) permit separate fieldwork activities or make combining work program items seem a sensible course of action (e.g., combining different sample levels).

HINTS AND TIPS

- Auditors must make sure that all Scopes relevant for the audit topic are included in the work program.
- During the audit, the work program should continually be monitored for completeness.

3.2.3 Process Elements: Risks and Internal Controls

KEY POINTS

- The risks and the internal controls identified for a process as a whole or for single process steps are an important part of the work program.
- Disclosures may be necessary as a result of legal requirements or general business process compliance.
- The individual risks should be in line with the risk categories of an implemented risk management system.

Starting Points

The risks and the internal controls identified either for a process as a whole or for single process steps are an important part of the work program. Depending on the given framework, there are two possible starting points for analyzing risk and internal controls: First, there are companies that do not (yet) have to comply with SOX or similar laws. These companies should, or have to, define audit content on the general basis of risk and internal control for each process step. Second, companies that are already subject to the above external rules of risk and control management have implemented systems that provide information on relevant risks and the necessary internal controls and transfer them into the work program. The risk and control management system may even be so well developed that, for a specific fieldwork activity, it is possible to refer from the work program or Scope to the relevant source documentation of an internal control system under SOX or a risk management system.

Main and Sub-Risk Categories

For companies that have a risk management system, the relevant risks correspond to the risk categories and sub-risk categories of the integrated operational risk management system used. As a general framework, the Scope shows the main risk categories, and the work program adds further detail by providing subcategories. Of course, in addition to the risk that can be planned for, unexpected risks may be identified at any time during fieldwork. Unexpected risks must be documented in the working papers but should not affect the risk allocation in the work program.

Significance of Internal Controls

The different types of internal controls can be used specifically to mitigate risks. Without laying claim to completeness or general applicability, the following individual assignments are possible.

Internal Controls and Creation of the Work Program

The internal controls contained in a Scope can either be used as they are when creating a work program, or adapted to individual audits. However, if SOX documentation is available, the already prescribed controls should be deemed mandatory. Additionally, the definition of controls may vary between Scope and work program because of special regional business practices or different laws and regulations.

Full Record of Internal Controls

The above combination of direct use and adaptation of the internal controls contained in the Scope is a good foundation for the creation of a complete record of all internal controls in the work program. This is intended to ensure that all significant business processes including their respective controls are fully covered. In addition, not only should all the risks of each process step be covered by internal controls, but their effect on the accounting and financial reporting system should also be considered. The audit procedures on the basis of process documentation that complies with SOX provide an important basis for this step.

Role of Internal Audit

Internal Audit can become involved in identifying and controlling risk only as part of its audit mandate. Internal Audit must not act as an exclusive control body and thus become part of operational process controls.

HINTS AND TIPS

- Auditors should also use informal discussions to get an overview of the internal controls in the company.
- In addition, auditors should get an idea of the company's value at risk. To estimate a value at risk, they have to assign the risks to the core business processes and analyze their impact.
- During an audit, auditors must always test the effectiveness of the internal controls.

3.3 Other Preparation Activities

3.3.1 Obtaining Background Information

KEY POINTS

- During audit preparation, auditors perform further tasks in addition to compiling the work program.
- To master a specific audit task, auditors need not only general audit expertise, but also a lot of specific and up-to-date information, which they obtain from internal and external sources.

- A back-up function provides technical experts for audit teams, and although these experts do not actively conduct audit activities, they perform content quality assurance in the background.

Necessary Knowledge Base

Apart from compiling the work program, there are a number of other tasks auditors must complete during audit preparation. It is important for auditors to familiarize themselves adequately with the audit topic. In addition to general audit expertise, comprehensive preparation usually requires up-to-date audit-specific information (see Section B, Chapter 3.3.2).

Basic Knowledge

An auditor's general expertise includes the fundamental facts of the audit segments identified in the company, irrespective of whether standard or special audits are planned. Auditors receive suitable internal and external training to acquire general auditor know-how and the specific knowledge relevant for specific audit segments. Coordinating training with the human resources department makes sense to assure systematic training in line with the requirements of Internal Audit.

Audit-Specific Information

As mentioned above, auditors have to obtain specific information about the audit at hand, beyond the general audit expertise that they already have. Possible sources include:

- Specialist publications and periodicals, publications of professional organizations, conferences, special training (see Section B, Chapter 3.3.2), workshops, etc..
- If the audit content suggests so, it is a good idea to contact the management of the area to be audited for advance information about certain topics and their importance. The audit lead and each audit team member should consider any requests or suggestions made by the auditees. Auditors should let employees making suggestions know that their input will be considered as far as possible without compromising the independence and objectivity of the audit.
- Valuable information can be obtained by contacting other corporate departments (Financial Reporting, Management Accounting, Risk Management, etc.), e.g., about reports and analyses, corporate guidelines that are currently applicable or under preparation, and frequent problems. Obtaining such information makes it easier to define focus areas for the audit.
- If the audit topic involves legal issues, recent judgments, comments, and recommendations given by the legal department should be taken into account. Even if Internal Audit is forced to rely on the knowledge of experts, auditors must assess all work done by others in terms of its reliability.
- For employee-related audit topics, the human resources department, employee representatives, the data protection officer, and the compliance officer should be contacted. However, for such audits it is difficult to obtain information because these audits are usually confidential. As a rule, Internal Audit needs very up-to-date information, but the process of getting current information must not reveal anything about the actual audit.
- It is also possible to exchange reports or information on audit focus areas with the external auditors.

In addition to gathering information before or at the start of an audit, information should also be obtained from the above sources during the audit.

Additional Capacity

Cooperation with employees outside the department is extended when it becomes clear that additional capacity is necessary or useful. Although anyone working in such a capacity is officially part of the audit team, the person's role is limited to indirect activities in the background, which are performed on request. Both external experts and internal employees can perform such a function, which normally involves content quality assurance. The confidentiality of the audit can be guaranteed by asking the person to sign a non-disclosure declaration.

LINKS AND REFERENCES ↗

- GRENOUGH, J. 2006. Seek and Ye Shall Find. *Internal Auditor* (October 2006): 65–69.
- MCCOLLUM, T. 2004. An Intranet Success Story. *Internal Auditor* (June 2004): 32–35.

3.3.2 Specific Training Needs

KEY POINTS •••

- In addition to general audit expertise and audit-specific information, Internal Audit employees also need technical knowledge, which they have to build up through training.
- Such training measures introduce new audit topics and content, bring the knowledge base up to date (including for software), and promote personal development.

Need for Specific Knowledge

In addition to their basic knowledge and the general information they obtain at the start of an audit, auditors may also need specific knowledge, and the necessary social and intercultural skills. Different audit topics generally require intellectual flexibility from auditors. By giving the audit department a regional structure and assigning audit topics to employees depending on their interest and expertise, auditors can achieve specialization. However, rotation may be useful or necessary over time, and new audit tasks may arise.

New Audit Topics

When shifts in content or new audit topics arise, auditors should be assigned to the relevant audits as soon as possible so that they can prepare themselves for the audit and obtain training if necessary. Such training can comprise both technical knowledge about the audit topic and information needed to deal with special local or regional peculiarities. For example, if company activities are moved to a different location, consideration for the applicable local rules, laws, and regulations must be given when planning the audit. The necessary knowledge should be acquired as part of the audit preparations.

Updating of Existing Knowledge

Even if the audit topics as such do not change, it is necessary to update the existing knowledge regularly. In particular, it is important to keep up with changes in legal requirements and professional guidance. The latest best practices should also be included in the training plan.

Software Knowledge

Auditors also need to be familiar with software relevant to the audit. Such software is either application software or audit-specific software. The rapid developments in this area make specific knowledge acquisition particularly important.

Personal Development

The social and cultural environment of an audit may lead to further audit-specific training needs. In addition to knowledge of local customs, this includes foreign language skills and supplementary training on information and communication behavior, team training, and various forms of cooperation.

Summary

Together, the three components – general audit expertise, information gathered for a specific audit, and training measures to acquire specific technical knowledge – ensure that auditors have the necessary knowledge level to be successful in their tasks (see also Section B, Chapter 3.3.1).

HINTS AND TIPS

- Auditors should compile the work program as early as possible so that they can identify any training requirements and schedule the necessary training.
- If possible, training needs should be assessed continuously with training scheduled regularly.

LINKS AND REFERENCES

- APPLEGATE, D. 2004. Training New Auditors. *Internal Auditor* (April 2004): 66–73.
- BAKER, N. 2006. A Checkup for the Audit Shop. *Internal Auditor* (August 2006): 88–92.
- CAMPBELL, D., AND S. DIONISI. 2001. Training as a Retention Tool. *Internal Auditor* (October 2001): 47–51.
- GLASCOCK, K. 2007. Reaching a Higher Level. *Internal Auditor* (February 2007): 20–25.
- INSTITUTE OF INTERNAL AUDITORS. 2002. *Practice Advisory 1230-1: Continuing Professional Development.* Altamonte Springs, FL: The Institute of Internal Auditors.

4 Execution
4.1 Fieldwork Activities
4.1.1 Introduction

KEY POINTS •••

- The opening meeting is primarily used to exchange information between auditees and Internal Audit about the audit.
- Fieldwork activities are subject to the materiality principle.
- Auditors must ensure that the work program is completed fully and consistently. All work program objectives must be achieved by suitable fieldwork activities.
- The audit activities and their results are documented in the working papers.
- Closing meetings are held to communicate audit results to the auditees.

Opening Meeting

At the beginning of fieldwork an opening meeting is held. At this meeting, Internal Audit presents, on the basis of the audit announcement, the audit objectives and audit contents to the auditees and to management. In addition to passing on information, a key objective of the opening meeting is to reach agreement on cooperation during and after the audit. Any unresolved questions can also be addressed and details of the audit can be defined, if this does not alter the nature of the audit. The audit lead must ensure that the opening meeting does not result in negotiation about audit content or the audit itself. The opening meeting should be properly structured, and minutes should be taken, especially if changes to the audit are made.

Materiality Principle

Fieldwork is subject to the materiality principle. For this reason, the auditors should always choose those items that are material to achieving the audit objectives. The auditors may vary the extent of the data to be examined and the work to be done, providing it leads to meaningful audit results. For this reason, the auditors should always consider the selection of fieldwork activities in the overall context of the audit concerned and define it in line with specific needs (for information on the main fieldwork activities, see Section B, Chapter 4.1.2).

Need for Fieldwork Activities

The aim of conducting suitable fieldwork activities is to produce evidence in order to meet the audit objectives. The selected sources and information carriers must be able to deliver reliable information on the audit object for the auditor. The extent and nature of the fieldwork must be carefully coordinated and aligned with the audit objective so that the fieldwork and the audit results can always be objectively traced. This makes it necessary to take a clearly structured approach to audit execution.

Definition on the Basis of the Work Program

Audit experience and reliance on the integrity and completeness of the information are not enough. On the basis of the work program, the auditors must specify in detail the type and extent of fieldwork to be conducted. One item in the work program may give rise to one or several different fieldwork activities (see Section B, Chapter 3.2.2).

Additions During the Audit

The audit process may necessitate additional fieldwork activities. Adjusting the pre-structured work program to actual audit processes increases the demand on the auditors' judgment, which is critical in ensuring that quality and quantity of the fieldwork conducted during the audit deliver sufficient audit evidence so that robust findings can be derived. It is not necessary to uncover every detail, but rather to provide evidence that the fieldwork activities performed are sufficient to arrive at audit results and prove that these results are correct. Often, the necessary evidence can only be provided by sensibly combining different fieldwork activities.

Positioning of Fieldwork Activities in the Audit Execution Phase

The diagram below shows how fieldwork activities are positioned in the audit execution phase. On one side they relate to the work program, and on the other to the working papers (see Section B, Chapter 4.2). The documentation in the working papers is the second aspect of audit execution. Here, the fieldwork activities and their results are stored in the documents provided for the purpose.

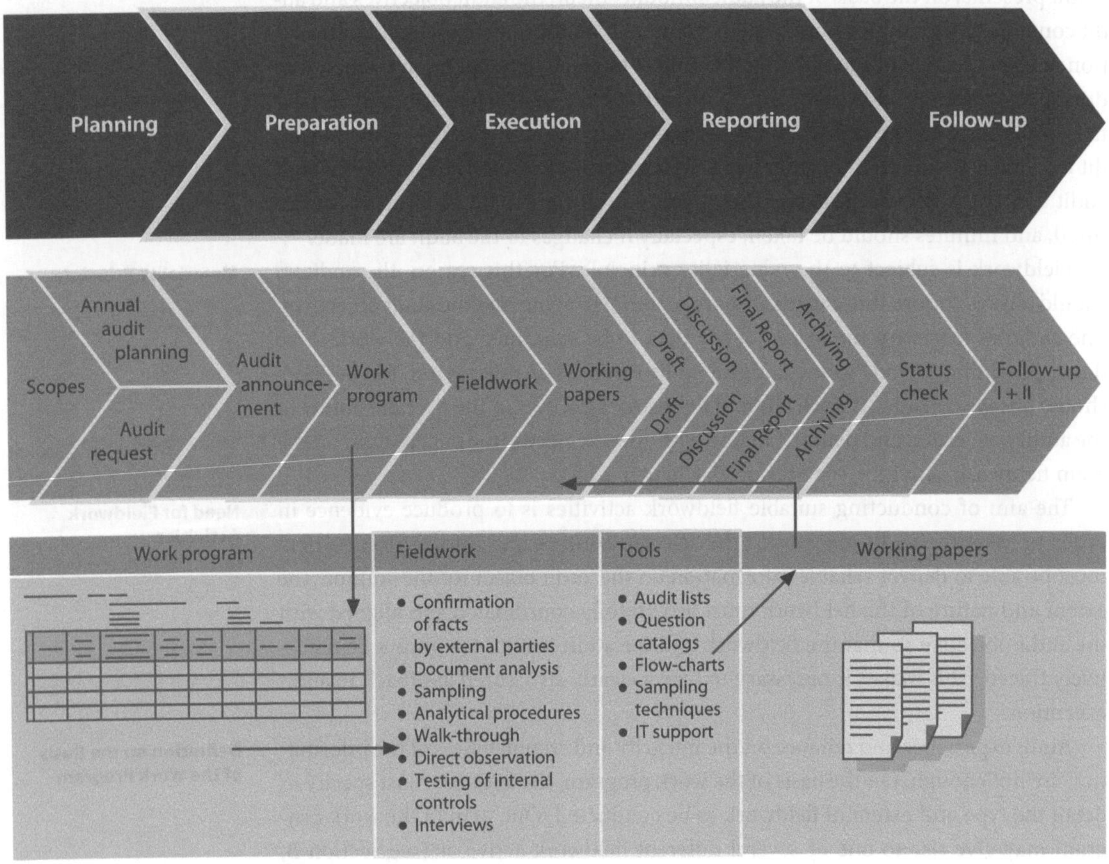

Fig. 12 Positioning of Fieldwork Activities in the Audit Roadmap

Basic Considerations Typical of an Audit

Audit execution requires clearly structured methods. Before the start, auditors therefore have to engage in some basic considerations typical of an audit and decide how they want to proceed with their work, including the following selected aspects: A test of individual documents may produce leads as to whether and how the fieldwork should be expanded. The same applies to testing inventories for accuracy and completeness and checking whether measurements comply with laws, guidelines, and instructions. Determining audit procedure also includes a decision on whether to use primarily formal (formal process compliance) or substantive (correctness of process content and results) fieldwork activities. Moreover, an audit can be approached from two directions: Either progressively (i.e., from the original document or transaction through processing to the final result of document processing), or retrogressively (i.e., by retracing the process from its end to its beginning, where the transaction originated or the document was entered). Section B, Chapter 4.1.2 gives details on fieldwork activity.

Extent of Audit

When determining the extent of an audit, the size of the basic data to be examined is the main parameter to be considered. The extent of the audit depends on the number of objects to be examined, the audit objectives, and the conclusiveness and reliability of the results. The full audit comprises all objects that meet the audit criteria. The alternative to a full audit is sample testing, which is used if the auditors can test a sample that is representative of the whole population.

Closing Meeting

Once the fieldwork and the documentation have been completed, a closing meeting is held with the auditees, at which the audit findings are discussed. If unresolved issues cannot be settled by mutual agreement, the auditors have to document them as disagreements in the implementation report (see Section B, Chapter 5.2.3). Especially for global audits or audits conducted within a very tight timeframe, draft reports may be available in time for the closing meeting, but normally they are the subject of a separate meeting.

HINTS AND TIPS

- Auditors must define at least one suitable fieldwork activity for each item of the work program.
- Each fieldwork activity should make a measurable contribution to the audit result.
- Auditors can use audit activities from past audits for practice. In doing so, they should ask themselves, why a specific procedure was chosen for the case in question, and whether they would have decided differently.

LINKS AND REFERENCES

- CRUMBLEY, L., Z. REXAEE, AND D. ZIEGENFUSS. 2004. *U.S. Master Auditing Guide*. 3rd ed. Altamonte Springs, FL: The Institute of Internal Auditors.

- INSTITUTE OF INTERNAL AUDITORS. 2002. *Practice Advisory 2310-1: Identifying Information.* Altamonte Springs, FL: The Institute of Internal Auditors.
- INSTITUTE OF INTERNAL AUDITORS. 2002. *Practice Advisory 2320-1: Analysis and Evaluation.* Altamonte Springs, FL: The Institute of Internal Auditors.

4.1.2 Main Fieldwork Activities

KEY POINTS •••

- Fieldwork activities comprise the gathering, analysis, and assessment of audit-relevant evidence on the basis of the work program.
- With the audit objective in mind, efficient fieldwork activities should be selected from a broad range of different options.
- The main fieldwork activities include external confirmations, document analysis, sampling, walk-throughs, direct observation, internal control testing, analytical audit procedures, and interviews.

Fieldwork Activities

Audit activities are also referred to as "fieldwork activities." They include the gathering, analysis, and assessment of audit-relevant evidence on the basis of the work program, i.e., the audit steps that have been taken and have to be documented in the working papers along with the conclusions and results.

Selection of Fieldwork Activities

A defined standard set of effective fieldwork activities has to be selected for Internal Audit from the large number of possible fieldwork activities. How this set is put together is determined by the audit topics and objects, the organizational and technical options, the audit objectives, and to a certain extent also by the skills and expertise of the parties involved. In addition, financial, time, and legal aspects must be taken into consideration, as well as access rights, data protection regulations, cultural practices, and corporate culture. The fieldwork activities described below represent a selection made with this in mind; audit or company-specific adjustments may be necessary. The auditors can also adapt fieldwork activities in terms of technology and organization in order to meet the audit requirements in each case. It is critical that the necessary content and procedures are maintained to ensure stable audit results.

Main Types of Fieldwork Activities

The following types of fieldwork activities are suitable for use in global audit departments and are therefore explained in this chapter:

- external confirmations,
- document analysis,
- sampling,
- analytical procedures,
- walk-through,
- direct observation,

- internal control testing, and
- interviews.

External Confirmations

Confirmation obtained from carefully selected external parties involves asking them to explicitly confirm a certain process, state of affairs, or its result to Internal Audit. Since these confirmations come from an independent party, such as a customer, this kind of evidence usually carries more weight as evidence than company-internal confirmations. There are two types of external confirmations: Negative confirmation only requires the external party to respond if it wants to object to the facts presented; explicit agreement is not necessary. In the case of positive confirmation, however, a response is required, irrespective of whether or not the facts are regarded as correct. To this end, the auditors can send the recipient either a blank form, asking for a description, or an agreement/rejection declaration regarding facts that have already been described. If the auditors do not get adequate responses, they must perform additional fieldwork activities to ensure that the audit objective is met.

Document Analysis

Document analysis is often recommended at the start of an audit. It tests whether the documents are conclusive and complete in order to get an overview of the audit topic. Document analysis may be sufficient in itself, or it may have to be followed by other fieldwork activities. Document analysis breaks down into different categories:

- contract analysis (completeness, signature authorizations, compliance, and accounting),
- analysis of guidelines (up-to-dateness, compliance, expedience, familiarity, understanding, and application),
- analysis of process descriptions (structure and workflows, internal controls, expedience, feasibility, and effectiveness), and
- analysis of supporting documentation (existence and authorizations).

To help with these tasks, the auditors can create audit lists or question catalogs, for example to guide them through a content-based or formal assessment of guidelines.

Test Procedures

Test procedures (see Section C, Chapter 3.1) used in audits include both analytical audit procedures and substantive testing. Test procedures form the qualitative and quantitative basis for providing strong and reliable evidence of specific circumstances in audits.

Sampling

As shown in the diagram below, when performing substantive testing there may be areas where audit reliability can only be obtained if all audit objects are tested in full. Possible examples include all purchasing processes that require Board approval, or the completeness of accruals. However, individual sample tests or combinations are used if the auditors want or need to limit the extent of testing. In all circumstances, the selected procedures must meet the requirements of a representative sample size to guarantee a meaningful conclusion. Sampling can be divided into purposive (or judgmental) sampling and random sampling.

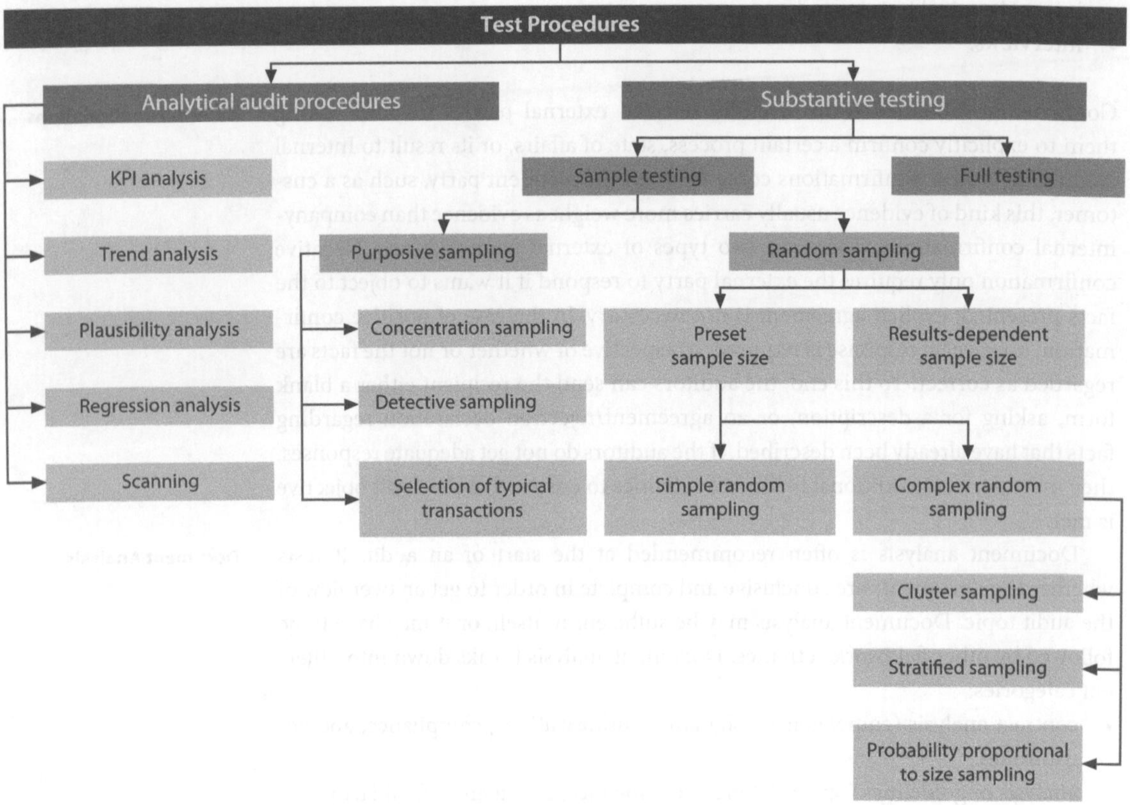

Fig. 13 Test Procedures

Purposive Sampling

Under purposive sampling, the sample is defined on the basis of audit experience and knowledge of the audit segment. The auditors use advance information, thresholds, risk factors, and error probabilities to decide which transactions are to be investigated.

- Under concentration sampling, the auditors base their selection on the absolute or relative importance of the transactions.
- Detective sampling focuses on those transactions where a high probability of errors is expected. The scale of the audit should be increased or reduced, depending on whether the audit detects more or fewer errors than expected.
- When typical transactions are selected, the investigation focuses on those transactions that are regarded as typical of the audit segment in question, with the aim of obtaining an audit result that is as representative as possible, even with a small number of transactions.

Random Sampling

In the case of random sampling, each object that meets the defined criteria has a specific, predefined mathematical probability of being included in the sample. Random sampling procedures break down into procedures with a preset sample size (the number of elements to be audited is determined before the audit) and procedures with a result-dependent sample size (determined only during the audit). The preset sample size procedure is in turn divided into:

- Simple random sampling, where each transaction has the same mathematical probability of being included in the sample.
- Complex random sampling, where all transactions have calculable, but different probabilities of being included in the sample. Since the populations are often very heterogeneous, there are different procedures for stratifying the sample more deeply through structuring attributes. Within each of these procedures, it is possible to look at further samples at the various levels.
  - Cluster sampling: The population is divided into clusters, or subsets, in such a way that the audit material of each subset is as representative of the total population as possible with regard to the expected proportion of errors. Individual clusters are randomly selected for a full test.
  - Stratified sampling: The population is divided into strata in such a way that the proportion of errors of the strata differs as much as possible from each other. Samples are again selected from each stratum, but the volume can normally be smaller than in the case of simple random sampling.
  - Probability-proportional-to-size sampling: The elements to be audited are selected from the population in proportion to their value.

Conclusions about the Population

The accurate testing of the selected sample is the first step toward producing a result. Distribution calculations or statistical testing can be used to extrapolate the attributes identified to the population as a whole, thus permitting conclusions about the population.

Analytical Audit Procedures

As mentioned earlier and shown in the diagram under test procedures, testing includes both substantive testing and analytical audit procedures (see Section C, Chapter 3.1). These activities should also lead to a conclusive statement about the quality of the underlying audit objects. The main objective in this regard is to verify the consistency and plausibility of all audit objects, e.g., entry and recognition of transactions or accounting figures. Cumulative figures can be used to detect or forecast irregularities that exceed set deviation ranges. To standardize the procedure, the following steps should be carried out:

- Define the expected test results.
- Determine the tolerable deviation range.
- Check the results for material deviations.
- Analyze material deviations.

Use of Analytical Audit Procedures

Analytical audit procedures can be used at any time during an audit. In particular, they serve to:

- identify critical processes and objects for auditing,
- identify the main audit contents,

- reduce or replace detailed testing,
- detect fraud,
- before an audit, define expectations about the financial figures to be audited, and,
- at the end of an audit, test the plausibility of accumulating findings and facilitate auditor judgment.

Distinguishing Between Analytical Audit Procedures

In terms of practical application, there are five different analytical audit procedures:

- Multi-period analysis or analysis of third-party key performance indicators (KPIs) should produce conclusive explanations in case of deviations or changes. Inability to provide explanations may indicate errors.
- Trend analysis looks at trends over several past periods and plots the course and extent of deviations. It also allows the auditors to check the plausibility with regard to trends.
- In plausibility analysis, figures or accounts of the current or of past periods are compared with the values expected when calculated in a model. This allows comparisons with budgeted targets.
- Regression analysis allows the auditors to quantify expected values in terms of size. This type of analysis looks at functional dependencies, such as the selling expenses to revenue ratio, for which approximate values can be determined mathematically on the basis of observations. Regression analysis is used above all when setting expected targets.
- Scanning, which is the systematic search for specific transactions, amounts, or special attributes, e.g., in accounts, allows experienced auditors to identify constellations that are prone to errors or possible fraud.

Walk-Through

In a walk-through, an individual transaction is followed through the entire system from beginning to end, encompassing all organizational steps, IT processes and reports, and their integration into the accounting system. This type of fieldwork produces a comprehensive insight into the process, including the controls and their importance for ensuring that the accounting system is compliant from end to end. In a walk-through, the auditees explain to the auditors each process step, their duties and responsibilities, and the internal controls implemented. The auditors compare them with existing guidelines and document all process steps, including the interviews with the auditees. The contents of walk-throughs make them particularly suitable for audits conducted under SOX and generally as the first fieldwork activity of an audit, because they help build a basic understanding. Walk-throughs also work well in combination with other fieldwork activities, such as interviews, internal control testing, and document analysis.

Direct Observation

Auditors perform direct observation when they watch the objects and processes to be audited while they are being carried out or take place in practice. Direct observation often complements other fieldwork activities. It is also suitable for helping auditors decide on further test procedures during an ongoing audit. At the start of an audit, direct observation is used to get an insight into the tasks of an auditee. Direct observation is also useful when assessing internal control mechanisms, because the auditors have to inspect the objects physically in order to arrive at a meaningful audit result and get sufficient evidence regarding the operational effectiveness of control procedures. For direct observation, the auditors can use a similar template as for the walk-through, because the information is essentially the same. This kind of documentation is especially useful if there is not yet any basic process description.

Internal Control Testing

Internal control testing involves auditing the internal control system of an organizational unit (department, entity, etc.). Internal controls should ensure that Internal Audit's objectives are met (see Section A, Chapter 1.2).

Use of Internal Control Testing

Testing the internal controls serves to ensure that transactions were recorded in line with accounting rules and to confirm the process, recording, and documentation of transactions, including the preparation of the annual financial statements. Another objective is to guarantee that the transactions entered do not lead to any misstatement or are fraudulent. Internal controls should above all be tested in combination with system tests or detailed tests of the entire internal control system. Audit lists, question catalogs, or IT applications can be used for support (see Section B, Chapter 4.1.3).

Procedure for Internal Control Testing

There are two different procedures for testing internal controls:

- Testing as part of the work program means that all test procedures listed in the work program must be performed. Weaknesses in the internal control system must be documented in the working papers.
- Testing as part of the compliance audit under SOX is intended to provide evidence of the effectiveness of the tests performed by management. In this regard, it is possible to compare the results of Internal Audit's tests with the test results obtained by management.

Interviews

Interviews are often conducted at the start of an audit in order to gather basic data or background knowledge on a specific audit topic. The results can also be used as a basis for additional fieldwork activities. Moreover, an interview may be useful for discussing the results of previous audits. The quality of an interview is substantially determined by the experience of the interviewer and the type of questions. Interview results can be summarized in writing. Interviews can basically be structured in terms of the following criteria:

- Direction of the information flow: Information is given to or requested from the interviewee.
- Interview structure: One-to-one or in groups.
- Form of communication: Verbal or written.

Types of Interviews

Additionally, interviews can be broken down by type:

- The standardized interview with clearly specified questions and a trend toward one-directional communication leads to clear, easily comparable responses. But there is a risk that important points not covered by the set questions are not addressed.

- The semi-standardized interview is supported by a question catalog and offers more freedom to tailor it to individual needs. This type of interview is normally used at the start of fieldwork activities to gather basic data and information.
- The unstructured interview deliberately refrains from using question catalogs and is only determined by the interview objective. The content and type of questions can be chosen freely, providing they serve the objective of the interview. The advantage of this form of interview is that all material aspects can be addressed, although it is hardly possible to compare its results with those of other interviews.

Basic Question Types

Irrespective of the interview type, interviews have three basic question types:

- the closed question, which has a limited choice of set answers (e.g., "How many people work in your department: Less than 10, between 10 and 20, more than 20?");
- the closed question with additional comments or the semi-open question (e.g., "What is the distribution of professional experience for the employees in the department?"); and
- the open question without specified response options (e.g., "How does the invoicing process work?").

Depending on the interview type, the interview process can be supported and simplified with question catalogs (for more information on question catalogs as an organizational tool, see Section B, Chapter 4.1.3.1).

Summary

The different fieldwork activities offer a broad range of options for conducting audits. The individual selection of the procedures and the judgment of the auditor responsible are critical to a successful audit process. In spite of the large choice of procedures, it is ultimately the auditor's wealth of experience that determines the conclusions to be drawn from the fieldwork activities and thus the audit results.

HINTS AND TIPS

- It is important to ensure that the fieldwork activities are structured so that they complement each other.
- Auditors can get detailed information on the selection and conduct of individual fieldwork activities by looking at past audits already completed.
- Auditors should ask themselves what fieldwork activities will lead to audit results most quickly and unambiguously, including the option to produce evidence.
- Auditors should note anything they want to avoid while conducting fieldwork activities (e.g., the excessive use of closed questions in interviews, etc.) and look at their notes as a daily reminder.

LINKS AND REFERENCES

- SEARS, B. 2002. *Internal Auditing Manual.* New York, NY: Warren, Gorham & Lamont.
- SAWYER, L. B., M. A DITTENHOFER, AND J. H SCHEINER. 2003. *Sawyer's Internal Auditing.* 5th ed. Altamonte Springs, FL: The Institute of Internal Auditors.

4.1.3 Technical Support

4.1.3.1 Organizational Tools

KEY POINTS

- Organizational, methodological, and IT-based tools are available for conducting fieldwork activities.
- Audit lists and question catalogs are organizational tools.
- There are different types of audit lists; they are particularly suitable for testing internal controls and single process steps.
- The basic patterns of question catalogs follow the interview techniques. They may be standardized or tailored specifically to the individual audit. When using question catalogs, the auditors should ensure that they are applied with the necessary flexibility.

Tools for Conducting an Audit

Organizational, methodological, and IT-based tools are available to provide technical support to the auditors. Some of these tools were already discussed in the context of fieldwork activities (see Section B, Chapter 4.1.2). This and subsequent chapters focus on and describe the techniques and tools relevant for practical audit work. The organizational tools are explained first. In this regard, it can be differentiated between audit lists and question catalogs. Audit lists are the preferred tool for non-verbal audit activities and question catalogs are more commonly used for verbal activities.

Audit List Structure

Audit lists allow the auditors to examine individual process steps or audit objects comprehensively and thoroughly. They consist of at least one question or statement and one response or check field. The check field can be expanded by entering a yes/no response or comment field for additional explanations.

Use of Audit Lists

Although audit lists can also be used for closed interviews, they have proven to be particularly useful in connection with auditing internal controls. When testing internal controls, the audit list is tailored to the control step, i.e., it contains the control step as such, the objective of the control, confirmation of its effectiveness, and a description of the test steps performed.

Forms of Question Catalogs

There are various forms of question catalogs. They are lists of audit-relevant questions and are therefore a valuable tool for structured audits. Since they are usually based on the interview technique used, they may contain closed, semi-open, or open questions. Question catalogs can be supplemented by providing multiple-choice answers. This may facilitate conducting the interview and make the audit results more clearly identifiable. For arriving at audit results, the auditors may find it particularly useful to compare the responses given either by different interviewees or at different times.

Content of Question Catalogs

Question catalogs may be structured purely in line with the technical area, in which case they are normally closely related to the contents of a Scope. If the auditors want to align the interviews with the particular situation or if they focus mainly on personal behavior, the question catalogs normally have to be specifically developed, or at least adjusted individually.

Structure of Question Catalogs

Since the auditors need special knowledge on the didactic structure to optimize question catalogs, they should make use of internal consultants or auxiliary tools. When designing question catalogs, the auditors should also consider additional options, such as combining different types of question catalogs, posing introductory, transitional, and concluding questions, using alternative languages, or changing contacts. Also, the importance of how the auditor delivers questions, how they are worded, and how specific the questions are, should not be underestimated for the success of the audit.

Flexibility of Question Catalogs

A question catalog should also allow for deviations from the interview plan. It should be possible to discuss additional issues. If the auditors keep to the question catalog too rigidly, the auditees may get the impression that Internal Audit is not quite sure of how to proceed. It is therefore important that auditors use the question catalog with confidence. They should be very familiar with the questions and take guidance from the way they are structured without letting this preclude the necessary flexibility.

HINTS AND TIPS

- Auditors can use existing templates and the results of earlier audits as a basis for developing audit-specific audit lists and question catalogs.
- Auditors should use external audit lists and question catalogs as samples or as control instruments.
- Auditors can only make flexible use of the question catalog if they know its structure exactly.

LINKS AND REFERENCES

- CRUMBLEY, L., Z. REXAEE, AND D. ZIEGENFUSS. 2004. *U.S. Master Auditing Guide*. 3rd ed. Altamonte Springs, FL: The Institute of Internal Auditors.
- WHATLEY, P. 2005. Easing Into Interviews. *Internal Auditor* (October 2005): 25–26.

4.1.3.2 Methodological Tools

KEY POINTS

- Methodological tools support audit activities by modeling audit content or assuring the procedure used.
- Flowcharts serve to standardize the visualization of audit content, especially processes.
- The use of audit activities is methodologically assured by using sampling procedures which guarantee the quality of a sample.

Methodological Tools

Methodological tools to model audit content or to assure the procedure applied during the audit are used to support fieldwork activities. It is of particular importance in this regard to standardize the applied methods throughout the company.

Modeling of Audit Content with a Flowchart

Flowcharts, which map the content and time dependencies of processes, are the most commonly used tool for modeling content. They can be produced either by hand or with software support. Suitable IT support is particularly recommended for standardizing the visualization of complex flow documents.

Use of Existing Data

For conducting audits, it is an advantage to obtain flowcharts in advance. SOX requires departments to produce process and control documentation that can be accessed during the audit. IT development departments also often use flowcharts for their work, so that the relevant documentation is normally available for use during system audits. But irrespective of any existing data, it may be expedient during an audit to structure and analyze processes and functional relationships in terms of form and content with the help of flowcharts.

Strict Formalism

The use of symbols in flowcharts is strictly formalized. This makes it possible to present complex relationships in a way that they can be uniformly understood and used in an international environment. Flowcharts focus less on the analysis of every detail, but on explaining an entire process that is conclusive within itself. If the process is mapped logically and consistently, any queries about the content can normally be answered by referring to the flowchart.

Sampling

Among the methodological tools, there are audit-related procedures and models, known as sampling procedures, which are intended to provide methodological assurance for the use of audit activities by guaranteeing the quality of a sample. By using such procedures, templates can be standardized and defined. For example, a collection of basic data can first be layered through an ABC classification before applying different sampling methods to make a selection within each layer (for a more detailed practical example on sampling, see Section C, Chapter 9).

HINTS AND TIPS

- Auditors should try to understand and document complex relationships by presenting them graphically in a flowchart.

- Auditors should familiarize themselves with the templates and rules according to which internal flowcharts are generated so that they can apply them appropriately.

LINKS AND REFERENCES ↗

- COLBERT, J. 2001. Audit Sampling. *Internal Auditor* (February 2001): 27–29.
- CRUMBLEY, L., Z. REXAEE, AND D. ZIEGENFUSS. 2004. *U.S. Master Auditing Guide*. 3rd ed. Altamonte Springs, FL: The Institute of Internal Auditors.
- MARTIN, J. 2004. Sampling Made Simple. *Internal Auditor* (August 2004): 21–24.

4.1.3.3 IT Tools

KEY POINTS •••

- IT applications are commonly used as technical support tools in conducting audit activities.
- The SAP Audit Information System (AIS) allows users to select and present financial data in particular.
- The internal control management tool supports all process documentation, including that of the internal controls in accordance with SOX.
- The risk management tool is used to document and track all risks reported throughout the company.

IT Applications as Technical Support Tools

IT applications are commonly used as technical support tools in conducting audit activities. The large number of different systems can be broadly split into two categories:

- Computer-based audit systems that allow users to process an entire audit must map and support all the phases of the audit process model used (see Section D, Chapter 4).
- In addition, there are a number of computer-based audit systems with functions that focus on specific tasks, for example data selection and analysis, process description, risk assessment, and the creation of audit reports. These functions form part of an overall computer-based audit system. They can generally be used in each phase of the Audit Roadmap, from planning and preparation through execution, reporting, and follow-up.

Main Tasks of the SAP AIS

The SAP Audit Information System (AIS), which is one of SAP's application programs, supports individual test procedures. The main tasks of the SAP AIS are:

- structured collection of the required data by presetting parameters for standard SAP reports and audit-specific analyses;

- tailored presentation and coordination of data;
- transfer of document data, account balances, and balance sheet data to user systems for further processing; and
- online controls to detect fraud.

Advantages of the SAP AIS

The functions of the SAP AIS allow auditors to improve the audit process and audit quality, particularly during the execution phase. It therefore serves as the auditor's toolbox in an SAP environment. For example, AIS has an on-screen menu with the most important reports and analyses structured for the purpose. Particularly for financial audits, it offers reporting programs with preset control parameters, which auditors can access through individual screen selection. One of the main functions of the AIS is to offer users the option to select and analyze documents, accounts, and balance sheet captions as part of financial audits.

Internal Control Management Tool

Another IT tool that can support fieldwork activities is the internal control management tool. In conjunction with the process documentation required under SOX, this tool helps meet the requirements of sections 302 and 404 in particular. This tool is also useful for assessing the controls identified in the Monitor and Evaluate domain of the COBIT® framework for IT governance. It primarily supports the documentation of business processes and of each process step, including the relevant internal controls, the status assessment, as well as manual and computer-assisted testing of the internal control system. In addition, the tool provides automatic reports and analytical diagrams, which are intended to help management understand the application of internal controls and track their effectiveness.

Functions of the Internal Control Management Tool

Main functions of the internal control management tool:

- documentation of all business processes and internal controls across the company's main areas of activity;
- annual assessment of the structure and content of the internal controls to test their effectiveness and efficiency;
- support for the detection of control weaknesses and monitoring of measures implemented to eliminate them;
- documentation of process and control changes;
- preparation of reports on internal controls; and
- support for the audit activities of external auditors.

Advantages of the Internal Control Management Tool

An important advantage of this application is that it consistently documents all business units and their business processes. The internal control management tool also defines a uniform documentation standard throughout the company and supports and monitors the central quality assurance and implementation of the internal control system to ensure compliance. The application also supports the reporting system required under SOX and provides management with a status report to confirm a functioning internal control system.

Support for Internal Audit from the IT Tool

The internal control management tool supports Internal Audit in auditing the implementation of SOX (see Section C, Chapter 8 and Section D, Chapter 14). This applies to all three areas related to SOX, such as support for process design and documentation, auditing the design of processes and implemented controls (design assessment), and testing the internal controls. The information from the tool helps create the work program and the working papers. In connection with reporting and follow-up audits, the tool can also be used to query, document, and monitor the present status of respective entity to reconcile Internal Audit's reports.

Risk Management Tool

Another IT tool for conducting audit activities may be an operational risk management tool. Such an application supports global risk management with standardized application functions (for details on the integration of Internal Audit and Risk Management, see Section D, Chapter 2.2). Based on the company's organization, it guarantees that those responsible are alerted to the various risks and thus able to respond adequately.

Main Objectives of the Risk Management Tool

Main objectives of the risk management tool are:

- The risk managers in the operational business units use the tool as a basis for applying standard rules throughout the company to identify, assess, and report risks and track them with the necessary measures.
- For this purpose, the tool has different views that allow comprehensive analysis of the organizational units, activities, and risks.
- The people responsible must continually reassess the risks on the basis of the risk management guidelines.
- In addition, management can assess those risks that are relevant from its point of view.

Advantages of the Risk Management Tool

To meet these objectives, risks are identified and assessed in predefined processes and activities. To this end, users define the response strategy and ongoing risk monitoring method in the system. Risk analyses allow them to generate risk summaries as well as the corresponding breakdown across all organizational units. To guarantee that the information it provides is always up to date, the risk management tool is fully integrated into the systems supplying the data.

Importance of the Risk Management Tool for Internal Audit

Internal Audit reports any risks identified during an audit to the responsible risk manager who enters them in the risk management tool so that they can be processed further, tracked jointly, and ultimately reviewed as part of the follow-up audit.

HINTS AND TIPS

- Auditors should always familiarize themselves thoroughly with the functions of the IT applications available. If needed, they should attend training courses.

4.2 Use of Working Papers

4.2.1 Requirements for the Documentation of Fieldwork

KEY POINTS •••

- The working papers map the fieldwork conducted and thus document the actual audit process.
- Working papers are either prepared by Internal Audit itself, or they are external source documents.
- The auditors have the main responsibility for preparing the working papers.
- Working papers can be filed according to different criteria.
- Due to the sensitive nature of the data they contain, working papers are subject to strict access control.

Basic Requirements

The results of audit activities must be documented truthfully, consistently, clearly, and completely, with a comprehensible description of all material details. This involves both the contents of a fieldwork activity and the procedure itself. This documentation of fieldwork activities is referred to as "working papers" to express its connection with the work results. The basic requirements for proper documentation apply to all types of fieldwork activities (see Section B, Chapter 4.1.2), although there are different types of documents, depending on the nature of the audit. In addition to the working papers which are mandatory, other documents can be created as optional extras; they contain information beyond the minimum information requirement.

Meeting of Obligations

Proper documentation ensures that Internal Audit meets three important obligations of audit work:

Independent Audit Findings

- In connection with the reports on the audit conducted (for details on reporting, see Section B, Chapter 5), the documentation in the working papers provides sufficient evidence, which can be accessed at any time. This gives the findings in the audit reports a verifiable content quality and makes the audit results clearly traceable, even for third parties. The audit thus becomes demonstrably separable from the person of the auditor. If there are claims that the auditor may be biased, they can be substantiated or refuted on the basis of the documentation.

Safeguarding of the Audit Method

- Proper documentation also ensures that the audit method complies with Internal Audit's principles. If a dispute were to arise with the auditees about the audit findings, it is always very important to have evidence that the principles of auditing have been observed.

Basis for Reporting

- The documentation not only records the actual fieldwork activities, it also forms the basis for reporting on the audit findings. The documentation thus also provides process support for large parts of the Audit Roadmap. For example, the documentation of pre-investigations can be used to prepare for the subsequent audit. In addition, the documentation may form part of the closing meetings.

The points that have been documented can also form the basis for expert discussions and the exchange of knowledge, especially in international teams.

Importance of the Documentation

The working papers are an indication of the audit quality in general. This needs to be considered because queries by different groups of addressees or their requests for information may often require access to this documentation. Accordingly, the working papers may serve as discussion or evidence documents, for example for queries from the Board, the unit requesting the audit, Internal Audit management, the Audit Committee, or the external auditors.

Direct and Indirect Documents

Working papers break down into primary, or direct, documents and documents that are secondary, or indirect, from Internal Audit's perspective. Direct documents are always prepared by Internal Audit itself, and indirect documents are source documents in the form of originals, copies, or references to sources. Indirect documents are subject to the same referencing, archiving, and retention requirements as direct documents. Since they are not created internally, indirect working papers must be included in the electronic archive as copies, with information such as "received from/distributed by," the date of receipt, and the auditor's initials (for referencing see Section B, Chapter 4.2.3; for archiving see Section D, Chapter 4.1.2).

Organizational Foundation

The preparation of working papers is subject to certain organizational requirements. Each auditor always has the main responsibility for preparing the documents, both during and immediately after fieldwork. Even though the audit lead and Audit Manager have ultimate responsibility for quality assurance, each auditor has to prepare and maintain the working papers with the necessary attention to detail. Working papers may be compiled by hand or entered directly into a system (which is normally more expedient, because it makes it easier to access the information again, e.g., to lift text blocks for the report).

Filing of Working Papers

During an audit, working papers can be filed according to different criteria, for example by organizational criteria or by subject. If the working papers are filed according to organizational criteria, they are assigned to the individual audit elements, such as reporting or the closing meeting. If they are structured according to subject, the auditor can distinguish between documents on licensing and documents on asset accounting, for example.

Access Authorization

All working papers should be available before the reports are compiled. Like almost all Internal Audit documents, they contain very sensitive data, which means that the auditors should control access to them strictly. While the audit is being conducted, only the relevant auditor and the audit lead should have access to the documentation. Once the audit has been completed, access can be extended to the Audit Manager and the CAE.

Documents with Special Value as Evidence

Documents with special evidentiary value must be considered separately. If necessary, they can be used in a court of law. In such cases, Internal Audit should cooperate with the legal department to ensure that all necessary information is disclosed and that it complies with the rules of legal practice. In this context, the attorney-client privilege should also be considered. Similar arrangements apply if parts of the documentation are to be used for other purposes, e.g., publication. The correct procedure in such cases must be coordinated with the legal department and the Board.

Permanent File

In the context of proper documentation, the question of a permanent file as a long-term documentation tool is often discussed in relation to a specific audit object. This form of documentation is useful in more static organizations. The organizational and process structures of internationally focused companies that operate in a fast-moving environment tend to change more frequently. For the longer-term perspective of Internal Audit, this means that the audit cycle (of around one to two years) carries more weight than the audit object. Providing they are comparable over several cycles, the documented cycles can be linked to each other with an index or cross-referencing.

HINTS AND TIPS

- During the entire audit, auditors should regularly coordinate the working papers with the audit lead and seek his or her feedback.
- Always compile the working papers during or immediately after fieldwork.

LINKS AND REFERENCES

- HUBBARD, L. 2000. Audit Working Papers. *Internal Auditor* (April 2000): 21–23.
- INSTITUTE OF INTERNAL AUDITORS. 2001. *Practice Advisory 2240-1: Engagement Work Program.* Altamonte Springs, FL: The Institute of Internal Auditors.
- INSTITUTE OF INTERNAL AUDITORS. 2001. *Practice Advisory 2240.A1-1: Approval of Work Programs.* Altamonte Springs, FL: The Institute of Internal Auditors.
- INSTITUTE OF INTERNAL AUDITORS. 2001. *Practice Advisory 2330-1: Recording Information.* Altamonte Springs, FL: The Institute of Internal Auditors.
- INSTITUTE OF INTERNAL AUDITORS. 2001. *Practice Advisory 2330.A1-1: Control of Engagement Records.* Altamonte Springs, FL: The Institute of Internal Auditors.
- INSTITUTE OF INTERNAL AUDITORS. 2001. *Practice Advisory 2330.A1-2: Legal Considerations in Granting Access to Engagement Records.* Altamonte Springs, FL: The Institute of Internal Auditors.
- INSTITUTE OF INTERNAL AUDITORS. 2001. *Practice Advisory 2330.A2-1: Retention of Records.* Altamonte Springs, FL: The Institute of Internal Auditors.

4.2.2 Structure and Content of Working Papers

KEY POINTS

- Standard templates for working papers ensure that fieldwork is documented fully and in a common format.
- There are mandatory working papers as well as working papers that are prepared only as needed.

Standard Templates

At GIAS, the working papers are designed as standard templates to ensure that fieldwork is documented fully and in a uniform format. However, for specific fieldwork activities, such as interviews over the internet or videoconferences, it is always possible to prepare specially structured minutes and a special agenda. If newly developed working papers prove useful, they are introduced as standard templates for future use. The existing working paper templates thus provide a basic set of tools to which further examples can be added as the auditors proceed.

Mandatory Working Paper

The work done sheets are the only working papers which are mandatory for each internal audit at SAP. Work done sheets contain the aggregated documentation of individual audit tasks and content and the associated fieldwork with regard to a main audit topic. In the work done sheet template, the audit title and number, the topic of the relevant work done sheet, and the creation date are specified. This information is followed by a list of the actual test procedures for each work package and the findings made; any risks are also stated and possible recommendations given.

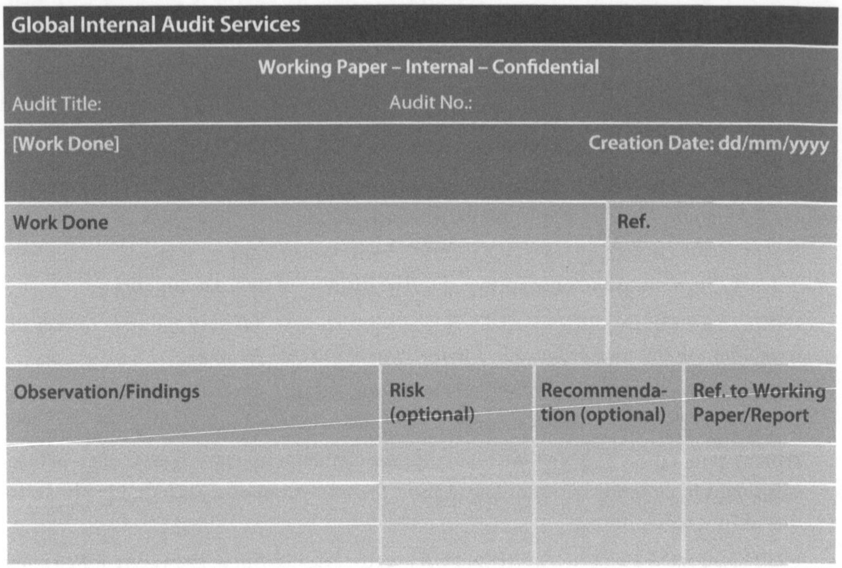

Global Internal Audit Services

Working Paper – Internal – Confidential

Audit Title:		Audit No.:	
[Work Done]			Creation Date: dd/mm/yyyy
Work Done			Ref.
Observation/Findings	Risk (optional)	Recommendation (optional)	Ref. to Working Paper/Report

Fig. 14 Work Done Sheet

Working Papers to Be Used as Needed

The individual work done sheets should be created even when no findings were made. In addition to these mandatory working papers, there are a number of other documents that are used only as required. GIAS currently has the following documents:

- The audit summary which gives an overview of all work done sheets ordered by the main audit topics covered in the audit.

- Interview records and minutes of meetings, which are often subject to the same formal rules from an auditing perspective. However, to record a general exchange of ideas rather than a specific meeting, auditors should use a blank form or create a new template.
- A form for audit notes, which auditors can use to record unusual or irregular events.
- A template to summarize the audit of a specific object, e.g., a contract, so that important information is readily to hand for comparisons.
- An overview of all documents prepared as part of an analysis.
- A memorandum for an internal status report or the creation of an interim report so that a decision on further audit steps can be taken.
- Question catalogs (see Section B, Chapter 4.1.3.1) as templates for the relevant fieldwork.
- A document for recording unresolved questions, intended as an aide-mémoire to plan further fieldwork or support the next test procedures.
- A list of contacts.
- A list of references (see Section B, Chapter 4.2.3).

Audit Summary

One of the more important working papers that are used only as needed is the audit summary. The audit summary gives an overview of all work done sheets according

Global Internal Audit Services			
Working Paper – Internal – Confidential			
Audit Title: Audit No.:			
Audit Summary [e.g. Consulting] Creation Date: dd/mm/yyyy			
Work Done Sheet			Ref.
Observation/Recommendation			
See individual work done items references			
Overall Conclusion	yes	no	
• okay/reasonable			
• smaller issues *(in case of yes, see individual work done items ref)*			
• in case of big issues, highlight issues below:			

Fig. 15 Audit Summary

to their topics. The audit summary template shown below gives the title, the audit number, the topic of the summary and of the work done sheets, and the creation date. In addition to the work done sheets, the audit summary also contains a summary of the observations and findings as well as an overall assessment and conclusion of the audit result.

HINTS AND TIPS

- Before writing the audit summary, auditors should agree the working papers on which the summary is based with their audit lead.
- Auditors should leave the working papers they have written for a while and critically review them later.

4.2.3 Referencing of Working Papers

KEY POINTS

- Referencing provides significant support for the administration of the working papers and other documents.
- To ensure a uniform procedure, SAP specifies both process-related and content-related standard references.
- This framework also allows for any kind of audit-specific referencing.

Need for a Referencing Framework

In order to provide a clear structure for the large number of working papers and other documents and to make these papers easier to handle, a reference framework should be defined. This gives the organization of the documents a uniform structure, which allows users to access individual documents at any time or to access a more detailed level while they are systematically working through the summary levels. Referencing also significantly facilitates and supports report analyses and quality assurance measures.

Referencing Technique

SAP uses referencing to link the individual working papers with each other. Referencing is a structured index, where each ID, or identification number, occurs only once and can be localized in any relation to the subordinated or supraordinated ID. The reference can be established during a subphase (e.g., working papers) or as a linking element between different subphases of the Audit Roadmap. This allows users to assign an interview record to a work done sheet, for example, and to make reference to the work program.

Referencing Requirements

To use referencing flexibly without compromising unique identification, the following points should be observed:

- A unique and self-explanatory terminology must be specified for all audits. The rules for identifying the relevant documents must have a globally uniform basis. To this end, it is a good idea to use the Audit Roadmap. Therefore an index for each phase of the process model was created at SAP:

- Audit planning and preparation: Reference A;
- Audit execution in general: Reference B;
- Specific audit execution: Reference C;
- Reporting: Reference D.

Global Internal Audit Services	
Working Paper – Internal – Confidential	
Audit Title: Audit No.: XX/200y	
Index	
	Reference
Audit planning/preparation	**A**
Audit announcement	A-1
Work program	A-2
Audit requirements (sent to auditees)	A-3
Opening meeting minutes	A-4
...	A-5
Audit execution	
General	**B**
Organizational chart	B-1
Commercial register information	B-2
External auditors' management letters	B-3
Risk Management information	B-4
List of company's legal advisors	B-5
List of company's tax advisors	B-6
Signing policies and bank authorized signatories	B-7
...	B-8
Audit execution	
Specific procedures	**C**
Consulting	C-1
Licenses	C-2
Example of referencing:	
Licenses audit summary	*C-2*
Work done 1	*C-2-10*
Working papers to work done 1	*C-2-10-100*
Work done 2	*C-2-20*
Working papers to work done 2	*C-2-20-100*
Working papers to work done 2	*C-2-20-200*
...	C-3
Reporting	**D**
Closing meeting minutes	D-1
Final audit report	D-2
Status check	D-3

Fig. 16 Referencing Structure

This structure, which follows the Audit Roadmap, provides significant support for the breakdown and assignment of working papers. It also makes it much easier for third parties to use the referencing system.

- The second dimension of referencing relates to content. The standard reference (first numeric classification) identifies the audit topic to be documented and/or the type of document or report. Standard references may have either a single digit or several digits.
- Within this standard reference framework, the lower-level referencing structure can be used freely, i.e., the audit-specific references are constructed in relation to the nature and extent of the working papers. This system has to work on a one-to-one basis so that each document can be uniquely assigned.

Use of Referencing

Since referencing is standardized to a large extent by linking the Audit Roadmap and audit contents, it allows users above all to create a uniform documentation system at a global level. Audit leads are still free to keep a regular check on referencing during the audit. This approach is recommended for audits involving several auditors.

HINTS AND TIPS

- Auditors must follow the standard referencing rules for all their working papers.
- Auditors must ensure that all documents are referenced consistently.

5 Reporting

5.1 Basics of Reporting

5.1.1 Professional Principles

KEY POINTS •••

- The results of the fieldwork conducted by Internal Audit are summarized and documented in an audit report.
- The reporting principles for external auditors apply also to Internal Audit's work.
- Impartial reporting must be complete, truthful, and clear.
- To ensure that the information is optimized, the reports should be made available as quickly as possible.
- Depending on the addressee, there are different reporting formats and writing styles.

Content of the Audit Report

The results of the fieldwork conducted by Internal Audit are compiled into a final audit report, which contains objective, expertise-based information on the results of the audit. At the same time, the audit report serves as a record of the work performed by Internal Audit employees. The IIA has issued professional guidelines for proper reporting.

Reporting Requirements

External auditors' reports must be complete, impartial, and accurate. The AICPA provides guidance for the completion of audit work and standardized reporting practices for external auditors. Internal auditors can follow these standards as well. The following paragraphs provide a brief explanation of main principles of reporting and communication, including completeness, truthfulness, and clarity.

Completeness

The requirement of completeness prescribes that all material findings be included in the audit report. Therefore, this requirement is very closely related to the materiality principle. Specifically, the auditors should include in the report all information that may influence the report addressees' assessment of the situation. In addition, audit findings must be supported by evidential matter.

Truthfulness

Internal audit reports meet the requirement of truthfulness when the present conditions are presented as they currently exist. Internal Audit must not include its own interpretations of the situation but should rely on facts.

Clarity

Audit reports that focus on clarity help the users to accurately interpret the information. Therefore, auditors should formulate the report so that it is coherent and clearly describes the current condition. In addition, the structure of the report has to be organized and logical, and the terms used must convey reality accurately.

Immediate Information

To ensure that the information is optimized, the reports should be made available in a timely manner, i.e., shortly after completion of the audit. This will help the auditees implement the recommended measures and derive a benefit from the audit quickly.

Report Formats and Styles of Writing

Audit reports may be issued to various levels within the organization. Auditors may use different reporting formats or styles for audit findings and recommendations when addressing these different audiences. Auditors should choose wording that matches the appropriate reporting style. The following chapters deal with these aspects in detail.

HINTS AND TIPS

- Auditors should read their reports critically to make sure that they comply with the relevant reporting principles.
- Auditors from other audit teams should also review the reports, e.g., for compliance with quality and readability principles.

LINKS AND REFERENCES

- BALAKRAN, L. 2007. A Solid Reporting Line. *Internal Auditor* (February 2007): 96.
- INSTITUTE OF INTERNAL AUDITORS. 2001. *Practice Advisory 2400-1: Legal Considerations in Communicating Results.* Altamonte Springs, FL: The Institute of Internal Auditors.
- INSTITUTE OF INTERNAL AUDITORS. 2001. *Practice Advisory 2410-1: Communication Criteria.* Altamonte Springs, FL: The Institute of Internal Auditors.
- INSTITUTE OF INTERNAL AUDITORS. 2001. *Practice Advisory 2420-1: Quality of Communications.* Altamonte Springs, FL: The Institute of Internal Auditors.
- INSTITUTE OF INTERNAL AUDITORS. 2001. *Practice Advisory 2440-1: Recipients of Engagement Results.* Altamonte Springs, FL: The Institute of Internal Auditors.
- INSTITUTE OF INTERNAL AUDITORS. 2001. *Practice Advisory 2440-2: Communications Outside the Organization.* Altamonte Springs, FL: The Institute of Internal Auditors.
- INSTITUTE OF INTERNAL AUDITORS. 2003. *Practice Advisory 2440-3: Communicating Sensitive Information Within and Outside of the Chain of Command.* Altamonte Springs, FL: The Institute of Internal Auditors.

5.1.2 Integration into the Audit Roadmap

KEY POINTS

- Reporting is one of the main phases of the Audit Roadmap.
- A clear link between the working papers and the individual findings in the report must be established.
- The audit reports form the basis for the follow-up phase.

Nature of Reporting

The fourth phase of the Audit Roadmap is the reporting phase. It forms a conclusion phase because, after the audit activities have been completed, the audit results are processed into the different audit reports which are then made available to the parties concerned. Reporting also represents the transition to the next phase of the Audit Roadmap: The follow-up phase starts when the final audit reports have been released.

Link to the Working Papers

The reports are primarily based on the working papers (see Section B, Chapter 4.2). Reference is made to both the work done sheets and the working papers on individual activities such as minutes, interview notes, and question catalogs. Secondary documents, i.e. original documents produced from notes by third parties, may also be used to create audit reports.

Audit Summary

The audit summary is the link between the working papers and the actual audit report (see Section B, Chapter 4.2.2). The audit summary lists the work done sheets, and from there the auditors can cross-reference to the individual documents. The links can be established uniquely through the name and number of the audit (see Section B, Chapter 4.2.3). The information is then incorporated into the individual findings of the implementation report and selectively into subsequent reports, e.g., the management summary.

Link to the Follow-Up Phase

The clarity and specificity of the audit findings form the basis for an effective follow-up process (see Section B, Chapter 6). Only if the recommendations are formulated comprehensibly and constructively can implementation and control be performed to an appropriate extent and with reasonable effort. The follow-up is thus based on reporting and is therefore dependent on the audit report, in terms of both time and content.

HINTS AND TIPS ●

- If the auditors have to communicate findings that are sensitive, they should consult with the Audit Manager or the audit lead before such findings are included in the report.
- When writing the report, auditors can already think of activities for the follow-up, i.e., possible measures to ensure that their recommendations are implemented.

5.1.3 Overview of the Main Report Formats

KEY POINTS ●●●

- All results of the audit activities must be adequately documented in the form of reports.
- There are audit-related and periodic reports.
- The audit-related reports provide an assurance of proper, comprehensive reporting tailored to individual needs.

Need for Different Report Formats All results of the audit activities conducted by Internal Audit must be documented without exception. The report format depends on the procedures applied during the audit, and on the audit objectives and thus the contents. For this reason, a specific predefined report format should be used to report on each type of audit.

Audit-Relevant Reporting System The diagram below shows the overall structure of the reporting system of Internal Audit at SAP. There are two main areas, individualized, audit-related reporting and standardized periodic reporting. Audit-related reporting covers primarily all reports that must be prepared within a clearly defined timeframe and relate directly to a specific audit. Calculations based on timesheets (see Section A, Chapter 4.7) have revealed that it takes on average around two to four weeks to write, coordinate, and distribute the reports. This applies particularly to all standard and special audits conducted on the basis of the Audit Roadmap. For ad-hoc audits, the reports are produced within a shorter time. Since information from ad-hoc audits is often required quickly, the reports usually have to be written within a matter of days. The preparation time for the audit reports also includes time to discuss the drafts. The actual writing of the report should be completed in a shorter time.

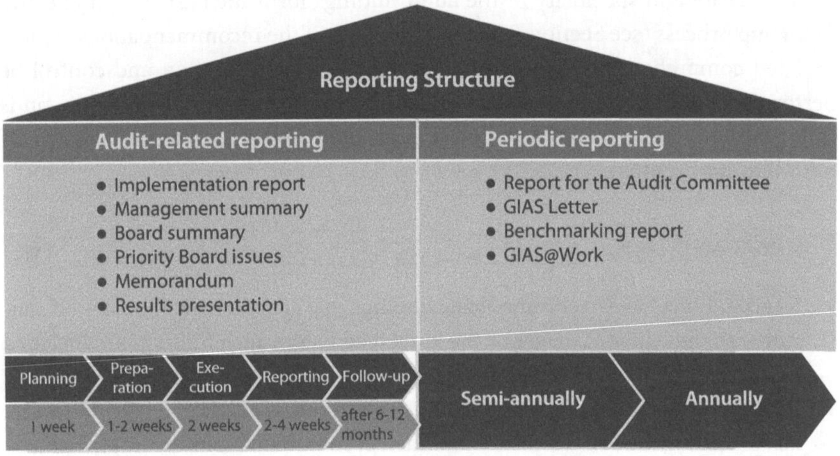

Fig. 17 Reporting Structure

Periodic Reports Periodic reports refer to all audits and other activities that Internal Audit has performed within the reporting period. Their main purpose is to present a summary of significant audit findings, key figures, and project content. Unlike the reports mentioned thus far, these reports do not relate to audits directly (for more information, see Section B, Chapter 5.4).

Important Report Formats Among the audit-related report formats presented above, the implementation report, the management summary, and the Board Summary are of particular importance (on the contents of these report formats, see Section B, Chapters 5.1.4, 5.2.3, 5.2.4, and 5.2.5). These reports form the core of Internal Audit's reporting and are therefore closely related to each other and are used for most audits (see Section B, Chapter 5.2). Although in terms of content they always refer to a single audit, they use different forms of presentation.

Different Target Groups

The various reports are tailored to their respective target groups, in terms of both detail and emphasis. In spite of these differences, a clear internal link must be maintained, i.e., the different report formats have to be consistent and the way they build on or relate to each other must be traceable.

Other Report Formats

The other reports mentioned in the above diagram cover further specific objectives. They include priority Board issues, the memorandum, and the presentation of results. These reports differ in results and format and generally respond to very specific information needs. Additional report formats may be specified at any time, for example review reports, activity catalogs, action plans, etc.

HINTS AND TIPS

- Auditors should be clear about the significance of each report format.
- It is advisable to summarize the specific criteria of each report format in a table.
- If possible, auditors should look at the reports of other companies, sectors, or audit institutes to identify best practices in reporting.

5.1.4 Overview of Report Contents

KEY POINTS

- For most audits, particularly important in terms of reporting are: implementation report, management summary, and Board summary.
- The reports are tailored to the situation and addressees by using reporting-specific terminology.
- The reports must present all the relevant content and explain findings and recommendations clearly and unambiguously.
- Because they have to deal with different target groups, all auditors must comply with certain rules when preparing an audit report, especially with regard to structure.
- It must be possible to trace the management summaries and Board summaries back to the individual items in the implementation report.

Types of Audit Reports

For audits across national and regional boundaries, the audit teams cooperate on a worldwide basis and jointly produce the necessary audit reports. Since the reports are produced and analyzed by different people, they should be standardized as far as possible so that all employees involved assess and interpret them in the same way.

It is therefore advisable to prepare them on the basis of standard rules that apply throughout the company. The standard report package created by GIAS includes the implementation report, the management summary, and the Board summary, each with a different emphasis, and may also include attached memorandums. They are briefly described below (for more details, see Section B, Chapter 5.2).

Description of the Results in the Implementation Report

The implementation report is primarily a description of observations and findings made during the audit. The circumstances are presented from an operational perspective, i.e. predominantly related to processes, controls, risks, and finance. The report is used to explain the audit results to the company's operational management. Each audit result is presented separately, the description of each finding broken down by topic. It should include the following elements:

- clear presentation of the issue identified during the audit,
- comparison of as-is and to-be situation, and
- result of the comparison of the current condition with the desired criteria.

Each of the above elements is structured according to process, control, risk, and financial impact. The report also states interactions in the risk constellation and the resulting consequences, two key items of information for identifying the risks and transferring them to the operational risk management system.

Recommendations in the Implementation Report

The implementation report also contains the audit recommendations, which set out what the auditees can do to change the current situation. The implementation report also has to make clear who must implement which action in what way.

Assignment

Each content element of an audit finding must have a one-to-one assignment to a recommended action. The auditors can also combine several points of a finding into one recommendation, or conversely, suggest several recommendations to respond to a single finding.

Wording of Recommendations

The way the audit recommendations are worded should not leave any doubt about their intended effect. There are a number of key terms that clearly express a suggested course of action. Criteria for selecting the appropriate wording include the degree of exposure and the significance of the finding for the audited area, as well as the financial impact of the problem identified. In addition, the overall effects and the influence on the audited unit's achieving its objectives are further considerations for how the recommendation should be worded.

Management Summary

The management summary is a condensed version of the original findings and recommendations of the implementation report, grouped by certain aspects of content. The above notes on the wording apply by analogy, but the auditors should choose a style suitable to management. One function of the management summary is to explain to management in general the responsibility for the findings and their impact. In this context, the auditors should focus in particular on how the findings are interrelated. The summary should also point out the consequences of failure to implement the recommendations and refer to any actions already resolved and/or introduced during the audit.

Link to the Implementation Report

The management summary condenses the findings in the implementation report relating to the same or similar topics. It must, however, be possible at any time to make a plausible link to the relevant audit result by using the correct reference.

Different Functions and Levels

It is important that the management summary reaches managers at different levels and in different functions, and the auditors should take this into account by tailoring the wording accordingly. A general summary of the audit result in the form of an overall conclusion for the audit should be included (for details, see Section D, Chapter 7.2.1).

Board Summary

The Board summary contains all the findings that are reported directly to the responsible Board members. Of course, the Board can at any time ask for the related reports to obtain more detailed information. In order to communicate the information effectively, the summaries should, as far as possible, be forwarded alongside the reports described above. Since the objective is to convey information on important findings as well as to provide an overall assessment of the audit, the reference must provide a direct link to each finding of the implementation report.

Content of the Board Summary

This aggregated report format provides a summary of findings and also reports selected individual findings from the implementation report. Often facts or developments are so significant that the Board must be informed immediately. It is important in such a case to give reasons for the assessment of the auditor (e.g., the effect on the company's image, potential legal risks, economic factors, etc.).

Memorandum

If additional information about the background of an audit engagement is required, a memorandum is also part of the report package. This may be the case, for example, for special audits or ad-hoc audit engagements. To integrate the implementation report and the corresponding memorandum, both reports are referenced accordingly (for more information see Section B, Chapter 5.3.1).

HINTS AND TIPS

- Auditors should check each finding for consistency to avoid contradictions.

5.1.5 Report Addressees and Distribution

KEY POINTS

- The confidentiality of audit reports is critical for many reasons, and careful consideration must be given to the parties who receive the report.
- Confidentiality must be maintained also during distribution. For this reason, the parties concerned receive their reports through clearly defined channels.
- These channels follow unique distribution lists based on the company's organization.

- All the reports are distributed by confidential e-mail. Management and the Board members additionally have access to the reports via the intranet.

Report Level Structure

Since audit reports are confidential, their distribution in the organization must be handled with sensitivity. The distribution is based on the current organizational structure. Although all information is of course strictly confidential, the contents of reports for management and the Board members are subject to an additional level of confidentiality. Specific distribution lists, which follow the structure of the report levels, contain the authorized addressees for each report. These distribution lists have to be kept up to date at all times by the Audit Manager or a central coordinator from Internal Audit, and access authorizations to each report must be constantly monitored.

Draft Distribution

Audit reports are normally distributed to those responsible in the audited area at the draft stage. This is particularly important for the implementation report and the management summary, but not for the Board summary, which is not distributed to the auditees. The persons responsible in the audited area have an opportunity to comment on the drafts, i.e., agree with or reject the draft, and make additions or corrections. Internal Audit has a duty to examine each comment carefully and incorporate it in the report if appropriate. Confidentiality must be fully maintained also during the drafting phase.

Timeframe

Final versions of the audit reports should be distributed within two to four weeks after the end of the audit. This meets an important requirement on the part of Internal Audit for timely implementation of the audit results.

Distribution of the Reports at SAP

Before the draft reports are distributed, the audit lead reviews their content and form, and the Audit Manager checks them for accuracy and completeness. Only then can the distribution process begin. To ensure that a standard procedure is followed, Internal Audit at SAP distributes the reports throughout the company using the following means:

- The audited area and the relevant operational managers receive the reports by confidential e-mail directly from the audit lead or the Audit Manager.
- Regional managers who are responsible for the area also receive the reports by confidential e-mail. At the same time, an Internal Audit employee makes the reports available to these employees on the company intranet.
- The CEO and the CFO have access to the Board summaries through an intranet-based management information system. All reports are linked to each other so that it is possible to get a detailed analysis at the level of the individual finding. Other Board members can also get access. If no special access has been authorized, the members of the Board are sent the relevant summaries by e-mail.

Other Report Addressees

In addition to the above groups of people, there may be other appropriate recipients for the reports, e.g., the legal department, the human resources department, or even the external auditors or other bodies in the case of legal matters (i.e., SEC, district attorney etc.). Distribution to these parties may be agreed with the CAE on a case-by-case basis and depends on content and necessity. Since audit reports always contain sensitive data, the CEO should be consulted before the reports are sent to any additional addressees. Before reports are sent to legal authorities, the legal department should be consulted. Under certain circumstances, it may be necessary to sign a non-disclosure agreement or the reports may be managed under the attorney-client privilege. It is furthermore necessary to etablish detailed rules for the distribution of reports to other units that are only indirectly affected by the audit (e.g., the legal department, the compliance office). Past audit reports can only be forwarded to new people responsible in the area to be audited if the CAE has given his or her approval.

HINTS AND TIPS

- Auditors must check the audit report distribution lists regularly and alert the people in charge of the necessary updates.

5.2 Standard Report Package for Audits

5.2.1 Audit Report Index

KEY POINTS

- The audit report index is the table of contents for the standard report package.
- It contains information on standard audit report components and appendices.
- Audit-specific details such as the audit name and number are entered in the header of the audit report index.

Table of Contents of the Standard Report Package

The standard report package starts with the audit report index. This index is a general overview of all report components of operational reporting (not including reports to the Board) on standard and special audits. It is the table of contents of the standard report package concerned.

Other Information in the Audit Report Index

In the header of the audit report index, the auditor enters the organizational unit and the number of the audit report, which has been assigned in the audit announcement. This number can be retrieved from the central data server at any time. The auditor also has to provide the title, which must be the same as that used in the audit announcement.

Components of the Standard Report Package

The standard report package comprises the following components:

- management summary to provide information to operational and regional management;
- implementation report which contains the audit findings; and
- classification and audit status overview, which are descriptive elements that provide important information in the standard report package (see Section B, Chapter 5.2.2).

Basic Audit and Follow-Up

The structure of the audit report index is the same for basic audits and follow-ups, but there are differences with regard to content. The following chapters relate to basic audit reporting (for follow-up audit reporting see B, Chapter 6.3).

Appendices

The audit report index contains standard suggestions of frequently used report appendices at SAP. The auditors can change appendices as required. Important appendices are lists and directories compiled by Internal Audit or original source documents such as organization charts and signature protocols. If appropriate, the decision as to whether to incorporate such documents should be made after consultation with the audit lead and the Audit Manager. The report packages should include (excerpts from) original source documents that provide evidence for transactions and audit objects and thus support the audit findings. However, the auditors should try to keep a reasonable balance between the size of the report and the size of the annexes.

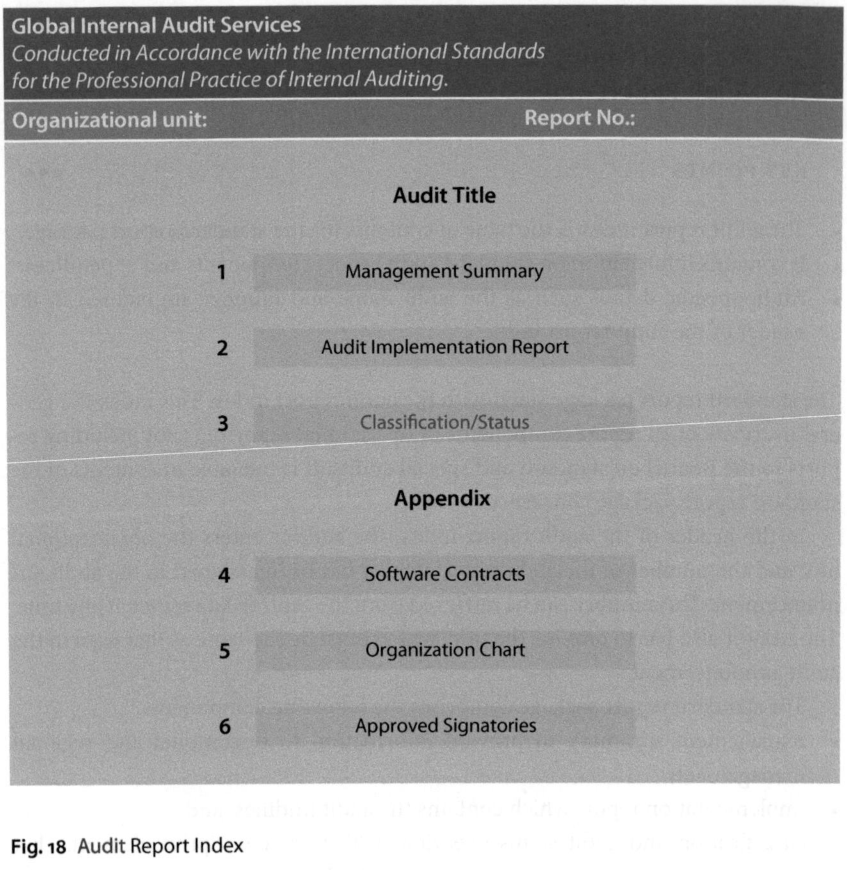

Fig. 18 Audit Report Index

HINTS AND TIPS

- After auditors have completed their reports, they should check that the information in the audit report index is correct and complete.
- Auditors can use previous audits to get a feeling for the nature and extent of the annexes used so that they can make an adequate selection when they conduct their own audits.

5.2.2 Classification

KEY POINTS

- Audit findings should be classified to make sure that they are implemented.
- A detailed system of indicators with weightings can be used for this purpose.
- Alternatively, findings may also be classified based on auditor judgment according to certain criteria.
- Whatever the method, the auditors should make sure that those responsible give proper attention to the findings and recommended measures.

Levels of Responsibility

When the findings and observations are classified as part of reporting, they are always assigned clear responsibilities to ensure that the recommendations are appropriately implemented. In doing so the relevant level of management responsibility is assigned to each item. The levels are as follows:

- The "Board" level represents findings relevant to the Board (identified with the letter B).
- The "Regional Management" level is for findings that fall under the responsibility of senior or regional management (identified with the letter R).
- The "Local Management" level comprises all other findings, which are the responsibility of operational management (of a single department or local subsidiary, identified with the letter L).

Assignment on the Basis of Indicators

When assigning findings and observations, the auditors must take into account a number of indicators, which are based on the structure of the risk categories used by risk management. Significant factors include the organizational unit, the area of responsibility, the number and assessment of the risks, the impact on other areas, the number of people involved, a possible link to fraud, external perceptions, and legal interests in the broadest sense. Additional classification by financial, organizational, structural, and product-related variables can also be useful. These criteria may be supplemented specifically for the audited area. In doing so, it may be helpful to weight the selected indicators with equivalencies. The resulting assessment matrix can be used to arrive at an overall weighting for each finding and thus assign it to one of the three levels of responsibility (for details, see Section D, Chapter 7.2.1).

Auditor Judgment

An alternative course of action is to make an assessment according to auditor judgment, using certain decision parameters. The breakdown into Board-relevant, regionally relevant, and locally relevant findings is based on the factors described below. These factors can be used in combination with auditor judgment to come to clearly motivated assignments.

Findings Relevant to the Board

Findings relevant to the Board include all findings that

- directly refer to guidance issued by the Board or global policies,
- relate to a risk the Board should be aware of,
- require a decision by the Board,
- necessitate action by the Board, or
- are regarded as relevant for the Board by Internal Audit management.

Regionally Relevant Findings

Audit findings are regionally relevant, e.g., if they

- refer to a guideline under regional responsibility,
- relate to a risk regional management should be aware of, or
- cause regional management to take a decision or action.

Locally Relevant Findings

All other findings are automatically assigned to local responsibility. For locally relevant findings, all the necessary decisions and actions can be taken by the audited area itself or by operational management. However, this does not mean that these findings are less important. All findings must receive the same attention, and their classification should not have any influence on the quality of the implementation measures. Assignment to a particular level of responsibility is only intended to ensure swift and efficient implementation of the measures at the appropriate level.

HINTS AND TIPS

- Auditors should request the audit lead or Audit Manager to classify the findings and compare the results.
- In addition, auditors should discuss the assignment with the people responsible for operations.
- Auditors should give thought to alternative courses of action in case the people responsible according to the classification fail to implement the recommendations and actions relating to the findings.

5.2.3 Implementation Report

KEY POINTS

- The implementation report is the core element of the reporting system.
- It is intended primarily for the audited area and managers with direct operational responsibility.

- It lists all the observations and findings and provides notes in separate columns on how to eliminate weaknesses.
- The implementation report consists of two sections: the actual audit results and the monitoring section for the implementation update of necessary actions.
- When creating the implementation report, the draft stage is very important, because this is where the final audit statements are agreed upon with the auditee in terms of form and content.

Main Part of the Audit Report Package

The implementation report forms the main part of the audit report package. It is compiled primarily for the audited area and its direct operational managers. After internal quality assurance by Internal Audit (see Section D, Chapter 5.3), a draft report is sent to the people in charge of the audited area to give them an opportunity to comment. Their comments may take the form of insertions, corrections, or additional evidence. Sometimes it is possible to present the draft reports at the closing meeting so that the findings can be discussed at the same time as the draft report. But normally discussion of findings and of the draft report are dealt with separately, unless there are specific reasons to combine them (e.g. travel requirements).

Global Internal Audit Services *Conducted in Accordance with the International Standards for the Professional Practice of Internal Auditing.*									
Audit Implementation Report No.: xx/200x					**Organizational unit:**				
Audit Status:					**Auditor(s):**				
Audit Items					**Monitoring**				
No.	**Classification**	**Observation/Finding**	**Risk Category**	**Recommendation**	**Action/ Management Responses**	**Responsible**	**Completion date**	**Status Local Management**	**Status GIAS**
1		Description: Risk condition: Risk consequence:							
2		Description: Risk condition: Risk consequence:							
3		Description: Risk condition: Risk consequence:							

Fig. 19 Structure of the Implementation Report

Report Structure

The above diagram shows the structure of the implementation report for a basic audit. First the audit lead enters the report number and the name of the audited unit, as well as the audit status and the names of the auditors involved. The actual report section follows this header information. The row structure is determined by the audit content. The individual items within each topic are shown in descending order of risk rating.

Presentation of Observations and Findings

Among the items listed, a differentiation is made between pure observations and findings. The findings are shown first according to their B (Board), R (Regional), and L (Local) classification (see Section B, Chapter 5.2.2). The observations then follow in the same order. The main difference between the two categories is the degree to which they are binding. Observations are identified weaknesses, although they cannot be benchmarked against any desired criteria. Findings, by contrast, are weaknesses identified always because of a deviation from required criteria. As a result, the implementation of the actions recommended as part of findings is more binding and therefore more important. The auditors should ensure that recommended actions are presented clearly (see Section B, Chapter 5.1.1). The following should be noted:

- Each finding is reported under a separate consecutive number. Headings or key words give the report a structure that is easy to follow. They are sourced in the working papers, especially the audit summary and the work done sheets.
- Depending on the circumstances, the auditors should also present positive aspects, at least in summary form. This puts the overall assessment into a more objective perspective and has a positive, motivating effect on the auditees.

Columns of the Implementation Report

The titles of the first two columns of the implementation report are consecutive number (No.) and Classification (see Section B, Chapter 5.2.2). The following main columns are next:

- Observation/Finding,
- Risk Category, and
- Recommendation.

They represent the core of the implementation report and thus the actual audit result. Under the heading "Observation/Finding" the audit results are described. In addition, a brief description of the risk condition and the risk consequence is given. Stating the risk category ensures that the risk attached to each finding is identified, thus preparing it to be incorporated in the risk management system. Capture in the risk management system furthermore requires entry of the risk in short form and any possible consequences.

Monitoring Section

The monitoring section is the second important block in the report structure. It has a column for "Action/Management Responses," where the management of the audited area can add comments. The following columns contain the names of those responsible for implementation and the completion date. The last two columns relate to the follow-up process and are therefore described in Section B, Chapter 6.3.

Importance of the Draft Stage

It has already been mentioned that the draft stage is particularly important for the creation of the implementation report. At this stage, content and wording are carefully coordinated, taking cultural aspects into account. This is a revolving, sometimes time-consuming process. Since this process leads to the presentation of the actual audit result, the auditors must complete it with a maximum of quality and objectivity. In addition to official quality checks, it is often advisable to perform internal quality reviews (see Section D, Chapter 5.3).

HINTS AND TIPS

- Auditors should consider carefully whether each audit result is an observation or a finding.
- It also makes sense to discuss the recommendations with auditors from other teams and to make comparisons with existing reports.
- If possible, auditors should wait at least two days after they have finished writing the report and then reread the complete document. If it then seems consistent and logical, they can send it to the audit lead.

5.2.4 Management Summary

KEY POINTS

- The management summary is used to present all audit items that are of interest or importance to operational and strategic management.
- In addition to information on the audit objectives and the overall audit statement, the auditors can include individual items of significance or summarize findings from the implementation report.
- Each item must be referenced against the findings in the implementation report.
- The overall audit statement for management is presented in the form of a traffic-light rating system.

Preparation of Audit Findings

The management summary is used to prepare all significant findings for presentation to operational and regional management. Only findings and observations identified by the appropriate classification are included (see Section B, Chapter 5.2.2 and Section D, Chapter 7.2.1). Items that are relevant for the Board or the region should be included in the management summary. Board-relevant items should be incorporated unchanged; regionally relevant items can (but do not have to) be summarized.

Information Included

The following figure shows the template for the management summary. The header shows the audit title and the report number. The second row provides information on the audit type (standard, special, or ad-hoc audit), audit status (basic audit, status check, follow-up I or II), and the execution (start) date of the audit. The next rows contain in the same order as listed:

- auditors involved, including guest auditors and consultants,
- manager responsible for the audited area,

- date of the closing meeting,
- participants in the closing meeting, and
- distribution list of report addressees.

An overview of the most significant specific audit objectives follows in the next row.

Global Internal Audit Services
Management Summary
Conducted in Accordance with the International Standards for the Professional Practice of Internal Auditing.

Audit Title:			**Audit Report No.:**
Audit Type:	Audit Status:	Basic Audit	Date of Audit:
Auditor(s):	Executive Responsible:		Date of Closing Meeting:
Participants of Closing Meeting:			
Distribution List:			
Overview/Audit Objectives:			

Audit Status (please tick)	Date	Audit Rating	Overall Audit Statement/ Scoring	Findings/Recommendations	Ref. Impl Report
Basic Audit ☐		●○○	☐ Substantial Weakness ☐ Weak		
		○●○	☐ Needs Improvement		
		○○●	☐ Meets Standard ☐ Exceeds Standard		
Status Check I ☐		R Y G			
Follow-up Audit I ☐		R Y G			
Status Check II ☐		R Y G			

# of findings: New: | In process: | GIAS Pending: | Open: | Reasonably controlled: | Done: | Mgmt. disagreed:

Fig. 20 Management Summary

Findings and Observations The header area is followed by a dated list of the findings and observations. The items listed here are based on the implementation report according to the classification mentioned above and are cross-referenced against the implementation report. The entries made in the "Findings/Recommendations" field are quoted unchanged or summarized. In the management summary, the overall audit statement (see Section D,

Chapters 7.2.1) is presented visually in the form of a traffic-light system as demonstrated in the figure above, assigning colors to the following categories:

- Red: "Substantial Weakness", "Weak".
- Yellow: "Needs Improvement".
- Green: "Meets Standard", "Exceeds Standard".

As the audit cycle proceeds, the management summary will also contain information on the status check and the follow-up (see Section B, Chapter 6) to show the entire history of the respective audit cycle.

HINTS AND TIPS

- Before sending the management summary for approval, auditors should review it with the Audit Manager in charge.
- Auditors should ensure that the contents of the findings correspond to the audit objectives.
- Auditors should keep a list, sorted by rating, of the audits they have conducted so that they can check the overall objectivity of their assessments by making comparisons.

5.2.5 Board Summary

KEY POINTS

- The Board summary presents all Board-relevant findings either for information, for decision, or for action.
- The Board summary is produced, distributed, and discussed with the CEO separately from the implementation report.
- Priority Board issues are reserved for matters that must be reported during an audit and allow Internal Audit to involve the Board actively.

Information for the Board

The Board must be informed of the audit results produced by Internal Audit. The classification into Board-relevant, regionally relevant, and locally relevant items (see Section B, Chapter 5.2.2 and Section D, Chapter 7.2.1) is a feasible method to filter out noteworthy items from a larger number of findings. All findings labeled Board-relevant must be incorporated in the Board summary.

Structure of the Standard Template

The header area of the Board summary template contains the title, number, and date of the audit. The overall audit statement (see Section D, Chapters 7.2.1) is shown as a traffic light status. The Board summary also states the audit objectives. The standard template has columns for the findings and recommendations, the manager responsible, and the reference to the appropriate item in the implementation report. The reference is particularly important if direct (online) access to the appropriate individual finding is required. A row at the bottom contains information on the priority, stating whether the finding is reported for information, for a deci-

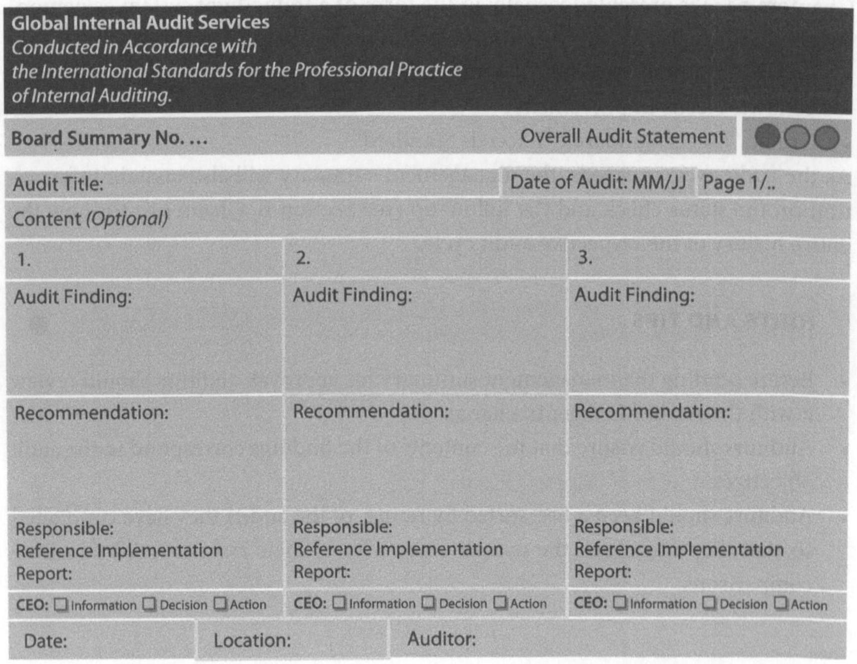

Fig. 21 Board Summary

sion, or for action by the CEO. The standard template is freely adaptable, which means that it can be set to one or two findings per page, for example. The footer area contains the creation date, the location of the audit, and the names of the auditors.

Full Reporting

To let the Board members know that the reports are complete and do not have any omissions, a Board summary must be created for each audit. If no findings of relevance to the Board were made during an audit, the Board summary should state this.

Communication to the Board

The Board summary and the completed implementation reports are compiled and distributed only after the reports have been discussed with the audited area. After the reports have been distributed, the audit results relevant to the Board are normally discussed at regular meetings between the CEO and the CAE. At these meetings, the CEO and the CAE also take the necessary decisions and initiate actions according to how the findings are labeled. After the meeting, executive management of the area is informed of the findings relevant to their area. Since audit findings are normally associated with financial risks, the CFO receives copies of all Board summaries.

Priority Board Issues

Priority Board issues complement the Board summaries. Their form and structure are the same as those of the Board summary, but they are created while the audit is still in progress or before the final report is submitted. Instead of audit findings, they record the status of matters and problems in progress. The recommendation contains suggested options for action. Priority Board issues thus contain highly confidential information about audits not yet completed and give Internal Audit the opportunity to report urgent matters to the Board in advance, agree decisions or actions on further test procedures with its members, and thus actively involve them in fieldwork. Memorandums are used if the information is more comprehensive (see Section B, Chapter 5.3.1). Since this type of report may compromise Internal Audit's independence, auditors should use it only in justified exceptional circumstances.

Global Internal Audit Services
Conducted in Accordance with the International Standards for the Professional Practice of Internal Auditing.

Priority Board Issues No. ...

Title:	Date of Audit: MM/JJ	Page 1/..
Content:		
1.	2.	3.
Issue:	Issue:	Issue:
Recommendation:	Recommendation:	Recommendation:
Date:	Auditor:	Ref. Impl. Report *(if applicable)*:

Fig. 22 Priority Board Issues

HINTS AND TIPS

- Auditors should write the Board summary last, after all the other report elements, because only then will they have a general overview of the logical and time sequence of the findings and how they interrelate.
- Auditors should align the contents of the Board summary with the contents of the other reports and, together with their audit lead, prioritize the actions that the Board needs to take.

- If priority Board issues are necessary, the auditors should be aware of the objectives and ask all members of the relevant audit team, the Audit Manager responsible, and the CAE to read them.

5.3 Other Report Formats

5.3.1 Memorandum

KEY POINTS •••

- Memorandums are used to present specific complex matters.
- Their purpose is to show the circumstances and the resulting action for a specific preliminary result.
- Memorandums can also be used to include supplementary documentation and to provide additional explanations.
- They are very adaptable and can be used for a variety of audit types and services.

Definition

There are a number of audits and other services for which conventional reports (see Section B, Chapter 5.2) are only rarely the appropriate form of communication. The reasons may be content (e.g., very complex circumstances) or the fact that it may be impossible to follow the Audit Roadmap. A memorandum may be used as an additional report format in such cases. The memorandum is a closed presentation of an individual topic that is normally complex in nature.

Reasons for a Memorandum

Memorandums are prepared especially in the following circumstances:

- The audit result can best be presented in the form of a description.
- The suggestions are of a general nature or relate to specific cases, so that explicit recommendations regarding the implementation of actions are not necessary.
- The information is confidential and should be sent to a limited number of addressees only.
- The findings presented in an implementation report or special report require additional verbal explanations.
- A preliminary result is to be reported.
- Detailed explanations of background facts or explanatory notes on related topics are necessary.

Use of the Memorandum

Memorandums are most suitable for certain types of services, such as pre-investigations, reviews, and certain support and consulting services (see Section A, Chapter 7). Memorandums may also be written in conjunction with regular reports, for example as a supplement to the Board summary.

Memorandum Structure

A memorandum starts with the usual header information, followed by the actual report section. Typically, a memorandum is structured as follows:

- background and current situation/request,

- audit content and objectives,
- summary of results,
- audit steps,
- results,
- required action, and
- further information.

Form of Presentation

As in all other report formats, it is important to present the information clearly. Especially for pre-investigations, a memorandum can include arguments for questions about further steps or pending decisions and actions. If further fieldwork is performed after the memorandum has been completed, the subsequent audit report must reference to the memorandum.

Memorandum and Implementation Report

An implementation report is additionally written if the auditors want to address the risk exposure of process steps in connection with a memorandum. In some cases, this course of action is advisable, because the implementation report created together with the memorandum will assign the required follow-up steps to each finding or recommendation.

Reporting Versus Working Papers

It should also be pointed out that the report memorandum described here should not be confused with the memorandum created at working paper level. Although the formats are similar, their contents are different.

HINTS AND TIPS

- An impartial colleague in Internal Audit should read the memorandum and check that it meets its communication objective.
- When preparing a memorandum, the auditors must decide whether an implementation report will have to be created in addition to the memorandum.

5.3.2 Results Presentation

KEY POINTS

- Results presentations are suitable for presenting the content of an audit if the auditors want to introduce results or test procedures to other parties or discuss them during or after the audit.
- The audit result should be summarized in a conclusive and meaningful way.
- A results presentation may also provide an interim status of audit work.
- Apart from audits, results presentations are particularly beneficial for customer project reviews and other internal projects.
- If the discussion of the results delivers new insights, they can be directly incorporated in the presentation.

Structure of the Results Presentation

Once the auditors have completed an audit, it may be helpful to condense the results in a presentation, in addition to all the other report formats mentioned already. To do so, the auditors should prepare a conclusive, meaningful summary of the key points of the audit. A results presentation often has the following structure:

- purpose of the audit,
- description of the audit execution,
- results of the audit,
- monitoring activities during the audit,
- cost impact,
- recommendations,
- alternatives for action,
- further steps, and
- explanations and diagrams.

The presentation must not reveal any details about how the audit was conducted or any confidential information.

Presentation of Interim Results

A results presentation may also give an interim report on fieldwork. By providing an interim report, the employees involved in an audit and those in charge of the audited area can be kept informed of the latest audit results and work progress. To keep such stakeholders informed, the content of the presentation is developed over a certain period. This gives presentations a twofold purpose: To communicate the results and to function as an audit tool. The information that has been condensed in a results presentation is more easily absorbed by the addressees, and the impact can be highlighted during the meeting, and placed in the relevant context.

Advantages of Results Presentations

The strength of a results presentation is enhanced through interaction between auditors and auditees, as well as in the way graphics and diagrams are used. Graphs and diagrams make content easier to visualize, and the audit results can thus be communicated more effectively. This makes results presentations particularly suitable for customer project reviews. In addition, results presentations can be used to communicate information on internal change management projects and complex, cost-intensive audits. For management, the audit results can be analyzed statistically and the processed data can be shown in condensed form. Presentations also allow larger groups of people to discuss the results, and different opinions can be identified during the presentation or provided to a larger audience for discussion.

Relation to Other Report Formats

Implications from a results presentation can be included in another report, such as the implementation report or a memorandum.

HINTS AND TIPS

- When creating a presentation, an auditor should obtain support from colleagues who have experience with presentations.
- It is a good idea to practice giving the presentation using the audit team as trial audience.

5.4 Periodic Reporting

5.4.1 Annual Report to the Audit Committee

KEY POINTS

- In addition to audit-related reports, Internal Audit also prepares periodic reports.
- The annual report to the Audit Committee provides a complete summary of the events that occurred in Internal Audit during a year.
- It should cover events that took place in the past as well as include forward-looking statements.
- The annual report to the Audit Committee, can also be sent to other units.

Periodic Reports

In addition to the comprehensive range of directly audit-related reports and analyses (see Section B, Chapters 5.2 and 5.3), the reports produced by Internal Audit also include periodic reports, although their structure differs from the actual audit reports in terms of presentation and information density.

Exchange of Information with the Audit Committee

Details of Internal Audit's relationship with the Audit Committee are provided in Section A (see Chapter 2.5.2). In addition to communicating details of audit events verbally to the Audit Committee at regular intervals or upon request in writing, the written annual report is the focal point of the information exchange.

Content of the Annual Report

The annual report to the Audit Committee has a defined structure covering the following main points:

- organizational structure of Internal Audit,
- audit performance record of the previous year,
- summary of significant findings and implementation actions from various audits,
- audit plan for the coming year,
- support actions, audits, and tests scheduled in accordance with SOX,
- fraud,
- safeguarding revenue recognition,
- support in other projects,
- internal projects of Internal Audit,
- cooperation, especially with the external auditors,
- special highlights in the department, e.g., significant innovations,
- long-term planning of Internal Audit, and
- major audit focus areas for the future.

Summarized Presentation

The different topics are presented in aggregated form. In addition, examples of one or two implementation reports should be attached to give the Audit Committee a feeling for the specific problems faced by Internal Audit. The report should also include a year-by-year comparison, which shows changes in Internal Audit's key figures over time (see Section D, Chapter 7).

Distribution of the Annual Report

Before the annual report to the Audit Committee is distributed, it is submitted to the Board member in charge. The Chairman of the Audit Committee then distributes the report to its members. Internal Audit archives the reports in chronological order. The reports play an important role for peer reviews (see Section D, Chapter 9), because they are a way for Internal Audit to document that it is meeting its reporting obligations. If required, the annual report to the Audit Committee can additionally be distributed to the external auditors. Alternatively, the external auditors may join the Audit Committee meeting during which the report is presented.

HINTS AND TIPS

- All auditors should keep in mind that their work will be included in the annual report to the Audit Committee.

5.4.2 Other GIAS Information Services

KEY POINTS

- The GIAS Letter is used to provide information to the Board and other decision makers; it contains information about Internal Audit activity during the last six months.
- The quarterly benchmarking report looks at selected key figures internally and externally and compares them to the previous year's figures for the purpose of internal control and informing specific areas of the company.
- GIAS@Work is a department-internal summary of the main work results of the last month. It is used within GIAS to exchange information among its employees.

Other Periodic Reports

In addition to the annual report to the Audit Committee, the following media are used at SAP to communicate information about the work of Internal Audit:

- GIAS Letter,
- Benchmarking report (see Section D, Chapter 7), and
- GIAS@Work.

All the above reports are issued periodically. They provide summarized information for specific target groups and thus give a quick overview of the latest events in Internal Audit.

GIAS Letter

The GIAS Letter is published twice a year; it contains summarized information for members of the Board and other decision makers. Apart from the recipients defined in the distribution list, this report may on a case-by-case basis be sent to other organizational units. The GIAS Letter is structured as follows:

- structure, distribution, and number of GIAS team members,
- audits conducted and other services performed, broken down into

  - scheduled audits,
  - ad-hoc audits,
  - safeguarding revenue recognition, and
  - support actions and audits in connection with SOX, each including the most significant audit findings and actions initiated,
- significant Internal Audit projects, and
- other support services provided by Internal Audit.

Benchmarking Report

The GIAS Letter only contains selected key figures. These are reported in much greater detail in the quarterly benchmarking report, which looks at key figures of Internal Audit internally and externally and compares them to the previous year's figures, thus highlighting important developments for ongoing control and planning. Benchmarking is used for the internal control of Internal Audit and to provide information to selected areas of the company (see Section D, Chapter 7).

GIAS@Work

GIAS@Work is used for department-internal communication. Under this banner, a one-page summary provides information on the main work results of each regional team as well as the SOX and the IT team, so that each Internal Audit employee can develop an understanding of the current tasks and results of other regional teams. It allows the department to identify quickly any synergies that can be exploited. At the same time, it provides a department-wide forum where employees can contribute their own results and signal their openness to cooperate with people experiencing the same or similar problems. Published monthly, GIAS@Work is a department-internal paper that must be treated with utmost confidentiality.

6 Follow-Up Phase

6.1 Basics of the Follow-Up Phase

KEY POINTS •••

- The follow-up phase serves to ensure that all recommendations given after the basic audit are implemented by the deadline.
- The follow-up phase breaks down into four sub-phases: status check I, follow-up I, status check II, and follow-up II.
- Different areas of responsibility are distinguished in the overall process.
- In addition to Internal Audit, other parties may be involved in the follow-up process.

Need for Implementing Recommendations

The release of the final audit report marks the conclusion of the basic audit. According to the Audit Roadmap, this is when the follow-up phase begins. The main objective of this phase is to test whether the auditees have actually implemented the recommendations that Internal Audit has made. The recommendations may involve actions that are so urgent that they need to be performed promptly. Other recommendations may only be implemented in the medium to long term. Staff shortages, changes in the organizational structure, or changes to the content of processes that impact the findings and recommendations already made may delay their implementation.

Definition

The follow-up phase is a process with which Internal Audit tests whether the implementation actions the management of the audited area has put in place are adequate and effective, and whether deadlines were met. The findings and recommendations documented in the implementation report (see Section B, Chapter 5.2.3) of the basic audit form the basis for the follow-up phase. These findings may also be based on information provided by external auditors and other parties, such as external consultants, independent experts, attorneys, etc., who may also be involved in the follow-up if necessary. The follow-up process may sometimes result in new fieldwork activities because the follow-up has raised new issues. A follow-up may therefore lead to fieldwork with regard to

- the actions implemented, and
- additional findings identified as a result.

In addition, fieldwork may also result from new independent audit topics that are audited during the follow-up.

Sub-Phases

The follow-up phase has four sub-phases: status check I, follow-up I, status check II and follow-up II. The specific purpose of each sub-phase is explained below (see Section B, Chapter 6.2).

Timeframe for Standard and Escalation Process

As shown in the figure below, the GIAS follow-up process distinguishes between a standard and an escalation process. During the standard process, the status check I (SC I) is performed 6-9 months after the end of the basic audit. Subsequently, the follow-up I (FU I) is conducted 12-15 months after the end of the basic audit and, if necessary, is followed by a status check II (SC II) after 18 to 21 months. The timeframe during an escalation process is tightened as shown in the figure below. Additionally, there is an optional follow-up II (FU II) audit included in this process.

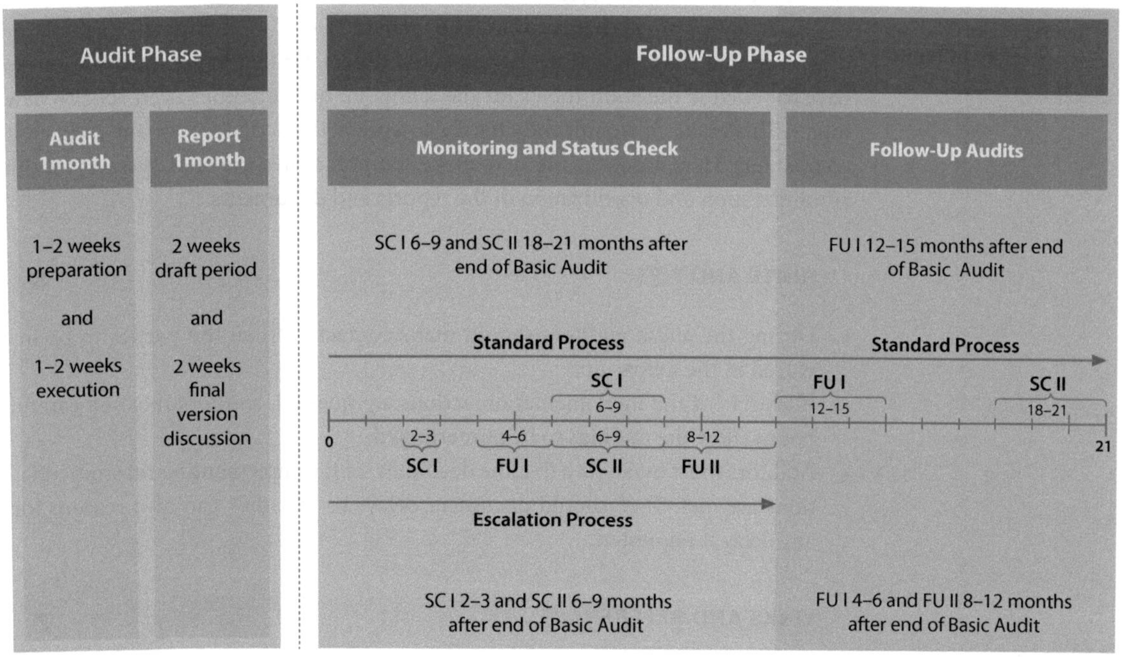

Fig. 23 Sub-Phases of the Follow-Up

Responsibilities

The basic audit is the exclusive responsibility of Internal Audit, but responsibility for the follow-up phase is shared: Management must implement the actions, and management and Internal Audit jointly monitor implementation. However, the follow-up audit is conducted exclusively by Internal Audit.

Involvement of Third Parties

Management has overall responsibility for implementing the recommendations made. The independent status of Internal Audit prohibits internal auditors from interfering with this process. At best, Internal Audit can monitor the actions while they are being implemented or provide consulting support. However, this function can also be performed by departments other than Internal Audit (e.g., Corporate Management Accounting or Corporate Financial Reporting). In such cases, Internal Audit is not, or only marginally, involved in the process.

Implementation Assessment

Internal Audit's next contribution is made when the implementation of the audit recommendations must be assessed from an assurance point of view, because Internal Audit is the only body that can do so objectively and independently. If other parties have been involved in the implementation of actions, the auditors should cooperate and consult with them closely.

Link with the Audit Roadmap

Each sub-phase of the follow-up phase takes place within strictly defined timeframes. The end of the follow-up II marks the end of the Audit Roadmap and thus also of the current audit cycle.

Changes to the Content of Audit Topics

Audit topics often change over time, primarily due to changing processes or organizational changes within the company. Whenever that happens, the auditors have to redefine the audit topics for the follow-up or sometimes even specify new topics. This makes it significantly harder to update the audit history and to keep it comparable. Here it may be useful to make comprehensive use of IT systems for the administration and organization of the reports and documents.

HINTS AND TIPS

- During the audit, auditors should make contact with all the parties to be involved in the follow-up.
- If aspects of the implementation actions are queried, auditors must be careful not to allow the findings to be reinterpreted.
- Auditors must make sure that the deadlines set for implementing recommendations are met. They should document delays so that they can give reasons for any delay if requested.

LINKS AND REFERENCES

- INSTITUTE OF INTERNAL AUDITORS. 2001. *Practice Advisory 2500-1: Monitoring Progress.* Altamonte Springs, FL: The Institute of Internal Auditors.
- INSTITUTE OF INTERNAL AUDITORS. 2001. *Practice Advisory 2500.A1-1: Follow-up Process.* Altamonte Springs, FL: The Institute of Internal Auditors.
- KEATING, G. 1995. The Art of the Follow-Up. *Internal Auditor* (April 1995): 59–62.

6.2 Follow-Up Phase in Detail

6.2.1 Status Check

KEY POINTS

- The status check gives senior management the opportunity to actively participate in the implementation monitoring process.
- The status check is normally performed in conjunction with the employees of the audited area.
- The aim is to receive information on the implementation status as indicated in the implementation report by the managers responsible.

- The status check forms part of the monitoring process and should be used as the basis for a long-term relationship with the audited areas.

Elements of the Status Check

The monitoring of the implementation of audit recommendations, i.e., the status check, is performed separately from the actual follow-up audit (see Section B, Chapter 6.2.2) in order to provide a clear structure and highlight the distinction. At SAP, the monitoring process breaks down into the following steps:

- The management responsible, in conjunction with the audited area, has to continually monitor the progress of implementation actions, based on Internal Audit's recommendations.
- Management enters the result of the monitoring activities in the "Status Local Management" column of the implementation report (see Section B, Chapter 5.2.3).
- The report with the filled column "Status Local Management" is sent to senior management:
  - Senior management must monitor and confirm the actions taken by the responsible management and sends the report to GIAS.
  - GIAS finally creates a status check report and makes an assessment based on "Status Local Management".

Operational Management's Status

The status of operational management can be classified as follows (see Section B, Chapter 5.2.3):

- Open: Recommendation has not yet been implemented.
- In process: The persons responsible have started to implement the recommendation.
- Closed: Implementation of the recommendation has been completed.

The status is not updated by Internal Audit, but by the operational management of the audited area. The background to and knowledge about the status check procedure is communicated to those who were assigned responsibility at the closing meeting of the basic audit (see Section B, Chapter 4.1.1). Another important point is that the "GIAS status" column of the report will not be used and updated during the status check (see Section B, Chapter 5.2.3).

Importance of the Status Check

During the implementation process, operational management ensures that the audited area assigns the appropriate importance to the implementation. The status check is performed by senior management and the risk management department in conjunction with the managers of the audited area. After the status check, there may be further exchanges of information between Internal Audit and the audited area, aimed at clarifying unresolved questions or incorporating changed environment conditions.

HINTS AND TIPS

- Auditors should try to clarify unresolved items directly and without official meetings.

- Auditors should make a note of especially critical points that should be implemented and discuss them with the audit lead.

6.2.2 Follow-Up Audit

KEY POINTS

- A follow-up audit is intended to ensure that all the recommendations from an audit have been implemented.
- It is a specific sequence of selected fieldwork activities.
- The follow-up assesses the implementation status of each recommendation.
- Sometimes, new aspects of a basic audit (new content) can be added to the follow-up.
- A second follow-up audit is scheduled if the first follow-up audit highlights results that do not meet the quality requirements.
- If the necessary implementation is delayed for a prolonged period, the auditors should think about instituting consequences.

Elements of the Follow-Up Audit

The follow-up process is one of the phases of the Audit Roadmap. The first follow-up audit should be scheduled around 12 to 15 months after the end of the basic audit. The following elements are feasible for a follow-up audit:

- follow-up fieldwork on the basis of previous findings and recommendations,
- individual processes or components of a basic audit (depending on the audit topic),
- important issues that the Board or regional/local management have flagged up since the basic audit, and
- other important issues that come to light during follow-up.

Need for the Follow-Up Audit

A follow-up must be conducted for each standard and special audit. Ad-hoc audits may also have follow-up audits. In case of only a few minor findings there is the option to close the audit cycle after status check I. A follow-up audit takes an average of two to three weeks to conduct. If the audit content is expanded, the time it takes to conduct the follow-up audit increases accordingly. The increase in auditing time should be in reasonable proportion to the standard follow-up time, i.e., the time taken should never more than double.

Activities During the Follow-Up Audit

A follow-up audit necessitates the following activities with regard to the findings and the implementation of recommendations:

- recording the actual implementation status of the recommendations on the basis of information or documents submitted by the auditees,
- gathering evidence that implementation has in fact taken place and the new situation is practiced on a day-to-day basis, and
- updating the audit report (see Section B, Chapter 6.3.1).

Internal Audit's Status

The last point of the above list is particularly important during the follow-up audit, where Internal Audit's status can be updated as follows:

- In process: Implementation of the recommendation has not yet been completed.
- Reasonably controlled: Internal Audit has performed a final test.
- Open: Recommendation has not yet been implemented.
- Done: A matter can be resolved conclusively.

Impeded Follow-Up Audit

For various organizational or content-related reasons, Internal Audit may be unable to determine if recommended measures have been implemented as required. Follow-up audits may be impeded by staff being unavailable, new guidelines having been issued, organizational structures having changed, or functions and processes no longer being applicable. In such cases, Internal Audit's status must be interpreted in the light of the latest circumstances in the audited area.

Follow-Up Audit Scenarios

In terms of content, two different scenarios are conceivable for a follow-up audit:

- The implementation report forms the working basis for all follow-up audit activities that result from findings of the basic audit. It thus replaces the work program of the basic audit. Depending on the particular requirements, fieldwork may have to be performed and working papers created. The follow-up audit should also have an opening and a closing meeting.
- If new aspects and issues are added to the follow-up audit, the Audit Roadmap should be applied by analogy to these new elements. This means that a separate work program must be compiled for the new aspects, which are then dealt with as part of a new basic audit conducted at the same time as the follow-up audit. This kind of add-on should, however, remain an exception. In the case of audits that require extensive traveling, there may be economic reasons for adding to the follow-up audit new topics that were not previously part of the basic audit.

Reporting on a Combination of Basic Audit and Follow-Up

Even if elements of basic audit and follow-up audit are combined, they must be presented in separate reports, because a clear distinction between aspects of the follow-up audit and those from the additional basic audit, i.e., between old and new elements, has to be made.

Follow-Up II

If the auditors find out during the follow-up I that the implementation of recommendations and actions is not having the desired success and if the rating of the basic audit was red the escalation process will proceed and after a status check II, the auditors will schedule a follow-up II according to the GIAS escalation process time schedule (see Section D, Chapter 6). The follow-up II deals exclusively with the items still outstanding.

Unsatisfactory Follow-Up

The follow-up II is only conducted if necessary and is therefore optional. If the traffic light status is red (see Section B, Chapter 6.3.2) at the follow-up I, a follow-up II is mandatory. The result of the follow-up II is final and should be reported as such. If the result is unsatisfactory, the Board should reprimand the audited unit. If even the follow-up II leaves issues unresolved, the auditors must decide on the basis of the case in question how to proceed further (see Section D, Chapter 6 on escalation).

Responsibility and Independence

Completion of the entire follow-up phase marks the end of the audit cycle. Internal Audit is responsible for conducting follow-up audits, and normally the team that conducted the basic audit will also perform the follow-up. In some cases, it may, however, make sense to use a different audit team to the one that conducted the basic audit. Likewise, it is possible to use guest auditors (see Section D, Chapter 10). This decision should in particular be made in light of independence considerations, because a different team of auditors means that implementation is not monitored by the same auditors who made the findings.

HINTS AND TIPS

- When preparing for a follow-up audit, auditors should familiarize themselves with changes in circumstances and other influencing factors.
- Auditors must agree any changes to the original audit recommendations with the audit lead.

6.3 Reporting During the Follow-Up Phase

6.3.1 Updating the Audit Report

KEY POINTS

- The results of the follow-up phase must be carefully documented.
- This applies to both the status check I and II and the follow-up I and II.
- The appropriate referencing must be included in the documentation.
- The management summary and the Board summary additionally contain remarks on the quality of the implementation status.

Documenting the Status Check

The results of the status check and the follow-up audit must be recorded carefully in the audit reports, i.e., the audit reports must be updated. First, the result of the status check is documented on the basis of the implementation report (see Section B, Chapter 5.2.3). This is done with a copy of the implementation report used as a template for the status check report. Only management's status is updated in this copy. However, the management summary is not changed. Audit lead and Audit Manager are responsible for distributing the status check report to the audited unit and operational management, the senior managers concerned, and the relevant members of the Board.

Documenting the Follow-Up Audit

The actual follow-up audit report plays a different role, as shown in the diagram below. The auditors should show a clear link to the previous reports by completing a separate reference column, where they enter the reference to findings made in previous reports. At the same time, the auditors should update the status of the findings transferred from previous reports. They can also include new findings in the report, initially without reference. In the management summary and the Board summary, the status of findings is shown in a separate column. Also note that the follow-up status is reported to the Board in a report template specifically developed for this purpose.

Global Internal Audit Services *Conducted in Accordance with the International Standards for the Professional Practice of Internal Auditing.*										
Audit Implementation Report No.: xx/200x						Organizational unit:				
Audit Status:			First Follow-up Audit			Auditor(s):				
Audit Items						Monitoring				
No.	ref. Report no. ref. Item	Clas-sifica-tion	Observation/Finding	Risk Cate-gory	Recom-mendation	Action/ Management Responses	Respon-sible	Com-pletion date	Status Local Manage-ment	Status GIAS
1			Description: Risk condition: Risk consequence:							
2			Description: Risk condition: Risk consequence:							
3			Description: Risk condition: Risk consequence:							

Fig. 24 Follow-Up Report Template

Documenting a New Basic Audit

In the case of a new basic audit, any unresolved findings are entered in advance in the new basic audit report. The auditors must point out that these findings come from an earlier audit cycle and that the recommended actions have not yet been implemented. Even if, because of extraordinary circumstances, the second basic audit immediately follows the status check and without first conducting a follow-up audit, the transfer of the unresolved findings must be clearly documented. Each finding must be documented without any gaps until successful remediation of the finding can be demonstrated.

HINTS AND TIPS

- Auditors should ensure that statements contained in earlier reports do not conflict with the current documentation.
- Auditors should always report to the management in charge and the Board when the status of significant findings and implementation actions has been updated.

6.3.2 Measuring Audit Outcome

KEY POINTS

- To guarantee that the results of the follow-up are reported accurately and clearly, an assessment and rating is produced for each finding, and thus for each report. This supports implementation monitoring.
- It is a prerequisite that the B, R, and L classification is maintained and the follow-up status is carefully and regularly updated.
- The rating of each finding produces an overall result and an overall rating for each follow-up report.
- The results are also presented in a traffic light system, indicating the status as green, yellow, or red.
- The rating of the results can also be used for benchmarking and trend analysis, which provides information on how those responsible have gone about implementing Internal Audit's recommendations.

Need for Measuring Success

To emphasize the importance of the follow-up phase, it is necessary to make the outcome of each of its sub-phases measurable and display it in diagrams or tables. If the implementation measures are clearly and transparently rated and visualized in a format that is easy to follow, it is easier for Internal Audit and the auditees to analyze the results of the follow-up phase.

Rating the Follow-Up

Rating the follow-up means:

- The status of the follow-up must be clearly defined.
- Each follow-up report is subject to a full rating process (see Section D, Chapter 7.2.3).
- Each finding in the follow-up report is therefore ranked according to an individual assessment and weighting.
- The B, R, and L classifications (see Section B, Chapter 5.2.2) are an important basis for determining the follow-up rating (see Section D, Chapter 7.2.3).

In the follow-up, the efficiency of the implementation process is measured while the overall audit statement for the basic audit shows the number and significance of audit findings in terms of content.

Monitoring Function of the Rating

The results of the follow-up and the respective follow-up rating support the monitoring process of the implementation. This monitoring function is an integral part of the follow-up phase. Reporting provides evidence of the implementation actions and thus ensures Internal Audit's own protection, because it ultimately demonstrates the success of the audit cycle. If a follow-up identifies completely new audit findings, they will be included in the assessment and benchmarking of the follow-up process.

Monitoring Result

Consistent, stringent monitoring ensures that:

- the sustainability of Internal Audit's recommendations is explained to those responsible,
- follow-ups can be measured and compared, thus making the overall success of the audit cycle measurable, and that
- all the people responsible, including management and the Board, are involved in the follow-up process.

Traffic-Light System

In the management summary and the Board summary the follow-up result is rated with a traffic light system of green, yellow, or red (for details of the rating, see Section D, Chapter 7.2.3). If the status is "red," explanatory comments must be added.

Updating and Adapting the Reports

Auditors maintain each report carefully and update it regularly to ensure that all items are included in the overall follow-up rating. Audit lead and Audit Manager are responsible for entering the relevant traffic light status in the reports.

Higher-Level Performance Measurement

The key indicators from the follow-up phase also form part of a higher-level performance measurement process for Internal Audit (see Section D, Chapter 7), where they constitute one of the key variables (average implementation rating), thus making a significant contribution to determining the effectiveness of the internal audit department. When this rating is benchmarked between different departments and against internal audit departments in other companies and analyzed over several years, it produces trend information on changes in the quality of audit implementation.

Quality Gates

The traffic light system for monitoring the follow-up process is a process-based quality control of the implementation process. All stages of the follow-up are of course subject to the same formal quality criteria as those of the basic audit, i.e., work progress is checked and approved on the basis of each quality gate (see Section D, Chapter 5).

HINTS AND TIPS

- Sometimes it may be necessary to clarify whether measures can realistically be implemented, or whether the necessary prerequisites are verifiably not in place.
- Information on slow implementation or reasons for delays should be documented in the working papers.

7 Special Audit Roadmaps

7.1 Objectives of Special Audit Roadmaps

KEY POINTS •••

- The Audit Roadmap is a framework that can be adapted to define modified procedures.
- These include further development of the standard Audit Roadmap and highlighting individual process models.
- There are many different reasons for special Audit Roadmaps: Increasingly complex topics, use of IT, different target groups, blurring of audit categories, standardization of alternative services, and modular breakdown of the services provided by Internal Audit.

Reasons for Special Audit Roadmaps

The ongoing development of the Audit Roadmap, which has to incorporate the topics presented in Section D, is one of the main long-term objectives of Internal Audit at SAP. This helps guarantee compliance with the auditing standards and the security of Internal Audit's own process and control checks under SOX. For a number of important audit topics, the standard Audit Roadmap only provides a framework of basic methods and techniques, in spite of its complexity. Elements of content and other influences, such as the regional aspects of an audit or the procedures that result from the relevant audit fields, make having additional or adapted Audit Roadmaps seem a good idea. The reasons are as follows:

Increasing Complexity of Topics

- The increasing complexity of topics often calls for specific question catalogs, testing procedures, and working papers. The resulting specialization moreover often entails additional audit steps or the involvement of external experts, which in turn require more consultation and documentation.

Use of Information Technology

- The growing use of IT and the increasing networking of modern communications have led to modified audit methods being used. However, for certain audit topics, confidentiality requirements allow for certain types of meetings, such as telephone or video conferences, only if additional non-disclosure declarations and security arrangements are in place.

Different Target Groups

- The rising number of different target groups (e.g., the Disclosure Committee, compliance departments) of an internal audit department also makes it necessary to use non-typical audit procedures. Examples include additional preliminary meetings, international consultation (e.g., with regard to international security standards), and special reporting requirements that take cultural aspects and interdisciplinary contacts into account.

Blurring of Audit Categories

- The increasing differentiation between local, regional, and global audits on the one hand, combined with the need to standardize these audits on the other, requires interfaces and consultation mechanisms to be defined among all employees involved. The different audit categories will have an increasingly diverse mix of topics in the future, making it ever more difficult to assign a specific audit to one category or another.

- **Range of Services** The different services that an internal audit department will offer in the future may require that some procedures are modified. To this end, special Audit Roadmaps for pre-investigations, reviews, and audit-related implementation support may conceivably be used; at their various stages they will require the use of specific procedures. For example, cataloguing the measures to be performed is an important aspect of reviews. Special procedures also have to be defined for the non-audit related services of Internal Audit. This may lead to overlap, as well as additions and interfaces with regard to other process models, e.g., the audit process model. However, as part of this process, the audit-specific content of the Audit Roadmap is not being subsumed into the process models of other corporate units, such as Risk Management. The dualism of the independence of the audit process and its integration into other procedure-based models is a major challenge of future process structures in audit-related areas.
- **Modular Breakdown** A certain amount of development time will still be necessary before Internal Audit's service profiles can be generalized for external use, but initial signs can be identified already. An important prerequisite is to break the Audit Roadmap down into modules. It would, for example, be possible to produce an internal and external audit service catalog of Internal Audit under which service packages are provided for planning, execution, and reporting in different legal systems, sectors of the economy, and industries. The Audit Roadmap is thus used as a structure to process specific audit content on an individual and sound scientific basis. This allows auditors to incorporate audit requirements, procedures, and responsibilities that are common in the sector, demanded by industry associations, or necessary in terms of security. The next step would be to create comprehensive service catalogs specific to each phase, which would also support a billing system for the services provided. This would create the prerequisites for Internal Audit to be structured and managed as a legally and/or commercially separate entity.

Development Perspectives The above reasons for developing special Audit Roadmaps explain that Internal Audit is turning into a service department and can thus meet different objectives and serve different target groups. They highlight long-term development perspectives, especially since issues such as compliance, process effectiveness, and safeguarding of internal controls are increasingly important in the international arena.

HINTS AND TIPS

- Auditors should discuss specific requirements on the Audit Roadmap with other team members and the Audit Manager.
- Auditors should analyze any existing Audit Roadmaps and use them for ideas so that they can define their own individual Audit Roadmaps when necessary.
- To this end, auditors should make a note of all noteworthy elements that could generally be used as criteria for individual Audit Roadmaps.

7.2 Audit Roadmap for Fraud Audits

KEY POINTS •••

- In the fraud audit field, a global audit department must respond reactively with ad-hoc audits and proactively with preventive audits.
- The Scope is based on processes and process weaknesses as well as fraud-related and compliance-related matters.
- Experience from SOX audits and fraud audits are incorporated in Internal Audit's risk-based annual audit planning.
- The preparation and execution of a fraud audit involves comprehensive fact gathering, which must identify and assess all aspects.
- The reports are based on the importance and impact of the fraud case and the need for a follow-up.

Fraud Audit Roadmap

The procedure for fraud audits differs from that used for other audits, which means that a special Audit Roadmap for fraud should be applied (for details on how Internal Audit handles fraud, see Section D, Chapter 13). Its content is different from the standard Audit Roadmap, because fraud audits require special preparation and focus on different views and work aspects. For ad-hoc fraud audits, it is necessary to gather detailed information within as short a period of time as possible. The information is usually substantially augmented by carrying out background research to shed light on and assess the situation. The rest of this chapter shows in detail for each phase what the standard Audit Roadmap and the Audit Roadmap for fraud audits have in common and where they differ.

Scope

Similar to the standard Audit Roadmap, the planning phase comprises the Scopes, audit planning, and, if applicable, the audit request. The Core Scope for fraud includes the Key Scopes defined for this audit field (see Section D, Chapter 13) which reflect the risk areas defined for fraud. They are also based on matters relevant under criminal and compliance law. The Key Scopes are the starting point for case-specific fraud audits and for the creation of individual work programs. They also form the basis for process-oriented preventive audits. The contents of the Scopes break down into internally committed fraud (fraud committed by employees) and externally committed fraud (fraud committed by third parties).

Annual Audit Planning

Audit topics connected with possible fraudulent activities are considered in the annual audit planning process (see Section D, Chapter 3). In line with the Audit Roadmap for fraud, the audit team responsible internally collects and assesses cases of fraud that have occurred in the course of the year. Sources may include the results of ad-hoc audits, weak-point analyses, SOX audits, and standard audits.

Annual Audit Planning: Preventive Audits

In addition, specific preventive audits (primarily process and transaction audits) may be included in the annual audit plan. Internal Audit may also receive reports of cases from various corporate units, such as the legal department, employee representatives, or the compliance department; these cases may also be turned into possible audit topics.

Audit Request

Ad-hoc audits are triggered by audit requests (see Section B, Chapter 2.3). When the request has been assessed by the relevant Audit Manager and discussed with the CAE, a case-specific ad-hoc audit or a preventive audit may be scheduled if appropriate. Such audits are immediately added to the execution planning.

Collecting Information During the Preparation Phase

During the preparation phase, Internal Audit must gather as much information as possible about the fraud case. If the fraud has been reported anonymously, this information must be analyzed with special care. Additional information may be obtained by using internal IT systems or questioning other employees: When investigating an anonymously reported case of fraudulent travel expenses, for example, Internal Audit can go through relevant data and documents in advance and obtain information about the accused employee by asking specific questions. In the best case, the allegation can be refuted by presenting the facts. However, if that is not possible, the auditors must take further steps, all of which have to be documented in a work program.

Work Program

The work program must be tailored to the situation in question and must be adaptable to all possible scenarios. Sometimes the main focus is on questioning employees, but at other times the auditors perform analyses in the internal systems. The work program should not be limited to the facts that are known already, but allow the auditors to take any action that gives them as comprehensive an overview of the situation as possible. New facts may cause the focus to shift at any time during the audit. Auditors may only draw conclusions after the completion of audit activities, once they have exhausted all ways of obtaining information. Here it may happen that detailed analysis of certain transactions reveals that no further action needs to be taken.

Other Preparations

Auditors should familiarize themselves with the facts of the matter during the preparation phase. They should compile question catalogs as preparation for interviews. The interviews will vary case by case and should therefore be newly prepared for each audit, although question catalogs from previous audits can be used for guidance. The auditors also should develop a strategy as to how and when to contact certain people and establish to what extent they can disclose the content of the audit, and whether some interviews must be coordinated with Human Resources and the legal department. They should always discuss these steps in advance in the audit team and with the Audit Manager concerned. A good way to prepare is therefore to hold a constructive meeting to gather and coordinate ideas in the audit team.

Audit Execution

The objective of audit execution is to gather facts, e.g., through interviews, system analysis, collecting background information, etc. Auditors can use internal and, as far as accessible, external systems for this purpose, either to collect data or to process data for analysis. It is important to make an accurate record in the working papers of the data analyzed and the results produced. The following are the main differences from a normal audit:

- Special data protection requirements must be observed.
- Since the matter is sensitive, the audit often has to be conducted covertly and the documentation adapted accordingly, including documents that may be used in a court of law.
- The entire audit must be conducted with the awareness that the results may have to be made available to external parties, such as the courts or the district attorney.
- There are uncertainties regarding the execution, outcome, and consequences of the audit, which may influence the behavior of individual auditors.

Detailed Documentation Detailed documentation supports the strength of the evidence provided by the audit results. To this end, the auditors should include as much individual data as possible and accurately trace the transaction history in order to prove any irregularities. In the case of posting a supplier invoice, for example, this includes:

- receipt of invoice,
- preliminary posting of document,
- invoice approval (date, name of authorizing employee),
- posting of invoice (accounts, posting text, posting date),
- release for payment (date, name of authorizing employee),
- payment (bank accounts, date), and
- archiving of supplier invoice (date, name of archiving employee).

Processes and Controls Audit execution also serves to find out whether further damage has been done or could be done in the future. Fraud audits therefore include recording the processes since most cases of fraud are possible only because the controls are weak or nonexistent. The combination of individual, normally person-related, one-time audits with process audits causes the elements of the traditional audit to mix with the special aspects of the fraud audit: The objective is to measure the extent of the damage and to build and strengthen the processes and controls.

Reporting Reports on fraud audits may be varied, depending on the type of fraud audit and the ensuing consequences. In the case of ad-hoc audits, the situation is presented in a memorandum, and the findings and relevant recommendations are embedded in an implementation report. The report format for preventive audits is the standard report package.

Follow-Up The follow-up process is the same as in the standard Audit Roadmap. However, in some cases of fraud audits, the follow-up must be conducted earlier or immediately after the report has been presented. This happens in cases, for example, where the auditors must ensure that the accounts are corrected immediately. Moreover, if measures by the human resources department are necessary, it may be important for Internal Audit to find out what measures have been taken. This may be important for reporting the matter immediately to the Board and for complying with deadlines or reporting requirements set by labor law. If a fraud audit has identified an immediate danger to the company, emergency measures may have to be introduced, which in turn must be tested immediately by Internal Audit.

HINTS AND TIPS

- Auditors always have to approach the situation to be investigated from an impartial angle.
- They should include all eventualities in their investigation.
- It is better to test something superfluously than to overlook something.

LINKS AND REFERENCES

- INSTITUTE OF INTERNAL AUDITORS. 2001. *Practice Advisory 1210.A2-1: Auditor's Responsibilities Relating to Fraud Risk Assessment, Prevention, and Detection.* Altamonte Springs, FL: The Institute of Internal Auditors.
- INSTITUTE OF INTERNAL AUDITORS. 2001. *Practice Advisory 1210.A2-2: Auditor's Responsibilities Relating to Fraud Investigation, Reporting, Resolution, and Communication.* Altamonte Springs, FL: The Institute of Internal Auditors.
- MCCONNELL, J., K. DONALD, AND G. BANKS. 1997. The New Fraud Audit Standard. *CPA Journal* (June 1997): 22–29.
- NYABUTO, S., AND B. MIIA. 2007. Intelligent Fraud Fighting. *Internal Auditor* (February 2007): 45–50.
- MOYES, G., P. LIN, AND R. LANDRY. 2005. Raise the Red Flag. *Internal Auditor* (October 2005): 47–51.
- ZWIRN, E. 2005. Sound Skepticism. *Internal Auditor* (February 2005): 73–77.

7.3 Audit Roadmap for Management Process Audits

KEY POINTS

- For management process audits, the standard Audit Roadmap should be adapted.
- Appropriate procedures and documents should be used to reconcile target group specific features to the methods and procedures of the standard Audit Roadmap.
- Important modifications and additions include the description of the Key Scopes, condensed documentation of audit objectives and process for management, special guidelines for execution, a modified reporting system, and a personal feedback discussion.
- In the future, international practices and requirements will have a particularly strong influence on audit procedures in the area of management process audits.

Reasons for the Modified Audit Roadmap Management process audits (see Section A, Chapter 6.2.2 and Section C, Chapter 5.4) are becoming increasingly important. A major reason for this is that the work of managers is becoming more and more the focus of external control and due care requirements. For Internal Audit, this results in the need to provide a clear definition of fieldwork in this audit field. In addition to creating a dedicated Scope, it helps to have in place a modified version of the procedural audit model, the Audit Roadmap. This modification gains in importance, complexity, and dynamics when the auditors look at management-specific interests at different management levels.

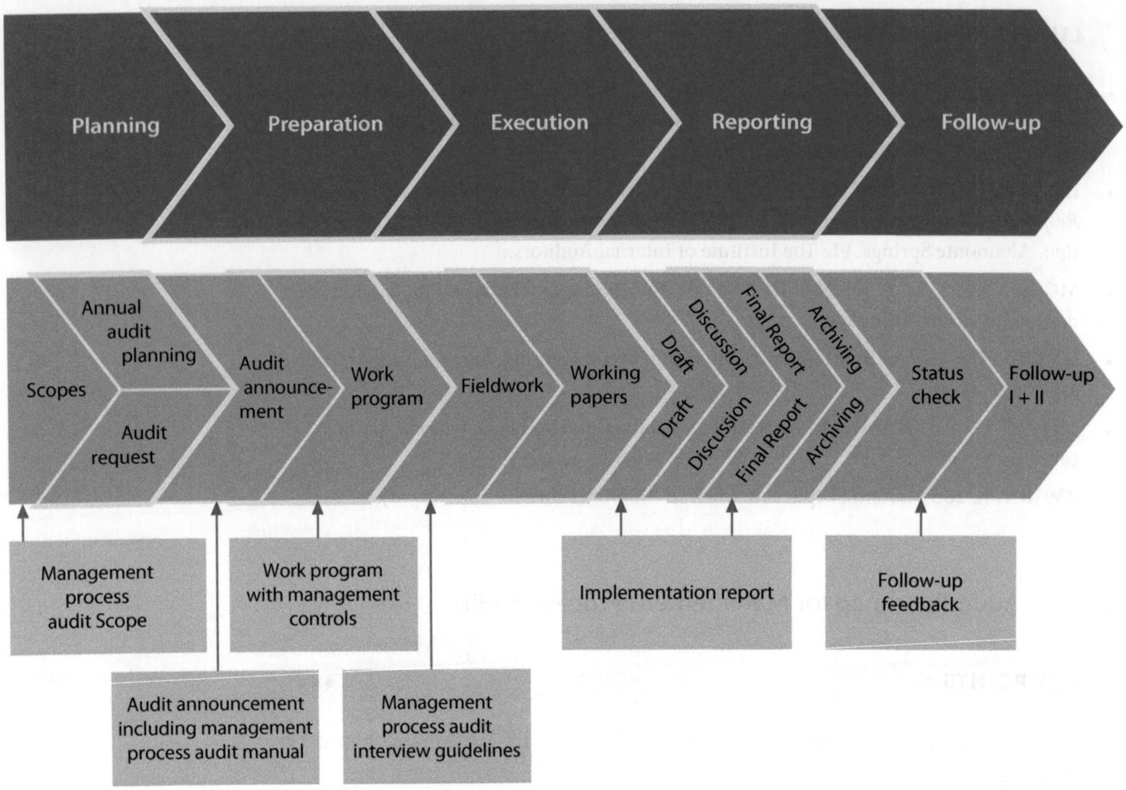

Fig. 25 Audit Roadmap for Management Process Audits

Main Features The familiar structure of the Audit Roadmap is not substantially changed for management process audits: The phases remain intact, and most of the sub-phases also occur. Still, it is advisable to adapt or expand certain procedures specifically for this audit field. More detailed analysis of the Audit Roadmap intended for this purpose reveals the following specific features:

- **Responsibilities** When describing the audit segments as detailed content, i.e., the individual Key Scopes, the auditors should pay particular attention to the responsibilities laid out e.g. in the management engagement model with its respective components (finance, compliance, operations, human resources). Here it may be an advantage to ask the manager concerned to confirm the responsibilities in writing after the auditors have discussed them with the manager.
- **Information for the Manager Concerned** In combination with the audit announcement, the managers concerned should be given a condensed document about the objectives, background, and execution of management process audits. This imparts knowledge and supports an open and constructive basis of trust.
- **Other Documented Control Systems** The work program also focuses on management controls. Here it is a good idea to create a link to other documented control systems, such as controls implemented under SOX, and to refer to them as appropriate.
- **Special Guidelines** For the execution of the audit, guidelines and question catalogs should be created that take detailed account of the social and personal components of this type of audit. This is to ensure that the relevant fieldwork activities, such as interviews with management, keep within a formal framework.
- **Further-Reaching Report Formats** When it comes to reporting, it is useful to provide further-reaching report formats. Reports for management are normally structured in stages, ranging from general to detailed views. Portfolio analysis, key indicator reports, and trend calculations are suitable for this type of presentation because they can be used to drill down to the level of individual findings and the underlying reasons. It is also possible to compile management audit reports even without separate recommendations for each finding depending on the management level and the significance of individual findings. The point of departure may be the overall audit statement for the management process audit, so that it can either be compared with other audits or a correlation can be established with the audit results of the other organizational units assigned to this manager.
- **Recommendations** Sometimes the auditee in a management process audit may be deemed responsible for suggesting the necessary recommendations and implementation steps for the findings and observations made during the audit.
- **Feedback During Follow-Up** Another feature of management process audits is that management can give feedback during the follow-up. To this end, Internal Audit should schedule a separate discussion that allows the manager to comment personally and in confidence on the audit results and give his or her opinion on the audit and its value added. It generally makes sense to conduct this dialog only between the manager and the audit lead.

Other Adjustments Depending on the management process audit concerned, it is up to Internal Audit to make specific additions to the above modifications of the Audit Roadmap. In the case of international management process audits, it remains to be seen to what extent such audits can also be conducted for responsibilities that span several countries. This could result in further adjustments, e.g., the inclusion of special interview techniques. In this context, Internal Audit must take cultural aspects into account because not all managers may regard it as their duty to give auditors from other countries or cultural groups information about their area of responsibility.

HINTS AND TIPS

- The planning of a management process audit should be based on the special Audit Roadmap as far as possible. Auditors should discuss the Roadmap in advance with the auditee.
- Auditors should suggest their own solutions for developing the modified Audit Roadmap further and discuss them with the audit lead.
- Auditors should also document their experiences with management process audits as an addition to the relevant templates.

LINKS AND REFERENCES

- TOROK, R. AND P. CORDON. 1997. *Operational Profitability: Conducting Management Audits.* Hoboken, NJ: Wiley & Sons.

7.4 Audit Roadmap for IT Audits

KEY POINTS

- For companies that rely heavily on information technology, the demands on IT systems, and IT security in particular, are of critical importance because they determine whether business success can be secured.
- The complexity in the area of information technology requires suitable audit activities.
- With the help of a documented security guideline, Internal Audit can quickly get an overview of the current status of IT security in the company.

Demands on IT Systems and Security

For organizations that rely to a great extent on information-technology, e.g. companies that use an enterprise system like SAP, the demands on IT systems, and IT security in particular, are of critical importance because business success depends on them. In order to meet basic business requirements, such a company must:

- ensure the integrity of the data stored in its computer systems,
- protect the confidentiality of sensitive data,
- guarantee that the information systems are always available, and
- comply with the relevant laws, regulations, and standards.

Definition of the Content of the Audit Object

Internal Audit must evaluate in IT audits whether the existing level of security meets the company's business requirements in terms of securing information against unauthorized use, disclosure, change, and accidental or malicious loss or damage.

Basis of the IT Scope

COBIT® is used as the basis for the IT Scope, because it covers almost all internationally recognized standards and recommendations. COBIT® is a model of generally applicable and internationally accepted IT process-related control objectives. It is used to guarantee that information technology is reliably applied. The framework has been developed for this purpose by the international Information Systems Audit and Control Association (ISACA).

Information Criteria under COBIT®

There are three categories into which the seven information criteria defined by COBIT® can be classified:

- IT quality control, which is determined by effectiveness and efficiency,
- IT security control, which is determined by confidentiality, integrity, and availability, and
- fiduciary control of IT, which is determined by reliability and compliance with legal requirements.

Audit Topics

Like all operating resources, IT resources must be planned, developed, implemented, operated, and monitored. The following four domains, i.e.,

- Plan and Organize,
- Acquire and Implement,
- Deliver and Support, and
- Monitor and Evaluate,

provide the basis for the audit topics of the IT and IT security audit field (see Section A, Chapter 6.2.5). COBIT® provides detailed guidance on processes within each of these domains. Each of the processes are linked to the basic business requirements for data: integrity, confidentiality, availability and compliance.

Audit Planning

Adequate planning is the first step necessary in the execution of an effective IT audit. Internal Audit should perform an overall risk assessment and then develop the annual audit plan, which contains the audit objectives and the actions required to meet these objectives (see Section D, Chapter 3). The Scopes relevant for the IT audit field must be described in detail. They form the basis for the design of IT work programs. The IT area may also require ad-hoc audits, e.g. with regard to urgent issues relating to access authorization and document security.

Audit Preparation

The procedure for testing internal controls is defined during audit preparation. The appropriate contact person(s) in the areas to be audited should also be determined, as well as the auditor's necessary technical skills and the resources required to meet the audit objective. For complex technical aspects, it may be sensible to use experts (e.g., database specialists) as guest auditors for support, e.g., during data analysis. The audit lead is responsible for coordinating the employees involved in the audit and must ensure that the audit objectives are met and the audit complies with all relevant standards.

Work Program

In addition to system analysis, organizational aspects are also evaluated during IT audits. Although following a specific sequence of procedures is not mandatory in IT audits, IT auditors will normally base their actions on a structured work program in order to understand the audit object and be able to assess and test the relevant control structures. The following are examples of what can be included in a work program for IT security:

- The design, implementation, and monitoring of access controls should be assessed to ensure the integrity, confidentiality, and availability of information.
- The security of the network infrastructure should also be evaluated to guarantee the integrity, confidentiality, availability, and authorized use of the network and the transmitted information.
- To avoid or minimize loss of information, it is important to assess the design, implementation, and monitoring of the control environment.
- Physical access controls should also be assessed to ensure that the level of protection for information and installations is adequate for meeting the company's business targets.

Audit Execution and Documentation

Audit execution is based on a work program. To obtain an initial overview, the auditors should use information sources relating to the execution of tests or documentation, such as flowcharts, guidelines, standards, and working papers from past audits. With the help of a documented security guideline, the auditors are able to record the current status of IT security in the company.

Reliability of Audit Documents

Although auditors can draw conclusions from any form of suitable evidence, some documents are more reliable than others. Factors that determine how to assess the reliability of audit documents include:

- Objectivity of the evidence: Objective evidence is more credible than evidence that requires subjective judgment. A system analysis carried out by the IT auditor is an example for objective evidence. Information that is based on discussions with certain employees requires subjective interpretation.
- Personal qualifications: Regardless of whether the information or documentary evidence is supplied by a company employee or a third party, IT auditors should always take the qualifications of the person concerned into consideration. This could apply also to IT auditors themselves, since test results are only reliable if the IT auditors have properly understood the test or control.

Communication of Audit Findings

Before communicating the audit results to the managers in charge, findings should be discussed with the employees of the audited area. Such a meeting should be aimed at obtaining the employees' agreement with the findings and their commitment to implement the recommendations. The weaknesses and potential areas for improvement identified should be appropriately documented and backed up with system analyses in order to avoid any disagreement.

Follow-Up Process

The follow-up for IT audits is not materially different from the standard procedure (see Section B, Chapter 6). Auditing the implementation of the recommendations relating to organizational processes sometimes requires substantial fieldwork. The implementation of system recommendations, on the other hand, is relatively easy to verify by analyzing the relevant settings. Especially for security-relevant system settings, which require immediate realization of the recommended modifications, the current status can be established quickly with a simple system analysis.

HINTS AND TIPS

- System analyses are more objective and thus more suitable for use as audit evidence than information obtained through interviews.
- Use internationally recognized guidelines for IT audits, such as COBIT®, to structure the work program.

LINKS AND REFERENCES

- INSTITUTE OF INTERNAL AUDITORS. 2005. *Global Technology Audit Guide 1: Information Technology Controls.* Altamonte Springs, FL: The Institute of Internal Auditors.
- IT GOVERNANCE INSTITUTE. 2007. *COBIT 4.1.* Rolling Meadows, IL: IT Governance Institute.
- OLIPHANT, A. 2004. *Auditing IT Infrastructures.* Mission Viejo, CA: Pleier Corporation.

C Examples from Audit Practice at SAP

1 Introduction

Structure and Content of Section C

Section C of this handbook provides practical examples of internal audit work at SAP. Chapter C.2 presents audit basics. Chapters C.3 and C.4 provide selected examples of financial and operational audits while Chapter C.5 gives details of combined audit topics. Chapters C.6 through C.9 deal with selected topics specific to SAP, and Chapter C.10 describes IT audits.

Selected Topics

The audit topics and examples presented in this section are not intended to represent the complete audit universe. They are a selection from the large number of tasks handled by Internal Audit at SAP. The selection is intended to cover traditional audit topics, while providing an insight into the company-specific realm of internal auditing. Further, the chapters provide specific information regarding the processes and accounting transactions that the internal auditors would review during a typical audit.

Fictitious Data

All practice-based examples given in the following chapters, including the figures quoted, are fictitious and are in no way related to real company data, figures, or information of SAP, its (local) subsidiaries, or other companies that have dealings with SAP.

Financial Reporting at SAP

SAP is listed on the NYSE, which means that SAP is subject to SEC oversight. The company therefore has an obligation to prepare consolidated financial statements in accordance with U.S. Generally Accepted Accounting Principles (US-GAAP) and SOX requirements. SAP's local subsidiaries prepare their financial statements according to US-GAAP based accounting guidelines. SAP AG and its local subsidiaries in the various countries recognize and report individual transactions between reporting dates (in the SAP system in periods 1-12 for the months January through December) uniformly in compliance with US-GAAP. Period 13 is used for year-end entries. The values carried forward to the new fiscal year are based on the closing US-GAAP balance sheet from period 13. Since January 1, 2007, the consolidated financial statements are additionally being prepared according to IFRS.

Relevant Accounting Principles

In the following chapters, the relevant financial reporting standards used will not be explicitly stated, because the focus is on the auditing procedure rather than on specific aspects of financial reporting. In some cases, we give details of the relevant US-GAAP rules in order to enhance understanding of the auditing procedure. The examples are based on US-GAAP and follow SAP's accounting guidelines.

Reports in the SAP System

GIAS uses the reports in the SAP system in all internal audits. Similar to other companies, SAP's auditors sometimes use application-based, SAP-specific reports and information, which is stored in the system. This section, however, does not explicitly deal with the various reports and paths in the SAP system.

LINKS AND REFERENCES ↗

- JARNAGIN, B. D. 2007. *US Master GAAP Guide*. Riverwoods, IL: CCH, Inc.
- NEW YORK STOCK EXCHANGE. 2003. *Final NYSE Corporate Governance Rules*. http://www.nyse.com/pdfs/finalcorpgovrules.pdf (accessed May 31, 2007).
- U.S. CONGRESS. 2002. *Sarbanes-Oxley Act of 2002. 107th Congress of the United States of America. HR 3763*. Washington DC: Government Printing Office.

2 Audit Basics

2.1 Overview of the Audit Process

KEY POINTS

- Before the start of standard and special audits listed in the annual audit plan, Internal Audit should send out audit announcements to the auditees.
- The work program is compiled with due consideration for the objectives of the audit.
- An opening meeting with the auditees is conducted before the fieldwork begins. A closing meeting is held after fieldwork is complete to review the results of the audit fieldwork.
- The audit report contains information on the objective, extent, and results of the audit.
- During the follow-up phase, Internal Audit checks whether the audit recommendations have been implemented.

Audit Roadmap

Internal Audit's audit work can be divided into five main phases according to the Audit Roadmap (for details, see Section B). The practical examples of internal audits at SAP are presented in the following chapters using the phases of the Audit Roadmap. However, since the planning phase is a process independent of the actual audits, it is discussed separately in Section B, Chapter 2 and Section D, Chapter 3. This chapter briefly explains selected aspects of the Audit Roadmap before providing an overview of the general basis of practical audit work at SAP (see Section C, Chapters 2.2 through 2.4).

Audit Announcement

Auditees are provided sufficient advance notice before the start of any standard or special audit listed in the annual audit plan (see Section B, Chapters 2.2 and 3.1). Ad-hoc audits generally become necessary due to sudden events or audit requests and must be investigated immediately (see Section B, Chapter 2.3). Therefore, ad-hoc audits are not scheduled in advance and usually no announcements are made before they begin.

Audit Objective

Before auditors can prepare for and conduct an audit, they must correctly and fully understand the topic and objective of the audit. For standard and special audits listed in the annual plan, the objective is defined in the audit announcement. For ad-hoc audits, the audit objective is usually defined in the audit request.

Time and Audit Steps

Before the start of fieldwork, Internal Audit sets the timeframe for the audit, selects the audit team and identifies the audit steps necessary to achieve the objectives of the audit. These audit steps are described in the audit work program.

Work Program

The work program is created within the existing framework (see Section B, Chapter 3.2). It includes the audit content and the specific audit steps necessary to ensure the internal audit team can meet the objectives of the audit.

Consultation with the Auditees

Before beginning the audit, Internal Audit should consult with the auditees to ensure that the employees responsible for the audit area will be available for interviews and the relevant working documents will be provided during the audit. Internal Audit should prepare a list of required information and documents for the audit and provide this list to the auditees ahead of time so that they may assemble the items. This facilitates the timely completion of the audit engagement.

System Authorization

The next step during audit preparation is to ensure that the auditors have all the necessary system authorizations to avoid time-consuming problems, which can significantly hamper audit execution.

Fieldwork

In simplified terms, fieldwork follows this sequence:

- opening meeting;
- audit execution on site:
  - analysis of the current condition of the processes and structures to be audited,
  - in-depth analysis of individual facts,
  - identification and definition of potential improvements,
  - agreement on the audit findings and recommendations with the employees responsible,
- closing meeting.

Opening Meeting

At the opening meeting, the internal audit team members introduce themselves and the internal audit department to the auditees and provide information about the audit process, explaining the main aspects of the audit objectives, content, and procedure. The management of the division being audited should be given the opportunity to contribute their own ideas and suggestions. Overall, this meeting should be used to create a basis of trust among those involved, especially the employees concerned.

Audit Execution

After the opening meeting, the various audit steps are taken as described in the work program. During fieldwork, the auditors collect and review relevant company policies, standards, guidelines, and similar documents, including rules of procedure, organization charts, process documentation, project definitions, and strategic and operational planning papers. The auditors should compare the existing condition of the audited unit to these criteria. The auditors derive various recommendations and improvement suggestions from this analysis if they have identified any weaknesses or opportunities for improvement.

Working Papers

The audit steps, observations, findings, and recommendations are documented in the audit working papers. The working papers also include any relevant documentation obtained throughout the course of the audit. Working papers must be accurately referenced and cross-referenced as necessary, such that an audit reviewer can easily navigate through the papers and understand the basis for the audit findings and recommendations (see Section B, Chapter 4.2.3).

Consultation

The results of the process analysis and the proposed improvements should be discussed with management first. Then the employees responsible for implementing the recommendations must agree to them. The internal auditors must have sufficient communication skills to convey the recommendations and their objectives such that they will be understood and carried out effectively. The audited unit should accept responsibility for and implement the recommendations. Finally, the auditees must agree to a plan to implement the recommendations (including a time frame for implementation).

Closing Meeting

A closing meeting takes place at the end of the audit. At this meeting, auditors discuss their observations, findings, and recommendations with those responsible in the audited unit.

Audit Report

The audit report, which is prepared after the audit, contains information on the objectives and extent of the audit, the audit results, the auditors' recommendations and the agreed measures (see Section B, Chapter 5). A draft report is sent to management of the audited unit for comment. Then the final version of the report is distributed according to the distribution list. The Audit Committee may receive the entire audit report or an executive summary of important findings.

Follow-Up

After the audit is completed, the internal audit team should perform a follow-up audit to ensure that agreed improvement measures have been implemented as planned. This can be achieved with a status check and with a follow-up audit on site (see Section B, Chapter 6).

LINKS AND REFERENCES ↗

- CASCARINO, R. AND S. VAN ESCH. 2005. *Internal Auditing: An Integrated Approach.* Lansdowne, SA: Juta and Co.
- SEARS, B. 2002. *Internal Auditing Manual.* New York, NY: Warren, Gorham & Lamont.
- SAWYER, L. B., M. A DITTENHOFER AND J. H SCHEINER. 2003. *Sawyer's Internal Auditing.* 5th ed. Altamonte Springs, FL: The Institute of Internal Auditors.

2.2 Tools Needed for the Audit

KEY POINTS •••

- During audit preparation, auditors assemble the required documents and working tools to ensure the audit can be performed efficiently and effectively.
- If a previous audit of the specific area has been performed, the internal audit team should familiarize themselves with the audit working papers and reports from those previous audits.

Preparation

Auditors must, of course, take the necessary working materials and documents to the audit. Normally these will include a laptop, notepads, dividers, files, pens, text markers, sheet protectors, and a calculator. In addition, they should think about other tools that may not be available on site. Auditors should also take their itinerary, the time schedule for meetings, and other documents created or collated during the preparation phase (e.g., work program, print-outs of annual financial statements, minutes of meetings with colleagues, etc.). It may also be useful to bring the audit announcement and/or audit request.

Prior Working Papers and Audit Reports

In addition, if previous audits of the specific audit area have been performed the internal audit team may bring the working papers and audit reports from those audits. These documents can provide guidance for the performance of the audit activities. Further, the internal audit team should compare the current condition of the audit area with the condition documented during past audits. This allows the audit team to determine if processes or control systems have changed.

HINTS AND TIPS

- Auditors should back up their working documents on a central file server or other storage device regularly throughout the audit.

LINKS AND REFERENCES

- CASCARINO, R. AND S. VAN ESCH. 2005. *Internal Auditing: An Integrated Approach.* Lansdowne, SA: Juta and Co.
- SEARS, B. 2002. *Internal Auditing Manual.* New York, NY: Warren, Gorham & Lamont.
- SAWYER, L. B., M. A DITTENHOFER AND J. H SCHEINER. 2003. *Sawyer's Internal Auditing.* 5th ed. Altamonte Springs, FL: The Institute of Internal Auditors.

2.3 Auditor Skills

2.3.1 The Right Tone

KEY POINTS

- An audit may be a difficult and stressful situation for the auditees.
- Auditors must be fair, objective, independent, honest, and reliable.
- The auditor should use a cooperative and diplomatic approach and should be sensitive to the concerns of the auditees to gain acceptance.

Audit Situation

An audit can be a difficult and uncertain situation for the auditees. No one likes to be audited, and the auditees may perceive the audit as a signal of mistrust. Although it is sometimes easier if the unit to be audited has already had experience with audits, the auditees may still be concerned and reluctant to cooperate.

Eliminate Prejudices

One of the auditors' tasks is therefore to provide balance in these situations. The auditors may face prejudices especially if Internal Audit and its employees are not yet known to the auditees. Often, Internal Auditors are perceived as "police" – only looking to find errors or fraudulent activities. The auditees may not realize that Internal Audit can also add value to the organization by providing recommendations to improve efficiency and effectiveness of operations and reduce risk. In such cases, the auditors should try to eliminate these prejudices in order to conduct a successful audit.

Communication Skills

Auditors need good communication skills. They must carefully consider their words to ensure they convey the appropriate message. The objective of audit work is not to issue orders and instructions or try to persuade the auditees, but to convince and to identify common ground.

Auditor Attributes

Above all, an auditor must be fair, objective, independent, honest, and reliable. A friendly and polite, yet professional, demeanor is essential for good cooperation. In this regard, it is helpful to give attention to the auditees and to be flexible – e.g., by working around their schedules (for details on the GIAS Code of Conduct, see Section A, Chapters 3.2 and 3.3).

Sensitivity

Auditors must always try to use the right tone for the employees of the division being audited. Sensitivity is an important and useful attribute that auditors can use to gain acceptance in a cooperative and diplomatic manner.

HINTS AND TIPS

- Auditors should put themselves in the position of the auditees and imagine how they would feel if their own unit was being audited.
- Auditors should treat the auditees in the same way as they would like to be treated in a similar situation.

LINKS AND REFERENCES

- CASCARINO, R. AND S. VAN ESCH. 2005. *Internal Auditing: An Integrated Approach.* Lansdowne, SA: Juta and Co.
- SEARS, B. 2002. *Internal Auditing Manual.* New York, NY: Warren, Gorham & Lamont.
- SAWYER, L. B., M. A DITTENHOFER AND J. H SCHEINER. 2003. *Sawyer's Internal Auditing.* 5th ed. Altamonte Springs, FL: The Institute of Internal Auditors.

2.3.2 Professional Auditor Conduct

KEY POINTS

- All auditors are responsible for the audit steps and associated work they perform.
- Every auditor should feel responsible for the overall success of the audit.

Responsibility of the Auditor

Each auditor has a certain level of responsibility, both for the audit and process steps that are taken and for the overall success of the audit. Overall success in this context means:

- The atmosphere between auditors and auditees is cooperative and constructive.
- All important issues are handled.
- The audit objective is met and the purpose of the audit is fulfilled.
- Internal Audit adds value to the audited unit and thus to the company as a whole.

Focus on What Is Important

With the purpose and objective of the audit in mind, auditors must remember that they must adhere to a preset time budget. Importantly, throughout the audit, various activities may be more time consuming than anticipated. For example, it often takes longer than expected to receive requested documents from the auditees. For this reason, the audit team must concentrate on material and particularly risk-prone audit objects. At the end of the audit, they must be convinced that they have covered and adequately audited all relevant aspects of the audited unit and that their audit has added value to the organization. This determination may be different for each audit. Therefore, the assessment should be made using the appropriate criteria for the specific audit (e.g. improvement of internal processes, monetary advantages, reputational benefits).

Documentation

Auditors have an obligation to ensure that their working papers are complete and consistent. All observations and results must be recorded in the relevant documentation (see Section B, Chapter 5). The audit working papers should include the following items:

- purpose of the audit step,
- description of the current condition (as-is) of the audit area,
- documentation of testwork, if applicable,
- assessment of the relevant control systems with regard to the risk that has to be covered,
- conclusion, including recommendations if applicable,
- the responsible auditor's name,
- the date of the audit work,
- evidence of review by the audit lead, and
- appropriate referencing and cross-referencing.

HINTS AND TIPS

- To save time, it is useful to request documents for different parts of the audit at the same time. This requires planning and coordination by the audit team.
- Auditors should develop professional skepticism and ask all the questions that have arisen during the course of the audit.

LINKS AND REFERENCES

- REDING, K. F., P. J. SOBEL, U. L. ANDERSON. et al. 2007. *Internal Assurance and Consulting Services.* Altamonte Springs, FL: Institute of Internal Auditors.

- CASCARINO, R. AND S. VAN ESCH. 2005. *Internal Auditing: An Integrated Approach.* Lansdowne, SA: Juta and Co.
- SEARS, B. 2002. *Internal Auditing Manual.* New York, NY: Warren, Gorham & Lamont.
- SAWYER, L. B., M. A DITTENHOFER AND J. H. SCHEINER. 2003. *Sawyer's Internal Auditing.* 5th ed. Altamonte Springs, FL: The Institute of Internal Auditors.

2.3.3 Team Work

KEY POINTS

- Audit work is usually team work.
- The entire audit team is responsible for the audit result.
- Regular communications and a continuous exchange of information among auditors are imperative for conducting audits successfully.

Audit Team

Audits are usually performed by at least two auditors, one of whom acts as the audit lead, although the choice of audit lead differs from audit to audit. The audit lead has operational responsibility for the audit (see Section A, Chapter 4.5), including facilitation of the opening and closing meetings.

Splitting Fieldwork

Usually, fieldwork is team work. Depending on the topic, the audit steps to be performed are assigned to the Internal Audit employees involved. Since the different audit topics may impact on each other, it is critical to forward the information gathered in the individual areas to all auditors.

Team Work

Team work includes:

- working together,
- sharing responsibility,
- helping and supporting each other,
- respecting and accepting each other,
- sharing knowledge,
- sharing information, and
- coordinating work efforts.

Communication

Permanent communication and a continuous exchange of information among auditors are important criteria for conducting audits successfully. The team as a whole is responsible for the audit result.

Cooperation

Cooperation within an audit team presents a challenge. Mutual respect, permanent communication and coordination are of particular importance in larger teams (of more than two or three members) or in multicultural teams in global audits.

HINTS AND TIPS

- Take into consideration that each auditor has special skills and know-how.
- For this reason, an important task within an audit team is to benefit from each other on the basis of acceptance, respect, and team work.

LINKS AND REFERENCES

- CASCARINO, R. AND S. VAN ESCH. 2005. *Internal Auditing: An Integrated Approach.* Lansdowne, SA: Juta and Co.
- REDING, K. F., P. J. SOBEL, U. L. ANDERSON. et al. 2007. *Internal Assurance and Consulting Services.* Altamonte Springs, FL: The Institute of Internal Auditors.
- SEARS, B. 2002. *Internal Auditing Manual.* New York, NY: Warren, Gorham & Lamont.
- SAWYER, L. B., M. A DITTENHOFER AND J. H SCHEINER. 2003. *Sawyer's Internal Auditing.* 5th ed. Altamonte Springs, FL: The Institute of Internal Auditors.

2.4 Scopes

KEY POINTS

- Usually for each audit object, Scopes are available (Core Scopes and Key Scopes) that represent a basic collection of all possible audit topics and provide detailed information about each topic.
- Scopes are used as a basis for compiling the work program during audit preparation.

Scopes as Audit Basis

At SAP, the preparation and execution of the different types of audit, such as standard, special, or ad-hoc audits (see Section A, Chapter 6.5) are performed on the basis of comprehensive standard documents known as Scopes (see also Section A, Chapter 5.3 and Section B, Chapter 2.1). Scopes contain detailed information about the audit area, including the processes, procedures, risks, and control systems. These documents are important tools used to perform efficient and effective audits. If a local subsidiary is to be audited, for example, auditors may prepare for the audit and create the work program by first reviewing the existing Core Scope from which they can select the topics to be audited (see Section C, Chapter 5.1). The Core Scope contains a basic collection of all possible individual topics that may be examined as part of auditing a subsidiary. Of course, an appropriate selection of objects to be audited must be made for a specific audit engagement on the basis of the time available for the audit, the size of the subsidiary, and the risk assessment. These objects are then transferred from the Scope to the work program of the audit.

Practical Application

The following chapters show successively how audits for different topics are structured and performed in practice. They mainly address those topics on which SAP's Internal Audit primarily focuses.

HINTS AND TIPS

- Apart from the tools used during audit preparation and execution, the auditor's most useful aids are common sense, logical thinking, experience, and analytical know-how.

3 Selected Financial Audit Topics

3.1 Analytical Procedures

KEY POINTS •••

- Analytical procedures consist of an analysis of figures and ratios and/or groups of figures and ratios and their development over a defined period.
- Analytical procedures are important tools for effectively performing any type of audit.
- There are different categories of analytical procedures, e.g., plausibility checks, trend analysis, and ratio analysis.
- Analytical procedures can be used during audit preparation, audit execution, and reporting.

Basics

As described in Section B, Chapter 4.1.2, analytical procedures are an important tool of audit work. The procedures consist of an analysis of individual figures and ratios and/or groups of figures and ratios. Analytical procedures also include analyzing the development of these figures and ratios over a defined period. The auditors' task is to use their judgment to examine critically any variances (or the lack of variances) between figures and groups of figures and assess the results. In this process, forecasts can be generated based on external market and sector information or company-internal information (strategy, processes, guidelines, budgets, prior-year figures, etc.).

Significance

Analytical procedures are important for the effective performance of any type of audit, because they help focus the extent of the audit work to be done. They can be used to obtain a comprehensive picture of the organization's situation and to design the work program (see Section B, Chapter 3.2).

Relation with Substantive Testing

Unlike substantive testing, analytical procedures can be used to cover several audit objectives simultaneously, such as completeness, correct assessments, and accurate statements. If executed properly, analytical procedures are as effective as substantive testing. Moreover, they can combine several audit topics and uncover errors that may otherwise be overlooked.

Types of Analytical Procedures

There are different types of analytical procedures: Internal Audit at SAP uses plausibility checks, trend analysis, and ratio analysis most regularly.

Plausibility Checks

Plausibility checks (also known as reasonableness tests) are used to compare financial accounting data with data from other areas to test the accuracy of financial accounting. The aim of such test calculations is to establish whether the amount of the recorded figures seems plausible and reasonable. The following fictitious example provides further clarification.

Fictitious Example of a Plausibility Check

Assume that the plausibility of personnel expenses of a local subsidiary (as of July 31, 2007) is to be examined on the basis of independent internal information supplied by the human resources department and various external information (e.g., sector salary and social security contribution levels). As a result of these analytical procedures, Internal Audit finds that personnel expenses have risen disproportionately. There are two reasons for this increase: First, social security contributions have risen from 24% to 27%, and second, total wages and salaries have increased by 7.7%. This is due to an increase in the number of employees in the local subsidiary and a corresponding increase in salaries. The following diagram shows the results.

	July 31, 2006	July 31, 2007	Increase	Increase
			absolute	%
Personnel expenses				
Wages and salaries	€ 4,141,667	€ 4,462,500	€ 320,833	7.7
Social security contribution	€ 994,000	€ 1,204,875	€ 210,875	21.2
Workforce	355	375	20	5.6
Personnel expense per head	**€ 14,467**	**€ 15,113**	**€ 646**	**4.5**

Information from HR department (independently of accounting system)
reconciled to list of totals and balances as of July 31, 2006 and July 31, 2007
Variance analysis: Social security contributions increased from 24% to 27%.

Fig. 1 Fictitious Example of a Plausibility Check

Trend Analysis

Trend analysis examines the development of a particular item, (e.g., an account or certain transactions) over time, and identifies trends. Using trend analysis, Internal Audit can determine the main drivers of the development. Trend analysis is used, for example, to estimate sales revenue on the basis of prior years or industry trends.

Ratio Analysis

Ratio analysis involves examining relationships between key variables, looking at changes in ratios in a company or region, or comparing two or more companies or regions.

Fictitious Example

In the following fictitious example, country A's six-month sales revenue (EUR 1,900,561) has fallen to less than half of the previous year's figure (EUR 4,141,667). Against expectations, trade accounts receivable has risen by EUR 502,174 and days sales outstanding (DSO) (see Section C, Chapter 3.2) has increased from 178 days in the previous year to 241 days as of June 30, 2007. The general bad debt allowance, however, has decreased by EUR 93,768. Internal Audit investigates and finds that the maturities in an important consulting project have been changed manually and invoices from 2006, which were due at that time, are no longer regarded as "due" on June 30, 2007. The project manager provides a satisfactory explanation of this situation. Additional analytical procedures, such as a plausibility check on the general bad debt allowance, can deliver further information. The need for further analytical procedures is established by auditor judgment.

	June 30, 2007	December 31, 2006	December 31, 2005
Sales revenue	€	€	€
Country A	1,900,561	4,141,667	4,462,500
Country B	437,129	952,583	1,026,375
Country C	1,710,505	3,727,500	4,016,250
Trade accounts receivable	€	€	€
Country A	2,544,640	2,042,466	1,833,904
Country B	679,978	626,356	506,158
Country C	1,140,337	1,276,541	1,430,445
DSO	Days	Days	Days
Country A	241	178	148
Country B	280	237	178
Country C	120	123	128
Country A	€	€	€
General bad debt allowance in €	559,821	653,589	623,527
General bad debt allowance as % of trade accounts receivable	22 %	32 %	34 %
Specific bad debt allowance	312,870	154,908	154,908
	Days	Days	Days
Region Y	80	76	77
Region Z	195	161	143
Reconciled to list of totales and balances			

Fig. 2 Fictitious Example of Ratio Analysis

Combinations

An analytical procedure may also comprise a combination of the above procedures or cover several periods. It is important that auditors have a good understanding of the relevant data relationships before selecting the analytical procedure to be used.

Purpose of Analytical Procedures

Analytical procedures help the auditors obtain an overview and an initial understanding of the information contained in the balance sheet and the income statement. What has changed and in which direction? How large is the difference? This kind of audit work supports the preparation for the audit and is particularly useful when compiling a risk-based work program. Analytical procedures are particularly important, because auditors can perform them while still in their office during audit preparation and not yet in the field. Thus, once the auditors arrive on site to perform the audit, they already have an understanding of the audited unit and some of the specific issues that may arise during the audit.

Options for Use during Audit Preparation

SAP always uses analytical procedures as part of risk-based audit preparation. At this stage, auditors do not yet have contact with the persons responsible for the audited area or access to local documents for analysis. Analytical procedures used during audit preparation identify audit content on which the fieldwork should focus and which must be added to or modified in the standard work program. During audit preparation, the analysis of the balance sheet and income statement helps gain an up-to-date understanding of the business processes of the area to be audited. In this context, it is important to include analyses performed by Accounting and Management Accounting.

Options for Use During Execution

In addition, analytical procedures can be used as an additional tool during audit execution. They can be applied to produce meaningful results, for example, when auditing specific areas such as license fees, social security expenses, and depreciation of noncurrent assets. They also help identify and uncover fraud.

Making Analytical Procedures Effective

The following aspects contribute to performing analytical procedures effectively. Auditors must:

- properly understand the objective of the analytical procedure,
- recognize the relationships among the data,
- analyze the data to the necessary level of detail,
- be satisfied that the underlying data is reliable, and
- use their judgment when assessing the results.

Meaningfulness of Results

The following factors determine how meaningful the results of analytical procedures are:

- data quality,
- precision of wording of the matter investigated,
- possibility to forecast the matter investigated,
- data collection, and
- type of analytical procedure used (e.g., plausibility checks can produce more accurate results than trend analysis).

Fictitious Example

The comprehensive fictitious example below shows how the standard work program for local subsidiary audits can be supplemented or modified on the basis of analytical procedures. It examines data from Company A's financial statements as of April 30, 2007. The latest available financials (in this case from the statements as of April 30, 2007) are compared with the previous annual financial statements and the relevant prior-year period (as of April 30, 2006). The income statement for the period ended April 30, 2007 is compared with the relevant figures for the period ended April 30, 2006. In addition, Internal Audit can also use the previous year's income statement for the twelve months prior to December 31, 2006, scaled down to four months, and compare the result with the actual figures as of April 30, 2007. To simplify, this fictitious example only mentions material variances and facts identified with analytical procedures.

Assets	
Result of analytical procedure	**Consequences for the work program**
Property, plant, and equipment: The amount as of April 30, 2007 (EUR 1,900,000) consists primarily of "leased vehicles" amounting to EUR 1,350,000. Vehicle leases are classified as capital leases.	Specific addition/modification to the work program: The correct classification and US-GAAP accounting treatment is to be checked for five selected leases.
Trade accounts receivable has fallen by EUR 4,530,000. This is partly the result of an increase in maintenance receivables by EUR 5,730,000, offset by a fall in software receivables by EUR 6,480,000.	This matter is covered by the standard work program.
The specific bad debt allowance on trade accounts receivable of EUR 100,000 has not changed from year to year. The specific bad debt allowance relates to Customer 1.	Specific addition/modification to the work program: An analysis must be performed to establish whether the specific bad debt allowance has been correctly measured and covers the full exposure.
In spite of a decrease in trade accounts receivable by EUR 130,000, the general bad debt allowance has increased.	Specific addition/modification to the work program: The trade accounts receivable included in the general bad debt allowance should be analyzed. Should items of the general bad debt allowance be reclassified to the specific bad debt allowance?
The specific allowance for returns, discounts, and rebates relates to Customer 2.	Specific addition/modification to the work program: An analysis must be performed to establish whether this specific allowance has been correctly measured and covers the full exposure.
Notes receivable of EUR 270,000 consist primarily of receivables from three customers.	Specific addition/modification to the work program: The auditors must establish how these notes receivable have arisen and test them for impairment.
Other taxes receivable consist primarily of tax deducted on license fee payments made in prior years amounting to EUR 1,500,000.	Specific addition/modification to the work program: The auditors must establish how these taxes receivable have arisen and test them for impairment.

Fig. 3 Fictitous Example of Possible Results from an Analysis of Assets and its Consequences for the Work Program

Liabilities	
Result of analytical procedure	**Consequences for the work program**
The provision for other taxes relates to other tax risks of EUR 900,000.	Specific addition/modification to the work program: The auditors must establish how these tax risks have arisen and whether the provision has been correctly measured.
The prepayment of other taxes in country B, which has been deducted from tax liabilities, includes tax withheld by third parties on export invoices.	Specific addition/modification to the work program: The auditors must establish how these tax receivables have arisen and test them for impairment.
Noncurrent lease obligations of EUR 1,800,000 include lease payments due with maturities of more than one year.	Specific addition/modification to the work program: The correct classification and US-GAAP accounting treatment is to be checked for five leases.

Fig. 4 Fictitious Example of Possible Results from an Analysis of Liabilities and its Consequences for the Work Program

Income Statement	
Result of analytical procedure	**Consequences for the work program**
Sales revenue has fallen by EUR 1,016,000. This is partly the result of a reduction in product sales revenue by EUR 2,250,000, partially offset by an increase in consulting sales revenue by EUR 1,300,000. Many consulting projects and software contracts have been concluded with the public sector.	Specific addition/modification to the work program: If there are indications of possible difficulties in the public sector of the country under review, the receivables have to be tested for impairment and it must be established whether all revenue recognition requirements have been met.

Fig. 5 Fictitious Example of a Possible Result from an Analysis of the Income Statement and its Consequences for the Work Program

HINTS AND TIPS

- Auditors should critically examine all results produced through analytical procedures.
- The meaningfulness of analytical procedures increases in proportion to the level of detail with which they are conducted.

LINKS AND REFERENCES

- ARENS, A. A., F. J. ELDER AND M. S. BEASLEY. 2006. *Auditing and Assurance Services: An Integrated Approach.* 12th ed. Upper Saddle River, NJ: Pearson Prentice Hall.
- CASCARINO, R. AND S. VAN ESCH. 2005. *Internal Auditing: An Integrated Approach.* Lansdowne, SA: Juta and Co.
- REDING, K. F., P. J. SOBEL, U. L. ANDERSON, et al. 2007. *Internal Assurance and Consulting Services.* Altamonte Springs, FL: The Institute of Internal Auditors.
- RITTENBERG, L. E. AND B. J. SCHWEIGER. 2005. A*uditing: Concepts for a Changing Environment.* Mason, OH: Thompson.
- SEARS, B. 2002. *Internal Auditing Manual.* New York, NY: Warren, Gorham & Lamont.
- SAWYER, L. B., M. A DITTENHOFER AND J. H. SCHEINER. 2003. *Sawyer's Internal Auditing.* 5th ed. Altamonte Springs, FL: The Institute of Internal Auditors.

3.2 Trade Accounts Receivable Audits

KEY POINTS

- A primary objective of auditing trade accounts receivable is to ensure that the timing of the recognition of receivables is appropriate.
- A second audit objective is to ensure that the receivables are correctly measured and fully disclosed.
- Although balance confirmations do not guarantee that the cash will be received, they do provide assurance of the existence and the amount of the receivable.
- Key activities of a trade accounts receivable audit include evaluating the timing of the recognition of the receivables, analyzing the open items, the ageing structure lists and the DSO list, examining bad debt allowances on receivables, and assessing currency translation.

Audit Objects

When auditing trade accounts receivable, the timing and appropriate recognition of receivables is critically important. One audit objective is to ensure that the receivables are measured correctly. Receivables must be measured based upon the amount of the expected cash inflow for the company, which means that they must be tested for impairment. The investigation should also include a check as to whether the trade accounts receivable are correctly and fully reported in the balance sheet, that is, whether they are classified into current and noncurrent receivables, domestic or foreign receivables, or local or foreign currency denominated receivables. The focus of Internal Audit's work includes both process and system analysis.

Audit Preparation

Local subsidiaries are audited at various times throughout the year (see Section C, Chapter 5.1). During audit preparation, the auditors must define the data they will examine during the audit. Generally, auditors use the figures from the latest interim financial statements as a basis for the audit. It is essential to also consider the figures of the latest annual financial statements, or even those from the prior year (for details of analytical procedures, see Section C, Chapter 3.1). SAP's corporate financial reporting department produces financial statement analyses for significant local subsidiaries between reporting dates. These analyses may provide valuable support during audit preparation.

Balance Confirmations

Since the audit of a local subsidiary is aimed at ensuring that trade accounts receivable are not impaired, Internal Audit may consider conducting balance confirmations, similar to those performed during the annual financial statement audit by the external auditors. To this end, Internal Audit should select a sample of debtors before the start of the audit. Although the confirmation of a balance does not guarantee that the cash will be received, it does provide assurance of the existence and the amount of the receivable.

Customer Contract Confirmation Round

In addition, SAP routinely conducts customer contract confirmations, by which it gathers information about existing software contracts (for details, see Section C, Chapter 9). These confirmations can also be used as evidence of the existence and the amount of trade accounts receivable and the correct timing of their recognition.

System Authorization and Segregation of Duty

Internal Audit must ensure that IT system authorizations grant maintenance rights for the customer master data to a restricted group of people only. Moreover, Internal Audit must enforce segregation of duty to ensure that the employee who updates the customer master data is not authorized to issue credit notes. Although the segregation of duty is more important when auditing liabilities (see Section C, Chapter 3.4), the principle of segregation of duty should also be examined when auditing trade accounts receivable. Depending on the IT system used, Internal Audit employees should use their auditor judgment to decide whether it is necessary to perform a reconciliation between sub-ledger accounts and the general ledger. In the integrated SAP live system, this reconciliation is performed continually in real time.

Important Aspects of Audit Execution

The following is a more detailed description of important aspects of conducting a trade accounts receivable audit:

- time when receivables are recognized,
- analysis of the open items list and ageing structure analysis,
- analysis of days sales outstanding,
- bad debt allowances on receivables, and
- receivables denominated in foreign currency/currency translation.

Time When Receivables Are Recognized

The recognition of trade accounts receivable is related to sales revenue recognition (for details, see Section C, Chapter 3.5).

Open Items List

To gain a general overview of the trade accounts receivable, it is useful to start by reviewing the receivables in an open items list. This step should be supplemented with an analysis of the ageing structure of the receivables. Based on the results, Internal Audit can then select individual receivables for further examination. The open items list contains all outstanding receivables per customer and provides an idea of the transactions that have been recorded. In the open items list, it should be possible to sort and analyze the data by criteria such as due date, customer name, and amount.

Accounts Included

The open items list allows analysis of the following current receivables (due within <12 months): "Trade accounts receivable, own country" (both local and non-local currencies from customers in own country) and "Trade accounts receivable, other countries" (both local and non-local currencies from customers in other countries).

Ageing Structure List

The ageing structure list provides critical indicators as to whether trade accounts receivable may be collectible or not. It is structured by maturity, providing a quick overview of customers with overdue receivables and the relevant amounts.

Business unit	Total receivables	Due ≤ 100 days	1% of amount due ≤ 100 days
A	80,000	78,000	780
B	60,000	30,000	300
C	8,000	1,000	10
D	130,000	30,000	300
Total	**278,000**	**139,000**	**1,390**

Fig. 6 Fictitious Ageing Structure List

Content and Structure of the Ageing Structure List

The ageing structure list identifies the outstanding receivables for each customer per business unit, broken down by the number of days overdue. Due dates and overdue thresholds can be set in the SAP system as required for individual customers. The ageing structure list is divided into business units and can be saved as a spreadsheet.

General Bad Debt Allowances

US-GAAP permits general bad debt allowances only if certain criteria are met. They are permitted if evidence can be provided from past experience or the current economic environment.

Bad Debt Allowances on Receivables

Receivables are measured at net sales proceeds. An allowance is recognized for all receivables in the amount at risk from non-collectibility. In essence, this is a specific bad debt allowance, i.e., each receivable must be assessed separately. The measurement of the allowance should be based on the best estimate. Allowances are offset against assets by deducting them from receivables.

Specific Bad Debt Allowances

The individual outstanding receivable can be examined using the information gained during analysis. The receivables to be reviewed are selected on the basis of auditor judgment or statistical sampling (see Section B, Chapter 4.1.2). Together with the employee responsible in the financial unit, Internal Audit must examine critically why there are overdue receivables and whether allowances should be recognized. In the case of payment difficulties, specific bad debt allowances must be recognized. Further, the auditors must establish whether customers are withholding payment because they are not satisfied with the product or service. To do this, auditors should contact the employees responsible in the business unit concerned and ask about their relationship with the customer. If payment is delayed because the customer is not satisfied, a specific bad debt allowance should not be recognized, instead a sales allowance, which is similar, should be used.

Specific Bad Debt Allowances Recognized by Local Subsidiaries

At least at the end of each quarter, each local subsidiary must review all specific bad debt allowances. The auditors should ask for the list of receivables for which specific allowances have been set up as of the latest annual financial statements audited by the external auditors and compare it with the local subsidiary's current list. Any variances, particularly reversals of specific bad debt allowances, should be discussed with the people responsible in the local subsidiary. Analysis of the above-mentioned open items list in conjunction with the ageing structure list may also provide indications as to the need for additional specific bad debt allowances.

Fictitious Example of General Bad Debt Allowance

The following fictitious example demonstrates how to set up a general bad debt allowance:

Total receivables (gross):	EUR 1,290,000
Less: receivables requiring a specific bad debt allowance (gross):	**EUR (100,000)**
Subtotal:	EUR 1,190,000
Less value added tax (19%):	**EUR (190,000)**
Receivables (net):	EUR 1,000,000
General bad debt allowance (1 %):	EUR (10,000)

The receivables for which a specific bad debt allowance has been set up are those receivables that were depreciated following separate evaluation. They do not necessarily need to be written off to zero, but the full amount of the specific bad debt allowances is deducted from the basis on which the general bad debt allowance is calculated.

Analysis of Days Sales Outstanding

Another way of analyzing trade accounts receivable is to examine the turnover rate of receivables measured in days. This is done using the days sales outstanding (DSO) list. DSO is the number of days from the invoice date through receipt of payment.

Country	Balance	Sales	DSO
A	16,000	93,000	62.8
B	500	4,000	45.6
C	50	500	36.5
D	20	200	36.5
E	0	400	0
Total	**16,570**	**98,100**	**61.7**

Fig. 7 Fictitious Example of DSO Analysis

Fictitious Example of How to Calculate DSO

The following fictitious example demonstrates how to calculate DSO:

Total receivables (net):	EUR 1,200,000
Total sales revenue for the period:	EUR 10,000,000

DSO calculation:
Total receivables (net) divided by sales revenue per day in period:

$$\frac{\text{EUR } 1{,}200{,}000}{\text{EUR } 10{,}000{,}000/365 \text{ days}} = 43.8 \text{ days}$$

The result 43.8 indicates how many days it takes customers on average to settle outstanding receivables.

Analysis of the DSO List

The DSO list therefore shows how long it takes a local subsidiary on average to collect its receivables. But this result alone is not very meaningful. Useful conclusions can only be drawn if the auditor compares the figure with that of other periods in the same local subsidiary, or with other local subsidiaries for the same period. The auditors should, however, only compare local subsidiaries that operate in a comparable economic environment, so that they can assume similar customer payment behavior. It would not make sense to compare the figure for a country with generally poor payment behavior with one where customers normally pay promptly.

Conclusions from the DSO List

Significantly high DSO values for overdue receivables may indicate process weaknesses in the debt collection procedures. High DSO figures also impact negatively on the liquidity of the local subsidiary in question. The reasons for high DSO values, therefore, must be investigated and any process weaknesses eliminated by the local subsidiary.

Assessment of Collectibility

Since the collectibility of receivables depends mainly on the solvency of the customer in question and the outcome of any litigation, Internal Audit must consult with the legal department concerned, the external local attorney, or the corporate legal department and obtain the relevant confirmations from the attorneys. This information is also useful when assessing the need for an additional provision for litigation costs (see Section C, Chapter 3.3). Auditors must ensure that they have used all available information sources in this context and that the lists are complete.

Uncollectible Receivables Due to Customer Complaints

Allowances due to customer payment difficulties must be distinguished from receivables that are uncollectible due to customer complaints. Separate sales allowances must be set up for receivables relating to goods or services with which customers are not satisfied and which they are therefore unwilling to settle or willing to settle only partially. The auditors should talk with the employees responsible in the audited unit to get a feeling for any projects where customers may be dissatisfied.

Receivables Denominated in Foreign Currency / Currency Translation

Receivables in foreign currency are measured at the current exchange rate. The measurement is performed at the end of each month. Currency translation results in foreign exchange gains or losses. Auditors should ask for a list of trade accounts receivable denominated in foreign currency and test a sample of accounts to determine whether the correct exchange rate has been used for measurement and whether any foreign exchange gains or losses have been taken to the income statement according to the company's accounting guidelines.

HINTS AND TIPS

- Auditors should not accept any statements without critically reviewing them first.
- The information obtained by analyzing the open items list and the ageing structure list should be used to select certain receivables for detailed testing.
- Auditors should be aware that assets are more susceptible to risk from overstatement than from understatement.

LINKS AND REFERENCES

- SEARS, B. 2002. *Internal Auditing Manual.* New York, NY: Warren, Gorham & Lamont.
- SAWYER, L. B., M. A DITTENHOFER AND J. H SCHEINER. 2003. *Sawyer's Internal Auditing.* 5th ed. Altamonte Springs, FL: The Institute of Internal Auditors.

3.3 Accrued Liabilities Audits

KEY POINTS

- When auditing accrued liabilities, one of the major objectives is to ensure that all material risks have been captured and measured as accurately as possible.
- During the audit, it is appropriate to focus on the main accrued liabilities. This includes, for example, vacation accruals, accruals for outstanding invoices,

bonus accruals, accruals for loss contingencies, other accruals (legal disputes, legal and consulting costs), and tax accruals.
- Currently, SAP primarily audits accruals as part of local subsidiary audits.

Setting Up Accrued Liabilities

When auditing the accounting units of local subsidiaries, Internal Audit must always consider the US-GAAP accounting principles. According to US-GAAP, accruals are reported under liabilities. The accruals account under liabilities on the balance sheet includes contingent liabilities, when the amount and/or basis of the liabilities are uncertain but an outflow of economic resources is probable. The recognition of accruals under US-GAAP depends on whether there is an obligation toward a third party (external obligation). Moreover, the following criteria must be met before an accrual can be recognized as of the balance sheet date:
- The cause of the obligation must be legal or financial in nature and result from a past event.
- The amount of the obligation must be determinable (i.e., the amount of loss can be reasonably estimated).
- The use of the obligation must be probable (i.e., loss is probable).

Each accrual should be measured as the best estimate of most probable use. If several values are equally probable, the lowest end of the most probable range is recognized under US-GAAP.

Audit Objectives

A major objective when auditing accrued liabilities is to ensure that all material risks have been captured and measured as accurately as possible. In addition, the focus of Internal Audit's work often comprises process and system analysis. Such process analysis is useful for annually recurring accruals such as for bonuses, vacation, etc.

Main Types of Accruals

It is appropriate to focus on the significant accrued liabilities during the audit. Materiality can be assessed under quantitative and qualitative criteria. This chapter deals with audits of the following types of accruals:
- vacation accruals,
- accruals for outstanding invoices,
- bonus accruals,
- accruals for loss contingencies,
- other accruals (legal disputes, legal and consulting costs), and
- tax accruals.

Audit Preparation

Accruals can be treated as a separate audit segment or examined as part of subsidiary audits. Internal Audit at SAP audits accrued liabilities primarily when auditing local subsidiaries. Those audits may be performed during the fiscal year (see Section C, Chapter 5.1). A significant aspect of audit preparation is to define the data to be examined. Normally it is expedient to use the figures from the latest interim financial statements and the comparable prior-year financial statements as a basis for the audit. In addition, the auditors should also consider the figures of the last two annual financial statements.

Analyses Before the Start of the Audit

SAP's corporate financial reporting department produces financial statement analyses for significant subsidiaries during the course of the fiscal year. These analyses may provide valuable support during preparation. Auditors should analyze the latest statement of changes in accruals and major movements on the relevant accrual accounts and discuss any material or unusual variances with the persons responsible within the local subsidiary. A statement of changes in accruals (accruals register) must be available at least once at the end of the fiscal year.

Vacation Accruals

Each local subsidiary must calculate its vacation accruals monthly, taking into account latest developments and changes, such as vacation days taken, salary increases, etc. The amount of vacation accrual depends primarily on the number of employees, the number of vacation days not yet taken (including any balances brought forward from the previous year), and the salary of each employee.

Testing Vacation Accruals

When testing vacation accruals, the auditors must consider the following aspects:

- They must ensure that all employees are included in the calculation of vacation accruals. Auditors can do this by asking the human resources department for a list of all active employees. This list is normally generated in the SAP-internal human resources system and compared with the list of vacation accruals. Generally, there should not be any variances, but any differences that do occur must be analyzed.
- Auditors also must ensure that all unused vacation days are accurately reflected in the calculations. Note that employees who joined the company in the course of the year will have a pro-rated vacation entitlement only. When calculating the accrual between reporting dates (e.g., for interim financial statements), the audit team should remember that the entitlement for the year to date is likewise a pro-rated figure. There may be country-specific differences at this point. In some countries it is normal to grant the full annual vacation entitlement if the employee joins before June 30 of a year.
- In addition to the number of unused vacation days, employees' salaries influence the vacation accrual. The audit team should examine a sample of employee records to ascertain whether the correct salary data is used to calculate the accrual. For each employee record included in the sample, the audit team should compare the salary data from the accrual to the data from the human resources system and the employment contracts. The team should ensure that any salary increases have been included.

Calculation of Vacation Accruals

The calculation of vacation accruals must include all salary components to which the employee has a firm entitlement. The auditors must also consider the social security contributions payable by the employer. It is useful to determine a daily rate for each employee and base the vacation accrual on this figure. Since the accrual expresses in monetary terms the vacation entitlement that employees have received but not yet taken, it is also important to calculate the expected number of working days per year. For example, the audit team in Germany uses 220 days per year as a guidance value. This figure of 220 days is calculated as follows: 365 days per year - 104 days for weekends = 261 days – 32 days average vacation entitlement = 229 days – 9 public holidays on average = 220 days. Individual local subsidiaries may have different figures because they may have different vacation entitlements and public holidays. During the audit, the auditors should establish whether employees are legally required to take their vacation by a certain date, because contraventions could have legal consequences for the employer.

Segregation of Duties

In general, the responsibilities of the human resources department must be separate from those of the accounting department (segregation of duties). It would not be appropriate if, for example, the accounting department were to originate and subsequently also process data that is included in the calculation of vacation accruals.

Fictitious Example

The following is a fictitious example describing how to calculate a vacation accrual.

Contractual annual salary:	€	60,000
Average employer-paid contribution to social security:	%	20
Average number of days actually worked per month:		18.3
Equals daily rate of: 60.000 € divided by 12 months divided by 18.3 days:	€	273
Plus 20% social security:	€	55
Total daily rate:	€	328
Pro-rated vacation entitlement already earned (incl. amount brought forward):	Days	25
Amount to be accrued: 328 € x 25 days = 8,200 €		

Fig. 8 Fictitious Example for Calculating a Vacation Accrual

Accruals for Outstanding Invoices

Accruals for outstanding invoices are similar to accruals for other obligations. The primary objective of setting up accruals for outstanding invoices is to accurately record those goods and services that a supplier has provided for the previous period but not yet invoiced.

Estimates Made by Local Subsidiaries

Each local subsidiary must be in a position to provide reliable and accurate estimates for any outstanding invoices. To record the amount of outstanding invoices for consulting services, local subsidiaries must have a functioning independent project control system, which they can use at least at the end of each month to report and analyze the latest project statuses (see Section C, Chapter 5.2).

Tests Relating to Outstanding Invoices

Two points are of critical importance for Internal Audit when auditing outstanding invoices:

- Testing of the relevant project control process: This examines the extent to which a local subsidiary has implemented a functioning and independent project control system. A process that allows reliable estimates of the amount of outstanding invoices must be in place.

- Detailed testing of accrual amounts: The auditors should ask for a list of unbilled services (e.g., those supplied by a subcontractor) for the review period that has just ended. To calculate the expected invoice total, the number of hours the consultants have spent on services is multiplied by the hourly rates agreed.

Comparison Between Calculated and Accrued Amount

Depending on the project in question, consultant hours for subcontractors and other local SAP subsidiaries can be entered in the SAP-internal service entry system. If so, auditors can call up the required information about hours entered directly in the IT system. The expected invoice total is compared to the accrual that has been set up. If there are material differences, they should be discussed with the person responsible. Accruals are also set up for separately billed travel expenses and non-deductible input tax.

Alternative Testing Option

Another option for testing accruals for outstanding invoices for consulting services is to compare accruals recognized with the invoices actually received for a specific project. Of course, the audit team can do this only for periods already ended, however, it allows the team to assess the reliability of accrual estimates for past periods.

Entries

Accruals for outstanding invoices are entered on the relevant accruals account. As soon as the invoice is received, the accrual must be reversed and a liability recognized on the vendor account.

Other Components of Accruals for Outstanding Invoices

In addition to the above-mentioned outstanding invoices for consulting projects, accruals for outstanding invoices also cover other expenses, such as telephone charges, lease service charges, and travel expenses. The exact amounts are very difficult to determine, so it is best to set up accruals based on usual monthly charges.

Bonus Accruals

Each local subsidiary can stagger bonus payments at its own discretion. The amount of bonus payment is based on the achievement of targets, which include individual employee targets and other components, such as departmental, unit, and local subsidiary targets. Each employee should have his or her own bonus agreement, which provides details of individual targets. The amount of target bonus can vary from unit to unit. Often, the variable component of target compensation is higher in sales-related departments than in administration departments. Bonus payments are normally subject to social security contributions.

Testing Bonus Accruals

Auditors should record the process of setting up bonus accruals and verify on a sample basis that the process controls are effective. Such controls can take the form of documents that set out the bonus agreements and the targets actually achieved and is signed by the employee concerned, his or her line manager, and an HR officer. The objective of the audit is to establish that realistic bonuses are agreed according to guidelines and that bonus achievement is adequately monitored and documented in writing by the line manager. Bonuses have to be paid in line with target achievement. To test the bonuses, the auditors should compare target achievement with the actual bonus payments made for the year. Often, a proportion of the bonus is paid to employees as an advance in the course of the year. If that is the case, the auditors must ensure that the advance payment does not exceed the maximum the employee can achieve. In this regard, it would be expedient for the line manager to analyze the employee's performance during the year.

Relevance of Company Performance

If company performance is relevant for the calculation of bonuses, the estimate of the annual result at the time the accruals are calculated should be compared with the target result for the year on which the bonus agreement is based.

Analytical Comparisons

In addition, it is useful to make analytical comparisons with the previous year and past quarters (see Section C, Chapter 3.1). Here the audit team can investigate, for example, whether bonus payments are developing in line with company performance and whether the bonus payments of each business unit are plausible.

Fictitious Example

The following is a fictitious example of how to calculate a bonus accrual as of September 30.

Specified target result of the local subsidiary:	€	200,000
Total local subsidiary bonus payable on 100% target achievement:	€	20,000
Forecast year-end result of the local subsidiary as of September 30: (forecast for December 31)	€	160,000
Year-to-date result of the local subsidiary as of September 30:	€	120,000

The accrual as of September 30 (if fiscal year is the same as calendar year) is calculated as follows:

I	$\frac{\text{Forecast year-end result as of September 30}}{\text{Specified target result for the year}} = \frac{160{,}000\ €}{200{,}000\ €} = 80\%$
II	$\frac{\text{Proportion of year-end result earned to September 30}}{\text{Forecast year-end result as of September 30}} = \frac{120{,}000\ €}{160{,}000\ €} = 75\%$
III	Amount to be accrued as of September 30: 80% (from I.) x 75% (from II.) x 20,000 € (total bonus payable) = 12,000 €

Fig. 9 Fictitious Example for Calculating a Bonus Accrual

Accruals for Contingent Losses

To describe the appropriate tests of accruals for contingent losses, customer-specific software development contracts are used in the following as an example. At the start of a development project, the project manager should draw up a detailed plan, including a costing of external and internal resources at fully absorbed cost. If there are signs that the costs of a fixed-price project (see Section C, Chapter 5.2), including any subcontractor costs, will exceed the contractually agreed revenue, the full anticipated loss from this project must immediately be recognized as an accrual for contingent losses.

Testing Accruals for Contingent Losses

Testing accruals for contingent losses includes the following:

- The tests must verify that the costing of the internal resources includes all direct and indirect costs. The elements of this costing are based on the budgeted figures and include any salary increases. The audit team should therefore use the approved budget as the basis. The basis for the figures should be reconciled and the calculations checked, taking any supplementary costs, e.g., travel, into account.
- The project costing should also reflect the terms and conditions agreed upon with any subcontractors. To verify these, the internal audit team must analyze the contracts carefully.
- The team must also ensure that the revenue assumptions are realistic by analyzing the signed contracts and reconciling the data the contracts contain to the project costing.
- Overall, auditors should get an overview of the status of the project in order to assess whether and to what extent project costs exceed projected revenue.

Other Accruals – Legal Disputes

When testing other accruals – e.g., for legal disputes or legal and consulting costs – auditors primarily check whether the local subsidiary's estimates are complete and the amounts realistic. To assess legal disputes, auditors must meet with local external attorneys and the corporate legal department before the start of the audit. They should request attorney confirmations from local external attorneys and also obtain tax consultant confirmations. In some cases it may be appropriate to obtain opinions from external experts. In addition, it is useful to analyze the customer accounts for any new accruals needed (see Section C, Chapter 3.2). Auditors should ensure that the legal disputes are correctly and fully captured in the balance sheet.

Other Accruals – Legal and Consulting Costs

Accruals for legal and consulting costs primarily comprise accruals for attorneys and external audit fees. Attorney fees can be clarified by requesting a letter from the attorneys or meeting with local external attorneys. The audit fees can be taken from the external auditors' engagement letter or contract. The previous year's fee can also be used for guidance purposes. Between reporting dates, costs should be reflected pro rata.

Tax Accruals

Testing of tax accruals includes trade tax and corporate income tax. The accrual is recalculated at the end of each quarter and adjusted accordingly. The parameters on which the calculation is based, e.g. operating profit before tax, should be checked. To do so, it is useful to ask for a reconciliation to the financial statements prepared under tax law. The country-specific total tax rate should be multiplied by the expected taxable income and compared with the accrual actually recognized. Advance tax payments and tax loss carryforwards must be deducted from the expected tax expense. For each type of tax, the audit team should examine whether the advance payment exceeds the expected tax payable. If so, the resulting receivable must be reported under other assets. Auditors must arrange a meeting with the local tax consultant, the local external auditors, and the corporate tax department so that they get an idea of any problems from an independent third party.

HINTS AND TIPS

- When auditing accruals, auditors should, above all, make sure that all accruals fully reflect anticipated volumes and values and follow US-GAAP requirements.
- Problems are often caused not by the accruals recorded in the balance sheet, but by those that have not been set up, although they should have been.

LINKS AND REFERENCES

- JARNAGIN, B.D. 2007. *US Master GAAP Guide*. Riverwoods, IL: CCH, Inc.
- SEARS, B. 2002. *Internal Auditing Manual*. New York, NY: Warren, Gorham & Lamont.
- SAWYER, L. B., M. A. DITTENHOFER AND J. H. SCHEINER. 2003. *Sawyer's Internal Auditing*. 5th ed. Altamonte Springs, FL: The Institute of Internal Auditors.

3.4 Trade Accounts Payable Audits

KEY POINTS

- Testing that trade accounts payable are fully captured, correctly measured and properly reported on the balance sheet is a significant audit object.
- When auditing trade accounts payable, it is very important to test the segregation of duties and correct period allocation.
- Completeness of trade accounts payable is crucial. Therefore, balance confirmations should be obtained.
- The following aspects should be considered when auditing current trade accounts payable: Time of recognition, reconciliation between sub ledger and general ledger, liabilities denominated in foreign currency/currency translation, liabilities to affiliated companies, critical authorizations and creation of master data, approval of purchase order requisitions, testing of substantive accuracy, approval of payment proposal lists, and effecting of payments.

Basics

This chapter deals with trade accounts payable audits. Accounts payable are broken down into current and non current liabilities. Current liabilities are due within twelve months. The timing of recognizing a liability is of critical importance. Testing that trade accounts payable are fully captured and correctly measured is a significant audit objective. US-GAAP requires that liabilities are recognized at present value. Current liabilities are always recognized at the invoice amount. Auditors should also examine whether the liability is correctly reported in the balance sheet. They also must ensure that only a restricted group of people has maintenance rights for the vendor master data in the IT system. When auditing trade accounts payable, it is therefore very important to test segregation of duties of the responsible employees involved.

Audit Preparation

A significant aspect of audit preparation is to define the data to be examined. Generally it is expedient to use the figures (e.g., current liabilities) from the latest monthly or quarterly financial statements as a basis for the audit and compare them with the previous year's figures. In addition, during audit preparation the auditors should also consider the figures of the last (or the last two) annual financial statements. SAP also conducts audits of local subsidiaries, which (can) include trade accounts payable audits, between reporting dates (see Section C, Chapter 5.1). SAP's corporate financial reporting department produces financial statement analyses for selected subsidiaries between reporting dates. These analyses may provide valuable support during preparation. In addition to financial data, the focus of Internal Audit's work comprises process and system analysis.

Balance Confirmations

When auditing a local subsidiary, the auditors should consider obtaining balance confirmations, as practiced during the audit of the annual financial statements. Unlike receivables, the selection of trade accounts payable to be confirmed is not based on the highest individual balances but on the highest sales that a vendor has made to SAP in the period under examination. The selection of vendors is thus derived from data in the financial statement. Alternatively, Internal Audit can test randomly selected samples (see Section B, Chapter 4.1.2).

Selected Aspects of Trade Accounts Payable Audits

The fieldwork activities are taken from the work program, which is compiled before the audit. This chapter deals primarily with the following aspects of auditing current trade accounts payable:

- point in time when liabilities are recognized,
- reconciliation between sub-ledger and general ledger,
- liabilities denominated in foreign currency/currency translation,
- liabilities to affiliated companies,
- critical authorizations and creation of master data, and
- approval of purchase order requisitions, testing of substantive accuracy, approval of payment proposal lists, and effecting of payments.

Time When Liabilities Are Recognized

Similar to receivables, trade accounts payable are broken down by maturity. Recognition in the balance sheet is related to the contract partner's receipt of the goods or services. While the invoice amount for the goods and services is not yet fixed, an accrual for outstanding invoices is set up (see Section C, Chapter 3.3). If the invoice amount is known, a liability for supplier invoices not yet received should be recognized. Trade accounts payable are normally reported under current liabilities.

Reconciliation between Sub-Ledger and General Ledger

The trade accounts payable in the general ledger (balance sheet accounts) are derived from the sub-ledgers. Entries are always made against the vendor itself. Depending on the IT system used, the auditors should use auditor judgment to decide whether to perform a reconciliation between sub-ledgers and general ledger.

Open Items List

In addition, the auditors should request an open items list, which complements the list of balances. It shows all unsettled invoices entered for a particular vendor. Auditors will use the open items list, for example, to test whether all vendor entries have been made in the correct period. It is useful to take a sample of vendors to check correct period allocation. Verify whether entry and delivery date are in the same period. If the auditors establish, for example, that the goods or services were provided in the previous period, but the invoice was only received in the subsequent period, they must ascertain whether an accrual for outstanding invoices was set up and the liability was recognized in the correct period. If the liability or accrual relates to expense items, the relevant effect on the income statement must be taken into account. If the goods or services are supplied in the previous period, but only recognized in the next period, the income for the previous period will be overstated.

Total for all company codes of accounts analyzed, in EUR (closing date: Dec. 31, XXXX)				
Total liability:	150,000 700,000 550,000 –	Debit Credit		
Per currency:	500,000 – 10,000 – 5,000 – 5,000 – 30,000 –		 AUD CHF GBP USD	 15,000 – 7,500 – 3,500 – 35,000 –

Fig. 10 Possible Structure of a Fictitious Open Items List, Broken Down by Currency

Vendors with Debit Balances

Vendors with debit balances should be examined critically and, if appropriate, items should be reclassified to receivables or other assets. Reasons that vendors may have debit balances could be overpayments, credits, or simultaneous, reversed payment obligations.

Liabilities Denominated in Foreign Currency/ Currency Translation

As can be seen in the above table, the open items list shows liabilities broken down by currency. Liabilities in foreign currency are measured at the current exchange rate. The measurement is performed at the current rate at the end of each month. This results in foreign exchange gains or losses. Once auditors have created an open items list in the IT system, they must use auditor judgment to decide if they should test whether the correct exchange rate has been used for measurement and any foreign exchange gains or losses have been taken to the income statement according to the company's accounting guidelines.

Liabilities to Affiliated Companies

When auditing trade accounts payable, the auditor must ensure that liabilities to affiliated companies are examined separately. Although liabilities to affiliated companies are also reported under current liabilities, they are normally captured separately. Liabilities are broken down by creditor groups on the face of the balance sheet, unless this is done in the notes to the balance sheet. The auditors should ensure that balances are reconciled regularly, at least annually at the end of the fiscal year.

Critical Authorizations and Creation of Master Data

Critical authorizations relating to the creation of master data are a particularly sensitive issue. Sometimes, employees are authorized both to update vendor master data and to effect payments. In such cases Internal Audit must consider the risk of fraud: If the employee is authorized to create vendors and also to make payments to vendors, fraud is theoretically possible. Auditors therefore must ensure that the same person cannot maintain vendor master data with banking information and also make payments. If there is not enough employee capacity to issue separate authorizations, additional internal control mechanisms must be in place (e.g., dual control).

Approval of Purchase Order Requisitions

In SAP's purchasing unit, various controls are mapped in automated IT process steps. This includes, for example, that employees request approvals for purchasing goods and services (purchase order requisitions) through the workflow. These purchase order requisitions are approved by the manager responsible and released as purchase orders (for details on purchasing, see Section C, Chapter 4.1). A purchase order number is created in SAP's system. Auditors should verify that an appropriate approval guideline exists and that the limits and approval procedures are reflected in the IT system.

Testing Substantive Accuracy

The "testing substantive accuracy" process control is examined in a separate step. The employee responsible should check each incoming invoice for factual correctness and release it into the workflow before it is added to the payment proposal list. The auditor should take a suitable number of samples to show that the checks have been made and documented. The auditor should also test whether the invoices have been correctly released and this is properly reflected in the live system. Auditors can also verify that the total invoice amount does not exceed the amount stated on the purchase orders.

Approval of Payment Proposal Lists

Once invoices have been examined for factual correctness, a payment proposal list is created. Controls should be in place to ensure that this list contains only invoices that have been factually checked. This list should, for example, be checked and released by the head of the finance department or the head of the accounts payable department. Auditors must verify that an appropriate process has been implemented and the controls have been carried out. Again, compliance with the dual control principle is absolutely essential.

Effecting of Payment

Payments are normally made by electronic bank transfer. As mentioned before, only a very limited group of employees should be authorized to trigger payments. The audit includes obtaining a written bank confirmation of the signing powers. The auditor should also reconcile the total of the payment proposal list to the total of the bank statement.

HINTS AND TIPS

- When auditing liabilities, auditors should ensure that all liabilities fully and correctly reflect actual volumes and values.
- Auditors should also make sure that the implemented processes have sufficient internal controls, e.g., the use of the dual control principle.

LINKS AND REFERENCES

- JARNAGIN, B.D. 2007. *US Master GAAP Guide*. Riverwoods, IL: CCH, Inc.
- SEARS, B. 2002. *Internal Auditing Manual*. New York, NY: Warren, Gorham & Lamont.
- SAWYER, L. B., M. A DITTENHOFER AND J. H. SCHEINER. 2003. *Sawyer's Internal Auditing*. 5th ed. Altamonte Springs, FL: The Institute of Internal Auditors.

3.5 Revenue Audits

KEY POINTS

- The revenue recognition regulations relevant to SAP under US-GAAP are primarily found in SOP 97-2 and SOP 81-1.
- The objective of revenue audits is to ensure that the revenues are classified correctly and stated in the appropriate amount and period.
- During audit preparation, Internal Audit should obtain a general overview of the largest revenue amounts recognized during the period under review. Offsetting account analysis is a good tool to use for this purpose.
- Moreover, revenue audits should include analytical procedures.

Revenue Recognition under US-GAAP

There are various general, as well as sector-specific, guidelines for recognizing revenue under US-GAAP. For the software sector, and thus also SAP, very important rules are contained in Statement of Position (SOP) 97-2 (Software Revenue Recognition), as amended by SOP 98-9 (Modification of SOP 97-2, Software Revenue Recognition, With Respect to Certain Transactions). Another set of guidelines relevant for software accounting at SAP is Accounting Review Bulletin (ARB) 45 (Long-Term Construction-Type Contracts), as interpreted by SOP 81-1 (Accounting for Performance of Construction-Type and Certain Production-Type Contracts). In addition to the above regulations, the following statements must be observed in the accounting system:

- Pronouncements that specifically comment on and explain certain sections of SOP 97-2.
- Pronouncements covering those transactions at SAP that are not regulated by SOP 97-2. Some of these are:

- Technical Practice Aids for SOP 97-2 (TPA) 5100.38 et seq.
- EITF 00-21: Revenue Arrangements with Multiple Deliverables.
- EITF 01-09: Accounting for Consideration Given by a Vendor to a Customer (Including a Reseller of the Vendor's Products).
- EITF 99-19: Reporting Revenue Gross as a Principal versus Net as an Agent.
- SAB 104: Revenue Recognition.

- SOP 81-1: Accounting for Performance of Construction-Type and Certain Production-Type Contracts. SOP 97-2 requires the application of the guidance provided by SOP 81-1 to elements to which SOP 81-1 is applicable in the case of contracts that either (a) require significant production, modification, or customization of the software, or (b) where the service element does not meet the criteria for separate recognition.

Revenue Recognition Criteria

Under SOP 97-2, revenue can be recognized for software sold without significant modification only when all of the following four criteria are met:

- Persuasive evidence of an arrangement exists.
- Delivery of the software has occurred.
- The fee is fixed or determinable.
- Collectibility is probable.

Audit Objective

The objective of a revenue audit is to ensure that the recognized revenue has in fact been realized, is correctly apportioned, and reported in full, and that the appropriate amount has been booked on the correct account according to US-GAAP and SAP's accounting policies. Revenue also must be classified correctly and must not be overstated or understated. Revenue audits are closely linked to audits of the corresponding business units. At SAP, revenue is mainly generated from Licenses and Maintenance (see Section C, Chapter 5.3), as well as Consulting and Training (see Section C, Chapter 5.2) which are therefore subject to revenue audits.

Offsetting Account Analysis

During audit preparation, the audit team should gain a general overview of the largest revenue amounts recognized during the period under review. This is done by analyzing the relevant revenue accounts, a task assisted by offsetting account analysis in the SAP system. Offsetting account analysis is a report of all entries made to a specific account in a certain period, with information on the offsetting accounts used for each transaction. On this basis, the audit team can determine how much revenue has been generated with which customers in the period under review for each revenue area. This allows the audit team to pre-select the revenues they intend to analyze more closely when on site. Offsetting account analysis also shows which other accounts have been used for entries in addition to customer accounts, e.g. VAT accounts, deferral accounts, accounts for revenue adjustments, etc. In addition, it also provides information and key figures that may be useful for detailed analysis, such as averages, percentages and the number of entries. A detailed study of the results of the offsetting account analysis is excellent preparation for the on-site work and will allow the auditors to conduct a well-structured audit.

Fieldwork

Customers, such as those with the highest revenue for the period, are selected for inclusion in the audit for each revenue area (Licenses, Maintenance, Consulting, Training) on the basis of the offsetting account analysis performed in advance. It is important to ensure that the business volume of each revenue area is sufficiently covered by audits. In addition, entries of revenue deductions are also examined (see Section C, Chapter 3.2). Any credit notes issued should also be analyzed because this allows the auditors to identify circumstances in which a revenue adjustment should have been recorded. The revenue audit also looks at US-GAAP adjustments and period-end deferrals.

Test Procedures in Detail

The specific revenues that have been selected are analyzed in detail, checking the transactions underlying the revenue from each customer. Again, the auditors should select data for a country, a region, or global data according to risk probabilities. The recognized revenue being analyzed may relate to a consulting project, a training event, a license agreement, or maintenance. Audits of the areas of Consulting, Licenses, and Maintenance are described in detail in the relevant chapters (see Section C, Chapters 5.2 and 5.3). In addition to revenue, the customer account entries must be examined for accuracy, receipt of payment and the agreed payment terms, any bad debt allowances, and revenue deductions. It is also important to perform additional analytical procedures (see Section C, Chapter 3.1) as part of the revenue audit, focusing on the following aspects:

- changes in receivables (compared with the previous year and changes since the start of the fiscal year),
- margin analysis,
- revenue-to-orders ratio,
- analysis of credit notes issued,
- analysis of write-offs and bad debt allowances,
- analysis of revenue distribution by business area (Licenses, Consulting, and Training) and of changes in revenue over time, and
- analysis of the bonus-to-revenue ratio.

Consultation Requirement

A revenue audit requires close consultation with other audit teams who are evaluating individual business areas. In addition to the SAP-specific areas mentioned above, this includes, for example, the auditing of accounts receivable (see Section C, Chapter 3.2), accounts payable (see Section C, Chapter 3.4), accruals (see Section C, Chapter 3.3) and, in the case of manufacturing companies, inventories. It is important that auditors exchange information all the time and ensure that the interfaces between individual audit segments are taken into account.

End of the Audit

Once the actual fieldwork has been completed, the regular reports are produced (see Section B, Chapter 5), followed, after a due period, by the status check and the follow-up audit (see Section B, Chapter 6). Revenue audits run through all the phases of the Audit Roadmap.

LINKS AND REFERENCES ↗

- ARB 45: Long-Term Construction-Type Contracts.
- EITF 99-19: Reporting Revenue Gross as a Principal versus Net as an Agent.
- EITF 00-21: Revenue Arrangements with Multiple Deliverables.
- EITF 01-09: Accounting for Consideration Given by a Vendor to a Customer (including a Reseller of the Vendor's Products).
- JARNAGIN, B. D. 2007. *US Master GAAP Guide.* Riverwoods, IL: CCH, Inc.
- SAWYER, L. B., M. A. DITTENHOFER AND J. H. SCHEINER. 2003. *Sawyer's Internal Auditing.* 5th ed. Altamonte Springs, FL: The Institute of Internal Auditors.
- SEARS, B. 2002. *Internal Auditing Manual.* New York, NY: Warren, Gorham & Lamont.
- SOP 81-1: Accounting for Performance of Construction-Type and Certain Production-Type Contracts.
- SOP 97-2: Software Revenue Recognition.
- SOP 98-9: Modification of SOP 97-2, Software Revenue Recognition, with Respect to Certain Transactions.

4 Selected Operational Audit Topics

4.1 Purchasing

KEY POINTS •••

- Purchasing audits can be conducted at a strategic or operational level.
- Purchasing audits should include a focus on fraud prevention.
- Supplier selection is also a primary focus of a purchasing audit. Proper documentation should be in place to allow the supplier selection process to be tracked.

Importance of Purchasing

The purchasing function (i.e., procurement) contributes to securing and enhancing a company's long-term potential for success by influencing critical success factors, such as costs, quality and time. Thus, audits of the purchasing process are especially important. The extent to which the purchasing process affects the success of the organization depends on the targets and objectives that management has set for purchasing, and whether the department is embedded within the company's supply chain management function, or whether it merely needs to meet the company's operational demands.

Formal and Technical Objectives

When assessing the purchasing function, auditors should begin with the objectives set for purchasing, which can be examined from several different perspectives. First of all, the objectives pursued by purchasing can be categorized as formal and technical objectives. The primary formal objectives of an organization include cost reductions and performance improvements. The key technical objective is to ensure the parts and supplies necessary for operations. For the long term, meeting these objectives includes both opportunities and risks for a company, because factors may change within the company or in the procurement market.

Strategic Objectives

The following strategic purchasing objectives of a company can be identified:

- securing the procurement market position,
- quality assurance,
- supply security,
- safeguarding the status of technology, and
- safeguarding flexibility.

These objectives can be condensed into groups as follows:

- cost reduction (reduction of prices, process costs, cost of materials and services),
- differentiation (quality and service improvements, participation in the expertise and image of the supplier or service provider), and
- supply security.

Role of Purchasing at SAP

At SAP, the purchasing function includes both operational requirements and the procurement of goods and services that may or may not be billed to customers. The procurement of goods and services, which are part of SAP's operational supply chain, make up a large percentage of SAP's purchasing volume.

Purchasing System

In a live (computerized) system, purchasing tasks can be processed with the Materials Management component or, in the B2B area, with an SRM (supplier relationship management) system. Materials Management (MM) is a fully integrated module of the SAP system.

Value Added Through Procurement with Minimized Expenditure

Over the past few years, the purchasing function has become increasingly important for company activities because the potential of the purchasing function to add value to company success has increasingly been recognized. One way that the purchasing function adds value is by procuring goods and services at minimized cost under total-cost-of-ownership criteria, which look at all cost drivers along the supply chain.

Other Forms of Value Added

In addition, the purchasing function can assist operating departments when they initiate purchases from third parties. This service adds value within the company, for example, because on the one hand, the exchange of information supports the development of or changes to products and services, while on the other hand, accurate market and price knowledge puts the company in a better negotiating position. By optimizing and securing supplies for the organization as a whole, purchasing also generates added value. Moreover, quality assurance in procurement is given high priority in every organization, mainly for reasons of product liability and the risk of adversely affecting sales success. This factor is becoming all the more noticeable because of the increasing importance of procurement for operating success. Specifically, procurement accounts for a high proportion of costs, ranging from 40% to 90% of sales depending on the sector.

Audit Preparation

The audit focus areas are defined during audit planning (see Section B, Chapter 2). Audit preparation varies according to these specific focus areas. When auditing strategic functions, the elements are subjected to spot plausibility and completeness checks. In the case of operational audits of purchasing, Internal Audit can examine either the purchasing process as a whole, or individual sub-processes.

Information of the Area to Be Audited

Before the initiation of the purchasing audit, the audit announcement informs the departments concerned of the impending audit (see Section B, Chapter 3.1). Depending on the circumstances, departments such as the purchasing unit of the subsidiary or the central unit of the parent company, Accounting, and/or the department placing purchase orders could be included in the audit. The audit can have its starting point in different areas and entail different approaches, depending on the circumstances of the audit and the audit objective. For example, the audit could begin with the purchasing process (e.g., purchase order, purchase requisition) or, on the vendor side by analyzing the vendor accounts. It is also possible to conduct an audit from the legal perspective with a focus on contract arrangements.

Sample Selection

Depending on the audit objective and audit object, it may be expedient to select a sample for testing in advance. At SAP, the selection can be made with the use of several data sources, e.g., the SAP-specific Global Contract Information Database.

Global Contract Information Database

This database contains various criteria by which contracts and master agreements can be selected for auditing. Criteria include the name of the supplier and the financial contract volume. Depending on the selection criteria applied, the system displays the relevant contracts, including all specific details and the original contract. Internal Audit can then select and audit individual purchase order requisitions, purchase orders, or invoices related to the selected contracts.

Purchasing Report

In addition to the above SAP-specific Global Contract Information Database, the Material Management Purchasing Area creates purchasing reports, which gives auditors many options for selecting purchase orders because the report is based on the data of the live SAP system, which contains all transaction data. The aim is to obtain an overview of all the purchase orders relevant for the audit segment concerned. The selection focuses on the same criteria as in the case of the Global Contract Information Database. Of course, there are other criteria that can determine inclusion in, and define the extent of, an audit, including details of the development of supplier relations or cost analyses.

Communicating the Sample

Once the sample has been determined, the departments to be audited should be informed so that all the necessary process documentation and records are available when the audit begins.

Scope and Work Program

A Core Scope (see Section B, Chapter 2.1) has been defined as the collection of all potential audit topics in relation to a specific audit area, including Purchasing. There may also be other Scopes (e.g., the Core Scope for Accounts Payable), that have an impact on the purchasing function. The exact specifications of the extent of the audit are included in the work program (see Section B, Chapter 3.2).

Need for Coordination

Purchasing can be audited either separately or as a sub-section of the audit of a subsidiary (see Section C, Chapter 5.1). For this reason it is important that internal audit teams consult with one another so that they can coordinate the audit topics and the relevant audit activities. The specific work program is then defined on the basis of this cooperation.

Preventive Audits

Often, audits are conducted in Purchasing with very specific work programs that are preventive in nature. For example, purchase orders with a certain order volume may be examined, particularly with regard to release and release strategies. Another preventive audit approach includes audits that focus on supplier selection and the related documentation. Supplier selection, which is a high risk area and very prone to misuse, is one of the most important elements of a purchasing audit (for details on fraud prevention, see Section D, Chapter 13).

Work Program

The combination of the end-to-end concept of the Scope and the adaptability of the work program is an ideal way of meeting all the requirements of audit planning and execution. The level of detail of the work program can also reflect and support specific nuances for each audit.

Tools and Templates

The Material Management Purchasing Area mentioned above is used to verify the sample selection in the SAP system and to earmark it for subsequent auditing. Various tools and templates are available to auditors for conducting the audit, including live system reports (purchase order analyses, G/L account analyses, one-time analyses) and/or the relevant purchasing and conduct guidelines.

Purchasing Guidelines of SAP

SAP's global purchasing policy provides the framework within which the strategic and operational processes relating to purchasing are managed. Important elements of these guidelines include the role of purchasing in the organization, the objectives of purchasing, etc.

Code of Business Conduct

The Code of Business Conduct applies throughout the SAP Group and must be signed by each employee. Contraventions of the Code may result in disciplinary action. For purchasing, the rules on accepting gifts and on customer and supplier relations are of particular relevance. Specifically, to ensure that employees do not favor vendors who provide lavish gifts, low monetary thresholds limit the value of gifts or favors (including meals) employees (or the company as a whole) may accept from vendors. Internal audits of the purchasing department will examine compliance with these policies.

Audits of Strategic Functions of Purchasing Management

The audit activities may also include the strategic purchasing functions. Purchasing is of strategic importance because of its responsibility for exploiting cost reduction and performance improvement potential. Purchasing is responsible for supporting the entire software development process, from the development of new products through shipping the final product.

Cost Savings Potential

Cost savings potential is the company's ability to reduce costs. This can be achieved with make-or-buy decisions, demand pooling, and strategic supplier relations. Moreover, process optimization and demand analysis can also deliver cost savings. The way in which purchasing is organized also unlocks savings potential in the purchasing area. For example, the cost savings potential of other divisions of the company can be influenced by centralizing purchasing.

Make-or-Buy Decision

When companies take make-or-buy decisions on the basis of strategic objectives, the decision is driven by their focus on core competencies. Before such a decision is taken, a number of analyses should be performed so that the core competencies can be determined conclusively. These include detailed cost analyses, competitor analysis, and customer profitability. In addition, the entire value chain should be examined to establish whether or not buying from a third party is potentially more profitable. Auditors primarily examine the plausibility of these analyses and the related documents.

Internal Potential of Purchasing

Because of their knowledge and experience, Purchasing's employees no doubt form part of its internal potential. Moreover, the design of the organizational and process structures also represents success potential. It is possible, as part of the process structure, to improve the quality of processes by specialization. Both the organizational and process structures of purchasing should be tested for effectiveness and efficiency.

Auditing Operational Functions of Purchasing Management

From Internal Audit's point of view, all tasks and phases of purchasing are eligible audit topics. The total procurement process can be broken down into several phases, to which individual tasks can be assigned: preparation, initiation, and award of contract.

Determining Demand

During the preparation phase, demand for materials or services arises either in the operating departments or as part of materials planning. For materials defined in the material master of the system, the system checks the reported inventory level and determines the materials to be reordered. Purchase requisitions can either be generated by authorized operating department employees or automatically by the system.

Determining the Procurement Source

The initiation phase starts with determining the procurement source. The SAP system supports operating departments in determining possible procurement sources, taking past purchase orders or existing contracts into account. This accelerates the creation of requests for quotations, which can then be sent directly to the required suppliers electronically. The quality of the supplier master data is an important element when auditing procurement sources. They should therefore be included in any audit, at least by way of samples, with a focus on suppliers with duplicate system entries that need to be removed. The SAP system can simulate pricing scenarios to facilitate comparing the quotations received and selecting a supplier.

Order Processing

The contract award phase begins with the processing of the purchase order. The SAP purchasing system takes the information from the purchase requisition and the quotation and generates a purchase order.

Order Monitoring

To monitor the ordering process, the SAP system checks the resubmission intervals and automatically prints reminders at the appropriate times. It provides the current status of all purchase requisitions, quotations, and purchase orders.

Goods Receipt and Inventory Management

The dispatch and goods receipt departments can confirm the receipt of goods by entering the order number in the system. Buyers are able to tolerate over- and under-deliveries within limits by specifying the permissible over and underdelivery tolerance levels.

Invoice Verification

The system also supports invoice verification: When auditors access order processes and goods receipt entries, they are alerted to any quantity and price variances.

Taking the Documentation into Account

As part of an audit, it should be possible to retrace all the above tasks of each phase of the procurement process. In relation to the size and workforce capacities of the SAP subsidiaries, the system-based purchasing process can be set up in the system in different ways. For this reason, the auditors should record the processes and the system before the audit. Further, the auditors should examine the relevant documentation for completeness and validity, and ensure that the system information agrees with the paper documents.

Auditing Release Strategies and Authorizations

When auditing the purchasing function, it is very important to include release strategies in the examination. Release strategies define who may grant approval for certain processes under what circumstances (depending on the goods and volume) and in what sequence. Within the purchasing process, there may be a number of release steps. From a control perspective, delegating the release of certain process steps should be restricted to a minimum and the dual control principle must be maintained. The audit focuses on the following:

- Approval for release: Has an approval for release system been installed for important processes? Approval for release requests are normally forwarded to the next higher-ranking level (e.g., cost center manager) in the workflow. It is also

possible to set up a second level for approval in the SAP system, e.g., financial control for releasing budgets for internal projects.
- Purchasing as a control body: In this context, purchasing employees examine the purchase requisitions of the operating departments before converting them into purchase orders, checking details such as supplier, quantities, specification, etc.
- Authorizations: Employee authorizations, which give them the power to release orders linked to the budget value, are an important control tool in the purchasing area.
- Release across several levels of hierarchy: The dual control system can also be maintained by involving several hierarchy levels. This may be sensible for high-value orders or for other specific instances defined by the company.

Information on Release Authorizations

Internal Audit should ask the global purchasing department for details of the relevant authorizations. It is also possible that an auditor may be authorized to obtain the relevant settings directly from the system. Depending on the audit focus, Internal Audit should examine all the authorizations for purchase requisitions and purchase orders of the local subsidiary as well as the release settings from the global purchasing department.

Auditing Procurement Control

Increasing process complexity has caused procurement control to change considerably in the past few years. The pure cost focus of the past has given way to a stronger process focus. Under the conventional approach, cost center expenses were compared to budgets and changes in material prices. More modern approaches strive to improve the cost structure and supplier performance, thus giving purchasing an increasingly strategic orientation. The changes have added to the tasks of procurement control, which now include the following:
- monitoring and ratio analysis,
- involvement in drafting target agreements,
- preparation for decisions,
- building of strategic procurement principles,
- analysis of the strengths and weaknesses of procurement potential,
- strategic comparison of to-be and as-is situations, and
- control measures in case of variance from targets.

Risk of Fraud

Every company is exposed to the risk of fraud (see Section D, Chapter 13). Fraud may be committed by employees at any level and under a large variety of circumstances. Company management must take all cases of fraud seriously. Fraud falls into two categories: embezzlement of company assets and misstating the company's financial position. In purchasing, the following processes are particularly exposed to fraud:
- supplier selection,
- changes of supplier master data, and
- payments and money transfer.

Fraud During Supplier Selection

During supplier selection, it is possible to give preferential treatment to certain providers, often by passing on internal information about the demand or the invitation to bid. The internal information is usually critical to the bidding process, e.g., prices, specifications, and the supply and payment terms of competitors. This may impact the company financially by way of less favorable terms and conditions because such insider action circumvents a truly competitive process. There is also a possibility of unauthorized signatures and contracts. Preventive measures may include the following:

- rotation of buyers' responsibilities,
- requirement for buyers to make a declaration about the supplier's independence,
- code of conduct and purchasing guidelines, and
- contract negotiation and contract awards in compliance with the dual control principle.

Manipulation of Supplier Master Data

The dual control principle helps minimize fraudulent changes to or manipulations of supplier master data, although Internal Audit should still examine this data for any changes made. The justification for any changes must be properly documented. Such changes can be tracked in the SAP system. Frequently, automated controls are part of the integrated SAP system.

Unauthorized Payments

Misuse of payment and money transfer systems is possible if controls are not in place or do not function properly. Various actions can be taken to prevent fraud, for example by implementing a "secure" process, i.e., a process where the necessary controls are in place. In addition, employees should be granted authorization rights selectively.

Supplier Tests

In purchasing, supplier tests are an additional preventive measure. Internal Audit can test the creditworthiness of the supplier by using general information or credit bureaus. The audit team can also check the supplier's reputation in the market on the basis of press reports entered in databases or through competitor surveys. It is also important to check the validity and existence of the supplier in order to detect the creation of fictitious suppliers. On-site supplier tests are often a criterion during supplier selection, because a supplier's readiness to allow a test for quality assurance purposes is seen as a positive sign when selecting the shortlist. On-site supplier tests can take the form of either a process audit or an IT system audit. If the focus is on processes, auditors check quality control, supplier resources, systems used, and employees of the supplier. An IT system audit involves a test of the supplier's IT systems. The way a supplier test is conducted on site is to a large extent determined by the agreements concluded at the time dealings commence with the supplier and by the relationship between customer and supplier. All persons involved in the process should take part in planning and executing such a test so that input is taken on board from different areas, such as procurement, quality assurance, and production.

HINTS AND TIPS

- Purchasing's documentation (e.g. of supplier selection), should never leave any gaps that are significant in risk and impact and should correspond to the information contained in the system.
- When conducting a purchasing audit, it is essential to have an overview of the purchasing organization and its processes.

LINKS AND REFERENCES

- JARNAGIN, B. D. 2007. *US Master GAAP Guide.* Riverwoods, IL: CCH, Inc.
- SEARS, B. 2002. *Internal Auditing Manual.* New York, NY: Warren, Gorham & Lamont.
- SAWYER, L. B., M. A. DITTENHOFER AND J. H. SCHEINER. 2003. *Sawyer's Internal Auditing.* 5th ed. Altamonte Springs, FL: The Institute of Internal Auditors.

4.2 Sales Processes

KEY POINTS

- The sales process is an important object of Internal Audit's work
- An important distinction is made between service contracts and license agreements.
- Sales processes can be tested for compliance using walk-through procedures.
- Before SAP enters into a sales contract with another party, the customer support officer and the sales manager perform a risk assessment.
- The SAP system provides certain tools and templates to ensure reliable audit execution.
- The objectives of a sales audit are to ensure that sales processes comply with policies and procedures and to identify potential risks in the sales entities.

Sales Process at SAP

The sales process is an important object of the audit work performed by Internal Audit at SAP. SAP's local subsidiaries are separate legal entities that act as sales companies. Internal agreements that govern the sale of software by local subsidiaries are in place. In addition, the local subsidiaries offer their customers consulting and training services. SAP products can also be marketed through resellers in the indirect sales channel. Under this type of arrangement, the resellers enter into contracts with the end customer, and the local SAP subsidiary is the reseller's contract partner.

Requirements on the Sales Processes

Local subsidiaries vary in size, which is reflected in the way they are organized. During the audit, Internal Audit must take account of the organization of the subsidiaries, as well as of local aspects and guidelines. However, for consolidated reporting purposes, the accounting treatment of all transactions must comply with US-GAAP. The sales process ranges from initial customer contact, through bidding and contract conclusion, to entering the transaction and providing ongoing support to the customer. Sales process audits are closely related to other audits and are often, at least partially, conducted alongside license or consulting audits. This means that they are, in part, an integral component of such audits, which in turn may bring up issues of revenue recognition. For more information on revenue recognition, refer to the description of revenue audits in Section C, Chapter 3.5, license audits in Section C, Chapter 5.3, and revenue recognition assurance in Section C, Chapter 9.

Test Procedures

Like all audits at SAP, sales process audits follow the general procedure of the Audit Roadmap. The basis is formed by recording and documenting the individual processes and comparing the current condition to the desired criteria. To do this, the audit team conducts interviews and reviews generally accessible or specifically requested documents and process descriptions. With this information, the auditors can conduct a walk-through to verify whether the documented process is followed in reality. In a walk-through, the auditors first select a document type from the described process, e.g., license agreements. Then they select a sample of documents (license agreements) from the total population and follow the complete process using the sample documents, to ensure compliance all the way through transaction entry, including the documented internal controls.

Testing of Individual Contracts

In addition, it is useful to examine individual license agreements (see Section C, Chapter 5.3). By reviewing original documents, the audit team can test their existence as well as formalities, including internal controls such as legal signatures.

Selection of Audit Objects

Since it is impossible, of course, to test all contracts, especially in larger subsidiaries, the auditors should select suitable samples (see Section B, Chapter 4.1.2). In addition to using statistical sampling methods, selection criteria such as the contract volume and the time of recognition are useful for choosing a judgmental sample.

Internal Control System

An important objective inherent in every internal audit is to test whether there is a functioning internal control system. This is of particular importance in a process that is as tightly managed, from a legal point of view, as the sales process. In detail, this involves ensuring that internal and external legal requirements are met in each phase. The sales area's internal control system is above all aimed at ensuring legal and accounting compliance. This is why each step of the sales process includes specific types of control and documentation (e.g. SAP's Global Contract Approval Form).

Relationship with the Sales Process

Sales process audits are always included in the work programs for local subsidiary audits (see Section C, Chapter 5.1). In addition, the sales process may also be in focus when ensuring that revenue is recognized correctly, e.g. in relation to compliance with the legal framework. This is particularly important when there are public invitations to bid. At the same time, the audit team must carefully consider internal rules, such as the code of conduct.

Contract Types at SAP

The contracts concluded with customers are an important element of sales process audits. A signed contract documents the result of negotiations. SAP has several types of contracts, including but not limited to contracts related purely to software and maintenance (license and maintenance agreements) or including software implementation and training (service contracts). SAP also concludes development cooperation agreements in the context of software development. These agreements can be concluded as separate contracts or under a master agreement.

License Agreements

License agreements include the extent of licenses, the customer's permitted level of usage, the price, and the payment terms (for more details, see Section C, Chapter 5.3).

Service Contracts

Service contracts are usually very complex and customized. They are based on a number of documents, such as feasibility studies, case studies, proofs of concept, etc. There are different options for the payment arrangements, depending on whether the project is billed on a fixed-price basis, on a time and material basis, or on a maximum price basis (see Section C, Chapter 5.2.1). In addition, this type of contract includes project plans, project target agreements, and function lists. The project target agreements set out clearly the project milestones for acceptance by the customer and the payment amounts and dates due to SAP (see Section C, Chapter 5.2.3).

Development Cooperation Agreements

Development cooperation agreements may relate to add-ons to be integrated into the software as a standard solution or to projects set up specifically for individual customers or partners.

Other Departments Concerned

Apart from the sales department, the audit of sales processes involves the contract department, the relevant finance unit, and Corporate Financial Reporting. The framework and requirements for the sales processes are specified and documented by the management of the sales area. The work of the employees responsible for implementing a sales process is also under scrutiny in the audit. The following paragraphs give a brief description of the positions involved in a typical sales process.

(Global) Customer Support Officer

The (global) customer support officer, who works under the sales manager, has overall responsibility for contract negotiations and the contract itself. It is likely that the sales manager may also review the work of the global customer support officer. Depending on the volume of the contract to be concluded with the customer, various SAP-internal approval steps must be complied with and risk assessments must be performed. The contracts must also be agreed with the contract and legal departments. These two departments are responsible for wording standard contracts, but if required they will also provide support for the design of individual contracts.

Head of Consulting

In the case of service contracts, the head of consulting is involved in the contract design and later provides information on project progress so that revenue can be recognized appropriately. In some instances, he or she controls this process in conjunction with the customer.

Product Support and Training Officers

If support and training services are offered, the product support and training officers are also involved in the contract design. They shape these offerings as part of the overall contract.

Customer and Sales Oriented Team

The virtual customer and sales-oriented team is made up of experts with knowledge of the product itself and on sector-specific solutions. This is of particular importance in global corporate groups with various contacts from different regions.

Risk Management

Risk management and the departments involved in it also play an important role in the overall sales process because they ensure that the requirements of risk management guidelines and processes are communicated and implemented and that the reporting system is compliant. Risk management is described below in this chapter as it relates to the sales processes.

Creation of Contract

The contract process consists of several separate stages, starting with contract development and ending with formal contract approval. The creation of the contract is based on the results of a formal assessment of the project and customer risks, such as their liquidity and creditworthiness. The risk assessment must be taken into account during the entire contract process.

Selection of the Sales Processes for Testing

When planning a sales process audit, it also is important for the internal audit team to review past events. Sales units that have had repeated problems in the past should be examined with greater priority. Likewise, current sales-related events may influence the selection of the process to be tested, e.g. restructuring in the sales area or knowledge of non-compliance with regulatory requirements. Internal Audit also must consider any partner companies involved in service performance.

Persons to be Audited

The group of persons affected by the audit depends on the process and is therefore not subject to any special restrictions. The (global) customer support officer, the head of consulting, the product support and training officers, and the virtual team supporting the relevant customer are all eligible for the audit.

Contract and Addendums

During a sales process audit, the internal audit team should review the following contracts and documents for accuracy and completeness:

- Contract: A distinction is made between license, service, and maintenance contracts. A contract can consist of several sections, which may be interdependent, thus mutually determining the amount and timing of the license revenue to be recognized.
- Bid: Customers request a bid from SAP, either directly or through a general invitation to bid.
- Non-disclosure agreement (NDA): This is a contract document that binds two contracting parties to confidentiality, thus ensuring that patent requirements, for example, are met.
- Addendums: Addendums are annexes to a contract. They can contain additional explanations or subsequent additions.
- Acceptance log: This type of document is signed by the customer in development or consulting projects according to the contract arrangements for each project milestone to confirm that the services have been duly performed.

Scope and Work Program

The Scope for sales process audits describes the general content and extent of such audits while the work program details the terms of specific audits. In addition, the Scopes and work programs of related audit segments and areas, e.g. for local subsidiary audits (see Section Chapter 5.1) or license audits (see Section C, Chapter 5.3), may contain further relevant audit specifications.

Aspects of Audit Execution

Most of the functions, processes, and objects to be audited can be taken from the overall sales process description. This description can be used to create the work program necessary for the audit, in combination with pre-defined and existing work programs. The audit can be conducted either independently or in connection with a license audit under a local subsidiary audit. In order to delineate the audit segments and coordinate the selection of contract samples, it is therefore important to agree with colleagues if any audit areas are to be added.

Obtaining and Evaluating Information

Audit-relevant data and information can be obtained in a number of different ways. It is, however, important to assess its relevance to the audit objective. Minutes of meetings, announcements, or the electronic archives of the department contain information that is easy to understand, but often unstructured. These sources may also provide information about the flow of information within a department. Compliance in the sales process is, to a considerable extent, assured with adequate internal controls. Independently of the contract itself, a contract supplement provides additional guarantees for all relevant aspects of the contract and involves those responsible in the approval and release process. This document is an important basis for audits conducted by Internal Audit.

Indications of Non-Compliant Processes

The achievement of goals defined as key performance indicators can provide information on process compliance, for example the percentage of risks in a project not previously identified in the risk profile.

Tools and Templates

The SAP system offers a number of options for retrieving different reports. During audit planning, each auditor should have, or apply for, the requisite system authorizations in order to access all relevant information.

Risk Management in Sales Processes

In addition to ensuring that sales processes are compliant, another important objective of the sales process audit is to identify potential risks in this area. The range of risk management covers the entire sales process. SAP's perspective is the primary focus of the audit, but as far as possible, the customer aspect should also be included, because customer risk may also lead to risk for SAP. Risk management in the sales area is part of global risk management and is subject to the methodologies, terminologies, processes and content requirements defined by SAP's global risk management department. Before a customer can be involved in a new project, the risk assessment and the preventive risk mitigation measures must be performed for this project. Internal Audit uses the specified risk process to test compliance with and implementation of risk management requirements in the sales process and how they have been documented in the form of risk profiles and risk summaries.

Risk Profile

The risk profile is a questionnaire to determine significant risks associated with a transaction. It must be compiled during the initiation and evaluation phase and approved and signed by the relevant level of management of SAP. The risk profile is used to identify potential risks that impact the profitability of the project and the contract itself, as well as functional and technical risks.

Risk Management During the Initiation Phase

Generally, with regard to risk management, two phases of customer relationships are distinguished in a sales cycle. Risk management during the initiation phase necessitates risk assessment during the bidding and contract phase. Risks that are identifiable in advance must be documented in the risk profile, and the results of the risk evaluation must be incorporated into contract design. There are technical and consulting services that can be used for proactive risk minimization during the sales process, including customer evaluation or project situation assessment on the basis of feasibility studies. Internal Audit should test the chronological and formal use of risk management, i.e., whether the risk minimization procedures were complied with before the bid was submitted and the contract signed. Significant changes to the contract situation always require the risks to be reassessed.

Risk Management during the Implementation Phase

Risk management forms an integral part of project management during the software implementation phase and could also cover the customer support phase. Internal Audit tests the accuracy of the risk management documentation of this phase with regard to form and content, such as the results of quality reviews or meetings of the project steering committee.

Risk Management for Partner Cooperation

Risk assessment is also important with regard to cooperation with partners during implementation projects. Such projects may give rise to various cooperation issues between SAP, its partners, and customers. This affects above all the roles and responsibilities to be defined as part of the project. The people involved must be specified across the various project objectives, work packages, tasks, and topics and assessed in terms of risk.

HINTS AND TIPS

- The selection of contracts to be audited should include different contract types.
- Auditors should check each document for possible inconsistencies with other documents.

LINKS AND REFERENCES

- JARNAGIN, B. D. 2007. *US Master GAAP Guide*. Riverwoods, IL: CCH, Inc.
- SEARS, B. 2002. *Internal Auditing Manual*. New York, NY: Warren, Gorham & Lamont.
- SAWYER, L. B., M. A. DITTENHOFER AND J. H. SCHEINER. 2003. *Sawyer's Internal Auditing*. 5th ed. Altamonte Springs, FL: The Institute of Internal Auditors.

5 Combined Audit Topics

5.1 Subsidiary Audits

KEY POINTS

- Subsidiary audits are preformed using a standard work program.
- Subsidiary-specific matters are added to this standard work program based on analytical audit procedures performed during audit preparation and the meetings held with colleagues from the various corporate departments.
- Significant audit topics in a subsidiary audit are: General topics, financial reporting, consulting, licenses, human resources, purchasing, and risk management.

Standard Work Program

As explained previously (see Section B, Chapter 3.2), a work program is compiled for each audit based on the relevant Scope. There is a standard work program for subsidiary audits, which comprises the basic audit topics and fieldwork activities that should be covered by a subsidiary audit. Matters specific to the subsidiary being audited are added to the standard work program. These specific matters are normally based on the results of the analytical audit procedures performed on the subsidiary's financial statements during audit preparation (see Section C, Chapter 3.1) and on information and documentation obtained in meetings with colleagues from various corporate departments.

Structure of the Standard Work Program

The standard work program for auditing a subsidiary breaks down into the following main areas:

- general topics,
- financial reporting,
- consulting,
- licenses,
- human resources,
- purchasing, and
- risk management.

In addition, GIAS' SOX audit team conducts separate audits to analyze SOX-relevant issues and circumstances (see Section C, Chapter 8; Section D, Chapter 14).

Audit Preparation

When preparing for a subsidiary audit, auditors should arrange a meeting with the local tax consultant and the local external auditors to get an idea of any issues and risks from an independent third party. In addition, audit preparation includes the following activities:

- performing analytical audit procedures on the financial statements of the subsidiary,
- examining the consulting and license contracts concluded in the period and select a sample in each case,

- gathering further information in meetings with colleagues from other corporate departments (e.g., Accounting, Management Accounting, Legal, Taxes, and Treasury)
- creating the specific work program by adding subsidiary-specific matters to the standard work program, and using a risk assessment to determine which audit topics to select and which fieldwork activities to conduct,
- dispatching a list of requirements to the head of accounting in the subsidiary and contact him or her; if the (consulting, license, etc.) contracts are not in a language the auditors understand well they should obtain translations,
- preparing for the opening meeting,
- discussing the work program with the Audit Manager and obtain approval, and
- assigning the audit topics to auditors.

Analytical Procedures on the Financial Statements

During audit preparation, the audit team should perform analytical audit procedures on the financial statements. They should compare the current balances of the balance sheet and income statement (as of the audit date) with those of the previous year and those of the previous balance sheet date (see Section A, Chapter 6.2.4 and Section C, Chapter 3.1).

Changes in Balances and Individual Accounts

By analyzing the financial statements for changes in balances, the audit team can obtain valuable initial information about the subsidiary, e.g. its business performance, special expenditure, changes in receivables and revenue, etc. The analysis may highlight areas that should be more closely examined when conducting the audit on site. During preparations it may also be expedient to take a closer look at specific financial statement accounts, such as provisions, receivables, liabilities, and revenue. It may also be sensible to review the central SOX process documentation before the actual audit.

Consulting Contracts

For the consulting and licenses topics, it is also necessary and useful to make preparations prior to the audit. The audit team should obtain a report from the IT system with all the consulting contracts concluded in the period under review. The SAP-specific consulting information system allows the audit team to generate reports on fixed-price projects and projects charged on a time and material basis. SAP also concludes maximum price projects with customers, which are similar to fixed-price projects from a risk point of view. For the sampling procedure and other possible fieldwork, see Section B, Chapter 4.1.2.

License Agreements

The audit team should also obtain a report from the IT system with all the license agreements concluded in the period under review. The SAP-specific Contract Information System (CIS) allows the auditors to call up reports for selecting license agreements. The license administration department of the subsidiary should have scanned all license agreements into the system, which can be tested during audit preparation.

List of Requirements

During audit preparation, after the audit announcement has been sent out, it is a good idea to make personal contact with and send a list of requirements, detailing the documents to be prepared, to the head of accounting for the subsidiary. At the same time, the audit team should arrange for meetings with the relevant contacts and officers from the different areas (managing director, head of accounting, head of license administration, head of consulting). A list of requirements may include the following items, for example:

- organization chart,
- risk management information,
- list of the subsidiary's attorneys,
- contact information for the subsidiary's tax consultants,
- signature policy,
- company guidelines (company cars, travel, cellphones, etc.),
- purchasing guidelines,
- sales process descriptions (consulting, licenses),
- intra-group contracts,
- extract from the commercial register, and
- authorized bank signatories.

Meeting with the Audit Manager

Before the start of the audit, the work program is discussed with and approved by the Audit Manager. This approval forms part of Internal Audit's quality assurance and thus represents a quality gate, i.e., a quality assurance procedure which must be performed to move the audit to the next phase (see Section D, Chapter 5.3).

Assignment of Audit Topics

Before the audit, the audit team lead assigns the topics to the different team members, possibly after consulting with the Audit Manager. The audit is conducted based on the specific work program, and each auditor completes the audit topics assigned to him or her.

Preparation for the Opening Meeting

At the opening meeting, the audit team introduces itself to the managing director and the head of accounting of the subsidiary and discusses the procedure for the audit. There is a template for the agenda of the opening meeting, which should be adapted to the specific audit content in question. Internal Audit also uses this opportunity to point out the audit survey (see Section D, Chapter 7.2.2), which the people responsible in the audited area use to give Internal Audit feedback after the audit.

General Topics

During audit execution, auditors look at general issues such as extracts from the commercial register, list of authorized signatories, and corporate guidelines (on travel, purchasing, signature policy, company cars, etc.). The basic data of the subsidiary is recorded first. This includes checking the existence and validity of the extract from the commercial register, examining minutes of shareholder or directors' meetings, and checking intra-group contracts and guidelines for plausibility, completeness, validity and conformity to group requirements.

Financial Reporting

In addition to the business units, an audit of a subsidiary's financial reporting also includes receivables, provisions, liabilities, cash, and bank balances. In other words, significant financial accounts are examined. Revenue is usually examined when the individual areas, such as licenses and consulting, are audited (see Section C,

Chapters 5.2 and 5.3). A sample of license agreements and consulting contracts are audited, as well as the US-GAAP receivables, provisions, and deferrals and accruals associated with these business units.

Insights from the Analytical Procedures

Additional accounts may be added on the basis of the insights gained during the analytical audit procedures. The analysis of the financial statements performed during audit preparation is a significant foundation for auditing financial reporting and provides additional information for further fieldwork activities. For example, if the analytical procedures find that receivables are significantly higher than in the previous year, but revenue is only up by a small amount, this may mean that customers are exceeding their payment terms and that the accounts receivable should be examined for overdue amounts (DSO analysis). The subsidiary's payment receipt monitoring and reminder processes should also be examined in this context. The auditors can also investigate the extent to which management from licensing, sales, and consulting are involved in this process and whether the incentive or target agreements of sales and consulting employees incorporate the target that customers settle receivables in a timely manner. In as far as these issues can be assigned to the audits of the respective SAP business areas (licenses, consulting, training), the necessary fieldwork activities should be performed when these topics are dealt with. The list of observations from analytical procedures performed on the financial statements could be continued at length (for more details, see Section C, Chapter 3.1).

Auditor Judgment

In addition to the financial accounts identified by the analytical procedures, auditors should, based on their judgment, add other accounts for testing, such as noncurrent assets, other assets, other liabilities, and equity.

Consulting

Consulting audits comprise aspects such as processes, fixed-price projects, maximum-price projects, consulting services provided by third parties, and consulting-specific risk management. The auditor records the processes and examines the projects on a sample basis, taking into account both fixed-price and maximum-price projects. In some cases, it may also make sense to include projects charged on a time and material basis. It is important for project audits to include:

- cost tracing,
- project monitoring,
- examination of the flow of information between Consulting, Accounting, and Management Accounting,
- consideration of the involvement of Risk Management in project initiation and processing,
- examination of the treatment (orders, processing) of third-party providers, and
- examination of the correct allocation of costs and revenues and period-end accruals.

For intra-group supplies, auditors must ensure that the internal costs are allocated correctly. For more details on auditing consulting contracts, see Section C, Chapter 5.2.

Licenses

License audits in the subsidiaries focus on recording the processes and testing the license agreements on a sample basis. In this regard, it is particularly important to ensure that pricing is correct, maintenance is billed correctly, contract data is appropriately entered in the system, the maintenance arrangements are properly reflected, and the relevant US-GAAP requirements are met (for more details, see Section C, Chapter 5.3).

Human Resources

An audit of the human resources function in a subsidiary should focus primarily on the basic arrangements for the subsidiary's incentive and compensation systems for employees. Auditors should obtain an overview of the methods the subsidiary uses. For example, the incentive system for sales employees should be linked to payments received from customers. The plausibility of the calculations for incentive payment provisions should be tested on a sample basis and individual items should be recalculated (see Section C, Chapter 3.3). In this regard the auditors should note, for example,

- on which process the correct incentive calculation is based,
- which internal controls are implemented,
- whether the flow of information between Human Resources, Accounting, and Management Accounting is working, and
- how the data from Management Accounting, Accounting, and Human Resources is linked to each other.

Purchasing

A subsidiary audit also includes the purchasing function. Unlike exclusive purchasing audits, audits of purchasing within the bounds of a subsidiary audit cannot achieve the same level of detailed analysis but instead must focus on the main points (for more details, see Section C, Chapter 4.1). The auditors should get an overview of existing guidelines and obtain the necessary authorizations, record the process, and conduct sample tests on different internal controls. It is also important to perform a general test in the system to establish which employees are authorized to edit vendor master data (for audits of IT security and system authorizations, see Section C, Chapter 10), the extent to which the same employees are authorized to edit bank master data and what control mechanisms are in place.

Risk Management

To examine risk management, the auditors should ensure that the company's global risk management guidelines are known, used, and implemented. Global Risk Management is a virtual form of organization that covers the entire company structure. Each region and subsidiary should have implemented the company's risk strategy and adapted it to local and regional circumstances and guidelines. Auditors should satisfy themselves that:

- there is a (local and/or regional) risk manager,
- the risk manager does not report directly to the head of consulting,
- the risk manager is involved in local strategic business decisions,
- the risk manager is involved in day-to-day business,
- project-specific risk analyses are performed, and
- any risks identified are entered and regularly updated in the appropriate SAP system.

Reporting and Follow-Up

Reporting and follow-up occur after the on-site subsidiary audit has been completed and documented in the working papers (for details, see Section B, Chapters 5 and 6).

LINKS AND REFERENCES ↗

- JARNAGIN, B.D. 2007. *US Master GAAP Guide.* Riverwoods, IL: CCH, Inc.
- SEARS, B. 2002. *Internal Auditing Manual.* New York, NY: Warren, Gorham & Lamont.
- SAWYER, L. B., M. A. DITTENHOFER AND J. H. SCHEINER. 2003. *Sawyer's Internal Auditing.* 5th ed. Altamonte Springs, FL: The Institute of Internal Auditors.

5.2 Consulting Project Audits

5.2.1 Classification of Consulting Projects

KEY POINTS •••

- Consulting projects can be categorized as short-term or long-term projects.
- A distinction is also made between fixed-price projects, cost-plus contracts (i.e., time and material contracts), and maximum-price projects.

Classification of Consulting Contracts by Maturity and Compensation

Consulting contracts at SAP cover an agreement between the company and the customer on the provision of consulting services in the area of software implementation. Consulting contracts can be classified by maturity into short-term and long-term contracts, and by compensation into fixed-price projects, cost-plus contracts, also known as time and material contracts, and maximum-price projects (i.e., time and material contracts with a cap). Normally, revenue is recognized on the basis of the services performed, taking certain criteria into account (see Section C, Chapter 5.2.3). Implementation support, (e.g., for a comprehensive software system), is normally a long-term consulting project. Long-term consulting projects are part of the family of long-term construction projects, similar to those undertaken in the construction sector. These types of consulting projects may begin in one fiscal year and be completed in the next fiscal year, or even in the year after that.

Fixed-Price Projects

Fixed-price projects are contracts under which defined consulting services are performed and for which the total compensation is contractually agreed from the start of the project. The following are typical characteristics of fixed-price projects:

- The project process is divided into individual milestones.
- SAP performs the individual services according to a defined plan, based on the milestones.
- SAP also invoices according to a contractually defined plan, which does not normally track project progress. This plan usually provides for an advance pay-

ment on contract signature, further payments as service components are performed and accepted, and a final payment after completion of the project.

- The provision of individual services and their acceptance by the customer are documented in acceptance logs.
- In some countries, it is common business practice to withhold part of the invoice amount (approx. 5 %) as a guarantee during the project term, until the project has been completed.

Time and Material Contracts

Cost-plus contracts (also known as time and material contracts) are contracts under which defined consulting services are performed, although the total compensation is not fixed in the contract, but relates to costs incurred. Under this type of contract, only a daily rate is specified for each consultant group (junior consultant, senior consultant, etc.). Similar to fixed-price projects, the provision of individual services and their acceptance are documented in writing. Depending on the contractual arrangement and country-specific business practice, time spent on the project is agreed in different ways, e.g. in the form of a signed log, by e-mail, or verbally. Internal Audit should verify whether the chosen form is recognized as legally binding in the country concerned and whether it has been carried out according to contract.

Maximum-Price Projects

Maximum-price projects are contracts based on time and material, but with an upper price limit agreed in addition. Similar to time and material contracts, a certain consulting service must be performed. The number of person days needed to complete the project is limited by specifying a maximum price. The daily rate for each consultant group (junior consultant, senior consultant, etc.) is contractually agreed upon before the inception of the consulting project. Similar to fixed-price projects and time and material contracts, the provision of individual services and their acceptance are documented in writing. Records of the time spent are agreed with the customer, according to what is stipulated in the contract.

HINTS AND TIPS

- Auditors must be clear about the category to which a consulting project is assigned, because this may provide indications about possible risks and appropriate accounting treatment.
- When individual contracts are tested, any relevant master agreements also must be examined.

LINKS AND REFERENCES

- JARNAGIN, B.D. 2007. *US Master GAAP Guide.* Riverwoods, IL: CCH, Inc.
- SEARS, B. 2002. *Internal Auditing Manual.* New York, NY: Warren, Gorham & Lamont.
- SAWYER, L. B., M. A. DITTENHOFER AND J. H. SCHEINER. 2003. *Sawyer's Internal Auditing.* 5th ed. Altamonte Springs, FL: The Institute of Internal Auditors.

5.2.2 Audit Preparation and Execution

KEY POINTS

- Before the start of an audit of consulting projects, auditors should use analytical procedures to gain an overview of the consulting projects to be examined.
- When auditing consulting projects, auditors first record the processes, then determine whether each process is carried out as designed, and finally assess consulting projects on a sample basis.
- The standard work program for consulting projects includes the following main components: Review of processes and the way they are organized, integration of the risk management system, and the project manager's role and cooperation with consulting control and the accounting department.
- Auditors also examine the profitability of consulting projects.

Audit Preparation

Analytical audit procedures (see Section C, Chapter 3.1) performed during audit preparation help the auditor gain an understanding of the company's situation and should be used as the basis for creating a specific work program for consulting projects. Such analysis not only provides a general insight into the company's current situation, it also reveals whether the company has concluded most of its consulting project contracts with the private or the public sector. This information may improve the auditor's assessment of contract complexity. The analysis also tells Internal Audit whether there are any customers with payment difficulties. The audit team should also ascertain the proportion of fixed-price projects, maximum-price projects, and time and material contracts the company has concluded in the period under review. Moreover, auditors need a general idea of project profitability (gross return on sales, from now on referred to as "profitability"). Projects that are barely profitable or loss-making should be included in the sample selected.

List of Requirements

Before the start of an audit, Internal Audit should send a list of requirements to the unit to be audited. This list covers the following main points:

- process description for consulting projects,
- documents regarding process and information flow,
- calculation of fully absorbed costs for the period to be analyzed,
- calculation of consultant market rates or standard daily rates for the period to be analyzed,
- signature policy for consulting projects and bids (Who must sign what, when, and why?),
- delegation of authority arrangements if the persons responsible for consulting projects and bids are unavailable (Who acts as delegate?),
- intra-group consulting contracts,
- significant contracts with consulting subcontractors,

- list of all consulting customers for whom a specific bad debt allowance has been recognized, and
- list of all consulting customers with payment difficulties.

In addition, the audit lead should arrange meetings with the persons responsible for consulting projects and with the head of the local finance unit. Also, Internal Audit should request input from Risk Management to obtain valuable information about projects exposed to risk.

Sample Selection

The auditors should use their judgment to select a sample of consulting projects for review (on sampling, see Section B, Chapter 4.1.2). Approximately four weeks before the start of the audit, the selection is presented to the head of the local finance unit so that he or she can make the relevant contracts available (in translation if necessary) at the start of the audit. The auditors may also need to have a translator on site during meetings.

Special Aspects of Sample Selection

It may be useful to include projects that have recently been completed or are scheduled to be completed shortly (within approximately one or two months from the time of the audit), or projects the profitability of which has fallen short of expectations. In addition, contracts with the public sector can be very complex and therefore should be included in the audit sample as well. For example, they may require compliance with EU competitive bidding regulations or observance of country-specific circumstances.

Scope and Work Program

The Key Scopes relevant to auditing consulting projects are selected from the total of all Scopes (see Section B, Chapter 2.1). The work program is developed based on these Scopes (see Section B, Chapter 3.2).

Audit Execution in General

When auditing consulting projects, the first step is to record the processes. Next, the auditors should determine whether the internal controls have been designed to adequately mitigate risk and whether each process is executed as designed. Finally, the auditors should examine the projects included in the sample. This last step can also be carried out when auditing process effectiveness. The standard work program for consulting projects includes the following main components (see below for details): review of processes and the way they are organized, integration of the risk management system, and the project manager's role and cooperation with consulting control and the accounting department.

Consulting Process and its Organization

As for many other areas, SAP has developed a process (ASAP Roadmap) for carrying out consulting projects which ensures a reliable internal control system. If the process is carried out as intended, information will flow reliably to and from the consulting department. At the same time, the integration of the risk management department, consulting control, the legal department, and the accounting department must be guaranteed and function effectively. Process organization should preferably follow the dual control principle and appropriate segregation of duties and should support the detection of fraud. Consulting control, which is an accounting function, also performs analyses on consulting projects, independently of Internal Audit, and is therefore able to produce reports on the basis of specific criteria. In addition, the consulting department prepares a brief quantitative summary of the most important points of each consulting contract for consulting control and the accounting department (e.g., cost planning, term, daily rates, free training or free consulting services, as well as project-specific topics such as information on whether the consulting services and know-how are essential for implementing the software product successfully).

Potential Indications of Deficiencies

Potential indications of poor process design and organization include:

- The process does not function as designed.
- The information flow between departments does not serve its purpose, is insufficient, subject to delays, or ineffective.
- The consulting department does not forward information on variances from the planned project procedure and the planned project costs to consulting control in a timely manner.
- Consulting control does not evaluate each project.
- The structure and design of the process organization do not follow the dual control principle.
- The control and approval procedures do not take place or are not performed according to the process description.

Auditor's Activities

Effective process design is not always achieved in practice. Internal Audit must analyze the processes of the audited unit carefully to establish whether there are any variances between the current situation and the prescribed processes. To do so, the auditors should familiarize themselves with the process description provided by e.g. the SOX documentation. Furthermore, they can meet with the risk manager and the person responsible for consulting projects to confirm their understanding of the process descriptions and clarify any other issues or questions. Auditors also need to assess whether, in their opinion, all significant controls are working effectively and whether the set up of the organization and functions is adequate. Findings and recommendations for improvement are documented in the working papers (see Section B, Chapter 4.2).

Involvement of Risk Management

The project manager should cooperate closely with the company's risk manager, who performs an independent assessment of any risks associated with the project, including probabilities and impacts, before a formal bid for consulting services is sent to the customer. The risk manager monitors this assessment during the course of the project and updates the risks if necessary.

Potential Indications of Deficiencies

The following criteria may indicate that the risk manager is ineffective:

- The risk manager's position in the overall organization does not allow him or her to perform an independent and effective evaluation of project risks.
- The risk manager does not have the necessary knowledge of consulting project management, the market, or the product to be able to identify all the risks effectively.
- The risk manager does not identify and evaluate the project risks in a timely manner.
- The risk manager's recommendations are not implemented in the company.

- The risk manager's reports are not completed in due time or are only of limited usefulness.

Auditor's Approach

In order to test whether the risk management system is adequately integrated into the consulting project process and the internal controls are working effectively, auditors should first obtain copies of the relevant project risk summaries for a sample of projects. In addition, they should identify the most important internal controls and test on a sample basis whether the controls were carried out and were functioning as intended. This involves assessing in particular whether most of the risks have been fully identified in a timely manner and properly evaluated before the start and during the course of the project. Findings and recommendations for improving the integration of the risk management system are included in the working papers.

Purpose of Consulting Control

For each consulting project, the order processing department creates an order in the consulting information system. The consulting controller checks whether this information has been entered correctly and in a timely manner. Control activities and the relevant posting records are supported by adequate IT tools, (e.g. the consulting information system for fixed-price projects in the SAP-internal live system). The function of consulting control is to perform regular checks on automatic accounting entries and on the quality of the system reports. This department also ensures that the order processing department creates invoices in time and that invoice and revenue blocking is in place in case US-GAAP criteria have not been met. The controllers are also responsible for checking that all consultant hours have been fully recorded, irrespective of whether they can be billed to the customer or not. For fixed-price projects, consulting control checks whether the percentage of project completion has been calculated correctly and whether the data entered reflect actual project progress. If necessary, and after consultation with the project manager, consulting control adjusts the amounts recognized.

Cooperation Between Project Manager and Consulting Controller

The project manager ensures that consultant hours have been recorded correctly, broken down into billable and non-billable services, and that they have been allocated to the appropriate project. The project manager forwards information on variances from the planned project procedure and the planned project costs to consulting control by no later than the end of the month. Consulting control, in conjunction with the project manager, checks that the consultant hours are fully recorded as of the end of the month and that the associated revenue and costs are properly recognized. Consulting control and project manager also have to ensure that all costs, e.g. those that can impact on the percentage of completion in fixed-price projects, are allocated to the correct period. Contract loss accruals are set up if necessary, i.e. when project costs exceed or are expected to exceed the fixed price for the project.

Importance of Consulting Control

The project manager's operational knowledge, (e.g. with regard to project delays, adjustments to total project costs, new customer requirements, availability of required resources, etc.) plays a very important role when it comes to taking all material aspects of the project into account correctly and in a timely manner. In this regard, the consulting controller's responsibility includes the correct assessment and recording in the internal information system of the financial impact that these aspects may have. This may result in adjustments to project revenue. For this reason it is essential that information between project manager and consulting controller can flow unhindered.

Potential Indications of Deficiencies

The following criteria may indicate that consulting control and the project manager are not working compliantly:

- The project manager does not regularly re-evaluate the total costs of each project.
- The project manager does not forward information on variances from the planned project procedure and the planned project costs to consulting control in a timely manner or does not evaluate such information correctly.
- The information flow is not timely or effective.

Cooperation between Accounting and Consulting Control

Consulting control and the accounting department are jointly responsible for determining the daily rates for each consultant group at fully absorbed costs and for updating them in the system. They also need to ensure that the projects are measured based on the internal accounting guidelines and that the necessary accruals for revenue are recorded in case that the consultant rates invoiced to customers do not correspond to standard market rates for consulting.

Potential Indications of Deficiencies

The following criteria may indicate that consulting control and the accounting department are not working compliantly:

- The consulting controller's reports are not completed in due time or are only of limited usefulness.
- The daily rates at fully absorbed cost and the standard daily rates are not reliably determined.
- The consulting controller's position in the organization does not allow him or her to perform independent and effective assessments of project performance and related costs.

Testing of Internal Controls

Auditors must identify the key internal controls in connection with consulting control activities and test a sample of contracts to determine whether the controls are effective. Auditors should also investigate whether all expected material control procedures relating to consulting control are fully and effectively addressed. Findings and recommendations for improvement are documented in the working papers.

Important Fieldwork Activities

Below is a list of the most important fieldwork activities and related documents that Internal Audit uses in auditing individual consulting projects. Auditors should analyze the contract in question, summarize its main elements, identify and evaluate all material risks, and coordinate or enhance (if necessary) their understanding of the project risks by talking to the project manager and the risk manager. Further fieldwork activities depend on the type of contract.

Important Fieldwork Activities for Fixed-Price Projects

When examining fixed-price projects, auditors should focus on the following questions, in particular:

- Is SAP able to determine reliably the total project costs and the percentage of completion of the project?
- Is SAP able to meet the project plan in terms of quality and deadlines?
- Does SAP incur contract penalties if milestones cannot be met in time?
- Does the customer have the option to query milestones already accepted from an overall perspective at the end of the project?
- Does SAP have the resources and the know-how to resolve project difficulties successfully?
- Does the project relate to the implementation of software products, for which a certain region, for example, temporarily has insufficient consultant capacity?
- Are consulting services for SAP software and the know-how essential for implementing this software product successfully (see Section C, Chapter 5.2.3)?
- Are the roles and responsibilities of both SAP and the customer clearly defined?
- Is SAP required to provide exceptional guarantees (for longer than usual, for exceptional amounts, or to an unusual extent)?
- Does SAP have the lead role in and control of the project?
- If not, is SAP able to determine adequately the percentage of completion and the total costs of the project?
- For fixed-price projects with customers where the services are provided by a subcontractor, has a back-to-back fixed-price agreement been concluded with the subcontractor?
- If the services of a project are performed jointly with other consulting firms, is there a separate agreement that clearly assigns the tasks and responsibilities and defines liability etc.?
- Are there fixed-price projects between companies in the consolidated group? Can transfer prices expose the company to tax risks?
- Are there acceptance logs approved by the customer?
- Has the customer already paid the most recent invoices?

Important Fieldwork Activities for Time and Material Contracts

When auditing time and material contracts, auditors should look at the following:

- Is the contract based on actual time and material costs, or has a maximum price been agreed?
- Is there a risk that the customer might not accept any of the consulting services performed?
- Are there acceptance logs approved by the customer?
- Has the customer already paid the most recent invoices?

Project Profitability

Auditors should obtain a copy of the consulting project's costing sheet, determine whether the schedule was created at the start of the project, and carry out a plausibility check. They should also note whether the project manager has signed the costing sheet to document that a review of the schedule has taken place as an internal control. Next, auditors should compare the planned project profit with the actual profit generated in different periods and determine any material variances that could be a sign of poor project control. The following diagram is a fictitious example of the structure of a consulting report.

Customer 1 Project A			
	Target	Actual	Actual/target
	€	€	%
Invoiced sales	1,300.00	400.00	30.77
Accrued sales		530.00	
Total sales	1,300.00	930.00	71.54
External (subcontractor) costs	520.00	450.00	86.54
Internal consulting costs	630.00	400.00	63.49
Total costs	1,150.00	850.00	73.91
Contribution margin	150.00	80.00	53.33
Profitability in %	11.54	8.60	

Fig. 11 Fictitious Consulting Report

Use of External Resources

Auditors should also gather information about whether and why resources from other local SAP subsidiaries or external subcontractors have been used in the project. If a project uses intra-group services, they must be accounted for according to SAP guidelines.

Invoicing

Fixed-price projects are invoiced according to the method agreed upon in the contract. In a fixed-price project, partial profit recognition on the basis of amounts already invoiced is not suitable for determining correct period allocation of revenue, because the invoices relate to the maturity of partial payments rather than overall project progress (see Section C, Chapter 5.2.3). By contrast, monthly invoices are normally produced for maximum-price projects and time and material contracts. The services to be invoiced on the basis of person days are agreed with the customer.

HINTS AND TIPS

- Analyze the contract to be audited carefully with regard to the conditions and obligations it contains and the possible project risks it poses.

LINKS AND REFERENCES

- JARNAGIN, B.D. 2007. *US Master GAAP Guide.* Riverwoods, IL: CCH, Inc.
- SEARS, B. 2002. *Internal Auditing Manual.* New York, NY: Warren, Gorham & Lamont.
- SAWYER, L. B., M. A. DITTENHOFER AND J. H. SCHEINER. 2003. *Sawyer's Internal Auditing.* 5th ed. Altamonte Springs, FL: The Institute of Internal Auditors.

5.2.3 Special Aspects of Consulting Project Audits

KEY POINTS

- Changes in project data of fixed-price projects may lead to larger or smaller fluctuations that impact the percentage of completion.
- Revenue from consulting projects is recognized according to effective project progress.
- Under multiple element arrangements, SAP offers maintenance, consulting, development, training, and other services together with software licenses. If a multiple element arrangement exists, software revenue is recognized according to the residual method.

Special Aspects in Day-to-Day Auditing

Complementing Section C, Chapters 5.2.1 and 5.2.2, this chapter provides details of special aspects the audit team may encounter when auditing different types of projects. First, the focus is on fixed-price projects and the percentage of completion method that must be considered for these projects.

Calculation of the Percentage of Completion

Calculating the percentage of completion is not always straightforward in practice. SAP uses the cost-to-cost method to calculate the percentage of completion by comparing actual costs to total estimated costs (budgeted costs). This method can be used either at overall project level or at sub-project/milestone level.

Fictitious Example

The following table uses a fictitious example to show the different results obtained when looking at a project at the overall project level as compared to the sub-project level (per milestone).

Sub-project/ milestone	Costs		Percentage of completion		Sales revenue			
	Budget	Actual	Calcu-lated	Actual	Budget	Actual (A)	Accrued (B)	Total (A + B)
	€	€	%	%	€	€	€	€
10	965	860	89.12	100.00	1,110	1,100	0	1,100
20	1,035	1,080	104.35	100.00	1,080	1,080	0	1,080
30	1,240	1,330	107.26	100.00	1,400	0	1,400	1,400
40	910	930	102.20	100.00	990	0	990	990
50	1,100	0	0.00		1,230	0	0	0
60	930	0	0.00		990	0	0	0
Overall project total	**6,180**	**4,200**	**67.96**		**6,800**	**2,180**	**2,390**	**4,570**
	Accrued at project level: (67.96% * € 6,800- € 2,180 = € 2,441)					**2,180**	**2,441**	**4,621**

Fig. 12 Fictitious Project A as of December 31, 2005

The percentage of completion at the overall project level of 67.96% has been calculated by comparing total costs incurred amounting to EUR 4,200 and total budgeted costs of EUR 6,180. If the project is analyzed at sub-project (milestone) level, the percentage of completion can be calculated for each sub-project. The mathematically calculated percentage of completion may differ from actual project progress. For example, the percentage of completion for sub-project 10 is calculated at 89.12%, although the actual percentage of completion is 100% (evidence provided, e.g. on the basis of sub-project acceptance by the customer).

Change in the Percentage of Completion

In the above example, project processing problems now require an adjustment to the budgeted costs (estimated total costs), from EUR 6,180 to EUR 9,860 as of March 31, 2006 (see figure below). This results in a change of the calculated percentage of completion to 50.61%.

Sub-project/ milestone	Costs		Percentage of completion		Sales revenue			
	Budget	Actual	Calcu-lated	Actual	Budget	Actual (A)	Accrued (B)	Total (A + B)
	€	€	%	%	€	€	€	€
10	860	860	100.00	100.00	1,110	1,100	0	1,100
20	1,080	1,080	100.00	100.00	1,080	1,080	0	1,080
30	1,330	1,330	100.00	100.00	1,400	0	1,400	1,400
40	930	930	100.00	100.00	990	0	990	990
50	4,760	790	16.60	16.60	1,230	0	204	204
60	900	0	0.00		990	0	0	0
Overall project total	**9,860**	**4,990**	**50.61**		**6,800**	**2,180**	**2,594**	**4,774**
	Accrued at project level: (50.61%* €6,800- €2180 = €1,261)					**2,180**	**1,261**	**3,441**

Fig. 13 Fictitious Project A as of March 31, 2006 after adjustment to budgeted costs

Other Consequences

In addition, an accrual for future project losses should be created, because the budgeted costs (EUR 9,860) exceed budgeted revenue (EUR 6,800) by EUR 3,060. The audit team must ensure that the appropriate departments are informed of any changes to project data in a timely manner.

Accounting Treatment of Consulting Projects

The rules of long-term construction projects are applied to consulting projects as appropriate. If the project is a fixed-price project, revenue is recognized according to effective project progress, if the following criteria are met:

- The company can provide reliable estimates of total revenue, total costs, and the percentage of completion.
- The contract clearly and unambiguously defines the services to be performed.
- Payment terms and project processing method have been determined.
- Payment for the services performed is probable (revenue can be realized).
- It is probable that the company performs the services agreed under the contract.

Fictitious Example of Accounting Entries

The following fictitious example shows possible accounting entries.

Milestone	Costs		Sales revenue		Percentage of completion
	Budget	Actual	Budget	Actual	
	€	€	€	€	%
10	950	900	1,100	1,100	30
20	1,050	600	1,200	1,200	50
30	1,000	1,200	1,200	1,200	90
	3,000	**2,700**	**3,500**	**3,500**	**100**

Fig. 14 Fictitious Fixed-Price Project B – Project Data

The relevant accounting entries for this project are as follows:

Account	Description	Balance sheet (assets/liabilities)		Income statement	
		Debit	Credit	Debit	Credit
Invoice for milestone # 10					
	Unbilled Accounts Receivable (Germany)	1,050			
	Revenue Accrual Fixed-Price Project				1,050
	Revenue Accrual Fixed-Price Project			1,100	
	Advance Payments		1,100		
	Accounts Receivable	1,100			
	Revenue Fixed-Price Project				1,100
Invoice for milestone # 20					
	Unbilled accounts receivable (Germany)	700			
	Revenue Accrual Fixed-Price Project				700
	Revenue Accrual Fixed-Price Project			1,200	
	Advance Payments		1,200		
	Accounts Reveivable	1,200			
	Revenue Fixed-Price Project				1,200

Fig. 15 Fictitious Fixed-Price Project B – Accounting Entries

Account	Description	Balance sheet (assets/liabilities)		Income statement	
		Debit	Credit	Debit	Credit
Invoice for milestone # 30					
	Unbilled Accounts Receivable (Germany)	1,400			
	Revenue Accrual Fixed-Price Project				1,400
	Revenue Accrual Fixed-Price Project			1,200	
	Advance Payments		1,200		
	Accounts Receivable	1,200			
	Revenue Fixed-Price Project				1,200
Closing					
	Unbilled Accounts Receivable	350			
	Revenue Accrual Fixed-Price Project				350
	Advance Payments	3,500			
	Unbilled Accounts Receivable		3,500		

Fig. 15 *(continued)*

If the above criteria are not met, the costs incurred are expensed. Under this method, revenue is not recognized until the project is completed or until all criteria for recognizing revenue according to effective project progress are met, whichever occurs first.

Account Entries for Time and Material Projects

If the project being examined is not a fixed-price project, but a time and material project, revenue is recognized according to service performance if the performance of the service is representative for the stage of completion. It is entered as shown in the following fictitious example.

Fictitious Example

The fictitious time and material project C has the following base data:

- Plan monthly service performance: 50 consultant days at EUR 20 per day.
- Actual monthly service performance:
  - Month 1: 50 consultant days at EUR 20 per day
  - Month 2: 30 consultant days at EUR 20 per day
  - Month 3: 70 consultant days at EUR 20 per day
- Project term: 12 month.
- Option A: Monthly invoicing and recognition of revenue.
- Option B: Quarterly invoicing and monthly recognition of revenue.

Option A: Customer is invoiced at the end of the month						
Account	Description	Balance sheet (assets/liabilities)		Income statement	
		Debit	Credit	Debit	Credit
Month 1					
	Customer 123	1,000			
	Consulting revenue				1,000
Month 2					
	Customer 123	600			
	Consulting revenue				600
Month 3					
	Customer 123	1,400			
	Consulting				1,400

Fig. 16 Fictitious Time and Material Project C, Option A: Accounting Entries for Time and Material Projects (Monthly)

Option B: Customer is invoiced quarterly					
Account	Description	Balance sheet (assets/liabilities)		Income statement	
		Debit	Credit	Debit	Credit
Month 1					
	Services not yet invoiced, time and material projects	1,000			
	Consulting revenue, time and material projects				1,000
Month 2					
	Services not yet invoiced, time and material projects	600			
	Consulting revenue, time and material projects				600

Fig. 17 Fictitious Time and Material Project C, Option B: Accounting Entries for Time and Material Projects (Quarterly)

Account	Description	Balance sheet (assets/liabilities)		Income statement	
		Debit	Credit	Debit	Credit
Month 3					
	Services not yet invoiced, time and material projects	1,400			
	Consulting revenue, time and material projects				1,400
Invoice at end of quarter					
	Customer 123	3,000			
	Consulting		3,000		

Fig. 17 *(continued)*

Recognition of Costs and Revenue

Normally, a final version of the consulting contract must be signed by the customer and SAP before any consulting revenue can be recognized. If the contract has not been finalized and negotiations with the customer are ongoing, no consulting revenue can be recognized. In such a case, the costs already incurred are expensed. If the contract is not signed within a specified period (e.g., three months), the auditors should follow up with management and review the process.

Multiple Element Arrangements

Another particular aspect of consulting projects may arise for auditors in relation to multiple element arrangements. Under multiple element arrangements, SAP sells maintenance, consulting, development, training, and other services together with software licenses. If a multiple element arrangement exists, software revenue is recognized according to the residual method at SAP. Under this method, revenue that will be realized in the future for maintenance, consulting, or other services still to be provided is determined on the basis of standard prices, deducted from the total license contract value, and recognized once the relevant service has been performed. The standard prices are market prices at which SAP offers goods and services individually. For goods and services that SAP has to date not offered on an individual basis, a standard price set by company management is used, providing it is probable that this price will not change. Any residual amount is allocated to software licenses and recognized as software revenue if all the other requirements of SOP 97-2 have been met.

LINKS AND REFERENCES ↗

- JARNAGIN, B. D. 2007. *US Master GAAP Guide*. Riverwoods, IL: CCH, Inc.
- SAWYER, L. B., M. A. DITTENHOFER AND J. H. SCHEINER. 2003. *Sawyer's Internal Auditing*. 5th ed. Altamonte Springs, FL: The Institute of Internal Auditors.

- SEARS, B. 2002. *Internal Auditing Manual.* New York, NY: Warren, Gorham & Lamont.
- SOP 81-1: Accounting for Performance of Construction-Type and Certain Production-Type Contracts.

5.3 License Audits

KEY POINTS •••

- A key aspect of audit preparation for license audits is defining the appropriate sample and testing the system data.
- During audit execution, auditors primarily test contract design and content, archiving, pricing, product delivery, approval procedures, and the accuracy of account entries.
- Because of the need to comply with US-GAAP requirements, the audit should also include revenue recognition criteria and any associated issues.

Software Licenses

When using software developed by SAP, the customer usually pays a one-time license fee and maintenance fees during the license term. The license fee is the price paid for using the software, and the maintenance fee is paid for technical support, upgrades and enhancements. Due to the variety of local requirements, market conditions, and special customer needs, there is a wide range of license contract types and contents.

Sales Channels

The software can be sold through direct or indirect channels, depending on the product and the market situation. Direct sale means the software is sold through one of SAP's local subsidiaries. If the customer buys the software through a third party (i.e., a reseller), it is called an indirect sale. In case of indirect sale, the customer concludes the license agreement directly with the reseller. SAP and the reseller have signed a master agreement. Depending on local requirements and procedures, the customer concludes the maintenance contract either directly with SAP or with the reseller.

Content of a License Agreement

In a license agreement, the following items are agreed upon with the customer:

- licensed product(s),
- license fee,
- maintenance fee,
- payment terms, and
- delivery procedures.

Annexes to the License Agreement

The following documents may be included as appendices to the license agreement:

- electronic costing sheet,
- customer-provided evidence regarding the use of the software for statistical business purposes (Solution Addendum Form (SAF)), and
- general terms and conditions.

Audit of License Agreements

License agreements can be audited in combination with other audit segments or as a separate audit topic. The license audit is part of every standard audit of a local subsidiary and, depending on the topic, may also be conducted as part of a special audit. The main audit objective of license audits is to assure correct revenue recognition and to ensure that all internal controls are in place to meet SOX and US-GAAP requirements. In addition to standard and special audits, Internal Audit also performs unannounced license audits and customer contract confirmations in the local subsidiaries (see Section C, Chapter 9).

Representative Sample of Contracts for Testing

The first step of the preparation process is to select a sample of contracts for testing, taking into consideration the period to be examined, the size of the local subsidiary, and the available auditing time.

Purposive Sampling

Information about the contracts concluded within the period to be examined should be obtained from the system. The audit team should export the data into an Excel spreadsheet in order to edit it according to the chosen sampling method. Under purposive sampling (see Section B, Chapter 4.1.2), the auditors should take the following criteria into account:

- contract volume,
- posting date in the SAP system immediately prior to the closing date for the month or quarter,
- type of contract (direct or indirect sales), and
- previous auditor experience.

Random Sampling

As an alternative to purposive sampling, auditors can choose from a number of statistical random sampling methods. Value-based statistical sampling is used for the customer contract confirmation process as part of revenue recognition assurance (see Section C, Chapter 9).

Core Scope for License and Maintenance Contracts

During audit preparation, auditors should get an overview of the Core Scope for license agreements, especially if they do not have any experience in this area. The Core Scope covers the key functions and processes that could enhance the auditors' understanding of this complex topic. See Fig. 18 for an excerpt from the "License Agreements" Core Scope.

Work Program

Derived from the Core Scopes for License Agreements and the relevant Key Scopes, the work program is the basis for the fieldwork and guides the whole auditing process from preparation through reporting (see Section B, Chapter 3.2). The work program should be adjusted for each audit according to the audit type and the local characteristics of the subsidiary to be audited.

Audit Lists and Question Catalogs

During audit execution, audit lists and question catalogs may facilitate the auditors' tasks (see Section B, Chapter 4.1.3.1). The extent to which such templates will be used is specified during audit preparation. If they are being used, they need to be filed as working papers for the respective audit. The following questions may be included in an audit list for license agreements:

- Is the contract available in original form?

- Do the amounts posted in the system match the original contract?
- Does the contract price conform to the local price list?
- Do the users and functionalities listed in the system match the contract?
- Did SAP and the customer sign the contract?
- Are the SAP signatories authorized to sign the contract (compared to local signing policy)?
- Is it clear who signed the contract (names also in block letters)?
- What is the signing date of the contract?
- Is there proof of software delivery?
- Was the software delivered before revenue was recognized?
- Are there any unusual clauses in the contract that may affect revenue recognition?

Content / Key Scope	Strategies/ Policies/ Procedures	Functions/ Business Processes	Processes	Objects
Bidding	Delegation of Authority, Contract Approval, Pricing Policy, Migration Strategy, Global Risk Management.	Technical Sales, License Agreement Administration, Accounting, Consulting Department, Training Department, Legal Department, Local Management, Executive Board, Sales, Development.	Bidding process, Free-of-charge services, US GAAP processing, Ramp-up process, Future functionality.	Maintenance fee, License fee, Discounts, Migration credits, Contract, Addendums, Bid, Master price list, Local price list, Product availability matrix, Costing sheet, Package specification, User specification.

Fig. 18 Excerpt from the Core Scope for License Agreements

Checking Data in the SAP System

To ensure efficient fieldwork, all data available regarding the selected license agreements should be collected in the preparation phase. The most important source of information on license agreements at SAP is the Contract Information System (CIS) reporting system, which contains all relevant contract data. This data is maintained by the license administration departments in the local subsidiaries. The auditors should print out all the information about the sample contracts selected, and examine previous contracts to gain an overview of the customer history. A copy of the original contract for each posting should also be scanned into the SAP system.

Audit Execution The following is a description of how an audit of license and maintenance contracts is conducted. Its structure is based on the work program derived from the Scope.

Archiving Auditors should note the following with regard to archiving important documents. The original contract, along with other legally relevant documents (e.g. annexes, addendums, and minutes), should be archived in a fireproof, locked cabinet, and only a limited number of persons should have access to the key. These documents should also be scanned and reflected in the system entries. The other relevant documents, such as delivery notes, correspondence etc., should be reasonably and systematically stored in the customer file.

Pricing The master price list for software is issued by the parent company. The local subsidiaries adapt the list to local circumstances. Auditors should check the adaptation and ensure that the contract prices agreed with the customer correspond with the current local price list.

Electronic or Physical Delivery Product delivery is a criterion for revenue recognition. Customers have access to the software they have purchased through electronic or physical delivery. In case of electronic delivery, the customers receive a password that allows them to download the product. In case of physical delivery, the product is sent on a CD or DVD to the customer. The date relevant for revenue recognition depends on the terms of the contract or the General Terms and Conditions. Proof of delivery is required for each license agreement.

Signing Policy To guarantee that sufficient internal controls are in place, each local subsidiary must have a signing policy and approval procedures. The signing policy should be based on the dual control principle and provide appropriate delegation of authority arrangements. During the audit of the license agreements, compliance with the signing policy must also be assessed. The current signing policy should be requested, checked, and filed among the working papers.

Entries in the SAP System The SAP system should contain all information about products and payment terms as agreed in the contract. Therefore, the auditors must test whether the information in the SAP system has been entered correctly. Incorrect entries and postings could lead to improper invoicing and incorrect revenue recognition.

Revenue Recognition Criteria According to US-GAAP, revenue from software sales can only be recognized when all of the following criteria are met:

- Persuasive evidence of an arrangement exists.
- Delivery of the software has occurred.
- The fee is fixed or determinable.
- Collectibility is probable.

If one or more criteria are not met, revenue must not be recognized (see Section C, Chapter 3.5). The main goal of the fieldwork is to ensure that all criteria were met at the time of revenue recognition. In the following, the above criteria are briefly discussed.

Evidence of Arrangement with Customer

There is evidence that an arrangement exists with a customer: A contract is available and signed by both parties before revenue recognition (contract signing date is decisive criterion).

Delivery Made

SAP must have delivered the software physically or electronically, and the software must be in functioning order. Written proof of delivery is needed.

Price Fixed and Collectibility Probable

At the time of delivery, the price must be fixed or determinable, and collectibility must be probable. To determine collectibility, the payment history of the customer, payment terms, cancellation privileges, acceptance provision etc. should be analyzed.

Multiple Element Arrangements

If SAP sells a combination of different products and services to its customers under one or more contracts, this may constitute a multiple element arrangement, which may have an effect on revenue recognition. During every license audit, the existence of a multiple element arrangement and its impact should therefore be reviewed (see Section C, Chapter 5.2.3).

HINTS AND TIPS

- Auditors should try to collect and analyze all possible information before the audit fieldwork begins.
- Auditors should use the IT systems available and clarify all unclear issues directly with the corporate departments. This will save time during fieldwork.

LINKS AND REFERENCES

- JARNAGIN, B. D. 2007. *US Master GAAP Guide.* Riverwoods, IL: CCH, Inc.
- SEARS, B. 2002. *Internal Auditing Manual.* New York, NY: Warren, Gorham & Lamont.
- SAWYER, L. B., M. A. DITTENHOFER AND J. H. SCHEINER. 2003. *Sawyer's Internal Auditing.* 5th ed. Altamonte Springs, FL: The Institute of Internal Auditors.
- SOP 81-1: Accounting for Performance of Construction-Type and Certain Production-Type Contracts.
- SOP 97-2: Software Revenue Recognition.
- SOP 98-9: Modification of SOP 97-2, Software Revenue Recognition, With Respect to Certain Transactions.

5.4 Management Process Audits

5.4.1 Basics of Management Process Audits

KEY POINTS

- A management process audit is the evaluation of individual management-related processes and the associated management skills.
- A management process audit provides important organization-related information that can be used as a basis for process optimization and an associated increase in efficiency.
- The focus of management process audits is on processes, controls, compliance, and risk management.
- Management process audits should not be used to assess the manager's personality or individual behavior.
- Such audits can be conducted independently, or as additional audit components in order to test management-relevant processes in detail whenever required.

New Audit Field

Management process audits are a relatively new audit field for Internal Audit and are increasingly incorporated into Internal Audit's activities at SAP. The requirements that SOX places on management have increased the importance of performing these audits (for details, see Section C, Chapter 8; Section D, Chapter 14).

Definition

A management process audit evaluates individual management-related leadership and decision processes and internal controls, as well as the management skills that are necessary during these processes. In addition to classic risk evaluations and the resulting support in minimizing risk, the core tasks in this audit field include advising management about untapped success potential in the company.

Distinction from Management Appraisal

Throughout SAP, the human resources department is responsible for assessing individual performance and personal management skills as part of management evaluation. Audits conducted by Internal Audit consequently do not focus on the manager or the manager's personality, but on the application and implementation of the management processes and controls represented by the manager. These audits are referred to as "management process audits" to make the distinction clear. In combination with the performance evaluation conducted by Human Resources, they can produce a complete picture of a manager's success factors (see Section A, Chapter 6.2.2).

Acceptance

In practice, the managers (i.e., the auditees) are likely to oppose management process audits. At least some of this opposition can be avoided by consistently referring to and designing the audit as a management process audit. Internal Audit uses the methods generally applicable for all audits to facilitate constructive cooperation with the auditee (see Section C, Chapter 5.4.2) and to ensure that objectivity is maintained. It is moreover important to distinguish between,

- audit documents that relate exclusively to processes, controls, and risks, and

- documents that permit drawing conclusions about the manager's personal conduct and qualities.

In the former case, documents can be treated according to Internal Audit's general reporting principles, but documents in the latter case are subject to special confidentiality requirements.

Objectives

Management process audits have the following objectives:

- providing important information on company organization as a basis for strategic decisions,
- ensuring compliance with laws, e.g., SOX, and with SAP-internal guidelines and principles, e.g., code of business conduct,
- testing the effectiveness and profitability of management processes in day-to-day operations,
- supporting management to improve management processes by identifying improvement potential in:
  - business processes and their implementation,
  - management skills,
- providing operational support to strategic departments, such as HR, or Management Accounting, if necessary,
- supporting communication and information flows in global and virtual teams by testing standard information exchange processes, and
- presenting ratio-based analysis for reporting on management process audits (performance indicators, balanced scorecard presentations, etc.) and for making the results comparable.

Motivation of Those Involved

There are different reasons for introducing and implementing management process audits, depending on those involved and the groups at which they are targeted. From Internal Audit's perspective, auditing management processes, including management's involvement in internal control processes, is becoming increasingly important. In addition, acts such as SOX or the provisions of the German Stock Corporation Act (see Section A, Chapter 1.3) have had a decisive impact on the control and risk monitoring function, thus making it necessary to incorporate management process audits into Internal Audit's work. Management process audits provide the Board with a more detailed overview of departments by showing how leadership processes are being used to implement existing guidelines based on external regulations. At the same time, they also map how these leadership and decision processes influence and guarantee the results of day-to-day business operations in terms of quality and quantity. Another related aspect is that this kind of audit shows whether the rules applicable to business activities exist only on paper or whether they are actually implemented in practice. Management process audits provide support to managers with regard to process optimization, because Internal Audit highlights critical processes in their areas of responsibility. In summary, the motivation of the main parties involved in management process audits can be shown as follows:

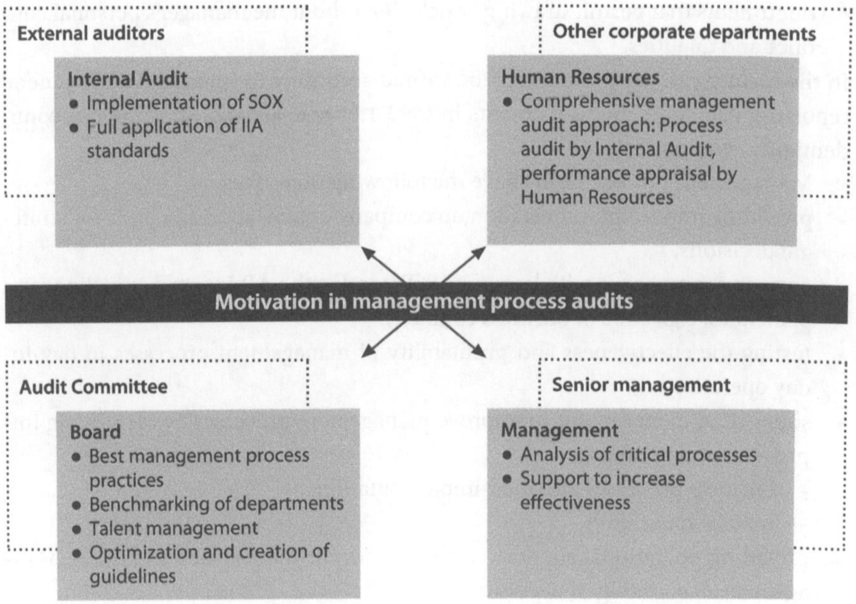

Fig. 19 Motivation of Parties Involved in Management Process Audits

Focus of Management Process Audits

Management process audits focus primarily on compliance and on efficiency achieved by implementing best practice processes. The result of a management process audit is the identification of improvement potential and support of any restructuring measures, if required. The areas to be investigated include processes, controls, and risk management. For a more detailed assessment, the auditors must consider that management results are driven by the following three components:

- performance of each manager,
- cooperation and performance in the management team, and
- functioning management processes in the organization.

A management process audit should therefore test the robustness of all three components and examine how they interact with each other. The transitions between the audited functions and processes are blurred, which is why Internal Audit and HR put different emphasis on them in their coverage.

Risk Management

It is also important to coordinate activities with Risk Management, with close cooperation being a key requirement, especially after the audit. Possible risks identified during a management process audit must be reported to Risk Management. Cooperation should also go the other way, that is, Risk Management should inform Internal Audit of units in the company that are particularly exposed to risk.

SOX

SOX audits are conducted by a dedicated SOX team, and again close connections and a high degree of overlap make it important for both groups to agree on a joint procedure. SOX regulations give rise to specific requirements for all strategic and operational levels of management (management controls, controls over management). Each manager is responsible for ensuring that all processes and controls applicable in his or her unit are fully documented and implemented, including any changes to the processes or controls. From this basic responsibility derives the obligation to provide the control bodies, as defined by SOX, with adequate evidence that the processes exist and the necessary internal controls are working (for details, see Section C, Chapter 8; Section D, Chapter 14). Internal Audit can test general compliance with SOX-related management responsibilities, either as part of SOX or management process audits. At SAP, testing management controls is an integral part of SOX work.

Audit Objectives

The audit is based on the relevant Core Scope for management audits. Since management processes make up the main object of the audit, appropriate process descriptions must be in place which can be used to specify targets for the audit. If the relevant descriptions are not available, the audit results may include a recommendation to create such descriptions. It must be possible to relate to recommendations that are based on experience and general application. For example, on the basis of practical working experience, a suggestion to hold regular coordination meetings to improve communication could make sense even if there was no hard and fast rule to that effect in the past.

Event Triggering the Audit

A management process audit can either be scheduled as a regular event or conducted as an ad-hoc audit to support decision finding if management quickly needs an objective presentation of the management-relevant processes of a department. A management process audit can be organized as a separate independent audit, but it can also be added as a component to department or local subsidiary audits (see Section C, Chapter 5.1). This requires close consultation and coordination in the relevant audit team and inclusion in the work program. The advantage is that strategic and operational areas of investigation are specifically divided into management processes and day-to-day business, and that Internal Audit's perception by management will be increased.

HINTS AND TIPS

- In a management process audit, auditors should first get a clear idea about the role of the manager responsible.
- During the audit, auditors should interact with the responsible managers constructively.

LINKS AND REFERENCES

- SAWYER, L. B., M. A. DITTENHOFER AND J. H. SCHEINER. 2003. *Sawyer's Internal Auditing.* 5th ed. Altamonte Springs, FL: The Institute of Internal Auditors.

• SEARS, B. 2002. *Internal Auditing Manual.* New York, NY: Warren, Gorham & Lamont.
• U.S. CONGRESS. 2002. *Sarbanes-Oxley Act of 2002. 107th Congress of the United States of America. HR 3763.* Washington DC: Government Printing Office.

5.4.2 Audit Preparation and Execution

KEY POINTS

- The relevant Key Scopes and the resulting work program form the basis for management process audits.
- Predefined questionnaires, which can be completed by the manager being audited for preparation purposes, increase the efficiency of the audit.
- A folder with information on the management process audit is provided to the manager being audited at the opening meeting.
- In management process audits, Internal Audit cooperates closely with other units, such as the HR department, thus a great deal of coordination is required.
- Management process audits aim at providing support for the audited manager.

Management Categories

A management process audit should produce forward-looking results that support management on issues such as filling a future vacancy or identifying potential for improvement in an existing position. In general, there are three levels of management:

- managers who manage employees,
- managers who manage managers, and
- managers who manage organizations.

Although in principle, these different management categories are subject to the same quality of management and decision processes, there are quantitative differences with regard to the level of detail and responsibility attached to the individual management functions, e.g., the size of the area managed. However, there are also management functions that exist exclusively within a specific management level, e.g. managing the overall information strategy in the management of organizations.

Breakdown of Core Scope

An important step is to define the extent of the testing for each of the above management categories. Using the list of audit segments relevant for this audit field, Internal Audit can make a qualitative and quantitative selection for each management level. The Core Scope for management process audits includes the following Key Scopes:

- Budget/Profitability,
- Cost Management,
- Approval Procedures,
- Methods and Method Knowledge,

- Communication,
- Management Development,
- Crisis/Emergency Management,
- Target Achievement,
- Performance Management,
- Human Resources Process Management, and
- Compensation Management.

Work Program

GIAS has compiled a standard work program on the basis of the Core Scope for management process audits. This program can be adapted to specific requirements and forms the basis of each audit conducted. The management process audit also follows internal principles and guidelines as well as external (legal) regulations, such as KonTraG or SOX. The audit should be referenced against desired criteria such as those detailed in specific corporate guidelines. These are set for the relevant operating departments and contain processes relevant to the departments and management-specific functions or aspects impacting them. For example, the product life cycle or the product innovation cycle would apply to development departments, and the customer business cycle would apply to Sales. Management programs such as "Global Management & Leadership" or "Management Excellence" and the "SAP Code of Business Conduct" (business principles for employees) have general validity.

Predefined Question Catalogs

Since management process audits must be as efficient as possible in order to make best use of managers' limited availability, Internal Audit at SAP has created predefined question catalogs to complement the work program (see Section B, Chapter 4.1.3.1). These catalogs allow auditors to work quickly toward their objectives and give managers an opportunity to get advance information on certain topics and to structure their response.

Information Folder

In addition, Internal Audit has prepared an information folder for management process audits, which provides an overview of Internal Audit and how the audit process works. It includes Internal Audit's charter and information on possible benefits the audit may deliver. This documentation is intended to minimize any resistance and facilitate the audit for the audit team. In general, good audit preparation and efficient procedures during execution will go a long way toward eliminating reservations about and resistance to a management process audit. The management process audit information folder is handed to the manager being audited at the opening meeting.

Document and Process Testing

The documents and processes to be audited are often of a strategic nature, and auditors therefore need a general understanding of the data and information they receive. For example, to assess performance indicators or a balanced scorecard system, auditors must be aware of the framework under which such systems have been defined. Individual objectives should dovetail into the overall corporate objectives, and the targets and objectives of a balanced scorecard must follow a defined method against which they can be tested. Further information may be found in the minutes of meetings, internal memos, or in department directories, which can provide details of the information flow in a department.

Use of Guidelines and Methods

Management knowledge and skills in the application of guidelines and methods are also investigated in the audit. For example, software development must base its operations on the product innovation cycle process and provide evidence that it has introduced and implemented this process. The sales and consulting organization must implement and document their tasks on the basis of the customer business cycle. Internal Audit tests in relation to the different requirements whether there is evidence that the guidelines have been implemented. At the Board and strategic management level, processes such as compliance with internal control management or contingency plans are audit-relevant. SOX-relevant processes (e.g. controls over management) are audited with the support of the SOX team (see Section C, Chapter 8).

Management Procedures and Knowledge

Another area to be tested is the manager's knowledge and use of generally applicable and SAP-specific management practices. These types of tests are intended to establish whether information is exchanged regularly with the different levels and whether the information is tailored to its recipients. Auditors must seek out this information, which is often qualitative, and make an appropriate assessment. A key prerequisite for them to be able to do so is that they have sound knowledge of the department's processes.

Management Performance

Since it is not always possible to distinguish clearly between personal factors and the implementation of performance-critical management processes, there is a need to coordinate the results of the management process audit with Human Resources. Likewise, Human Resources' evaluation of managers may provide useful information for a management process audit. However, Internal Audit invariably focuses on the relevant processes, although they may also have an effect on the manager's or department's performance.

Audit Result

The communication and assessment of the fieldwork results should predominantly be made with the aim of providing support for the manager. These results, which are highly confidential, are intended to identify weak points, but also strengths, in the manager's area of responsibility. The results of management process audits will only identify serious weaknesses if the auditors find that the manager has clearly circumvented guidelines. If that is the case, Internal Audit must follow the rules and also report the audit result to the Board.

Feedback

Generally, feedback from a management process audit should also be regarded as possible support from an independent body, which tests the relevant processes objectively and draws conclusions about any optimization potential. This efficiency-enhancing effect should be acknowledged during the closing meeting and in the reports that follow, but generally the auditors should not leave the feedback until the end of the audit, instead they should keep the manager informed about the status of findings. Although this kind of interaction takes more time, it facilitates cooperation because auditors also must rely on the manager's willingness to share information.

HINTS AND TIPS

- Wherever possible, experienced auditors should be selected to conduct management process audits.
- Ahead of the audit, auditors can also obtain personal information about the managers so that they can prepare themselves for their dealings with them.

LINKS AND REFERENCES

- SEARS, B. 2002. *Internal Auditing Manual.* New York, NY: Warren, Gorham & Lamont.
- SAWYER, L. B., M. A. DITTENHOFER AND J. H. SCHEINER. 2003. *Sawyer's Internal Auditing.* 5th ed. Altamonte Springs, FL: The Institute of Internal Auditors.

6 Business Review

KEY POINTS

- The business review is not one of Internal Audit's traditional audit tasks.
- Projects with customers (consulting or development) or other matters arising from SAP's relations with customers or partners may be examined during a business review.
- The review focus may differ, depending on the circumstances and the specific request. Its focus may be one of the following: Pure implementation performance, contractual and financial aspects, or the nature and design of business relations.
- A business review normally involves several rounds of meetings between the customer and the relevant management at SAP, where the current status, interim results, proposals, and actions are discussed.
- Finally, a report is created for the Board member in charge and for the customer, explaining the matters identified and the action proposals discussed.

Business Review as a Special Form of Review

The business review is not one of the traditional audit tasks of Internal Audit (for the distinction between audit and review, see Section A, Chapter 6.2.7). At SAP, this special, innovative form of review has its origins in day-to-day audit work. Projects with customers (consulting or development) or other matters arising from SAP's relations with customers or partners may be the objects of a business review. Depending on the complexity of the request, a review of this kind can take several weeks. This chapter deals with conducting business reviews in practice (for details on business audits, see Section A, Chapter 6.2.7). Above all, a business review examines an as-is (current) situation. The review involves fewer fieldwork activities than an audit and focuses more on conclusions or drafting solutions jointly with colleagues from other departments in order to achieve an improvement of the situation. In this regard, reviews help prevent escalations, especially since they are conducted by Internal Audit and are thus intended as intervention by the Board with a focus on de-escalation (for more on escalation, see Section D, Chapter 6).

Request

Business reviews are normally requested ad-hoc and therefore not included in the annual audit plan (see Section B, Chapter 2.2). In this case, Internal Audit receives a request, for example, from the CEO to investigate certain aspects of day-to-day business.

Preparation

Preparation differs, depending on the circumstances and the specific request. For example, the review of a customer consulting project for pure software implementation requires different preparation from a review of contractual or financial aspects of business relations. Often, it is not easy to keep these matters separate, but a review request may result in different emphases.

Support Provided by Other SAP Departments

Irrespective of the type of request and the resulting emphasis during the review, Internal Audit consults with relevant colleagues in the customer support (sales) and consulting departments. The relevant customer support officer in sales is responsible for answering inquiries on all customer matters and the general business relationship with the customer. For a consulting project, Internal Audit's contacts may include the head of consulting and the local project manager, and for a development project the contact will be the respective project manager from the development unit. From a general perspective, Corporate Risk Management is also an important contact.

Use of the SAP Systems

Further information on the customer and the project or situation concerned, such as customer master data, license revenue, consulting revenue, payment behavior, etc., can be retrieved from the SAP system.

Implementation Review

If the review focuses on software implementation, Internal Audit should consider incorporating into the audit team consulting colleagues who are familiar with implementing the specific SAP system components (e.g., finance and purchasing). These consultants can provide Internal Audit with technical support throughout the review. In such cases, Internal Audit assumes control and coordination of the technical project review. In addition, Internal Audit investigates contractual, legal, and financial aspects of the project.

Review of Contractual and Financial Aspects

For a review focusing on contractual and financial aspects, Internal Audit first examines the contracts with the customer concerned for existing obligations and performs a detailed analysis of the financial project data from the SAP system.

Review of Business Relationship

If the request asks for the review to focus on customer and business relations, the auditors will also need to gather a variety of information ahead of the review, e.g., on the sector of industry, size of the customer, the relevant contacts, or the quality of the customer relationship. This information can be obtained by conducting interviews with the relevant customer support officer, the head of consulting, or the project manager, and by analyzing the legal and financial data contained in the contract documents and the SAP system.

Other Involved Parties

The following table shows other parties that may be involved in a business review and their responsibilities, depending on the request and circumstances:

Allocation of roles & responsibilities	Board	Internal Audit	Sales/account management	Active global support	Global Risk Management	Review program	Legal & Contract department	Compliance Office
Customer account management	if significant enough	no	yes	no	no	no	no	no
Coordination of service delivery	if significant enough	no	yes	no	no	no	no	no
Partner management	if significant enough	no	yes	no	no	yes	yes	no
Risk management	if significant enough	yes	yes	no	yes	yes	yes	no
Commercial issue resolution	if significant enough	yes	yes	no	no	yes	yes	no
Technical issue resolution	if significant enough	no	yes	yes	no	yes	no	no
Code of Business Conduct issues	if significant enough	yes	yes	no	no	no	no	yes

Fig. 20 Responsibilities of Parties Involved in a Business Review

Aspects and Procedures

On the basis of the pre-review preparations, auditors analyze specific matters on site. At this stage, the focus is also on contact with the customer. In discussions with the customer, Internal Audit investigates and analyzes the circumstances and situation on site. This entails various interviews with the project manager and the customer's project team and also with members of the SAP project team. Different solution proposals are prepared on the basis of the information obtained.

Requirements for Internal Audit Employees

Not least because of the direct contact with customers, a business review requires that the whole team and the individual Internal Audit employees approach the matter with the necessary diplomacy and sensitivity. Internal Audit's task is to draft a solution from a neutral, objective, and impartial point of view, or to support and control the development of a solution based on the insights gained from the review and to communicate the results achieved. The drafted solution must satisfy all parties involved, meeting their needs and ensuring that the project objective is achieved.

Review Steps in Detail

In detail, a business review consists of the following steps:

- Analysis of the legal situation/contract analysis:
  - The legal situation and basis are analyzed and potential risks and obligations highlighted.
  - The status quo of the project is reviewed on this basis.
- Analysis of the financial situation/project analysis and costing:
  - project costing,
  - comparison of current condition and desired criteria,
  - comparison of the performance agreed and performance delivered, and
  - attainment of milestones and appropriate evidence.
- Analysis of the technical project status (if necessary with support from colleagues from Consulting or other areas):
  - Internal Audit selects a team with knowledge of the relevant software applications.
  - This team examines on site the current implementation status in terms of project fulfillment and quality.
- Analysis of the customer-project relationship on the basis of interviews and discussions with project managers and project team members, as well as the customer.

Information Provided by the Customer

At the meetings between Internal Audit and the customer, the current situation is discussed and the customer's opinion is established. The customer's suggestions for improvement, complaints, requests, and criticism regarding the existing business relationship are collected and examined for possible implementation. The results of these meetings are included in the business review reports to the managers responsible at SAP, including the Board.

Reporting

The reports on this type of review usually differ from Internal Audit's regular reporting (see Section B, Chapter 5). A business review normally involves several rounds of meetings with the customer and the relevant management at SAP, where the current status, interim results, proposals, and possible actions are discussed. Finally, a report is created for the Board member responsible and for the customer, explaining the matters identified and the action proposals discussed. Different report formats can be used, depending on circumstances (for more on the possible report formats, see Section B, Chapter 5).

7 Global Audits

KEY POINTS

- As the trend towards globalization continues, Internal Audit must respond by conducting global audits.
- Internal Audit must be able to handle global topics adequately, however, a special process model for global audits is not necessarily needed.
- Global audits entail greater coordination and communication efforts.
- In global audits, GIAS can use its strengths with regard to global presence under centralized management with decentralized operations.
- Global audits present special challenges for each auditor, which can have a positive effect on his or her personal career development.

SAP as a Global Company

SAP is a global company in many respects. SAP currently has customers in over 120 countries and offers software solutions in 31 languages. Indeed, there is worldwide demand for SAP products and services. For this reason, the company now generates a large proportion of its revenue in countries outside Europe, particularly the United States. Further, the Asian market as well as countries like India, Russia, and Brasil have gained considerably in importance. SAP's shareholders are also international. Most of the company's individual shareholders are based in the United States. In addition, SAP's global orientation is reflected in the international composition of its workforce. Approximately 40% of SAP's employees are currently based in Germany. The remaining 60% are distributed among SAP subsidiaries in over 50 countries.

Tension between Local and Global Aspects

Some of SAP's local subsidiaries act fairly independently. Often, it is sensible to maintain local independence and culture as part of the overall company organization so that business activities can be tailored to the market and customers. However, the parent company must always be in a position to enforce necessary changes globally in order to implement global values, standards, and strategic decisions in all parts of the company. This means that global companies must balance the tension between globally focused corporate management and strategy and the specific local requirements and cultures.

Support for Enforcing Global Standards

Internal Audit helps ensure that global companies can implement globally mandated standards in their various locations, without forsaking local needs and requirements. In addition, local standards and regulations may also affect a global company as a whole. For example, in the U.S. it is widely accepted (and currently protected under SOX 806) that employees can report illegal or unethical activities occurring within their organization to the appropriate authorities. As organizations become global, regional practices and customs, such as whistleblowing, are being widely recognized throughout the organization.

Support for the Implementation of Management and Control Functions

In addition, globalization entails the need to adapt quickly to change on a worldwide scale. It refers not only to the purely geographical spread of a company with global operations, which require business activities to be conducted in all parts of the world, but also to the growing trend toward outsourcing and the virtualization of business relationships. This includes new business and company models, which pose a number of different demands on the organization. It is becoming increasingly difficult to tell where a company starts and where it ends. Due to its position in the company, Internal Audit can support executive management in performing the necessary management and control functions.

Embedding Global Audits in Internal Audit's Organization

If a company has a global orientation, Internal Audit also must have a global structure. This requires not only that the department have a global presence, but also that the audit method can adequately cover global topics. However, this does not mean that there should be a special audit model for dealing with global topics. Like other audits, global audits include all the phases of the Audit Roadmap (for a detailed description, see Section B). They follow the same typology, i.e., they can be conducted as standard, special, or ad-hoc audits, and they can run through the entire audit cycle, from basic audit through status check and follow-up. Nevertheless, for global audits to be successful, they need to have special attributes, which will be discussed in more detail in this chapter.

Special Attributes of Global Audits

Global audits relate to global topics, issues, and processes. While in some cases, the relevant responsibilities are clearly defined, in most global audits they are not. Under normal circumstances, Internal Audit is rarely asked to investigate global topics that have clearly assigned responsibilities and therefore high-quality processes. Instead, its services are usually required for audits of processes whose global orientation causes local and central competences to overlap (e.g., audits of the risk management function).

Global Audits in the Case of Worldwide Responsibilities

A typical scenario of a global audit looks at a global business unit, which has the sole mandate for a global process but in practice must rely on informal cooperation with a number of other business units. It is important that the responsibility is genuinely global, i.e., these business units have direct reporting lines to their globally distributed employees. These employees therefore do not report to their local business units, but to a global management unit. This is the case, for example, where the head of the regional purchasing organization is directly responsible for his or her region, but at the same time reports directly to the head of Global Purchasing. Many central business units, typically the administrative units of the parent company, do not meet this criterion. Although such units often control central processes and have to rely on global cooperation, they operate without assuming direct operational responsibility. Day-to-day management is therefore the responsibility of the local units.

Global Approach of Internal Audit

When investigating global audit topics, Internal Audit should use local expertise while managing the audits centrally. For global audits, the audit lead should be appointed from the region that has global responsibility for the process to be audited. Global audit teams consist of members from different regions and often work on an audit project mainly on a virtual basis under central management (see Section A, Chapter 4.4). In this way, Internal Audit operates truly globally, combining its central audit model under central supervision with regional expertise so that it can investigate global topics properly.

Advantages of the Global Approach

This global approach not only helps the immediate audit process, but Internal Audit also benefits as a department. Global audit teams help Internal Audit employees bond and exchange practice-based experience of audit methods and procedures. In addition, global audits present demanding challenges, which provide the auditors the opportunity to gain specific experience. The successful completion of a global audit is therefore an important step in an auditor's personal career development (see Section A, Chapter 4.6).

Involvement of the CAE

Since global audits are of great importance internally and externally, the CAE should be directly involved in conducting the audit, e.g., by appointing the audit lead personally and asking for regular audit progress reports.

Special Aspects When Conducting Global Audits

Global audits follow the general process model of the Audit Roadmap. However, the above special aspects and the complexity of such audits entail that each phase meet special requirements, as explained below.

Audit Planning

Global audits are conducted by global audit teams. This means that the regional and global staffing plans must be closely coordinated (see Section D, Chapter 3.4). In the first instance, this means that all team members must recognize that the audit is truly global and therefore must be designated and treated as such. Global audits are time-consuming, not least because they typically relate to more complex issues than local or regional audits. Moreover, they require greater communication and coordination efforts (e.g., a centralized reconciled issue-logging), such that Internal Audit should allow more time for the planning phase of such audits. Since the audit lead will therefore be required to perform additional communication and coordination tasks, this should be taken into consideration when compiling the regional execution plan.

Audit Preparation

Audit preparation (see Section B, Chapter 3) mainly includes the audit announcement and the compilation of a work program. For global audits, defining the extent of the engagement is of particular importance. Global topics tend to be more diffuse and less straightforward and normally affect several business units and responsibilities. It is therefore essential that all auditors involved have a thorough and complete understanding of the matter. This is necessary for defining the focus areas for the audit. Audit leads must therefore be given an opportunity to familiarize themselves with the topic before distributing the audit announcement, which includes an initial list of focus areas for the audit.

Cooperation of the Global Audit Team

If possible, the members of the global audit team should have an opportunity to meet in person at a preparatory conference. This meeting can be used to add detail to audit topic definitions and to fine-tune the work program as part of a genuinely collaborative process. The investigation of global issues in particular requires the use of different experiences, views, and skills. In this context, it is important to ensure that auditors are aware of all relevant global guidelines. But the meeting should also deal with practical aspects, such as specific staffing plans, the assignment of audit segments, and the definition and mandating of milestones. Other practicalities include the coordination of itineraries, the authorization of IT access for all auditors involved, the creation of a shared archiving structure, and agreement on virtual cooperation (e.g., telephone and video conferencing). At the end of the meeting, all audit team members must understand the contribution they must make in order to turn the global audit into a success.

Communication with the Auditees

The members of the audit team are not alone in needing clear-cut agreement on procedure. This is also important for the global units being audited, which is why the audit lead should engage them in dialog at an early stage. Information about the organization of the audit must be communicated in a structured and timely manner. Cooperation between Internal Audit and the auditees is mostly of a virtual nature, so that clearly structured and unambiguously formulated documents, e.g., presentations, are an advantage when exchanging information.

Audit Execution

When conducting the audit (see Section B, Chapter 4), audit leads have to make sure that the work program is strictly followed. They will only have limited opportunity for personal meetings to obtain certainty about the audit progress. It is therefore all the more important that each auditor complies with the agreed documentation requirements and immediately reports any delays or problems. The members of the global audit team may be based in different time zones, which may delay the audit lead's response. Not all the team members will be able to communicate in their native language, so that misunderstandings may arise that must be cleared up. Because of the increased communication and coordination requirements, global audits need a great measure of diligence in their execution to make them successful.

Reporting

With regard to reporting, audit leads must make sure that the audit findings are consistently and uniformly documented and motivated (see Section B, Chapter 5). In global audits it is often difficult to find the right addressees for the findings and to identify the people responsible for resolving them. Audit leads must ensure that they address recommendations to those who are directly responsible. It is also their duty to conduct the closing meeting and prepare the final report. This also includes ensuring internally on a global basis that the audit documents are centrally archived in a standardized way.

Follow-Up Phase

The special aspects presented above also apply to status checks and follow-ups (see Section B, Chapter 6) in connection with global topics. In addition, the auditors must remember that a global audit will require meeting with or contacting a number of people responsible in various locations to obtain information about the implementation of the audit recommendations made.

HINTS AND TIPS

- Communication is very important in global audits, i.e., there should be an active exchange of information.
- Each auditor should practice using virtual working methods at an early stage, e.g. preparing for and conducting telephone conferences, net meetings, etc.
- Members of a global audit team must be very flexible with regard to time, because the audit may span several time zones.

LINKS AND REFERENCES ↗

- CASCARINO, R. AND S. VAN ESCH. 2005. *Internal Auditing: An Integrated Approach.* Lansdowne, SA: Juta and Co.
- REDING, K. F., P. J. SOBEL, U. L. ANDERSON, et al. 2007. *Internal Assurance and Consulting Services.* Altamonte Springs, FL: The Institute of Internal Auditors.
- SAWYER, L. B., M. A. DITTENHOFER AND J. H. SCHEINER. 2003. *Sawyer's Internal Auditing.* 5th ed. Altamonte Springs, FL: The Institute of Internal Auditors.
- SEARS, B. 2002. *Internal Auditing Manual.* New York, NY: Warren, Gorham & Lamont.
- U.S. CONGRESS. 2002. *Sarbanes-Oxley Act of 2002. 107th Congress of the United States of America. HR 3763.* Washington DC: Government Printing Office.

8 SOX Audits

KEY POINTS

- There are three types of SOX audits: audits of the implementation of SOX in each of the company's units, audits of the quality of SOX work undertaken locally, and audits of various SOX-related process groups, processes, and control systems.
- Preparation for a SOX audit for process groups is of crucial importance and should include the following steps: review of the available documentation regarding the processes to be audited, review of the results of design assessments and testing procedures, and discussion of issues with the local SOX champion and the central SOX team.
- The execution of the SOX audit for process groups includes reviews of design assessment tests, control effectiveness tests, and of the existing flowcharts.
- Auditors must ensure that the population and any samples have originated in the current fiscal year. Samples taken from the previous year cannot prove that the controls are effective at the time of the audit.
- Auditors must document the sampling method so that the audit can be reperformed.

Introduction

SOX audits focus on section 404 of the Sarbanes-Oxley Act (Management Assessment of Internal Controls). This section requires that management provide an assessment of the effectiveness of internal controls as part of the annual financial reporting process. With regard to section SOX 404, there are three possible types of audit that Internal Audit may perform (for details, see Section D, Chapter 14):

- audits of the implementation of SOX 404 in the company's entities (local SOX project audits),
- audits of the quality of SOX 404 measures implemented in the entities (focusing on compliance with the formal criteria and quality assurance standards of the SOX process), and
- audits of various SOX-relevant process groups, processes, and controls in the entities.

This chapter deals with the third type of audit: the audit of various SOX-relevant process groups. This audit precedes the external audit of the company's financial statements. It should be conducted to ensure that all critical areas of individual process groups have been identified at the local level and have been properly documented and assessed. The following assumes that a company has an internal control framework based on the COSO Framework (see Section A, Chapter 1.3 and Section D, Chapter 14.1.2).

Procedures Necessary for Audit Preparation

The Scope of a SOX audit for process groups is clearly defined. The audit relates only to the process groups identified in the annual investigation as relevant with regard to SOX 404. Specifically, the audit focuses on those processes which affect the financial reporting of the organization. The audit examines the required documentation, the associated control objectives and risks as well as the related financial statement accounts related to those process groups. To prepare properly for the audit, the audit team should complete the following steps:

- Contact the local SOX champion to obtain a status update of the process groups being audited and to ensure that the process documentation is up-to-date. If a central tool is used for this purpose (e.g., at SAP, the internal control management tool; see Section B, Chapter 4.1.3.3), the documentation does not have to be reviewed on site, but can be accessed in the system prior to the start of the audit. If this is not the case, the local SOX champion should provide the auditor with electronic copies of any process group documentation.
- Review and understand the process documentation, the possible risks, and the financial statement accounts for the process groups to be audited.
- Review the testing results for design assessment and control effectiveness documented by the local SOX champion for the process groups to be audited. This may only be possible on site if no centralized tool is in use.
- Contact the company's central SOX team to discuss any concerns or issues they may have with the local entity being audited.
- Prepare the process group templates required to complete the audit.
- Prepare the opening meeting presentation.
- Divide the responsibilities for the various tasks required during the audit execution phase among the audit team members.
- Review past Internal Audit reports relating to the same group of auditees.

Examination of the Process Documentation

Once the process groups have been selected, the auditor should review process and control descriptions to become familiar with the local processes. The focus here should be on obtaining a basic understanding of what steps are taken as part of the process and where the internal controls are located. A detailed analysis of the process documentation will be performed during audit execution (more details below).

Preliminary Risk Review

The auditor should also complete a preliminary review of the risks associated with the process groups to be audited. Such a review is aimed at establishing what risks exist and how significant they are. This gives the auditor an initial impression as to whether these risks have been adequately addressed within the process.

Financial Statement Review

A review of the financial statement accounts will allow the auditor to determine which accounts are significant for the process groups to be audited. An account is significant if there is a probability that it contains misstatements that individually, or when aggregated with others, could have a material effect on the financial statements.

Review of the Results Documented Locally

The process and control design assessments and control effectiveness testing procedures and results must be documented by the local managers responsible. Prior to arrival, the auditor should analyze the procedures and results documented to ensure conformity with quality assurance standards set by the company. A second reason to perform this review before the audit execution phase is to obtain an idea, in advance, of how detailed or how plausible the work performed locally is and where there may be potential weaknesses that need extra focus during the audit.

Process Group Templates

Once the preparatory review is completed, the auditor should complete the process group templates. GIAS has prepared special spreadsheet templates for each process group for documenting the following: design assessment, risks, financial statement accounts, testing procedures, testing issues, and the associated findings. Individual process and control steps should be copied to the template, preliminary questions should be formulated concerning the process descriptions, and testing procedures should be documented for the controls to be tested.

Test Procedures

After preparation, the audit execution phase begins. Here, the auditor reviews the procedures already carried out by the SOX champion. This may include the following steps:

- detailed desk review,
- control walkthrough,
- review of the individual control designs,
- review of the overall process design,
- review or re-performance of the internal control effectiveness testing, and
- review of any relevant flowcharts.

Details of each procedure are given below.

Design Assessment

In order to guarantee control effectiveness, internal controls must be designed adequately. The adequacy of the internal control design must be assessed both internally by the local organization as well as by its external auditors. The design assessment should determine whether the internal controls are operating as intended. Additionally, the design assessment should test whether the necessary controls are in place to provide reasonable assurance of accurate account entries. When performing the design assessment, the auditor should follow the procedure described below.

Desk Review

A desk review is performed first. It serves to obtain a general overview of the process – what are the risks, what are the internal control objectives, where have the significant controls been integrated, etc. The following steps should be taken when completing the desk review:

- Check if control description is clear, comprehensive, and complete.
- Check for preventive and detective controls.
- Check for manual and automated controls.
- Check for significant controls. If such controls seem to exist, ask whether they are really significant or whether the process group under review does not have any significant controls (significant controls must be designed in such a way that they can prevent or detect errors or fraud that could lead to material misstatements in the financial statements).

- Check if the internal controls fully cover all known risks.
- Check if significant and accounting-relevant assertions are covered by the internal controls.
- Identify points in the process where material misstatements and/or fraud could occur.
- Check whether the controls within a process are positioned properly.
- Assess the existing documentation of the controls to establish whether it is adequate to test the effectiveness of these controls.
- Develop a list of questions and information necessary for conducting a walk-through.

Now follows a detailed description of the first six steps of a desk review.

Internal Control Description (Step 1)

The internal control descriptions should be reviewed to ensure compliance with company quality assurance standards. Control documentation should enable the addressee to understand the flow of activities required to initiate, authorize, record, and process transactions, as well as create the necessary reports. Consequently, it is vital that the control descriptions accurately explain how the activities are performed. The best way to ensure clear descriptions is if they answer questions like "who?," "what?," "how?," "when?," "where?," and "why?."

Control Attributes (Steps 2–4)

After reviewing the process and control descriptions for clarity and consistency, the auditor should examine the attributes of each identified control. Examples of a standard set of control attributes that are utilized to further enhance the control descriptions are shown below.

Attributes	Values
Significance	Significant control, standard control
Purpose of control	Preventive, detective
Automation	Automated, semi-automated, manual
Date or event driven	Date-driven, event-driven
Frequency (if date-driven)	Continuous, daily, weekly, biweekly, monthly, quarterly, semi-annually, annually
Event description (if event-driven)	Description of event that triggers the process step or control

Fig. 21 Control Attribute Values

The following table summarizes the definitions of the control attribute values of significance, control purpose, and automation.

Attributes	Values	Definitions
Significance	Significant control	If the control fails, a misstatement is very probable.
	Standard control	Supporting control.
Purpose of control	Preventive	Errors are prevented.
	Detective	Errors are retrospectively identified and corrected.
Automation	Automated	The control is performed automatically by a computer or enforced by the system settings.
	Semi-automated	Automatic control, but requires manual start or validation.
	Manual	The control is effected exclusively by persons.

Fig. 22 Definition of Control Attribute Values

Audit Focus

When reviewing the general attributes, the auditor should look for an appropriate balance of control characteristics. The auditor should be able to clearly distinguish between standard and significant controls. Additionally, a good process design will contain a balanced mixture of preventive and detective as well as manual and automated controls.

Control Review (Step 5)

If an internal control is well described, the auditor should be able to clearly determine the business risk that the control is designed to mitigate. The process owners are required to map the correlation between identified internal controls and inherent business risks. The auditor's task is to verify that there truly is a correlation between the described control and the business risk to which it has been mapped.

Risks Without Internal Controls

A failure to map all the risks to internal controls does not necessarily indicate an inadequate control level. There may be legitimate reasons why no internal control has been assigned to a defined risk. The general business risks identified by the company do not always apply to all locations. Often, risks within one process group will be mitigated by controls in another process group. In this case, an explanation should be provided within the process design assessment results. Additionally, the local entity may have internal controls in place that have not been documented. A finding should only be made in the event that a relevant business risk has been identified that is not mitigated by an internal control.

Control Assertion Review

In addition to mapping the correlation between identified internal controls and inherent business risks, the process owners must also determine which of the assertions listed below is assured by the internal control in relation to the risk. Every internal control should cover one or more of the following aims:

- Completeness: All information is captured during the course of transactions, process steps, and activities.

- Accuracy: The factual and formal correctness of the data and documents used for the affected process step is guaranteed.
- Validity: Verification that the data or objects of given transactions truly exist (by either an authorized person or the system itself).
- Restricted access: Users only have access to data and functions that are relevant to their responsibilities and their roles.

As with the general control attributes, a good process description should contain an appropriate balance of control assertions.

Review of Account Mapping (Step 6)

Having mapped the internal controls to their respective risks and control assertions, process owners must then determine the correlation between the internal controls and the corresponding financial statement accounts they affect either directly or indirectly. The company should have identified financial statement accounts that are relevant to each process group on a consolidated group level. Once auditors have identified the significant accounts for the local entity, they must then ensure that each of these accounts is mapped to an internal control.

Financial Statement Assertions

The process owner should also map each internal control to a corresponding financial statement assertion. Every control should cover one or more of the following assertions:

- Existence or occurrence: Assertions about existence or occurrence address whether assets or liabilities of the entity exist at a given date and whether recorded transactions have occurred during a given period.
- Completeness: Assertions about completeness address whether all transactions and accounts that should be presented in the financial statements are included.
- Valuation or allocation: Assertions about valuation or allocation address whether asset, liability, revenue, and expense components have been included in the financial statements at appropriate amounts.
- Rights and obligations: Assertions about rights and obligations address whether assets are the rights of the entity and liabilities are the obligations of the entity at a given date.
- Presentation and disclosure: Assertions about presentation and disclosure address whether particular components of the financial statements are properly classified, described, and disclosed.

Walk-Through Review

Once the desk review has been completed, the auditor should examine each control design individually. The most effective way to conduct this review is to re-perform the walkthrough. The local SOX champion should have documented the procedures used during the walk-through, and the auditor will now test these procedures. The purpose of the walkthrough is to confirm with the process owner the overall accuracy of the process documentation. It should establish whether the number and type of controls in a process are sufficient to minimize business risks efficiently. The following steps should be performed:

- The process owner should explain the process to the auditor so that the results of the desk review can be verified.

- The auditor should focus on the potential risks and form a preliminary agreement with process owners on what those are.
- The main emphasis should be on significant internal controls. Suitable risk minimization measures should be agreed upon with the process owner.
- For each internal control, the auditor should randomly select one or more transactions from the appropriate population.
- The auditors should trace the transactions from the beginning to the end of the process. They should check to determine whether there are interfaces to other processes and to ensure that no transaction-related information is transferred by mistake.
- The auditors should ask questions concerning the operation of any significant controls that are in place to detect or prevent material misstatements (confirmation of the account mapping).
- It is necessary to obtain supporting documentation demonstrating that the control is working as documented. The auditor should note whenever the actual process deviates from the documented version.
- Auditors should obtain screenshots for any part of the process that involves computer input or other computer procedures.
- The auditors should prepare the internal control testing phase and file the collected results in binders.

Internal Controls Maturity

On the basis of the desk review and walk-through results, the auditor must determine whether or not the control maturity rating assigned by the SOX champion is appropriate. The following table shows an example of a possible rating.

Unreliable	Informal	Standardized	Monitored	Optimized
Control activities are not designed or in place. The environment is unpredictable.	Control activities are designed and in place, but they are not adequately documented.	Control activities are designed, in place, and adequately documented.	Controls are standardized. There is periodic testing for effective design and operation with reporting to management.	Controls are integrated. There is real-time monitoring by management and continuous improvement.

Fig. 23 Internal Controls Maturity Framework

Review of the Control Design Assessment

Once the desk review and walk-through have been completed, Internal Audit must review the control design assessment made by the SOX champion. This requires the following steps:

- Ensure the control description is clear, comprehensive, and complete.

- Examine the internal controls to ensure they are sufficient to fully address risks. Make notes of any deficiencies.
- Examine how risks have been assigned to the financial statement accounts.
- Assess the coverage of financial statement assertions.
- Assess the documentation of the controls to establish whether it is adequate to audit the effectiveness of these controls.
- Assess the ability of the control owner to perform control (skills, training, etc.).
- Describe the assessment made.

Review of the Process Design Assessment

Having completed their assessment of each individual control within a process, the SOX champions must then provide an assessment of the adequacy of the overall process design. The process design assessment should be a cumulative evaluation of each of the control assessments within the process. The result of this assessment may be as follows:

- Adequate: All controls within the process are standardized, or risk-minimizing controls exist.
- Deficient: One or more controls within the process are missing, informal, or unreliable.
- Significantly deficient: Significant controls within the process are missing or unreliable.

Not all Controls Conform to Standard

If a single control assessment does not conform to the standard, it does not mean that the whole process design is deficient. Often, informal or unreliable standard controls are mitigated with overriding significant controls. However, an adequate rating should not be given to a process design where a significant control is unreliable.

Process Design Assessment Steps

Once the auditors have analyzed the results of the SOX champion's process design assessment, they perform their own review. In general, a thorough assessment should include the following steps:

- Assess the adequacy of the documentation, verifying that it is clearly written and contains sufficient detail to enable a third party to evaluate the control design and to test the operating effectiveness.
- Check if the mix of preventive and detective as well as manual and automated controls is sufficiently balanced to mitigate process-inherent risks.
- Test the significant internal controls.
- Examine how risks have been mapped to the financial statement accounts (including the explanation of process risks not addressed).
- Check whether controls within a process are located in the right place.
- Verify that each risk of potential material misstatement as well as the risk-minimizing controls are documented.
- Identify controls implemented to detect or prevent unauthorized acquisition, use, or disposition of company assets.

Documentation During the Design Assessment Phase

The SOX champion must document the process and control design assessments in detail. In addition, the auditor should document the following in the process group templates based on the internal control design review:

- procedures performed,
- expected results,
- audit evidence, and
- conclusion drawn from the assessment.

Findings

If the auditor determines that the design rating for a process or control is either "deficient" or "significantly deficient," then an appropriate finding must be reported. Findings are documented in the process group template. It may be useful to use standardized findings categories for analytical purposes on a company level. In the process of reporting findings, the auditor must assign a priority. Again, it may be helpful to have standardized priority levels (e.g., high, medium, and low) as well as a guideline explaining in what cases each priority applies. It may not be necessary to document a detailed remediation plan for every finding that is noted. For example, the company may determine that detailed remediation plans are only required for issues that cannot be corrected within four weeks. However, there may be specific topics (e.g., findings relating to revenue recognition under US-GAAP) that always require remediation plans.

Need to Test the Effectiveness of Internal Controls

The control and process design assessment is followed by tests of the effectiveness of the internal controls put in place to ensure that these controls operate as planned. By performing such tests, the auditor can show that an internal control process may not function adequately, even if its design is adequate. This situation usually occurs when internal controls are not properly monitored or implemented.

Review of the Tests Performed by the SOX Champion

Internal Audit must determine whether the techniques the SOX champion has used to test internal control effectiveness are reliable. In addition, they must ensure that the testing techniques are compliant with the standards established by the company (preferably, in conjunction with the external auditor). Lastly, a random sample of significant controls should be re-tested to ensure that the results are consistent with those of the SOX champion.

Reliable Testing

There are four levels of appropriate testing techniques:

- interviews with competent persons,
- observation of processes in the company,
- testing of the relevant documentation, and
- re-performance of the control.

The level of security increases with each level. A reliable testing procedure should have a balanced mix of these techniques.

Introduction of Mandatory Parameters

In addition to proper testing techniques, a company should also consider using mandatory testing and re-testing parameters. These parameters must be adhered to in order for the external auditors to be able to rely upon the work performed locally. The first set of parameters deals with the number of controls tested per process group. In all cases, all significant controls should be tested. However, a company may also decide, for example, to test 10% to 20% of standard controls, just to have additional assurance within a process group. The second set of parameters deals with the number of samples selected per test. In general, the number of testing samples increases directly with the frequency with which the control is performed. A fictitious example of specific parameters for selecting testing and re-testing sample sizes is illustrated in the chart below:

Control frequency	Sample size	Number of errors	Findings	Re-testing	No. of additional errors	Findings
Annually	1	1	Yes	After correction	Not applicable	Not applicable
Quarterly	2	1 to 2	Yes	After correction	Not applicable	Not applicable
Monthly	3	1 to 3	Yes	After correction	Not applicable	Not applicable
Weekly	10	1	No	5 additional, immediately	1 or more	Yes
		2 to 10	Yes	After correction	Not applicable	Not applicable
Daily	20	1 to 2	No	10 additional, immediately	1 or more	Yes
		3 to 20	Yes	After correction	Not applicable	Not applicable
Several times daily	30	1 to 3	No	15 additional, immediately	1 or more	Yes
		4 to 30	Yes	After correction	Not applicable	Not applicable

Fig. 24 Special Parameters for Selecting the Sample Size

Procedure for Event-Driven Controls

Usually, it is not possible to determine sample sizes for event-driven controls in advance. When testing event-driven controls it is useful to proceed according to the same specifications as in the case of date-driven controls. The more often the event occurs, the larger the sample size should be. The ultimate value is based on a date-driven sample size. It must therefore be determined how often the event occurs on average (e.g. quarterly, weekly, daily) and the corresponding sample size taken.

Tester Independence and Experience

When reviewing the effectiveness of testing procedures, auditors should consider the testers' independence and experience. In general, testers should always be independent of the processes which they are testing. That is, the test should not be performed by the process owner. However, the tester should be experienced and familiar enough with the process to be able to form a well-founded opinion regarding the effectiveness of the controls.

Test Documentation

Before testing can begin, a set of testing procedures should be documented locally by each owner. This allows the auditor to understand exactly how controls were tested for effectiveness. Internal Audit should also document these procedures in the process group template. The following items are of particular note:

- sample size,
- sample selection,
- testing approach and mix of testing techniques, and
- expected results (type of result, formal and factual accuracy).

Fictitious Examples of Internal Control Testing Procedures

The following are fictitious examples of procedures for testing internal controls:

- The auditors obtain a list of all purchase order requisitions created in 2005. Using interval sampling, they determine the interval for choosing the requisitions at random. The auditors note the requestor, cost center, cost center manager, actual approver and PR content. They then document the results and copy the first page of each purchase order requisition as audit evidence. They reference the documentation and file it in the testing binder.
- The auditors obtain copies of the quarterly reports for two quarters within the current year. Together with the process owners, they review the reports to determine what is to be checked here. The procedure is as follows:
  - The documents to be examined are copied and referenced, or
  - the exceptions are copied and the quarterly reports are captured electronically. The exceptions and the electronic document are referenced. The documentation is filed in the testing binder.

Once the testing procedures have been completed, the results should be documented.

Fictitious Examples of Documenting Test Results

Examples of how the results of testing the internal controls can be described are as follows:

- All items in the sample met the required criteria. No exceptions were found. This provides evidence that an effective control exists. Supporting documents have been cross-referenced and filed in a testing binder.
- Out of 30 requisitions reviewed, ten had some form of exception. Either there was no formal approval for the order (five times) or requestor and approver were the same (five times). All exceptions and documents reviewed were copied, referenced and filed. This control is significantly deficient.

Content of Working Papers

SOX audits also require the preparation of working papers as audit evidence. They must make the following items transparent:

- how the testing was performed (responsible employees interviewed and the substance of the inquiries, including additional corroborative results),

- the control results (any documents examined and an identification of the samples selected for testing, e.g. invoice no. 1234, no. 2345 etc. were selected and assessed for accuracy of signature according to the approval matrix),
- the results of the testing (information includes the number and description of any exceptions, e.g., all samples selected have been accurately signed with the exception of invoice no. 2345 where the approval signature is missing),
- the nature of any re-performance of tests, and
- recommendations for improvement, where appropriate.

Document Filing

Testing results and evidence in the form of working papers are collected in testing binders. The results and evidence should be referenced so that a link can be made to the control step tested. In addition, specifying the date that the document was copied or received and the source of the document helps ensure that the documentation can always be traced back to the owner.

Closing Meeting

Finally, at the end of each testing phase, a meeting should be held with each process owner and/or process group owner in order to confirm all the results (including any findings and planned remediation). Once an agreement has been reached with the process owner on a finding and the correction of its cause, the exceptions can be finalized and corrected in the process group template.

Flowchart Review

In addition to verbally describing their internal control structures, the process owners should also prepare process flowcharts (one per process group). A company may have defined standard symbols and formats that should be used when preparing these documents. The auditor must verify that these flowcharts comply with the company's quality assurance standards. As an example, a process group flowchart may consist of the following three levels:

- Level 1: Overview of the process group.
- Level 2: Breaking process groups down into key processes.
- Level 3: Breaking processes down into key transactions and describing workflows and controls.

Flowchart Requirements

In general, a well organized and properly prepared flowchart should:

- use the standard symbols correctly,
- be clear, simple, and concise,
- clearly identify the controls, including their input and output,
- demonstrate the chronological sequence of events,
- use descriptive text concisely and sparingly and be properly referenced to provide further explanation, and
- clearly indicate who is performing the controls.

HINTS AND TIPS

For design assessments:

- Auditors must ensure that the control assertions of completeness, accuracy, validity, and restricted access are addressed in each process (not only in the process group).
- In general, each process must have at least one significant control.
- If a control covers a number of risks, it is probably a significant control.
- For control steps that include system input or output or systematic procedures, the relevant transaction codes and result reports must be specified.

For control effectiveness tests:

- When using the test procedures, auditors must make sure that they are testing the control actually described.

LINKS AND REFERENCES

- COMMITTEE OF SPONSORING ORGANIZATIONS OF THE TREADWAY COMMISSION (COSO). 2003. *Enterprise Risk Management Integrated Framework.* New York, NY: AICPA.
- DELOITTE. 2005. *Optimizing the Role of Internal Audit in the Sarbanes-Oxley Era.* www.deloitte.com/dtt/cda/doc/content/us_ERS_Internal%20Audit%20POV.pdf (accessed May 31, 2007).
- HAUSER, D., R. HOPKINS, AND H. LEIBUNDGUT. 2004. The Sarbanes-Oxley Act and the Role of Internal Audit. *Der Schweizer Treuhänder* (December 2004): 1057-1065.
- INSTITUTE OF INTERNAL AUDITORS. 2004. *Internal Auditing's Role in Sections 302 and 404 of the U.S. Sarbanes-Oxley Act of 2002.* Altamonte Springs, FL: The Institute of Internal Auditors.
- PUBLIC COMPANY ACCOUNTING OVERSIGHT BOARD (PCAOB). 2004. *Auditing Standard No. 2: An Audit of Internal Control Over Financial Reporting Performed in Conjunction With an Audit of Financial Statements.* http://www.pcaobus.org/Standards/Standards_and_ Related_Rules/Auditing_Standard_No.2.aspx (accessed May 31, 2007).
- PUBLIC COMPANY ACCOUNTING OVERSIGHT BOARD (PCAOB). *Staff Questions and Answers: Auditing Internal Control over Financial Reporting.* http://www.pcaob.org/standards/staff_questions_and_answers/2005/01-21.pdf (accessed May 31, 2007).
- REDDING, K., P. SOBEL, U. ANDERSON, et al. 2007. *Internal Assurance and Consulting Services.* Altamonte Springs, FL: The Institute of Internal Auditors.
- RITTENBERG, L. E. AND B. J. SCHWEIGER. 2005. *Auditing: Concepts for a Changing Environment.* Mason, OH: Thompson.
- SAWYER, L. B., M. A. DITTENHOFER, AND J. H. SCHEINER. 2003. *Sawyer's Internal Auditing.* 5th ed. Altamonte Springs, FL: The Institute of Internal Auditor.
- SEARS, B. 2002. *Internal Auditing Manual.* New York, NY: Warren, Gorham & Lamont.
- U.S. CONGRESS. 2002. *Sarbanes-Oxley Act of 2002. 107th Congress of the United States of America. HR 3763.* Washington DC: Government Printing Office.

KEY POINTS

- The GIAS revenue recognition assurance program supports the company in ensuring compliance with revenue recognition rules.
- This concept includes, for example, customer confirmations and unannounced license audits that are used in addition to regular audit activities.
- Internal Audit's general quality assurance program has been adapted to the special requirements of revenue recognition assurance work.

Concept

Compliance with revenue recognition rules is an important audit topic. For this reason, SAP's Internal Audit has developed an additional program, which provides special work programs for this issue. Under this revenue recognition assurance program, Internal Audit conducts unannounced audits of license agreements and obtains contract confirmations from customers. Unannounced license audits largely follow the procedure for standard license audits (see Section C, Chapter 5.3). Customer contract confirmations involve writing to customers, asking them to confirm the components and terms and conditions of contracts. The objective of these tests is to ensure that the contract documentation is complete and to exclude the existence of any supplementary agreements that are not documented or taken into account, as well as to ascertain the amount of revenue recognized.

Customer Contract Confirmations in General

Internal Audit conducts three customer contract confirmation cycles per year in each region on a global basis. These three cycles cover contracts signed in the first quarter, contracts signed in the second and third quarters, and contracts signed in the fourth quarter respectively. Each confirmation cycle spans approximately eight to ten weeks, from contract selection through final report. In addition, the external auditors also obtain customer contract confirmations every quarter. However, Internal Audit conducts its customer contract confirmation cycle independently of the external auditors' confirmation process.

The Customer Contract Confirmation Process

The entire customer contract confirmation cycle consists of six main process steps: Preparation, distribution, inquiry I, inquiry II, alternative audit work, and reporting. If all the contracts are properly confirmed by customers, alternative audit work is not necessary. Details of each of the main process steps of the confirmation cycle are provided below.

Preparation

To prepare for customer contract confirmations, the internal audit team selects the countries to be audited through a risk assessment. Internal Audit conducts this risk assessment once a year in November/December with the involvement of other departments within the company. For example, Corporate Financial Reporting or the regional finance managers are asked to give their risk assessment. On the basis of the feedback received and the risk assessments made, each regional unit of Internal Audit selects different countries for each cycle, in relation to the size of the region. Additionally, the results of this risk assessment are reviewed before the start of the next customer contract confirmation cycle to establish if the risk evaluation is still up to date.

Cooperation with the External Auditors

Since SAP's external auditors also obtain contract confirmations, the internal audit team has to ensure that a customer is not contacted twice about the same contract. Therefore, after selecting the countries, Internal Audit requests a list of contract confirmations sent out by the external auditors. Once this information is available, Internal Audit selects contracts for review. In return, Internal Audit then passes the corresponding information to the external auditors.

Contract Selection

Contract selection involves a combination of individual selection according to auditor judgment and random selection. First, a complete list of all customer contracts should be compiled. To facilitate selection, this list must be sorted by contract value in descending order. Two groups of contracts are created on the basis of the selection model: Group A includes all contracts whose accumulated volume makes up 80% of the total contract volume on the list for the selected period. Group B contains all other contracts.

- Selection from group A: Inclusion of all contracts above a certain threshold is mandatory. This threshold should be around twice the average contract value in group A. Below this threshold, internal auditors initially use their own discretion to select further contracts. Additional contracts are randomly selected until 50% of the remaining value of the contracts not already selected is reached in relation to contract volume (remaining value of contracts not already selected = group A – contracts above the threshold – internal auditor selection – contracts selected by the external auditors not yet included by the internal auditors).
- Selection from group B: The contracts are selected randomly and/or according to internal auditor judgment for up to 20% of the total volume of group B.

Based on this selection model, at least 75% of total contract volume is examined (including the contracts selected by the external auditors).

Announcement

Once the contracts have been selected, the local and regional managers are informed by e-mail, which also serves as audit announcement (see Section B, Chapter 3.1). Soon after the announcement, the Internal Audit employee responsible for assuring revenue recognition contacts the local subsidiary, requesting the necessary customer and contact information, e.g., customer contact person, telephone number, and date of first delivery (including delivery documents).

Language Problem

Because of the many different languages, the customer contract confirmation cycle is normally supported by the local external auditors if Internal Audit cannot cover the relevant language internally. They provide Internal Audit with translations of the customer contract confirmation requests and of the main points of the selected contracts.

Distribution

Once preparations have been completed, i.e., all the information and translations are available, Internal Audit writes the contract confirmation letter for distribution to customers. Each customer gets an English and a local language version.

Documentation

Process steps 2 (distribution) through 6 (report) are documented in a monitoring working paper, which replaces the working papers normally used.

Audit Tasks during Customer Contract Confirmations

The following audit tasks should be performed and documented during the customer contract confirmation cycle:

- The following standard audit work is performed before the customer contract confirmation letter is returned:
  - System accounting entries are checked.
  - License payments are checked.
  - Maintenance payments are checked.
  - Deliveries are checked.
  - Necessary accruals and deferrals are checked.
- Calls to customers (inquiry I).
- On return, the customer contract confirmation letter is checked for completeness and accuracy (inquiry II).
- All audit steps conducted during alternative audit work.
- All information received or audit steps taken between the alternative audit work and the report.

Inquiry I

Approximately two weeks after the confirmation letters are sent to customers, all customers who have not returned the contract confirmation should be contacted by telephone. If possible, Internal Audit should obtain and document verbal confirmation this way. If Internal Audit cannot obtain a proper confirmation, the contract should be earmarked for alternative audit work.

Returned Confirmation Letters

All contract confirmation letters received from customers must be examined for completeness and accuracy. If there are exceptions, the following audit steps should be taken:

- If possible, the exceptions should be clarified with the customer by telephone.
- Contact the local subsidiary's accounting department, contract administration department, and/or sales executive for clarification.

If the exceptions cannot be clarified, the internal audit team should earmark the contract for alternative audit work.

Inquiry II

Approximately two weeks before the date scheduled for alternative audit work, Internal Audit evaluates the customer contract confirmation status. The result is written into a report and distributed to the managers responsible in the local subsidiary (at least to the head of the accounting unit). If one or more contracts have not been confirmed, the sales executive responsible in the local subsidiary can assist the internal audit team in contacting the customer. All contracts of a confirmation cycle that are not confirmed to Internal Audit by the customer as of the scheduled starting date of the alternative audit work must be examined locally in the subsidiary.

Alternative Audit Work

The following information is updated during alternative audit work:

- License payments are checked.
- Maintenance payments are checked.
- Credit notes issued are checked.
- The Global Contract Approval Forms (GCAF) are checked.
- It is checked if sales confirmation letters have been signed by the responsible sales executive.

In addition, all further relevant information received in the meantime should be processed and documented. All available documents relating to unconfirmed contracts must be reviewed locally in the subsidiary, particularly the original contract, the documents held by the license administration department, and the customer file with any correspondence.

Reporting

The final report is the last process step of the customer contract confirmation cycle. There are three different reporting levels (local, regional, and global). The local reports are distributed to local management. The regional reports include an overview of all countries selected for auditing in the region concerned, and additional information from the local report. These reports are sent to regional management. The global reports are prepared and distributed by the global coordinator for the GIAS revenue recognition assurance program. The global report includes a global overview and the regional reports. The report is sent to the members of the Board and other affected parties, e.g. corporate departments and the external auditors.

Customer Contract Confirmation Findings

If the customer contract confirmations result in findings that require follow-up, an internal implementation report (GIAS only) is compiled in addition to the report on the confirmation cycle for use as a basis for the follow-up.

Quality Assurance During Customer Contract Confirmations

In addition to Internal Audit's general quality assurance concept (for details, see Section D, Chapter 5), a specific quality assurance program has been developed and introduced for the customer contract confirmations, intended to guarantee the following:

- effectiveness of the confirmation cycle,
- compliance with SAP-specific standards set by Internal Audit,
- compliance with international standards for Internal Audit, and
- continuous process improvement.

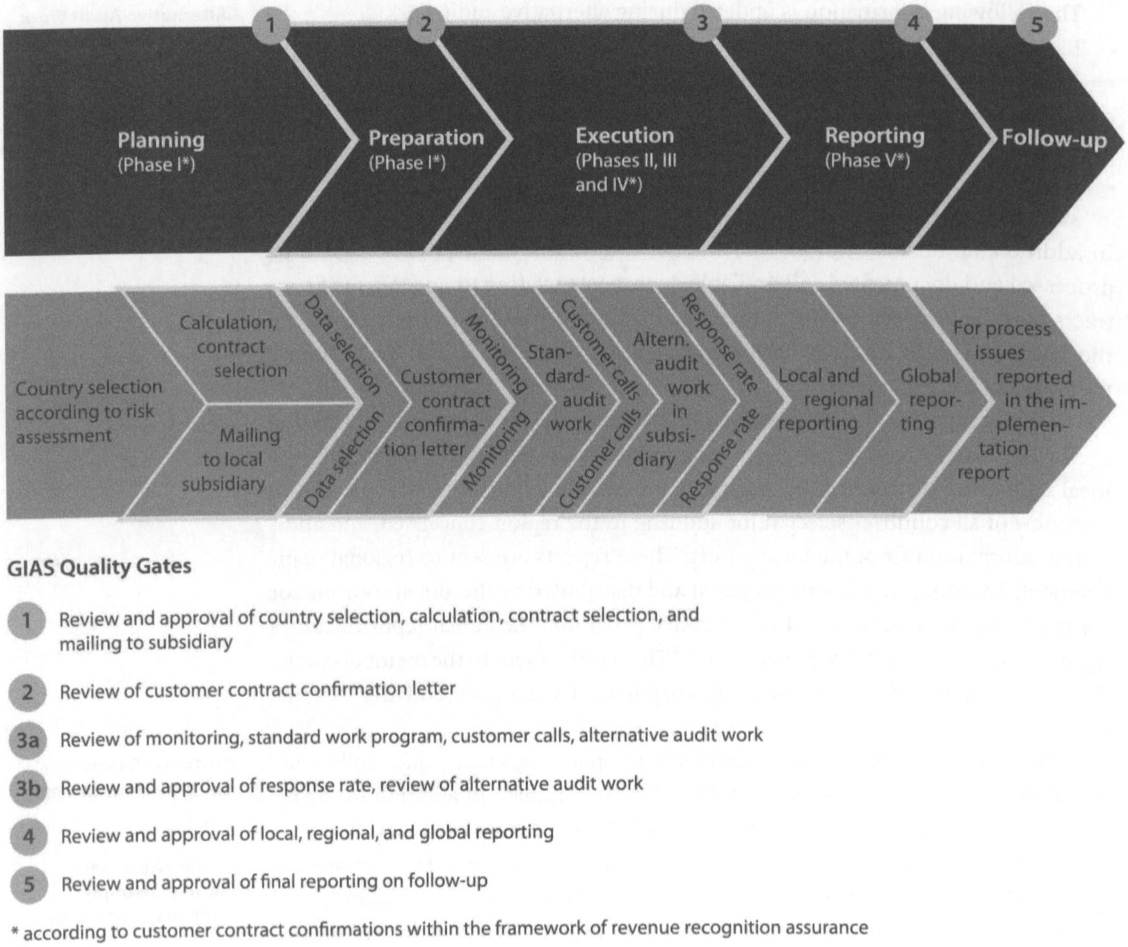

Fig. 25 Quality Gates during Customer Contract Confirmations

Quality Gates

The above figure shows the quality gates that have been defined for the customer contract confirmation process. The measures relating to quality gates are defined as follows:

- Review: The audit object is finalized before it is forwarded for final approval.
- Approval: This authorizes the completion of the current audit phase.

All quality gates must be documented at least electronically.

Unannounced License Audits

Besides customer contract confirmations, unannounced license audits are the second component of the revenue recognition assurance program. Unannounced license audits are normally ad-hoc audits and largely follow the standard work program for license audits (see Section C, Chapter 5.3). Every year, between three and six unannounced license audits are conducted in each region. Depending on the size of the local subsidiary, the audit takes three to five days if two auditors are appointed.

Execution of Unannounced License Audits

The execution of unannounced license audits is largely the same as license audits conducted as part of a basic audit, e.g. the selection of the local subsidiary to be audited is subject to the same risk assessment process as for customer contract confirmations. However, there are differences during preparation and execution:

- Contract selection: The contracts are selected two days before the start of the audit. The contracts are selected from a specific period before the audit date. Out of these, 50% of the contracts are selected on the basis of contract volume (i.e., large-volume contracts). The other 50% of contracts are determined by auditor judgment.
- Announcement: The audit is not announced to the local subsidiary. However, it is acceptable to inform the head of the accounting unit approximately one hour before arrival.
- Closing meeting: The closing meeting should be attended by at least the head of the accounting unit. The head of the local subsidiary should also be informed. Depending on the nature of the results, additional participants may be included in the closing meeting.

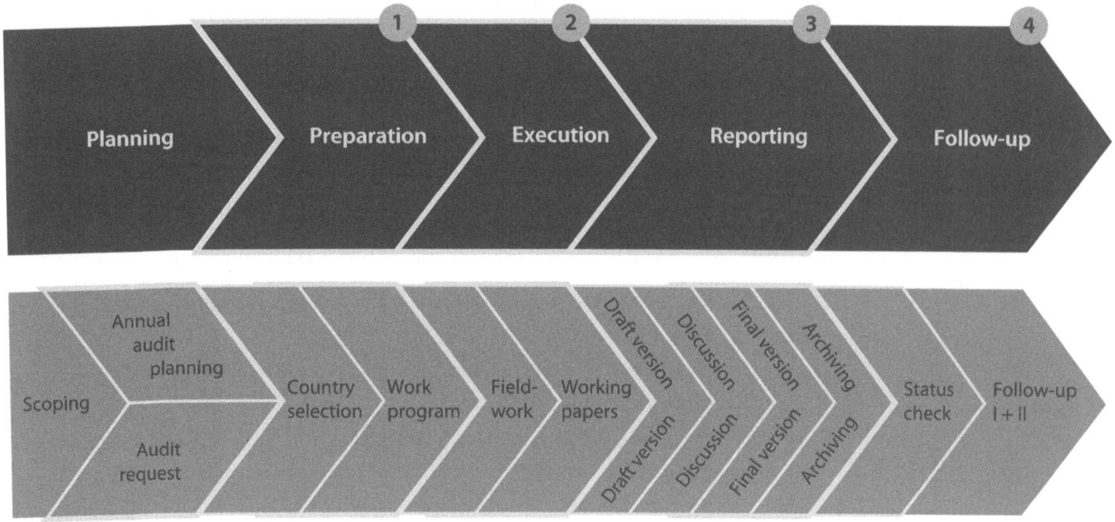

Quality Gates

1 Review and approval of country selection and work program

2 Review of all mandatory working papers before sending draft report to auditees

3 Publication of audit report (draft and final version)

4 Only in case of relevant results (process issues etc.)

Fig. 26 Quality Assurance during Unannounced License Audits

- Reporting: The standard report template is used for unannounced license audits to produce the report. For findings that entail a follow-up, the same follow-up process applies as for regular audit engagements (see Section B, Chapter 6).

Quality Assurance during Unannounced License Audits

The quality assurance concept for unannounced license audits is based on the general quality assurance guidelines for the Audit Roadmap (see Section D, Chapter 5), but has been adapted to take account of the different audit process.

Quality Gates

The first quality gate includes a review and approval of the countries selected and the work program. The review is optional for the regional Audit Manager, but the approval is mandatory for the global coordinator for the GIAS revenue recognition assurance program. If the standard work program has been changed by the audit team, it must be examined by the regional revenue recognition assurance officer. It is mandatory for the regional revenue recognition assurance officer to check the working papers of the second quality gate. This review is optional for the global revenue recognition assurance coordinator and the regional Audit Manager. Acceptance of the above two quality gates should be documented on paper, or at least by e-mail. The last two quality gates in Fig. 26 are broadly the same as those in the general quality assurance program of Internal Audit at SAP (for more on quality assurance see Section D, Chapter 5).

HINTS AND TIPS

- When making a conscious selection of contracts, auditors should take into account criteria such as posting date and contract type.

LINKS AND REFERENCES

- CASCARINO, R. AND S. VAN ESCH. 2005. *Internal Auditing: An Integrated Approach.* Lansdowne, SA: Juta and Co.
- KIESO, D. E., J.J. WEYGANDT, AND T. D. WARFIELD. 2004. *Intermediate Accounting.* 11th ed. Hoboken, NJ: Wiley.
- REDING, K. F., P. J. SOBEL, U. L. ANDERSON, et al. 2007. *Internal Assurance and Consulting Services.* Altamonte Springs, FL: The Institute of Internal Auditors.
- RITTENBERG, L. E. AND B. J. SCHWEIGER. 2005. *Auditing: Concepts for a Changing Environment.* Mason, OH: Thompson.
- SAWYER, L. B., M. A. DITTENHOFER, AND J. H. SCHEINER. 2003. *Sawyer's Internal Auditing.* 5th ed. Altamonte Springs, FL: The Institute of Internal Auditors.
- SEARS, B. 2002. *Internal Auditing Manual.* New York, NY: Warren, Gorham & Lamont.

10 IT Audits

10.1 Basics and System Configuration

KEY POINTS

- Internal and external compliance and reliability requirements on financial reporting must be supported by a company's information technology.
- The extent of the IT audit is influenced by the domains of Plan and Organize, Acquire and Implement, Deliver and Support, and Monitor and Evaluate.
- Possible risks for an IT system include non-compliance, inconsistent data, user error, uncontrollability, and unreliability.
- In addition to system tests, the organizational analysis of the IT system is a key component of IT audits.

IT Audits at SAP

Section A (see Chapter 6.2.5) provides information about the significance of Internal Audit for companies that rely heavily on information technology. Especially in global software groups such as SAP, the reliability of information technology for the support of business processes is a key prerequisite for the achievement of corporate objectives. In addition, there are external requirements that place clear demands on information technology to ensure that the company's financial reporting is compliant. IT auditors must observe various internal and external rules, including country specific rules, relating to the proper operation of IT systems, effective system controls, and the way in which computers, programs, and data are used.

Information Technology Criteria

COBIT® (see also Section A, Chapter 6.2.5) identifies the basic criteria for quality, security, and compliance in information technology as follows:

- confidentiality,
- integrity,
- availability,
- reliability,
- effectiveness,
- efficiency, and
- compliance with legal requirements.

Focus of the IT Audit Process

COBIT® also identifies four domains of IT governance. These domains influence the extent of an IT audit in ensuring that the operation of the IT system is compliant. They are:

- Plan and Organize,
- Acquire and Implement,
- Deliver and Support, and
- Monitor and Evaluate.

Each of these domains represents a separate audit object, which is successively integrated into audit planning following its evaluation. While COBIT® provides initial guidance by presenting key measures for processes within each of the domains, the utilization of these measures and the identification of additional measures depend on the extent of the audit and the sophistication of the technology. In an IT structure as complex as that of SAP, responsibility for the different systems and applications is distributed among various organizational departments. Some departments have their own audit teams for the different domains in order to guarantee that internal guidelines are observed and external requirements and customer requests are met. Many IT units at SAP are ISO certified for this reason. Although this information is useful during audit planning, IT auditors still need to form their own independent opinion as to whether an IT system is compliant and how the different organizational units interact.

Focus on System Audit

The following description is not intended to provide a detailed picture of all the elements of IT audits but it explains the procedure of a system audit, using an audit of the classic SAP systems as an example. New technologies such as the Netweaver® platform require special fieldwork activities, which will be an additional focus of IT audits in the future and will therefore have to be scheduled and prepared for accordingly. This is part of another major challenge for IT auditors: to respond with adequate audit measures to the ever faster developments in the world of IT.

Audit Preparation

The audit-relevant areas must be defined during audit preparation in order to establish whether the system is compliant. The following IT system risks have to be taken into account:

- non-compliance,
- inconsistent data,
- user error,
- uncontrollability, and
- unreliability.

Scope and Work Program

The requirements as to how and to what extent a system audit must or can be conducted are described in the general Scope (see Section B, Chapter 2.1). The actual fieldwork activities to be included in the specific work program are derived on this basis. The audit guidelines for SAP systems developed by the Audit Working Group are among the documents used as a basis for creating the work program. The work program for an SAP system audit takes the following into account:

- system configuration,
- transport system,
- table access and logs,
- security and access protection in user administration,
- interfaces, and
- job award procedure and documentation.

According to the procedure under the COBIT® framework, the above items are assigned to the Deliver and Support domain (see Section B, Chapter 7.4).

Technical Aspects

An SAP system audit requires that attention is paid to a large number of security and audit related aspects. For a meaningful audit, IT auditors must at least have a basic understanding of the complex structure of the SAP system. The most important technical aspects of the system from an auditing point of view include:

- transactions,
- ABAP (programming language of the SAP system),
- programs,
- tables,
- files,
- authorizations,
- authorization profiles and user master records,
- data media, and
- other safeguards, e.g., table categories, separation of different clients (clients are the top-level organizational unit in the SAP system).

SAP AIS

SAP provides the role-based SAP AIS system to support auditors. The description of the procedure and content of an IT system audit in this chapter are in part based on the SAP AIS. The SAP AIS accesses reports and transactions that exist in the SAP system. Auditors should make use of this option to support their fieldwork, especially with a view to saving time, because much of the information they need can be generated from the system at the push of a button.

System Configuration

Apart from the technical aspects of the system audit, organizational analysis of the SAP system is also of crucial importance, because it determines the effectiveness of technical measures implemented to guarantee proper data processing. The existence of meaningful documentation has to be checked in relation to the organizational status of the system. The system summary must be supplemented with user samples (e.g., regarding the treatment of user authorizations), system documentation samples (e.g., regarding program and table documentation), and system environment samples (e.g. regarding the general handling of the system in case of system terminations).

Responsibilities

Auditors should get an overview of overall responsibility for the systems and the responsibilities regarding

- critical data and tables,
- authorizations,
- programs and interfaces, and
- changes to the above.

The ongoing audit will further enhance the insights gained from this overview.

Systems in Use

Auditors must establish what systems are in use and which of them are used for live operations, or for development, testing, acceptance, or training purposes. Auditors must test in the live system (audits of which are the main focus of the following description) what clients are active in this installation.

System Authorizations for Auditors

Auditors should be given direct system access with the appropriate authorizations. Auditor authorizations should be limited to read access to all applications and basic functions to ensure that auditors do not change any data. In addition to displaying active data, auditors should also be able to view change documents. SAP ships standard profiles with read-only access. For conducting IT audits, this type of access is sufficient. If access is granted to personal data, the provisions of data protection legislation (e.g. the Health Insurance Portability and Accountability Act (HIPAA) and the Gramm-Leach-Bliley Act in the U.S. or the data protection acts of other countries such as the German Data Protection Act) as well as works or collective bargaining agreements must be observed.

Necessary Transactions, Tables, and Reports

All data in the SAP system is managed on the basis of tables. Any information displayed that does not require interactive user entries is referred to as an ABAP report. Here follows a list of transactions, tables, and reports required for an SAP system audit.

Transactions necessary for an SAP system audit:

- general table display,
- ABAP program execution,
- display of system change options,
- table maintenance,
- display of dumps (system terminations),
- display of update task terminations,
- display of jobs, and
- display of batch input sessions.

Tables necessary for an SAP system audit:

- clients,
- company codes,
- business areas,
- plants,
- storage locations,
- table of prohibited passwords,
- technical table data,
- technical description of all systems, and
- WBOT: Order header.

ABAP reports necessary for an SAP system audit:

- table analysis including history administration,
- analysis of table log database,
- list of change documents relating to authorizations,
- list of superusers created,
- list of all users with critical authorizations,
- list of change documents relating to users,
- list of change documents relating to profiles,
- list of change documents relating to authorizations,
- history of system change options, and
- definition of basic system parameters.

Business Structure

The first step in a system audit is to record and analyze the structure implemented in the SAP system within each live client. To map the structure, SAP makes available to users the data and access structure hierarchy in

- client,
- company code,
- business area,
- plant, and
- storage location.

HINTS AND TIPS

- Auditors should include the AIS as a support tool in fieldwork because it can help improve the audit process and thus audit quality.
- IT auditors should allow sufficient time before the audit to ensure they have the necessary authorizations for system access.
- Existing recognized IT audit guidelines (e.g., COBIT®) are useful for audit execution and should be used.

LINKS AND REFERENCES

- DSAG AUDIT WORKING GROUP. 1997. *FI Audit Guide for SAP-R/3*. www.sap.com/germany/company/revis/pdf/plf-fi-e-30d.pdf (accessed May, 31 2007).
- INSTITUTE OF INTERNAL AUDITORS. 2005. *Global Technology Audit Guide 1: Information Technology Controls*. Altamonte Springs, FL: The Institute of Internal Auditors.
- IT GOVERNANCE INSTITUTE. 2007. *COBIT ® 4.1*. Rolling Meadows, IL: IT Governance Institute.
- PFLEEGER, C., AND S. L. PFLEEGER. 2003. *Security in Computing*. 3rd ed. Upper Saddle River, NJ: Prentice Hall.
- U.S. CONGRESS. 1999. *Gramm-Leach-Bliley Financial Services Modernation Act. Public Law No. 106-102, 113 Stat. 1338*. Washington DC: Government Printing Office.
- U.S. CONGRESS. 1996. *Health Insurance Portability and Accountability Act of 1996. Public Law 104-191*. Washington DC: Government Printing Office.
- U.S. CONGRESS. 2002. *Sarbanes-Oxley Act of 2002. 107th Congress of the United States of America. HR 3763*. Washington DC: Government Printing Office.

10.2 SAP Workbench Organizer and Transport System

KEY POINTS

- The SAP Workbench Organizer and the Transport System (WBOT) are used to register and fully document all changes to system objects.
- They also prevent parallel changes to a system object.
- Possible risks associated with making system changes include the validity of system objects, incorrect settings in the corrections transport system, system instability, or manipulation.

Workbench Organizer and Transport System

The SAP Workbench Organizer (a tool for the administration of central and decentralized development projects) and the Transport System (WBOT) are used to register and document all changes made to system objects (development objects). This includes, for example, elements in the Data Dictionary (e.g., tables), ABAP programs, screen templates, interface definitions, documentation components, and application-defined transport and customizing objects. They are also used to prevent parallel changes to the same system object by different developers and to regulate the transfer and release of development objects between different SAP systems or different clients within the same SAP system.

Purpose of the Workbench Organizer

WBOT consists of the Workbench Organizer and Transport System components. The Workbench Organizer guarantees that there is only one original object for each existing system object within (networked) SAP systems. Changes are normally only made to this original object and transferred to other SAP systems via the Transport System. The Workbench Organizer stores all changes to Data Dictionary elements and ABAP programs. Old versions can be restored and compared with the latest version. The Workbench Organizer is activated automatically as soon as a user attempts to change an object. Users can only create or change objects if they have first created a change request in the Workbench Organizer or are using an existing change request. While a task is being entered, the objects are blocked for all other developers to prevent parallel changes. The block is only removed once the request has been released.

Purpose of the Transport System

On release, the tasks are transferred to the Transport System, which is to guarantee that system objects and customizing settings are transported safely and with a traceable record. The Transport System is system-independent, i.e., the system objects can be transported between all operating systems supported by SAP systems. Any necessary conversions are carried out automatically.

Function Changes

Changes to tables and programs cause changes to the system functions. One control objective is therefore the implementation of procedures which ensure that only approved changes become effective and overall functionality is maintained. Another control objective is to document all system changes without exception and thus make them retraceable. Changes must always be made using WBOT, taking the following into account:

- Adequate mandatory rules must be in place for placing orders (e.g., for the creation of an ABAP), carrying out changes, as well as for testing, acceptance, and transfer into the live environment.
- Each change must be described in adequate detail and formally approved by the data owner. Approval is required for program changes as well as for data transfers.
- Since system objects are normally valid throughout the system, the test system must be separate from the live system.
- WBOT uses a blocking mechanism to prevent parallel changes to an object by several developers.

- When using the Workbench Organizer, changes to system objects are recorded in the history by the system, i.e., old versions of a program can be recovered, for example.
- The SAP naming conventions (name range for customer objects) must be observed in order to avoid problems with future release changes or system corrections.
- Self-defined system objects must be adequately documented.
- Acceptance procedures should follow the dual control principle, i.e., they should normally be carried out by the user department, independently of the programmer.
- In case of program changes, it should be established, by comparing the result with the source code, whether modifications are in fact limited to the program section to be updated.
- The acceptance test should be performed in an SAP system that is separate from the live environment (quality assurance system), using a customizing that is similar to the live system and a suitable dataset.
- There must be an organizational assurance that no subsequent changes are possible once changes/new developments have been accepted.
- Acceptance and transfer into the live system must be documented in writing.
- The relevant evidence (e.g., order and release form) must be archived in accordance with the applicable legal or internal regulations.

Coordination of Components

The Workbench Organizer and the Transport System are perfectly coordinated with each other. At the start of development, a change request and one or several tasks for all employees involved are created. Then the affected objects are created or modified, and this is registered on the request. At the end of the development, the developers release their task(s), and thus, by releasing them, export the change request and all modified objects from the source system. The object is then transported to the relevant target system at operating system level. It is possible to combine several change requests into a single transport request.

SAP Systems

For the purposes of the corrections transport system, the SAP system consists of one or more SAP systems in the same version and of the same database system. To distinguish between these systems, SAP uses the following terminology:

- (Special) development system: Separate development of critical project components in an isolated environment.
- Integration system: Development of non-critical applications and system tests.
- Consolidation system (quality assurance): Backs up development levels and acts as a distributor for subsequent recipient systems.
- Recipient system (live system): Automatic transfer of software from consolidation systems. The term “recipient system” covers all of the system level transferred to the customer.

System Landscape The current standard is to use one system landscape with three clients. The following diagram is a graphical representation of the system landscape with transport routes:

Fig. 27 Standard System Landscape Including Transport Routes

If development work is performed on system objects, one system with several clients for development, testing, and release is not sufficient, because system objects normally affect all clients and any modifications can have an immediate impact on the live system. It may therefore be necessary to use several systems.

Execution of Transports The generation of a transport request leads to the creation of an auxiliary file at operating system level with the relevant transport content, which the transport program analyzes when the file is imported into the target system. If the SAP systems have a shared transport directory, a test import is performed automatically when the transport requests are exported from the source system to the target system. The authors of the transport request are notified of the success or failure of the export or test import. Transport logs can be displayed by using the information system.

Validity of Development Objects Maintenance may expose the systems to different risks. Since system objects are generally valid throughout the system, the modification of an ABAP, for example, may affect all clients of the SAP system in question. Authorizations to modify system objects in the live system must therefore be handled very restrictively (e.g., no programming authorization).

Instability The SAP system consists of different changeable components, which depend on each other in the overall scheme of the system. Due to this complexity, improper changes may in some cases lead to uncertainty and instability, for example:

- Errors cannot be detected immediately.
- Data is not processed, processed incompletely, or processing is duplicated.
- The required availability of system functions is not always guaranteed.
- There are delays in the execution of functions (process flow reliability).
- It may no longer be possible to execute controls, which are thus rendered ineffective.

This makes the system unreliable. It is clear that this bears significant risks.

Manipulation Uncontrolled changes can lead to processing errors, which could be misused. If adequate control mechanisms are not in place, there is a possibility in principle that data will be further manipulated.

Recording the System

During fieldwork on program maintenance procedures, auditors must first review the overall list of user-defined system objects and all relevant corrections/repairs performed on SAP objects. In this context it is important that a clear description of their function is available. Then the system is recorded and, if required for the audit, the system maintenance and release procedure is documented.

Testing the Concept

The above SAP system requirements form the basis for auditing the concept recorded. In addition, a general test is performed with regard to the objectives and risks formulated above, paying particular attention to an adequate segregation of functions during development, release, and transport.

Compliance with the Concept

Compliance with the concept is tested on the basis of a sample of development requests and associated test and release logs. These tests are performed both top down (i.e., going from change request to system object in the live environment), and bottom up.

Fieldwork on the System

On the system, the auditors must test the settings for WBOT and system change options. Auditors also have to examine how the applied method for the organization's change procedures was determined, and how the users authorized to create and release a transport request are determined in the case of corrections and repairs.

No Development Directly in the Live System

Development must never be carried out in the live system, but must run through a transport system. Table analysis is used to test whether programs have been created in the live system.

Other Test Procedures

Other test procedures include determining the users who can perform imports into the live system, establishing what rules are applied to the use of the correction and transport system, checking as to whether these rules are followed, and testing for manual intervention in tables.

Changes to Customizing Settings

Changes to customizing settings made in the test or development system and transported to the live system with WBOT are only logged in the test system. If the auditors need to trace any such changes, they should consult the change logs there.

System Change Options

The SAP system has two distinct areas of system changes: firstly, the ABAP Workbench and customizing across all clients, and secondly, client-based customizing. Change options can be set for either area. Modifications to the ABAP Workbench and customizing across all clients are regulated through global system change options.

Table Settings

In the live system, the setting should be "Global setting: No changes possible." In the table it can be specified which objects can be changed. That way, it can be ensured that new objects and object changes can only get into the live system through the transport system. In emergencies (e.g., serious system errors), this setting can be changed temporarily. Such emergencies must be handled by way of a standardized, documented procedure, replicated in the development system, and transported to the live system through the transport system.

HINTS AND TIPS

- IT auditors can use the AIS to test system settings.
- Before starting a test of the system settings, auditors should obtain an overview of the system landscape by asking the IT manager responsible for a detailed technical system description. They should make sure that the description refers to the systems currently used.

LINKS AND REFERENCES

- SAP online documentation of Workbench Organizer and Transport System.

10.3 Table Access and Logs

KEY POINTS

- The objective of the table change procedure in the SAP system is to ensure that the table settings are correct and all changes are traceable.
- All relevant changes to table content must be logged.
- An authorization concept must be in place whose functions include regulating which user IDs are authorized for table maintenance.
- Table maintenance audit objects include the test and release procedure, the responsibilities and the authorization system for table changes, and the settings of the table logging procedure.

Definition of a Table

A table is a two-dimensional matrix that describes a relationship in the database system. It consists of a header, which defines the fields (attributes), and a variable number of similarly structured rows, which contain the data values (data records). A data record is divided into a primary key and a functional part. The primary key uniquely identifies the data records within a table. It can be composed of several attributes.

Types of Tables

The following different types of tables can be distinguished:

- tables with system control data,
- tables with basic business data,
- tables with company structure data, and
- tables for application data.

Tables with System Control Data

Tables with system control data are intended to enable company-specific adaptations to standard software without modifying the programs. They contain variable parameters for:

- flow control systems (e.g., account assignment),
- logic tests (e.g., only certain value entries permitted),
- calculation routines (e.g., calculation of value added tax),

- automatically generated events (e.g., posting of cash discount income), and
- screen modifications (e.g., mandatory entry into a field).

Table Change

The objective of the table change procedure is to ensure that the table settings are correct and all changes are traceable. The term "changes" in this instance refers to changes to table content in tables with system control data of the following delivery classes:

- C – customizing table: user organization maintenance only, no SAP import.
- G – customizing table: users permitted to insert only.
- E – system control table: SAP and user organization have their own keys.
- S – system table: SAP maintenance only, change = modification.
- W – customer's system table.

Changes to table structures are made under the control of the Workbench Organizer and the Transport System.

Logging

From an auditing perspective, tables must meet certain requirements. All (relevant) changes to table content (data records) must be logged. In addition, changes to the structure, i.e., changes in the Data Dictionary (data directory) caused by corrections or repairs must be updated. Logs for "critical" tables, e.g., those that control the volume and value flow, such as account assignment and valuation, should be tested on a sample basis. It must be possible to make table changes readable within a reasonable period of time. The legal retention period for evidence of table changes should be identified for each relevant geographic region (e.g. ten years for Germany).

Access Protection

An authorization concept must be in place whose functions include regulating which user IDs are authorized for table maintenance. SAP has created a default portfolio of authorization groups and assigned tables and views to the relevant authorization groups. The authorization groups are in turn stored in tables. Table maintenance requires the following authorizations:

- authorization for the authorization group of the table and the "table maintenance" action, and
- global authorization for client-independent tables.

The global authorization test applies to all tables of delivery classes C (customizing), G (customer tables with SAP entries), and E (system tables that the customer can change). This global authorization is always necessary because changes to a client-independent table can impact other clients entered in the system.

Work/Organization Instructions

To reduce dependence on the knowledge of individual persons and to increase the security of a correct table setting, work/organization instructions should exist for critical tables, with information like:

- naming conventions,
- occasion and reason for a table change, and
- consequences of a table change.

Request for changes to critical tables must be subject to the release procedure and performed by using the correction and transport system. It must be possible to provide evidence that a table change has been made.

Securing the Information Flow The high level of integration of the SAP system can lead to unintended side-effects (e.g., in other modules) when table changes are made. For this reason, a mandatory procedure should be in place to ensure that information is sent to anyone affected by a change to "critical" tables.

Table Access The installation of a system should follow the implementation guide because this ensures that all system set-up work is fully completed. Possible ways of accessing the table for table entries:

- implementation guide,
- customizing menus,
- direct table maintenance,
- correction and transport system, and
- ABAP.

System Settings for Logging Changes to table content must be logged. Technically, this requirement must be implemented by means of two system settings:

- For relevant tables, the "table logging" field must be activated in the Data Dictionary (technical setting).
- In the SAP start profile, the "rec/client" parameter must be initialized to the client(s) to be logged.

The start parameters can be analyzed with the RSPARAM report.

Analysis of Table Changes Table changes can be analyzed with special ABAP reports. Important tables in financial accounting include:

- clients,
- company codes and company code control,
- document types and texts,
- charts of accounts,
- tax codes,
- blocking reasons for automated payments,
- house banks,
- fixed account table,
- account assignment,
- payment transactions,
- foreign currency valuation methods,
- changed reconciliation accounts,
- special general ledger accounts,
- account groups,
- tolerance limits for invoice verification,
- document change rules,
- foreign exchange rates, and
- customer tables.

Changes to Table Structures Changes, through corrections or repairs, to table structures entered in the Data Dictionary are made under the control of the correction and transport system (if activated). The system keeps a history, so that modifications of this kind can be traced.

Risks

Since the tables in the SAP system have a central control function, there are obvious risks associated with an inadequate procedure for changing table content:

- There is a risk of incorrect settings.
- Changes made to a table can have unintended side effects elsewhere.
- The integrity of the dataset and the functionality may be violated. Authorizations defined in the tables could be changed. There is a risk of non-traceable system changes.
- Change documents could be deleted without archiving.

Other special risks include:

- "rec/client" parameter not initialized,
- incorrect table entries,
- important tables not logged,
- system settings of the upstream system (feeder system to the live system from where objects are entered through the transport system), and
- copy functions between clients, which overwrite table settings without updating the history.

Necessary Test Procedures

The following test procedures are necessary for table access and logging:

- Determine the procedure for changing tables.
- Evaluate the procedure on the basis of the requirements listed above.
- Test compliance with the requirements on the basis of samples.

Other tests include establishing the extent of archiving (before deletion) and monitoring the change frequency of important tables.

Audit Objects

Audit objects include:

- test and release procedure,
- responsibilities and authorization system for table changes, and
- system settings for table logging, especially the technical settings in the Data Dictionary and the SAP start profile.

The settings in the tables must also be examined. The change documents will show whether changes were made to the level of recording during the period under review.

HINTS AND TIPS

- To get an initial overview of table logging, test the "rec/client" parameter.
- In the SAP system, documentation on each table is available in report RSSDOCTB. The documentation includes the structure and the field descriptions.

LINKS AND REFERENCES

- Audit Guidelines for SAP systems. www.sap.com/germany/company/revis/infomaterial/index.epx (accessed May 31, 2007).
- SAP online documentation.

10.4 User Administration

KEY POINTS

- An access protection system that can be used to grant individual authorizations ensures that only authorized persons get access to the system and specific data.
- Assessing the procedure for assigning authorizations may be included in an IT audit.
- To improve security, maintenance and activation of authorizations are segregated in the system.
- Passwords must conform to the syntax prescribed by the system.
- There are standard users with predefined rights in the SAP systems. The handling of these standard users is also an object of an IT audit.

Access Protection System

An access protection system with the option of granting individual authorizations has four main objectives:

- to protect confidential data from unauthorized access,
- to protect data from unauthorized (including accidental) changes or deletion,
- to create system transparency to the extent that it is possible to trace who had which authorizations at what time, and
- to ensure that applications can be audited.

These preventive control measures in the internal control system are intended to prevent breach of the legal prohibition on amendment of entries and guarantee traceability in order to make sure that no unauthorized, incomplete and incorrect data gets into the system, or that data is assigned to the wrong period or transaction in the system.

Requirements on an Access Protection System

Access protection must ensure that only authorized persons gain access to the system and specific data. It must be possible to hide the necessary keys (passwords) during entry. The system should ensure that:

- only passwords of a specified minimum length are accepted,
- it is impossible to use character sequences that are easy to guess,
- passwords can be created and changed only by the user,
- mandatory password changes are triggered at definable intervals, and
- passwords are kept secret from anyone except the user.

Minimal Authorization Policy

The authorization concept must make it possible to restrict the rights of users to those activities and accesses in the system that they absolutely need within the bounds of their position and responsibility in the company (minimal authorization policy). This means that it should be possible to implement the most detailed degree with regard to:

- the type of data access (read, create, edit, delete),
- programs,
- data and files, and
- functions (menus, menu lines),

while using any combination of these levels as far as possible.

Assignment Procedures for Authorizations

Since the compliance of the SAP authorization concept is influenced to a significant degree by the procedure for assigning authorizations, the assignment procedure is also included in an IT audit. This procedure should be documented in organizational terms, well structured, and traceable. Compliance with the procedure should be monitored. Finally, it must be ensured that user master records, authorizations, and profiles are newly created, edited, or deleted in the quality assurance (test) system and then transferred to the live environment through the correction and transport system.

Authorization Concept in the SAP System

By granting authorizations, it can be defined which business objects the company's employees may edit and what editing functions are permitted in this regard. The authorization concept allows granting and controlling user access to the SAP system accurately and flexibly. In line with this concept, a user can be given different authorizations for different company codes, for example edit access in company code 01 and read only access in company code 02. The authorization concept also includes security measures, which restrict unauthorized logon or unwarranted interference with user master records, profiles, and authorizations.

Administration of User Master Records and Authorizations in the SAP System

The administration of user master records and authorizations in the SAP system is organized as follows. User master records and authorization components are dependent on clients, which means that separate user master records and authorization components must be maintained for each client in the SAP system. The protection of objects (e.g., data, tables, etc.) is described by authorizations or global authorizations assigned to the objects to be protected, similar to locks fitted to doors. They contain values for fields defined in an associated authorization object. The users are given authorization profiles, similar to keys, and/or global authorization profiles, similar to bunches of keys, which are entered in their user master records. The check as to whether a user's authorization profile matches an authorization, i.e., whether a key fits a lock, is performed either in dialog mode during runtime or if the key word "AUTHORITY CHECK" appears in an ABAP, for example.

Segregation of Maintenance and Activation

Maintenance and activation of profiles and authorizations are segregated in the system to improve security. Only the active version of a profile or authorization is effective in the system. A person's maintenance authorization can be restricted to certain users, profiles, and objects.

Upstream Security Systems

Security checks must take the following levels into account:

- PC level,
- network level,
- operating system level, and
- database level.

The remainder of the audit is conducted on the SAP application level.

Possible Security Risks

The high flexibility of the SAP authorization and user administration concept can lead to security risks if used improperly. It is possible to influence work processes and/or account entry tasks. For example, the recording of change documents (master data, documents, control tables) could be fully or partially suppressed, or the authority check in programs could be removed.

Risks of Standard Profiles

SAP ships large volumes of what are known as standard profiles tailored to diverse operational functions. Due to the complexity of the authorization concept, many users implement these profiles unchanged, which may expose them to certain risks:

- The standard profiles do not sufficiently cover operational requirements.
- If the standard profiles are adapted to operational requirements, this may give rise to new risks (e.g., by expanding the authorizations granted).
- If the SAP names of the profiles are retained, even though the profiles have been changed (e.g., by granting additional authorizations), the ability to audit the profiles may be at risk.

Importance of Assigning Authorizations

The above example shows that the security, and ultimately the compliance, of the entire system directly depends on the authorizations assigned. The assignment of authorizations therefore requires particular attention. Before auditing the processing results, the auditors first must test the user authorizations to ensure that processing results are based on authorized routines and entries.

Fieldwork Activities Regarding User Administration

The following organizational and system based fieldwork activities are significant with regard to user administration:

- Obtain information about the organization of user authorization assignment (application and approval procedure, segregation of duties) and internal instructions put in place for this purpose.
- Clarify whether there are written instructions on issuing and changing user authorizations.
- Verify that organizational measures are in place to ensure that, when employees leave the company, their user authorizations are cancelled and test whether these measures are utilized.
- Test whether new user authorizations or changes and deletions must be approved by an employee in charge.
- Examine whether control procedures are applied by the user departments responsible when a new user master record is created or when a user's access rights are changed.

- Test whether user access rights are changed by a system procedure:
  - when the users' responsibilities in the company change and their user master records have to be changed as a result (risk of multiple access rights if responsibilities in the company change frequently),
  - when employees leave the company.
- Test on a sample basis whether the authorization profiles of employees match their job tasks.
- Test on a sample basis whether the authorizations actually granted match the authorizations approved.
- Test whether profiles and authorizations are changed by a compulsory procedure when an authorization object is changed. An authorization object consists of up to ten authorization fields, which are checked during an AND operation, testing whether a user is permitted to perform a specific action.
- Test whether changes within the user authorization concept are documented and the corresponding documents are retained for at least as long as the legal retention period.

Analysis of Superusers

There are standard users with predefined rights in the SAP system (superusers). The initial passwords for these types of users are generally known and should be changed after each installation and after each client copy.

Other Fieldwork Activities

Fieldwork activities required in this regard include:

- Test whether new logon is necessary after the user has been inactive for a while (system parameters or external security software).
- Ensure that all authorizations of the general SAP user have been canceled and transferred to a secret emergency user.
- Ensure that the standard password of the DDIC (data dictionary) user, which is normally necessary for installation and maintenance work, has been changed in the active clients.
- Ensure that the comprehensive authorizations in DDIC are made available only temporarily.
- Critically examine the authorizations of IT employees, who should be granted edit access to data only in exceptional circumstances.

Special Users

A special user with comprehensive system authorizations should be defined for emergencies. Any activity by this user must be logged in a traceable way, observing the dual control principle.

Manipulation Risk

A risk of manipulation exists when unauthorized access is made to those user master records the owners of which have never logged on to the system and for which no password change has been enforced yet. In such cases, it is possible to manipulate data under a false name. In this context, the auditors should examine whether a setting has been specified in the system that requires the standard password to be changed within a certain number of days and blocks the user if it has not been changed (also possible for any other password).

HINTS AND TIPS

- From an auditing perspective, IT auditors should pay particular attention to the existence of a central user administration. Above all, they should test the organizational and system-based internal controls.
- The use of special auditing software provided by other vendors for the SAP system may be effective when auditing complex authorization combinations.

LINKS AND REFERENCES

- Audit Guidelines for SAP systems. www.sap.com/germany/company/revis/infomaterial/index.epx (accessed May 31, 2007).
- INSTITUTE OF INTERNAL AUDITORS. 2005. *Global Technology Audit Guide 1: Information Technology Controls.* Altamonte Springs, FL: The Institute of Internal Auditors.
- IT GOVERNANCE INSTITUTE. 2007. *COBIT 4.1.* Rolling Meadows, IL: IT Governance Institute.
- PFLEEGER, C., AND S. L. PFLEEGER. 2003. *Security in Computing.* 3rd ed. Upper Saddle River, NJ: Prentice Hall.
- SAP online documentation.

10.5 Batch-Input Interfaces and Background Processing

KEY POINTS

- Batch input is normally used to import data from external systems into SAP systems, or to transfer data between SAP systems.
- The objectives of the job-order process are to protect company and personal data, to maintain the integrity of data and functions, and to protect resources.

Batch-Input in SAP Systems

Batch input is normally used to import data from external systems into SAP systems, or to transfer data between SAP systems. The source system uses a transfer interface for the data transfer, which is provided by an SAP application in the target system. The interface program of the application then generates a batch-input session.

Batch-Input Session

A batch-input session consists of several transaction calls, to which a program has added user data. Normally, the system executes the transactions in a session without any further user intervention. This allows to import a large volume of data into the SAP system within a very short period of time. A session simulates the online entry of transaction codes and data, generally using the same procedures as in dialog mode. The data entered in the screen fields through a session are subject to the same consistency checks as data entered in dialog mode. Batch-input processing is called with certain transactions. Batch-input sessions are usually not started interactively. At regular intervals a background job starts sessions that have not yet run. Sessions are normally processed interactively only for testing and correction purposes.

Requirements on the Batch-Input Process

The legal framework, which requires data to be recorded, stored, and processed fully, accurately, and in a timely and structured manner and which stipulates that the data must not be falsified in case of changes, also calls for controls in the batch-input process. The prerequisites for the creation of effective controls include the organization of workflows, the segregation of incompatible functions, as well as control measures and bodies.

Internal Control System

The nature and extent of the IT organization and its workflows have a significant impact on the effectiveness of the internal control system. Such a system must achieve a compulsory sequence of processes, and any deviation from this sequence should produce an error that must be noticed by a control unit. An effective internal control system involves the segregation of duties, which should distinguish between planning, executing, and monitoring functions.

Authorizations

Generally, batch-input sessions are subject to the usual user authorization checks performed by the system. When a session is processed online, the authorizations of the processing user apply.

Processing Types

There are three processing types to choose from:

- Invisible processing: Under this processing type, a session is processed immediately.
- Visible processing: Incorrect transactions can be corrected interactively and any transactions not yet executed can be processed successively.
- Display errors only: This processing type is similar to the "visible processing" type, except that error-free transactions not yet executed do not run interactively.

A session contains an error if it causes a type E (error) or type T (termination) error message. Other messages are ignored and have no impact on the processing of a session.

Logs

For each batch-input session, there is a log that can be displayed in the system. It contains all error messages relating to session transactions. The log also shows batch-input error messages relating to problems with the processing of transactions, including the relevant transaction code and the screen on which the error occurred. In addition, the log contains overall session processing statistics. A log for a batch-input session will exist only once this session has been processed according to one of the above three types. When a session is processed, the error-free transactions are entered, and marked as processed in the session. Transactions with errors are not entered, and marked as incorrect. If a session contains incorrect transactions, it can be processed more than once, with each repeat only reprocessing those transactions marked as incorrect. For each processing run, the SAP system generates a session log, which overwrites the existing log. The log contains only those messages that occurred during the last processing. Apart from error messages, posting messages are also logged. There is at least one message for each transaction processed.

Risks In the case of feeder systems that are independent of SAP, there is a risk that plausibility checks are used that differ from the SAP tables. This can affect master and transaction data. If session names are not plausibility checked, it is possible that authorized persons start, correct, or delete (depending on the authorizations assigned) the processing of batch-input sessions of other departments.

Analysis of the Display The analysis of the readout of the batch-input sessions provides an overview of all sessions stored in the system. The entries in the "incorrect" register are of interest to auditors.

Audit Objects Auditors should ask the following questions on the basis of the control requirements:

- Is there an overview of all batch-input interfaces with SAP software, specifying details such as issuing application area, data content, file name, period, session name, processing job, relevant tables, reconciliation group, and responsibility?
- Which users are allowed to create, start, correct, or delete sessions?
- Is there an overview of which session names are reserved for which department (transaction SM35)?
- Who coordinates the posting data of the processed sessions?
- Who checks that the data from feeder systems is imported fully, correctly, and in a timely manner?
- Are internal controls in place between feeder systems and ongoing processing?

Job-Order Process Jobs are sequences of programs that regularly run one after the other in the system. The job-order process has the following main objectives:

- to protect company and personal data,
- to ensure the integrity of data and functions, and
- to protect resources.

Job Documentation and Logs The objectives of the job documentation are:

- to ensure smooth processing,
- to achieve independence from the detailed knowledge of specific persons, and
- to ensure that the IT-technical processing can be checked by an expert third party within a reasonable period of time.

Job logs are necessary to provide evidence of compliant processing, i.e., compliance with the job-order process in particular.

Requirements on the Job-Order Process The job-order process must always contain clearly defined processes and responsibilities for assigning orders, execution, postprocessing, and output distribution. Since a user department can generate and start a large number of jobs in the SAP system, the relevant process documentation in the respective department's application manual is normally sufficient.

Requirements on the Job Documentation When jobs are generated by an SAP system, the documentation is automatically generated at the same time. When users create their own jobs (native job generation, e.g., sessions), they must also create the necessary documentation. The retention period for job documentation depends on the applicable legal retention periods for each relevant geographic region.

System Logs

Job logs have to provide evidence as to when which job was processed with what parameters. The job logs generated in the system must be specially protected, and in sensitive areas there must be separate reporting on the basis of the system logs.

Jobs in the SAP System

In general, a specific job (e.g., dunning run) is automatically generated by the system on the basis of a job-specific user command. Access to a job generation command can be protected as part of the general authorization concept. A job can consist of several steps. There are two different types of jobs: One-time jobs, which are to be executed immediately or according to a schedule, and periodic jobs. A job is started by the system when a defined event has occurred (e.g., a point in time or the end of another job). This allows building job networks. A job is in exactly one of the following states: scheduled, released, ready, active, completed, or terminated.

System Logs in the SAP System

The following logs are available as system logs in an SAP system:

- job logs,
- system logs,
- database logs,
- operating system logs, and
- workload logs.

Risks

The following risks must be considered:

- unauthorized (read) access to company and personal data,
- unauthorized, uncontrolled, undetected changes to data and programs,
- high load on resources as a result of inappropriate program configuration,
- user error, especially in exceptional circumstances (error handling), and
- dependence on the knowledge of individuals.

Fieldwork Activities

During the audit, the current status of the procedures must be recorded. To this end, the auditors must record and document (to the extent necessary for the audit) the desired requirements for job-order processes, job documentation, and the creation and handling of system logs. When auditing the procedural concepts, the desired requirements recorded earlier are to be examined on the basis of the requirements and risks discussed in this chapter. Compliance with the desired requirements is tested by reviewing the documents and analyzing the log files and logs.

HINTS AND TIPS

- When auditing batch-input sessions, auditors should also check the existence of process instructions.
- To test who is permitted to delete batch-input sessions, auditors should check the relevant authorizations.

LINKS AND REFERENCES ↗

- Audit Guidelines for SAP systems. www.sap.com/germany/company/revis/infomaterial/index.epx (accessed May 31, 2007).
- SAP online documentation.

D Special Topics and Supplementary Discussion

1 Documentation in Internal Audit

1.1 Basics of Documentation

1.1.1 Objectives, Requirements, Sources, and Responsibilities

KEY POINTS •••

- Documentation is a key element of each audit.
- Important objectives of documentation include providing evidence that the audit work is compliant, ensuring readiness to give information, and presenting the audit history across audit cycles.
- This results in a number of different tasks, including ensuring the completeness of the information, the traceability of the findings and recommendations, and providing a safeguarding function.
- The audit lead has to assess and take adequate account of the different sources of information and how balanced they are.

Importance of Documentation

The concept of auditing is inseparable from documentation that is focused and accurate. Documentation is one of many processes accompanying audit work, and its main objective is to lay out in writing all activities and facts relating to an audit. It is one key to the success of every audit. Clear and comprehensive documentation is particularly important for audit compliance. Documentation makes audit work itself auditable.

Documentation Objectives

Documentation in Internal Audit has three main objectives:

- Its first objective is to provide detailed descriptions of all the operational audit processes and process steps, as outlined in the Audit Roadmap (see Section B). It documents that the structure of Internal Audit is compliant in relation to processes and their associated internal controls. For this reason, all relevant process steps, internal controls, and (if appropriate) their links with financial reporting must be recorded, taking SOX requirements into account. The documentation guidelines must be applied consistently to all audits to provide audit evidence to prove that the audit principles have been complied with and the requirements of SOX have been met (see Section C, Chapter 8; Section D, Chapter 14).
- Standardized audit evidence is necessary to ensure that Internal Audit is able to corroborate the information it provides to all internal and external parties at any time. To guarantee that conclusions and recommendations can be substantiated, Internal Audit documentation must be complete, truthful, readily available, traceable, and as detailed as necessary. Since Internal Audit has different information levels and therefore different levels of detail, the documentation must be consistent betweeen these different levels.
- Another important objective is to provide an audit history. Given the dynamic changes in business life, the monitoring of audit results on the basis of documents is an important task for Internal Audit. It is ultimately the only way to

provide evidence of compliant audit cycles. References to earlier results, the identification of trends, long-term comparisons, and the identification of priorities and courses of action for the future can also be important sub-objectives under this heading.

Documentation Tasks

These central objectives lead to different documentation requirements:

- No information should be lost during an audit. It is therefore necessary to create documentation guidelines on the information to be included and on how this information should be recorded. Such guidelines should be structured by information type and documentation type. They should offer guidance for preparing uniform and comprehensible documentation throughout Internal Audit.
- A safeguarding function may also be important for Internal Audit in certain circumstances (e.g., in fraud audits). If required, key documents (e.g., e-mail correspondence, working papers, draft reports) should be made subject to the attorney-client privilege by signing a legally binding declaration.
- Documents themselves may be audit objects and be subjected to specific fieldwork activities.
- Another major item is the traceability of findings and recommendations. The documentation should ensure at all times that each audit finding is supported by reliable audit evidence and free from assumptions, contradictions, or speculation.
- Audit documentation is also used to exchange information. Consequently, it should be readily available to all parties concerned.
- Another documentation requirement results from the increasing internationalization of business processes. Multilingual documentation of facts helps to prevent misunderstandings. Accurate translations are particularly important in relation to legal matters.

Documentation Sources

The question of documentation sources is important with regard to the requirements of the documentation. Documents may:

- result from Internal Audit's own fieldwork,
- arise from certain advance output such as pre-investigations,
- be consulted from audits conducted earlier,
- be provided by the auditees,
- be made available by other units of the company, or
- come from external information sources.

Responsibility for Documentation

An important task in each audit is to apply the materiality principle to make a correct, meaningful selection from the large number of available sources of documentation. For this reason, the auditors should allow sufficient time for creating and reviewing the documentation. The audit lead is ultimately responsible for the adequacy of the documentation. However, each auditor should make sure at all times that the documentation is compliant.

HINTS AND TIPS

- During an audit, auditors should document all observations in their working papers and evaluate their materiality at a later stage.
- Auditors have to check all documentation for completeness, consistency, and comprehensibility. They should ensure this through plausibility checks questioning each finding to ensure that it can be supported in detail and does not contradict other results.

1.1.2 Legal Requirements

KEY POINTS

- The IIA has issued guidance and recommendations for document retention policies.
- Laws and regulations may influence the documentation requirements for Internal Audit. They may include data protection provisions, archiving regulations, and document retention requirements.

Direct Legal Requirements

There is no specific legal guidance in the U.S. for Internal Audit regarding documentation retention beyond the necessity to have documentation as part of a functioning financial accounting and reporting system as required by the Foreign Corrupt Practices Act and SOX. The IIA has issued guidance on documentation retention, but it only requires that an internal audit department have a document retention policy that is consistent with the organization's requirements. The guidance does not specify minimum retention requirements. However, the IIA recommends that a minimum of five years of data be available for peer reviews.

Comprehensive Documentation Policy

A comprehensive documentation policy can include the introduction of document management, electronic archiving, and data processing systems and should give consideration to data security management to prevent the disclosure of confidential employee or customer information. In this context, data protection laws such as the U.S. Data Protection Act of 1998 or EU data protection regulations must be considered.

Data Protection Requirements

Internal auditors should consult with legal counsel to determine specific document retention requirements in their jurisdiction and to establish a feasible time for which documents should be retained.

HINTS AND TIPS

- Auditors should familiarize themselves with pertinent documentation requirements.

- In the case of documents containing personal information, Internal Audit should check that confidentiality is protected, involving the legal or the human resources department if necessary.
- Internal Audit's documentation concept should be discussed with the company's data protection officer.

LINKS AND REFERENCES ↗

- FILIPEK, R. 2006. Guidance Promotes Sound Records Management. *Internal Auditor* (August 2006): 16–17.
- INSTITUTE OF INTERNAL AUDITORS. 2001. *Practice Advisory 2100-2: Information Security*. Altamonte Springs, FL: The Institute of Internal Auditors.
- INSTITUTE OF INTERNAL AUDITORS. 2001. *Practice Advisory 2100-5: Legal Considerations in Evaluating Regulatory Compliance Programs*. Altamonte Springs, FL: The Institute of Internal Auditors.
- INSTITUTE OF INTERNAL AUDITORS. 2001. *Practice Advisory 2330.A1-1: Control of Engagement Records*. Altamonte Springs, FL: The Institute of Internal Auditors.
- INSTITUTE OF INTERNAL AUDITORS. 2001. *Practice Advisory 2330.A2-1: Retention of Records*. Altamonte Springs, FL: The Institute of Internal Auditors.
- INSTITUTE OF INTERNAL AUDITORS. 2001. *Practice Advisory 2330-1: Recording Information*. Altamonte Springs, FL: The Institute of Internal Auditors.
- LANGE, J. 2005. Curse of Prior Workpapers. *Internal Auditor* (August 2005): 26–27.

1.1.3 Important Documentation Criteria

KEY POINTS •••

- The documentation of an internal audit department should be organized in a basic structure.
- The documentation system should be based on the Audit Roadmap and a number of additional criteria.
- Documentation medium, document filing, retention periods, document archiving, and responsibilities and authorizations must be considered.
- Internal Audit should define consistent rules for the treatment of documents according to each documentation type. This ensures that unique document selection is possible.

Documentation Criteria

In order to define the characteristics of effective, forward-looking documentation, the main tasks for each documentation type must be determined. The tasks can be phase-specific or span several phases along the Audit Roadmap. The following criteria must be taken into account for comprehensive and general, but also flexible and specific documentation:

Documentation Medium

- The documentation medium is the first criterion to consider. Nowadays, almost all documents in IT-based systems are stored on hard disks, shared network drives, internet-based systems, or external storage media. This applies to both documents Internal Audit itself has produced as well as various source documents, which are increasingly generated in electronic form or are available as scanned documents or electronic faxes. Electronically available information can be supported by plausibility checks (e.g., keyword indexes, reference systems, and search algorithms), processed and condensed automatically, and included in comparisons and analyses. However, the auditors should keep hard copies of at least the audit reports. Doing so provides additional security, but also defines original versions, signed copies of which are labeled as such and stored as documentary evidence. The documents stored electronically can be write-protected in order to prevent subsequent modifications.

Document Filing

- The filing of documents is based on how the internal audit department is organized. If it consists of one local unit, documents can be filed uniformly and centrally in a single location. With increasing decentralization of the department, data storage and filing have to be arranged individually for each document type (see Section D, Chapter 1.2). On the basis of classifying attributes, such as auditor, audit year, or audit method, individual searches can be performed thus allowing many kinds of analyses. This is supported by document-specific folder directories, in which the auditor can conduct searches and make selections by documentation type, by content within a type, or across different types.

Document Archiving

- Document archiving is aimed at permanently storing information either as printed copies or on special data media such as online archives, external storage media (e.g CD, DVD) and operational IT systems. The documents must be filed individually according to how current and significant they are. The fact that the information needs to be available and up to date means that storage and resource usage have to be organized efficiently, i.e., both the timeliness of accessing the information and storage efficiency have to be optimized. Since many companies use servers with integrated databases, the data will often be stored centrally on an online-capable medium. All information should be stored with write protection.

Retention Periods

- Two aspects are significant with regard to retention periods: external requirements resulting from laws and external guidelines, if applicable (see Section D, Chapter 1.1.2), and periods imposed internally to ensure a sensible audit process.

Responsibilities and Authorizations

- Responsibilities and authorizations primarily pertain to the creation, checking, and release of documents, as well as their administration in general. Authorizations are defined and granted through a clear assignment system. Specifically, the following must be defined:
  - Who is given read access to files?
  - Who can create, edit, and delete documents?

- Who is responsible for organizing the filing, archiving, and distribution?
- Who grants access authorizations?

Taking All Criteria into Account

When designing a documentation concept, equal consideration must be given to each of the above criteria. None of the criteria must be left out, because otherwise Internal Audit will not be able to provide a comprehensive guarantee that its document management is reliable and complete.

HINTS AND TIPS

- Auditors should archive the audit documents at the time they officially conclude the audit.
- Auditors should create a keyword index of all the topics they have covered and assign the documents to the relevant keywords.

1.2 Documentation Along the Audit Roadmap

KEY POINTS

- In addition to the documentation criteria and the focus on the process structure of the Audit Roadmap, the documentation concept is influenced by Internal Audit's organizational structure.
- The criteria of the documentation concept should be applied to each document type and every audit cycle along the Audit Roadmap.
- Although general rules are advisable, the need for separate retention periods and storage media must be considered.

Documentation Concept Along the Audit Roadmap

GIAS' documentation concept manifests itself in the implementation of the documentation criteria described in Section D, Chapter 1.1.3. These criteria apply to each document type and every audit cycle along the Audit Roadmap (see Section B). Closer examination of the documents reveals the following:

Scope

- The Scope is a central document, which is normally created by the person responsible for the topic. This document should be stored electronically to make it available and accessible to all Internal Audit employees. It should be archived online for five years. All Internal Audit employees should have read access to the Scopes. Changes may only be made by the person responsible for the Scope after consultation with management, i.e. the Audit Manager in charge and (especially in the case of new Scopes) the CAE. For some audits – especially ad-hoc audits – for which no Scope exists, responsibility for the creation of a Scope lies with the audit lead and the Audit Manager, both of whom review the Scope as part of the quality assurance program (for details on quality assurance for the individual documents, see Section D, Chapter 5.3).

Audit Request

- An audit request can be sent to Internal Audit electronically as an e-mail attachment or as hard copy by internal mail. Any hard copies received should first be scanned. The relevant audit team files the audit request and the other audit documents, which together comprise the audit-related documentation, for a period of three years in a decentralized location. In addition, Internal Audit should keep the request on an external storage medium, e.g., a CD, for a period of seven years. All Internal Audit employees should get read access, but authorization to edit the request document should not be granted.

Audit Announcement

- The audit announcement is converted into a non-editable storage format and then e-mailed to the auditees. The document is filed electronically in a decentralized location for three years. The document should not be changed or edited thereafter, and only the authorized persons, i.e., audit lead, audit team, and Audit Manager, are given read access. In addition, the audit announcement is stored on a CD for seven years.

Work Program

- The work program is created and stored electronically. The document is filed electronically in a decentralized location for three years and centrally in the online archive for five years. Documentation should be accessible by audit and by topic. Moreover, it makes sense to store the documents externally on a CD for seven years. All Internal Audit employees should get read access, but authorization to change and edit the work program is reserved for the audit team.

Working Papers

- During audit execution, the auditors produce the working papers in addition to the source documents. The source documents are available electronically or as hard copies. The auditors should scan any hard copy documents. Source documents and working papers should be filed in a decentralized location for three years and externally on a CD for seven years. All Internal Audit employees should get read access, but only the audit team may change and edit the documents. In addition to the various working papers, the audit summary and the work done sheets should be stored electronically. These documents should be retained in a decentralized location for three years, in an online archive for five years, and on CD for seven years.

Reporting

- All reporting documents are normally created electronically, but the final report should always be available electronically (e.g. as a pdf-file) and as hard copy. The printed version must be kept for two years. Reports should be filed in both a decentral and a central location. In addition, they should be filed according to audit object in a central location assigned to the relevant audit topic. The recommended retention periods are three years in a decentralized location, five years in the online archive, and seven years on an external storage medium (e.g., CD). The auditors should make sure that any changes are reflected consistently across all storage locations. Only the audit team can edit the reports. All other Internal Audit employees will have read access.

Audit Survey

- Once an audit has been completed, the auditees are asked by way of an audit survey to give their assessment of Internal Audit's work (for details, see Section

D, Chapter 7.2.2). The questionnaires, which the audit lead e-mails to those concerned, are returned electronically. After receipt by Internal Audit, the audit lead can add comments and then saves the document so that it is write protected. The document is filed by Internal Audit management in a decentralized location for three years, in the online archive for five years, and on CD for seven years. All internal auditors are given read access, but no changes are allowed.

Follow-Up

- The follow-up documentation is treated in the same way as the documentation for the basic audit.

Documentation According to Audit Cycle

If the monitoring mandate issued to Internal Audit necessitates further audits in the same unit beyond the follow-up, the whole audit process repeats itself, and thus also the documentation process. At the end of the documentation processes, after the retention periods have elapsed, the documents must be deleted. The following diagram shows how the described process steps relate to each other.

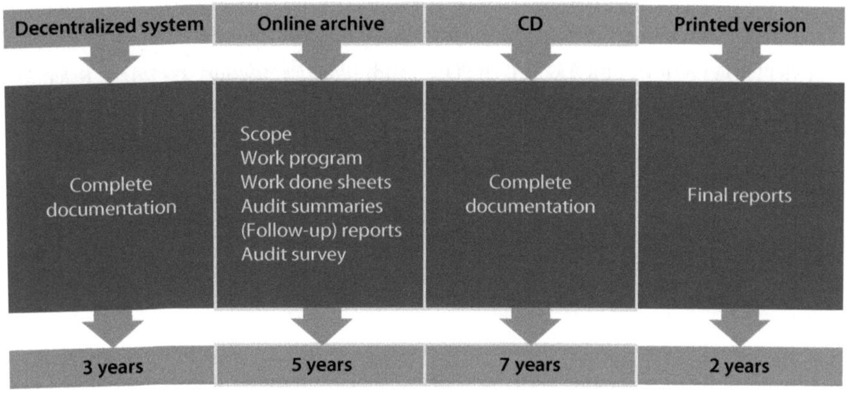

Fig. 1 Documentation within GIAS

Significance of the Organizational Structure

In addition to the documentation criteria and the focus on the process structure of the Audit Roadmap, the documentation concept is influenced by Internal Audit's organizational structure. The structure provides the framework, which ensures that adequate documentation control is maintained over time. Especially if Internal Audit has an international organization, a clear documentation strategy must be pursued, with deviations between legal systems as harmonized as possible. The objective is to achieve a documentation concept that takes equal account of each documentation type, of the general criteria, the phases of the Audit Roadmap, the structural attributes of audit and audit object, and the organizational structure.

HINTS AND TIPS

- A documentation concept can only provide a general framework. Individual adjustments must be possible to accomodate specific audits.
- For the duration of an audit, auditors should make personal copies of every important document and store them in a confidential directory.
- Auditors should test the availability of data and reports for ongoing as well as completed audits.
- The archiving of documents should be logged.
- If auditors notice that audit documents are missing, they must immediately notify the Audit Manager in charge.

LINKS AND REFERENCES

- INSTITUTE OF INTERNAL AUDITORS. 2001. *Practice Advisory 2100-2: Information Security.* Altamonte Springs, FL: The Institute of Internal Auditors.
- INSTITUTE OF INTERNAL AUDITORS. 2001. *Practice Advisory 2330-1: Recording Information.* Altamonte Springs, FL: The Institute of Internal Auditors.
- INSTITUTE OF INTERNAL AUDITORS. 2001. *Practice Advisory 2330.A2-1: Retention of Records.* Altamonte Springs, FL: The Institute of Internal Auditors.

2 Cooperation

2.1 Communication and Information Flow

KEY POINTS •••

- Communication and information exchange are important components of the work of an internal audit department.
- The confidentiality of information must be observed at all times.
- The correct tone and style of communication are as important as the right timing.
- Internal Audit has to conduct itself professionally and objectively in verbal and written communication.

General

An important part of the work of an internal audit department in a corporate group is to obtain and process internal and external information. Relevant information may, for example, be obtained from the internet, professional publications, or through communication with cooperation partners. For Internal Audit to be effective, it is essential to be open to information from many different channels within the company and in different formats.

Confidentiality of the Information

There are various criteria for communication and information flows, which have to be met to achieve effective cooperation. For example, the confidentiality of the information transferred – irrespective of flow direction – must be guaranteed. Auditors must observe Internal Audit's special rules for the distribution of information and the corporate guidelines on the treatment of confidential information, i.e., they must mark all audit reports as "confidential" when sending them out. In addition, the applicable data protection regulations and legal requirements must be complied with.

Information Flow Matrix

It is important that a company maintains a mutual exchange of information internally. SAP's Internal Audit has mapped the necessary relationships in a matrix (described below), which has been discussed with the respective departments. The tasks of audit management include constantly updating and implementing the matrix. The matrix has to be adapted to the individual regions and also has to be coordinated with the other departments or individuals, such as the responsible Board members. Region-specific matrices have to be discussed with the CAE before they are implemented. This discussion represents a quality check, rather than control over regional information flows.

Communication within the Team

Of course, there are also information flows within the Internal Audit teams and across regions between team members and the Internal Audit management in charge. This information flow is very important especially with regard to audit-related issues. In addition, contact at a personal level also serves to strengthen the team spirit. Good team spirit is particularly valuable when a global audit team is put together and the auditors have to get used to each other's working style in a short period of time. Annual departmental meetings, which bring together all Internal Audit employees in one place, also have a positive effect on team spirit.

Global information flow

Recipient / Sender	Internal Audit	Accounting	Management Accounting	Legal	Global Risk Management	Tax	Regional finance org.	External auditors
Internal Audit								
Accounting								
Managerial Accounting								
Legal								
Global Risk Management								
Tax								
Regional finance org.								
External auditors								

Fig. 2 Information Flow Matrix

Right Tone and Style

It is important to use the right tone and an appropriate style when exchanging information. A different tone should be used when communicating within the company than when dealing with external partners or other companies. But even internally, auditors must ensure that all other parties perceive Internal Audit as professional and objective. The type of information exchange – verbal or written – is important in this regard. For electronic and paper-based written communication as well as for direct contact, there are special conventions that should be observed. When information is, for example, passed on in writing, particular attention should be paid to form, clarity, and completeness of content. In this regard, it is the responsibility of audit management to specify the correct tone and style of communication for the department.

Timing

Another important aspect of communication is timing. First, there is a periodic exchange of information, which has to be arranged with other departments. And second, there are occasional exchanges of information as the need arises. In such cases, timing is important so that information is not communicated too early or too late.

Creation of a File Note

For verbal communication (face-to-face, via telephone, video conference, net meeting etc.), it is usually a good idea to create an internal file note to have a written record of the discussion. There are standard templates, such as interview or meeting logs, in the working papers for this purpose (see Section B, Chapter 4.2). In the day-to-day flow of information, the decision of whether the creation of a file note is appropriate or not depends on the substance and importance of a discussion. As with other working papers, the purpose of the file note is to have a record of the conversation available on request. Especially if there are queries from the people involved in the audit or in relation to other fieldwork activities and report preparation, it is useful to make the Audit Manager or CAE aware of the file note or to forward a copy. If there is a dispute about what was said at a meeting, the written file note protects those who took part in the discussion.

Format

When information is exchanged in writing, the auditor has to decide on an appropriate format for each case (e.g., minutes or memorandum). In addition, it must be specified whether subsequent changes are to be allowed, and if so, who is authorized to make them.

HINTS AND TIPS

- When communicating with others, auditors must always remember that they represent the company's internal audit department.
- Sometimes it may be useful to ask colleagues to read an e-mail before sending it out.
- Auditors should observe the information flow matrix.

LINKS AND REFERENCES

- CLIKEMAN, P. 1999. Improving Information Quality. *Internal Auditor* (June 1999): 32–33.
- INSTITUTE OF INTERNAL AUDITORS. 2001. *Practice Advisory 2050-1: Coordination.* Altamonte Springs, FL: The Institute of Internal Auditors.
- INSTITUTE OF INTERNAL AUDITORS. 2001. *Practice Advisory 2310-1: Identifying Information.* Altamonte Springs, FL: The Institute of Internal Auditors.
- INSTITUTE OF INTERNAL AUDITORS. 2001. *Practice Advisory 2410-1: Communication Criteria.* Altamonte Springs, FL: The Institute of Internal Auditors.
- KOLETAR, J. 2006. Intelligence Gathering and the Future of Internal Audit. *The CPA Journal* (April 2006): 16–17.
- ORSINI, B. 2000. Improving Internal Communications. *Internal Auditor* (December 2000): 28–33.

2.2 Global Risk Management

2.2.1 Integration Overview

KEY POINTS •••

- Risk Management and Internal Audit are closely related functions.
- The close relations between the two units are evident from various perspectives.
- Despite their closeness, they should be separate organizational units.

Risk Management and Internal Audit

Risk management is one of internal auditing's most closely related partner disciplines, and the two areas are significant interrelated instruments of corporate management. Historically, the risk management function and the internal audit function have developed with different objectives in mind. In the past, the risk management function was often almost fully included in the internal audit function, but today the two functions are usually separated. This means that in terms of function and organizational integration, Risk Management is a separate unit from Internal Audit, even though the two areas are closely interrelated. Different relationship levels are shown below.

Fig. 3 Network of Relations between Internal Audit and Risk Management

Risk-Based Procedure

Quite clearly, it is an objective for Internal Audit to identify and address potential risks in every audit. This minimum requirement of a risk-based procedure can be implemented step by step in all the phases of the Audit Roadmap, until a risk-based audit approach is ultimately achieved (see Section A, Chapter 6.3). When this approach is aligned with the Audit Roadmap, a risk relation can be derived for each audit step in terms of quality, and sometimes quantity, i.e., each risk can be localized and analyzed. The aim is to use audit findings to identify relevant business risks, to deal with them according to predetermined rules within the audit process, and to make information about them available to Risk Management.

Risk Management as a Separate Audit Object

In addition, Risk Management represents a separate audit object, because, like any other organizational unit of the company, this area has its own guidelines and principles. Certain structural and process-related approaches to working are based on these guidelines and principles and are naturally included in Internal Audit's work focus, along with communication and information flows.

Separate Risk Management Process Model

Effective risk management must have an independent process model, i.e., a separate Roadmap. In the context of mutual integration, Internal Audit can contribute to generating and updating such a Roadmap. There is possible overlap between the steps of the risk management process model and the Audit Roadmap. The aim of the cooperation from Risk Management's point of view is to obtain all the information required for effective risk control. Internal Audit can be a useful partner in this regard by providing all audit-related risk information.

Integration versus Independence

Essentially, Risk Management is intended to help the areas with potential risks in identifying and controlling them on the basis of a standardized method and quality assurance system provided by a neutral corporate function. If the integration approaches shown above are combined, then it becomes clear that Risk Management and Internal Audit are closely related units and should cooperate closely. The processes of each department should therefore be highly integrated. However, the sometimes different nature of the work, different perspectives, and the need for independence from each other necessitate the existence of two separate organizational units.

HINTS AND TIPS

- Every auditor should try to keep in touch with Risk Management.
- Whenever appropriate, risk managers should be involved in an audit. In particular, a risk manager should be invited to the closing meetings.

LINKS AND REFERENCES

- INSTITUTE OF INTERNAL AUDITORS. 2001. *Practice Advisory 2050-1: Coordination.* Altamonte Springs, FL: The Institute of Internal Auditors.
- INSTITUTE OF INTERNAL AUDITORS. 2003. *Practice Advisory 2110-1: Assessing the Adequacy of Risk Management Processes.* Altamonte Springs, FL: The Institute of Internal Auditors.
- INSTITUTE OF INTERNAL AUDITORS. 2003. *Practice Advisory 2110-2: Internal Auditor's Role in the Business Continuity Process.* Altamonte Springs, FL: The Institute of Internal Auditors.

2.2.2 Risk Management Along the Audit Roadmap

KEY POINTS

- The implementation of the risk-based audit approach as a framework concept is an integral process component of the Audit Roadmap.
- Every phase of the Audit Roadmap is conducted under risk aspects.
- The cooperation between Internal Audit and Risk Management must be coordinated in detail.

Overview

The implementation of the risk-based audit approach as a framework concept (see Section A, Chapter 6.3) is an integral process component of the Audit Roadmap. Risk-based audit planning assigns pre-defined Key Scopes to each audit topic. The main risk category is one of the items indicated in the Key Scope. This general assessment of risk is specified for the associated item of the work program by noting the risk sub category. The subsequent audit will reveal whether or not these risk assumptions are confirmed. Once the audit has been completed, each finding relating to an item in the work program will be connected to the identified risk in the audit report. This information will be passed on to Risk Management for further evaluation, assessment, and monitoring.

Audit Planning

The audit topics identified during audit planning include information about risk-prone areas related to the topics (e.g., organization, finance, etc.), determined on the basis of the common risk catalog of the risk management system. This catalog forms the basic structure of all known risks. During the annual planning phase (see Section B, Chapter 2.2 and Section D, Chapter 3), Internal Audit assesses all relevant audit topics from a risk perspective. Risk Management is also involved in this risk assessment procedure. Similar arrangements apply to ad-hoc audits, where an individual risk assessment is made at the time an audit request is accepted or submitted.

Audit Execution

During field work, the main focus is on testing whether internal controls are active and effective in avoiding or limiting risk. If they are not, new internal controls will have to be defined. The audit object on which the finding is based will have to be questioned, and the risk flagged as an existing, though potentially avoidable, risk. As part of these testing activities, different risk categories are analyzed for interrelations among each other and for their actual, independent existence. Often, more than one risk is assigned to a finding.

Working Papers

For each finding, the information relating to the relevant risks is added to the working papers, especially to the work done sheets. Accordingly, every finding has to relate to at least one risk. At the same time, it is possible to make appropriate recommendations, which may relate exclusively to the treatment of the risk or in addition include other facts mentioned in the finding, such as non-compliance with internal guidelines.

Audit Report

The findings which are pre-structured in the working papers, including risk identification, are ultimately included in the audit report, and the final recommendations are prepared. By following this procedure, a report will be created that provides details on the risks actually assigned to a finding, including the relevant recommendations.

Effect on Risk Management

On the basis of the audit results, Risk Management will, if appropriate, create the relevant activities and items in the risk management system. Risk Management assesses the risks transferred into the risk management system, analyzes them with a focus on loss probability and potential impact. Risk Management clarifies and monitors all further information, especially the steps taken to minimize risk.

Follow-Up

Follow-ups may give rise to additional Internal Audit and Risk Management activities, such as testing and risk-based evaluation of newly implemented internal controls. These activities must be coordinated with operational management. The objective of all activities is to achieve adequate risk control. Since overlap between the activities of the individual areas is probable, it is necessary to coordinate tasks.

HINTS AND TIPS

- If possible, the identification of risks during fieldwork should always be coordinated with a risk manager.
- In preparation for an audit, it may be useful for the auditor to review risk management reports on specific risks.

2.2.3 Risk Management Audits

KEY POINTS

- The risk management audit breaks down into the central organization and the decentralized functions of the risk management organization.
- Certain focus areas must be taken into account when auditing Risk Management.

Risk Management Audit and Audit Roadmap

Risk management audits are a separate audit task for Internal Audit. Such audits also pass through all the phases and sub-phases of the Audit Roadmap.

Possible Audit Structure

SAP's central risk management department is supplemented by a decentralized organization with local and regional risk managers, and the actual decision makers and process owners in the risk management process. It thus seems sensible for Internal Audit to structure risk management audits along these levels, but without neglecting the integration of these areas and the communication between them.

Audit Focus Areas

The focus areas of a risk management audit are as follows:

- organizational structure, responsibilities, and Risk Management's integration into the overall corporate governance complex,

- formal flow of information, communication, and reporting paths, especially to the Board,
- basic structure of the risk management process, consisting of identification, assessment, control, monitoring, and reporting,
- functionality and compliance of the IT solution the company uses for risk management,
- processes, information, and communication flows between the central department and the decentralized units, as well as among the separate decentralized units,
- decentralized structure of the risk managers in charge,
- objectives, tasks, and cooperation of the risk managers vis-à-vis the decentralized units responsible and among each other, and
- Risk Management's cooperation with other functions to ensure compliance in the company, e.g., Internal Audit and compliance management.

In addition, individual risks will be audited by analyzing the entire population or a sensibly chosen sample. Evidence of the efficiency and correctness of the risk management process has to be provided on the basis of these risks. Compliance with the requirements of SOX is also tested. A review of the direct assignment of specific internal controls to individual risks completes the audit.

Network of Responsibilities

Breaking the audit down into centralized and decentralized aspects helps differentiate audit findings in terms of responsibility. Often, individual responsibilities are interrelated with each other. This kind of responsibility network is addressed by a structured audit, making it easier to detect and eliminate any unclear responsibilities.

Detection of Additional Risks

A risk management audit may detect additional risks that were not known previously. Internal Audit treats and documents such risks according to the Audit Roadmap.

HINTS AND TIPS

- The work program for a risk management audit should be discussed with a risk manager.
- The special relationship between Internal Audit and Risk Management, especially with regard to their independence, has to be taken into consideration.

LINKS AND REFERENCES

- INSTITUTE OF INTERNAL AUDITORS. 2001. *Practice Advisory 2010-1: Planning.* Altamonte Springs, FL: The Institute of Internal Auditors.
- INSTITUTE OF INTERNAL AUDITORS. 2003. *Practice Advisory 2110-1: Assessing the Adequacy of Risk Management Processes.* Altamonte Springs, FL: The Institute of Internal Auditors.

- INSTITUTE OF INTERNAL AUDITORS. 2003. *Practice Advisory 2110-2: Internal Auditor's Role in the Business Continuity Process.* Altamonte Springs, FL: The Institute of Internal Auditors.
- INSTITUTE OF INTERNAL AUDITORS. 2003. *Practice Advisory 2140-4: Internal Auditing's Role in Organizatons without a Risk Management Process.* Altamonte Springs, FL: The Institute of Internal Auditors.

2.2.4 Internal Audit as Part of the Risk Management Process

KEY POINTS •••

- A particular challenge for Internal Audit and Risk Management is to harmonize their two process models.
- This ensures that both parties can guarantee the necessary mutual integration while maintaining their respective self-image.

Process Model for Risk Management

As mentioned earlier, a well developed risk management function should have its own process model, i.e. a Roadmap. In different phases, this model represents the platform for appropriate cooperation between the two compliance units, Risk Management and Internal Audit. In general, the risk management process consists of five operational phases: risk planning, risk identification, risk analysis, risk control, and risk monitoring.

Cooperation of Internal Audit and Risk Management

These five operational phases provide the risk management function with an action framework that facilitates close interaction between Internal Audit and Risk Management. The fact that each department mirrors some of the other's activities results in overlap, which requires coordination. Despite special perspectives and a different focus, it pays to identify as many commonalities as possible and to consider them in daily operations.

Coordination with the Risk Manager

Once risks have been identified, they have to be discussed with the relevant risk manager in a timely manner. In critical cases, an automatic information mechanism should be triggered. The risks are analyzed and assessed by the process owner with support from Risk Management. This assessment includes in particular the development of an appropriate risk control strategy, which has to be discussed with operational management. It is possible and desirable to establish substantial links to the recommendations made by Internal Audit.

Link to the Follow-Up

Risk control is closely linked to the follow-up (see Section B, Chapter 6) conducted by Internal Audit, because in addition to a risk review by Risk Management, this control phase simultaneously requires the results from Internal Audit's follow-up to be coordinated and updated. In addition, all relevant facts have to be communicated to Risk Management to be entered in the risk management tool. Maintaining this tool is the responsibility of Risk Management.

Joint Responsibility All risk management activities should always be conducted in close coordination with the people responsible in the operating unit. Generally, operational management is responsible for risk control. Internal Audit takes on a control function by checking the implementation of recommendations and thus the minimization of risks. The collaboration of all parties is an important element of a successful and standardized risk management process.

Shared Objective A critical factor is that Internal Audit and Risk Management understand that they can effectively function as compliance tools only if they act together. This requires joint efforts and a sensible degree of frankness with each other, in spite of the stringent need for confidentiality. This places particular demands on the managers in Risk Management and Internal Audit to create the necessary prerequisites to guarantee the flow of information.

HINTS AND TIPS

- If possible, auditors should take part in risk strategy meetings between Risk Management and employees with operating responsibility.
- Auditors should have read access to Risk Management's risk data base for their current audit. The status of the data has to be monitored continually together with Risk Management.
- Especially before a follow-up, auditors should obtain information from Risk Management about its assessment of the audit objects that the auditors want to work on.

LINKS AND REFERENCES

- INSTITUTE OF INTERNAL AUDITORS. 2001. *Practice Advisory 2010-1: Planning.* Altamonte Springs, FL: The Institute of Internal Auditors.
- INSTITUTE OF INTERNAL AUDITORS. 2003. *Practice Advisory 2110-1: Assessing the Adequacy of Risk Management Processes.* Altamonte Springs, FL: The Institute of Internal Auditors.
- INSTITUTE OF INTERNAL AUDITORS. 2003. *Practice Advisory 2110-2: Internal Auditor's Role in the Business Continuity Process.* Altamonte Springs, FL: The Institute of Internal Auditors.

2.3 Global Quality Management

KEY POINTS

- Companies must be able to rely on the quality of their products and services, because risks and defects can have a serious impact on their success.
- A risk-focused internal audit function therefore must ensure that product quality is monitored.

- When assessing the operational quality management system, it is useful to collaborate with company-internal testing bodies, because they normally have the required expertise.
- In this context, SOX has led to increased demands on a company's internal control system.

Introduction

Every company has to ensure that its customers are satisfied with the quality of goods and services it delivers. A consistently high level of quality cannot be achieved by merely engaging in final checks on the products supplied to customers and making corrections as necessary. Rather, a comprehensive quality management, which includes requirements for the internal processes (process standards) and for the functionality of the products (product standards) is necessary. Ultimately, this customers-focused view of quality should be an integral part of the management philosophy of every company. If customer satisfaction plays a central role, it stands to reason that quality management will be given similar priority. Most employees of the company have to be involved in quality management, an approach referred to as total quality management.

Need to Assess Quality Management

Quality management has two consequences for Internal Audit. First, Internal Audit itself has to be focused on quality and design its own internal processes accordingly. And second, quality defects on products or services can lead to considerable financial losses, which may even impact the company's going concern. Such losses must be avoided. Any internal audit department that claims to work with a risk focus cannot afford not to assess quality management.

Internal and External Quality Standards

The performance output in the company should meet both internally specified quality targets, and external quality standards. The most commonly used external standards are the ISO 9000 series. In addition, every company should adapt its quality management system to its specific needs and define its own internal quality targets independently of external standards.

Special Issues at SAP

When implementing a quality management system, software companies such as SAP have to allow for the fact that their products are intangible and quality measurement therefore poses particular challenges. Furthermore, the focus of this type of company is not on traditional production and supply processes, but on the relevant software product development processes. These include in particular:

- Project management (Are project targets being achieved?).
- Requirements management (What performance is expected of the product?).
- Configuration management (Which version is being shipped? How does it fit into the company's existing product portfolio? How can the product be maintained and updated if necessary?).

SAP's main development processes and certain support processes are regularly certified according to the ISO standard by external certification bodies. In addition, SAP uses Six Sigma methods (SAP Sigma) and has implemented a comprehensive internal quality management system to ensure that software quality is of a consistently high standard.

Documentation of the Quality Management System

Generally, quality management procedures should be documented in writing, (e.g., in a quality management manual). The documentation should properly structure the processes, define significant quality variables, and assign the relevant responsibilities clearly. When assigning responsibilities, a careful distinction should be made between "quality management" and "quality assurance," because each term covers different tasks. Quality management refers to all coordinated activities to manage and control an organization with regard to quality, but quality assurance represents operational measures aimed at meeting the quality requirements. Given the enormous importance of high-quality products and services for company success, Internal Audit should also involve itself with quality assurance.

Internal Audit and Quality Management

The following procedures are feasible for quality management audits, depending on the design of the quality management system in a company:

Independent Audit of Quality Management as a Whole

- When the entire quality management is audited, Internal Audit examines all elements of the quality management process. This includes the company's basic quality policy and concept, the processes, responsibilities, etc. Auditors do not always have the necessary knowledge to do this, because in software companies, this requires expertise in software architectures, development landscapes, as well as coding and configuration details. Without this knowledge, it is difficult for auditors to assess compliance with process and product standards. For this reason, the auditors should cooperate with quality experts and testers (see Section D, Chapter 10).

Cooperation with Internal Technical Testing Bodies

- To audit quality management, Internal Audit can also collaborate with technical testing bodies from within the company, if available. These bodies, known as quality control, should have the required independence (ideally such a department will report directly to executive management) so that any quality defects can be identified. The cooperation can be beneficial for both parties, because it perfectly complements Internal Audit's work from a more technical angle. Since both parties share an auditor's view and way of thinking, a coordinated procedure should be easy to achieve.

Cooperation with Quality Officers in Project Groups

- Another option for Internal Audit is to cooperate with quality officers on individual projects. Quality assurance in projects is not primarily a task of higher-level quality control but it is part of the responsibility of each employee. Many smaller project groups or departments are unlikely to have independent testing bodies. Instead, the role of quality officer is assigned to specific employees who have the necessary technical and process knowledge and social skills for this job. Cooperation between Internal Audit and these quality officers is important when specific major projects are investigated. When Internal Audit is requested to get involved, projects are often:
  - particularly prone to risk, or
  - problems have already been reported.

In both cases, the quality officers are among Internal Audit's main contacts.

Quality-Related Audit Documents

In its fieldwork, Internal Audit can primarily rely on documented information. Particularly, the following quality-related documents should be available and assessed:

- a quality manual, which documents in writing the entire quality management system as practiced by the company,
- individual quality plans, which document the quality management system for a specific product or project,
- requirement specifications (or quality criteria), which set out the requirements to be met,
- process and work instructions, which describe in detail the processes to be applied,
- practice-based guidelines, which include recommended implementations and best-practice solutions for clarification, and
- notes to provide evidence of the quality-related steps taken or the quality results achieved.

Impact of SOX

SOX also has an impact on the quality management system of a company (see Section D, Chapter 14). Under SOX 302, the management of the company must ensure that information of relevance to investors is made known fully and correctly. This requirement goes beyond the pure financial reporting criteria of SOX 404. The question is not so much whether the information is of a financial nature, but whether or not it is material to stakeholders. Stakeholders therefore must be informed of material defects in a company's quality management system. In addition, under SOX 302 executive management is personally responsible for certifying the effectiveness of internal controls. Company officers must confirm directly that they are also responsible for the internal controls in quality management and that the controls are effective.

HINTS AND TIPS

- Auditors should familiarize themselves with the company-internal documentation of the quality management process.

LINKS AND REFERENCES

- INSTITUTE OF INTERNAL AUDITORS. 2004. *Practice Advisory 1300-1: Quality Assurance and Improvement Program.* Altamonte Springs, FL: The Institute of Internal Auditors.
- INSTITUTE OF INTERNAL AUDITORS. 2004. *Practice Advisory 1320-1: Reporting on the Quality Program.* Altamonte Springs, FL: The Institute of Internal Auditors.
- INTERNATIONAL ORGANIZATION FOR STANDARDIZATION. 2005. *ISO 9000: Quality Management System.* http://www.iso.org/iso/en/ (accessed May 31, 2007).

2.4 Corporate Security Function

KEY POINTS

- Communication between Internal Audit and Corporate Security takes place according to a predetermined information flow for fraud prevention and investigation.
- Information can be exchanged between the two parties at departmental meetings and workshops.
- Information can also be transferred in the form of minutes of departmental events and monthly updates about matters relevant to corporate security.

Relations between Internal Audit and Corporate Security

In many cases, Corporate Security and Internal Audit cooperate on fraud prevention and specific fraud investigations. In addition, they communicate according to criteria defined in the information flow matrix (see Section D, Chapter 2.1). The cooperation between Internal Audit and Corporate Security may lead to improved working practices for both departments, because it allows information to be exchanged and improvements for future procedures to be proposed and evaluated.

Communication between Internal Audit and Corporate Security

SAP's internal audit department has access to the tools for reporting security-relevant incidents and fraud, which are developed and maintained by Corporate Security. This creates a permanent exchange of information between the two departments. Internal Audit's team in charge of fraud investigation and prevention is in direct contact with Corporate Security employees. Both groups cooperate closely during ongoing investigations especially regarding IT security and infrastructural security (e.g., facilities). In addition, Internal Audit provides information, which has a direct impact on the work performed by those responsible for corporate security and leads to improved security in the company. If required, the incidents reported in the reporting tool are discussed and necessary actions are taken. This may lead to an ad-hoc audit being conducted or information being referred to the compliance team, for instance.

Information Flow from Internal Audit to Corporate Security

To pass information from Internal Audit to Corporate Security, employees from Corporate Security can be invited to departmental meetings or events held by Internal Audit, for example the global department workshop, which takes place once a year at SAP. At these events, participants can discuss particular issues of cooperation, such as fraud allegations, protection of the company, internal data protection, etc.. Information can be transferred in one direction or exchanged between parties. This further builds the expertise of the employees in both departments. If Corporate Security is involved in audits conducted by Internal Audit, all audit-specific processes must of course be discussed, and the investigation of Corporate Security must also be coordinated with that of Internal Audit. Meetings have to be arranged to agree the details of the joint procedure and for preparation and post-audit activities.

Information Flow from Corporate Security to Internal Audit

Information can also flow from Corporate Security to Internal Audit. Corporate Security can invite Internal Audit employees to its departmental events and workshops, where aspects relevant to corporate security are discussed. As previously mentioned, these events can be used either to provide or to exchange information. Apart from these joint meetings, Corporate Security can also forward to Internal Audit a monthly status summary of security incidents that have occurred and have been processed, either informally by e-mail or formally at meetings of the heads of these departments. At personal meetings, the individual circumstances can be discussed in detail. In this case it is important to forward such information to the employees of Internal Audit. In addition, Corporate Security can forward to Internal Audit minutes of security committee meetings, which SAP holds regularly. If necessary, Internal Audit will ask for clarification of certain matters.

HINTS AND TIPS

- Auditors must always be aware that the information transferred is confidential.

2.5 Management and Supervisory Bodies

KEY POINTS

- Internal Audit has to rely on close cooperation with the company's management and supervisory bodies so that it can perform its audit services independently and objectively within the company.
- Different corporate laws in different countries shape the way in which Internal Audit cooperates with corporate management and supervisory bodies.
- In Germany, the Executive Board with the managing directors is normally responsible for Internal Audit and is therefore the main point of contact for all audit-related needs.

Country-Specific Cooperation Partners

Because of its prominent organizational position and its importance with regard to monitoring and control processes, Internal Audit has to cooperate closely with other control bodies in the company. German stock corporations have a two-tier board system with an Executive Board, comprised of the managing directors, and a Supervisory Board, comprised of shareholder representatives and employee representatives. While the Executive Board manages the company, the Supervisory Board oversees the Executive Board and nominates its members. Internal Audit cooperates with both bodies. In countries with a monistic management system (board system), e.g., the United States, management and supervision are performed by a single body or a combination of executive (inside) directors and non-executive (outside) directors. In this case, cooperation takes place with the Board of Directors, senior management and the Audit Committee.

Relations Between Internal Audit and Executive Board

Since in Germany, Internal Audit reports directly to the Executive Board, the Board is almost always the main point of contact for Internal Audit's operational needs. This includes primarily taking note of the annual audit plan, the discussion of additional audit requests and of Board summaries, and the provision of the resources that Internal Audit needs. Cooperation between Internal Audit and Executive Board means that Internal Audit has to establish itself as a tool of executive management. It is important that Internal Audit takes a proactive approach, because this is the only way in which it serves as a forward-looking management instrument. Examples of cooperation on corporate management tasks include participation in the risk management system or audit-related KPI systems, from which forward-looking statements can be derived. For example, an accumulation of audit findings or their particular nature helps operational management focus its work. Internal Audit must be able to respond flexibly to requests outside the annual audit plan, such as pre-investigations, ad-hoc audits, requests for comment, and support projects.

Duties of the Supervisory Board

Since SAP AG is a German corporation, GIAS is, however, also responsible for providing information to the Supervisory Board. The main duties of the Supervisory Board include the monitoring of executive management, also with regard to risk handling. The Supervisory Board also has to check whether executive management has implemented an adequate internal control system for this purpose, and whether it uses the system as intended and monitors its effectiveness and efficiency. Executive management's audit approach and the results it produces are important indicators for the Supervisory Board's monitoring tasks. If the Supervisory Board has established an Audit Committee, this body is mainly responsible for monitoring the company's financial reporting and the related internal controls and for budgeting and monitoring the external auditors. At SAP, the Audit Committee asks for regular reports on the work of Internal Audit (see Section B, Chapter 5.4.1).

Form of Organization in the United States

There is a different form of organization in the United States. All companies listed on the NYSE are required to have an internal audit function. This means that SAP has the duty to establish such a function. However, these tasks can also be assigned to third parties. There are no additional rules on how Internal Audit has to be integrated in the company organization. The recognized best practice is to segregate the reporting lines into administrative and functional branches. This means that the CAE commonly reports to the executive directors about day-to-day administrative needs and to the Audit Committee about functional issues.

Cooperation with the Board

Generally, the cooperation between Internal Audit and the Board is arranged differently in different companies. For example, companies can specify that the Audit Committee asks for regular reports on the work of Internal Audit, although this may sometimes lead to conflict between executive management and Internal Audit in its duty as a monitoring body.

HINTS AND TIPS

- Internal Audit should communicate regularly with the Board and the Audit Committee.
- For the benefit of stakeholders, auditors should include in their work information that the company has published externally.

LINKS AND REFERENCES

- BARRIER, M. 2002. Relating to the Audit Committee. *Internal Auditor* (April 2002): 29–30.
- INSTITUTE OF INTERNAL AUDITORS. 2001. *Practice Advisory 2060-1: Reporting to Board and Senior Management*. Altamonte Springs, FL: The Institute of Internal Auditors.
- INSTITUTE OF INTERNAL AUDITORS. 2002. *Practice Advisory 2060-2: Relationship with the Audit Committee*. Altamonte Springs, FL: The Institute of Internal Auditors.
- INSTITUTE OF INTERNAL AUDITORS. 2004. *Practice Advisory 1320-1: Reporting on the Quality Program*. Altamonte Springs, FL: The Institute of Internal Auditors.
- INSTITUTE OF INTERNAL AUDITORS. 2001. *Practice Advisory 2500-1: Monitoring Progress*. Altamonte Springs, FL: The Institute of Internal Auditors.
- INSTITUTE OF INTERNAL AUDITORS. 2001. *Practice Advisory 2600-1: Management's Acceptance of Risks*. Altamonte Springs, FL: The Institute of Internal Auditors.
- LEITHHEAD, B. 2000. In Touch with the Top. *Internal Auditor* (December 2000): 67–69.

2.6 External Auditors

KEY POINTS

- There is a certain amount of overlap between the tasks of Internal Audit and those of external auditors.
- However, there are also differences. For example, external auditors primarily focus on past events, but internal auditors also focus on forward-looking topics.
- Both parties have an interest in a functioning internal control system and are therefore natural cooperation partners.
- Apart from regular coordination meetings, additional arrangements between Internal Audit and the external auditors encourage good and trusting cooperation.

Introduction

Internal and external auditors should cooperate to ensure proper coverage and minimize duplication of effort. The tasks of Internal Audit and the external auditors overlap whenever Internal Audit deals with audits of the financial and accounting system and audits of the internal control and monitoring system on which the financial and accounting system is based.

Looking Back versus Looking Forward

However, aside from commonalities, there are significant differences between the two functions. The external auditors primarily conduct reviews as of a specific closing date and therefore tend to focus on the past when determining fieldwork activities. Internal Audit, on the other hand, also performs forward-looking work, always with the aim of improving business processes in the company as a whole.

Independence

Internal Audit at SAP is primarily instituted by executive management and remains an integral part of the company, even though it has a great extent of internal independence. Therefore, Internal Audit cannot achieve the same form of independence as external auditors appointed by the Supervisory Board.

Regulatory Cover

Another difference is the regulatory framework that represents the basis for the work of the external auditors and Internal Audit. In contrast to the increasingly stringent regulations on external company monitoring, e.g., as a result of SOX and the establishment of an oversight board for external auditors in the United States (PCAOB), there is a considerable amount of freedom for the organizational design of an internal audit function. Although the PCAOB clearly states that the absence of an internal audit function can be regarded as a significant deficiency in the internal control system, and legal requirements also stipulate the existence of an internal audit function, the actual design is undefined. This means that there must be an internal audit function in a company, but unlike the external audit function, it has greater freedom in terms of design.

Cooperation from the External Auditors' Perspective

Given the similarities between the fieldwork of Internal Audit and that of the external auditors, it seems sensible to avoid duplication, for example by using the audit results produced by Internal Audit for the audit of the financial statements and vice versa. It is important to ensure, however, that the external auditors ultimately have sole responsibility for the statutory audit of the financial statements. They cannot share this responsibility with Internal Audit and may not include current Internal Audit employees in their audit team. The findings of Internal Audit cannot replace the external auditors' own fieldwork activities. This applies in particular to those transactions considered material for the annual financial statements and to those requiring a greater degree of subjective assessment (e.g., the measurement of accrued liabilities). However, this does not mean that the external auditors should ignore the results of Internal Audit's work. They should rather take them into account in their own work, providing Internal Audit's technical qualification and (internal) independence are assured.

Internal Control System

Internal Audit is one of the core elements of a company's internal monitoring system, the effectiveness of which in turn determines the extent of fieldwork to be performed by the external auditors. As part of their audit planning, the external auditors have to test carefully to what extent they can rely on the existing internal control system when determining their fieldwork activities. If external auditors conclude that the system functions adequately, they can, within the framework of SOX, concentrate their fieldwork for example on material transactions. But if they conclude that the internal control system is too weak, they also have to focus on routine transactions in their fieldwork.

Access to Internal Audit's Reports

It is important for external auditors to have access to Internal Audit's reports, because they provide a good insight into the audit focus areas and procedures as well as the results achieved. If based on a longer-term period, they also show the degree of commitment with which the recommendations resulting from the audit findings have actually been implemented in the company.

Cooperation from Internal Audit's Perspective

Conversely, Internal Audit should, as far as permissible, be informed of all significant insights established by the external auditors. This information may influence the audit topics as well as the risk-based audit planning. Even though Internal

Audit employees cannot be integrated into the team of external auditors, they should be able to get access to the external auditors' work. Looking for a good co-operation with the external auditors with regular meetings and discussions may help improve external and internal auditors' efficiency and effectiveness.

Procedure at SAP

Also in view of increasing company complexity, both Internal Audit and the external auditors are currently facing particular challenges with regard to their roles as (joint) guarantors of an effective corporate governance system. It is therefore obvious that the two parties should coordinate their work to the extent permissible. SAP's internal audit department strives to make arrangements beyond the regular coordination meetings with the external auditors in order to guarantee a smooth exchange of information.

Information Supplier / Addressee	Internal Audit	External Auditors
Internal Audit		• Audit reports • Report summaries such as those for the Audit Committee
External Auditors	• Professional publications and pronouncements • If appropriate, ad-hoc reports on important findings	

Fig. 4 Information Flow Between Internal Audit and External Auditors

LINKS AND REFERENCES ↗

- AICPA. 1991. *SAS No. 65: The Auditor's Consideration of the Internal Audit Function in an Audit of Financial Statements.* New York, NY: AICPA.
- BRODY, R. G., S. GOLEN,. AND P. M. J. RECKERS. 1998. An Empirical Investigation of the Interface Between Internal and External Auditors. *Accounting and Business Research* (Summer 1998): 160–171.
- INSTITUTE OF INTERNAL AUDITORS. 2001. *Practice Advisory 2050-2: Acquisition of External Audit Services.* Altamonte Springs, FL: The Institute of Internal Auditors.
- INSTITUTE OF INTERNAL AUDITORS. 2001. *Practice Advisory 2440-2: Communication Outside the Organization.* Altamonte Springs, FL: The Institute of Internal Auditors.

2.7 External Institutions and Other Interested Parties

KEY POINTS •••

- There are numerous external partners who can support Internal Audit with technical collaboration, professional advice, and provide an external perspective.
- An active exchange with these cooperation partners keeps Internal Audit informed of the latest developments.
- The special aspects associated with Internal Audit's work (e.g., auditor acceptance and skills, treatment of sensitive issues and confidential data) impose limits on the extent of these types of cooperation.

Introduction

Internal Audit should seek cooperation with parties that could support it in providing its services. However, since the department has to compete for internal company resources, Internal Audit must demonstrate and document the benefits of these services, to get necessary funds approved. A number of institutions and service providers are eligible as external cooperation partners.

Significant Cooperation Partners

The following entities are among the significant external cooperation partners for Internal Audit. Possible aspects of cooperation are explained afterward:

- company-external providers of audit services,
- professional associations,
- education and science, and
- networks with other internal audit departments.

Cooperation with Audit Service Providers

Internal Audit's cooperation with external providers of audit services can take many different forms, ranging from equal exchanges of knowledge and experiences to outsourcing or co-sourcing of internal audit services.

Outsourcing Option

Certain provisions governing Internal Audit, such as listing requirements of the NYSE, merely stipulate that a company must have an internal audit function. It is therefore permissible, and in smaller companies even expedient, to outsource the internal audit function to a third party. Before an outsourcing decision is made, the benefits and costs of such a decision must be analyzed carefully. However, a pure cost-benefit analysis might not be sufficient as acceptance and skills issues and a lack of familiarity with corporate culture, etc. are factors that can derail an outsourcing attempt.

Hybrid Model

A hybrid model may be a good compromise, under which Internal Audit would in principle remain within the company, buying in external capacity at times of peak demand or when special expertise is needed. Internal Audit takes on a monitoring and coordinating role in such cases, while resources are added as needed. These additional resources can be external guest auditors or non-audit employees from elsewhere in the company (see Section D, Chapter 10).

Procedure at SAP

SAP has opted for the hybrid model. Internal Audit at SAP regards certain audit segments, such as revenue audits in sales and consulting business (see Section C, Chapter 3.5), as its core competency. These types of audits are always conducted by GIAS employees. For specific other topics, especially if special technical or legal expertise is required, it is sensible to involve experts. This enhances Internal Audit's acceptance among the auditees. GIAS has accordingly put suitable measures in place to implement this cooperation in daily auditing practice. For example, special non-disclosure agreements are concluded to ensure that sensitive data is handled correctly. In addition, financial control for the audit object gives the audit lead the necessary overview of the costs an audit has accumulated.

Benchmarking

Normally, Internal Audit should have sufficient confidence in its abilities to seek comparison with other audit departments. Comparison is a good way of drawing attention to its own strengths. Benchmarking also identifies Internal Audit's potential for improvement. The benchmarking process has to be uniform and objective. External consulting firms offering such comparisons are typically best suited to achieve this.

Cooperation with Professional Associations

Cooperation with professional associations such as the IIA has a number of benefits for Internal Audit. First, they normally offer their members a broad range of training options. In the United States, the AICPA also offers support to Internal Audit employees. Cooperation with these institutions is useful, for example to derive guidance from best practices. The IIA even offers the internationally recognized qualification of "Certified Internal Auditor." In addition, the associations present a forum for discussing practical issues of audit work with professional colleagues. The AICPA, for example, maintains its own program for auditors in industry with different audit-related focus topics.

Cooperation with Education and Science

Cooperation with education and science, such as university departments focused on auditing, is aimed at keeping Internal Audit's method-based approaches abreast of the latest developments. An external perspective should help auditors avoid getting professionally blinkered and make them receptive of innovation. At the same time, it enables Internal Audit to explain its importance and to share its knowledge with a wider audience, e.g. through publications or organized events. The exchange of knowledge with education institutions is also aimed at offering new talent the opportunity to supplement their academic education with practical experience. SAP offers students the opportunity to cooperate on specific audit projects for periods between three to six months. In addition, SAP regularly awards audit-related thesis topics to undergraduate and graduate students.

Networking

A rather informal exchange among internal audit departments of different companies at professional association level should be intensified by establishing a network. Especially for issues that concern a specific group of companies, for example global software companies listed on stock exchanges in two countries, such as SAP, it would be useful to focus on this type of cooperation. Practical topics, such as organizational structures, should be given priority in such networks. In any case a competitive situation between different internal audit departments should be avoided.

HINTS AND TIPS

- Professional associations are a good starting point when looking for suitable cooperation partners.
- If possible, Internal Audit should make use of existing partner programs within the company.

LINKS AND REFERENCES

- INSTITUTE OF INTERNAL AUDITORS. 2001. *Practice Advisory 2050-2: Acquisition of External Audit Services*. Altamonte Springs, FL: The Institute of Internal Auditors.

3 Annual Risk-Based Audit Planning

3.1 Inventory of Possible Audit Topics

3.1.1 Identification of Possible Audit Topics

KEY POINTS

- A large variety of sources may help identify possibly auditable topics.
- Internal sources include Internal Audit itself and other corporate departments as well as the Key Scopes defined by Internal Audit.
- Among the external sources for auditable topics are the external auditors, and other internal audit departments.

Theoretically Possible and Practically Feasible Audit Topics

At GIAS, the annual risk-based audit planning phase is divided into the following sub phases: creation of risk profiles for all possibly relevant audit topics, compilation of the audit inventory, and creation of the annual audit plan. However, the foundation of the actual planning phase is an ongoing, more or less formalized process of identifying possible audit topics. Generating audit topics is most prolific when focused on what are theoretically possible and at the same time practically feasible topics, i.e. topic and content must be plausible and have a relevant practical application. A large variety of sources may be tapped for identifying possible topics, e.g., Internal Audit itself, corporate functions, all members of management, and employees from different parts of the company.

Key Scopes

Audit topics can also be derived from the audit segments defined on the basis of Key Scopes. The Key Scopes provide a structured collection of topics and help to take into consideration operational needs such as core business processes. At the same time, Key Scopes establish a direct link between audit content and the physical audit. Possible audit topics may also arise from ad-hoc requests.

Audit Topics of Other Departments

Besides Internal Audit itself, other compliance-based departments may be a possible source of topics. Internal Audit's discussion of individual cases with, or general issues relating to, the risk management department, the legal department, the human resources department, or the compliance department may also lead to auditable topics.

External Sources

External sources can also supply additional data such as information provided by the external auditors, changes in laws or new legislation, or information derived from exchanging ideas with internal auditors from other companies. In addition, customers, partners, and vendors may also provide initial impulses for generating audit topics. It is important, however, to investigate such topics from an internal perspective since not all information from external sources may be relevant to the organization.

Annual Audit Planning Process

The identified possible audit topics are analyzed, structured, and assigned to recognizable entities. In this context, the term "entity" comprises all different organizational units (e.g., subsidiaries, departments) as well as all types of projects, initiatives etc. with clear structures with regard to responsibilities and accountability.

In the course of the annual audit planning, a risk profile is created for each entity, and the risk assessed entities are added to the GIAS audit inventory (see Section D, Chapter 3.1.2). The audit inventory in turn is the basis for the compilation of the annual audit plan (see Section D, Chapter 3.2) and the subsequent execution planning (see Section D, Chapter 3.3).

HINTS AND TIPS

- Auditors are encouraged to submit their own audit topic suggestions.

3.1.2 Risk Assessment and Audit Inventory

KEY POINTS

- The risk assessment of all auditable entities marks the start of the annual audit planning.
- For each auditable entity a risk profile is created taking in consideration all relevant SOX process groups and risk indicators.
- On the basis of the risk profile, an overall risk rating is produced for each entity and its relevant SOX process groups.
- The result of the risk assessment is an audit inventory which contains all auditable entities and their respective risk ratings.
- The risk assessments of all entities should be reviewed at least once during the year at the end of the second quarter.

Risk Profile

Every annual audit planning cycle starts with a risk assessment for all auditable entities identified. The term "entity" comprises all different organizational units with specific responsible persons, e.g. subsidiaries, departments, as well as all types of projects, initiatives, and other units. The basis of the risk rating methodology is the GIAS risk profile which is created for each auditable entity. The main objective for creating risk profiles is the identification of all significant risk indicators for each entity and their allocation to the entity's SOX process groups. Each risk profile is structured as a matrix with the vertical dimension containing all currently documented SOX process groups per entity and the horizontal dimension denoting the relevant risk indicators.

Risk Indicators

The risk indicators are grouped into main risk categories such as strategic risks, financial risks, compliance risks, operational risks, etc. as defined by the global risk management department. The focus is set primarily on the overall risk indicators facing SAP. Each risk indicator should describe a potential risk exposure and must be identifiable and measurable. Common indicators include the profit and loss situation, sales performance and forecasts, as well as change management measures.

Status descriptions or attributes must be defined for each indicator, denoting clearly whether or not these indicators apply. It is thereby possible to specify accurately the conditions under which the indicators do or do not impact the organization. For each process group of an entity, each relevant risk indicator is classified as either low impact (1), medium impact (2) or significant impact (3) indicating the existence of a specific risk. This approach allows GIAS to clearly determine the impact of each of the available fifteen indicators.

SOX Process Groups

The GIAS risk profiles also include the SOX process groups relevant for each auditable entity. All significant risk indicators are classified as described above and allocated to their respective SOX process groups.

Overall Risk Rating

On this basis, a calculation is performed that determines an overall risk rating (i.e. low, medium, high, or extremely high) on both the process group and the entity level. In the event that an auditor's personal judgement differs from the specific risk rating determined by the calculation, the risk level can be adjusted if an appropriate explanation for the change is given. The objective of the risk assessment is to develop a preliminary understanding of the potential risk exposures facing each entity based upon individual risk indicators and, if necessary, on auditors' judgement. The indicator-based approach to annual audit planning also allows GIAS to support its ratings for each auditable entity in detail.

Audit Inventory

All entities evaluated through the GIAS risk rating methodology are included in the GIAS audit inventory together with their respective risk rating. To obtain an independent risk assessment, GIAS provides the total inventory comprising all regional, global, IT, SOX, and revenue recognition assurance (RRA) entities to the global risk management department. Global Risk Management then performs its own risk assessment based on the general rating methodology low, medium, high and extremely high considering the main indicators such as financial risks, strategic risks etc.. Global Risk Management's rating is returned to GIAS, a weighted average of the results (25% Global Risk Management to 75% GIAS) is compiled, and the respective global, regional, IT, SOX, and revenue recognition assurance (RRA) inventories are finalized.

Iterative Planning

The compilation of the annual audit plan should be started with a preliminary comparison of the total auditable entities and the available headcount. Taking the GIAS timesheet as reference (and, in the future, the GIAS performance measurement results), the average auditing times for all entities with a risk rating of "extremely high", "high" and of some rated "medium" are added up and compared at an aggregate level with GIAS' available personnel capacity. The intention is to test the feasibility of the audits and, if necessary, prioritize the audits according to their risk assessment (iterative planning process). The outcome of this process is a risk-based ranking of auditable entities, which is regarded as the basis for compiling the annual audit plan.

Risk Assessment Review

One of the most important aspects of the risk-based audit planning approach is the ongoing review of the risk assessments during the fiscal year. This review should include the entire audit inventory in order to obtain a complete picture of the current risk exposure of all auditable entities. Ideally the re-assessment should be performed on a quarterly basis. However, since this might not be possible due to time constraints, a half year re-evaluation is mandatory. The re-assessment is performed as follows:

- The review should commence before the end of the second quarter.
- As previously mentioned, the entire content of the inventory should be subject to review.
- All re-assessments of risks should be performed only on the level of risk rating (either low, medium, high or extremely high) and should not be performed based on risk indicators.
- In case of a change in risk-level, the background and the reason for the adjustment must be documented. There is no need to adjust the corresponding risk profiles.
- Based upon the revised GIAS audit inventory, the annual audit plan and thus also the audit performance record is adjusted accordingly.

Ad-hoc Requests Besides being updated on the basis of the half-year re-assessment, the annual audit plan is also influenced by the continuous reconciliation of the risk exposures from ad-hoc requests with those from previously scheduled audits. From a risk perspective, determining the priority of ad-hoc requests versus previously scheduled audits is one of the biggest challenges facing audit management.

LINKS AND REFERENCES ↗

- BEASLEY, M, R. CLUNE, AND D. HERMANSON. 2005. ERM – A Status Report. *Internal Auditor* (February 2005): 67–72.
- GRAMLING, A. AND P. MYERS. 2006. Internal Auditing's Role in ERM. *Internal Auditor* (April 2006): 52–58.
- INSTITUTE OF INTERNAL AUDITORS. 2001. *Practice Advisory 2010-1: Planning.* Altamonte Springs, FL: The Institute of Internal Auditors.
- INSTITUTE OF INTERNAL AUDITORS. 2001. *Practice Advisory 2010-2: Linking the Audit Plan to Risk and Exposures.* Altamonte Springs, FL: The Institute of Internal Auditors.
- INSTITUTE OF INTERNAL AUDITORS. 2003. *Practice Advisory 2110-1: Assessing the Adequacy of Risk Management.* Altamonte Springs, FL: The Institute of Internal Auditors.
- MCNAMEE, D. 2004. Risk Reflections. *Internal Auditor* (October 2004): 75–79.
- ROTH, J. 2006. An Enterprise Risk Catalyst. *Internal Auditor* (February 2006): 81–87.
- SOBEL, P. 2006. Building on Section 404. *Internal Auditor* (April 2006): 38–44.
- WÜSTEMANN, J. 2004. Evaluation and Response to Risk in International Accounting and Audit Systems: Framework and German Experiences. *The Journal of Corporation Law* (2004): 449–466.

3.2 Annual Audit Plan

KEY POINTS •••

- The annual audit plan is determined by two factors: by including the firmly planned audit engagements and by adding new audit engagements resulting from the risk assessment.
- Including fixed audits limits the available audit capacity for the year and thus reduces the volume of additional engagements that can be included as a result of the risk assessment.
- Certain thresholds should be observed in this regard to avoid neglecting one of the scheduling options.
- After scheduling the fixed audits, the annual audit plan is filled with risk-based audit engagements transferred from the audit inventory.
- An overall plan is then compiled and coordinated, checking it especially against available net capacities.

Risk Assessment and Audit Inventory

The annual audit plan (see Section B, Chapter 2.2) is derived from the audit inventory based on the priorities identified by the risk assessment (see Section D, Chapter 3.1.2). Generally equal consideration should be given to fixed engagements which are already scheduled and newly added engagements resulting from the risk assessment. An audit performance record is used to capture a summary view of all planned audits. It is the basis for audit monitoring and control.

Structure of the Annual Audit Plan

The annual audit plan consists of three different sections:

- Part A: The projected annual audit plan based on the current personnel capacity of the department.
- Part B: All entities with high risk exposure that are not included in the annual plan due to personnel restrictions.
- Part C: Strategies to compensate missing headcount including a calculation of additional headcount needed.

Part A should contain all significant audit topics that cover risks from a corporate governance and compliance perspective. Therefore, part A of the annual audit plan is created according to the following procedure.

Fixed Audits

The firmly planned audits, which are included in the annual audit plan as fixed, can be categorized in several different types:

- **Special Audits** First, special audits (see Section A, Chapter 6.5) must have a firm place in the annual audit plan. In the context of revenue recognition assurance (see Section C, Chapter 9), customer contract confirmations and unannounced license audits are included in the annual audit plan as fixed audits. In addition, global audits and SOX audits are firmly scheduled engagements.
- **Ad-hoc Audits** Around 30% to 40% of the available net audit capacity in a year is reserved for ad-hoc audits on the basis of audit requests (see Section B, Chapter 2.3). This percentage should be reviewed (and adjusted if necessary) annually, taking historical requirements into account.

Follow-Ups

- Next, the follow-up audits (see Section B, Chapter 6) that fall into the planning period must be scheduled as fixed audits. The auditors must observe the deadlines within the follow-up cycle. Follow-up audits are due within specified periods following the basic audit. In addition, second follow-up audits are scheduled as fixed audits if the status of the first follow-up is red or according to auditor judgment when it is yellow (see Section B, Chapter 6.2.2; Section D, Chapter 7.2.3).

Audits Brought Forward from the Previous Year

- Another important item is audits postponed or carried over from the previous year. A risk assessment should be made to determine whether there is still a need to conduct these audits. If there is still a valid reason to conduct the audits, these topics are included in the current audit plan, in combination with other topics if appropriate.

Newly Scheduled Audits

In addition to the firmly planned audits, the annual audit plan should also include newly scheduled highest-priority topics identified in the risk assessment (see Section D, Chapter 3.1.2). Taking into account the fixed audits already entered as well as the planned capacity for ad-hoc audits, the net budgeted audit time for new risk-based topics can be calculated according to the following formula:

	Total available net audit time
–	Audit times already assigned to fixed items (global audits, SOX audits, revenue recognition assurance, and other fixed engagements)
–	Time reserved for ad-hoc audits
=	**Net capacity for new risk-based topics**

Fig. 5 Calculating the net audit capacity for new risk-based topics

Entry in the Annual Audit Plan

The annual audit plan includes time allocations as per timesheet for each audit engagement. This means that for each basic audit, status check, and follow-up, the currently applicable time factor is used. The planner can avoid overscheduling by comparing the already scheduled time to the available time during the planning process. As soon as the maximum available time is reached, the phase of risk-based inclusion of audit engagements in the annual audit plan is completed.

Credibility

The planner must be able to demonstrate that the plan has been compiled with an emphasis on optimization and that the selection of engagements is not a result of arbitrary decisions. This is of particular importance for Internal Audit's credibility, because it evidences objectivity and independence.

Parts B and C

The above planning process ensures that part A of the annual audit plan contains all significant audit engagements with regard to corporate governance and compliance. Part A is broken down according to GIAS' team structure. Part B follows the same structure showing all relevant audit engagements that cannot be covered due to restricted personnel capacity. If during the year additional engagements are needed to cover available capacity, the topics from section B should be considered for inclusion. Part C should give a clear picture of which audits are not covered due to capacity constraints and of the way potential risks could be treated. Alternative solutions could include reduced audit extent, combined audit engagements, and additional headcount if possible.

Final Consolidation

The draft of the annual audit plan is presented to the CEO, the CFO, and the head of the Audit Committee for their concurrence. After gathering their input, GIAS assesses their comments independently and finalizes the annual audit plan. The final version of the GIAS annual audit plan must be approved by the CAE. The parties mentioned before receive a copy of the final audit plan for their information. Then the respective GIAS regional teams commence with the execution planning.

HINTS AND TIPS

- Auditors should check whether the annual audit plan contains the required follow-up audits and audits carried forward from the previous year that relate to them.
- Auditors should make sure that their capacity is sufficient for the audits to which they have been assigned.

LINKS AND REFERENCES

- INSTITUTE OF INTERNAL AUDITORS. 2001. *Practice Advisory 2010-1: Planning.* Altamonte Springs, FL: The Institute of Internal Auditors.
- INSTITUTE OF INTERNAL AUDITORS. 2001. *Practice Advisory 2010-2: Linking the Audit Plan to Risk and Exposures.* Altamonte Springs, FL: The Institute of Internal Auditors.
- INSTITUTE OF INTERNAL AUDITORS. 2003. *Practice Advisory 2110-1: Assessing the Adequacy of Risk Management.* Altamonte Springs, FL: The Institute of Internal Auditors.

3.3 Execution Planning

KEY POINTS

- During execution planning, the topics of the annual audit plan are assigned to possible auditors and time slots.
- This process typically occurs in stages, because a number of personal, technical and time-related interactive effects must be taken into account.

- Once planning has been completed, the results are discussed with the team members.
- In addition, the head of the Audit Committee has to concur to the plan, and the CEO is informed.

Operational Planning

Once the annual audit plan has been approved, the respective Audit Managers are responsible for the execution planning. Separate planning steps must be taken for each regional team so that the different audit teams can be designated, following the procedure outlined below.

Fixed Topics

First, the timelines for those topics included in the plan as fixed items (see Section D, Chapter 3.2.1) should be specified in detail. Depending on whether the items in question are follow-ups or topics carried forward from the previous year, Internal Audit management has to make certain assumptions and set priorities, relating for example to urgency or period closing dates, etc. Team colleagues are then tentatively assigned to each topic, taking into account their responsibility, expertise, interests, etc.

Newly Scheduled Audits

Next, the new risk-based audit topics are arranged into a logical planning order, finding the right balance between risk assessments (see Section D, Chapter 3.2.2), the situation of the auditees, and availability of the auditors to be deployed. This is normally an iterative process, because often repeated coordination is necessary, using alternative planning scenarios. Now the previously rough estimates of the time requirements for each audit are worked out in detail, using the data from the timesheets. Simple estimations reveal the total time required for every item in the annual audit plan and allow the Audit Manager to reconcile this with the actually available working days.

Team Structure

In addition to identifying the audit team members, the team structure is determined, i.e., the positions of audit lead and auditor are assigned. The position of audit lead should be filled in a timely manner for each audit, because this person must perform certain activities before the start of the audit. Moreover, external audit team members and guest auditors (see Section D, Chapter 10) may have to be added to the schedule.

Buffer Times

When drawing up the plan, buffer times should also be included and distributed as evenly as possible. These buffers will allow the Audit Manager to accommodate additional requests for audits to be conducted during the year, in addition to those already scheduled. The same applies to meetings and workshops, for example. The Audit Manager should also enter planned vacation and training in the execution plan since they can have a considerable impact.

Overall Check

Lastly, the feasibility of the execution plan is checked. All planned audit and buffer times are added up and compared to the total net working time according to the timesheet. If the variance is 5% or less in either direction, the plan can be regarded as stable. This overall feasibility check is also referred to as final planning consolidation.

Starting Point for Audit Leads

On the basis of the parameters now available, the key data for each audit can be planned, including the precise audit period, the audit announcement, the reporting date, and the opening and closing meetings. The audit leads in charge can start their audit planning well in advance based on this data.

Shared Working Basis

Once the execution plan has been completed, the regional teams should discuss the results in detail. This allows auditors to identify and resolve any issues or errors at this early stage. The team members should voice their general agreement with the plan. Comments on team formation or unclear audit topics should be discussed. This process turns the plan into a shared working basis, which all involved parties can agree to.

Information to the CEO and Concurrence of the Audit Committee

Finally, at the end of operational planning, the CEO should be informed of the result, and the head of the Audit Committee should concur with the plan. This will signal the implementation of the annual audit plan and provide an opportunity to comment.

HINTS AND TIPS

- Auditors should make a note in good time of the relevant key data of the audits for which they have been scheduled.
- Auditors should seek involvement in the plan for topics that are relevant to them.

3.4 Interrelation of Global and Regional Planning

KEY POINTS

- Global and regional audits must be planned in close coordination with the various teams involved.
- Global audits should be planned first in order to determine the resources required and to facilitate the subsequent planning of regional audits.
- For this reason, global teams are put together and the audits coordinated in outline with those responsible at an early stage.

Need for Global Coordination

An important annual planning issue for global internal audit departments is the interrelation between regional and global audits. Since the audit plan is ultimately subject to central responsibility, regional plans have to be coordinated among each other with consideration given to the global audits.

Avoidance of Duplicated Planning

Especially in light of global audits, the contents and timelines of the audit plans of regional teams must be coordinated to avoid multiple scheduling of topics and double-booking of auditors. The optimal sequence for dealing with the topics and selecting the teams has to be examined. The time needed for global engagements must be included in the timesheet.

Time Sequence

Global audits must be planned ahead of regional audits, since global audit teams are normally composed of members of different regional teams. First, the global audit lead has to be nominated, since he or she has the right to influence the composition of the global audit team to a significant extent. Especially the overall execution of global audits takes longer than that of regional audits (for details, see Section C, Chapter 7). For this reason, it is recommended that the Audit Manager perform a first check of the execution planning once all the global audits are scheduled. If there is insufficient capacity to cover them, the Audit Manager will normally have to supplement them with external resources. In global audits, external support may be necessary to deal with complex topics as well as different legal systems and cultures.

Cooperation with the Board and Risk Management

In addition, global audits should be closely coordinated with the manager of the units to be audited and – in extraordinary circumstances – with the CEO. Often, matters concerning the company's strategy and mission can determine the success of an audit, because due to their nature, global audits are also requested by the Board. Global Risk Management should be involved so that, if necessary, they can provide feedback about the urgency of the audits in question and possible regional priorities.

Global Coordination Process

This requires the global planning process to be closely coordinated with the global planning organization and the regional teams. Any changes or subsequent adjustments have to be communicated to all parties involved, because they may have far-reaching consequences. This is the only way to maintain the stability of execution planning at a global level.

HINTS AND TIPS

- If possible, the execution plan should allow each auditor to take part in a global audit at least once a year.
- Auditors should regularly exchange their global audit experience with their colleagues.
- Auditors should also use global audits to build their networks.

4 IT Environment of Internal Audit

4.1 Structure of a Global IT Environment of Internal Audit

4.1.1 Decentralized Use of IT

KEY POINTS

- Work templates are provided on a central server for the operational level of the audit, allowing auditors to copy the documents they need for further processing.
- Standard commercial software, IT tools for data selection, and all SAP application systems, including their audit-specific components, are available for supporting audit work.
- From a formal perspective, IT use should be standardized in the form of internet-based audit software.

Integrated IT Solution

In order to institutionalize Internal Audit's methodical approach in a uniform manner, the utilization of IT has to be organized accordingly. The provision of an integrated IT solution for Internal Audit can require considerable effort and resources. It is no longer sufficient merely to provide the means to capture, process, and transfer data. IT technology is now required to deliver much more besides: IT is changing from a local application perspective to an overall global technical concept. Although the individual IT tools remain a significant component of the total IT landscape, they have to be integrated into a higher-level overall structure.

IT Support at the Operational Level

The operational level of the Audit Roadmap is the initial focus for IT support. Although auditors work locally, they have to be able to do so in a way that allows as much coordination and networking as possible among each other. The templates are stored and maintained centrally on a server, based on the phases of the Audit Roadmap. Auditors can copy the templates they need to their workstations for further processing. They can use standard IT programs or audit-specific programs. In addition to standard commercial software, GIAS auditors primarily use IT tools for data selection and all SAP application systems, including their audit-specific components (see Section B, Chapter 4.1.3.3).

Formally Standardized Use of IT

The formal aspects of IT use should be standardized. All defined work templates should be based on the same audit software system in order to simplify the exchange of work results and reports. For this reason, the templates have to be developed, maintained, and used in a standardized manner. The decision on which systems to use should be taken on the basis of their availability at all company locations, the degree to which they are known, and their flexibility and adaptability. The available functions should in all instances include word processing, spreadsheet, and graphics functions. For local storage, different storage systems, e.g. databases, can be used.

Content-Related Aspects of the IT Application

Apart from formal standardization, the content-related aspect of the IT application is also significant for the different phases of the Audit Roadmap. Special IT tools, e.g., for data selection, are available, in particular for audit execution. However, these IT tools do not cover the entire audit process, because they do not support networking beyond the relevant databases or internet-based applications. This restricts their data transport options and means that, although they are important for audit work, they do not meet the requirements of an integrated IT system for Internal Audit.

Requirements on a Comprehensive IT Solution

The applications currently available offer only limited access options and often provide only rudimentary support (if any) for the necessary cross functions. Phase-based quality assurance is an example of such a cross function. Workflows on the basis of local applications therefore are to be used to network the auditors and Audit Managers involved. It should also be possible to monitor the time, work progress, and, if relevant, the budgets and costs of audits on an integrated basis. There should also be an IT application that supports a centrally standardized documentation concept. The above presents a tangible starting base for a comprehensive IT solution for Internal Audit.

HINTS AND TIPS

- Before editing a document, auditors should always make sure that they are using the latest template version.
- Auditors should carefully select the IT tools for audit support and sensibly integrate them into the audit process.
- Confidential information should be stored in a separate protected area.

LINKS AND REFERENCES

- OLIPHANT, A. 2004. *Auditing IT Infrastructures.* Mission Viejo, CA: Pleier Corporation.

4.1.2 Central Filing Structure

KEY POINTS

- During the audit, the documents are stored in decentralized systems.
- Once the audit has been completed, they should be stored centrally according to the criteria of the general documentation concept.
- Arrangements must be made for compliance with security regulations. Exceptions with regard to access rights must be handled restrictively and documented accordingly.

Decentralized Storage

It is a matter for discussion whether Internal Audit should have a decentralized or a central document filing system. During the audit, the documents for processing are stored in individual decentralized systems. During this phase, auditors have to have the latest versions of their documents readily accessible at any time. In addition, a back-up copy should be saved to the central audit server at least twice a week. The back-up copies stored by the audit team members give the audit lead the opportunity to get an update of audit progress and of the most important results.

Central Storage

With this in mind, it may be useful to store centrally certain information or documents of more general interest during the audit. This allows all auditors involved in the audit to keep themselves informed about observations and findings and to update and supplement this data (e.g. through maintaining a central issue log file). However, this should apply only to information of interest to other auditors working on the audit. In general, only completed portions of the audit documentation should be made available centrally to all auditors concerned. For a certain period after the audit, however, auditors may still store the data locally. This may be useful in case of queries, subsequent amendments, etc. Ultimately, auditors have to take this decision based on their own judgement or in consultation with the audit lead.

Central Storage Structure

When stored centrally, the documents should be stored in a manner that allows them to be retrieved using different criteria. Step-by-step access along the audit database storage structure should therefore be possible in all circumstances: The audit keywords (e.g., audit number, audit type, report number, etc.) allow users to call the information at the relevant level on the central server. By specifying the parameters of an audit, e.g., the consecutive number or match code, i.e., with a parametric search key, the title, the auditor, or the period, it is possible to make the relevant documents available. Audit-related documents in this regard are the audit request, the audit announcements, the work program, and the various reports. However, the documents can also be structured according to the phases of the Audit Roadmap by assigning them to the relevant phase and classifying them by any further criteria at this level, e.g., fiscal year, audit parameters, or auditees. This may be very useful especially in the case of summaries per individual Roadmap phase (e.g. the percentage of completion of all working papers as of a certain cut-off date).

Other Documents

The central storage of audit documents must be coordinated with the way other documents are stored, e.g., external sources or source texts. Here relevant summaries will lead from the reports to the descriptive elements, e.g., the audit summaries, and vice versa. Keywords, keyword indices, or referencing may be useful in this regard.

Security Plan

A comprehensive security plan must be implemented for the central audit data server, covering issues such as:

- anti-virus protection,
- internet security,
- archiving,
- data protection, and
- access authorization.

Internal Audit and IT Security should agree on procedures to implement the above issues, which are also important from an IT control perspective. In particular, unauthorized access to centrally stored data of Internal Audit must not be possible. For this reason, access paths and the documents that can be accessed by each authorization group must be defined precisely. In exceptional circumstances and after consultation with the Board or the Audit Committee, it may be decided to make certain parts of the information on the central data server accessible to other parties. This must, however, remain the exception and any such authorization must be documented accordingly.

Data Archiving

The final archiving of the data and the physical removal of data that has been deleted logically, follows the requirements set out in the documentation concept. This is where appropriate parameters for the documentation medium, the retention periods (see Section D, Chapter 1) etc. must be defined.

HINTS AND TIPS

- Auditors should test access to the centrally stored audit documents in the creation of which they have been involved.
- The auditor responsible should inform the audit lead when central data storage has been completed.

4.1.3 Decentralized Reporting System

KEY POINTS

- The decentralized distribution of Internal Audit reports must meet the information requirements of all parties affected by the audits.
- All parties receive the reports as soon as possible and with the necessary level of confidentiality.
- A comprehensive administration system ensures that report distribution follows due process.

Central Storage as a Prerequisite

Central storage of the documents of Internal Audit is an important prerequisite for globally standardized data management. This ensures that complete and coordinated documents are available for every audit. Central storage and archiving forms the basis for report distribution that is fully scalable. The different target groups affected by an audit receive these reports on the basis of their responsibilities, with a guarantee that they receive them soon after the audit and that the information is complete.

Distribution Administration

The distribution of the reports has to be centrally administered in the IT audit system, and it must be guaranteed that the reports reach their recipients in the specified way and within the agreed time. This should be ensured by using checklists and completeness records. Generally, one or two Internal Audit representatives should be nominated for global report distribution, and the audit leads should forward their reports to them for distribution. To ensure that reports are always distributed properly, the entire distribution concept, including all authorizations and target groups, should be critically analyzed at least once a year.

Distribution According to Purpose

The reports must be made available to their target groups based on their role in the audit process. The parties directly affected by the audit receive the reports by e-mail under confidential cover. They include the operational managers of the audited unit and the senior managers in charge of the region or unit. The reports are distributed as report packages (see Section B, Chapter 5).

Distribution to the Board

At SAP, the Board receives the Board summary and the associated detailed reports through an intranet-based reporting and analysis system. Online access allows the Board members to get immediate and direct information about the audit results in question. All other report addressees receive their audit reports by encrypted e-mail or through access to an appropriate portal.

Prerequisites for Report Distribution

A number of prerequisites must be met before the reports of Internal Audit are distributed. Firstly, the reports must be complete, cover all report types, and contain all the information necessary for each audit. As soon these prerequisites are met, Internal Audit's central report administration is informed. A formal quality check is performed at this stage, and if any data is missing or incorrect, report distribution is stopped. This affects all reports distributed through an internet-based information system. The initial distribution of the reports, i.e., immediately after completion is the responsibility of the audit lead and the Audit Manager. Again, this is preceded by a formal quality check.

HINTS AND TIPS

- On the basis of spot inquiries, auditors should check whether the addressees have received the reports relevant to them.

4.1.4 IT Tools for Data Analysis

KEY POINTS

- The use of computer-assisted auditing techniques benefits auditors when analyzing large volumes of data, where manual processing would entail disproportionate effort and error risk.
- Auditors should therefore consider using software-assisted tools in order to attain audit objectives.
- Computer-assisted auditing techniques include general audit software, software for online audits, and special audit software.

Need for Computer-Assisted Auditing Methods

Auditors must collect relevant and meaningful evidence during audit execution. The findings and summaries must be supported by the relevant analyses and interpretations of the audit results. Today's information processing systems have to meet special requirements in this regard, because much of the documentary evidence exists electronically and can only be audited by using the relevant technical tools. IT landscapes that consist of different hardware and software systems and contain different data structures, formats, and functions make it virtually impossible for auditors to collate and analyze data without the use of a software tool. Moreover, the sheer volume of large stores of data exceeds the capacity of a manual audit. Computer-assisted auditing techniques reduce the effort and error risk associated with manual processing. The data quality of the information source used determines the reliability of the audit findings made in this regard. Computer-assisted auditing techniques include general audit software, software for online audits, and special audit software.

General Audit Software

Auditors need to know the exact capabilities of the audit software in order to use it efficiently. General audit software simplifies system access to data for analysis purposes and allows auditors to read information directly from different database systems, file systems, and data formats. It can also be used to facilitate mathematical calculations, statistical analysis, follow-up checks, access control, and calculation methods. General audit software supports the following functions:

- File access: The software allows users to read different formats and file structures.
- File organization: The software allows users to index, sort, mix, and combine files.
- Data selection: The software allows the use of general filters and selection criteria, including higher-level criteria, for example to describe the relationship with external sources.
- Statistical functions allow the use of sampling techniques, stratification, as well as frequency and trend analysis.
- Arithmetic functions allow users to calculate ratios.
- Search functions enable keyword searches.
- Automated processes help with document analysis.

Software for Online Audits

Another primary application of computer-assisted auditing techniques is the capability to conduct continuous online audits. This method allows auditors to test system reliability during normal operation. In this way, the operation and functioning can be monitored continuously and selected audit evidence can be extracted from the IT system.

Special Audit Software

The SAP AIS audit software is a system-supported IT tool for audits in the SAP environment (see Section B, Chapter 4.1.3.3). Its use can help improve the audit process and audit quality in the SAP environment. SAP AIS can be used in the areas of internal and external auditing, tax audits, and data protection. It provides a large number of individual roles, i.e., defined user profiles with a clear task portfolio, and offers a structured collection of preset SAP report programs. Its structure is based on the standards and requirements of internal and external audits. For this reason, the analyses and reports for a typical fieldwork activity, e.g., in a tax or financial statements audit, are presented with a meaningful structure and content, thus providing the data necessary for further fieldwork. The use of SAP AIS is expedient for the following fieldwork activities:

- online checks in the areas of process-related and financial reporting-related audits, and
- export of document data and account balances, e.g., to text files.

HINTS AND TIPS

- When compiling a work program, auditors should ascertain the possible uses of IT tools.
- During audit preparation, it is useful to conduct a test run to assess the IT tools.

4.2 Globally Integrated IT Solutions

4.2.1 Requirements on a Fully Integrated IT Solution

KEY POINTS

- The various functions that a fully integrated IT solution for Internal Audit needs to provide result in a number of technical and content-related requirements.
- A system that meets the requirements should incorporate the internal control management tool and SAP AIS.

Central Database

A number of core requirements can be derived from the functions that a fully integrated IT solution needs to have. As already discussed in Section D, Chapter 4.1.2, it must be possible to maintain the work templates and documents as well as the working papers and documentation data of all audits centrally and in a standardized way. This is of critical importance to provide a clear, uniform information base on the basis of standardized and up to date documents for all those involved in an audit. Accordingly, the documents have to conform to Internal Audit's statutes.

Online and Offline Processing

Another central requirement is that online and offline processing is possible simultaneously. Depending on the audit in question, audit teams may work either centrally or locally. For this reason, it must be guaranteed that both types of IT use are available and are linked to each other perfectly. Online processing should be used wherever possible.

Role Concept

Internal Audit's IT system authorization profile must be role-based. It is necessary to define user profiles clearly and unambiguously for Internal Audit and its different functions and management levels. Roles should also be defined for third parties (e. g., guest auditors) involved in audits. Authorizations or authorization groups must be assigned to these user profiles for certain system functions so that unique roles can be defined.

Integration and Networking

A high level of integration and networking with other users in the compliance area as well as all other business application systems will considerably enhance the data transfer options. Intelligent search and analysis functions can be built on this basis, which can use historical analysis and current results to identify trends and thus generate prioritized audit suggestions for the future and consequently support preventive audits.

Flexible Information Analysis

Another important aspect is the flexible analysis techniques for analyzing the information and data generated by Internal Audit. This applies as much to the treatment of findings and recommendations across different summarization levels, rankings, and links as it does to the generation of audit-process-based ratios.

Ratio Analysis

In addition, there may need to be a closer link between the reporting system and the results of ratio analysis. This can be achieved with absolute ratios, benchmarking concepts, or balanced scorecard systems (see Section D, Chapter 7). Detailed analysis must then be possible on the basis of the ratio as well as on the basis of the underlying findings, reports, and thus audits.

Information Databases

Audit experience and best practices of Internal Audit and of the auditees can be used to help resolve current issues by collecting them in separate databases and making them available through search functions, e.g., keyword searches. Internet-based networking with internal guidelines and process descriptions as well as external rules, regulations, and statutes provides a broad information base for Internal Audit.

Specific Audit Tool

An integrated audit tool that is tailored to the specific requirements of an internal audit department has to meet all the above criteria. SAP's AIS application and the internal control management tool described earlier (see Section B, Chapter 4.1.3.3) should be integrated at this juncture, with due consideration for the Audit Roadmap.

HINTS AND TIPS

- Internal Audit employees should discuss ideas for improving IT use.
- Routine evaluation of completed audits can contribute to the continuous improvement of the audit processes.

4.2.2 Concept for a System Structure of an Integrated IT Solution

KEY POINTS

- Integrated IT software for Internal Audit must offer a solution flexible enough to allow multiple audit teams to exchange data and collaborate through IT systems.
- In addition, flexibility of content and form has to permit individual use of the system, so that system control can be optimized for different types of audits.
- In this regard, the requirements of a defined auditor role have to be combined with the needs of system-optimized function control (control principles, predefinition, etc.).

Comprehensive IT Solution

The detailed concept of the Audit Roadmap defines a number of content-related criteria for a meaningful structure of a comprehensive IT solution for Internal Audit. However, this concept has to be specified in greater detail, especially with regard to application-related aspects such as predefined standard content, full search functions, automatic data replication, etc. The focus of the technical solution is what is known as the master database.

Master Database

The master database centrally stores the latest applicable versions of all documents, templates, guidelines, and work instructions along the Audit Roadmap. It forms the basis for the creation of audit-specific Roadmaps, a process that is triggered when a planning item is reached in the annual audit plan or when an approved ad-hoc audit request is set up. Both transactions generate an audit master record in the system, including all important information relevant to the audit, ranging from audit title and number, scheduling and responsible auditors through information about the auditees. On the system side, this master record in turn triggers the creation of a copy of the Audit Roadmap on the target server, intended for the audit lead. This is where the documents needed for the audit are stored. The extent of the documents filed here can be set with system parameters in the customizing. This ensures that the relevant documents are configured specifically for the relevant audit.

Audit Preparation and Execution

Once the audit lead has added further audit-related information to the data, he or she has to define work packages, assigning specific tasks to participating auditors, who receive them as individual work program items into their local databases through the workflow. At the same time, they are given access to all the necessary documents and templates. The auditors can now edit the audit steps in the system directly online, or offline without having to access the server.

Definition of Roles

For each phase of the audit, users can configure in detail, on the basis of their role definitions, a unique combination of possible functions. However, some standard settings are made at group level, e.g., per audit type. This also includes the customizing of interfaces, i.e. what data is transferred in which way to Internal Audit's software from neighboring systems. A distinction should be made in this regard between system parameter settings for integrated software and data transfers from third-party IT applications, because different plausibility checks have to be initiated there.

Quality Assurance

Once the auditors have completed their working papers, the finished documents are replicated on the audit lead's server, either one by one or in a single transaction. This also allows the audit lead to monitor the process continually. This is not only a check of each audit step, but also provides all the information necessary for a full and reliable audit status for each phase of the Audit Roadmap and continuously for the entire audit. The structure of the Audit Roadmap is therefore very important for quality assurance. As soon as a certain phase is reached, completeness checks are automatically performed according to the parameters set in the system. Then messages and process steps are generated for the approval levels and the appropriate logging and automatically forwarded to the relevant audit leads and Audit Managers. When all the feedback has been received, the system automatically triggers the start of the next audit phase.

Unplanned Activities

Another important aspect is the control of activities that arise during the audit. It must be possible, in terms of both content and capacity, for the audit lead and individual auditors responsible to schedule and perform expanded or alternative fieldwork activities for a work package. In such cases, work packages may be processed simultaneously, and this will require automatic IT support.

Flexibility

Even though the contents of the system are networked, there has to be flexibility and an appropriate degree of independence between the individual phases of an audit. It has to be possible to exchange working papers between work program items, reassign findings and recommendations that have already been allocated, and to map the results to any report format or even multiple formats. A change on one level will automatically reflect on the other levels, e.g., in the working papers, audit reports, etc.. This means that the assignments must not be static, although a link should always be created by means of referencing.

Updating of Ratios

The system should update ratios and costs automatically and break them down by relevant criteria. It should also guarantee that the latest information is available at any time to those responsible for control and monitoring purposes.

Graphic User Interface

The entire IT application should have a consistent graphical user interface, through which all functions are accessible with a mouse click. Only data should be entered alphanumerically, but even here references to key words and standard texts can be used. It should also be possible to simulate audits, which is usually only possible with a minimum of effort, if there is an easy-to-use interface.

HINTS AND TIPS

- Auditors should make suggestions on how IT auditing tools can or should be integrated into Internal Audit's IT landscape.
- Auditors should check the contents of the Audit Roadmap for ways in which they could be supported by IT.

4.2.3 Proposed Solutions in Terms of Corporate Governance and Compliance

KEY POINTS

- The audit universe combines in a standardized IT system all the foundations and implementation measures for meeting corporate governance requirements in general and compliance criteria in particular.
- In this regard, the following levels can be identified: General principles of Internal Audit, documentation, knowledge database, and Audit Roadmap.

- These levels can be combined into an application portal, which is an internet-based application and also allows access to other sources of audit-relevant data.

Compliance and Corporate Governance Tool

An IT solution for Internal Audit not only implements the Audit Roadmap, but can also make available the methods used by Internal Audit as a tool to meet compliance and corporate governance requirements. In a global audit universe (see Section A, Chapter 5.5), this results in an IT solution that transcends the pure process perspective. It includes the components described below.

General Principles of Internal Audit

The fundamentals of Internal Audit provide a solid basis for the resulting overall concept. The mission, the rules contained in the GIAS Code of Conduct, and the general audit mandate of the department provide the framework for all significant activities performed by Internal Audit to guarantee compliance in particular and corporate governance in general. Guidelines for compliance with SOX, COSO, COBIT® and numerous laws, acts and regulations should be included. All these guidelines should be stored in a database in text format and also as check tables in order to document the degree of their fulfillment. In this regard, there can also be system-based links between the check tables and the individual audit types, so that evidence can simultaneously be provided that the rules defined there have actually been implemented in the system. The ultimate objective is also to ensure that Internal Audit is compliant itself.

Documentation

The second logical level contains all the documents, guidelines, rules, and instructions that define and describe how the audit process per se is being implemented – including in its support function to ensure the compliance of other corporate units. Together with the principles of Internal Audit, this level forms the basis of the two primarily operational levels of a comprehensive audit universe.

Knowledge Database

The data storage level for all audit process results includes performance indicators, best practices, audit archives, and statistics. It also contains documents from external sources that have arisen during auditing. Taken in its entirety, this material provides a type of knowledge database: Portal access can turn this database into a valuable information source for every employee interested in Internal Audit.

Audit Roadmap

The actual operational level is primarily made up of the Audit Roadmap with all its documents and templates. This level is controlled according to the rules and processes defined in Section B. The other levels get data and information (including updates) mainly from this working level.

Application Portal

All the data stored and processes modeled are ultimately combined into an integrated interactive application portal. All the levels described above are addressed through this portal. In addition, it is possible to make the content accessible through the internet or to create a link to other audit-internal and external sources so that data and information from there can be integrated and utilized.

Combination of All Factors

The rules and system functions must, however, be supplemented in that every auditor and manager contributes their experience and know-how in their daily work to the best of their ability. Only the combination of these factors can ultimately guarantee that Internal Audit makes an optimal contribution to maintaining compliance and corporate governance.

HINTS AND TIPS

- Auditors should collect as many relevant pieces of external information or sources on internal audit as possible.
- Auditors should regularly review Internal Audit's documents to make sure they are complete and up to date.
- If possible, auditors should clearly show for all significant fieldwork activities how they are linked to compliance and corporate governance.

5 Quality Assurance for Internal Audit

5.1 Quality Assurance in General

KEY POINTS

- Quality assurance is important for every internal audit department so that it can provide the best possible services.
- Organizations such as the IIA or AICPA have integrated quality assurance into their standards and recommendations.
- The benefits of a quality assurance program include consistent application of processes across global, regional, and local audits, standardization and completeness of documentation, and reporting reliability.
- Continuous process improvement (CPI) is also part of the quality assurance program. It is one of the key requirements for Internal Audit to meet expectations successfully.

Objectives of Quality Assurance

How does a company ensure customer satisfaction? How does it ensure customer loyalty? How does any service department such as Internal Audit develop the reputation of a "trusted advisor" within the company? What ensures that added-value services are delivered to customers? The answer is a comprehensive quality assurance program. Quality assurance is of such importance for every company that organizations such as the IIA and AICPA have integrated quality assurance recommendations into their work in different ways, e.g., as an integral part of their standards or in the form of specialist internal working groups.

Approach of Internal Audit at SAP

Internal Audit at SAP has responded to these challenges and developed a comprehensive quality assurance program, which is documented in detail. The main purpose of this program is to provide clear procedures and thus ensure compliance within Internal Audit itself. As part of the quality assurance program, different so-called quality gates have been established for the Audit Roadmap. These quality gates define responsibilities and necessary activities in connection with feedback, reviews, and approval for the different process steps. They also ensure that Internal Audit's customers always get the best possible service. Internal Audit's quality assurance program therefore also includes a number of department-specific quality steps embedded in the process and organizational structure.

Benefits

One of the major benefits of having a quality assurance program is consistency in the application of the process model across global, regional, and local audits. A well designed quality assurance program increases the effectiveness of the supervisory function and enhances the reliability of Internal Audit reporting. It also ensures, among other things, standardization and completeness of documentation, completeness of fieldwork activities according to the work programs, adequate linkage of audit recommendations to working papers, and consistency in items presented in the implementation report, management summary, and Board summary.

New Challenges for Internal Audit

Due to its consistent quality assurance program, Internal Audit at SAP is able to face new challenges arising from the increasing demands by internal customers and external partners. Due to factors such as globalization and corporate scandals, the role of (internal and external) auditors has increased considerably in recent years from providers of pure audit services to internal consultants, trusted advisors, risk identification experts, fraud prevention or early detection champions, SOX experts, users of the latest information technology, and much more. Quality assurance helps auditors meet these new roles by improving their work through continuous process improvement (CPI). The quality assurance program that GIAS has implemented includes methods for the continuous updating and improvement of the steps in an iterative process model, i.e., the Audit Roadmap (for details on the Audit Roadmap, see Section B).

HINTS AND TIPS

- The quality assurance process requires the assignment of an owner or champion responsible for continuous monitoring and updates.
- The quality assurance champions should educate the other employees and involve them in their work in order to achieve the desired results.

LINKS AND REFERENCES

- AICPA. *AICPA General Standards.* http://gaqc.aicpa.org/Resources/Audits+Performed+Under+Government+Auditing+Standards/General+Standards (accessed May 31, 2007).
- BRINKLEY, M. 2006. Health Check for the Audit Brand. *Internal Auditor* (June 2006): 79–83.
- FABRIZIUS, M. AND R. SERAFINI. 2004. Initiating a Quality Assessment can help an Internal Audit Group come out on Top. *Internal Auditor* (February 2004): 38–43.
- INSTITUTE OF INTERNAL AUDITORS. 2004. *Practice Advisory 1300-1: Quality Assurance and Improvement Program.* Altamonte Springs, FL: The Institute of Internal Auditors.
- LIEBESMAN, S. 2005. Quality in the Mix. *Internal Auditor* (October 2005): 73–77.
- MARKS, N. 2005. Maintaining Control. *Internal Auditor* (February 2005): 36–38.
- WHITEPAPER. 2006. Quality review. *The CPA Journal* (March 2006): 12–20.

5.2 Definition of Terms

KEY POINTS

- A quality gate is a procedure in which a completed process step is assessed to establish whether it has been completed properly and whether the audit is ready for advancement to the next phase.

- In addition to the quality gates, the overall audit process has additional internal controls, which monitor the audit process continuously.
- All quality gates are also internal controls, but not all internal controls are necessarily quality gates.
- The quality assessment can be made by way of feedback, review, or approval, following the sequence of the controls.

Terms Used

To enhance the understanding of the structure of Internal Audit's quality assurance program at SAP, this chapter explains the terms normally used to describe the quality gates and quality assurance procedures.

Quality Gates

Quality gates are key components of quality assurance. In general, a quality gate is a procedure in which a responsible team member assesses whether a completed process step has been dealt with properly and whether the audit can proceed to the next phase. In other words, to go to the next phase or sub-phase of the Audit Roadmap, the previous phase must have successfully passed the quality gate. The actual audit execution, for example, can only start once the work program has been completed. The quality assessment of each process step is represented by feedback, review, and finally the approval of the party responsible.

Internal Controls

In addition to quality gates, the overall audit process has further internal controls, which monitor the process continuously. All quality gates are internal controls, but not all internal controls are quality gates, although both are used to achieve quality assurance. For example, the feedback, review and approval process related to the audit work program is both an internal control and a quality gate whereas an internal control that guarantees that the quality gates are passed through properly during the entire audit process would be considered an internal control but not a quality gate (see Section D, Chapter 5.4).

Feedback

The quality assessment can be made by way of feedback, review, or approval. Feedback means suggestions that should be considered for subsequent activities, although their application is not mandatory. For example, the quality gate for the annual audit plan includes receiving mandatory feedback from Global Risk Management and the regional GIAS team members. It also includes receiving optional feedback from the CEO or other groups. When preparing the annual audit plan, it is important to obtain, consider, and (if determined necessary by Internal Audit) incorporate feedback from such groups into the annual audit plan. This process is intended to minimize the risk of excluding relevant audit topics from audit planning.

Review

Review means ensuring that the audit object is complete (including the feedback) prior to submission for final approval. A review is more binding than feedback, because it directly addresses the review partner, who has to perform the set task. However, unlike a withheld approval, a negative review result cannot stop the process from moving forward. For a draft report, for example, Internal Audit employees will only be asked for feedback, but the auditees will have to perform a review of the draft, i.e., their opinion has to be obtained. The comments from the review should be incorporated into the report.

Approval Approval authorizes advancement to the next stage of the overall work process. Approval of the work program, for example, leads to the start of audit execution.

Sequence If all three steps are necessary, the normal sequence is for feedback to be obtained first, followed by the review, and approval is given last. Section D, Chapter 5.3 deals with testing compliance with quality gates and the relevant documentation.

HINTS AND TIPS

- The auditor must request feedback if it is mandatory, because failure to obtain feedback poses a risk to the compliance of the entire audit process.
- Important documents should not be submitted for approval without a review.

LINKS AND REFERENCES

- INSTITUTE OF INTERNAL AUDITORS. 2004. *Practice Advisory 1300-1: Quality Assurance and Improvement Program.* Altamonte Springs, FL: The Institute of Internal Auditors.

5.3 GIAS Quality Assurance Structure

KEY POINTS

- The GIAS quality assurance structure includes quality gates along the Audit Roadmap and departmental quality measures.
- For each phase of the Audit Roadmap, there may be mandatory or optional arrangements regarding feedback, review, or approval by other parties.
- GIAS' overall quality assurance program ensures a continuous improvement of the audit process.

Need for the GIAS Quality Assurance Program The quality assurance program developed by SAP's internal audit department comprises internal controls, quality gates for the Audit Roadmap, and other quality assurance activities. The quality assurance program defines the minimum standards of quality checks that all GIAS processes need to pass. The GIAS quality assurance program follows the structure shown in Fig. 6.

Audit Roadmap and Quality Gates Internal Audit has developed both Roadmap-specific and departmental quality measures. The five quality gates shown in Fig. 7 are intended for the phases of the Audit Roadmap. They are explained below. Each quality gate defines the parties involved and requires either an optional (O) or a mandatory (M) task for the feedback, review and approval of the different GIAS critical processes.

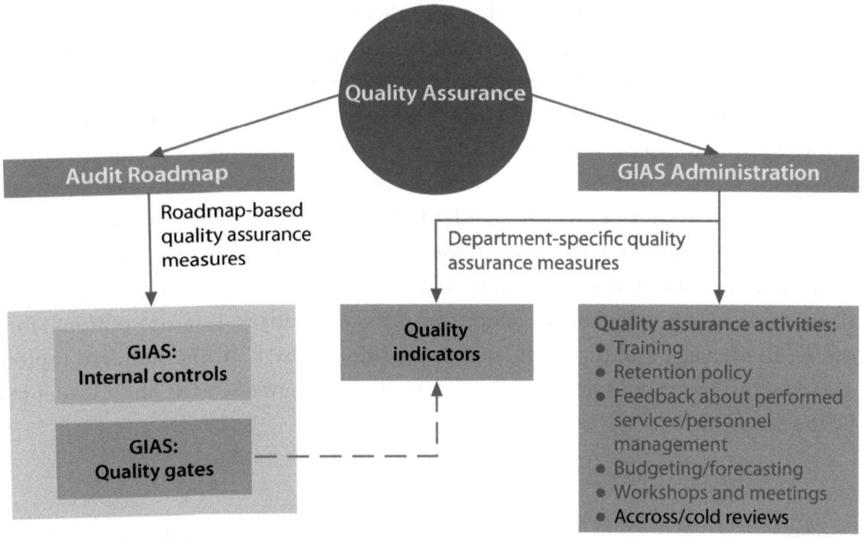

Fig. 6 GIAS Quality Assurance Structure

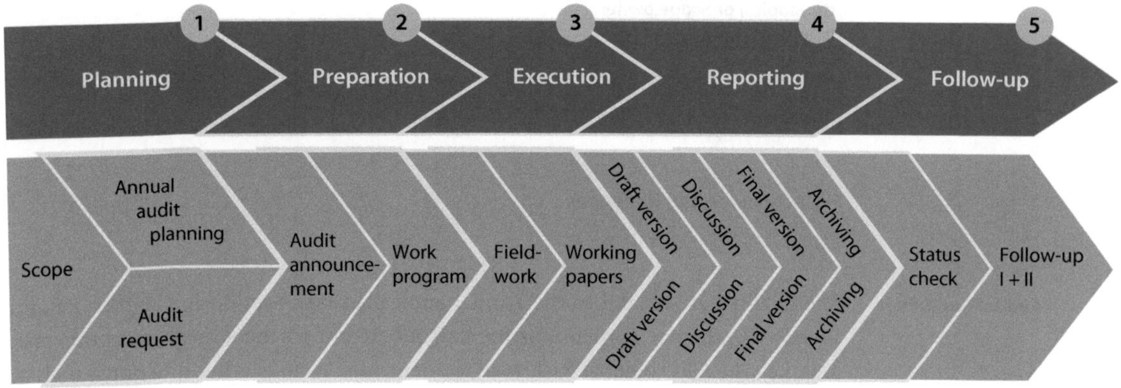

GIAS Quality Gates

		Global	Regional
1	Review and approval(1): Scope, annual audit planning, and audit request (if applicable)	X	
2	Review and approval(1): Audit announcement and work program	X	X
3	Review and approval(1): All mandatory working papers, before sending draft report to auditees		X
4	Release of the audit report (draft and final)	(X)	X
5	See quality gates 1 2 3 4 as additional quality assurance cycle		

(1) Physical signature if possible, otherwise by e-mail

Fig. 7 Audit Roadmap and Quality Gates

Scope

The quality gate for audit planning includes feedback, review, and approval regarding the Scope, annual audit plan and audit request (for more on planning, see Section B, Chapter 2). With regard to Scopes, there are two scenarios: One for regularly recurring audit topics, for which a Scope already exists, and one for non-recurring or new topics. The scenario for new or non-recurring topics relates to the minimum requirement of creating a Table of Key Scopes, but the scenario for standard topics relates to existing standard Scopes that have been assigned already, irrespective of audit type. For new or non-recurring topics, it is mandatory for the audit lead to review and for the Audit Manager to approve the Scope, but it is optional for the CAE to review the Scope and provide feedback. It is also optional for the Audit Manager and the audit team to provide feedback. In the standard topics scenario, the Scope does not necessarily have to be reviewed by the audit lead, but by the Scope owner.

Scopes	Feedback	Review	Approval
CAE	O	O	
Audit lead (new/non-recurring topics) or Scope owner (standard topics)		M	
Audit Manager	O		M
Audit team	O		

Fig. 8 Quality Gates for Scopes

Annual Audit Plan

The quality gate related to the annual audit plan (see Section B, Chapter 2.2 and Section D, Chapter 3) mentions the key interaction partners involved in this process, i.e., the CEO, Global Risk Management, and various other functions, such as regional finance officers and corporate departments, ensuring that all opinions are reflected in the annual audit plan. This quality gate defines that while the Board member responsible has to concur with the plan, he or she also has as an option to provide feedback. On the other hand, Global Risk Management and the GIAS regional teams are required to provide feedback. The review tasks must be performed by the GIAS planning champion, the GIAS regional teams and the CAE. Prior to the CEO's concurrence, the CAE must approve the final proposal of the annual audit plan. This quality gate ensures that at the end of the process, GIAS develops a very comprehensive audit plan.

Annual audit plan	Feedback	Review	Approval
CEO	O		
Global Risk Management	M		
Other finance officers and corporate departments	O		
CAE		M	M
Planning champion		M	
Regional GIAS teams	M	M	

Fig. 9 Quality Gates for the Annual Audit Plan

Audit Request

The quality gate related to audit requests indicates that when an audit request is received, the Audit Manager and the CAE must review the request. The employees of Internal Audit could also get involved by providing feedback. Once this quality assurance process is completed, the audit request must be presented to and discussed with the CEO, before GIAS can process it further.

Audit request	Feedback	Review	Approval
CEO		M	
CAE		M	
Audit Manager		M	
Audit team	O		

Fig. 10 Quality Gates for the Audit Request

Audit Announcement

The audit preparation phase of the Audit Roadmap includes the audit announcement and preparation of the work program (see Section B, Chapter 3.2). Both documents are mandatory for the audit process and have to be available to enter the next phase of the Audit Roadmap. Feedback on and review of the audit announcement prepared by the audit lead are optional for the audit team. For regional and local audits, the Audit Manager must approve the audit announcement, but in the case of global audits, the CAE is responsible for approving the audit announcement.

Audit announcement	Feedback	Review	Approval
Audit Manager (regional and local audits)			M
CAE (global audits)			M
Audit team	O	O	

Fig. 11 Quality Gates for the Audit Announcement

Refusal to Approve the Audit Announcement

The approval of an audit announcement may be refused for formal or content-related reasons. Formal reasons include incomplete information, incorrect timings, etc. Content reasons could be incorrect or ambiguous information on audit content. If approval is refused, the audit announcement is returned to the audit lead, who corrects the document within the specified timeframe.

Work Program

The quality gate related to the preparation of the work program gives the CAE and a GIAS employee not involved in the audit the option of reviewing the work program. Once the work program has been prepared, the audit lead must review it. In addition, the Audit Manager must approve the work program. Creation, review, and approval have to be documented in a dedicated folder, the work program folder. This includes entering in the file the date and the name or initials of the people who have created, reviewed, and approved the work program. During the audit, if a step of the work program is deemed not necessary, an explanation must be provided in the "comments" section, with the name of the auditor and date.

Work program	Feedback	Review	Approval
CAE		O	
Audit Manager			M
Audit lead		M	
Peer from GIAS		O	

Fig. 12 Quality Gates for the Work Program

Refusal to Approve the Work Program

Refusal to approve the work program may jeopardize the entire audit process. For this reason it is recommended that, in the case of comprehensive work programs, the preparer forward any completed sections for approval as early as possible. This may become particularly relevant for ad-hoc audits, for example, where the work program has to be compiled and approved immediately.

Audit Execution

The execution phase of the Audit Roadmap refers to the fieldwork activities and their documentation in the working papers (see Section B, Chapter 4.2). Working papers are evidence of the auditor's work and support the audit results that give rise to the recommendations. It is advisable not to leave quality assurance to the end, but to carry it out concurrently. This means that the audit lead should check the working papers regularly to make sure that they:

- clearly and adequately support audit results and recommendations,
- have been filled correctly,
- are complete in terms of type and extent,
- have been written clearly and carefully, and
- are properly cross-referenced.

Working Papers

The quality gate relating to the working papers indicates that the audit lead must review the working papers prior to sending the draft audit report to the Audit Manager. The Audit Manager can review the working papers and explicitly approve them. Evidence of the review and approval must be documented in the working papers with initials or name and date or by e-mail.

Working papers	Feedback	Review	Approval
Audit Manager			O
Audit lead		M	

Fig. 13 Quality Gates for the Working Papers

Reporting

Quality assurance is particularly important for reporting, since the ultimate objective of the reports is to document Internal Audit's work correctly in terms of content and form. The reporting phase of the Audit Roadmap (see Section B, Chapter 5) relates to the distribution of the draft audit report, obtaining feedback from the auditee, and releasing and archiving of the final audit report. Depending on the specific case and audit type, audit reporting will include as a minimum the Board and management summaries and the implementation report. The distribution of the audit survey (see Section D, Chapter 7.2.2) is another quality assurance measure. Since the auditees are best suited to assess Internal Audit's work after audit execution, the audit survey should be sent out after the execution phase, ideally together with the draft report.

Draft Report

It is the responsibility of the audit lead to ensure the accuracy, coherence, and completeness of findings and recommendations in the draft version of the audit report. The check must also ascertain whether sufficient audit evidence has been provided. This is why the quality gate related to the report's draft version indicates that it is mandatory for the audit lead to review the draft. The CAE has the option of approving this draft report and team members have the option of reviewing it. All obligations, including the audit lead's review and the Audit Manager's mandatory approval, must be completed prior to sending the draft to the auditees for review.

Auditee Review

When GIAS obtains from the auditees the reviewed draft implementation report, the "Action/Management Responses," "Responsible," and "Completion Date" columns must have been completed by the auditees. This is a critical step because discrepancies with GIAS' findings and recommendations need to be discussed, clarified and accepted during the reporting process. For this reason, open communication is very important if the auditors want to achieve the best possible result. In some cases, it is necessary to discuss openly the reason for and purpose of a finding. Sometimes, this discussion may establish that a finding is not a finding at all. Audit recommendations must be examined to ensure that they can be implemented. When the report is discussed internally, the person in charge can also work out targets for the follow-up and add them to the report. An arbitrating body should be available for controversial issues (for escalation see Section D, Chapter 6).

Draft Report	Feedback	Review	Approval
CAE			O
Audit Manager			M
Audit lead		M	
Audit team		O	
Auditees		M	

Fig. 14 Quality Gates for the Draft Report

Final Audit Report

The basis for the final audit report is the reviewed and approved draft report. In other words, the final audit report should have at a minimum all audit results, recommendations and management's commitment as per the draft report. The audit lead, together with the Audit Manager, is responsible for verifying the completeness, accuracy and clarity of the report content. The quality gate related to the final version of the audit report stresses the importance of the review, final approval for release, and approval for distribution processes. All tasks of these processes are mandatory for the identified key interaction partners. This is necessary because the final version of the audit report is the final product delivered to the auditees and to senior management. This quality gate also indicates that the reporting champions, i.e., the audit lead and the Audit Manager, must review the final version of the audit report for compliance with GIAS standards prior to final distribution and archiving. The same quality gate applies to the Board summary.

Final report	Review	Release approval	Distribution approval
Audit Manager	M	M	
Audit lead	M	M	M

Fig. 15 Quality Gates for the Final Report

Need for Additional Quality Gates

The quality assurance process is not only useful for conducting standard audits but also for special, and ad-hoc audits (see Section A, Chapter 6.5). Additional quality gates have been developed to guarantee a minimum quality standard for these services. All GIAS audits are ultimately based on the Audit Roadmap. Thus, quality assurance for non-standard audits is also determined to a large extent by the general quality assurance procedures of the Audit Roadmap. Additional quality gates are included in the audit process as needed. The assurance of revenue recognition is a good example. The concept developed to this end includes unannounced license audits and customer confirmations. For more information of quality assurance during revenue recognition audits see Section C, Chapter 9.

Departmental Quality Measures

In addition to the Roadmap-specific quality measures detailed above, Internal Audit at SAP also has departmental quality measures, which not only provide fieldwork support for Internal Audit employees, but also encourage continuous process improvement. To this end, GIAS has developed extensive documentation. Another reason for establishing departmental quality measures is to ensure that internal processes from areas such as human resources, communications, IT infrastructure, and administration are transparent and clearly defined. The following are examples of departmental quality measures:

- Human Resources:
  - job descriptions,
  - timesheets,
  - training,
  - performance feedback, and
  - professional development plans and career path at GIAS.
- Communication:
  - GIAS intranet pages,
  - GIAS reporting system,
  - GIAS Letter/annual report for the Audit Committee,
  - audit request form,
  - global workshops, and
  - audit survey.
- IT Infrastructure:
  - computer equipment,
  - use of the SAP-internal live system,
  - access authorization,

- audit tools,
- shared servers, and
- video conferencing/telecommunication equipment.

- Administration:
  - charter,
  - organization chart,
  - strategy,
  - mission,
  - objectives,
  - GIAS Principles,
  - planning system,
  - benchmarking initiative,
  - budgeting process,
  - cost center reporting, and
  - ratios and indicators.

Job Descriptions

The ultimate goal of departmental quality measures in the Human Resources area is to recruit, develop and retain auditors who possess the knowledge and skills needed to perform their individual tasks. GIAS has complete statements of job requirements for every position. This departmental quality measure ensures that, when searching for audit professionals, the effort is concentrated on recruiting personnel who meet specific job description requirements. Detailed job descriptions (see Section A, Chapter 4.5) with accurate role definitions ensure that GIAS auditors know exactly what their functions and responsibilities are and that they can execute their jobs successfully.

Training

In-house and external training, e.g., in accounting, fraud prevention, and technology, ensures that Internal Audit employees have the appropriate knowledge and technical skills to perform their tasks.

Professional Development Plan

The professional development plan includes specific development objectives, tailored to each GIAS team member, such as obtaining professional certifications, involvement in global audits, and specializing in key topics such as revenue recognition.

Timesheets and Career Development

Along with the professional development plan, the timesheet (see Section A, Chapter 4.7), and the professional career path (e.g., Internal Auditor, Senior Auditor, Global Auditor, Audit Manager, CAE; see Section A, Chapter 4.6) are in place to ensure the retention of all members of the GIAS team.

Communication

Departmental quality measures regarding communication are geared toward achieving the most effective way of exchanging information between Internal Audit and other interested internal and external parties. As much as possible, GIAS promotes direct communication. This is why, when needed, GIAS uses telephone and video conferencing. Communication among team members and with internal customers, Board members, and other departments ranges from telephone calls, e-mails, etc. through workshops and meetings (informal or formally requested). GIAS also has an intranet site which is a central repository and communication hub for all processes, policies, procedures, audit reports, news, and additional departmental documentation. The site also provides contact information and specific forms, e.g., the audit request.

Audit Survey

After completing an engagement, GIAS uses audit surveys to request from the auditees their feedback regarding the quality of the service performed by the employees of Internal Audit. This facilitates GIAS' continuous improvement process (see Section D, Chapter 7.2.2).

IT Infrastructure

Departmental quality measures related to IT infrastructure ensure that employees have access to modern hardware and telecommunication equipment, such as laptops, cellphones, and video conferencing technology. In addition, GIAS has established for team members specific user authorization profiles not only to restrict the access of unauthorized persons to sensitive data but also to gain access to financial and operational data and data analysis in the SAP-internal live system.

Administration

GIAS has developed very comprehensive and complete documentation as part of its departmental quality measures for administration. In this area, auditors find the charter, the mission statement and the objectives and principles that guide Internal Audit. There are also policies, procedures and templates that standardize the work of Internal Audit throughout the SAP Group. The departmental quality assurance systems also include:

- the planning system (e.g., audit inventory, risk assessment of GIAS and managers responsible, risk rating, annual audit plan, implementation plan),
- audit activities (e.g., methods to collect and capture evidence during the audit),
- benchmarking (e.g., an assessment system that facilitates comparison among auditees), and
- ratios and indicators (e.g., number of recommendations made, number of recommendations implemented, and cost savings resulting from implemented recommendations).

Up-To-Date Documentation

All the above departmental quality measures are live documents and processes that are constantly being reviewed and updated by GIAS to improve the service provided and to accommodate changing needs.

HINTS AND TIPS

- Since quality assurance measures take time, the person in charge should schedule a sufficient buffer to accommodate them.
- In order to provide maximum assurance, auditors should also make use of the optional steps of the quality assurance process.

5.4 Process and Documentation

KEY POINTS

- Evidence of compliance with quality gates must be gathered and archived in the working papers.
- A quality assurance monitoring sheet supports the work process.

Quality Assurance Monitoring Sheet

For a successful quality assurance process, it is essential that all quality gates are passed through in full. GIAS has developed the quality assurance monitoring sheet, a document that consists of two sections. The header section describes in detail basic data (e.g., audit title, number, team member responsible, start and end dates, closing meeting date, audit type, audit status, Scope). The monitoring section lists all the quality gates along the Audit Roadmap. There are also specific areas where review and approval are to be documented for each quality gate, stating by whom and the date. The document also compares the actual timelines to the plan. Based on these factors, the auditors, the Audit Manager or an external reviewer can determine if the audit process has passed each quality gate or not. If not, there is a field on the monitoring sheet to justify the reason for non-compliance with a quality gate.

Evidence Through the Working Papers

Although the quality assurance monitoring sheet supports the audit lead and the Audit Manager in performing their monitoring tasks, the evidence required for each quality gate to confirm feedback, review, and approval still needs to be provided in the form of working papers. These working papers are proof that the individual quality gates have been passed. For example, if for an audit announcement, approval by the CAE or the Audit Manager has been given by e-mail, and this e-mail has been archived in the working papers (as hard copy or electronically), it provides evidence that this process has in fact taken place.

HINTS AND TIPS

- Internal Audit should have electronic copies of as many documents as possible, since this will enable a smoother quality assurance process on a global level.

5.5 Quality Assurance Monitoring

KEY POINTS

- The IIA has developed two standards, one for internal (IIA Standard 1311) and one for external (IIA Standard 1312) assessments of quality assurance programs.
- Internal assessments of Internal Audit at SAP can be either announced or unannounced.

Assessment of the Quality Program

As a general rule, processes in a company should be monitored to determine if the rules are being complied with, whether the respective processes are achieving the expected results, and whether any adjustments are required. The IIA recommends assessing and reporting on Internal Audit's quality program.

IIA Standard 1311

According to IIA Standard 1311 internal assessments should cover in particular the following aspects:

- ongoing reviews of the performance of the Internal Audit activity as determined by quality gates, and
- periodic reviews performed through self-assessment or by other persons within the organization, e.g., with regard to SOX requirements, taking knowledge of internal auditing practices and the IIA's Standards into account.

Cold Review and Across Review

In response to IIA standard 1311, Internal Audit at SAP has created the "cold review," which is an unannounced cross-team quality review of compliance with quality gates for a randomly selected audit engagement. GIAS has also created the "across review" program, which also tests compliance with quality gates, but as opposed to the cold review the across review is announced.

Team Members Responsible

Both reviews are performed by Internal Audit employees (preferably from different regions). The independent team member for the across review is selected at the beginning of the audit and carries out the independent review on a continuous basis from the beginning to the end of the audit. In addition to the quality assurance performed by the Audit Manager, the across review is another form of control.

IIA Standard 1312

IIA Standard 1312 recommends that external assessments such as quality assurance reviews should be conducted at least once every five years by a qualified, independent reviewer or review team from outside the organization (for more information on peer reviews see Section D, Chapter 9). GIAS has committed itself to carry out 25% of its internal assessment work each year over a four year period to be prepared for the external assessment in the fifth year.

LINKS AND REFERENCES ↗

- DELOITTE. 2005. *Optimizing the Role of Internal Audit in the Sarbanes-Oxley Era*. www.deloitte.com/dtt/cda/doc/content/us_ERS_Internal%20Audit%20POV.pdf (accessed May 31, 2007).
- INSTITUTE OF INTERNAL AUDITORS. 2004. *Practice Advisory 1310-1: Quality Program Assessments*. Altamonte Springs, FL: The Institute of Internal Auditors.
- INSTITUTE OF INTERNAL AUDITORS. 2004. *Practice Advisory 1311-1: Internal Assessments*. Altamonte Springs, FL: The Institute of Internal Auditors.
- INSTITUTE OF INTERNAL AUDITORS. 2004. *Practice Advisory 1312-1: External Assessments*. Altamonte Springs, FL: The Institute of Internal Auditors.
- INSTITUTE OF INTERNAL AUDITORS. 2004. *Practice Advisory 1312-2: External Assessment – Self Assessment with Independent Validation*. Altamonte Springs, FL: The Institute of Internal Auditors.

- JOHNSTON, W. AND D. KIRCH. 1996. Benchmarking Peer Reviews. *Internal Auditor* (December 1996): 42–47.
- MCCABE, K. 2007. Continuous Improvement. *Internal Auditor* (February 2007): 83–87.

5.6 The GIAS Quality Assurance Program Compared to the Requirements of the IIA

KEY POINTS

- IIA Standard 1300 relates to quality assurance in an Internal Audit department.
- GIAS' quality assurance program conforms to IIA Standard 1300.

Minimum Quality Assurance Requirements

Internal Audit at SAP has developed comprehensive guidance for its quality assurance program, which supports the entire quality assurance process for the department. This chapter compares the SAP-internal quality standards to the requirements set out in the standards of the IIA. The IIA has established Standard 1300 "Quality Assurance and Improvement Program" as the minimum guidelines for quality assurance and improvement programs for an internal audit department. This standard assigns responsibility for the development and maintenance of a quality assurance and improvement program to the CAE. The quality assurance and improvement program should cover all aspects of Internal Audit activity and continuously monitor its effectiveness, particularly when it comes to adding value through recommendations for improving the organization's operations.

Comparison of GIAS and IIA Standards

The table below shows a comparison between the quality assurance program implemented by GIAS and Attribute Standard 1300 of the IIA.

GIAS	IIA 1300
Cold review and across review	Internal assessment
Peer review	External assessment Reporting of external assessment
Audit survey	Survey of audit customers
Quality gates along the Audit Roadmap	Audit working papers
Quality gates along the Audit Roadmap	Audit report
Departmental quality measures	Review by Internal Audit

Fig. 16 GIAS' Quality Assurance Program vis-à-vis IIA Standard 1300

The above table shows that the GIAS quality assurance program meets the requirements of the IIA (for information on peer reviews, see Section D, Chapter 9).

HINTS AND TIPS

- The IIA offers training on quality assurance.
- Auditors can broaden their horizon and collect valuable experience by voluntarily showing commitment to quality assurance.

LINKS AND REFERENCES

- INSTITUTE OF INTERNAL AUDITORS. 2004. *Practice Advisory 1300-1: Quality Assurance and Improvement Program.* Altamonte Springs, FL: The Institute of Internal Auditors.

6 Escalation Procedure

KEY POINTS

- Escalation processes may result from (1) a red traffic light status in the overall audit statement, (2) the fact that recommendations have not been implemented, or (3) from a disagreement about some of the audit findings or recommendations.
- During escalation, all responsible parties, including the Board, are informed directly.
- The overall audit statement for a basic audit is primarily intended to assess the quality of the findings, but the overall follow-up rating looks mainly at the effectiveness of the implementation process.
- If there is any disagreement, the audit team, the audit lead, and/or the Audit Manager should attempt to de-escalate the situation or reach a consensus with the auditee without varying the original audit finding.
- However, if the disagreement persists, a "management disagreed" classification is added to the audit report and the Board summary.

Audit Procedure

Internal Audit should ensure that the actual execution of audits is done in a manner that is agreeable to everyone involved. To ensure such agreement, audit results should never be used for anything other than the intended purpose, as required by the standards and codes of conduct of the international audit institutes. Relations between Internal Audit and auditees should always be based on a transparent and professional audit, rather than on possible consequences of an audit, because this could have a negative impact on long-term cooperation and trust.

Need for Escalation

Nevertheless, audit work may sometimes give rise to situations that require special notification of all those responsible, including the Board. This form of reporting exists outside the normal reporting system and depends on the particular situation. It is known as escalation, because it is used to make those responsible aware of problem situations in a clear and unmistakable manner. The objective is to identify problem focused solutions quickly and to implement them effectively. Escalation should not be interpreted as a penalty, but as a way of getting to the necessary solutions quickly and securely in order to ensure a smooth audit and to maintain the interests of the auditees and their organizations.

Escalation According to Classification

During the escalation process, the classification of audit findings into locally, regionally, or Board-relevant has to be observed in all instances. If audit findings classified as local are escalated, the auditors must decide whether such findings should be reported directly to the Board. The auditors should first attempt to resolve the matter with regional management, but if agreement cannot be reached, the auditors should change the classification and report the case to the Board. For significant audit findings, the classification is immediately set to "Board-relevant."

If a finding is serious and Board-relevant, the auditors can also inform the Board immediately through a priority Board issue (see Section B, Chapter 5.2.5), asking the Board to take a decision or to intervene.

Escalation Hierarchy

Escalation should always take the issue to the next higher level of the hierarchy, the audit lead escalating to the Audit Manager, who in turn escalates to the CAE, who ultimately informs the Board.

Scenarios for an Escalation Process

In general, Internal Audit distinguishes between three different scenarios that can trigger an escalation process:

- escalation due to an inadequate overall audit statement (red traffic light; see Section D, Chapter 7.2.1),
- escalation because recommendations have not been implemented (follow-up), and
- escalation because management does not agree with certain findings

If an audit is escalated, the sub-phases of the follow-up phase must be executed in a shorter time frame (see Section B, Chapter 6.1).

Escalation Stages

At GIAS, the escalation procedure for audits identifies two escalation stages. The chart below shows when escalation stages I or/and II are initiated. The actions that are performed during an escalation process are explained in more detail in the following.

	Status		Escalation Stage I	Escalation Stage II
Report Type	Overall Audit Statement/Scoring R	Management Disagreed	CEO Alert (from CAE office)	Escalation Process
Basic	X	Na	X	Na
	Na	X	X	Na
	X	X	X	X
Follow-up I	X	Na	X	X[a)]
	Na	X	X[1)]	X[2)]
	X	X	X	X
Follow-up II	X	Na	X	X
	Na	X	X[1)]	X[2)]
	X	X	X	X

a) In case where **Basic Audit** Overall Audit Statement/Scoring has a RED traffic light.
1) For new Findings
2) For Findings from Previous Audits
Na Not applicable
X Applicable

Fig. 17 Escalation Process

Criteria for Escalation Processes

The GIAS escalation procedure is characterized by a number of criteria:

- The CEO must be informed, either at a personal ad-hoc meeting with Internal Audit and/or with an e-mail sent by the Audit Manager or the CAE.
- The CEO will ask the management in charge to ensure an adequate sequence of actions regarding the unresolved items.
- If other Board responsibilities or business units are affected, the Board member in charge of the operational area must be involved in the discussion of the problem.
- The regional and/or local manager proposes an action list, including timelines, for eliminating the problems.
- During the follow-up phase, the auditees must provide clear evidence of the results and actions taken.
- Every quarter, GIAS prepares the GIAS escalation report and distributes it to the Board.

Red Overall Audit Statement Traffic Light

The following applies to the escalation scenarios related to the overall audit statement:

- The overall audit statement is always considered inadequate if the rating was "weak" or "substantial weakness" (see Section D, Chapter 7.2.1). Such a rating directly leads to a red traffic light status. Once the overall audit statement has been issued, the relevant sections of the management and Board summaries are updated.
- These reports are forwarded directly to the regional and local heads of the finance unit, regional and local risk management, and the corporate departments.
- These parties are then directly involved in the findings identified as R (relevant to regional/senior management) or B (Board relevant) by way of a joint implementation process and an immediate examination of the results by Internal Audit.

Follow-Up Scoring

The overall audit statement is a qualitative evaluation of the findings. The follow-up scoring (see Section D, Chapter 7.2.3) measures the implementation and effectiveness of the actions taken in response to an audit. In case of any new findings the assessment of the implementation of the recommendations and the new findings are be rated separately and then combined into a final rating. This means that in every audit cycle a quality history is created, i.e., a grading of substantive and formal quality, which provides a qualitative overview of the auditees and their management. For measuring the subsequent actions, it is therefore important to find out whether none or few problems have been resolved in response to an audit, i.e., if most of the recommendations are still open or in process. Escalation may follow if recommendations are not implemented, resulting in the following action:

- The auditors must enter "open" or "in process" in the "GIAS status" column of the implementation report (see Section B, Chapter 5.2.3).

- The status in the management and Board summaries is updated on the basis of the details given in the implementation report.

Different Opinions

The results of audit activities are continually communicated and discussed with the responsible managers. In exceptional cases, differences of opinion about audit findings may arise at the closing meeting or when the draft audit report is prepared. Ideally, management will voice a differing opinion during the audit or no later than the closing meeting. The audit lead is responsible for trying to reconcile differing opinions and to reach a consensus if possible. However, if no consensus is reached, escalation may ensue.

Acceptance of the Audit Finding

Two basic options can be pursued if the differences of opinion between Internal Audit and the management of the audited unit cannot be resolved. Management either accepts the audit finding under dispute, despite differing opinion, or it does not accept it. If management does accept it, it can explain its view in the "Management action/response" column of the draft audit report and document its differing opinion. The audit lead should make it clear that, although management's comments are noted, the relevant recommendations have to be implemented. This has to be documented in the working papers, preferably also in the "Management action/response" column. The follow-up will specifically look at the implementation of such audit findings. In such cases, it is normally possible to resolve differences by de-escalation.

Management Disagreed

If in spite of intensive exchanges of views and discussions of a finding or recommendation, Internal Audit and the auditees do not agree the audit lead should initially try to resolve the issue. Should such a resolution not be possible, the Audit Manager must be informed. If the problem persists, it is flagged by inserting "management disagreed" under Internal Audit status in the implementation report. This shows that Internal Audit and management have not reached agreement. In line with Internal Audit's cooperative approach, the auditor should, however, adopt a cautious and considerate attitude, because Internal Audit will be more successful if it can convince rather than enforce.

Dropping Audit Findings

The audit lead may only drop a finding if it can be convincingly refuted. For example, if compelling documents or evidence are submitted that were not included in the audit and now contradict Internal Audit's findings, the relevant findings in the audit report will either be reworded or omitted. This must be documented in the working papers.

Further Reasons for Escalation

In addition to the scenarios already mentioned, there may be other situations that trigger an escalation process:

- Management accepts the audit finding but not the recommendation.
- The management of an audited area agrees with the audit findings and recommendations, but regional management does not, or vice versa.

The auditors should try to resolve differences of opinion before distributing the final audit report.

Diagram The following diagram shows the escalation process at the time of reporting with and without consensus and acceptance.

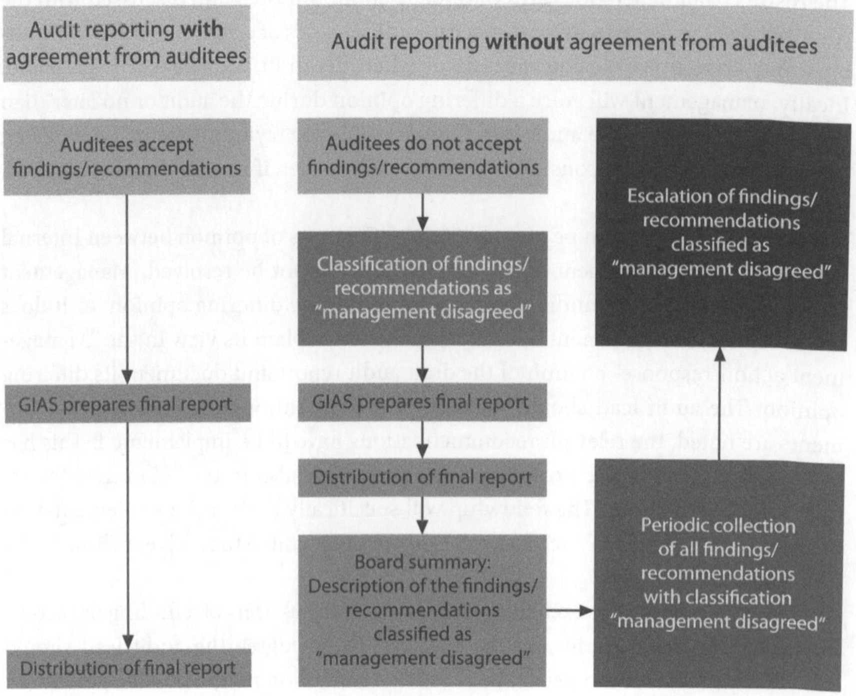

Fig. 18 Different Procedures with or without Agreement about Audit Findings and Recommendations

Escalation Unavoidable In spite of all the efforts outlined above, it is possible that escalation may be the only option left. This means that, in addition to the above steps, the following action will have to be taken:

- The persons responsible in Corporate Financial Reporting and Corporate Risk Management (and in other corporate departments if appropriate) assess and process the items under dispute.
- Internal Audit assesses the status of actions during the follow-up and changes the status to "done" if the cause of the finding has been eliminated.
- If the follow-up status shows that the disagreement persists, the issue must again be escalated to the Board and to the Audit Committee.
- After a follow-up, any problems unresolved due to lack of agreement should again be reported to the units mentioned above.

Escalation Unrelated to Findings and Recommendations

Some matters may be escalated irrespective of the audit findings and recommendations made, for example, if the auditees have identified inappropriate auditor behavior or defects have been found in the auditors' fieldwork. In this case, the auditees can escalate directly to the audit lead and/or Audit Manager. Moreover, the audit team's assessment in the audit survey (see Section D, Chapter 7.2.2) may trigger escalation. The Audit Manager and/or the CAE are responsible for determining the causes of escalation and for de-escalating the matter.

HINTS AND TIPS

- Auditors should be considerate of the approach taken by the auditees in the situation concerned.
- The communication of critical audit findings requires consideration and judgment to decide between immediate escalation and an attempt to convince management.
- Auditors should always offer their help in dealing with audit findings.

7 Performance Measurement System

7.1 Basic Principles of an Internal Audit Approach Based on Key Performance Indicators

7.1.1 Content, Objectives, and Structure

KEY POINTS

- Performance indicators and ratios serve a variety of different purposes in Internal Audit.
- The available data material is very complex and offers many different levels for comparison and analysis.
- Internal Audit can define comparisons in the form of benchmarking or a balanced scorecard.

Information Processing

An examination of Internal Audit from a modern corporate management perspective invariably requires consideration of different business concepts, e.g. benchmarking, to establish whether they can be used for Internal Audit. The analysis of past audits yields an almost limitless wealth of information, which can be used for targeted and focused control and monitoring with the help of benchmarking methods. The objective is to capture, process, and report information from the audit process in such a way that it produces a condensed yet meaningful and comprehensive summary of the audit services performed. The purpose is:

- to facilitate management's navigation through the report structures,
- to show the ranking and distribution of the underlying data and derive from it comparisons, trends, and forecasts regarding certain statistics,
- to allow a qualitative and quantitative assessment of audits, and
- to support external comparison.

Introduction of Key Performance Indicators and Ratios

For data analysis, it yields important insights to express the large amount of information in the form of ratios and key performance indicators (KPI). Internal Audit can use different sources, methods, and summary criteria to define the substance of each indicator in relation to the subject matter it describes. The indicators and ratios can be produced directly by counts and measurements based on organizational and process structures, or they can be calculated arithmetically. Each of them expresses proportions or mutual relationships, which permit conclusions about the underlying subject matter, thus providing firstly an indication of size in relation to other variables and secondly a measure of quality.

Objectives of a KPI System

The objectives of a KPI system in Internal Audit include the following in particular:

- Fieldwork generates a lot of different information, which is made more accessible by structuring it both in aggregated and in disaggregated form. Ratios and performance indicators provide insights about audit content (e.g., the number of high-risk findings relevant to financial reporting) as well as process-related statements (e.g., number of rejections/approvals per audit step and audit type at the quality gates). Moreover, important information is presented by overall indicators such as the overall audit statement and the audit survey rating (see Section D, Chapter 7.2.2). All indicators and ratios can be used to monitor and analyze audit results, thus forming the basis for additional audit planning.

- Indicators and ratios can also be determined as classification attributes, allowing the auditors in the context of audit findings or recommendations to calculate variables for accounts, customers, suppliers, and even contracts, either per audit object or as averages. This allows the auditor to obtain additional information about error causes and weaknesses in the organization of the auditees.
- Other indicators can be used to benchmark organizational units against each other, e.g., departments or local subsidiaries, comparing and ranking the number of audits, audit results, follow-up results, etc. This makes organizational units comparable in terms of organizational weaknesses.
- Another objective of indicators in this regard is to control and measure the performance of Internal Audit itself. These performance indicators can relate to the department, teams, or individual auditors and rate both their audit work and the results achieved.

Creation of a Systematic KPI Structure

These indicators, initially as absolute figures, provide first clues that permit statements about Internal Audit at a summary level. If read as individual variables, they can stand alongside other results of the audit. In a second step, the indicators can be integrated into a benchmarking system. Internal Audit benchmarking is primarily about organizing the variables in a sensible structure and grouping them in a way that they can be compared against other objects and periods (see Section D, Chapter 7.3). The balanced scorecard is an advanced way of using and controlling key performance indicators for business processes. It structures the indicators on operational levels, according to perspectives and critical areas of success, such as the financial and internal business perspectives (see Section D, Chapter 7.4).

HINTS AND TIPS

- All auditors should discuss ways of using different ratios and indicators with their colleagues.

LINKS AND REFERENCES

- KATHY, S. AND R. MCKAY. 2002. Balanced Scorecard. *The CPA Journal* (March 2002): 20–25.
- LEANDRI, S. 2001. Improving Financial Performance Through Benchmarking and Best Practices. *The CPA Journal* (January 2001): 44–48.
- REDING, K, C. BARBER, AND K. DIGIROLAMO. 2000. Benchmarking Against. *Internal Auditor* (August 2000): 41–46.

- SCHMIDT, C. 2005. The Driver's View. *Internal Auditor* (June 2005): 29–32.
- ZIEGENFUSS, D. 2000. Measuring Performance. *Internal Auditor* (February 2000): 36–40.

7.1.2 Structure of the Key Performance Indicators

7.1.2.1 General Criteria

KEY POINTS •••

- **In order to define and treat the large number of possible ratios and indicators in Internal Audit according to standard criteria, all indicators must be determined unambiguously and consistently.**
- **A distinction can be made particularly between content-related, organizational, and formal criteria.**
- **Moreover, value and time aspects as well as the intended target group must be considered.**
- **Indicators and ratios must be measured, recorded, and presented consistently.**

Content-Related and Organizational Aspects of Indicators

Key performance indicators and ratios in Internal Audit can be based on different aspects. If audit content is used as the guiding principle, indicators can be defined at different levels, ranging from individual findings and audit objects to the entire audit and the audited unit (e.g., the number of internal controls within a specific process). From an organizational point of view, the focus is more on the relationship with the audit organization, i.e., these types of indicators compare the audit or audit findings to other audit teams or the average performance of the entire internal audit department (e.g., average duration of an audit).

Value-Based and Time-Based Indicators

In addition, indicators can also be defined according to different value bases, because comparisons are based on budgeted and actual values, as well as on averages or external values, e.g., statistics issued by audit institutes or other companies. Closely related to this is the period perspective, under which all forms of possible time horizons, from pure closing date analysis through period analysis between reporting dates and year-to-year comparisons can be analyzed. Time intervals comprising seasonal variation, for example due to business cycles or restructuring processes, are particularly interesting. It is important to distinguish accurately between period and cumulative values, i.e., whether the data relates to one specific period or represents aggregate values for several individual periods.

Formal Aspects of Indicators

Furthermore, there are formal aspects that influence the selection of a suitable indicator by the auditor to establish which type of indicator to use, i.e., whether absolute or relative variables are best suited to describe the subject matter. On the basis of statistical considerations, indicators can be shown as individual values, distributions, time series, or in the form of correlations or trends. The form depends on the addressee's expectations. A KPI-based summary can present aggregated comparisons as well as a breakdown into underlying base information.

Key Performance Indicators for Different Target Groups

The target group Internal Audit wants to address is another criterion for tailoring the different indicators. For example, indicators intended for the Board level have to meet different requirements than indicators for operational management or the auditees. At the Board level, strategic information is more important, i.e., if a guideline has been breached, the Board will investigate whether the guideline serves its purpose and is appropriate for the company, whereas operational management will be interested in the cause of the contravention to be able to put adequate internal controls in place for the future. Selecting the right form of presentation can be vital in communicating effectively and in ensuring that any analysis is met with acceptance throughout the company.

Ways of Stating the Indicators

The units of measurement for stating the indicators must be clear and consistent. The way decimal points or large figures are shown (1,000,000, 1,000 thousand, 1 million), the treatment of rounding and the resulting differences, as well as units of measurement themselves have to conform to international standards or prevailing local customs. A written definition of form and content can considerably facilitate consistent application and a common interpretation of the indicators.

Measurement and Recording of Indicators

Indicators can be measured and recorded in different ways. In general, indicators are the result of counting, calculations, or correlations. The recording process can sometimes be automated or defined as an additional function of the operational or planning process. The time aspect is important, i.e., whether recording is continuous or the figure relates to a specific date. Internal Audit also has to ascertain to what extent the recorded base data has to be made comparable, i.e. standardized by adjusting it (e.g. discounting). This may be necessary for financial data with different interest due dates or maturities.

Consistent Guidelines for Presenting Indicators

It is important for companies to have consistent guidelines for presenting performance indicators. There has to be a company-wide standard as to how, where, and when specific indictors are used. This applies to both indicators and ratios at the operational report level and management summaries. Consistent rules help avoid misunderstandings about indicators.

HINTS AND TIPS

- Auditors should think of criteria that are to be mandated for all key performance indicators of the internal audit department and discuss them with their colleagues.

LINKS AND REFERENCES

- ETTER, A., AND P. TURNER. 2006. Collecting Performance Data. *Internal Auditor* (October 2006): 89–93.

- INSTITUTE OF INTERNAL AUDITORS. 2001. *Practice Advisory 1311-2: Establishing Measures (Qualitative Metrics and Qualitative Assessments) to Support Reviews of Internal Audit Activity Performance.* Altamonte Springs, FL: The Institute of Internal Auditors.

7.1.2.2 Selected General Standard Key Performance Indicators

KEY POINTS

- When designing a KPI system, Internal Audit must set priorities with regard to the target groups that will receive this information.
- Setting priorities is the basis for defining the indicators and the required base data.
- Indicator content must be defined according to purpose so that the indicators can be used appropriately.
- This ensures that the ratios and indicators create measurable added value for Internal Audit's work.

Selection of Specific Indicators

When creating a KPI system for Internal Audit, Internal Audit has to decide on a specific set of indicators. This pre-selection has to be made with the distinctions presented in Section D, Chapter 7.1.2.1. If possible, the person in charge should consider the interests of all involved parties, from the CAE, Audit Managers, and audit leads to audited units, their managers, and members of the Board equally.

Possible Indicators

A KPI system is regarded as a decision and argumentation tool and it therefore serves as a management instrument. General standard indicators and ratios and specific, more complex variables should be considered to be included in a KPI system for Internal Audit. This chapter defines general indicators and ratios; Section D, Chapter 7.2 deals with more specific performance indicators variables.

General Standard Indicators

The general broad standard indicators for an internal audit department include the following:

- number of auditors per department, audit team, and audit,
- number of auditors for every 1,000 employees, every 1 million euros of revenue, and every 1,000 euros of Internal Audit budget,
- Internal Audit cost structure ratios in each region,
- time percentages taken up by the phases of the Audit Roadmap and the correlations between them,
- number of different audit types compared to the total number of audits,
- proportion of global, regional, and local audits, and
- auditor capacity utilization as a proportion of net available working time.

All indicators should be either measured or calculated based on the audit process. Indicators can be created by bringing other indicators in relation to each other to enhance comparability, values can be combined in any way required, or additional different coordinates can be included in the calculation.

Presentation of General Indicators

The question of how to present indicators arises from the underlying requirements. First of all, indicators and ratios can be presented on the basis of a suitable structure, e.g., the Audit Roadmap. They can likewise be supplied as specific, detailed information in addition to the relevant findings and recommendations. Furthermore, it may be useful to tailor the presentation of indicators to the particular target group by preparing a special KPI summary. This means that, since indicators are derived variables, they should always be presented in relation to the underlying data as well as the relevant target group, e.g., a comparison of the numbers of SOX-related findings for each of the Board areas.

Significance of the General Indicators

Internal Audit management is responsible for ensuring that the indicators are complete and correct, both in terms of base data reliability, and their meaningful integration in the audit processes. Determining indicators is only one aspect, communicating them within the company is another equally important aspect. Taking both factors into account is the only way to achieve the objective of creating an understanding for the indicators and thus prepare the way for further applications, such as benchmarking and the balanced scorecard.

HINTS AND TIPS

- Auditors should arrange, in order of importance, the indicators they have identified as critical for an audit.
- Auditors should analyze the informative value of each indicator and suggest alternatives if appropriate.
- If an audit produces unusual results, a comparison of indicators may shed light on the irregularities and thus provide arguments to assure the findings.

7.2 Selected Special Key Performance Indicators

7.2.1 Overall Audit Statement

KEY POINTS

- The overall audit statement makes the audit results comparable. It can make one organizational unit measurable against another in the company.
- It can also be included in the company-wide risk model.
- An overview of the overall audit statements gives the Board a clear understanding of the organizational units audited in the company.
- The overall audit statement is based on the classifications of the audit findings in the audit report, to which end a classification has to be assigned to each audit finding.
- Audit observations are not rated.
- In order to standardize the classification process, the classification of audit findings is based on the risk categories adopted from global risk management.

- The overall audit statement is shown in five categories and is visualized with a traffic light system. The quantitative result is calculated in the first step, and the qualitative aspect added in the second.
- Any result in the substantial weakness category has to be escalated immediately.

Globally Consistent and Objective Opinion

The overall audit statement provides a universally consistent and objective opinion on the audit object for the auditees as well as for regional and senior management. It forms part of the audit report, making the audit results along the Audit Roadmap measurable and comparable. The assessments are consistent, because all audit teams have to apply the same assessment standard.

Ranking

An overview of overall audit statements helps the Board to develop a clear understanding of the qualitative process compliance of the organizational units audited in the company. The overall audit statement helps make an organizational unit comparable against another organizational unit in the company. This benchmark can be used to produce a ranking, which should comprise organizational units with similar contents and objectives. The overall audit statement can also be used in connection with the corporate risk model, especially when assessing the risks for the different audit topics during selection for the annual risk-based audit planning.

Compliance with Audit Standards

By establishing the overall audit statement, Internal Audit complies with IIA Standard 2410.A1, according to which final communication of engagement results should, where appropriate, contain the internal auditor's overall opinion and/or conclusions.

Classification of Audit Findings

The classification method is based on a logical calculation model, which ensures that a consistent procedure is followed. This avoids an individual assessment of the classifications according to regional team assessments and also creates a globally consistent procedure within Internal Audit. The overall audit statement is based on the classifications of the audit findings in the audit report, which are as follows:

- L = locally relevant,
- R = regionally relevant, and
- B = Board-relevant.

A classification must be assigned to each audit finding. Audit observations are also classified according to this system. Internal Audit distinguishes between audit findings and observations as follows:

- Audit finding:
  - verifiable facts supported by objective evidence, and
  - proven non-compliance with internal or external rules.
- Audit observation:
  - improvement potential identified in certain areas, and
  - no factual proof that indicates an audit finding.

Only audit findings are included in the calculation of the overall audit statement.

Description of the Classifications

The following diagram provides a description of the L, R, and B classifications. Of course, in some cases individual decisions on classifying an audit finding have to be made.

Classification	Finding	Example
B (= Board/CEO)	All findings that • directly refer to a guideline of the Board • relate to risks the Board should be aware of • require a decision by the Board • demand Board action • the CAE and Audit Managers consider relevant for the Board	• Breach of policies and guidelines • Management issues • Fraud • Significant US-GAAP/ revenue recognition issues • …
R (= Regional/ senior management)	All findings that • refer to a guideline of regional responsibility • relate to a risk regional management should be aware of • prompt regional management to make a decision or take action • are relevant for regional management according to the auditors and Audit Managers	• Breach of policies and guidelines • Change management • Shared Services • Significant US-GAAP/ revenue recognition issues • …
L (= Operational/ local management)	Any other finding	All other issues

Fig. 19 Classification

Risk Assessment of the Audit Findings

In order to standardize the classification process, the classification of audit findings is based on the risk categories adopted from Corporate Risk Management. The ten risk categories are:

1. Economy,
2. Market,
3. Strategy,
4. Personnel/employees,
5. Organization and control,
6. Communication and information,
7. Finance,
8. Products,
9. Projects, and
10. Other operational risks.

These risk categories are broken down into further levels, which simplifies the assignment of the content of audit findings.

Point System Rating

Each of the ten risk categories is rated per audit finding on a scale of 1 to 3 points:

- 1 – low impact,
- 2 – medium impact, and
- 3 – high impact.

Thus maximum of 30 points can be reached per audit finding. This produces the following classification:

- L: 1 to 10 points,
- R: 11 to 20 points, and
- B: 21 to 30 points.

Documenting the Calculation

The way the classification has been calculated has to be documented in a working paper (available as a standard template) and filed with the working papers of the audit.

Detailed Description of the Overall Audit Statement

The above calculation of the classification forms the basis for the overall audit statement, which is expressed in one of the following five categories:

- Exceeds standards: Adequate, efficient and effective internal controls are in place. No operational and/or accounting weaknesses and/or errors have been identified.
- Meets standards: Adequate, efficient and effective internal controls are in place. Only minimal weaknesses and/or errors have been identified.
- Needs improvement: Identified weaknesses and/or errors must be eliminated in order to minimize the risk of financial loss and improve operational effectiveness and efficiency.
- Weak: The weaknesses and/or errors identified pose risks to the company. There is a risk that fraud can be committed and remain undetected. Identified variances from existing guidelines cannot be accepted. The situation has to be escalated to management immediately and remedied quickly.
- Substantial weakness: The weaknesses and/or errors identified pose significant risks to the company. Fraud cannot be ruled out. The company is not protected from financial loss. The matter must immediately be escalated to management and the Board and corrective action must be taken immediately.

The five categories are visualized in the audit report with a traffic light system. The first two categories lead to a green traffic light status, the needs improvement category is shown as yellow. The last two categories trigger a red traffic light status.

Quantitative and Qualitative Assessment

The overall audit statement is determined quantitatively and qualitatively:

- Quantitative statement: The categories described above are rated according to the number of audit findings.
- Qualitative statement: Since a rating on the basis of the number of audit findings alone would distort the overall picture, a weighting according to the L, R, and B classifications is performed.

Viewed as a whole, this leads to the following matrix.

Quantitative		Qualitative			
Audit result	Audit statement	Audit result			Audit statement
Number of findings	Preliminary rating	Classification			Final rating
		B	R	L	
0	Exceeds standards	–		–	Exceeds standards
1 – 4	Meets standards	0 – 50% 51 – 80% 81 – 100% Fraud		–	Meets standards Needs improvement Weak Substantial weakness
5 – 14	Needs improvement	0 – 50% 51 – 100% Fraud		–	Needs improvement Weak Substantial weakness
15 – 24	Weak	0 – 100% Fraud		–	Weak Substantial weakness
25 or more	Substantial weakness	0 – 100%		–	Substantial weakness

Fig. 20 Rating System

Examples

The diagram below shows how the rating is calculated, using fictitious examples.

Example	Number of findings	L	R	B	% of R – B	
1	0	No findings				Exceeds Standards
2	4	4			0–50%	Meets Standards
3	4	1	2	1	51–80%	Needs improvement
4	12	4	5	3	51–100%	Weak
5	1	Employee defrauds around EUR 1 million from accounts payable.			–	Substantial Weakness

Fig. 21 Calculation Examples

Increasing the Extent of the Engagement

If the work program must be expanded during the audit due to new circumstances outside the area of responsibility of the management being audited, the audit lead must ensure that these circumstances are not included in the assessment of the original audit. For this reason, the new circumstances have to be reported and rated separately. This report can make direct reference to the original report or get a new report number.

Escalation in Case of Substantial Weakness

Any result in the substantial weakness category must be escalated (see Section D, Chapter 6) through the Audit Manager and, depending on the circumstances, the CAE directly to the Board. The time aspect takes on a special importance in this regard. The audit lead is responsible for completing and distributing the (draft and final versions of the) audit report as quickly as possible. Depending on the circumstances under audit, the CAE may have to submit a preliminary report to the Board immediately. The risk manager in charge is also informed. Completion of the "comments/reasons" field in the management summaries is mandatory. A detailed follow-up plan must be submitted to the Audit Manager and the CAE.

Deviation from the Calculated Rating

In isolated cases and after consultation with the Audit Manager, the audit lead can adapt an overall audit statement, depending on the circumstances and the documentation at hand. This means, that the calculated result can be varied if there are compelling reasons to do so. The reasons for the deviation have to be documented in the audit report, and a detailed motivation for the adaptation should be filed with the working papers.

Reporting

The overall audit statement is reported in the management summary using the traffic light system. The result is also incorporated into the Board summary. The findings and recommendations describe in an aggregated way the overall audit status. The development of the status in the course of the audit cycle with regard to the audit object is also important, because it gives the overall audit statement its dynamics for a comprehensive, continually updated history.

Alternative Model for Calculating the Overall Audit Statement

The overall audit statement also can be determined by calculating the financial impact of each finding. The calculation is based on the actual or estimated financial consequences and is adjusted by the probability of the occurrence. Depending on the auditor's ability to give a reliable estimation of the financial impact, two categories of findings can be defined: quantifiable and non-quantifiable (i.e., qualitative) findings. In case of non-quantifiable findings, an average theoretical financial impact is calculated based on the size of the audited entity. The overall audit statement (red, yellow, or green traffic light) is the sum of the financial impact of each finding. The materiality and thresholds for the traffic lights are determined once a year by using the financial figures (e.g. yearly revenue, assets) of the different entities. The feasibility of this new model for calculating the overall audit statement is currently being evaluated by GIAS during a six month pilot phase. If the new calculation model proofs to be feasible in practice, it will eventually replace the old model.

HINTS AND TIPS

- As soon as auditors notice that the overall audit statement will probably produce a red traffic light status in the audit report, they should inform the Audit Manager.

LINKS AND REFERENCES

- INSTITUTE OF INTERNAL AUDITORS. 2001. *Practice Advisory 2410-1: Communication Criteria.* Altamonte Springs, FL: The Institute of Internal Auditors.

7.2.2 Audit Survey

KEY POINTS

- After every engagement, Internal Audit sends an audit assessment questionnaire (audit survey) to the audited or supported unit.
- There are two different templates available: one for standard audit engagements and one for ad-hoc audit engagements.
- The audit survey has three sections. The middle section, which is the main part, consists of ten questions about the audit. The questionnaire for ad hoc audits consists of nine questions.
- The audit survey helps determine Internal Audit's value for the company and facilitates the assessment of its work.
- Asking for feedback increases the department's credibility.
- The audit lead and Audit Manager are responsible for obtaining feedback.

Purpose of the Audit Survey

After every engagement, Internal Audit sends an audit assessment questionnaire to the audited or supported unit. This document is used to rate the technical and administrative performance of the audit team. The audit survey helps Internal Audit management understand how the audit team's work and results have been received. This allows drawing inferences about the performance of the audit lead and each individual auditor. This feedback helps Internal Audit managers with performance appraisals and allows them to coordinate training measures for individual auditors if weaknesses have been identified. If the survey has flagged any problems, Internal Audit management can remedy the situation and identify improvement potential for future audits. The audit survey also measures the quality of audit work and is therefore suitable for setting departmental performance targets.

Value Argument

There are several reasons for introducing an audit survey: First, part of Internal Audit's mission is to add value by developing management-focused solutions. The audit survey has been introduced to measure the benefits delivered by Internal

Audit and to give managers the opportunity to assess audit performance in a structured and standardized way. It provides an opportunity to measure Internal Audit's standing within the company. A performance indicator is derived on this basis and can be used for internal presentations. It also helps respond to question about the value that Internal Audit adds in the company. Internal Audit's value cannot always be measured in full, because its activities are too varied, but the audit survey can help give the auditees an easy-to-use way of assessing the audit work.

Compliance with the Quality Program

IIA Practice Advisory 1310-1 (Quality Program Assessments) recommends implementing a method to demonstrate and measure the value and benefit that Internal Audit generates for the company. SAP has responded to this recommendation by introducing the audit survey.

Credibility

The audit survey shows Internal Audit's commitment to having its performance assessed outside of the department. In principle, Internal Audit has to fulfill its audit mandate irrespective of the auditee's level of satisfaction and produce objective, accurate and meaningful audit results. It is nevertheless a question of corporate culture to what extent the auditee's opinion is being considered. Internal Audit should be open to constructive criticism as an opportunity to identify potential improvements. The audit survey demonstrates the department's willingness to accept and process feedback and to respond appropriately. Internal Audit also demonstrates the company that it welcomes input and is prepared to accept and implement recommendations within its own department.

Structure of the Audit Survey

The audit survey consists of three sections. The header contains administrative data for the audit. The middle section has ten (or nine for ad-hoc audits) questions, which are answered by checking one of the following six ratings:

- strongly agree,
- agree,
- neither agree nor disagree,
- disagree,
- strongly disagree, or
- not applicable.

In a third section, there is room to add comments on specific questions or responses. The bottom section is for the audit team to add any comments or remarks as free text. The completed audit survey is sent to the Audit Manager electronically and then forwarded to the CAE.

Alerting to the Audit Survey

The opening and closing meetings are good occasions for making auditees aware of the audit survey. It is enough to refer to the survey briefly at the opening meeting, but the auditors should present and explain the questionnaire at the closing meeting. The auditors can, of course, also present and explain the audit survey in e-mails or discussions during the preparation phase.

Distribution of the Questionnaires

The questionnaires should be sent out at the same time as the draft report, because the audited unit will have had recent exposure to Internal Audit's work, and its responses will reflect the entire audit execution. The distribution of the survey is a quality gate for Internal Audit and must be documented. Internal Audit offers the opportunity to hold a separate meeting with the audited unit to discuss the draft

Audit Survey

Recently GIAS has conducted an internal audit within your unit/area of responsibility. This survey is part of GIAS' continuous improvement process. We would be very grateful if you could support our efforts by completing this survey and returning it to the audit lead or Audit Manager.

Audit No. and Title as per Audit Announcement:		Executive Responsible:	
Audit Lead:		Survey filled out by:	
Audit Manager:		Survey filled out on:	
Date of Audit:			

#	Question	Strongly agree	Agree	Neither agree nor disagree	Disagree	Strongly disagree	n/a	Comments (if any)
1	Contact with GIAS ahead of the audit helped to prepare well for the audit.							
2	The announcement was received in a timely manner and was understandable.							
3	The audit timeline, objectives, content, and procedures were well explained at the opening meeting.							
4	I was able to address any issues and concerns to the audit team.							
5	The audit was performed in a fair, co-operative and constructive manner.							
6	I was continuously informed and involved during the audit.							
7	Audit results were clearly and understandably communicated during the closing meeting.							
8	In the audit report, the results were presented in a clear, concise, and objective manner.							
9	Audit management was responsive and provided adequate oversight and support.							
10	Overall, the audit added value to my operations.							

Other comments and suggestions (what was best about the audit, what wasn't so good?)

Thank you for your feedback!

Input by Audit Lead/Audit Team:

Fig. 22 Audit Survey for Standard Audit Engagements

audit report in detail. This meeting provides another opportunity to ask the auditees to complete the audit survey, particularly since it is sometimes difficult to get the completed questionnaire back within the Audit Roadmap timeframe. The latest time for sending out the questionnaires is when the final audit report is distributed.

Responsibility of the Audit Lead

The audit lead decides whether the questionnaire is sent to several people or just one person. Sending the questionnaire to several people may be necessary for regional and global audits, for example. The audit lead is also responsible for making auditees aware of the audit survey, sending out the questionnaires, and asking for the completed questionnaires to be returned. The audit lead is responsible for making the auditees aware of the fact that the audit survey is not anonymous, but that the results will be treated confidentially. The audit lead and the Audit Manager should agree who the addressee of the survey should be and send the questionnaire to the appropriate person (e.g., the local finance officer in the case of a local subsidiary). The audit lead can normally add comments to the audit survey, e.g., if the opinion voiced requires the audit lead to state his or her point of view or if additional facts have to be presented.

Information Value of the Audit Survey

The audit survey helps the Audit Manager improve audit quality continuously. At the same time, it can also document good performance and thus motivate the audit team and the whole department. To prevent the rating of individual auditors, the questions in the survey focus on audit execution, not on the performance of individuals.

Results of the Audit Survey

The results of the audit surveys can be compiled monthly, but no less frequently than quarterly. Results can be broken down by region and/or audit level. The CAE consolidates and analyzes the results. They are rated on a scale of 10 (best) to 1 (worst) and communicated to Internal Audit management, the CEO, and the Audit Committee.

LINKS AND REFERENCES ↗

- INSTITUTE OF INTERNAL AUDITORS. 2004. *Practice Advisory 1310-1: Quality Program Assessments.* Altamonte Springs, FL: The Institute of Internal Auditors.

7.2.3 Follow-Up Rating

KEY POINTS •••

- The follow-up assesses the extent to which the measures recommended as a result of the preceding audit have been implemented.
- Each audit finding is rated according to a set scale.
- New findings during a follow-up are rated as well.
- The overall follow-up rating is reported in the management and Board summaries as a traffic light status.

Follow-Up Scoring

The follow-up audit assesses the extent to which the measures agreed during the preceding audit have been implemented. It thus evaluates the effectiveness of the implementation process resulting in the follow-up scoring. The status is reported using a traffic-light system (red, yellow, green). Each audit finding is rated according to a set scale. The points system in the diagram below forms the basis for the follow-up scoring.

Status / Classification	Open	In process	Done/Reasonably controlled
Board	Red/ 12 points	Red/ 6 points	Green/ 0 points
Regional	Red/ 6 points	Yellow/ 3 points	Green/ 0 points
Local	Yellow/ 3 points	Yellow/ 1 point	Green/ 0 points

→ New findings of the follow-up are not included
→ Report rated (red, yellow, green) on the basis of the points total

Fig. 23 Points Matrix for the Follow-Up Scoring

Example for the Implementation Rating

The following examples illustrate the scoring process:
- A finding that was classified as Board-relevant at the preceding audit, but has not yet been implemented at the time of the follow-up audit is rated twelve points.
- A finding that was classified as relevant to regional management at the preceding audit and that is still in process is rated three points.
- A finding that was classified as locally relevant at the preceding audit and has been fully implemented is rated zero points.

The aggregated scoring, is classified as follows:
- Green status: 0 to 11 points.
- Yellow status: 12 to 23 points.
- Red status: 24 or more points.

New Findings Rating and Overall Follow-up Rating

New findings made in the course of the follow-up are rated separately using the rating system for the overall audit statement (see Section D, Chapter 7.2.1). Finally, the follow-up scoring (for the implementation) and the follow-up new findings rating are combined into an overall follow-up rating (see Fig. 24).

Reporting

The overall follow-up rating is reported in the management and Board summaries as a traffic light status. If the status is red, a brief explanation has to be added to both documents. The Board summary contains a table, which shows a points summary for each status. In the audit report, the points are added up and automatically transferred to the management and Board summaries. The results of the overall

Overall Follow-up Rating

FU Scoring \ FU New Findings Rating	Exceeds Standard (green)	Meets Standard (green)	Needs Improvement (yellow)	Weak (red)	Substantial Weakness (red)
Green	Green	Green	Yellow	Red	Red
Yellow	Yellow	Yellow	Yellow	Red	Red
Red	Red	Red	Red	Red	Red

Fig. 24 Rating Matrix for the Overall Follow-Up Rating

follow-up rating depend on the degree of implementation and the quantity and quality of the new findings. If a follow-up I audit results in a red traffic light status, a second follow-up audit must be performed. If the traffic light status is yellow, the audit lead and Audit Manager decide whether a second follow-up is necessary. If a follow-up II audit is conducted, the rating is performed in the same way as for the follow-up I audit. If the second follow-up produces another red traffic light status, the conditions for "heightened escalation" are met, which leads to the CEO's or Board's intervention (for more information on escalation see Section D, Chapter 6).

HINTS AND TIPS

- The status of each audit finding has to be kept up to date meticulously so that the overall follow-up rating can be reliably calculated.
- The overall follow-up rating in the audit report must always agree with that stated in the Board summary. Auditors should therefore align the two documents.

LINKS AND REFERENCES

- INSTITUTE OF INTERNAL AUDITORS. 2001. *Practice Advisory 2410-1: Communication Criteria*. Altamonte Springs, FL: The Institute of Internal Auditors.

- INSTITUTE OF INTERNAL AUDITORS. 2001. *Practice Advisory 2500-1: Monitoring Progress.* Altamonte Springs, FL: The Institute of Internal Auditors.
- INSTITUTE OF INTERNAL AUDITORS. 2001. *Practice Advisory 2500.A1-1: Follow-up Process.* Altamonte Springs, FL: The Institute of Internal Auditors.
- LAROSA, S. 2005. ERM-based Audit Reports. *Internal Auditor* (December 2005): 73–75.
- MCCUAIG, B. 2006. ABCs of Reporting on Controls. *Internal Auditor* (October 2006): 35–39.

7.3 Benchmarking Structure

KEY POINTS •••

- Benchmarking is a systematic comparison of key performance indicators and ratios with corresponding values from other periods or sources.
- For benchmarking, the indicators need to be structured with the target group in mind.
- Benchmark comparisons must be standardized and performed, maintained, and quality assured by a benchmarking champion.
- Variances are treated according to different strategies.
- The results are normally prepared specifically for management.

KPIs and Benchmarking

A benchmarking concept is the starting point for enhancing the meaningfulness of simple key performance indicators and ratios. This means that indicators are compared to benchmarks and presented in alternative ways, i.e., in multicolored diagrams or tables. For an overview, all the indicators should be grouped by content. Depending on the target group different perspectives must be considered. This may result in different indicator rankings. From Internal Audit's perspective, the following structure is recommended:

- Indicators relating to the internal audit department and its organization should be considered first.
- They are followed by the ratios and indicators that analyze Internal Audit's service portfolio, i.e., the various audit-related and non-audit-related services.
- Then, indicators that measure the content of the audits should be included: These are indicators that are related to a single audit object, e.g., a contract, and those that relate to the entire audited unit, e.g., a local subsidiary.

Definition of Suitable Benchmarks

The next step is to define benchmarks for the various indicators and ratios. Indicators always have an absolute and a relative value, and the benchmark selected determines how accurate they are. The appropriate benchmarks have to be selected specifically for every situation, ranging from closing-date values, averages, and percentage distributions through intervals and series, which can be compared with each other. It is ultimately the expected or required substantial meaning that determines the selection.

Possible Categories for Comparison

The following are the main comparison categories of interest for Internal Audit:

- benchmarks from the previous year or averages from several prior years,
- benchmarks from other corporate units, e.g. Management Accounting, if available,
- benchmarks from external sources (e.g., auditing institutes, industry associations, other companies),
- benchmarks defined in terms of business targets, especially as part of cost-benefit analysis, e.g. in relation to project results, and
- benchmarks in terms of outcomes expected by management.

Regular Control of the Indicators Used

Benchmarking rarely uses all the above values at the same time. The focus is rather on selected values, because the effort required for generating the data is considerable. In addition, it is advisable to test whether the selected data is comparable in terms of both form and content. Internal Audit should nominate a benchmarking champion, who centrally examines benchmarking quality and form. If no such control is implemented on a regular basis, then there is a risk that the indicators follow diverging rules and are no longer consistent.

Extent of Benchmarking in Internal Audit

The actual control function of benchmarking is based on identified variances. For example, if variances occur in comparison to external values, it is necessary to first analyze the quality and origin of these benchmarks. It should also be tested whether the indicators are plausible in relation to past development. Past development is then extrapolated into the future. This means that ultimately data comparison and trend analysis form part of Internal Audit's benchmarking analysis. An explanation for variances also has to account for interdependencies.

Presentation of Results

Benchmarking should be presented at different management levels, for information purposes and to ease navigation through the underlying data material. The addressees will normally absorb the benchmarking results better and faster if they are presented graphically.

HINTS AND TIPS

- Auditors should comment the indicators they have determined, e.g., to indicate whether there are positive or negative variances.

LINKS AND REFERENCES

- ALLAN, M., H. TONKIN, AND R. RUNDLE. 2002. *Benchmarking the Internal Audit Function Follow-on Report.* www.anao.gov.au/WebSite.nsf/Publications/5527C42C327C50E1CA256C5C001BA5D5 (accessed May 31, 2007).
- INSTITUTE OF INTERNAL AUDITORS. 2001. *Practice Advisory 2500-1: Monitoring Progress.* Altamonte Springs, FL: The Institute of Internal Auditors.

7.4 Structure of a Balanced Scorecard Approach

KEY POINTS •••

- The balanced scorecard (BSC) approach is a KPI system that utilizes and incorporates different perspectives and views integrating them with strategic approaches.
- The BSC structure can be applied to Internal Audit, and the predefined indicators are set as strategic objectives.
- These can be used to derive measures, which in turn lead to indicators and comparisons of to-be and as-is values.

Balanced Scorecard and Key Performance Indicators

The balanced scorecard approach takes the key performance indicators and ratios discussed earlier one step further. It makes them part of corporate operations, expressed in different action fields and perspectives creating a network-like structure of directly and indirectly linked indicators, which has to be understood and treated as a whole.

Attributes of the Balanced Scorecard

The following should be noted:

- A balanced scorecard can be defined both strategically at the corporate level and operationally at the departmental level.
- The balanced scorecard approach integrates financial and non-financial performance measures on four dimensions. The general dimensions are financial performance, process indicators, customer satisfaction, and innovation.
- The indicators are chosen to capture the company's main areas of activity and decision levels.
- Every indicator is compared against targets, action tracking, as-is measurements, and feedback.

Focus on Internal Audit

Internal Audit has special requirements for the design of a balanced scorecard structure. The starting point in choosing components of the balanced scorecard is a clear mission, from which visions and objectives can be derived, which in turn are the different dimensions that are to be integrated in the balanced scorecard. Internal Audit's specific dimensions are financials, employees, the audit process (including audit objects), and auditees. Appropriate indicators are defined for these dimensions. They are specified, controlled, and monitored in terms of overall target achievement by the managers in charge.

Control with the Balanced Scorecard

The metrics can be lead or lag indicators. At Internal Audit, a classic example of a lead indicator is risk assessment, and a typical lag indicator is the number of actual audit findings. The number of actual audit findings can in turn be used as input for a new risk assessment and thus become a lead indicator. This makes indicators important as both planning and analysis tools. As lead indicators, they can be used in planning, and as lag indicators, they serve to document developments. The balanced scorecard tracks different indicator meanings and their interdependencies across various perspectives. Due to its comprehensive nature, especially the inclusion of quality aspects, the balanced scorecard concept enables KPI-based control of Internal Audit. The department's mission, visions, and objectives are integrated into the concept and mapped through quality-focused indicators. Since efficiency is an important point to consider, the financial perspective should be tied into a comprehensive analysis.

HINTS AND TIPS

- Auditors should familiarize themselves with the balanced scorecard concept using indicators they have selected.
- Auditors should be aware of the benefits of the balanced scorecard approach and the value it adds compared to benchmarking.

LINKS AND REFERENCES

- CALLAGHAN, J., A. SAVAGE, AND S. MINTZ. 2007. Assessing the Control Environment Using a Balanced Scorecard Approach. *The CPA Journal* (March 2007): 58–63.
- KAPLAN, R., AND D. NORTON. 1996. Using the Balanced Scorecard as a Strategic Management System. *Harvard Business Review* (74): 75–85.
- KATHY, S., AND R. MCKAY. 2002. Balanced Scorecard. *The CPA Journal* (March 2002): 20–25.

8 Integrated Cost Management (Cost of Internal Audits)

KEY POINTS •••

- To allow Internal Audit to perform its tasks effectively, the organization must provide adequate resources to guarantee that the department's capacity is fully utilized and it produces the best possible results.
- A tracking system can be used to allocate costs to Internal Audit's activities and thus measure resource utilization.
- A time management system is an important tool for allocating the cost of time and effort spent to audit activities. By recording time Internal Audit management can also analyze how employees use their time.
- Internal Audit's total costs may include time and effort, direct audit-related costs, direct non-audit-related costs, and indirect costs.
- An effective cost monitoring process also supports Internal Audit's billing process.
- There are several different cost transfer models that can be used. Selection of the appropriate model depends on the administrative burden created by the billing process and the nature of the audit activities conducted in the company.
- Internal Audit's performance should be assessed from both a financial and non-financial perspective.

Cost Management

When it comes to cost management, Internal Audit is no different from other corporate departments. To allow Internal Audit to perform its tasks effectively, the company must ensure it has appropriate resources available to ensure that the department's capacity is fully utilized and it produces the best possible results. It is also important to ensure that the costs of Internal Audit's activities do not exceed the annual budget.

Compiling an Annual Budget

According to guidance from the IIA, the CAE should compile and submit an annual budget to the Board of Directors and senior management for approval at the beginning of each fiscal year. The annual budget should be compiled after the Audit Committee has concurred with the annual audit plan, because the budget should cover the costs of the activities that Internal Audit has planned for the next fiscal year.

Cost Elements Included

The normal budget for Internal Audit primarily includes employee-related and audit-related cost elements. Other costs to be included in an internal audit budget include training costs, the cost of audit-related literature and publications, audit technology, expert advice, and the engagement of independent specialists. These costs must be included in the budget calculation so that Internal Audit can perform its tasks efficiently and effectively.

Budgeting Method

For the compilation of a realistic budget, it is essential to develop a method of recording all significant audit-related costs incurred as a result of the department's work. At SAP, GIAS' budget is produced using timesheet data (see Section A, Chapter 4.7) and actual prior-year figures. Using this method, it must also be possible to adequately allocate the costs to the activities that drive them. Based upon these allocations, Internal Audit's performance can be measured in terms of how resources (e.g., auditor time and corporate funds) are used for the various activities.

Advantages of Performance and Cost Analysis

By determining Internal Audit's performance and the costs of its activities, Internal Audit management can gain an overview of the department's effectiveness and efficiency. It is also possible to make regular comparisons of the budgeted and actual costs of audit activities for certain periods of a fiscal year and to establish whether a specific audit has remained within budget.

Profit Center

An internal audit department can be transformed from a cost center into a profit center, where the auditees and customers are billed for the audits conducted by Internal Audit (see Section A, Chapter 2.5.5). However, it cannot be Internal Audit's objective to generate revenues. Internal Audit's costs are managed primarily so that business efficiency and productivity, as well as resource utilization and budget compliance, can be measured and thus contribute to increasing efficiency.

Cost Centers at GIAS

The costs incurred as a result of Internal Audit's activities are recorded in the SAP system and then allocated to the defined cost center. These costs include personnel costs, travel expenses (flights and accommodation), and allocations for the use of IT equipment and offices. GIAS must administrate the cost centers carefully so that Internal Audit's performance can be measured at the global level. This includes not only allocating the costs to individual profit centers, but also analyzing and measuring costs while considering possible cost transfer. GIAS does not currently bill customers for the costs it incurs in connection with audits. The remainder of this chapter describes how cost transfers could work.

Time Management

One of the most important factors in calculating the costs of internal audits is the time auditors spend performing actual audit work. Therefore, for most internal audits, time management systems are an important information tool to help allocate costs to audit activities. Time management reports provide information to Internal Audit management about how efficiently and effectively the employees involved in an audit use available time. These reports can also be used to support performance analysis, which is important for a number of performance targets. The reports can be produced regularly, or for specific events or purposes.

Time and Effort Costs

The following describes the different types of costs that are incurred in Internal Audit's work and should be measured and documented to produce a realistic summary of total costs. As previously mentioned, the costs for the time and effort spent by the employees involved in an audit are one of the most important cost elements. An internal audit is a service provided by trained and qualified auditors. By recording the time they spend on an audit, the internal audit function can analyze how time is distributed among the different audit activities and how efficiently they are carried out.

Time Recording

The normal procedure for determining the time and effort spent on an audit is to record the time spent in time records, which all auditors complete regularly (e.g., monthly, fortnightly, or per audit). Generally, every auditor completes his or her own time record. The data shows, how each auditor's working time has been spent during the period. It is important to record the time actually spent on each audit activity. Time may also be spent on administration or training. These periods also must be recorded carefully, so the department's time record is not distorted.

Advantages of Time Recording

Accurate time recording has the following advantages:

- Quantitative support for time management at employee level: Accurate time recording for all audit activities in the current year facilitates future timesheet calculations and thus realistic preparation of future budgets and audit plans. It also allows auditors to make sensible plans for specific audits.
- Control of audit activities: The audit lead and Audit Manager responsible can use direct time records to compare actual to budgeted times and thus effectively analyze whether the audit is progressing according to schedule and how far the audit is from completion. This allows forward-looking planning of employee engagements. These can be broken down into the phases of the Audit Roadmap, which in turn leads to greater planning accuracy. Moreover, auditors are motivated to conclude the audit project according to schedule and meet quality standards.
- Increased productivity: Analysis of the time actually spent on auditing (audit-related time) compared to time spent on administrative and other activities (non-audit-related time) facilitates monitoring resource utilization.

Important Time Record Data

The completion of the time records is an essential prerequisite for meaningful analysis. The following time record data is useful for Internal Audit management:

- time that the audit team spends on each audit activity,
- exceeding of the estimated time required,
- non-billable time per month (e.g., for training or administration),
- proportion of budgeted time to actual time spent on each audit activity, and
- proportion of non-billable to billable time per auditor.

Time Recording Procedure

Normally, time is recorded for each audit during the reporting period (monthly or twice monthly). Every audit activity that can be clearly determined is first assigned to a cost center code so that times can be recorded without problems.

Check by the Audit Manager

The annual audit plan allows a certain period for conducting the audit activities. For effective monitoring, every auditor records the time he or she has actually spent on an audit object. The responsible Audit Manager should review and approve the times recorded to ensure that the time and effort for the reporting period have been captured properly. The Audit Manager needs the following information to review the recorded times:

- approved audit object budget,
- time recording datasheets where the times spent on conducting the audit activities have been accurately recorded, and
- regular reports on billable hours generated from the system.

Allocating Costs to Time Spent

If the time spent on auditing tasks can be measured, Internal Audit management can allocate the costs for the time spent to the audit activities on the basis of the compensation of each employee involved in the audit. Another way to allocate time and effort cost is to multiply the number of auditor hours spent by the appropriate hourly rate. The hourly rate is the average hourly cost billed for the services of an Internal Audit employee. This rate should cover the costs of providing the service, at least in part. To ensure efficiency, the hourly rate should also cover overhead costs (operating costs and personnel costs). The hourly rate for individual auditors is set by Internal Audit management. Normally, a higher hourly rate is charged for a Senior Auditor than for a less experienced auditor, which means that the hourly rates generally reflect the job hierarchy in the department.

Direct Audit-Related Costs

In addition to time and effort, direct audit-related costs represent another significant cost of internal audits. Direct audit-related costs are costs incurred as a direct result of identifiable audit activities in an audit project. Internal audits usually incur direct audit-related costs such as travel expenses, including flights and local accommodation for auditors. They can also include subsistence, local transport, or telecommunication expenses. Costs for time and effort and direct audit-related costs together account for the majority of audit-related costs.

Direct Non-Audit-Related Costs

In addition to direct audit-related costs, there are other direct costs that Internal Audit incurs as a result of activities not directly related to an audit. Examples include departmental events, initiatives, or projects, and Internal Audit employee participation in external events.

Third-Party Costs

Third-party costs, e.g., for legal advice, are also significant and should be included. If these types of costs are incurred in direct relation to an audit activity, they should be classified as direct audit-related costs. If not, they are treated as direct non-audit-related costs. Internal auditors must ensure that the costs of non-audit-related activities are within budget, because they can hardly be billed to customers. These costs can, however, be charged, if the costs billed to customers are made up of the actual costs incurred and a mark-up. Distinguishing between direct audit-related and direct non-audit-related costs creates greater cost-driver transparency.

Documentation and Analysis

The costs incurred must be accurately analyzed and classified. Occasionally, direct costs may be incurred that can be allocated to more than one audit activity, (for example, if the costs of a flight are related to two independent audit activities performed by Internal Audit). For this reason, it is important to track these types of costs to facilitate subsequent analysis and accurate cost transfers to auditees.

Indirect Costs

In addition to time and effort costs and the other direct costs, Internal Audit's activities also incur costs that cannot be clearly allocated to a specific audit or a non-audit-related activity. These costs are also referred to as indirect costs or departmental overheads. They are necessary for Internal Audit to perform its central function as an internal audit body. Indirect costs are normally carried by the department as a whole and not allocated to an individual auditor or audit engagement. In return, the advantages generated with these costs benefit the whole department.

Indirect costs are incurred, for example, for the use of office space, office materials and IT equipment.

Billing of Indirect Costs

Internal Audit also incurs indirect costs in the process of performing the necessary audit services. Thus, all service users should pay for their share of these costs. Commonly, these costs are (partially or fully) recovered through the hourly rate determined by Internal Audit.

Billing Models

Careful cost monitoring is also critical to the billing process of the internal audit department. The models presented below consider how the costs of Internal Audit can best be billed. In doing so, Internal Audit must consider the reasons and motives for charging specific costs. The following billing models are presented below:

- actual cost model,
- cost-plus model,
- revenue model, and
- hybrid model.

Actual Cost Model

The actual cost model is relatively simple to use. Under this model, the auditee is billed one-to-one (e.g., without mark-up) for all direct audit costs and all billable time and effort costs using cost allocation and following cost accounting principles. This model is based on the principle that the auditees should assume the costs of the audit project, because they are using the services of an internal department. The idea is that internal audit costs are unavoidable costs for ensuring compliance, which the auditees must cover as part of their business activities. If the auditees carry the costs of internal audits, they can in return expect certain outputs from Internal Audit, such as improved efficiency, increased productivity, and fraud detection.

Advantages of the Actual Cost Model

One of the advantages of the actual cost model is that it is easy to administrate, because the invoiced costs are directly measurable and transparent for the auditees. Moreover a functioning cost monitoring system (e.g. through time recording and cost center reporting) allows Internal Audit management to easily determine the total costs to be allocated and billed to the auditees as part of its administrative duties.

Suitability and Limits of the Actual Cost Model

However, the actual cost model is only suitable for audits included in the annual audit plan and agreed upon by the Board of Directors or Audit Committee. Since the annual audit plan has been prepared and approved based upon a risk analysis of all corporate units, it is easier to explain to the auditees that audits are necessary and therefore the auditees should be responsible for all associated costs. It is, however, difficult to get the auditees to accept the costs of spontaneous, unplanned audits (e.g., process reviews or investigations into fraud and anonymous allegations).

Cost-Plus Model

Another billing model for invoicing is the cost-plus method. This model includes all actual costs incurred in conducting the audit activities (similar to the actual cost model), plus a mark-up of, say, 5% to 10%, which is billed to the auditees. The mark-up is billed mainly to cover the indirect costs incurred by Internal Audit.

Using Internal Audit's Services

Internal Audit is often used for a variety of reasons. For example, the company as a whole may value its services and be prepared to pay for them. Also, Internal Audit employs experts and has extensive knowledge of the corporate units, so that its activities can add value. The auditees must decide whether it is necessary to ask Internal Audit to investigate operational matters in the company and whether the costs are justified. By contrast, irrespective of whether the actual cost or cost-plus method is used, Internal Audit must reconcile the need to bill its services with the company's overall objectives. If the fact that Internal Audit bills for its services deters potential auditees from engaging Internal Audit, so that fraud, for example, may go undetected and thus unpunished, Internal Audit fails in its obligation to act in the company's interest. For this reason, when using the cost-plus model, audit management should make sure that the billing of audit services does not have a negative impact on the relationship between auditees and Internal Audit.

Determining the Mark-Up

Depending on the annual budget, the mark-up can be fixed at different levels from year to year. If required, Internal Audit and the auditees should conclude a service level agreement each year, which establishes the mark-ups (for the year in question) and Internal Audit's services on which the mark-up is based.

Revenue Model

The revenue model is another alternative for cost transfers. Under the revenue model, the costs of internal audits are billed on the basis of fixed or variable percentages of the revenue generated by the auditees. This model is not related to direct or indirect costs incurred by Internal Audit. Revenue can, for example, be calculated on the basis of six-month moving average revenue or on the basis of the latest annual sales figure. For the concept of the revenue model to be understood, the involved parties must understand how Internal Audit fits into the company as a whole: Internal Audit is regarded as an in-house corporate function, because the services it provides benefits all the units of the company. As for all in-house functions, the corporate-wide costs are allocated using an appropriate formula.

Determining the Percentage Charged

The percentage charged must be determined such that Internal Audit's direct and indirect costs are covered. However, this is not easy to implement, because, depending on the percentage determined earlier, Internal Audit may recover more or less than the costs it has actually incurred, resulting in a profit or loss, respectively.

Suitability and Limits of the Revenue Model

The revenue model is suitable for planned internal audits. It can also be used for units that must be audited at least annually, units that are exposed to significant risks, or those that are of central importance. The fixed or variable percentage used should be an indication of the risk profile of the auditee. A high percentage can mean that the unit is exposed to high risks, so that the higher rate of recovery has to finance the additional resources that Internal Audit may have to use as a result of the high risk. This gives the auditees an incentive to manage their unit with a view to reducing the risk so that the percentage charged falls over time. Moreover, the revenue model facilitates administration for Internal Audit, because the auditees are billed at a previously agreed rate, irrespective of the actual costs incurred by the audit activity. The tracking of costs in such a case serves to monitor total costs and audit progress within the audit budget. There are, however, some units, such as shared service centers, for which this model is less suitable because they do not generate revenue.

Hybrid Model

Besides the models described so far, Internal Audit can also use a hybrid model. As the name suggests, the hybrid model is a combination of the models described above: Depending on the nature of the audit activities conducted, Internal Audit uses a combination of suitable models to bill the auditee. Using these models for billing will turn Internal Audit into a true profit center, reporting profits at least for parts of its activities.

Departmental Budget

As mentioned earlier, the departmental budget is derived from the department's objectives, which are set annually. Based on an existing cost transfer structure, Internal Audit can determine whether the department has kept within or exceeded budget. Although Internal Audit is not a revenue-generating department, it should ensure that it meets its budget. With the overview that the budget provides, Internal Audit management can analyze whether the existing cost transfers are based on reasonable parameters. It can also regularly (e.g., quarterly) monitor budget utilization compared to cost recovery. Such regular checks help initiate any necessary corrective action immediately. In addition, at the end of the year, Internal Audit should analyze the variances between the actual figures and the budget for the year.

Annual Reports

Internal Audit management should check Internal Audit's annual cost reports to establish whether the reported figures are in line with standard values or budget (see Section D, Chapter 7). The following are examples of reports that can be made available to Internal Audit management:

- summary of the published reports and their results,
- summary of billable project hours,
- list of non-billable hours, e.g., for general administration,
- summary of the audit surveys,
- absenteeism statistics,
- current status of all outstanding audits, and
- audits that have exceeded their time schedule.

Indicators

In addition to Internal Audit's costs, the department must also analyze its performance from both a financial and non-financial perspective. Variance analysis is not the only way of determining the efficiency and effectiveness of the department's resource utilization. It is also possible to assess productivity by analyzing the results of peer reviews. Internal Audit's performance can also be assessed through specific indicators and ratios, such as number of audits per auditor, number of findings per audit, number of audit requests, percentage of costs in excess of audit budget, proportion of non-productive and productive time per auditor, and direct audit-related costs as a proportion of total costs per audit project. These indicators and ratios allow Internal Audit to take effective measurements of the quantitative and qualitative aspects of all audit activities.

HINTS AND TIPS

- The time spent on an audit should be recorded immediately and analyzed as soon as possible.

LINKS AND REFERENCES

- INSTITUE OF INTERNAL AUDITORS. 2001. *Practice Advisory 2020-1: Communication and Approval.* Altamonte Springs, FL: The Institute of Internal Auditors.
- REDING, K. F., P. J. SOBEL, U. L. ANDERSON, et al. 2007. *Internal Assurance and Consulting Services.* Altamonte Springs, FL: The Institute of Internal Auditors.
- SAWYER, L. B., M. A. DITTENHOFER, AND J. H. SCHEINER. 2003. *Sawyer's Internal Auditing.* 5th ed. Altamonte Springs, FL: The Institute of Internal Auditors.

9 Peer Review

KEY POINTS •••

- A peer review, also known as a quality assurance review (or QAR), is the evaluation of an internal audit department by independent professionals in the same field as required by the IIA.
- A peer review examines the internal audit department's compliance with professional standards and suggests improvements in order to align the department with best practices recognized in the profession.
- Generally, internal audit departments can decide for themselves whom to select as audit partner.
- The peer review goes through the normal phases of an audit project, i.e., planning, preparation, execution, reporting, and follow-up.

Definition

A peer review is the evaluation of an internal audit department's work by independent professionals in the same field. Other terms commonly used for this process include "quality assessment", "quality assurance review" or "QAR." In a peer review an external party examines the strengths and weaknesses of the internal audit department, usually including organizational and operational structures. Peer reviews must be conducted by qualified persons who have relevant professional expertise, are not connected with the company, and have no conflicting interests. Peer reviews are concluded with a written report.

Peer Review and Public Accountants

In recent years, recognition and public scrutiny of auditors has increased, enhancing the importance of independent peer reviews. As a result, the AICPA has revised its Practice-Monitoring Program and issued new standards with effect from January 1, 2005.

Peer Review and Internal Audit

Likewise, internal audit institutes have enhanced their peer review programs. IIA Standard 1312 (External Assessments) advises that a peer review should be conducted by an independent body once every five years. Further, since this standard came into effect on January 1, 2002, every internal audit department seeking accreditation for its activities according to the International Standards for the Professional Practice of Internal Auditing must conduct a peer review by December 31, 2006. The IIA has issued additional guidance on peer reviews in Practice Advisories 1312-1 (External Assessments), 1312-2 (External Assessments Self-Assessment with Independent Validation), and 1320 – 1 (Reporting on the Quality Program). In addition, the IIA updated its Quality Assessment Manual in 2006.

Peer Review Objective

The main objective of a peer review is to improve audit quality as a whole. Such an assessment is a good way of evaluating, documenting and reporting on the effectiveness and quality of an internal audit department to internal (e.g., corporate management, Board of Directors) and external bodies (e.g., external auditors). It also provides valuable suggestions for improving internal audit practices. Although the professional practice standards form the basis for a peer review, they are normally supplemented by the experience of the peer review providers. This process is therefore not only about compliance with standards and about finding out if auditors adhere to their own processes. It is also about aligning Internal Audit with the profession's recognized best practices.

Objectives of the Peer Review at SAP

In 2005, Internal Audit at SAP initiated a peer review process with the following objectives:

- to obtain objective confirmation from professional third parties that the audit procedures practiced by GIAS conform to IIA standards,
- to gain a certified substantive basis for the development of an SAP software solution for audit management,
- to enhance the profile and status of GIAS both within SAP and among third parties,
- to gain credibility among contacts as well as internal, and external customers by reversing the roles (auditing the auditors),
- to allow Internal Audit employees to gather valuable personal experience throughout the process,
- to facilitate benchmarking against internal audit departments of other companies, and
- to motivate Internal Audit employees because the peer review should give them confidence that they are using an internationally recognized and effective audit model.

Development of the Peer Review Concept

The development of the peer review concept involves preliminary considerations and general planning for conducting a peer review. These considerations comprise the following:

- initial assessment of the project to obtain a clear understanding of the expected benefit,
- appointment of an internal project team,
- presentation of a first project plan to the entire department to establish its basic readiness to conduct a peer review,
- definition of the period to be reviewed, and
- testing of the internal quality assurance program which is the basis for the processes to be subjected to peer review.

Selection of the Peer-Review Partner

The professional standards of the IIA only require that external quality assurance reviews be conducted by qualified, independent auditors. To a large extent, the internal audit departments can decide for themselves whom to select for this task. However, in terms of content and topic, a peer review should be conducted according to IIA principles, because they represent the current best practice in the profession.

Possible Peer-Review Partners

Many consulting firms offer quality assessment reviews as part of their audit-related services. The professional internal audit institutes also offer peer review services. The quality assessment can be made either mainly by a third party, or in the form of self-assessment, followed by a review of the results by a third party. The IIA commonly provides and also performs quality assessment services.

Partner Selection at SAP

As is the case for most purchasing decisions, bids for comparison should be invited when selecting a peer-review partner. GIAS considered several bids in this regard from the IIA as well as from external consulting firms of different sizes and eventually decided on the IIA as a review partner.

Company-Specific Decision

Each internal audit department must make its own decision regarding the benefits and suitability of the different providers. But unlike external consulting firms, the professional organizations generally rely on practicing professionals making themselves available on a voluntary basis. These professionals are members of the profession and certified as such, but they do not receive any fees; only their expenses are reimbursed.

Preparation for the Peer Review

Once the internal audit department has selected a suitable peer-review partner, the actual preparation phase begins. At this stage Internal Audit should match and compare the IIA standards with the department's current processes and rules.

Preparatory Steps at SAP

It is of critical importance that an internal audit department be knowledgeable of its own processes before undergoing an external review. Internal Audit at SAP took the following measures to prepare for its peer review:

- Developed a detailed definition and clear documentation of its own quality assurance concept (see Section D, Chapter 5).
- Used cross-team auditors to assess internally whether the existing quality assurance concept is complied with.
- Conducted a department-internal employee survey: A standard questionnaire, which is based on IIA questionnaires, was used to ask employees to give their personal assessment of the quality of the Internal Audit function.
- Conducted a pre-investigation in conjunction with the selected peer-review partner. A one- or two-day meeting provides the opportunity to discuss preliminary results from internal review steps in advance and, if appropriate, agree the first corrective measures.

These results were communicated to all Internal Audit employees immediately before the actual peer review so that they could look forward to the subsequent external review with confidence and a positive attitude, or rectify any shortcomings, if possible.

Execution of the Peer Review

The internal audit department being reviewed has little influence on the execution of the actual peer review, but it can play a key role in helping the process succeed by providing support and explanations to the reviewers. It is particularly important to ensure that the peer review auditors are able to communicate with the company's management bodies and Internal Audit's other main contacts, because a quality review often involves open and structured interviews with managers, auditors, and other employees (e.g., from Corporate Legal or Corporate Risk Management).

Main Focus Areas of the Peer Review

The peer review mostly focuses on assessing the following aspects of audit work:

- Organizational positioning and structure of Internal Audit: Here, the organizational fundamentals of the department are considered (e.g., on the basis of the Charter, mission, target agreements, and the audit handbook).
- Definition and implementation of a risk-based audit approach: This involves reviewing the audit reports, working papers, and audit planning documents as part of the assessment of the audit approach and project management.
- Personnel management within Internal Audit (i.e., the qualifications, training plan, and career development of its employees).
- Definition of and compliance with quality assurance programs as defined by the IIA standards.
- Audit of IT-related issues.

Communication

The peer-review partner should keep Internal Audit informed about the progress of the review. Like all other audits, the success of a peer review relies upon trusting, transparent cooperation between the parties involved.

Reporting

At the conclusion of a peer review a report describing the results is written, which, if applicable, will confirm that Internal Audit complies with the IIA standards. In addition to confirming compliance, the reports should also suggest improvements by highlighting best practices. It is also important to inform those responsible for Internal Audit in the company of the results of the peer review (e.g., CEO, Audit Committee).

IIA Assessment

The peer review results in an overall assessment of Internal Audit's activities. The IIA allows for three possible ratings, i.e. "generally conforms", "partially conforms", and "does not conform". In 2006, GIAS was awarded the "Generally conforms" status by the IIA.

Internal Audit's Response

Internal Audit should have the confidence to communicate the peer review results within the company. This is the only way the peer review can achieve one of its main objectives: to strengthen Internal Audit's standing in the company.

Implementation of Recommendations and Follow-Up

The minimum objective of a peer review is to confirm that the internal audit department reviewed performs its activities in accordance with the IIA standards. If this objective is not met, the peer-review partner should specify corrective actions and deadlines within which the actions are to be implemented. If the minimum objective has been met, Internal Audit should continue aligning itself with recognized best practices. For this purpose the peer review partner can point out potential for improvement and, if possible, specific steps to best tapping this potential. These recommendations should then be implemented in a sustainable way as part of a structured follow-up process, i.e., with firm responsibilities, deadlines, and escalation procedures if necessary.

HINTS AND TIPS

- Internal Audit's professional associations provide comprehensive peer review guidelines.
- Many consulting firms also offer detailed guidelines on this topic.

LINKS AND REFERENCES

- INSTITUTE OF INTERNAL AUDITORS. 2004. *Practice Advisory 1312-1: External Assessments.* Altamonte Springs, FL: The Institute of Internal Auditors.
- INSTITUTE OF INTERNAL AUDITORS. 2004. *Practice Advisory 1312-2: External Assessments Self-assessments with Independent Validation.* Altamonte Springs, FL: The Institute of Internal Auditors.
- INSTITUTE OF INTERNAL AUDITORS. 2004. *Practice Advisory 1320-1: Reporting on the Quality Program.* Altamonte Springs, FL: The Institute of Internal Auditors.
- INSTITUTE OF INTERNAL AUDITORS. 2002. *Standards for Professional Practice.* Altamonte Springs, FL: The Institute of Internal Auditors.
- INSTITUTE OF INTERNAL AUDITORS. 2006. *Quality Assessment Manual.* 5th ed. Altamonte Springs, FL: The Institute of Internal Auditors.
- SAWYER, L. B., M. A. DITTENHOFER, AND J. H. SCHEINER. 2003 *Sawyer's Internal Auditing.* 5th ed. Altamonte Springs, FL: The Institute of Internal Auditors.
- SEARS, B. 2002. *Internal Auditing Manual.* New York, NY: Warren, Gorham & Lamont.

10 Guest Auditors

KEY POINTS •••

- Guest auditors may be used in all types of audits.
- The use of guest auditors may be necessary or desirable when specialist know-how is needed, capacity problems exist, or employees have to be trained.
- There are qualitative and quantitative criteria for the selection of guest auditors.
- At SAP, the selection of guest auditors follows a set procedure.
- Guest auditors should be integrated into the audit team from an organizational and technical point of view.
- Before the start of the audit, basic auditing procedures should be explained to guest auditors during a training day.
- The relationship with the guest auditor should be maintained even after the end of the audit.
- Cost allocation for the use of guest auditors must be clarified before the audit, and all costs have to be budgeted.

Introduction

At SAP the audit lead or the Audit Manager is responsible for deciding whether to include one or more guest auditors in a GIAS audit team. This chapter shows that the use of guest auditors may be considered for a variety of reasons. The general term "guest auditor" is used in this context to refer to any persons with significant involvement in an audit who do not directly belong to the internal audit department. In practice, more than one guest auditor may be used, depending on the particular audit in question, but an audit team must never consist exclusively of guest auditors, i.e., care has to be taken to involve at least one permanent Internal Audit employee in the audit. While guest auditors are used infrequently at SAP, in some organizations resource constraints require consistent use of guest auditors in formal co-sourcing or out-sourcing arrangements, where part or all of the internal audit field work is performed by outside auditors.

General Need for Guest Auditors

The environment in which Internal Audit operates has become increasingly complex. Sometimes this gives rise to situations where Internal Audit employees cannot cover certain audit content with their own expertise, and the appropriate training would take too long to complete. However, in other parts of the company and also outside the company, there may be experts who will have the relevant background and required knowledge. Internal Audit must recognize and tap into the wealth of knowledge and experience of these experts. This will allow Internal Audit to conduct complex, specialized audit activities in line with requirements.

Quantitative Reasons for Guest Auditors

There can also be capacity reasons for employing guest auditors. For example, if the resource schedule does not provide sufficient capacity to staff a team for an audit that cannot be postponed, (e.g., because of instruction from the Board of Directors) it is possible to add one or more guest auditors. Extraordinary situations like that must be agreed with the relevant Audit Manager and the CAE.

Training and Recruitment

In some cases, it may be possible to include an inexperienced guest auditor, e.g., a university student, in an audit. The selection depends on the time and resource schedule for the audit concerned. In such cases, the focus is not on co-opting technical expertise, but on providing training for inexperienced Internal Audit employees and people who may join the department in the future.

Deployment Options

Guest auditors can be used in standard and special audits, as well as in ad-hoc audits. It is the responsibility of the audit lead and the Audit Manager to identify the need to deploy a guest auditor. Since audit leads are aware of engagements well in advance (see Section B, Chapter 2.4), they are in a position to start the resource procurement process if necessary. Due to the short notice given for ad-hoc audits, guest auditors may become involved in such audits on short notice.

Definition of Terms

Guest auditors should be involved in audit work from the beginning of the audit. At SAP they work according to the GIAS Roadmap (see Part B) and cooperate closely with the Internal Audit team. However, third parties involved in audit work for a specific task that relates only to a certain function are not classified as guest auditors. Such parties, known as assessors (e.g. medical experts, private detectives, members of the police service, lawyers) are co-opted for dealing with very specific tasks in the audit. In certain circumstances, the Audit Manager and the audit lead must decide, in consultation with the legal department if necessary, whether to involve an assessor to give an expert opinion.

Qualitative Selection Criteria

When selecting guest auditors, it should be ensured that they meet the technical requirements of the audit in question and are able to contribute the necessary know-how. The guest auditor's technical qualifications and experience should be considered relative to the Scope on which the audit is based. If the audit is complex, for example in the case of fraud audits, it is advisable to involve an auditor who already has experience in this area.

Selection at SAP

SAP has formalized the use of guest auditors within GIAS audit teams according to the following process, which distinguishes between internal guest auditors (SAP employees) and external guest auditors.

- Internal guest auditors:
  - The Audit Manager and the CAE agree on the use of a guest auditor so that his or her deployment can be approved.
  - The Audit Manager informs the CAE of the costs (working days and travel expenses).
  - An internal order is created and the internal order number is forwarded to the audit lead.
  - The audit lead creates a staffing list for the guest auditor (necessary for SAP-internal cost transfers), which records the relevant personal and order-related data.
  - The guest auditor must sign a non-disclosure agreement, also arranged by the audit lead.
  - The audit lead requests a new drive on the data server (group share) on which the guest auditor can work. After the audit, the data is transferred to

the general GIAS group share. The reason for the separate drive is to protect sensitive data on the Internal Audit drive from access by the guest auditor.

- External guest auditors:
  - The Audit Manager and the audit lead must obtain at least two different price quotes for guest auditors.
  - The Audit Manager and the CAE agree on the use of a guest auditor so that his or her deployment can be approved.
  - A purchase order and an internal order are created.
  - An external user ID is requested for the guest auditor in order to give him or her access to predefined systems. This task is carried out by the audit lead in cooperation with the personal assistant of the CAE.
  - The external guest auditor must sign a non-disclosure agreement, again arranged by the audit lead.
  - For the same reason as in the case of the internal guest auditor, the audit lead applies for a new drive on the data server (group share) on which the guest auditor can work. After the audit, the data on this drive is also transferred to the general GIAS group share.

Technical and Organizational Assignment

The assignment of guest auditors to a certain role within the audit team presents a particular challenge for the Audit Manager and the entire team. The guest auditor's technical and organizational assignment must be defined before the audit and communicated clearly to all involved. It is also possible to appoint the guest auditor as audit lead. This decision is made by the Audit Manager, in consultation with the CAE. A guest auditor may be used as the audit lead when there is a shortage of resources at the time the staffing plan is drawn up. However, at SAP at least one auditor from the internal audit department must be involved in every audit.

Training

Whatever the circumstances, it is essential to introduce the guest auditor to Internal Audit's audit approach and basic auditing procedures. To this end, it is useful to schedule a training day in order to familiarize the auditor with these topics. The audit lead is responsible for preparing the training. At SAP such training deals in particular with the GIAS standard Roadmap, basic audit procedures, the creation and filing of working papers, communication with employees of the area being audited, and the creation of the audit report.

Integration into the Team

The audit lead is responsible for the guest auditor's smooth integration into the audit team. This means knowing the guest auditor's technical background and communicating this to the rest of the team. Conversely, it also requires informing the guest auditor about the audit team and the technical qualifications and/or preferences of its individual members. In addition to the technical background, the personal aspect also plays an important part when integrating the guest auditor into the team. Audit lead and Audit Manager should recognize and take into consideration the guest auditor's strengths and weaknesses to enhance cooperation. They also should ensure that the guest auditor's arrival in the team does not give rise to any (personal) conflict in the team and eliminate any difficulties as soon as possible, ideally before the actual audit work begins. If possible, the audit lead should schedule and prepare for a meeting of the entire audit team before the audit begins.

Conclusion of the Audit

At the end of the audit, the guest auditor should be given an appropriate "farewell." This refers to the extent to which the relationship with the guest auditor established during the joint audit work should be maintained beyond the end of the engagement. A distinction should be made in this regard between external third parties and guest auditors from elsewhere in SAP. Clarification, from both an organizational and a financial perspective, should also be sought as to whether the guest auditor will continue to be involved in any audit follow-up activities. It must also be clearly defined to what extent contact with the guest auditor will be maintained. Depending on the cooperation in the audit team, this may vary between rather formal and more relaxed forms of contact. Whatever the case, the guest auditor should be available for queries and information relating to the audit, because there will invariably be questions after the audit or meetings with the auditees. If these meetings raise topics covered by the guest auditor, he or she should also attend.

Guest Auditor Costs

The use of guest auditors incurs both internal and external costs. The costs are charged to the GIAS cost center conducting the audit and are therefore under the Audit Manager's responsibility. The costs of external auditors can easily be identified and assigned on the basis of the invoice.

Internal Cost Transfers

If the guest auditor is an SAP employee, cost allocation may be more complicated. Two different cost categories are possible. Travel expenses and the guest auditor's labor. Travel expenses are charged to the relevant GIAS cost center on the basis of the internal order and the associated staffing list. In certain circumstances, SAP-internal guest auditors, consultants for example, may wish to charge their hours to the internal order according to the charge-out rates assigned to them. In such cases, the audit lead and the CAE have to decide whether the guest auditors will be compensated for the hours worked and the costs actually charged to the relevant GIAS cost center.

Budgeting

For both internal and external guest auditors, the costs must be budgeted and included in the overall budget of the appropriate GIAS cost center. If they are not appropriately budgeted, there may be delays in acquiring the guest auditor, which in turn may impact the audit and GIAS generally. The Audit Manager is responsible for avoiding such impact.

HINTS AND TIPS

- Make sufficient allowance in your budget for the possible employment of guest auditors.
- Start selecting suitable guest auditors well in advance.

LINKS AND REFERENCES ↗

- INSTITUTE OF INTERNAL AUDITORS. 2001. *Practice Advisory 1210-A1: Obtaining Services to Support or Complement the Internal Audit Activity.* Altamonte Springs, FL: The Institute of Internal Auditors.
- INSTITUTE OF INTERNAL AUDITORS. 2002. *Standards for Professional Practice.* Altamonte Springs, FL: The Institute of Internal Auditors.

11 Management of Internal Audit

11.1 Operational Audit Management

KEY POINTS •••

- Audit management is influenced by the different management levels within the internal audit department and their respective focus on different tasks.
- Audit management consists of different components: audit planning, quality management, performance management, and audit control.

Internal Audit Management Levels

Management of the internal audit function is influenced by the various management levels within the department as well as management's focus on different tasks. The CAE keeps track of the implementation of the annual audit plan and of audit control as a whole, while the Audit Managers perform management tasks during the audit execution. Audit leads are responsible for the audit process from their specific perspectives.

Orientation of Tasks

The type and complexity of the tasks to be monitored by audit management should also be considered. Strategic tasks, such as the introduction and use of a benchmarking system, require as much management control as a complex audit itself. Management tasks include cooperation and the joint identification of solutions with the parties concerned when bottlenecks or other problems occur. This requires the cooperation of all management levels within Internal Audit and with the auditees.

Audit Management Disciplines

Different disciplines can be included under the general heading of audit management:

- audit planning,
- quality management,
- performance management, and
- audit control.

Audit planning (see Section B, Chapter 2 and Section D, Chapter 3) and quality management (see Section D, Chapter 5) form an integral part of the Audit Roadmap and have been firmly established as operational audit management elements of Internal Audit's process. The two other audit management disciplines, performance management and audit control, can be seen as overall management functions of Internal Audit management, especially since they are monitoring tasks rather than operational activities. Performance management in Internal Audit has two components, the audit performance record and employee management, i.e., line management and control, including performance feedback (for details, see Section A, Chapters 4.5 and 4.6).

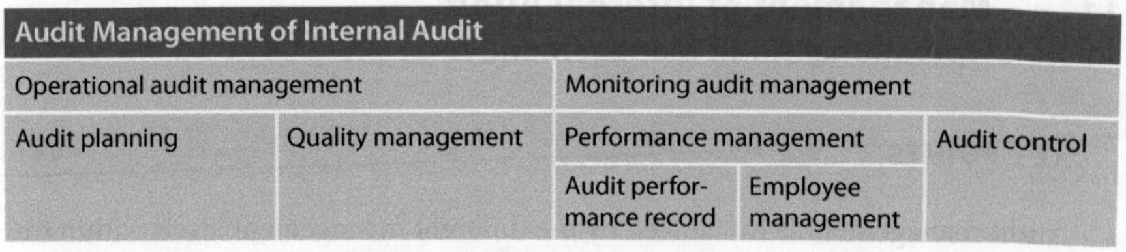

Fig. 25 Audit Management Disciplines of Internal Audit

HINTS AND TIPS

- Audit Managers should use their own initiative to contribute to operational audit management processes, for example, by completing optional quality gates.
- Audit Managers should also regularly discuss the potential for improving operational audit management.

LINKS AND REFERENCES

- REDING, K. F., P. J. SOBEL, U. L. ANDERSON, et al. 2007. *Internal Assurance and Consulting Services.* Altamonte Springs, FL: Institute of Internal Auditors.
- SAWYER, L. B., M. A. DITTENHOFER, AND J. H. SCHEINER. 2003. *Sawyer's Internal Auditing.* 5th ed. Altamonte Springs, FL: The Institute of Internal Auditors.
- SEARS, B. 2002. *Internal Auditing Manual.* New York, NY: Warren, Gorham & Lamont.

11.2 Monitoring Audit Management

11.2.1 Audit Performance Record as Part of Performance Management

KEY POINTS

- The audit performance record provides an overview of target achievement for all planned audits.
- It contains all the relevant information from the start through the end of the year, documenting the actual time sequence of every audit.
- Internal Audit management is primarily responsible for the audit performance record.

Function of the Audit Performance Record

The purpose of the audit performance record is to monitor and control the implementation of the annual audit plan. It is used as evidence to show all those involved in Internal Audit and all other responsible units that the annual audit plan has been duly implemented and any amendments have been documented and can be traced. Thus, the focus is less on the individual audit per se, which will be monitored in the context of audit control (see Section D, Chapter 11.2.2).

Starting Base

Once audit planning has been completed, the firmly scheduled audits are entered in the audit performance record. This forms the basis for updates with the aim of having full control of progress and any changes made in the course of the year. The Audit Managers continuously monitor each item of the plan.

Vertical Structure

The items included in the plan are structured vertically and break down into:

- global audits,
- regional and local audits, and
- special audits, such as customer confirmations and SOX audits.

In addition to this basic structure, further differentiation is possible for each item. In the course of the year, ad-hoc audits are added to the items already planned.

Horizontal Structure

In addition to the vertical structure, there is also a horizontal structure, according to which Internal Audit should differentiate audit engagements by audit type, auditor responsible, and execution date. Internal Audit also should state whether an engagement has been returned to the audit inventory, whether an audit has been postponed until the following year, or whether the engagement has been canceled (with reasons given). Since the annual audit plan is a target agreement between the Audit Committee and Internal Audit, any change must be made in consultation with the CAE and explicitly and clearly justified.

Basic Audit Performance Record Pattern

At the end of the year, the audit performance record concludes with items to be carried forward to the following year. On this basis, Internal Audit can assess the implementation of the annual audit plan and the efficiency of Internal Audit. Further, Internal Audit can include other information in the audit performance record, e.g. information on any audit surveys received (see Section D, Chapter 7.2.2).

Responsibility for Data Maintenance

The Audit Managers of Internal Audit and the relevant audit leads are responsible for correctly maintaining and monitoring the audit performance record. Together with the Audit Manager concerned, the audit leads should be aware of their responsibility and maintain the data accordingly. The accuracy of the information that the audit leads pass on depends on their own judgment and on the information individual auditors have given them. This means that an accurate audit performance record is the responsibility of all involved and should be interpreted in this way.

Discussion of the Audit Performance Record

The CAE and the Audit Managers should discuss the audit performance record regularly and analyze the results at least once each quarter. The latest status of the audit performance record should also be discussed during team meetings. By including the opinions and suggestions of individual auditors, Internal Audit will ultimately arrive at a comprehensive, objective picture for each audit team and for Internal Audit as a whole.

HINTS AND TIPS

- Auditors should let the audit lead and Audit Manager responsible know about any circumstances and changes that could have an impact on the audit plan.
- Auditors should regularly check the plan about the status of audits in which they are involved.
- Auditors should discuss any discrepancies with the Audit Manager responsible.

11.2.2 Audit Control

KEY POINTS

- Audit control focuses on detailed planning and monitoring of an individual audit.
- The minimum requirement under this process is to plan the necessary times, resources, and budgets for each phase of the Audit Roadmap and to monitor them based upon defined milestones.
- The relevant correction and control measures are closely related to this requirement.
- Another important element of audit control is the measurement of the efficiency of the final audit result.
- The audit lead and the Audit Manager are jointly responsible for audit control.
- For each audit, audit control can be mapped along the Audit Roadmap on the basis of figures and can be reported to the Audit Committee and the Board through key performance indicators and a standardized evaluation system (such as the traffic light system).

Detailed Monitoring

Audit control is a sub-discipline of audit management and deals with the detailed planning and monitoring of audits. It affects all categories and types of audits. As explained previously (see Section B, Chapter 2.2), an annual audit plan is compiled first. This plan defines the time periods scheduled for all audits and assigns auditors and an audit lead to each. This perspective looks at the audit as a whole. However, to ensure closer monitoring of an audit, it is necessary to plan and analyze the specific phases of the audit, always depending on the audit concerned, and especially the audit type. To establish comprehensive audit management, an internal audit department should define some standard grids or templates to assist the planning process. These grids can be used to structure individual audits quickly and securely according to operational project management principles.

Required Definitions

Before introducing audit control, Internal Audit should set a number of basic parameters, for example the way in which time is recorded. It is also necessary to clearly define how these variables are used in employee evaluations and salary reviews. Internal Audit should clarify possible interrelations and the exchange of information with Human Resources, the data protection officer, and Managerial Accounting. Internal Audit should decide the extent to which recorded working times can and may be used as a basis for cost transfers (see Section D, Chapter 8). Another closely related issue is the treatment of overtime, including the resulting alternative billing options (e.g., higher rates charged for time worked outside normal hours). Internal Audit must determine how to differentiate the data to be captured (i.e., whether the information is to be recorded per auditor and audit or whether aggregates are sufficient). Here Internal Audit must consider data protection regulations in the interest of individual employees as well as the need to conduct objectively successful audits without running the risk of making mistakes during audit work due to time and cost constraints.

Basic Elements of Audit Control

Irrespective of the attributes of the individual audit, the following basic components can be specified for audit control:

Time Required

- Every audit task requires a certain amount of time. The timesheet can be used to specify a time schedule for every audit by setting milestones. For each phase of the Audit Roadmap or even within a phase, these milestones are used to check whether an audit step or work package has been completed. The percentage of completion is then compared to the costs incurred and the time taken up to that point.

Planning Unit

- Detailed audit planning can be carried out at the activity level (i.e., process step) or the auditor level. The overall perspective is achieved by summarizing the auditor values in relation to certain activities or an audit. For global or longer-term special audits, the most suitable planning unit will probably be the auditor level, and for standard audits the activity level will tend to be more suitable because the necessary audit processes are usually standardized in this case.

Comparison of Actual and Budgeted Times

- As part of monitoring, actual times are compared with budgeted times, and the milestones reached are set against plan. If there are any variances, suitable measures are defined, e.g. adjustments to the extent of the audit and/or the number of auditors deployed, or an extension of the time period for individual phases or audit steps. In order to enable this comparison, the audit times should be recorded according to an activity catalog. Activities in this context could be the phases of the Audit Roadmap or individual process steps, such as the creation of the work program. Internal Audit should record actual times for each activity, divided into core time and overtime. This makes actual times directly comparable to budgeted times.

Organizational Prerequisites

- A clear definition of individual processes within Internal Audit is an important prerequisite for organizational implementation of audit control. The definition specifies the method and period of time recording, auditor or management responsibility, the internal controls and approvals, and the planning unit. Thus, Internal Audit should also specify the account assignment, i.e., the system used for assigning performance data, and the different updating levels (per audit, per audit period, type, etc.).

Cost Monitoring and Budgeting

- The recorded times are used to assess auditor performance. Different billing methods can be used for a detailed allocation of costs incurred to the individual audits (for details, see Section D, Chapter 8). Different options generally exist also with regard to budgeting. Although Internal Audit should aim for audit-related budgets, they will generally be achieved only for certain strategic or global audits, if at all. For this reason, collective budgets are set up, which include, for example, budget figures per region or audit type.

Audit Result Check

- It is also important to examine the audit results based on planned and actual times, resources, budgets, and costs. Internal Audit should examine critically whether and how the results correlate with these variables. At the same time, Internal Audit should compare the planned audit objectives with those actually achieved. This allows Internal Audit to evaluate the substance of the audit and also guarantee that the audit result is in reasonable proportion to the resources used.

Benefits of Audit Control

Audit control can be mapped along the Audit Roadmap for every audit. Variances can be shown either through key performance indicators or a traffic light system (where "red" indicates the variance is too large, "yellow" indicates medium – moderate difference and "green" means the variance is acceptable). Aggregated information on individual audit types, periods, regions, etc. is of particular interest. Thus, audit control is also enabled to perform analyses according to different dimensions. For example, budgeted and actual times can be aggregated per phase for certain audit types, or by topic and region, in order to obtain a more accurate basis for planning. This allows Internal Audit to allocate resources quickly and provides the ability to exercise better control over audit efficiency. Moreover, it forms a good basis for an integrated benchmarking system and a balanced scorecard (see Section D, Chapter 7).

Responsibilities

The audit lead and the Audit Manager in charge are responsible for audit control. The Audit Manager must stay involved in monitoring the progress of audits and intervene if there are significant variances. To this end, Internal Audit can define thresholds within the department to specify at what stage the Audit Manager and the CAE have to be informed or take action. Internal Audit also should consider to what extent the Board and/or the Audit Committee should be involved. Generally, summarized information regarding audit progress should be provided to these bodies at least twice a year, using an overall status report that lists all conducted and ongoing audits (see Section B, Chapter 5.5).

HINTS AND TIPS

- Auditors should always record costs as accurately as possible and allocate them to the specified planning units.
- Auditors should regularly review the results of audit control analysis together with the audit lead in charge and discuss the causes of any unusual items.

12 Marketing of Internal Audit

12.1 Internal Marketing

KEY POINTS •••

- By providing quality audit results quickly and making objective and useful recommendations, Internal Audit can effectively market itself throughout the organization.
- To reach all those with an active or passive interest, Internal Audit should offer different forms of information.
- Internal Audit should use the company's intranet, distribute printed documents, hold information events, and draw attention to its work in publications.
- Audit surveys are also part of Internal Audit's internal marketing.

Audit Quality

Internal Audit performs its activities as staff department of the Board and provides audit results to the auditees on a confidential basis. The best form of marketing for Internal Audit is to make the results of any type of audit available as quickly as possible and in the best possible quality. The reliability and objectivity associated with such a practice are recognized by the organization and help the department build a relationship of trust. Compliance with the audit principles and a convincing reporting system help safeguard the department's reputation across all levels of the organization.

Recommendations

A second internal marketing technique, which should occur naturally as a result of an effective audit process, is the implementation of all the recommendations from the audit report. If the audit results are integrated into corporate processes as expertly motivated and objectively value-adding propositions, they will have a positive influence on how Internal Audit is perceived throughout the company.

Communication

Internal Audit cannot exist outside today's networked communication and media landscape. In order to reach all those with an active or passive interest, Internal Audit must offer different forms of information. Sometimes other employees in the company are not aware of the existence of an internal audit department or they may have the wrong impressions of how the department works and are therefore reluctant to engage it for certain tasks. Therefore, Internal Audit should actively promote the fact that it is available to help with many types of problems and can be involved in finding a solution. To this end, all the instruments that can build communicative relationships should be used.

Use of the Intranet

The intranet is of particular importance in this regard because it can be used to provide the following:

- information about the department,
- services offered,
- audit principles and standards,
- process model,

- forms, e.g., an audit request, and
- reports for the Board members and strategic management.

This ensures that all levels in the company can use the intranet to get information about Internal Audit as needed.

Printed Documents

Other information media used for internal marketing include printed documents, such as the Internal Audit charter or a white paper, which contains a short summary of important information about Internal Audit. A comprehensive internal audit handbook is another internal marketing instrument, as is a peer review of the department, including certification and publication of results (see Section D, Chapter 9).

Events

Training and information events showcasing Internal Audit are also important. They can take the form of employee training or specific department presentations. These events should provide general information about audit work to as many employees as possible in order to highlight the value specific to their unit that Internal Audit can add and encourage them to cooperate actively with the department.

Publications

Another form of internal marketing is the publication of articles in in-house communication media. At SAP, publications that support internal marketing include the GIAS Letter and the annual report to the Audit Committee (see Section B, Chapter 5.4.1). Senior management circulars should also be used to provide information about general audit results and/or present Internal Audit's involvement in higher-level issues. In order to protect employees and safeguard their interests, audit results should be used as a basis for new guidelines, with reference to Internal Audit if appropriate.

Audit Surveys

Audit surveys, which the auditees complete after the audit has been conducted, are also part of Internal Audit's internal marketing (see Section D, Chapter 7.2.2). A Board summary of the results the department has achieved in the audit surveys can also promote Internal Audit's work. Consolidated results can also be included in presentations for other departments.

HINTS AND TIPS

- Auditors should check whether publications about internal auditing can be used for in-house communication.
- Auditors should determine what, in their view, are the most important information channels and optimize their use by Internal Audit.

LINKS AND REFERENCES

- SEARS, B. 2002. *Internal Auditing Manual.* New York, NY: Warren, Gorham & Lamont.

12.2 External Marketing

KEY POINTS •••

- By cooperating with external institutions, Internal Audit can demonstrate its compliance with external requirements and also contribute to developing these requirements further.
- Other significant external marketing instruments of Internal Audit are the publication of papers, the development of software solutions for internal auditing, and participation in benchmarking studies.
- Training events are also a good way to present the internal audit department outside the organization.

Cooperation with External Institutions

Internal Audit's processes are not only governed by internal requirements, but are also subject to significant external influences, such as laws, guidelines, and statutes. By cooperating with the relevant external institutions, Internal Audit can demonstrate its acceptance of and compliance with these requirements and also contribute to developing them further. By presenting and publishing papers, and holding workshops, Internal Audit can draw attention to important issues and provide critical support as it drives the development of possible solutions. This is an important element of this department's external marketing, because it also supports new trends in higher-level company-wide positioning, e.g. thought leadership, corporate citizenship, and reputation management.

Professional Journals

Contributions to professional journals generate interest and promote understanding for the functions of Internal Audit, even beyond the group of people who are directly affected. In addition, Internal Audit's external marketing may include compiling comprehensive scientific publications and recommending them as practice-based audit standards in the form of an internal audit handbook. Other information media, such as CDs or DVDs with didactic content and practical examples support such concepts.

Software for Internal Audit

Under certain circumstances, some internal audit departments may also consider the option of developing standard software for internal auditing. A successful market launch would result in marketing the company's internal audit department, because it will have piloted the software. The pilot version would be used to define a standard application for internal auditing. It would therefore be regarded as reference for subsequently introducing the software in other companies.

Benchmarking

Participation in sector-based or cross-sector benchmarking activities through key performance indicator analysis and appropriate studies is another form of external marketing because it shows how Internal Audit is positioned within its own company and in comparison to other companies. Participation in benchmarking studies is also a commonly used method to identify strengths and weaknesses.

Training

Training offerings such as courses, seminars, and information events are also popular marketing instruments. Internal Audit can make important contributions regarding topics such as compliance, SOX requirements, and fraud prevention. Offering auditor training contributes significantly to enhancing the positive perception of an internal audit department. Information events and papers presented at universities simultaneously provide an opportunity for the department to recruit future employees.

Developing an External Marketing Concept

A comprehensive marketing concept should always be developed in cooperation and agreement with the public relations department of the organization. In order to disseminate the relevant information and content successfully in different international linguistic and cultural groups, Internal Audit will normally need to co-opt media experts with publishing experience. In addition to Internal Audit, a company also has other important instruments and institutions to ensure compliance, which may also be the subject of external interest. Accordingly, it is an important function of a consistent external marketing concept to achieve a balanced public perception of all the components and their interaction.

HINTS AND TIPS

- Auditors should seize any opportunity for external marketing, e.g., giving talks on Internal Audit's special subjects.
- Auditors should also contribute to the writing and publication of papers on audit topics with which they are familiar.
- Regular participation in external working groups is recommended.

13 Fraud Prevention

KEY POINTS

- Fraud can be committed in any company. Therefore all companies should prepare their process structures for such an eventuality.
- Fraud should be identified and evaluated reactively and proactively. All measures should also be taken for adequate prosecution of those who commit fraud.
- An organization should have a clear, unambiguous code of conduct.
- Guidelines and instructions must be comprehensible and accessible to all employees.
- An organization should have a shared set of values and clearly communicate the consequences that fraud entails.

Dealing with Fraud

Every company must face the subject of fraud, first because many companies have experienced the negative impact of fraud in the form of financial losses and damage to their image, and second because this has been necessitated by legal requirements such as SOX. Thus, it has become increasingly important to equip the company adequately so it can deal with such problems. Within its area of responsibility, Internal Audit investigates and assesses very different types of incidents and suspected fraud. Internal Audit is an integral part of the company's handling of fraud, although other departments, such as Corporate Legal and Corporate Security are also involved. To effectively deal with fraud it is important to have a clearly structured organization, which immediately deals with the relevant circumstances of fraud and triggers, coordinates, and performs the necessary activities quickly, accurately, and reliably.

Role of the Corporate Legal Department

The corporate legal department is the organizational center dealing with fraud at SAP and is also known as "fraud filter." This is where all the reporting lines come together and are consolidated. This global function is primarily responsive in character, because it initiates action on the basis of information and reports, followed by measures taken in the different departments. The corporate legal department is also responsible for central coordination. Due to its central administrative function, it also has statistical information at its disposal, which is included in the fraud prevention process.

Fraud Evaluation Committee

When a fraud is suspected the Fraud Evaluation Committee should convene immediately, depending on the significance and urgency of the information or report. At SAP, this committee is made up of employees from Internal Audit, Corporate Legal, and Corporate Security. The committee decides which department is to take what action and when. In addition to such ad-hoc meetings, the Fraud Evaluation Committee should meet regularly so that all important matters can be discussed in this communication forum.

Fraud Filter

With its global mandate, SAP's fraud filter is connected to different communication channels, which supply information within the organization. All SAP employees can access incident reporting mechanisms and the whistleblowing function via the intranet and use these tools without restriction. The global compliance organization provides another important communication medium.

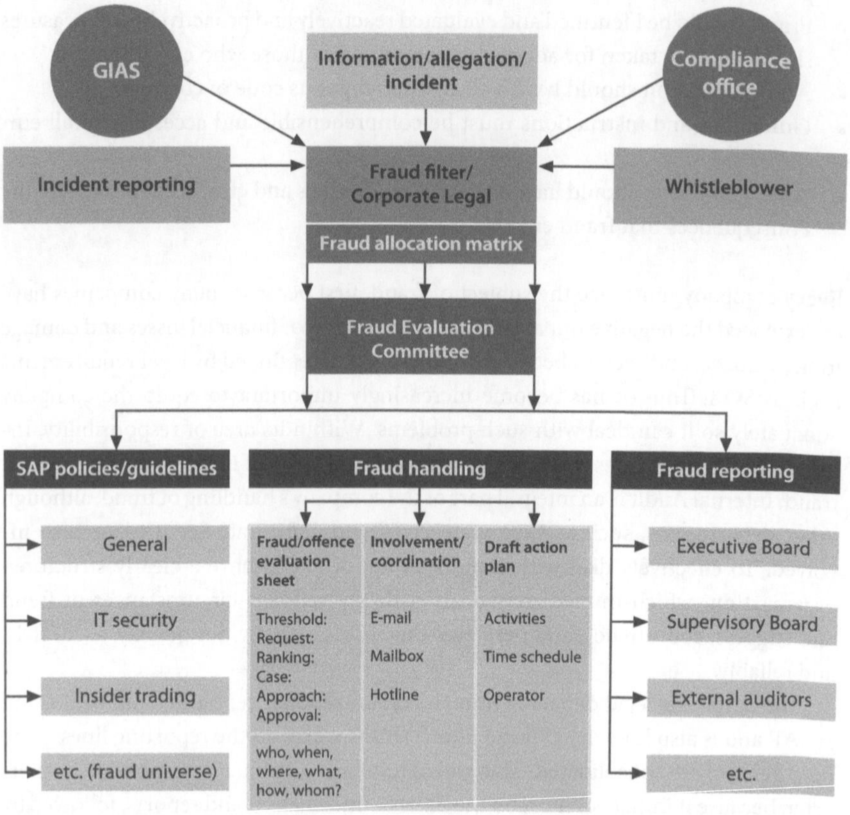

Fig. 26 SAP Fraud Filter

Incident Reporting

Incident reporting is an intranet-based reporting tool that employees can use to report incidents, although they cannot report anonymously through this tool. The standardized structure of the report covers all aspects of possible threats, from hacker attack through asset theft. There are also free-text fields, where any description can be added. Depending on the circumstances, the recorded incidents are reported to Corporate Legal and/or Corporate Security and handled accordingly.

Internal Audit has read access to all incident reports received. Incidents reported through this system form the main basis for Fraud Evaluation Committee meetings.

Documentation of Reported Incidents

Once the reported incidents have been investigated, they can be used to develop measures to prevent fraud in the future. At SAP, the incident report documentation is also used for the reports to the Board and the external auditors.

Whistleblower Facility

The whistleblower facility is a SOX-compliant anonymous reporting tool available to SAP employees on the intranet. It is intended for reporting irregularities with regard to revenue recognition and other financial data of SAP (see Section A, Chapter 2.6).

Global Compliance Team

The global compliance office is another point of contact for employees and managers that assesses and handles very diverse matters. In essence, the global compliance team drafts the code of conduct within SAP and ensures employee compliance. Contraventions of this code can be reported to the corporate legal department and may also be dealt with by Internal Audit, depending on the seriousness of the circumstances.

Fraud Allocation Matrix

The fraud allocation matrix is the working foundation of the fraud filter. It embodies the filter function, because one axis lists the possible threats and the other the departments responsible or to be informed. All possible risk scenarios are listed here, from theft through corruption, so that the response can be as rapid and focused as possible. The scenarios exist in overview format and in detail for each department.

Departments Involved

At SAP, Internal Audit, Corporate Legal, and Corporate Security are the primary departments involved in fraud investigations. Like a rapid response group, the audit teams of Internal Audit are in a position to act promptly whenever necessary in any local subsidiary or business unit of SAP. In special circumstances, Internal Audit can also engage external persons and service providers, usually detectives, forensic experts, or attorneys.

Prevention Model

SAP's fraud prevention model forms an integral part of its organizational and operational structures. From Internal Audit's perspective, the fraud prevention model's company-wide elements, such as the SAP Code of Business Conduct, play as critical a role as its audit-specific elements. The basic stages of the model have been institutionalized, for example through global guidelines and the Code of Business Conduct, and are coherent and comprehensible for all employees of the organization. This is important, because it is impossible to implement or comply with guidelines that are not known or understood. Overall, the fraud prevention model should be regarded as a cycle, because the process is driven and supplemented to a significant extent by past experience. Any weaknesses that occur must be eliminated as part of the process and lead to an overall improvement at the various levels. This reflects the model's top-down and bottom-up approach, which gives it the necessary flexibility.

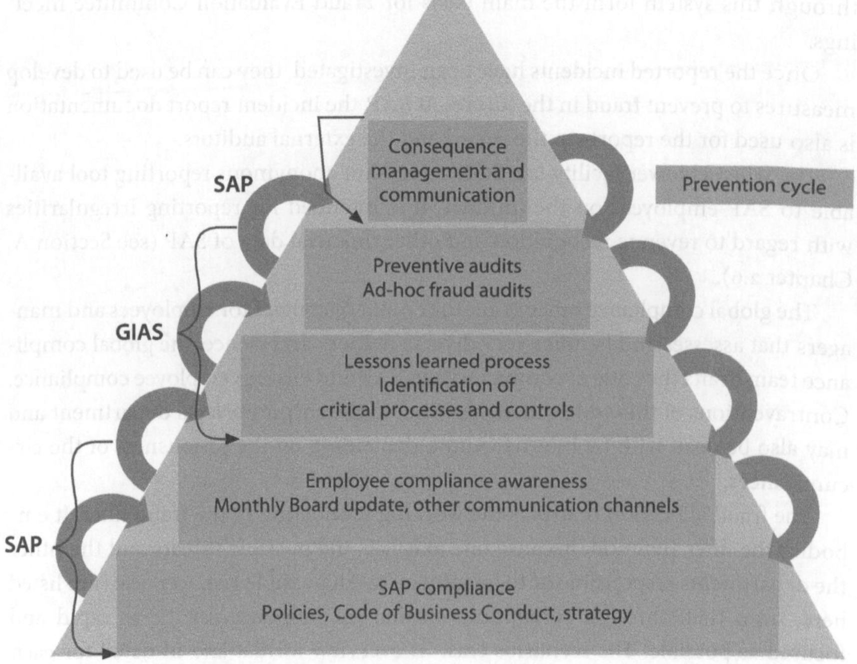

Fig. 27 Fraud Prevention Model Overview

Guidelines

Organizational guidelines provide a framework of conduct for an organization and its employees. They should provide instructions for all business units, transactions, and organizational units and must not contravene prevailing laws and regulations. In addition to the actual instructions, the following items should be made clear and documented accordingly:

- objective,
- benefits,
- strategic contribution,
- risk in case of non-compliance,
- area of application and target group,
- confidentiality,
- consequences of non-compliance,
- implementation and enforcement, and
- responsibility for the guideline.

SAP's guidelines, such as the Code of Business Conduct, are accessible to all employees on the intranet, and the persons responsible for the relevant guideline are available for queries. The rules provided therein are subject to a permanent updating process and represent the latest version. This transparency and availability facilitates audit work significantly, because the guidelines provide a fixed point of reference.

SAP Code of Business Conduct

The SAP Code of Business Conduct applies to all SAP employees around the globe. It assesses and regulates how to deal with potential conflict relating to employees, customers, partners, and suppliers. The code of conduct also provides guidance on how to resolve conflict that arises from related-party dealings.

Employee Awareness

In addition to the fundamental guidelines and instructions, another important criterion is whether and to what extent employees are aware of matters relating to fraud. An organization must use different communication elements to alert employees of fraudulent activities or rules regarding fraud adequately. Information and communication that comes from the Board receives special priority and attention. Any communication generally should conform to the corporate philosophy and culture. It is also important to highlight clearly the consequences of any contravention of the guidelines.

Importance for the Fraud Filter

Knowledge of communication channels, such as incident reporting or the whistleblower facility, heightens employees' awareness of the guidelines. The communication channels to the fraud filter, which activates the organization's response system, will only function once the guidelines have been positioned in a clear and comprehensible way and the employees are aware of their responsibility.

Prevention by Internal Audit

The work of Internal Audit, which acts by conducting specifically designed audits, is based on the cornerstones described above. Due to Internal Audit's proactive approach, the department forms part of SAP's prevention program. Internal and external empirical values are one basic element of proactive audits, and the results of testing internal controls in accordance with SOX are another source of information.

Focus of Preventive Fieldwork

Furthermore, preventive audit fieldwork focuses on the following processes and content elements:

- income statement, expenses, and costs,
- accounts receivable,
- accounts payable,
- purchasing, procurement, invitations to bid,
- capital expenditure,
- payroll,
- external services and service contracts, and
- areas where bribery and corruption is possible.

Consequence Management and Communication

Consequence management and its communication in the organization form the apex of the prevention model. The reports and memorandums of Internal Audit are the starting point for consequences and the resulting communication. In addition to any criminal charges, the consequences of economic crime or incidents that cause loss to the company are mostly of a disciplinary or organizational nature. Consequences must be applied uniformly, without favoritism and irrespective of hierarchy levels. The line taken on consequences is communicated throughout the organization and thus creates a fixed set of values on which the entier fraud prevention model is based.

Anti-Fraud Process Structure

SAP's internal audit department is part of the anti-fraud process structure, because it takes on key tasks in investigating cases of loss caused to the company. Internal Audit conducts audits proactively as part of the annual audit plan under the fraud prevention model, but also reactively when initiated by a request. Such a request can be made through the communication media mentioned earlier or, most commonly, directly through the fraud filter. Reactive audits are normally conducted ad hoc and require fieldwork to be started immediately. Depending on the circumstances, Internal Audit can also merely initiate a pre-investigation. This procedure is mapped in an Audit Roadmap developed specifically for this purpose (see Section B, Chapter B.7.2).

Scope and Work Program

The fraud Scope is an intentionally comprehensive presentation of all potential circumstances that are conceivable in relation to actions that cause loss to the company. In outline, the Scope has both a process orientation and a fraud orientation, allowing Internal Audit to identify potential risks at process level as well as vulnerable organizational units and accounts at fraud level. Based on the Scope, a flexible work program is adjusted or supplemented for each audit. Specific emphases can also be reflected in and supported by the level of detail of the work program. Work programs are compiled and implemented for both reactive and proactive audits. There are pre-drafted work programs for particularly vulnerable processes, which merely need adjustment to the specific circumstances. This makes it easier to prepare for reactive audits and saves time.

Action Guide

When the audit team begins fieldwork without knowing the details of a fraud case, the extent of loss, or the persons involved, an appropriate action guide should be followed first. This guide is used to collate facts and carry out structured research and investigations. As details of the incident are entered, an initial picture of events emerges. The action guide is a structured method of giving the audit team an initial overview. Individual issues complete the picture and signal the next action and audit steps. The action guide can also be used as a documentation vehicle and subsequent working paper and fraud summary, even if the facts are not yet known. The action guide collates the following information:

- persons and companies involved,
- relationships and links among persons and companies,
- timeline of events,
- documents and systems affected,
- quantification and qualification of extent,
- accounting estimate, and
- link to previous or similar incidents.

Interviews

Internal Audit interviews the people who are affected or involved in the incident. Throughout the investigation, suspected employees can also be questioned. If the interviews reveal that employees are guilty and have directly or indirectly admitted their guilt, the result of the interviews is of critical importance for reporting and documenting the case. Interviews should always be conducted by two auditors in order to ensure that the evidence is authentic.

Contact with External Third Parties

In the course of their fieldwork, auditors may have contact with external third parties, e.g., the police or the district attorney's office. It is important to conduct these talks, or at least prepare for them, together with the corporate legal department. The employees' privacy must be protected, which is why Internal Audit does not publicize the suspected fraud or voice any suspicions, but rather hands over the collected facts relevant for the case.

Background Checks

In addition to interviews and system tests, which are primarily performed in SAP AIS, depending on the specific case, background checks on the facts, and the people and companies involved are also important. Taking the relevant data protection regulations into account, the data sources for background checks include:

- commercial register,
- national and international internet databases,
- press databases,
- solvency checks, and
- detective agencies and credit bureaus.

Reporting and Documentation

All documents related to the allegations or the matter being investigated must be filed. They should be available at all times and presented in such a way that they can be understood by third parties. Internal Audit's reports always conform to the normal reporting guidelines. This requires that Internal Audit produce implementation reports or memorandums, which at SAP are forwarded to the CEO, the respective Board member and any other involved parties. However, other reports may also be used, particularly in cases of fraud and their solution. These include:

- expert reports and surveys,
- analyses of forensic investigations,
- analyses of (backed-up) data,
- legal reports,
- witness statements,
- background and research reports, and
- reports from third parties, e.g., detectives.

These reports are normally produced and commissioned in consultation with the corporate legal department and are protected by the attorney-client privilege. The legal department also helps clarify and ascertain that they can be used in a court of law and criminal prosecution.

HINTS AND TIPS

- Auditors must understand clearly that fraud can occur anywhere any time.
- Functioning communication structures and clearly assigned responsibilities are very important with regard to fraud prevention and investigation.

LINKS AND REFERENCES ↗

- ANDERSON, U. AND A. DAHLE. 2006. *Implementing the Professional Practices Framework.* 2nd ed. Altamonte Springs, FL: The Institute of Internal Auditors.
- INSTITUTE OF INTERNAL AUDITORS. 2006. *Practice Advisory 1210.A2-1: Auditors Responsibilities Relating to Fraud Risk Assessment, Prevention and Detection.* Altamonte Springs, FL: The Institute of Internal Auditors.
- INSTITUTE OF INTERNAL AUDITORS. 2006. *Practice Advisory 1210.A2-2: Auditors Responsibilities Relating to Fraud Investigation, Reporting, Resolution and Communication.* Altamonte Springs, FL: The Institute of Internal Auditors.
- INSTITUTE OF INTERNAL AUDITORS. 2002. *Standards for Professional Practice.* Altamonte Springs, FL: The Institute of Internal Auditors.

14 Services Provided by Internal Audit Relating to the Sarbanes-Oxley Act

14.1 General Principles

14.1.1 Legal Framework

KEY POINTS

- SOX was passed by the United States Congress in 2002 with an aim to protect investors and restore the public's confidence in the capital markets.
- Among the many provisions of SOX, sections 302 and 404 of SOX are of particular importance to internal auditors.
- SOX section 302 makes management, particularly the CEO and the CFO, responsible for the compliance of the company's financial reports.
- To meet these obligations, SOX section 404 requires management to provide evidence that all core business processes relevant to the financial reports, including the internal controls, are documented and effective.
- In addition, SOX has created the Public Company Accounting Oversight Board, or PCAOB.

Loss of Trust

In recent years, there has been a marked increase in uncertainty among investors, especially small investors, about the compliance of financial reports and the management of companies. In part, this is because of several highly publicized cases of companies manipulating financial statements and collapsing as a result. In many cases, it was shown clearly that the causes were mismanagement and fraudulent acts, resulting in severe losses for shareholders. These events led to a serious loss of trust among investors in capital markets around the world. In the United States, these developments are of particular importance, because equity investments play an important role in the pension arrangements for the entire population. At the same time, they damaged the public's confidence in companies in general and their corporate governance structures. The U.S. government responded in 2002 by passing the Sarbanes-Oxley Act (SOX).

Purview of SOX

The purview of SOX covers all U.S. companies registered with the U.S. Securities and Exchange Commission (SEC), including their foreign subsidiaries, as well as foreign companies listed in the United States (e.g., foreign private issuers, such as SAP). Although U.S.-based companies have had to fulfill the provisions of section 404 of SOX (see Section C, Chapter 8) since November 15, 2004, certain concessions apply to foreign private issuers, requiring them, among other things, to apply SOX 404 only to fiscal years ending after July 15, 2006. The act contains detailed requirements on reporting, also with regard to the effectiveness of internal controls, sets new standards for management responsibility and accountability, increases transparency, and lays down rules for proper business conduct. The application of SOX is to ensure compliant reporting and restore the confidence of all stakeholders in good corporate governance and management.

Significance for Internal Audit The introduction and establishment of this sophisticated set of rules poses new challenges for Internal Audit. Often, its provisions lead to the restructuring or re-alignment of individual areas of responsibility and the associated tasks. As an NYSE-listed and therefore SEC-registered company, SAP – and by extension also GIAS – must face the challenges of implementing SOX.

Key Requirements In this context, two sections of SOX are of key importance to Internal Audit:

- **SOX 302** SOX section 302 ("Corporate responsibility for financial reports") mandates that internal control procedures are established, maintained, and evaluated to ensure full and accurate financial disclosure that effectively reflects the financial position of the company. A prerequisite for this is that all information is captured properly and in a timely manner so that the CEO and CFO have access to this data in time to enable them to certify that the financial reports are compliant. Both officers are required to sign an affidavit to confirm the effectiveness of these controls and procedures and make known every incident of fraud that affects management or other employees materially involved in the internal control system, irrespective of its seriousness. By signing the affidavit, these officials assume personal responsibility for the accuracy of the company's financial information as published in all annual and interim financial statements.
- **SOX 404** The implementation of SOX section 404 ("Management assessment of internal controls") requires the greatest effort to ensure compliance with the regulation. It requires management to produce an internal control report that affirms that management has established and monitors an internal control system and documents and assesses the effectiveness of the internal controls. This is to ensure that all financial statements are produced according to the applicable accounting principles and misstatements in the financial statements are avoided. SOX section 404 covers all internal controls relating to financial reporting. Evidence of the effectiveness of this control system must be provided annually as part of a process specifically instituted for this purpose. A management report confirming the effectiveness of the internal control system, certified by the external auditors, must be submitted annually to the SEC.

PCAOB The Public Company Accounting Oversight Board (PCAOB) has also been introduced as a result of SOX. Newly established by SOX section 103 ("Auditing, quality control and independence standards and rules") in 2002, the PCAOB is a private-sector, non-profit corporation to oversee both U.S. and foreign auditors of public companies. All auditors and public accounting firms that prepare audit reports for issuers governed by SOX must register with the board. This ends the self-regulation of public accountants in the United States. The PCAOB is supervised by the SEC and takes on investigative and disciplinary powers over public accountants: Under the provisions of SOX, it monitors compliance with the existing standards of a profession, but it also has far-reaching powers to formulate new standards, i.e., it can set auditing, quality control, ethics, and independence standards, which must all be complied with. In addition, the PCAOB can conduct quality inspections of registered auditors and public accounting firms.

HINTS AND TIPS

- Auditors should familiarize themselves with the main elements of the relevant sections of SOX.
- In the future, auditors will need to focus even more on the completeness of the internal controls, especially with regard to risk cover and financial reporting.

LINKS AND REFERENCES

- DELOITTE. 2005. *Optimizing the Role of Internal Audit in the Sarbanes-Oxley Era.* www.deloitte.com/dtt/cda/doc/content/us_ERS_Internal%20Audit%20POV.pdf (accessed May 31, 2007).
- GRAY, G. L. 2004. *Changing Internal Audit Practices in the New Paradigm: The Sarbanes-Oxley Environment.* Altamonte Springs, FL: The Institute of Internal Auditors.
- HAUSER, D., R. HOPKINS, AND H. LEIBUNDGUT. 2004. The Sarbanes-Oxley Act and the Role of Internal Audit. *Der Schweizer Treuhänder* (December 2004): 1057-1065.
- INSTITUTE OF INTERNAL AUDITORS. 2004. *Internal Auditing's Role in Sections 302 and 404 of the U.S. Sarbanes-Oxley Act of 2002.* Altamonte Springs, FL: The Institute of Internal Auditors.
- PUBLIC COMPANY ACCOUNTING OVERSIGHT BOARD (PCAOB). 2004. *Auditing Standard No. 2: An Audit of Internal Control Over Financial Reporting Performed in Conjunction With an Audit of Financial Statements.* http://www.pcaobus.org/Standards/Standards_and_Related_Rules/Auditing_Standard_No.2.aspx (accessed May 31, 2007).
- PUBLIC COMPANY ACCOUNTING OVERSIGHT BOARD (PCAOB). *Staff Questions and Answers: Auditing Internal Control over Financial Reporting.* http://www.pcaob.org/standards/staff_questions_and_answers/2005/01-21.pdf (accessed May 31, 2007).
- ROTH, J. AND D. ESPERSON. 2003. *Internal Audit's Role in Corporate Governances: Sarbanes Oxley Compliance.* Altamonte Springs, FL: The Institute of Internal Auditors.
- U.S. CONGRESS. 2002. *Sarbanes-Oxley Act of 2002. 107th Congress of the United States of America. HR 3763.* Washington DC: Government Printing Office.

14.1.2 COSO Requirements

KEY POINTS

- The COSO Internal Control framework is a non-binding recommendation for establishing an internal control system.
- Visually, the model is presented in the form of the COSO cube to illustrate the overlapping relationships between the objectives, components and levels of the organization.
- An implemented internal control system should cover all COSO components in order to meet the requirements of SOX 404.

COSO Framework When the Committee of Sponsoring Organizations of the Treadway Commission (COSO), founded in 1985, conducted a study of fraudulent financial reporting in 1992, it developed a concept that provides a non-binding, generally applicable framework to support companies in establishing, using, monitoring, and assessing their internal control systems. It specifies a standard definition of an internal control system, thus ensuring that financial reports are comparable and of high quality. Under the COSO framework, an internal control system has three key objectives:

- effectiveness and efficiency of operations,
- reliability of financial reporting, and
- compliance with applicable laws and regulations.

Internal Audit also pursues these objectives as part of the internal monitoring system (see Section A, Chapter 1.2).

COSO Cube The following diagram shows a modified version of the COSO cube. It demonstrates that an internal control system is shaped by the characteristics of different internal control components, which are necessary to achieve the above key objectives. The components are:

- Control Environment,
- Risk Assessment,
- Control Activities,
- Information and Communication, and
- Monitoring.

The third dimension comprises all the processes and company units for which the achievement of objectives must be ensured through the operative control components.

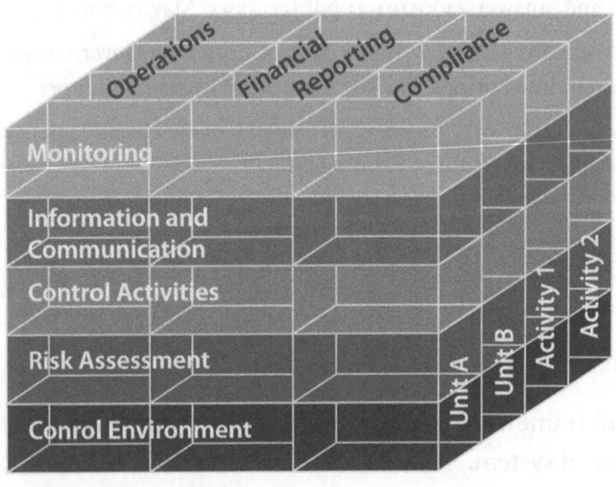

Fig. 28 COSO Cube (COSO IC)

Adapted from SOX-Online, www.SOX-online.com/COSO_cobit_COSO_cube-old.html

Copyright © 1992 by the Committee of Sponsoring Organizations of the Treadway Commission

COSO IC and COSO ERM

The COSO Internal Control framework (COSO IC) provides a comprehensive view of the dimensions of the internal control system and its implementation activities. COSO IC represents a global standard for the internal control system to be established under SOX and ensures that the installed systems are consistent, measurable, and comparable. An expanded model, the COSO Enterprise Risk Management framework (COSO ERM) has since been developed, specifically defined for the interests of a comprehensive risk management system in the company (see Section A, Chapter 1.3). The main additions relate to objectives of the organization (e.g., strategic objectives have been added) and the internal control components (e.g., objective setting, determining risk appetite, and event identification have been added).

Control Environment

The control environment is the foundation for the other four components. It reflects the corporate culture and the monitoring activities performed by the supervisory bodies in order to influence the control consciousness of the company's people. Control environment factors include integrity, ethical values, management's operating style, delegation of authority systems, as well as the processes for managing and developing people within the organization.

Risk Assessment

A precondition to risk assessment is the identification and establishment of consistent internal objectives. All risks that can affect the achievement of business targets must be identified, documented, and evaluated during risk assessment, and appropriate actions for mitigation must be specified. This comprehensive risk assessment concept is a prerequisite for determining how the risks should be managed.

Control Activities

Control activities are the policies and procedures that help ensure management directives relating to risk identification and control are understood and carried out within the company. The actual implementation and documentation of these controls are a prerequisite for an effective response to risks and also serve as concrete evidence of control activities for the external auditors. For this reason, control activities are a key component of the SOX 404 provisions.

Information and Communication

Intra-company communication of relevant information guarantees appropriate decision-making by management, on the basis of the results produced by the internal control system. All employees must be aware of this with regard to their area of responsibility within the internal control system. A functioning internal control system is thus only possible if there is a suitable information system.

Monitoring

In view of the constantly changing parameters for the internal control system, the system must be permanently monitored to ensure it is effective at all times. This process involves above all management, the Board of Directors, Internal Audit, and all responsible employees.

Link Between SOX and COSO

SOX requires that organizations implement a formal internal control framework. While COSO IC is not explicitly required, it is suggested and recommended as an example of an appropriate framework. Further, survey evidence suggests that this framework is the most commonly adopted by companies that must comply with SOX. In order to meet the requirements of SOX 404 with regard to the confirmation of the effectiveness of the internal controls, it is important that an installed internal control system covers all the above components of the COSO framework. These components therefore form the basis for understanding SOX 404.

HINTS AND TIPS

- Audits of the internal control system should be guided by the components of the COSO cube.
- Auditors should try to incorporate, directly or indirectly, all the components of COSO in the work program in order to guarantee that the requirements of SOX 404 are met.
- In every audit, internal auditors should establish the link to the objectives of the internal control system.

LINKS AND REFERENCES

- ANDERSON, S. A., M. H. CHRIST AND K. L. SEDATOLE. 2006. *Managing Strategic Alliance Risk: Survey Evidence of Control Practices in Collaborative Inter-Organizational Settings.* Altamonte Springs, FL: The Institute of Internal Auditors.
- COMMITTEE OF SPONSORING ORGANIZATIONS OF THE TREADWAY COMMISSION (COSO). 1992. *Internal Control Integrated Framework.* New York, NY: AICPA.
- COMMITTEE OF SPONSORING ORGANIZATIONS OF THE TREADWAY COMMISSION (COSO). 2003. *Enterprise Risk Management Framework.* New York, NY: AICPA.
- DELOACH, J. 2000. *Enterprise-wide Risk Management: Strategies for Linking Risk and Opportunity.* London: Financial Times Management.
- PUBLIC COMPANY ACCOUNTING OVERSIGHT BOARD (PCAOB). 2004. *Auditing Standard No. 2: An Audit of Internal Control Over Financial Reporting Performed in Conjunction With an Audit of Financial Statements.* http://www.pcaobus.org/Standards/Standards_and_ Related_Rules/Auditing_Standard_No.2.aspx (accessed May 31, 2007).
- PUBLIC COMPANY ACCOUNTING OVERSIGHT BOARD (PCAOB). *Staff Questions and Answers: Auditing Internal Control over Financial Reporting.* http://www.pcaob.org/standards/staff_questions_and_answers/2005/01-21.pdf (accessed May 31, 2007).
- U.S. CONGRESS. 2002. *Sarbanes-Oxley Act of 2002. 107th Congress of the United States of America. HR 3763.* Washington DC: Government Printing Office.

14.1.3 Impact of SOX on Internal Audit

KEY POINTS

- The introduction of SOX entails new challenges and demands for Internal Audit.

- It is important to strike a balance between safeguarding the audit principles and making the greatest possible contribution to the SOX processes without putting the independence and objectivity of Internal Audit at risk.
- However, none of these considerations must detract from the fact that management has the overall responsibility for the compliance of the SOX processes.
- There are many ways in which Internal Audit can perform an important support function.

Transformation of Internal Audit

The tasks of Internal Audit have undergone a major transformation in recent years and their overall significance has increased (see Section A, Chapter 2). The stringent requirements that SOX has placed on internal control systems have accelerated this development because Internal Audit, as part of the internal monitoring system and acting on behalf of company management, is also responsible for monitoring the internal control system.

Responsibility of Company Management

It is ultimately the sole responsibility of top management to ensure compliance with SOX sections 302 and 404, and this responsibility cannot be transferred. Company management must satisfy itself at least once a year that sufficient internal controls over financial reporting processes are in place and working effectively by conducting internal control tests. This is the only way to ensure that the certification of the financial statements required under SOX can be made with the necessary confidence about its content and form. But company management can additionally delegate control tasks required by SOX to the next management level and, by cascading them down, illustrate the responsibility of all managers involved in the internal control system. Internal Audit can provide assistance to company management in essentially two ways: by offering support services and by providing actual audit services (see Section D, Chapter 14.3). However, the critical factor is that the CEO and CFO ultimately must certify that the internal controls are working effectively, and SOX section 904 specifies strict legal penalties that may befall these executives if the certifications are not truthful, including large monetary fines and prison sentences.

Maintaining Independence and Objectivity

There is general consensus that Internal Audit must protect its independence and objectivity at all times. Thus, it cannot assume separate and final responsibility for anything other than auditing – in this case with regard to the process of providing and preserving evidence according to SOX. As a result, Internal Audit must find a careful balance between its audit mandate and its support functions. In this context, the IIA has developed possible solutions and evaluated them with regard to the audit principles of objectivity and independence. It is for every company to decide whether to regard these proposals as useful guidance and to implement and apply them in line with its in-house possibilities.

Roles of Internal Audit

In relation to SOX activities, Internal Audit can assume the following roles:

Consulting Body

- Internal Audit's role as a consulting body means that it supports the company in identifying, evaluating, assessing, as well as eliminating risks. Provided Internal Audit limits itself to making recommendations or giving assessments of processes and controls, this role does not give rise to concerns regarding the principles of independence and objectivity.

Testing and Documenting Body

- Internal Audit's testing and documenting role allows management to involve the department in testing the effectiveness of the internal control system and to muster its support in the documentation of the processes and internal controls. This does not interfere with the principles of independence and objectivity as long as management retains the authority to decide on process and control design and to assess the effectiveness of the internal control system.

Main Project Lead

- If Internal Audit acts as main project lead, the auditor assumes the role of lead project manager during the implementation of SOX 404. If the auditor's function is restricted to administrative tasks, there is no conflict with the independence and objectivity principles. However, as soon as the auditor performs management tasks and thus has special decision powers, compliance with these principles can no longer be fully guaranteed.

Trainer and Know-How Carrier

- Due to Internal Audit's knowledge of company-internal controls, it makes sense for Internal Audit to assume the role of trainer and knowledge leader in the handling of controls. Auditors are uniquely positioned within the organization to offer support and training for activities necessary as part of the internal control system. This does not give rise to any conflict with the principles of independence and objectivity.

Expert Assessor of the Internal Control System

- Internal Audit can also be consulted by management as an expert in assessing the effectiveness of the internal control system. This expertise allows auditors to support management in its assessment by providing training and information without infringing upon the independence and objectivity principles. A conflict would only arise if the auditors were to perform these assessments under their own responsibility.

Accreditation Body

- As an accreditation body, Internal Audit performs accreditations and is involved in assessing the internal control system. It can only do so in a supporting and consulting role, which must not involve taking on any responsibility, because this would put Internal Audit's independence and objectivity at risk.

Summary

If the different roles are combined, Internal Audit can take on an important position in the SOX scenario. Special procedures must be developed, although they should be based on the formal parameters of the general audit process. This is the only way to ensure that all Internal Audit engagements are handled properly and the expected results are correct and comparable.

HINTS AND TIPS

- Auditors must ensure that their SOX-related activities do not conflict with the audit principles of independence and objectivity.
- Auditors should develop their own SOX skills, i.e., acquire knowledge of the implementation methods and the consequences of SOX-related activities.

- The classic audit process should always be examined for overlap with the SOX requirements.
- Auditors should document everything that could in any way influence the design of the internal control system.

LINKS AND REFERENCES ↗

- GRAY, G. L. 2004. *Changing Internal Audit Practices in the New Paradigm: The Sarbanes-Oxley Environment.* Altamonte Springs, FL: The Institute of Internal Auditors.
- INSTITUTE OF INTERNAL AUDITORS. 2004. *Internal Auditing's Role in Sections 302 and 404 of the U.S. Sarbanes-Oxley Act of 2002.* Altamonte Springs, FL: The Institute of Internal Auditors.
- INSTITUTE OF INTERNAL AUDITORS. 2005. *Practical Considerations Regarding Internal Auditing Expressing an Opinion on Internal Control.* Altamonte Springs, FL: The Institute of Internal Auditors.
- PUBLIC COMPANY ACCOUNTING OVERSIGHT BOARD (PCAOB). 2004. *Auditing Standard No. 2: An Audit of Internal Control Over Financial Reporting Performed in Conjunction With an Audit of Financial Statements.* http://www.pcaobus.org/Standards/Standards_and_ Related_Rules/Auditing_Standard_No.2.aspx (accessed May 31, 2007).
- PUBLIC COMPANY ACCOUNTING OVERSIGHT BOARD (PCAOB). 2004. *Staff Questions and Answers: Auditing Internal Control over Financial Reporting.* http://www.pcaob.org/standards/staff_questions_and_answers/2005/01-21.pdf (accessed May 31, 2007).
- REDING, K. F., P. J. SOBEL, U. L. ANDERSON, et al. 2007. *Internal Assurance and Consulting Services.* Altamonte Springs, FL: Institute of Internal Auditors.
- ROTH, J. AND D. ESPERSON. 2003. *Internal Audit's Role in Corporate Governances: Sarbanes Oxley Compliance.* Altamonte Springs, FL: Institute of Internal Auditors.
- U.S. CONGRESS. 2002. *Sarbanes-Oxley Act of 2002. 107th Congress of the United States of America. HR 3763.* Washington DC: Government Printing Office.

14.2 Integrating SOX Organization and Internal Audit

14.2.1 Management of Internal Controls

KEY POINTS •••

- In order to meet SOX requirements, management must scrutinize the business processes and the underlying accounting transactions.
- The organization must identify the relevant internal controls for all financial accounts related to the financial statements and their control objectives.
- The internal control management tool helps meet the requirements of SOX 302 and 404.
- All core business processes and the information necessary for a comprehensive SOX approach are stored in a central process catalog.

- The process groups are divided into individual processes, which in turn comprise different process and control steps.
- Significant controls, in particular, must be identified and described accurately.

Involvement of Internal Audit

The main purpose of this chapter is not to present basic information about the SOX procedures, but the way in which Internal Audit is involved and fully integrated into this audit-related process. Some of the fundamentals have already been described, at least in outline, in earlier sections of this handbook (see Section A, Chapter 2.6). With reference to the introduction to the internal control management tool (see Section B, Chapter 4.1.3.3), details of Internal Audit's involvement in the SOX process are now provided. This will make it easier to classify Internal Audit's various SOX approaches and to assess their significance for compliance with the provisions of SOX.

Business Processes as Starting Point

One of the main objectives of SOX is to ensure that the significant financial data disclosed in the financial reports presents an accurate and complete picture of the financial health of the organization. The reports are based on national laws and international standards, which provide rules on how to present transactions in the accounts. The purview of SOX not only includes events that follow the entry of an incoming document in the accounting system, but also the underlying business processes that precede entry. The accounting system is scrutinized to establish whether a transaction is verified by sufficient controls, i.e., whether it has in fact been triggered by bona fide business processes and its nature and amount are based on actual business operations.

Internal Controls

From the perspective of the financial accounts, materiality is an important criterion, that is, it is established whether adequate controls exist for those accounts that are relevant to the financial statements. Internal controls normally relate to clear control objectives in order to cover the corresponding risks and ensure that the business processes are compliant overall. This is to ensure that, from the perspective of the financial accounts, all values entered have been duly confirmed by controls based on clearly described business processes and that these controls cover, or at least mitigate, the risks associated with these processes.

IT Tool

As mentioned earlier, SAP has developed an IT tool for analyzing and evaluating the internal controls, which is intended to support compliance with the requirements of SOX 302 and 404. Specifically, it helps:

- confirm that the figures in the interim and annual financial statements and the relevant publications are correct,
- document, establish, and implement the controls and process steps required,
- assess the effectiveness of the controls and process steps and create a report summarizing the results, and
- show in periodic reports all changes to the internal controls, including all material weaknesses that have occurred since the last assessment.

Process Catalog

A central process catalog is a key component of this IT tool. This catalog contains all the process groups and processes relevant to SOX 404, including all relevant control objectives and risks, as well as the affected accounts. The process groups are based on the core business processes of the high-tech industry that have a direct or indirect impact on the figures reported in the financial statements. Depending on the organizational structure, some process groups are relevant only to corporate departments, others only to local subsidiaries, although some are relevant to both. Here follows a list of selected process groups by way of example:

- Managerial Accounting,
- Accounts Receivable,
- Purchasing
- Internal Audit,
- Corporate Financial Reporting,
- Accounts Payable,
- Marketing, and
- Sales.

It is important to ensure that each process group is separately identified in the IT tool so that the relevant processes can be assigned unambiguously and administered correctly.

Processes within the Process Groups

Each process group is in turn divided into separate processes. Here follow as an example the individual processes of process group "General Purchasing" (PR G), identified numerically in increments of ten:

- PR G 10 Contract,
- PR G 20 Purchase requisition,
- PR G 30 Purchase order,
- PR G 40 Control and reports.

Process and Control Steps

Each process consists of different process and control steps. Although the process groups and processes have centrally standardized definitions, the process and control steps are determined individually for each organizational unit. They are identified by the process number, divided into individual step numbers, as shown in the following example for the "Contract" and "Purchase requisition" processes from the "General Purchasing" process group:

- PR G 10.01 Goods/service selection,
- PR G 10.02 Supplier selection,
- ...,
- PR G 20.01 Preparation of purchase requisition,
- PR G 20.02 Creation of purchase requisition.

The specific details of this example may vary in different companies.

Significant Controls

The assessment of the significance of a control is often subjective, but there are a number of criteria to help decide whether or not a control should be regarded as significant. Significant controls normally occur at the beginning (e.g., monitoring of access authorizations) and at the end (e.g., contract signed by two signatories) of a process. Specifically, they include the following:

- controls relating to the preparation of the annual financial statements and the figures to be disclosed, especially all controls of process steps that trigger or report account movements,
- controls intended to prevent fraud,
- controls on which other controls depend, e.g., management control of operational controls, such as the dual-control principle,
- controls on significant, non-routine, non-systematic transactions (e.g., accounts, including measurements/assessments and estimates, such as the approval of an impairment loss on an asset or the reversal of an impairment loss), and
- controls on periodic closing processes in financial reporting, including controls on individual process steps, such as
  - entry of totals in the general ledger,
  - entry of journal values in the general ledger, and
  - recording of recurring and non-recurring adjustments in financial reporting, e.g., in connection with deferrals, accruals, etc.

HINTS AND TIPS

- Auditors should familiarize themselves in detail with those process groups that are important for their fieldwork.
- If auditors identify any issues, they should inform the person responsible for the process group.
- When creating Scopes and work programs, auditors should use the process catalog as a guideline and, wherever possible, take into account in their fieldwork interrelations and interfaces between process groups.

LINKS AND REFERENCES

- DELOITTE. 2005. *Optimizing the Role of Internal Audit in the Sarbanes-Oxley Era.* www.deloitte.com/dtt/cda/doc/content/us_ERS_Internal%20Audit%20POV.pdf (accessed May 31, 2007).
- INSTITUTE OF INTERNAL AUDITORS. 2004. *Internal Auditing's Role in Sections 302 and 404 of the U.S. Sarbanes-Oxley Act of 2002.* Altamonte Springs, FL: The Institute of Internal Auditors.
- PUBLIC COMPANY ACCOUNTING OVERSIGHT BOARD (PCAOB). 2004. *Auditing Standard No. 2: An Audit of Internal Control Over Financial Reporting Performed in Conjunction With an Audit of Financial Statements.* http://www.pcaobus.org/Standards/Standards_and_Related_Rules/Auditing_Standard_No.2.aspx (accessed May 31, 2007).
- PUBLIC COMPANY ACCOUNTING OVERSIGHT BOARD (PCAOB). *Staff Questions and Answers: Auditing Internal Control over Financial Reporting.* http://www.pcaob.org/standards/staff_questions_and_answers/2005/01-21.pdf (accessed May 31, 2007).

14.2.2 SOX Lifecycle Process Model

KEY POINTS

- The SOX lifecycle, which is a specific process model, forms the basis for all SOX-related activities.
- Within the SOX lifecycle, two main phases, design assessment and testing of the internal controls, are particularly important.
- An IT tool is used for the administration and documentation of all the steps in the SOX lifecycle.

SOX Lifecycle as Basis for Integration

The SOX lifecycle, which is a specific process model, forms the basis for all SOX-related activities. It contains the different steps that a company must perform to comply with the requirements of SOX. This process model also shows why and how Internal Audit can be involved in or monitor this process. The different approaches of Internal Audit can be mapped according to the general process and the resulting roles. The many, sometimes complex, issues are discussed in the next chapter (see Section D, Chapter 14.2.3). They form the basis for the approaches Internal Audit takes to its SOX integration, described in Section D, Chapter 14.2.4.

Design Assessment

The process documentation must be compiled, reviewed, and supplemented annually. This means that the process owner must evaluate, on the basis of the process catalog, whether all processes meet their purpose and objectives and are correctly and fully organized and documented. This also includes a complete examination of all the mapped risks and controls. To this end, the process owner can use descriptive text as well as flowcharts, tables, and matrices. Within the design assessment phase, two areas are distinguished (for details, see Section C, Chapter 8):

- During control design assessment, the controls are scrutinized to establish whether they are theoretically able to minimize or prevent the relevant risks and whether they are suitable for ensuring that the amounts stated on an account are correct.
- During process design assessment, on the other hand, the material risks of a process are analyzed to determine whether all are effectively covered by the defined controls. This involves establishing whether the controls are working correctly and positioned as specified, and whether significant controls are missing.

It is important to ensure that every process has at least one significant control (also referred to as key control) and that each control covers at least one of the following criteria: completeness, accuracy, validity, and restricted access.

Design Assessment Result

The design assessment will either confirm that the processes and controls are correct or find exceptions or errors that should be discussed with their owners. If no exceptions are identified and all controls are regarded as effective, the design of the processes and controls can be rated as adequate. If exceptions are identified, the rating depends on their significance, either in relation to the individual exceptions

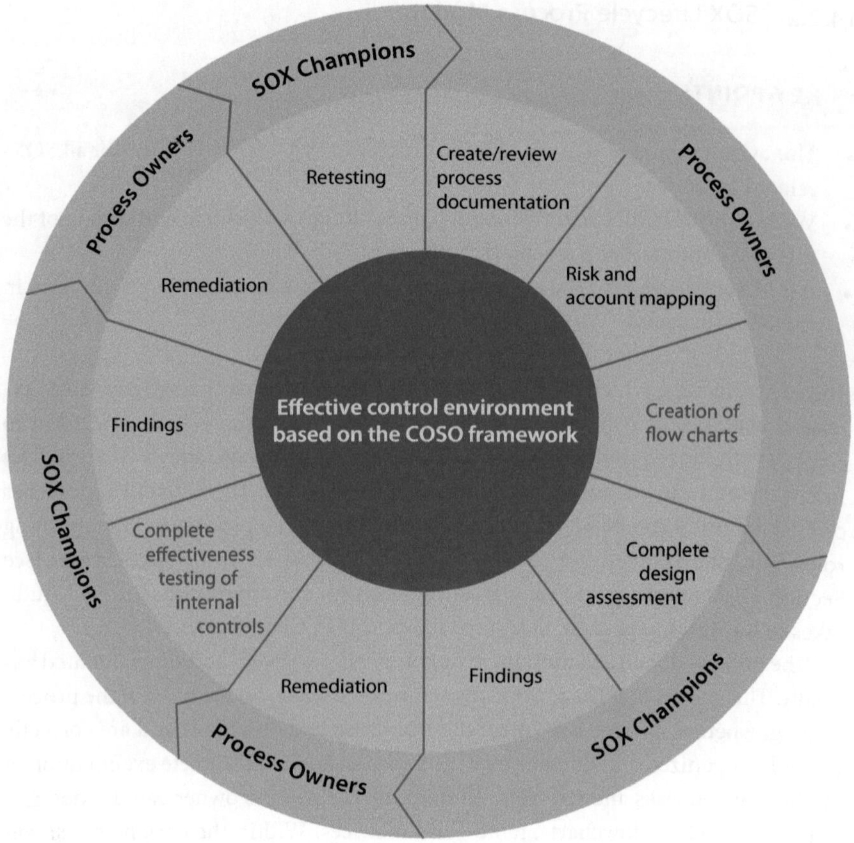

Fig. 29 SOX Lifecycle

or aggregated with other control exceptions in the specific process or in relation to their effect on other processes. In such a case, the process and control design can still be rated adequate, or it may be rated insufficient. There are a number of similar criteria (e.g.: Is the number of controls sufficient? Are the controls independent? Do they cover the material risks?) to assess the adequacy of both the controls (e.g., the control reduces the risk to an acceptable level) and the processes (e.g., all controls are correctly positioned).

Documentation of the Result

The results of the design assessment are documented in the internal control management tool, where detailed information, such as the assessment steps taken, the expected results, the evidence obtained, and the conclusion, is recorded. Any exceptions should be appropriately reported using predefined issue categories such as "Inadequate control design" or "Control not performed." A closely related issue is the prioritization of the findings according to:

- high priority (e.g., if the exception found could trigger a misstatement in the financial reports),
- medium priority (e.g., if the exceptions found could have an impact on the accuracy of the financial data), and
- low priority (e.g., if the exception found is offset by a documented and successfully tested control).

The SOX champion also must decide whether to create a specific remediation plan. It is normally advisable to develop a remediation plan, if remediation will take longer than four weeks to eliminate the identified weakness or if the finding relates to the application of the US-GAAP accounting guidelines (e.g., with regard to revenue recognition) or to a missing control.

Testing the Effectiveness of the Internal Controls

The second important stage of the SOX lifecycle is the testing of the internal controls (see Section C, Chapter 8). The company is obliged to carry out such tests and to examine different aspects of internal control, including, for example, the type of control. The method, timeframe, and extent of testing must be defined accordingly once a year, and in particular, evidence must be provided to ensure that the internal controls are effective for all important financial accounts. The internal controls can be tested in different ways, e.g., through interviews, direct observation, walk-throughs, or document analysis.

Extent of the Tests to Be Performed

The extent of the tests to be performed is of particular importance (see Section B, Chapter 4.1.2; Section C, Chapter 8). The samples should be selected using a reasonable procedure. Depending on the requirements of the external auditors, it can be specified, for example, that all significant controls and 10% of all standard controls must be tested. On the basis of such parameters a structured sampling procedure can be determined. A sample selection criterion can be the frequency of use of the internal control (annual, monthly, daily, etc.).

Documenting Test Execution

When testing the effectiveness of the internal controls, certain information must be stored in the IT tool, including the sample size, the type of sampling, the test procedure or combination of testing methods, and the expected results (type of evidence, formal and substantive accuracy). The actual test results also must be documented. The test results and the appropriate evidence are collected in a folder, referencing the test steps and items of evidence to the relevant control steps in the process documentation. At the end of the test phase, a meeting is held with the process owners to discuss the results and findings. After the meeting, the test results should be documented in the IT tool, using the appropriate categories for describing any exceptions.

Retesting

After the remediation phase for the exceptions found, the controls are retested, focusing on whether the control weaknesses identified have been eliminated and whether the CEO, the CFO, and the external auditors will be able to confirm the compliance of the financial data on the basis of an adequate internal control system.

HINTS AND TIPS

- When compiling work programs, auditors should, if possible, incorporate the results of the SOX lifecycle.
- In particular, auditors should assess the documented and tested internal controls from Internal Audit's perspective.
- Internal Audit employees should ask to be included in the relevant distribution lists so that they receive regular updates on SOX procedures.
- All documented process steps and controls must be carefully referenced.

LINKS AND REFERENCES

- COMMITTEE OF SPONSORING ORGANIZATIONS OF THE TREADWAY COMMISSION (COSO). 2003. *Enterprise Risk Management Framework.* New York, NY: AICPA.
- COMMITTEE OF SPONSORING ORGANIZATIONS OF THE TREADWAY COMMISSION (COSO). 1992. *Internal Control Integrated Framework.* New York, NY: AICPA.
- INSTITUTE OF INTERNAL AUDITORS. 2006. *Sarbanes-Oxley Section 404: A Guide for Management of Internal Control Practitioners.* Altamonte Springs, FL: The Institute of Internal Auditors.
- PUBLIC COMPANY ACCOUNTING OVERSIGHT BOARD (PCAOB). 2004. *Auditing Standard No. 2: An Audit of Internal Control Over Financial Reporting Performed in Conjunction With an Audit of Financial Statements.* http://www.pcaobus.org/Standards/Standards_and_ Related_Rules/Auditing_Standard_No.2.aspx (accessed May 31, 2007).
- PUBLIC COMPANY ACCOUNTING OVERSIGHT BOARD (PCAOB). 2004. *Staff Questions and Answers: Auditing Internal Control over Financial Reporting.* http://www.pcaob.org/standards/staff_questions_and_answers/2005/01-21.pdf (accessed May 31, 2007).
- U.S. CONGRESS. 2002. *Sarbanes-Oxley Act of 2002. 107th Congress of the United States of America. HR 3763.* Washington DC: Government Printing Office.

14.2.3 Roles and Responsibilities

KEY POINTS

- The procedures for SOX compliance comprise complex arrangements and affect a number of parties.
- In addition to the process owners, the SOX manager, and the SOX champions, Internal Audit, the external auditors, the CEO, and the CFO are all involved in SOX compliance.
- Cooperation between these parties must be clearly defined and coordinated.

- Internal Audit's activities are primarily focused on sharing information and process experience.
- A closely related task is the development and optimization of best practices as standards for the core business processes.

SOX Cooperation

The procedures for SOX compliance comprise complex arrangements of organizational functions and affect a number of parties, ranging from process owners and the actual SOX organization through Internal Audit and the Board of Directors and management, who sign the certification of the financial statements. To ensure successful cooperation, it is necessary to clearly define and coordinate the roles of all the parties involved. Due to the complexity of the tasks and responsibilities, it is only possible to deal briefly with each of the parties.

Process Owner

A process owner should be selected for each process or process group (if applicable). Typically, process owners are the managers or the employee responsible for the process on a day-to-day basis. That is, the process owner is someone who is intimately familiar with the process. Process owners are responsible for ensuring that the documentation of the processes and controls is always up to date, the processes serve the intended purpose, and the controls are adequate and sufficient. Thus, process owners serve as quality managers and experts for the processes and controls assigned to them. For the entire duration of the SOX lifecycle, the process owners are the main contacts for all other parties, but, to ensure independence, they should not assume direct responsibility for performing design assessments or testing internal controls. This is the job of the SOX champion. The SOX champion works very closely with the local manager, whose management duties include verifying that the internal controls are working.

SOX Manager

Within the actual SOX function, the SOX manager, who is part of the corporate risk management function, is available as the first point of contact. He or she reports to the head of the corporate risk management function. The most important task of the SOX manager is to monitor and, if necessary, coordinate the whole SOX process from an overall global perspective.

SOX Champion

The SOX champions are another important group within the SOX function. They are responsible for SOX coordination at the local level, i.e. within the entity concerned. Together with the internal and external auditors, they ensure that all SOX-related activities are carried out properly. This includes training process owners, monitoring the quality of data in the IT tool, holding coordination and status discussion meetings, and preparing the regular reports for the SOX manager. Moreover, the SOX champions carry the main responsibility for large parts of the SOX lifecycle, especially design assessment and support for testing the effectiveness of the internal controls.

SOX Auditors in Internal Audit

Internal Audit's integration into the SOX compliance procedures gives SOX auditors the opportunity to gain a comprehensive understanding of all SOX-relevant core processes (for more on how Internal Audit is involved in the SOX procedures, see Section D, Chapter 14.2.4). Best practices can be identified and defined on the basis of the different forms the processes take, with due regard for business and cultural differences. At SAP, the SOX auditors are organized as a separate team within Internal Audit. They contribute audit expertise and provide a consistent knowledge base for the global SOX process, thus facilitating the introduction of standardized testing methods and the communication of process recommendations. At the same time they support management in developing, improving, and applying internal controls. The SOX auditors can provide important information about how global guidelines are met to Internal Audit's other regional teams, the SOX manager, the Board of Directors, and the corporate departments concerned. Their knowledge of suitable processes, systems, and structures qualifies SOX auditors as a competent source of information on issues of company organization. But SOX auditors also fulfill an important role in passing their knowledge and experience on to other departments and local subsidiaries: For example, SOX auditors can pass their knowledge of SOX-relevant transactions, system settings, and process designs on to other local subsidiaries or inform other audit teams of specific process and system details relevant for their audits. Since it deals with so many different aspects, the SOX audit team is an ideal starting point for new employees: First, it introduces them to the basics of auditing, and second, because they must familiarize themselves with many different process groups, they have the opportunity to acquire comprehensive expertise within only a few years. For this reason, Internal Audit should develop an appropriate training program.

External Auditors

The external auditors are responsible for preparing the annual SOX certification. According to the prevailing audit guidelines, they must consider the design assessment and the effectiveness testing of the internal controls and assess the quality of the company's internal SOX evaluation process. If the external auditors' assessment has found that the internal testing is reliable, the external auditors can base their SOX audits on Internal Audit's work results. This means that the extent to which the external auditors must test the internal controls can be reduced in terms of quantity (although not quality).

CEO and CFO

The CEO and the CFO ultimately carry the overall responsibility for confirming the effectiveness and compliance of the internal control system (see Section D, Chapter 14.1.1). They must satisfy themselves personally that the internal controls are working by getting involved in the SOX process, especially with test activities. Internal Audit can support the Board in some aspects of this task, although this can be no substitute for taking action of its own.

HINTS AND TIPS

- Auditors should look for opportunities to be included in SOX-related activities.
- During process audits, auditors should interact closely with the SOX audit team.
- Internal Audit's employees should share best practice suggestions based on their fieldwork with the SOX auditors and SOX champions.
- Auditors should keep up to date with SOX activities in their audit areas by keeping in contact with the relevant SOX champions.

LINKS AND REFERENCES ↗

- INSTITUTE OF INTERNAL AUDITORS. 2006. *Sarbanes-Oxley Section 404: A Guide for Management of Internal Control Practitioners.* Altamonte Springs, FL: The Institute of Internal Auditors.
- PUBLIC COMPANY ACCOUNTING OVERSIGHT BOARD (PCAOB). 2004. *Auditing Standard No. 2: An Audit of Internal Control Over Financial Reporting Performed in Conjunction With an Audit of Financial Statements.* http://www.pcaobus.org/Standards/Standards_and_ Related_Rules/Auditing_Standard_No.2.aspx (accessed May 31, 2007).
- PUBLIC COMPANY ACCOUNTING OVERSIGHT BOARD (PCAOB). *Staff Questions and Answers: Auditing Internal Control over Financial Reporting.* http://www.pcaob.org/standards/staff_questions_and_answers/2005/01-21.pdf (accessed May 31, 2007).
- REDING, K. F., P. J. SOBEL, U. L. ANDERSON, et al. 2007. *Internal Assurance and Consulting Services.* Altamonte Springs, FL: The Institute of Internal Auditors.
- RITTENBERG, L. E. AND B. J. SCHWEIGER. 2005. *Auditing: Concepts for a Changing Environment.* Mason, OH: Thompson.
- U.S. CONGRESS. 2002. *Sarbanes-Oxley Act of 2002. 107th Congress of the United States of America. HR 3763.* Washington DC: Government Printing Office

14.2.4 Overview of Internal Audit's SOX Services

KEY POINTS •••

- There are two basic ways in which Internal Audit can be involved in the SOX compliance procedures: By providing support services and by carrying out audit engagements.
- Different forms of services, which cover specific topics according to the SOX lifecycle, are possible.
- However, the SOX organization, the process owners, and the relevant managers are responsible for ensuring that the SOX lifecycle is completed.

Dedicated SOX Audit Team

This chapter provides an overview of the different ways in which Internal Audit can be involved in the SOX compliance effort. Subsequent chapters will discuss each in more detail and with a greater focus on the Audit Roadmap. Especially during the first years of SOX implementation, it is advisable to assign Internal Audit's SOX compliance activities to a dedicated SOX audit team. This allows specific expertise to be built faster and controlled according to requirements. In addition, the risk of neglecting Internal Audit's other audit work is eliminated.

Two Types of SOX Services

Provided that a dedicated SOX audit team has been designated, Internal Audit can approach the SOX process in two ways: either by providing support services or by carrying out audit engagements. The aim of support services is primarily to help the departments and subsidiaries affected by SOX, especially during the preliminary phases of implementation. The ultimate objective of audit services is to test existing SOX processes as part of a "classic" audit, to report any weaknesses, and provide recommendations for improvement. The procedure is largely the same as that for other types of audits. The differences are described later (see Section D, Chapter 14.3). Whenever Internal Audit is involved in the SOX lifecycle, the principles of independence and objectivity must be maintained. The following diagram illustrates the different SOX services.

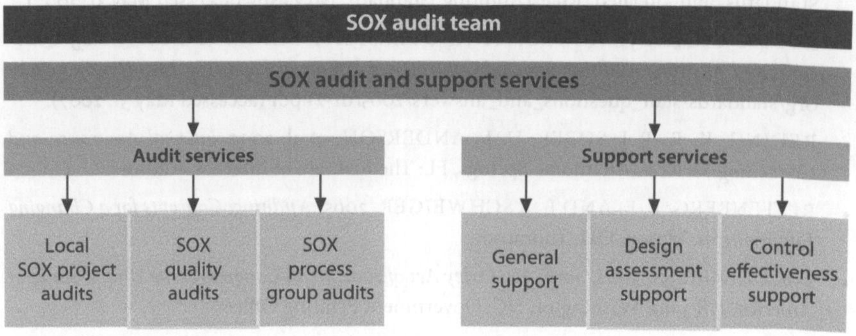

Fig. 30 Overview of SOX Services

Support Services

Support services are described as follows:

- The main purpose of general support services is to provide help as requested, e.g. training, document creation, process reviews, etc. Every organizational unit affected by SOX sections 302 and 404 is eligible for these types of services. The time it takes to provide the support depends on the extent of services requested, but it should not exceed 30 days per auditee unit. Several auditors can work simultaneously during this period. The time restriction is imposed to limit responsibility and ensure independence for subsequent audits.
- Design assessment support services provide help in performing a complete process assessment of specific process groups. This concerns every unit that must comply with SOX sections 302 and 404. The time provided for design assessment support should also not exceed 30 days per auditee unit.
- From the GIAS' perspective, control effectiveness support for specific process groups is the most typical form of support Internal Audit can provide because it is very closely related to auditing. This concerns all subsidiaries subject to SOX sections 302 and 404, and the 30-day time limit also applies.

Audit Services

The following forms of audit services are possible:

- Local SOX project audits should establish how SOX processes have been implemented in a unit from an organizational perspective. These audits should include new subsidiaries that must comply with the SOX requirements for the first time. The maximum timeframe for these audits should be 20 person days.

- SOX quality audits are aimed at testing the quality of SOX activities in a subsidiary. They affect all units that have already completed the SOX lifecycle and focus on compliance with the formal criteria of the SOX process. From a practice point of view, we recommend a timeframe of no more than 5 through 15 person days to prevent these audits from evolving into a support engagement or a full-blown process group audit (see Section D, Chapters 14.3.1 and 14.3.2).
- For SOX process group audits, specific process groups are selected for a full SOX review, ranging from design assessment through testing. They again affect all units that have already completed the SOX lifecycle. Depending on the complexity, a timeframe of 30 through 40 person days is recommended.

Main Responsibility

Although the support services are normally optional and should be viewed as a "start-up" service during the first two years of SOX implementation, the SOX audit services will be an integral part of Internal Audit's annual audit plan. Each company must decide for itself whether these services should continue to be offered by a dedicated audit team, or whether they should be partially or gradually assigned to regular audit teams. However, the main responsibility related to design assessment and testing remains with the SOX organization, the process owners, and the managers responsible. Internal Audit's involvement must be limited to that of an independent staff department.

HINTS AND TIPS

- If at all possible, auditors should be involved in Internal Audit's SOX support or audit services, even if they do not belong to the SOX audit team.

LINKS AND REFERENCES

- HAUSER, D., R. HOPKINS, AND H. LEIBUNDGUT. 2004. The Sarbanes-Oxley Act and the Role of Internal Audit. *Der Schweizer Treuhänder* (December 2004): 1057-1065.
- INSTITUTE OF INTERNAL AUDITORS. 2006. *Sarbanes-Oxley Section 404: A Guide for Management of Internal Control Practitioners.* Altamonte Springs, FL: The Institute of Internal Auditors.

14.3 Integration along the Audit Roadmap
14.3.1 SOX Support Model

KEY POINTS

- GIAS' SOX support is based on both the SOX lifecycle and the phases of the modified Audit Roadmap.
- A SOX auditor can assume a supporting role in reviewing the SOX documentation and in assessing and testing the controls.

- The support work can be performed throughout the phases of the Audit Roadmap.
- Although SOX support is not an audit, a report should be sent to the Board.

Support Task

The integration of Internal Audit into SOX process design allows Internal Audit to provide support to the organizational units concerned, both during preparations and when implementing the provisions of SOX section 404. The SOX audit team should ensure that the SOX champion and the relevant process owners understand their duties and are able to perform their tasks correctly and carefully.

Audit Roadmap and SOX Lifecycle

When providing SOX support, a service in the non-audit-related category (see Section A, Chapter 7.3), Internal Audit bases its activities on the standard process model of the Audit Roadmap (see Section B). Specific elements are added where required by the SOX support. The SOX lifecycle is another reference framework for Internal Audit's activities (see Section D, Chapter 14.2.2). Both elements should be reconciled and aligned with each other. When providing SOX support services, special factors arise in relation to each phase of the Audit Roadmap. These factors are explained in the following.

Audit Planning

When planning SOX engagements, Internal Audit's support services are also taken into consideration. This affects primarily the local subsidiaries and the process groups that are subject to the provisions of SOX. Two types of SOX support can be distinguished: support that Internal Audit has identified as necessary during annual audit planning and support that the local subsidiary or local SOX champion requests from Internal Audit.

Scope

The extent of the support services to be provided depends on the requirements of the organizational unit concerned. All activities are based on the process documentation recorded in the internal control management tool (see Section D, Chapter 14.2.1). The preparations for SOX support comprise two main steps: The support announcement and a detailed definition of the necessary activities.

Support Announcement and Definition of Activities

The support announcement must give reasonable notice to the organizational unit concerned, i.e., it should not be made later than one month before activities are scheduled to start. Then the SOX support lead, in consultation with the local SOX champion, determines the process groups to be given support.

Execution

The SOX auditors carry out the SOX support largely according to the procedures of Internal Audit. In doing so, they assess existing (partial) work results on the one hand, and on the other they close any gaps and provide useful examples for design assessment and test procedures. The support provided is documented in the working papers in a structured format; for the control test phase in particular, the sampling method must be accurately documented.

Reporting

Once the support work has been completed, a closing meeting is held at which the SOX champion and the local CFO are informed of the results. If they accept and agree with the results, the final report is handed to them, as well as to all those responsible in the SOX organization and Internal Audit. The final report contains the findings for each process group and indicates the relevant status. A Board summary is also prepared, which gives a traffic-light status and highlights the most serious problem areas. A copy of this summary is also sent to those responsible in Internal Audit. If the status of the report is red, the results are discussed with the CEO. In addition, the Board should be given a separate quarterly report, which summarizes the results.

Follow-Up

After reporting, the follow-up phase begins with the remediation of the findings. The findings describe the current status, listing the weaknesses identified for remediation as a basis for further action. Then the SOX champions retest the process and control design and the effectiveness of the internal controls. Normally, this task is not included in Internal Audit's remit, and it is generally the process owner's responsibility to resolve any problems. Once this task has been completed, the process or control has to be left to do its work for at least one month before the SOX champion performs another test. This is to ensure that the weakness has in fact been eliminated and no further problems have occurred. If necessary, Internal Audit can support the organizational unit again during retesting.

HINTS AND TIPS

- Auditors should try to incorporate the results of SOX support activities into their work programs.
- Auditors should regularly exchange information about the SOX quality status in the various local subsidiaries with colleagues from other audit teams.

LINKS AND REFERENCES

- HAUSER, D., R. HOPKINS, AND H. LEIBUNDGUT. 2004. The Sarbanes-Oxley Act and the Role of Internal Audit. *Der Schweizer Treuhänder* (December 2004): 1057-1065.
- INSTITUTE OF INTERNAL AUDITORS. 2006. *Sarbanes-Oxley Section 404: A Guide for Management of Internal Control Practitioners.* Altamonte Springs, FL: The Institute of Internal Auditors.

14.3.2 SOX Audit Model

KEY POINTS

- Internal Audit's SOX procedure is based on the standard Audit Roadmap.
- Appropriate additions and modifications should be made for specific phases.
- Internal Audit must apply special procedures for the preparation and execution of SOX audits.
- Special procedures must be applied for SOX audits because of the deep structure of the processes and objects to be audited and the alignment with the internal control management tool.

Modified Audit Roadmap The general Audit Roadmap forms the basis for all SOX-related audit activities. This applies to all engagement types (see Section D, Chapter 14.2.4) and serves to ensure that Internal Audit always meets the compliance requirements of international audit institutes. For SOX-related audit activities, parts of the standard Audit Roadmap are modified.

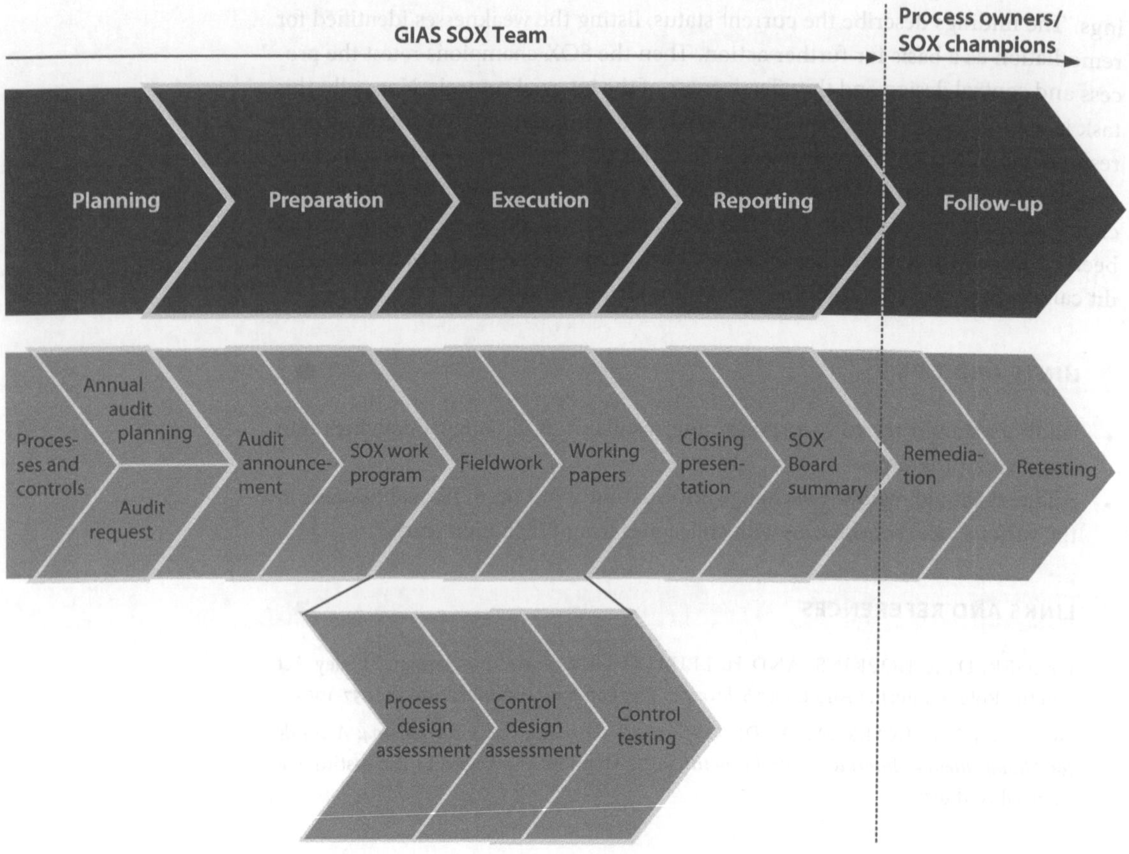

Fig. 31 SOX Audit Roadmap

Audit Planning Since resources and capacities for possible SOX audits are limited, the units to be audited should be assessed, analyzed, and selected according to risk (see Section D, Chapter 3), in the same way as during the general audit planning process (see Section B, Chapter 2). To be able to weight audit objects of equal standing, the classic risk assessment formula or determined risk level is further qualified by a weighting factor (e.g., in relation to sales). In addition, SOX audits can also be included in the audit plan in response to audit requests (see Section B, Chapter 2.3). Similar to other audits, SOX audits should have an opening meeting. SOX auditors should also use the internal control management tool during the planning phase, because it provides them with a good overview of the substance and status of the SOX processes in the organizational unit concerned.

Scope

The definition of a Scope is predetermined by the necessary comprehensive process and control documentation. Since the SOX documentation describes the content in detail, it is not necessary to create a special Scope for SOX audits. The audit steps can be transferred to a work program on the basis of the described processes.

Audit Preparation

The next step is the development of the SOX-specific work program, which consists primarily of a project-related audit list and allows the auditors to test each individual SOX process step, from documentation through certification of the financial statements. Since activities focus on independent tests of the design assessment and the internal controls, the work program contains details of these steps, with reference to the relevant categories in the IT tool. In this context, it is a good idea to analyze the audit preparation and execution phases in close correlation, because they build on each other.

Different Audit Types

There are different types of audits: Local SOX project audits, SOX quality audits, and SOX process group audits. SOX project audits follow the classic procedure. They are used by preference when a subsidiary is introducing the SOX processes. The objective is to find out whether the subsidiary is sufficiently prepared for the SOX compliance procedures. The aim of SOX quality audits is to gain as comprehensive an overview as possible of how well the SOX processes comply with the quality standards. Process group audits focus on various SOX-related process groups (for more information see Section C, Chapter 8).

Audit Execution

Audit execution passes through the entire SOX lifecycle in detail. A distinction must be drawn between the comprehensive audit section and the individual case, selected by sampling (see Section B, Chapter 4.1.2). The relevant templates for recording the test results from the design assessment review and control testing are suitable for use as working papers (for details, see Section C, Chapter 8).

Closing Meeting

The SOX audit activities are officially concluded at a closing meeting, where the results are presented and discussed. This includes the process group review, a summary of the significant findings for each process group, a preview of the Board summary, and the clarification of any unresolved issues. All involved parties from the SOX organization and, if appropriate, also the process owners should attend this closing meeting.

Reporting

The Board summary is a significant reporting element. For each audit segment, it provides the summary status on the basis of Internal Audit's findings. This report should also be sent to all involved parties in the SOX organization and all those responsible in Internal Audit.

Follow-Up

The last remaining step is the normal follow-up phase. During this phase, the auditors, in consultation with the SOX organization, investigate when and to what extent Internal Audit's recommendations have been implemented by taking appropriate action. The follow-up is preceded by setting timeframes within which these investigations are to take place. This has to be closely coordinated between Internal Audit and the SOX organization.

Extent of Internal Audit's Involvement

The extent of Internal Audit's involvement in the SOX processes depends on a number of factors. In the long term, Internal Audit cannot by itself ensure that the SOX provisions are properly implemented. For this reason, other operational parties must carry the main responsibility by conducting assessments and tests. But this can only be organized if there is no overlap of responsibilities and no conflict of interest regarding the control functions. If this works properly, Internal Audit may depend on these results and verify them with qualified samples.

HINTS AND TIPS

- When preparing for SOX audits, auditors should also try to consult the results of other audits.
- Auditors should establish at an early stage whether the SOX process documentation is complete.

LINKS AND REFERENCES

- COMMITTEE OF SPONSORING ORGANIZATIONS OF THE TREADWAY COMMISSION (COSO). 2003. *Enterprise Risk Management Framework.* New York, NY: AICPA.
- INSTITUTE OF INTERNAL AUDITORS. 2006. *Sarbanes-Oxley Section 404: A Guide for Management of Internal Control Practitioners.* Altamonte Springs, FL: The Institute of Internal Auditors.
- PUBLIC COMPANY ACCOUNTING OVERSIGHT BOARD (PCAOB). 2004. *Auditing Standard No. 2: An Audit of Internal Control Over Financial Reporting Performed in Conjunction With an Audit of Financial Statements.* http://www.pcaobus.org/Standards/Standards_and_ Related_Rules/Auditing_Standard_No.2.aspx (accessed May 31, 2007).
- PUBLIC COMPANY ACCOUNTING OVERSIGHT BOARD (PCAOB). 2004. *Staff Questions and Answers: Auditing Internal Control over Financial Reporting.* http://www.pcaob.org/standards/staff_questions_and_answers/2005/01-21.pdf (accessed May 31, 2007).
- U.S. CONGRESS. 2002. *Sarbanes-Oxley Act of 2002. 107th Congress of the United States of America. HR 3763.* Washington DC: Government Printing Office.

14.3.3 Coordination of SOX Activities

KEY POINTS

- Internal Audit's involvement in SOX certification activities includes introducing the SOX regulations and long-term task assignment.
- Efficient cooperation between the different audit teams within Internal Audit is necessary right from the start of SOX implementation.

- In the long-run, Internal Audit must leave the units to perform the operational aspects of SOX and concentrate on the actual audit task.
- The tasks and responsibilities are gradually being redistributed among the different audit teams within Internal Audit.

Short-Term and Long-Term Involvement

As described earlier, Internal Audit's involvement in the SOX activities affects the whole department in a variety of ways. The early years of SOX implementation differ from the longer-term focus and distribution of tasks, because during the SOX introduction phase, the objectives and deadlines can only be met if all the involved parties pool their efforts.

Responsibilities

Existing responsibilities should be discussed as follows:

- The process owners and the SOX organization have central responsibility for the current process documentation, and must guarantee not only that the financials are correct, but also that the internal control system is working. The Board must ensure that the significance of this responsibility is clear to all involved, and the annual tasks under the SOX lifecycle must be an integral component of their activities to ensure that the entire organization is compliant with SOX.
- Internal Audit should be responsible for monitoring the implemented controls. Internal Audit can use different forms of auditing: Either a full audit or a sample-based audit. Only if operational units cooperate and audit work is focused effectively can the necessary assurance be reached for certification by management and the Board.

Assignment of Tasks

Internal Audit must also determine how the SOX-related tasks are assigned within the department. It should generally be assumed that, as process audits, SOX audits form a long-term component of a "normal" standard audit and tie in with the other long-term components accordingly.

Cooperation Between SOX Audit Team and Regional Team

The SOX audit team primarily conducts audits on the basis of a SOX work program, examining the local subsidiary-specific results, test standards, and significant internal controls. The team then forwards the results to the regional audit teams for further assessment and auditing if appropriate, or for incorporating them into an audit already scheduled. The regional audit teams also conduct audits on the basis of a standard work program, which allows them to test significant internal controls. The results are made available to the SOX team so that it can assess them and conduct further SOX-specific audits, if appropriate. The mutual exchange of audit results must be precisely timed and coordinated in order to avoid duplication and exploit synergies.

Task for All Audit Teams

Although it is sensible to form a dedicated SOX audit team during the early phase of SOX implementation, in the longer term, the tasks will tend to spread among all audit teams. In general, this is done in the interest of time, but also relates to the content of the audits. With regard to time, the SOX activities are tied into a fixed timeframe, (i.e., the audit cycle must be completed within one fiscal year). SOX audits conducted by Internal Audit must comply with this timeframe to produce usable results. This should be reflected in the annual audit plan, if organizational units earmarked for auditing are subject to the SOX provisions. If this is the case, Internal Audit should consider whether the audits should follow the modified SOX Audit Roadmap rather than the standard Audit Roadmap (see Section D, Chapter 14.3.2). In the longer term, Internal Audit can also use the internal control management tool to address and conduct the SOX audits of process groups using the standard work program and document the results in the tool. This would turn the SOX-relevant audit procedures into an integral part of a standard audit, with the difference that the audit would be conducted exclusively by the regional audit teams and no longer by two independent audit teams.

HINTS AND TIPS

- Significant SOX-related audit results should always be shared with all Internal Audit colleagues to maximize the learning effect.

LINKS AND REFERENCES

- INSTITUTE OF INTERNAL AUDITORS. 2006. *Sarbanes-Oxley Section 404: A Guide for Management of Internal Control Practitioners.* Altamonte Springs, FL: The Institute of Internal Auditors.

14.4 Impact of Introducing SOX

KEY POINTS

- The introduction of SOX has many different consequences for the affected companies, both internally and externally.
- SOX supports Internal Audit's development into an active management instrument.
- Internal Audit's focus on supporting compliant SOX certification, the quest for best practices, and its universal audit mandate make it a competent partner for many parties.

Significant Aspects

The introduction of SOX has external and internal consequences for the various organizational units. From Internal Audit's perspective, these consequences can be summarized as follows:

Opportunity to Play Key Role

- The introduction of SOX presents an important opportunity for Internal Audit to play a key role in the certification process. This is justified because of Internal Audit's knowledge of the internal control system. Internal Audit should use this opportunity, while making sure that it complies with the department's own principles and fulfills its general audit mandate.

- As a result of Internal Audit's role in the certification process, the Board of Directors and management will take greater notice of Internal Audit. This supports Internal Audit's efforts to develop into an active management instrument. The attention it receives as a result of SOX can enhance Internal Audit's acceptance as a management instrument. **Perception as Management Instrument**
- There are further consequences for Internal Audit itself in that it must cooperate with additional partners and reorganize its task structure, at least partially. These internal effects should not be underestimated, because they may entail changes to the entire process flow. This also involves closer cooperation with all parties affected by SOX, including the external auditors. **Increased Cooperation**
- Internal Audit also derives various other benefits from SOX. For example, a comprehensive internal control system makes the processes more self-regulating, which means that Internal Audit can be even more focused on significant audit content, because automated procedures help reduce the extent of auditing. A closely related aspect is the quest for best practices, which can be maintained centrally and in a standard format for the entire Group or transferred to the service organizations. **Additional Benefits of SOX**
- SOX certification ensures both internally and externally that the processes of the organization are compliant. This also guarantees that the financial statements are reported correctly and without omissions, which creates a reputation of trust and security among stakeholders. The effect this has, especially on business partners such as customers, suppliers, and banks, must not be underestimated. **Certification as Basis of Trust**

Effects on Business Success

Moreover, SOX certification completes the image of a successful company. Although they do not directly generate sales or profits, the positive effects – especially increased investor confidence resulting from the confirmation of internationally recognized compliance – can boost business success. An efficient and effective procedure is a prerequisite in this regard.

Trendsetter

If a company wants to take a leading role among national and international competitors, it must stay abreast of the latest developments. Thus, SOX can and will act as a trendsetter and lead to further developments for companies not (yet) directly affected, as they will not be able to escape this trend.

HINTS AND TIPS

- When preparing reports on SOX audits or support services, auditors should highlight any best practices.
- In the management summaries, they should establish a link to the SOX requirements and their implementation.
- Information about Internal Audit's SOX activities should be made available to all stakeholders.

LINKS AND REFERENCES ↗

- DELOITTE. 2005. *Optimizing the Role of Internal Audit in the Sarbanes-Oxley Era*. www.deloitte.com/dtt/cda/doc/content/us_ERS_Internal%20Audit%20POV.pdf (accessed May 31, 2007).
- INSTITUTE OF INTERNAL AUDITORS. 2006. *Sarbanes-Oxley Section 404: A Guide for Management of Internal Control Practitioners.* Altamonte Springs, FL: The Institute of Internal Auditors.
- REDING, K. F., P. J. SOBEL, U. L. ANDERSON, et al. 2007. *Internal Assurance and Consulting Services.* Altamonte Springs, FL: The Institute of Internal Auditors.
- RITTERBERG, L. AND P.K. MILLER. 2005. The Good News About Compliance. *Internal Auditor* 62(3): 55–60.

E Conclusion

Perception of Internal Audit

For many years, Internal Audit stayed on the sidelines of day-to-day business operations and was generally perceived as a group of "box-checkers," feared rather than valued as a control body at the behest of corporate management. We hope that the exploration contained in this handbook has changed this perception and, using the developments at SAP as an example, refuted it at least in part. Even if some elements of these original views persist, the first important steps toward a changed perception of Internal Audit have been taken.

Limits of Further Development

The reorientation is not about totally reinventing Internal Audit, because much of what has long been accepted as good and correct still applies to this day. Traditional audit activities at the day-to-day working level will always form part of the audit work carried out to achieve the desired results. The requirements for documentation and reporting, for example, have not lost their significance. In addition, a healthy measure of respect for Internal Audit within the company may be expedient, because Internal Audit would otherwise not be able to fulfill its audit mandate in the interest of company management and all employees. Therefore, Internal Audit's further development should continue to be integrated into the framework and basic principles of audit work and the auditors' self-image and into every company's own corporate governance system. Any attempt to change or redefine this radically should be resisted. Internal Audit's roots must not be forgotten, irrespective of overall economic or business developments.

Changed Framework

Many aspects of Internal Audit have started to change. The internal audit framework and its changes, which we have covered extensively in this handbook, will shift the tasks of Internal Audit further toward ensuring holistic entrepreneurial compliance and business efficiency in the future. As our discussion has shown, a number of approaches and methods already exist at SAP. The implementation of the Audit Roadmap, internal and external cooperation models, increasing internationalization, strong involvement in the implementation of and compliance with the provisions of SOX, but also the increasing requirements in terms of audit-related additional services are all factors that are influencing and changing Internal Audit's self-image for the long term. These issues affect not only large corporations, but increasingly also medium-sized companies.

Customer Focus

In the age of enhanced customer focus, Internal Audit also must develop its role as a service provider. As an instrument of corporate management, it is first and foremost responsible for monitoring the implementation of and compliance with policies and guidelines. Since the application of these rules can contribute to securing the company's continued existence, Internal Audit must perform its task with consistent determination. At the same time, it should develop different types of tasks and topics and cooperation models and fulfill its primary mandate with the appropriate customer focus.

Software Solution for Internal Audit

The question of a comprehensive software solution that is integrated into the company's IT processes will pose another challenge for Internal Audit in the future. The discussion in the preceding sections can make a valuable contribution here, because in many respects, it covers the principles needed for a comprehensive, internationally applicable audit concept. In the future, there should be special consideration for auditing with automatically generated Scopes, audit plans, etc. and for continuously identifying audit topics, in-process, on the basis of thresholds or risk assessments. This entails that Internal Audit will adopt a proactive role, which requires support from an integrated system of audit software and application software.

Highlighting Additional Benefits of Internal Audit

Another focus for Internal Audit in the future will be on highlighting the additional benefits the department can deliver. It is easy to show on the basis of a single finding whether the implementation of an audit recommendation has led to an improved situation or process. An individual assessment like this can be made easily and accurately. The greater challenge, however, is to demonstrate the results of audit work throughout the company. This is a very complex issue, because it is difficult to accurately trace improvements back to the work of Internal Audit. These achievements are measurable effects, expressed as cost savings or enhanced benefits. However, these results should be aggregated on the basis of meaningful structures, e.g., responsibilities or processes.

Development of Findings over Time

Another important aspect of internal audit work is the development and examination of findings over time. Findings should be aggregated across the company so that trends can be identified as to whether the work of Internal Audit promises results in certain areas and the processes and internal controls have in fact improved. If the same findings are made repeatedly, either the existing arrangements pertaining to the finding are not or only barely applicable, or communication or the speed of change is not adequate. In such cases, information events or training may be needed to ensure the requirements are clear to all employees. Thus, error frequency and control weaknesses must be analyzed in detail, because their root may be found in the organization, the process, or even among employees or company management. Lasting improvements can only be made if the cause has been identified.

Fraud

The treatment of fraud remains a significant issue. It is important to establish whether a fraud happened unintentionally or was committed deliberately, and whether it was a one-time or a repeated occurrence. As part of its preventive activities, Internal Audit can help investigate combinations of topics, such as the perception of injustice among employees, the extent of compliance awareness in the company, and the need for appropriate guidelines. The main challenge for Internal Audit in the future will be to coordinate its activities closely with other corporate units, e.g., the global compliance organization, Risk Management, Human Resources, as well as operational management.

Future of Internal Audit

Two aspects are of key importance for the future of Internal Audit:

- First, Internal Audit must define its own strategic reporting system, which goes far beyond current reporting levels. Currently, reports have a strong operational focus, and those prepared for management provide summaries rather than analyses and forecasts. Internal Audit should identify trends and future (focus) areas for action on the basis of its experience with regard to these and other factors.

This can relate to the audit topics per se or, more importantly, to the resulting areas of action for corporate management and the relevant supervisory bodies. Possible instruments in this context include, for example, portfolio analyses and forecasts of the distribution and development of audit topics and findings. This enhanced reporting allows Internal Audit to demonstrate its ability to add value by identifying areas for improvement preemptively.

- Second, Internal Audit must cooperate with other parties, both within and outside the company. Internal Audit's tasks can no longer be accomplished in isolation. The complex requirements of the company and of external stakeholders and regulators can only be met efficiently with internal and external cooperation. Importantly, this includes cooperation with other companies, professional associations and government institutions as a suitable means to develop a globally consistent interpretation of compliance.

Outlook

Important first steps have been taken, but there is no doubt that much work is still required to adapt the significance, position, and function of Internal Audit to the changed framework. There is still a long way to go before these objectives can be achieved. Thus, this book is certainly not the end of the journey but hopefully a significant milestone.

F Subject Index

D

E

System requirements

Processor: Intel® Pentium® II or faster processor with 450 MHz (or equivalent)
Hard drive: 128 MB RAM
Operating system: Windows® 2000 or Windows® XP
Sound-System: MS Windows® compatible
Browser: Internet Explorer® 5.5 or higher (6.0 or higher recommended),
Firefox 1.0.2 or higher
Monitor resolution: 1024 × 768 with 16-bit video card or higher
Software: Microsoft® Office 2000 Professional
Adobe® Acrobat® Reader 5.0 or higher

Starting the application

The application will start automatically after inserting the CD in the CD-ROM drive. If the autorun function is deactivated, open the "Start.exe" file in the CD's main directory. Setup is not required. The CD starts in full screen mode. Use ESC to reduce screen.

Note

You will need administrator authorizations for installing plug-ins.

Supplementary CD for the Internal Audit Handbook

The Audit Roadmap, the process model of internal auditing developed at SAP®, can be a central tool in managing the tasks of an internal audit department. Section B of this handbook gives an in-depth description of the structure of the Audit Roadmap and its application in day-to-day operations. The CD provides an overview of the main points discussed in Section B and thus helps to easily become acquainted with the individual phases of the Audit Roadmap.

The description of the Audit Roadmap is supplemented by 32 templates, which are available in two modes:

- View: to gain a quick overview.
- Edit: for downloading the templates as Word®, Excel®, or PowerPoint® files.

Contents:

- Welcome
- Audit Roadmap (Planning, Preparation, Execution, Reporting, Follow-up)
- Quality Assurance
- Additional Information
- Audit Management Solution
- Help
- Publisher details and contact information

Return or exchange only possible
when packaging unopened

MIX
Papier aus verantwortungsvollen Quellen
Paper from responsible sources
FSC® C105338

If you have any concerns about our products,
you can contact us on
ProductSafety@springernature.com

In case Publisher is established outside the EU,
the EU authorized representative is:
Springer Nature Customer Service Center GmbH
Europaplatz 3, 69115 Heidelberg, Germany

Printed by Libri Plureos GmbH
in Hamburg, Germany